Enjoying American History

Revised

HENRY ABRAHAM
IRWIN PFEFFER

Dedicated to serving

AMSCO

our nation's youth

When ordering this book, please specify:
either **R 273 P** *or* ENJOYING AMERICAN HISTORY, PAPERBOUND

Amsco School Publications, Inc.

315 Hudson Street / New York, N.Y. 10013

Henry Abraham is former chairman of the social studies department at William Cullen Bryant High School
in Long Island City, N.Y. Irwin Pfeffer is former chairman of the social studies department at Thomas Jefferson High School in Brooklyn, N.Y. The two men are
coauthors of *Enjoying Global History.*

Cover: Joseph Pickett, *Manchester Valley* (1914–18?),
oil with sand on canvas, 45 1/2 × 60 5/8 inches; Collection, The Museum of Modern Art, New York. Gift
of Abby Aldrich Rockefeller.

Cover and Text Design: Harkavy Publishing Service
Maps: Kathe Kelleher
Illustrations: Don Sibley
Cartoons: Irene Trivas
Graphs: J & R Graphics

ISBN: 0-87720-634-1

Printed in the United States of America

Preface

Over the years, some of our students have complained that their history courses are dull and lifeless. "Why can't history be interesting?" they asked.

ENJOYING AMERICAN HISTORY, like its companion text ENJOYING GLOBAL HISTORY, was written to show students that the study of the past is not just memorizing names, dates, battles, and treaties. History is all of these things, of course, but it is also people. Real people made history—our past was their present.

ENJOYING AMERICAN HISTORY presents a history of America from the pre-Columbian period to the present day. To make history come alive, we have written 124 stories about the people and events of the past and present. Many of the characters in our stories are or were real people. Some of the incidents in the stories are fictional, but many actually did happen. Those incidents that are imaginary are based on solid historical evidence. Most of them might very well have occurred.

We have used a variety of literary forms—short stories, plays, newspaper reporting, interior monologues, letters. Many of the illustrative materials—maps, graphs, cartoons, line drawings—are the motivations for comprehension questions in the exercise sections following the stories.

Each story is a self-contained entity. It is introduced by a fact-filled, comprehensive historical narrative that sets the time and place and explains the story's political, social, and economic perspectives. The stories add human interest to the factual materials and provide the basis for a clearer understanding of American history. Most stories are followed by postscripts that tell the outcome of the events or situations or bring them up-to-date.

The sixteen units are introduced and concluded by conversations between a history teacher, Mr. Miller, and a student, Jack. These conversations preview the content of the units and give a summary of the major ideas. We have also created classmates for Jack. They present biographical reports about Americans of many backgrounds who contributed to the development of our country. These "Who Built America?" pieces come at the end of 11 units. The conversational exchanges among the class members in the reports are designed to motivate students to do further research into the lives of the highlighted Americans.

Another feature is a series of chapters called "The Growth of the Constitution." These chapters, placed at the end of 10 units, demonstrate how the Constitution has continued to be a living document, accommodating the needs and attitudes of the people of each historical period.

Thought-provoking questions for homework follow each story, as does a variety of short-answer questions. In addition, the "Activities and Inquiries" sections offer opportunities for student research and development of social studies skills.

It is our hope that the stories in ENJOYING AMERICAN HISTORY will interest students and give them insight into the forces that have shaped the lives of Americans over the centuries. We also hope that students will gain confidence in their ability to cope with future events.

We wish to convey our gratitude to two editorial associates, Norman Lunger and Barbara Ryan, for their creative contributions to the text.

To our wives, Elsa Abraham and Gloria Pfeffer, we express our appreciation once again for their encouragement and understanding.

Henry Abraham
Irwin Pfeffer

Contents

UNIT ONE

Americans Before the Arrival of Columbus

Mr. Miller, a history teacher, met Jack in the hall of the school. Jack is not fond of history, although he did well in Mr. Miller's World History class last year.

"Say, Mr. Miller," said Jack. "I didn't know you were teaching American History."

"That's right, Jack. I have a class the fifth period."

"Well," replied Jack, checking his schedule, "you're going to have to put up with me for another year!"

"That's not so bad. You'll have to listen to me again. I can stand it if you can. See you later!"

"Wait a minute, Mr. Miller. I've been through World History. Isn't that enough for one person? Besides, I took American History in junior high. Who needs it again?"

"Do you think you understand everything about the history of our country?"

"Not everything," replied Jack. "But I can get by. Look, I've read about the exploration of America and about the colonies and the Revolution. And I know that this is a democracy."

"Fine, Jack. That's a good beginning. What else do you know?"

"I remember that people worked hard; they struggled. And, well, our country has turned out to be in pretty good shape."

"If only it were that simple," said Mr. Miller with a sigh.

"I know there were problems along the way—war and depression, crime and corruption, hunger and prejudice. But, Mr. Miller, I've had it! I don't want to hear any more about that stuff."

"I know how you feel," said Mr. Miller, "but the bad often comes with the good. Think for a minute. Do you know how the American people were able to live through the tough times?"

"I guess we were strong," answered Jack slowly.

"True, but what makes us strong? What makes Americans the kind of people we are? And what's American democracy all about?"

"Gee, Mr. Miller, I can't answer those questions. I'm not sure."

"Wouldn't you like to be able to answer them?" asked Mr. Miller.

"Okay, you win. I'll see you in class. I suppose it's back to Christopher Columbus for openers."

"No, Jack, further back than that. First we'll take a look at the people who lived in America before Columbus came."

1 Honor to the Great Sun

America's story opens between 25,000 and 50,000 years ago. At that time Asian peoples began to move eastward across the Bering Strait into what is now Alaska in search of food. Many traveled by foot across a land bridge that once connected northeast Asia and North America. This land bridge disappeared into the sea about 10,000 years ago.

Settlers from Asia also found their way across the Pacific Ocean. People from what is now Japan may have sailed to Ecuador about 3000 B.C. Other people probably sailed eastward from the Polynesian Islands.

These first Americans were mainly hunters. They dressed in animal skins and used weapons of stone and bone. Spreading out from their points of arrival, they gradually settled most of North and South America.

By the time Columbus arrived in the New World, there were millions of people here. He called them "Indians" because he believed he had found the Indies in Asia. The early Americans called themselves many different names but not Indians. Today they are often referred to as Native Americans.

Early Indians spoke many different languages and followed many sets of customs. They belonged to many tribes. A tribe is a group of related people who all speak the same language and follow the same customs. Indian tribes are sometimes called "nations."

Most early Americans led simple lives, using crude tools and moving from place to place to hunt. But some, such as the Aztecs of present-day Mexico, developed complicated ways of life. They and the Mayans, in neighboring Central America, built great stone cities. The Mayans were also experts in mathematics and astronomy (the study of stars and planets). They created an accurate calendar, a system of writing, and beautiful paintings and stone carvings.

Whether they lived in forests, mountains, or plains, Native Americans lived close to nature. Their wonder about nature led them to develop religions to help explain nature's ways. Native Americans believed that people must work with nature, rather than try to conquer nature. They prayed for success in the hunt and begged forgiveness from the animals they were about to kill. They also thanked the spirits for the wonderful gift of life. Most tribes had legends (stories about the past) that dealt with nature's mysteries. The legends were handed down from parent to child by word of mouth.

Native Americans got their food in many ways. Some tribes came to be mainly farmers. Other tribes lived mainly by hunting or by gathering foods that grew wild.

Indian farmers grew crops unknown to Europe and Asia at the time. They raised corn, squash, and beans. Among their other important crops were potatoes, tomatoes, peanuts, peppers, and avocados. These foods were not introduced into Europe until after the first European voyages to America.

Native Americans knew about healing drugs. They invented canoes, sleds, hammocks, and moccasins. In spite of their many advances, however, they never discovered the wheel. Most travel was by foot or by boat. Nor did they use metals for weapons or tools.

The responsibilities of men and women varied from one tribe to another. In some tribes, the men did such work as hunting. They taught their sons to hunt and to live with nature. The women cooked, dried meat, cured skins to make leather, and sewed clothing. They cared for the children, built homes, gathered wood, and made fires. They also tended gardens. In some groups, such as the Pueblo, men and women worked side by side tending the fields. Hopi men wove the family's clothing.

Indian governments also varied. In the Northeast, all members of a tribe held hunting territories in common. Five tribes banded together into a powerful Iroquois League with a democratic governing council. In the Southeast, tribes did not join together—in fact, they turned against one another.

The Natchez had a powerful ruler who was called the Great Sun because the sun was said to be his ancestor. Other tribes gave their chiefs less power. They picked men with special courage or wisdom to be their chiefs. In most cases, a chief's power was limited to giving advice. His followers sometimes went against his advice.

The Indians of present-day Arizona and New Mexico lived in fairly large towns. Some tribes, like the Pueblos, built apartment-house-like dwellings on ledges in cliff walls or on top of mesas (steep-sided, flat-topped hills). These buildings were easy to defend against enemies. They were made of adobe (sun-dried earth and straw), and many still stand today.

Other tribes lived in small villages near their farmlands and hunting areas. Their homes might be made of tree bark, animal skins, logs, or grass. Hunting tribes often had separate villages for summer and winter.

One large group of Native Americans was known as the Mound Builders. They were divided into many tribes. The Mound Builders lived in the Ohio and Mississippi River valleys from the Great Lakes south to the Gulf of Mexico.

From about A.D. 1300, these Indians farmed in the clearings, hunted in the thick forests, and fished in the rivers and the gulf. They played ball games and a game called *chunkey* that involved throwing sticks through a stone ring.

What made the Mound Builders different from other Indian groups was their custom of creating great earthen piles. Many were burial mounds, filled with carvings, pottery, and the bones of chiefs. Today, scientists are digging up the burial mounds and other mounds on which temples once stood. The objects taken from the mounds tell scientists much about the way of life of the Mound Builders.

The Natchez Indians, who were among the Mound Builders, lived along the lower Mississippi. Their society had a definite class system. At the top of the social ladder was the chief—the Great Sun. He was both ruler and high priest. His wife, children, and other close relatives were called Little Suns. Below them were the Nobles, followed by the Honored People. At the bottom of the ladder were people of the Lower Class.

Some rules of the Natchez gave women special power. One rule was that every Little Sun had to marry someone in the Lower Class. The children of female Little Suns and male Lower-Class members became Little

Indian Culture Areas in North and South America, About A.D. 1400

Suns. The children of male Little Suns and Lower-Class females became Honored People. By marrying a woman from a higher class, therefore, a man could expect his children to have a higher rank than he did. As you will see, female Little Suns were especially important.

The following story takes place more than 600 years ago in a Natchez town called The Hickories. Some people of the Lower Class are building a burial mound. What would you find if you could dig into that mound today? Are the Natchez burial customs like any others you have heard about?

The Hickories, about 1380

It is early morning in The Hickories. Beyond the high wooden fence, the vines and moss that drape the huge trees sparkle with dew. Morning birds sing in the deep forest as Harvest Moon, dressed in a deerskin skirt, begins her day.

Harvest Moon looks across the village from the door of her house made of sun-dried mud and straw. Workers have almost finished hauling dirt for the burial mound they began two days ago, when the Great Sun died. At the foot of the mound, people are gathering gifts of food, pottery, and bone carvings. The gifts will go with the Great Sun to the next life.

Harvest Moon calls to her husband, Yellow Corn. He is coming from his field with a bone hoe on his shoulder. Hearing her call, Yellow Corn moves more quickly toward the house. His wife is a Little Sun, and he is only a Lower-Class farmer. When she calls, he comes.

The woman studies Yellow Corn as he approaches. His head was carefully shaped when he was a baby to come to a point at the top. Harvest Moon thinks Yellow Corn's head is handsome. So are the tattoos covering every inch of skin that shows above his white breechcloth and outside his sleeveless shirt. The children he will give her will make beautiful Little Suns.

"What is it, Harvest Moon?" The man bows very low at her feet.

"I want to know when the burial is to be. Go and find out for me."

He bows again and then strides toward the mound. If only Yellow Corn were a Noble, thinks Harvest Moon, he would have been a brave warrior. He could have captured women and children to serve the couple as slaves. Then Yellow Corn would not have to work in the garden beside the Great Muddy River.

Now Yellow Corn runs toward her, and Harvest Moon senses the sudden bustle in the village.

"The Little Suns are ready, honored wife. It is time to bury the Great Sun." He helps her down the steps from the house, high up on log pillars. With the crowd, they hurry toward the clearing. Everyone steps back and bows, letting Harvest Moon go ahead. Her husband falls back with his class.

Around Harvest Moon now are her relatives, the Little Suns. They are excited and happy that their ruler is about to make the wonderful journey to a "new land."

On Harvest Moon's right side are the female Little Suns like herself. Tonight the women will meet to select a new Great Sun. Harvest Moon finds that power almost as exciting as the Great Sun's "voyage."

A great shout goes up. Slaves come near, carrying the body of the ruler on the litter he used to ride. On the ruler's head is a beautiful crown of swan feathers with red tassels. On his shoulders is a feathered cloak, symbol of his ancestor the Sun God.

The people of all classes are beside themselves with joy for their departing priest and leader. They shout and throw flowers. Slowly the litter bearers make their way to the mound and disappear inside. In a few minutes, they return empty-handed.

Now, from the temple mound, come the Great Sun's wife, children, and closest advisers. In a moment they, too, will die in order to travel with him and serve him. Their heads are high, and their eyes shine. The village honors them with clapping and singing. Proudly they march into the burial mound to be drugged and strangled. Then, after all the gifts have been put beside the dead chief, workers shovel dirt into the opening. The merrymaking ends, and the village people return to their duties.

Yellow Corn goes off to the garden by the river. Harvest Moon walks back to her house, thinking about the Little Suns. One of them must be the new Great Sun. How to pick one? She was a very little girl at the last burial of a leader. Most of her life she honored the Great Sun they have just buried. She has never bowed, touching her face to the ground, to anyone else. Now she must help choose a new leader, whom her future children will be pleased to honor. It is a heavy duty but a proud one, too.

Then Harvest Moon remembers that soon it will be time for the harvest and the Green Corn festival. Her people will sweep and clean everything in the village, break their pottery, and make everything new. It will be a good time for a new Great Sun to take charge of The Hickories. The Sun God is wise to arrange things so well. Harvest Moon's heart leaps. She is happy and proud to be a Natchez.

POSTSCRIPT

The highly organized Natchez way of life continued for 300 years after the time of Harvest Moon. Then the French came to The Hickories and other Natchez villages. Some Indian leaders helped the newcomers; others fought them. The newcomers brought many changes. The Natchez way of life ended when the French captured a last small group of surviving Indians. The French killed some of these Indians by burning them and sold the rest—even the Great Sun—as slaves in the West Indies. A few escaped and fled to other Indian tribes, where they lived out their lives as medicine men.

Homework Questions

1. How did the first Americans get here, and where did they come from?
2. Describe three different ways of life among Native Americans.
3. Why are the Natchez called Mound Builders?
4. Why did the Natchez bury food, pottery, and carvings with their rulers?
5. Describe what happens during the Green Corn festival.

Understanding the Story

A. Write *T* for each statement that is true and *F* for each statement that is false.
   1. The Mayans of Central America were experts in mathematics.
   2. The first Americans believed that people must conquer nature.
   3. All chiefs had absolute power over their tribes.
   4. A democratic council governed the Iroquois League.
   5. Everyone in The Hickories was equal.
   6. All Little Suns had to marry Lower-Class Natchez.
   7. A Natchez child was born into his or her father's class.
   8. People in The Hickories lived in buffalo-hide tepees.

B. Complete each of the following sentences by filling in the missing word or words.
   1. The earliest Americans used weapons of _____ and _____.
   2. The _____ of present-day Mexico were a group of Native Americans who had an advanced culture.
   3. Among Indians of the Northeast, hunting land belonged to _____.
   4. Native American inventions still used today include _____, _____, and _____.
   5. A _____ body was beautiful to the Natchez.
   6. Each Natchez Indian was part of a definite social _____.
   7. Upper-class _____ selected the leader.
   8. The Natchez disappeared after the _____ came.

C. The U.S. President, like the Great Sun, is elected to office. Are there other ways in which a President is like a Great Sun? In what ways is a President different?

Activities and Inquiries

1. Do you think present-day Americans look upon nature in the same way early Indians did? Explain your answer.
2. Using your library, write a report about digging into an Indian mound or about the way of life of another Mound Builder tribe.
3. List reasons why you would like to be a close adviser to the Great Sun. Then list reasons why you would *not* like to be such an adviser.
4. If you had the duty of selecting the things to be buried with a Great Sun, what would you select? Why?
5. Why, in your opinion, did Harvest Moon think that choosing a new Great Sun was a "heavy duty"? Do you think it is fair for one group of people (the Little Suns) to choose a ruler for a larger group (all of the Natchez)? Why or why not?

2 Possessions and Power

Along the Pacific Coast lived Native Americans whose customs and ideas differed from those of other tribes. One group, the Tlingits, lived in what is now southeastern Alaska. South of them were Haidas, Nootkas, Chinooks, Kwakiutls, and dozens of other tribes. To the north lived the Eskimos of the Alaskan Arctic.

The fiercest of the Northwestern Indians, the Tlingits, were seafarers. By hollowing out great logs, they made boats as long as 60 feet. These warships carried raiding parties across the cold northern waters to nearby islands. There Tlingit warriors took what they wanted, including many slaves. Smaller boats were used for fishing and for hunting seals and otters.

Because of plentiful fish, game, and berries and because of frequent raids, the Tlingits became rich. Important families carved figures (called totems) on tall poles put near the doorways of their houses and at the graves of honored persons. The designs of animals, humans, and supernatural beings told passers-by about special events in a family's or a person's life. Chiefs had their own special totem poles.

Because the Tlingits did not have to work hard to get food, they had time to develop arts and crafts. They used wood, ivory, and bone to make jewelry. They wove soft bark threads and wool into blankets and coats. Later they learned to make complicated designs on thin sheets of copper.

As do all groups of people, the Tlingits had special ceremonies. One of these, used by many Northwestern tribes, was a type of party called a potlatch. Such parties were held for various reasons. One reason was to bring honor to a particular person or family.

In our story, a chief is giving a potlatch that he hopes will live in the memory of his people forever. Do you think that his hope is realized? Why or why not?

Tlingit village, 1400

Smiling with pride, White Bear looks around the big room of his new house made of cedar planks. There are many guests at this feast, which he has been planning for months. He claps his hands and signals to his slaves. They walk among the guests, offering smoked salmon, roasted sea birds and bear, sweet roots, berries, and many other special foods. White Bear knows that he has much more food than his guests can eat. Again and again he sends the tired slaves around with bowls and platters.

Finally everyone refuses more food. No one can eat another bite.

White Bear is delighted. He stands up to begin the next part of the potlatch.

First he sings a long song about his family and himself. He boasts of the fame of his ancestors and of his own bravery. He sings of his strength at rowing boats and of the size of the fish he has caught. He boasts of the canoes he has carved, which fly across the waves faster than sea eagles. He sings about the beauty of the women in his family and the goodness of his daughters. More verses tell about the wisdom of his son, who will one day be a great chief. The song goes on and on.

Since he was a little boy, White Bear has heard songs like this one. He has seen one chief after another try to give the best potlatch possible. He grew up knowing that a potlatch was a "giving." The man who offered the greatest feast and gave away the most wealth became the most honored man in the tribe.

Tonight he will give away so much that he will make his rivals feel small and insignificant. Many will try in the months ahead to outdo his giving. Spouting Whale, sitting there by the fire, is an especially bitter rival. But he and all the others will never match White Bear's generosity. White Bear's rivals will feel as unimportant as a captive Haida or Kwakiutl slave.

White Bear claps his hands again. His slaves parade around the room with fur robes—sea otter, seal, deerskin, and bearskin. White Bear gives all the robes away to his guests. Then he looks at Spouting Whale. What's this? The rival is still calm. Envy has not yet stung Spouting Whale. White Bear frowns and turns to summon more gifts.

The slaves bring heaps of blankets woven of shredded cedar bark and the wool of mountain goats. The visitors gasp at their bright colors and unusual designs. They laugh with joy when White Bear hands each guest a blanket. Pictures woven into some of the blankets tell stories of White Bear's family. The pictures go all the way back to legends of a long march from a forgotten home, across a narrow stretch of land that later vanished.

After the blankets, White Bear gives away coats and headdresses covered with seashells. Surely Spouting Whale knows now that he cannot match this generosity. But the guest's leathery face is still calm.

Carvings come next—long boats, spirit totems, ivory nose rings. Then come beautiful copper plates pounded into rich designs. Spouting Whale watches silently. He must be planning his own potlatch, White Bear thinks. Spouting Whale will have his slaves build a bigger house, weave more cloth, carve more totems, make more gifts.

How can White Bear make sure his potlatch tops all others? He remembers that at one potlatch, years before, the host had given away all his gifts. Finally, late in the night, he picked up a club and killed his most valuable slave. Is that what White Bear should do?

First he will try something else. He remembers his father's "grease feasts."

White Bear picks up a seal bladder full of oil. In an icy northern winter, no man is wealthier than one who owns plenty of oil. White Bear will burn his whole supply tonight. He'll awe Spouting Whale with such daring generosity. The oil will burn with great heat, forcing Spouting Whale to move away from the fire. That will be a sure sign of White Bear's greater strength.

As White Bear flings the greasy skin filled with oil into the fire, a trail of the liquid spills across the floor. The oily bag bursts into flames, and everyone—even Spouting Whale—has to move back to avoid being burned. Suddenly the grease spits tongues of fire into the room as the spilled oil catches fire. In a flash, robes and dry wood erupt in flames. Guests scramble out into the night. The house that slaves built for this night becomes a crackling bonfire.

From a distance, White Bear watches the building collapse. He is happy. His "grease feast" was better than he dared to hope. How could any rival show more strength or riches? Surely the Tlingits will carve White Bear's face into the tribal totems forever.

POSTSCRIPT

Soon Spouting Whale gave a potlatch, but he could not outdo White Bear. Shamed by his failure, Spouting Whale went off to war, hoping to die. Many chiefs outdone by a rival's potlatch did the same. But a shamed chief's people often planned another potlatch that would embarrass the one who had caused the shame.

Thus the practice, which seems so wasteful to us, went on. Potlatches had at least one good result. They spread wealth among members of the tribe, so that many people could enjoy more comfort. But potlatches could also cause suffering. For example, a family that gave away its wealth might have to go hungry and cold throughout the winter. Wars sometimes started because of the embarrassment caused by potlatches.

Homework Questions

1. Why did the Northwest Coast Indians put up totem poles?
2. Give one reason why Tlingits gave potlatches.
3. Describe four kinds of food Tlingits ate.
4. What did White Bear sing about to his guests?
5. What problems could potlatches cause?

Understanding the Story

A. Write *T* for each statement that is true and *F* for each statement that is false.
   1. The Tlingits lived in what is now Alaska.
   2. Food was scarce in the Tlingit territory.
   3. The Tlingits developed arts and crafts.
   4. At a potlatch, guests gave gifts to the host.

5. No one enjoyed the food at White Bear's party.
6. The Tlingits lived a peaceful life.
7. White Bear felt bad about losing his new house.
8. White Bear hoped the tribe would carve his face on totem poles.

B. List the numbers of the statements White Bear made or might have made.
1. I will be honored in death as in life.
2. I do not care what anyone thinks about me.
3. I will wear my oldest clothes to the potlatch.
4. People will remember my celebration for a long time.
5. Pouring oil on the fire will make my guests move back.
6. I do not want to tell about the wonderful things I have done.
7. I will hire someone to sing at my potlatch.
8. Spouting Whale is a greater chief than I am.

C. In the United States today, political candidates sometimes host free barbecues or picnics during election campaigns. In what ways are such events like potlatches? In what ways are they different?

Activities and Inquiries

1. Imagine that you are a reporter. Interview some of White Bear's guests. What questions do you ask? What answers do they give?
2. As a reporter, speak to White Bear. How does he justify giving away his wealth? Will he be a poorer man as a result? Explain.
3. Using your library, prepare a report comparing the lives of the Tlingits with those of another Northwest Coast tribe.
4. White Bear's potlatch tells us what matters most to him. What is it?
5. Describe how the Tlingit way of life was like that of the Natchez. How was it different?

3 Life in a Sky City

In the dry land that we know as Arizona and New Mexico, early people raised corn, cotton, beans, and tobacco along the rivers. They lived near their small farms in houses made of adobe and wood.

Built on mesas or under overhanging cliffs, clusters of such dwellings could house a thousand or more people. Some dwellings were two to six stories high. They were the first apartment buildings on our continent.

Most Pueblo tribes were peace-loving and gentle. The name of one Pueblo group, the Hopi, means "peaceful ones." The Pueblos were also hardworking. There were no rich or poor among them. They shared equally, believing that every person was as good as every other.

One reason for the calm good humor of these Indians was the religion that directed their lives. Religious societies were their only real government, and men spent half their time in religious duties. A council advised the people; a civil priest and a war priest divided the power. The whole village celebrated special times with one feast after another, all year long. Most of the special times had to do with the planting and harvesting of crops.

Another reason for good humor was the gentle way in which parents treated their children. The threat of punishment by spirits was the worst that would happen to a boy or girl who misbehaved. This gentleness produced people who hated not only war but also competition and loud voices. They thought that these were evil things that caused their world to be out of harmony.

One of the oldest Pueblo villages is Acoma, a "sky city" on a high, flat-topped mesa in New Mexico. It was built about A.D. 1150. Sheer cliffs protected it from surprise attack by nearby Mohave or Navajo tribes.

In the story that follows, a 12-year-old boy becomes a man by joining a religious society. From this day on, his life will center on the society's kiva. A kiva is a ceremonial room in the cluster of houses that make up a pueblo, or village. The kiva is as familiar to the Pueblo man as his own home.

What will the future be like for the boy? How do you think the girl in the story feels about her brother's new place in village life?

Acoma, about 1540

Squash Blossom stands in the shade of her mother's adobe house. She watches the kachinas (men dressed as kindly spirits) as they dance through the pueblo. She hears the rattle of their gourds, the beat of their drums, and the toot of their flutes. The kachinas are leading a parade. Behind them are clowns turning handsprings. Then come the pueblo boys who are to become men today. One is Painted Sand, Squash Blossom's brother.

Suddenly the parade is over. The men and boys disappear into the kiva, a round room dug into the mesa floor. The women return to their grinding stones inside a special house.

Squash Blossom kneels at her stone and spreads her long cotton dress to cover her bare feet. She pours corn kernels onto the stone. Then she presses down with a smaller stone. Back and forth and around she moves the top stone, grinding the kernels to flour.

Painted Sand is in the kiva now, learning the secrets of the Pueblo religion. Little brother is becoming a man! Squash Blossom looks at her mother, kneeling at the stone next to hers.

"It is strange, Mother, to think that Painted Sand is no longer a boy. I will miss seeing him playing ball with the younger boys in the plaza."

Her mother nods. "He will still weave our cloth, Squash Blossom, and help your father in the fields by the river. Things will not be so different."

"When the kachinas dance again, my brother will be with them, wearing a mask. He will be one of the gods."

Squash Blossom knows that the figures in the strange masks are men of the village and not gods. But everyone likes to believe that the dancers are kindly spirits who have come to live in the village and make the crops grow well. They come, the legend says, from a pit in the ground. Out of that opening, goes the legend, the Indians first climbed from an ancient underground world into this one.

The older woman nods her head, and her long braids bounce. "Yes, he will dance as a kachina and carry a feathered prayer stick. Perhaps he will hold a live rattlesnake in his mouth at the next Rain Dance. But he will also farm and hunt rabbits in the desert with the rest of us, just as before."

Squash Blossom finds in herself other feelings besides pride and sadness. "Right now Painted Sand is learning secrets I will never learn, in a room I will never see. Today I feel younger than he is, though I am two summers older."

"It has always been so, Squash Blossom. Our ancestors, the Basket Makers, believed that women should make baskets and pottery, gather berries, and build adobe houses. The men should raise the

"Painted Sand is learning secrets I will never learn, in a room I will never see."

crops and weave the cloth. They should be our civil and war priests. Our religion is in them."

For a few minutes the women are silent as they work. The stones grate, and a lizard flashes across the sandy floor.

Then Squash Blossom speaks. "Mother, why do we need a war priest at all? I do not remember a war. Not in all my 14 summers."

"That is true, Squash Blossom. Our people do not want war. But even our peaceful people do not always get along. I have heard tales of some Pueblo people who argued very bitterly. It is shameful, but at times this brings war. Sometimes a quarrel has sent hundreds of people away from a village. Villages can die because too many people move away to other lands."

"I see." When Squash Blossom moves her head in agreement, the heavy rolls of dark hair circling her head catch the light.

"Besides," continues her mother, "there are tribes a long way from Acoma that love war. They do not see, as we do, that fighting is evil. We must always be prepared to defend our villages if others attack us. But, daughter, there is another reason to have a good war priest in Acoma."

Now the older woman's voice drops low. Squash Blossom can hardly hear the words. "Tongues are wagging about strange beasts from the south. The gossips say that these animals are coming toward our village. Every day they come closer."

Squash Blossom's dark eyes widen. "What are these beasts like?"

"Tall as two men, I hear, with four legs. On top they are silver like the river in moonlight. Below they have fur and long tails. They can run faster than any man and throw sharp claws at people who get in the way."

"Mother! What can we do about these monsters? Can we keep them off our mesa?"

"Of course. Our war priest is a good man. Besides, no one has ever set foot on our mesa without our permission. These strange—"

A sudden hum of voices and the rattle and beat of music interrupt her. The men and boys are returning from the ceremony. The mother stands and goes out toward the sound. But Squash Blossom stays on her knees. She is worried.

If the terrible beasts come across the desert to Acoma, her brother will be among the men who will have to drive them away.

POSTSCRIPT

The "monsters" were Spanish explorers. They rode the first horses the Pueblos of Acoma had seen. They wore armor that shone in the sun. Their "claws" were guns, swords, spears, and daggers. With the Spanish were Indians the Pueblos had never come across before.

By the time Painted Sand was 16 or 17, the newcomers reached Acoma. But they did little to change Pueblo life. They were looking for gold, and

Acoma offered none. The Spanish generally left the quiet, hard-working Indians alone. Sometimes the Spanish took Pueblo men on expeditions. Spanish missionaries were sent to teach the Pueblos about Christianity.

Then, in what was a very short time in Pueblo history, the Spanish went away. Desert winds blew the sands over the marks of their horses' hooves, and Pueblo life went on much as it had for thousands of years.

Homework Questions

1. Give two reasons why the Pueblos have a peaceful nature.
2. How is a boy's life different from a girl's life in Acoma?
3. What are kachinas? What do they do?
4. Why is Squash Blossom afraid of the strange beasts?
5. What might the Pueblos learn from the Spanish?

Understanding the Story

A. Write *T* for each statement that is true and *F* for each statement that is false.
   1. Acoma stands in a forest.
   2. The Pueblo Indians believe that kachinas are friendly spirits.
   3. The boys grind the corn for the family.
   4. Squash Blossom wears a leather dress.
   5. Pueblo men weave cloth for the family.
   6. Religion is important to Pueblo peoples.
   7. The Pueblos choose a war priest because they love fighting.
   8. Squash Blossom fears the Spanish and their horses.

B. Complete each of the following sentences by filling in the missing word or words.
   1. Pueblo homes were America's first _____ buildings.
   2. Hopi means _____.
   3. Pueblo parents were _____ with their children.
   4. The special room for men only was called a _____.
   5. Both men and women hunted _____ in the desert.
   6. The _____ were ancestors of the Pueblos.
   7. Kachinas made music with _____, _____, and _____.
   8. _____ explorers were the first white people the Pueblos met.

C. What special ceremonies do young people in the United States today go through to become adults? In what ways are these ceremonies like those of the Pueblos? In what ways are they different?

Activities and Inquiries

1. Pueblo Indians believed that they came to this world from an underground place. Using your library, describe one other idea about humanity's beginnings.
2. Does the presence of a war priest mean that a village is warlike? Explain your answer.
3. Tell how the Pueblos divided the work of the tribe.
4. Compare a Pueblo house in Acoma with your own dwelling.
5. Do you think you would like to have been a Pueblo boy or girl? Explain your answer.

4 Changes in Mohawk Ways

Near the joining of two great rivers, the Mohawk and the Hudson, in what is now New York State, lived the Mohawks. They were part of the Eastern Woodland group of Native Americans. Like many related tribes, the Mohawks spoke the Iroquois language. Together, these tribes made up the Iroquois people.

The story that follows takes place in a Mohawk village in a forest clearing. The clearing is surrounded by a fence made of three rows of logs, put up for defense against attack. Within the fence are some 50 buildings—long, wide, windowless structures with rounded roofs. These buildings are called longhouses. Each one is about 100 feet long and 16 feet wide. Nine or ten families live in each longhouse, their spaces set apart by hanging hides. All the families in each longhouse are related to the oldest woman in the house.

The village buzzes with chatter and laughter. Outside, dogs are barking. Inside one longhouse, White Moon and her husband, Chief Red Jacket, sit beside a fire in the center of the building. They talk about the news that messengers have just brought to the village.

What kind of life do these Mohawks lead? How do they divide the work of the village? What are their feelings about other tribes?

Mohawk Valley, 1569

White Moon stirs food that is cooking in a clay pot over the fire. "This is a strange message, Red Jacket. The chief of the Onondaga nation has never sent words of peace before. Can we trust the Onondagas?"

The tall, well-built man answers slowly. "I do not know, White Moon. The chief says that Deganawidah, the Huron medicine man, wants all Iroquois to join together and promise not to fight among themselves. That is not the way of our fathers."

Looking down the long, smoky room, White Moon sees hundreds of fish hung up to dry. There are many animal hides. At each fire, women are stirring pots of meat stew. Laughing children dart about, playing games.

White Moon speaks. "The Master of Breath has been good to the Mohawks. We win many battles against Oneidas and Senecas. We have plenty of food and many captive slaves. Why should we risk divine anger by making peace with our old enemies?"

"You are right. Our fathers' way was good. It made others—even the powerful Algonquians—fear and respect us. No one interferes with the Mohawk."

"I think about my family, too." As the eldest woman in the long-house, White Moon is responsible for her family. "Our son will soon go on a long hunt and bring back big game. When he does, he will be a man. How will our young men earn tattoos and prove themselves as warriors if there are no war parties in the valley?"

"The Onondaga chief says that Mohawk braves will fight alongside other Iroquois to defeat outsiders. We will all wear the same paint."

White Moon shakes her head. "It is hard to believe. And what about Little Fawn? She has seen 12 summers and should soon be promised to a brave. I would not like to have to bargain with people outside our own village to find her a husband."

"There are many things to think about before we answer the Onondagas. But, White Moon, I am not completely against the joining together of all Iroquois."

"What good do you see in it?"

"Last year our gardens gave us fewer beans and squashes than usual. The corn ripened late, and the crop was poor. The land is tired."

"Yes, the women complained that they must work much harder in the gardens for little return. They grumble that the men should help when the land is so bad."

"No brave will work in the garden. We hunt and fish. The digging stick and the hoe are women's tools. But in a year or two, we will have to move the village to a place where the land is good. Then the braves will clear new gardens for the women to plant. They will have to find new fishing places and hunting areas. They can do that quickly if they do not have to go off in war parties. Our people will not go hungry waiting for food."

"We Mohawks have always survived before and still raided our enemies. Why can we not manage again?"

"Perhaps we can."

"How do we know that the chief of the Onondagas will not get us to put away our tomahawks and then raid our village?"

"We cannot know."

"Red Jacket, I am afraid that the Holder of the Heavens will not smile on us if we turn away from the old ways."

"Very well, White Moon. I will do what my father did when he was in doubt. I will fast from food for three days and then go into the woods alone. The Great Spirit will send me a vision, as he did when I was a boy. I will come back and tell our chiefs what my vision tells me to do."

White Moon nods her agreement. The old ways are best.

POSTSCRIPT

About 1570, five tribes that spoke the Iroquois language (Mohawks, Oneidas, Onondagas, Cayugas, and Senecas) joined forces to form the Iroquois League of the Five Nations. Later the Tuscaroras joined them, forming the Six Nations of the Great Peace.

The League Council met each summer at an Onondaga village. Its 50 sachems, or wise men, served for life. Only a woman who was head of a family could cause a sachem to lose his power in the council. If she did not approve of his actions or decisions, she could force him to resign. The oldest woman in each family might also choose another chief to represent her group in the council. These chiefs could speak in meetings but could not make decisions. No action could be taken until all of the sachems agreed on it.

The League generally avoided talk about the internal problems of each tribe. It helped the six tribes to get along in peace. They learned to fight only common enemies and not one another. For 200 years the Great Peace united the Iroquois, making them the strongest known union among Native Americans.

Homework Questions

1. How does the work of Mohawk men and women differ?
2. How does the Onondaga chief propose to end war among the Iroquois?
3. Give three names used by White Moon and Red Jacket for higher beings or gods.
4. Why does Red Jacket think that the village will have to move in a year or two?
5. How will the League Council make its decisions?

Understanding the Story

A. Write *F* for each statement that is a fact and *O* for each statement that is an opinion.
   1. The Mohawk Indians live in longhouses.
   2. The Mohawks fight many wars.
   3. The Mohawks are better than neighboring tribes.
   4. The Mohawk chiefs should pay attention to Red Jacket's vision.
   5. Mohawk women grow corn and beans.
   6. All Mohawk men are brave.
   7. Mohawks make slaves of their captives.
   8. The Iroquois League is a wise solution to wars among the Iroquois.

B. List the numbers of the statements White Moon made or might have made.
   1. I am not sure we should trust the Onondagas.
   2. I do not want our son to be a warrior.
   3. Men should help us work in the garden when the land is poor.
   4. Our son needs to attack the enemy to prove himself as a warrior.
   5. I am glad to change the old customs.
   6. Mohawks have always lived in peace with other tribes.
   7. I want our daughter to marry a Mohawk.
   8. The women should hunt and fish.

C. Imagine that you have been asked by the President of the United States to work out ways to avoid future wars. Does the Iroquois League suggest an approach that might be useful? Why or why not?

Activities and Inquiries

1. Compare White Moon's position in her tribe with that of Harvest Moon (Natchez) or Squash Blossom (Pueblo).

2. Compare Mohawk and Pueblo houses.
3. Compare Mohawk and Pueblo food.
4. Using reference sources in your school or your public library, write a report on the Iroquois League. Why, in your opinion, was it so strong?
5. Why does White Moon like the old ways best? Do you yourself prefer old ways or new ways? Explain your reasons.

5 Horses and Buffalo

Indian culture varied widely from place to place. Each tribe had its own customs and myths. Land features, climate, and food supplies also helped to make the tribes different from one another. But when we think of Native Americans, the image that usually comes to mind is of the Plains Indian. Books, movies, and television have carried around the world two models of this original American. The first is the silent, noble man in a feathered headdress and leather leg coverings, sitting on a horse. The other is a cruel raider who burns the homes of settlers, scalps people, and attacks wagon trains and forts.

Few Plains Indians fit either of these models. Most Sioux, Osage, Crow, Arapaho, Comanche, and other Plains peoples were no more noble or cruel than any other humans. By today's standards, their lives were fairly simple and uncomplicated. They were centered around food gathering, seasonal ceremonies, and concern for their families and members of their tribes.

In the following story, Cheyennes in what is now Wyoming are celebrating their yearly Sun Dance. What does the storyteller teach us about his tribe? Which of the Cheyenne beliefs will clash with the beliefs of the settlers?

Cheyenne village, 1750

On this clear summer day, heat waves shimmer above the wide, flat plain where a Cheyenne village stands. Tepees cluster in a big semicircle, opening toward the east, the rising sun. The tepees are made of poles covered with buffalo hides.

The Sun Dance festival, with its races, games, dances, and tests of courage, is the high point of the Cheyenne year. For four days, people will laugh, eat, smoke, and compete with one another.

A pony race ends in a flurry of dust, shouts, and laughter. Roaming Elk, the young winner, leaps down from his pony and runs to tell his grandfather, Forest Hunter.

The old man sits cross-legged at the opening of the family's brightly painted tepee, smoking his pipe. Once tall and strong, he is now small under his large feathered headdress. But Roaming Elk knows that his father's father has a memory as sharp as an eagle's claws. He is the tribe's storyteller. For as long as the boy can recall, even the chiefs have sat at Forest Hunter's feet to hear his tales of Cheyenne legend and history.

"Grandfather, I won! I won the race!"

Forest Hunter smiles at the boy's excitement.

"I rode better than Mountain Deer and all the others. Next winter, my pony and I will ride out after buffalo. I'll bring you meat and hides. Wait and see!"

The storyteller reaches down to smooth the dirt at his knees. He presses his thumbs into the spot, then touches one thumb to his forehead. Roaming Elk's eyes brighten. This is the signal of Forest Hunter's connection with Mother Earth. It means that he is about to tell a story.

"May the Mother Earth listen to my words and be proud of her people."

The boy sits down silently. He loves the tales that reach back into the mists of his people's beginnings.

"You ride, Roaming Elk, as though you and your pony are one being. You go as fast as the wind off the blue mountains to the west. But you should remember that the horse was not always with the Cheyenne. When our people came from a far-off land, they traveled on foot. Later, when we lived in earth lodges in the woods where the Great River rises, we had no horses. On our long journey from the forest to these prairies, we walked. Dogs pulled our belongings on frames of bone and wood. Sweet Medicine, who gave us our laws and our Cheyenne way of living, never saw a horse. When he got the Sacred Arrows from the Black Hills, there was no horse in our world."

Forest Hunter stops and draws on his pipe. Roaming Elk cannot help asking questions.

"Then what, Grandfather? When did the horse come to us? Where did it come from? Do you remember when there were none?"

Slowly the storyteller answers. "Who can say where the mountains came from or men or horses? All are one, all are part of Mother Earth."

"But do you remember? When did you first see a horse?"

Forest Hunter turns and points to a scene painted on the tepee. It shows a line of Cheyennes marching toward a range of mountains.

"In those days, I was not much older than you are now. We walked many suns to the dry land in the south to trade with the Utes and Navajos there. We gave our buffalo hides for their pottery and beads. On the way back, we were crossing a narrow lake when we saw a strange animal. I remembered what my own grandfather had told me about Sweet Medicine's promises. Sweet Medicine said that we would see animals with round hoofs and shaggy manes and tails. Men, he said, would ride on their backs. So we caught the animal with a rope. Our people call that place Horse Creek."

"So you brought it back to our village. And then we caught others?"

"Before long every nation had horses to trade. The Arapahos, the Sioux, the Crows—everyone had horses."

"But we are the best riders, aren't we, Grandfather? The Cheyennes are the best?"

"We have learned well, Roaming Elk. So have the Sioux and other peoples."

"And isn't the horse a good thing for us, Grandfather? We can kill many more buffalo because we can travel far to their feeding grounds. And we can count coup in a battle because we have horses."

Counting coup, thought Roaming Elk, brings the greatest honor to a Cheyenne warrior. To touch an enemy in the midst of battle and escape unharmed means more than killing him or taking his scalp.

"Horses have brought us good things, Roaming Elk. But they have changed the Cheyennes, too. We used to live in one place. Now we wander without a special home. Our braves fight more often in order to steal horses and grow wealthy. These changes I do not like."

"But some things have to change. We still grow beans, corn, and squash as our fathers did. But we have more meat now, because there are buffalo here and none in the forests. Some changes are good."

"It makes me sad, Roaming Elk."

"Why?"

"When Sweet Medicine was an old man, as I am now, and ready to return to the gods, he looked into the future. He made a prophecy."

The old man rocks back and forth. His voice rises to a singsong as he recites Sweet Medicine's prophecy:

"'A time is coming when many things will change. Strangers with light skins called Earth Men will come, bringing great power and different languages and ways. They will kill all the buffalo and you will learn to eat the meat of a smaller animal with smooth hair and no hump.'"

Roaming Elk laughs. "What a funny animal, Grandfather!"

"Hear the rest of Sweet Medicine's words: 'Your sons will change from the ways of our ancestors. They will lose their beliefs and respect for their leaders. They will begin to live the Earth Man's ways and forget my laws.'"

Roaming Elk shakes his head. "Impossible, Grandfather! There are not enough Earth Men to make us change. We will never turn away from our own ways."

The old man does not reply, but he looks sad. He reaches down and smooths the thumb marks out of the dirt.

POSTSCRIPT

The Cheyennes and other Plains tribes thrived in the centuries before outside settlers took over the West from Native Americans. Life on the Plains changed greatly after the Spanish introduced horses from Europe. Forest Hunter saw the arrival of the first horses among the Cheyennes. Roaming Elk lived to see the arrival of white and black explorers. His sons watched as settlers took over the Indians' land and killed the buffalo.

With neither land nor buffalo, the Plains Indians could not live the kind of life they liked. They were herded onto reservations—plots of land set aside solely for Indians. Although they did not like a life that depended on farming, they had no other way to provide food for themselves. They even had to eat the meat of animals "with smooth hair and no hump"—that is, cattle. Settlers from the East brought metal tools, knives, rifles, cloth, and wagons. The Indians wanted these items and dropped old ways to make use of them.

Homework Questions

1. How did the horse change the Cheyenne way of life?
2. Which prophecies of Sweet Medicine came true?
3. What part does a tribal storyteller play in the life of the Cheyennes?
4. Describe the importance of "counting coup."
5. What useful items did the Plains Indians get from settlers?

Understanding the Story

A. Write *T* for each statement that is true and *F* for each statement that is false.
   1. Cheyennes live in tepees.
   2. Roaming Elk does not know how to ride.
   3. The Cheyenne have always lived in the plains.
   4. The Indians care about their tribal history.
   5. Forest Hunter worries about changes the horse has brought.

6. The buffalo is not important to the Cheyennes.
7. Forest Hunter believes Sweet Medicine's prophecies.
8. Roaming Elk will live to see that Sweet Medicine was mistaken.

B. Complete each of the following sentences by filling in the missing word or words.
1. The Cheyenne grow _____, _____, and _____.
2. Tepees are arranged in a _____.
3. The Sun Dance is a _____, lasting _____ days.
4. The storyteller makes a sign to show his connection with _____.
5. When the early Cheyenne moved, _____ pulled their belongings on frames of _____ and _____.
6. A warrior's proudest act is _____.
7. Sweet Medicine prophesied that the Cheyennes would ride _____ and eat _____.

8. Settlers from the East brought _____, _____, _____, and _____ to the plains.

C. What do you think Forest Hunter might like about life in modern America? What might he dislike?

Activities and Inquiries

1. Using your library, compare the lives of the Cheyenne at the time of the story with those of Plains Indians living on reservations today.
2. Did you read things in the story that surprised you? If so, make a list of the surprises.
3. Imagine that you visit with Roaming Elk in his village. What would you tell your friends about the Cheyenne way of life?
4. Would you want to visit for a long time or to hurry home? Explain.
5. Using a library, make a list of ways in which Plains Indians used the buffalo.

"Well, Jack, what did you think of our first unit?"

"Neat, Mr. Miller. It really surprised me. I guess I thought all Indians were pretty much alike. But they were at least as different as—well, as the French and the Germans."

"How do you suppose you got the idea that they were all the same?"

"Probably from the movies. That's where I got my first notion of Native Americans. But cowboy-and-Indian films weren't fair to the Indians."

"What do you mean?"

Jack answered slowly. "They made Indians seem threatening and, well, primitive. Actually, some tribes were pretty well organized. Like those Natchez, with their different levels of society and rules about marriage and burials. Indian history is really part of the history of all Americans, isn't it?"

"Yes. And we are finally waking up to that fact."

"Why now, Mr. Miller? After so many years?"

"For one thing, we are only now realizing how important it is to care for the earth's natural resources. We see now that we waste and abuse what Forest Hunter called Mother Earth. In some ways, the Indians were wiser about the natural world than the conquerors were. If we learn more about Indian ways, we may come to understand how to use our resources more intelligently."

"I'm interested in learning more about the Spanish who brought horses from Europe. And I want to know about the settlers who moved in on the Indians."

"The next unit will tell you, Jack."

UNIT TWO

The Age of Exploration

"I've heard all about the explorers," Jack announced. "'In 1492 Columbus sailed the ocean blue'—things like that. Who needs more?"

"I'm sure you have read a little about the exploration of America," Mr. Miller agreed. "But what do you know about the explorers themselves?"

"I know that they sailed over here from Europe. They were looking for some kind of a shortcut to Asia."

"Very good, Jack. But you haven't really answered my question. What kind of person sails thousands of miles across uncharted seas in a tiny ship?"

"I think you'd have to be very brave and willing to take all kinds of chances," Jack replied. "Danger would mean nothing to you."

"But why?" Mr. Miller persisted.

"Oh, by taking risks you might become famous or rich—or both. Or maybe you could do something that no one else has done before."

"Now you're beginning to see the light," Mr. Miller said.

"Sure, today it would be exciting to discover a new use for a product or a different way of tossing a Frisbee," Jack added.

"Or a new shortcut to a friend's house."

"But an explorer—I mean a *real* explorer—must need something more," Jack said thoughtfully.

"Right, Jack, it's time for you to discover what the explorers were really like."

1 Columbus: To the Indies

Other explorers may have arrived in America before Columbus. For example, Eric the Red, a Norseman from Iceland, started a colony in Greenland in the late 900's. In the year 1000, while Eric's son Leif was sailing from Norway to Greenland, his ship was blown off course. He found a land where, as he said, "wild grapes grow."

Historians are not sure where Leif landed. They guess that it was the coast of what is now eastern Canada near the Gulf of St. Lawrence. Leif Ericson may have been the first European to find North America. But Europeans in general knew nothing about the discovery. For almost 500 years more, from 1000 to 1492, the Indians had America to themselves.

During most of those 500 years, merchants in Italy carried on a very profitable trade with countries in Asia. They brought spices, diamonds, silks, porcelain (fine china), and other goods over land routes and across the Medi-terranean Sea into Europe. Naturally, business people in other parts of Europe were also eager to trade with Asian countries—what are now China, Japan, India, and Indonesia. How could these people get a share of the profits without following the trade routes of the Italians?

They wanted to find another way to Asia, or the Indies, as some called the area. The new route would have to bypass the Mediterranean Sea to avoid Italy and its merchants. The goal, then, would be to find an all-water route either south around Africa or west from Europe to Asia.

In our story we see how Christopher Columbus spent most of his life planning voyages to find a western route to Asia. Ask yourself these questions: Why was Columbus so sure that Asia could be reached by sailing west from Europe? Did he deserve to be called Admiral of the Ocean Sea? What happened as a result of his voyage?

Spain, 1493

You are Christopher Columbus. As you rest after a long sea trip, you are thinking about your life. You had a dream that by sailing west from Europe you could reach the Indies. You know the earth is round, not flat like a table top. If you keep sailing in one direction, you can return to the place where you started. You can't fall off the edge of the world, as many people without much education believe.

You were born in Genoa, Italy, in 1451 and have spent your life learning about the sea. Far-off places fascinated you so much that

26

you read all the geography books you could find. Of special interest was the story of Marco Polo's travels to China. Marco Polo told of rubies as thick as a person's arm and palaces with roofs of gold. You filled the margins of his books with your remarks. Some day, you promised yourself then, you would see these things for yourself.

There was nothing for you in Genoa, so you went to Portugal, the greatest sea power of Europe. Its ships sailed all the seas that people knew about. Weren't the Portuguese looking for a sea route to China and India? True, they thought the shortcut was to sail south around Africa. You talked to King John III of Portugal and showed him books and maps to prove that the best way to Asia was to the west, not to the south.

The Portuguese could not be convinced. But you would not give up your dream. You had a strong faith that a westward voyage to Asia was God's plan for you.

You saw that your future was not in Portugal. So you studied more and drew maps. In 1484 you moved to Spain.

Two years later you met with King Ferdinand and Queen Isabella. You carefully planned what you would say to each of them. Since Isabella was very religious, you told her that a voyage would spread Christianity through all the lands you would discover. Ferdinand was more interested in wealth. You told him about the gold you would find for him. Then, for Isabella, you added that this gold could be used to win back Palestine, the Holy Land, from the non-Christian Turks.

Isabella was pleased, so you thought victory was just around the corner. But Ferdinand was not so sure about approving your trip. Your dreams tumbled down. Ferdinand wanted a team of scholars to look into the voyage. They studied the idea and said, "No!" They did not like your plan.

All seemed lost. Then Isabella said that she would still think about the voyage. There remained a small hope that your dream might come true. But first, the two monarchs had to push the Moors—Muslims from North Africa—out of Spain.

For six long years, you did not stop trying. You wrote to King Henry VII of England. He rejected your plan to sail to the Indies. You wrote to King Charles VIII of France. He was not interested. Failure after failure haunted you.

Finally, on January 2, 1492, Granada, the last Moorish city in Spain, was defeated. Now Ferdinand and Isabella had no more excuses. They called you to the palace and said, "You will sail west to find the Indies and China and even Japan. The ships are yours."

But you were not completely satisfied. You wanted something more. The words spilled out, "I must be made a nobleman so people will call me 'Don.' I also wish to have the title 'Admiral of the Ocean Sea.' I must be made the governor of all the islands and continents I discover. I want to keep 10 percent of all the wealth I find. All of these rights and powers must pass to my children."

"You are an ungrateful man," said Ferdinand and Isabella. "Our treasury is empty. We cannot let you go under these conditions."

But you knew better. You knew that they would agree to your conditions—and they did.

You went to the port of Palos to see your three ships. You were excited because you had become the commander of a fleet. Although the ships were small, they looked good to you. There were your flagship, the *Santa Maria* (85 feet long), the *Pinta* (75 feet long), and the *Niña* (70 feet long). You watched the men caulking the ships to make the seams watertight. Although you complained that they were doing a sloppy job, they refused to do the work over. You had to accept the ships as they were and pray that there wouldn't be too many leaks.

Finally, Friday, August 3, 1492, arrived. On board the *Santa Maria*, half an hour before sunrise, you gave the order to lift anchors. You set your course for the Canary Islands. In the Canaries you made sure that there would be no shortage of food, fuel, or water. Nothing was overlooked. Then, you set sail again, heading due west from the Canaries.

You worried about your sailors because you knew how afraid they were of the unknown. Sailors fear the emptiness of the sea. They like to see land every few days. As the days passed and you still saw nothing but water, your crew grew restless. Why couldn't the men believe that you would find land, that you would take them to the Indies? You knew you would. They should have trusted you.

The first man to sight land will get a large reward, you told them. Day after day birds were seen. The sailors got excited because birds usually mean that land is near. One day a flying fish leaped out of the water onto the deck of the *Santa Maria*. The sailors were confused. How could fish fly like birds? Where was the land? How could there be all of those birds and no land?

On October 10, 1492, your men complained and shouted, "Mutiny! Down with Columbus! Throw him overboard!" Somehow you calmed them.

They wanted to go back to Spain. You talked to them quietly and explained that land had to be very close. They did not believe you because they had not seen anything but sea and sky for five weeks. "Turn back," they demanded.

You could argue no longer. Finally you said, "Let us keep going for three more days. God will help us find the Indies. I know we will find land. Give me just three more days." The men quieted down and hoped you were right.

Every man became a lookout, even at night in the moonlight. Suddenly, at 2 o'clock in the morning of October 12, 1492, there came a shout, "Tierra! Tierra! Land! Land!" A few miles to the west, you could see a shoreline in the moonlight. You could hardly wait for the dawn.

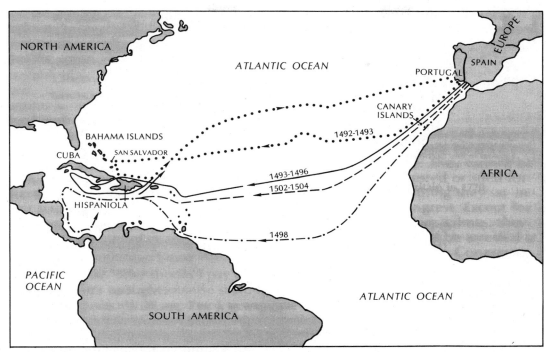

Columbus's Voyages to the New World

As the sun came up, you saw an island that appeared to be about 13 miles long. You named it San Salvador. Carrying the royal flag, you were rowed ashore, where naked people greeted you. When you landed, you pushed the flagpole into the ground and claimed the land in the names of the king and queen of Spain.

POSTSCRIPT

When Columbus returned to Spain, Ferdinand and Isabella named him Admiral of the Ocean Sea, just as he had asked. Three more times, between 1493 and 1504, Columbus sailed to the west. He came upon more new lands that he continued to think were the Indies. In fact, he called the people who lived in these lands Indians.

Part of Columbus's dream did come true. By sailing west he did come to rich lands—not the Indies, China, or Japan, but an area unknown to Europeans. Others would name these lands the Americas. From them would come great riches. Columbus did not share in many of these riches nor did he realize how important his voyages would be. But his dream and his voyages changed the world forever.

Homework Questions

1. Why did Italian merchants trade with Asia?
2. What was Columbus's goal in sailing west from Europe?
3. Why did Columbus move from Italy to Portugal and then to Spain?
4. Why did Columbus's sailors want to return to Europe?
5. What happened on the morning after the sailors sighted land?

Understanding the Story

A.   List the numbers of the statements that are true.
   1. Columbus discovered Greenland.
   2. America was left to the Indians from 1000 to 1492.
   3. Columbus was looking for a westward route to the Indies.
   4. Columbus lived all of his life in Spain.
   5. Columbus sailed for King Ferdinand and Queen Isabella of Spain.
   6. Columbus's flagship was the *Santa Maria.*
   7. Columbus's sailors trusted him to find land.
   8. Columbus gave the name San Salvador to the first island he saw in the New World.

B.   Number the following events in the order in which they took place.
   1. Columbus read about Marco Polo's travels.
   2. Columbus wrote to the king of England.
   3. Columbus landed on San Salvador.
   4. Columbus lived in Genoa.
   5. Columbus sailed west from the Canary Islands.
   6. Columbus was turned down by the king of Portugal.

7. Columbus met Ferdinand and Isabella.
8. Columbus was named Admiral of the Ocean Sea.

C.   Imagine that you are living in 1492. Columbus is hiring a crew to sail west to the Indies. Would you sign on? Why or why not?

Activities and Inquiries

1. Study the map of Columbus's voyages on page 29. Then choose the term or phrase that best completes each statement.
   a. On his voyages of exploration, Columbus sailed west across the (*1*) Mediterranean Sea (*2*) Atlantic Ocean (*3*) Pacific Ocean.
   b. Columbus touched the continents of (*1*) Europe and South America (*2*) Asia and Africa (*3*) North America and Greenland.
   c. The voyages all started from (*1*) Italy (*2*) Spain (*3*) Portugal.
   d. Columbus's second voyage started in (*1*) 1492 (*2*) 1498 (*3*) 1493.
   e. Columbus's last trip ended in (*1*) 1498 (*2*) 1496 (*3*) 1504.
2. Imagine that you have been given the job of preparing a report card on Columbus. Grade each of the following items as Excellent, Average, or Poor. Write a sentence explaining each grade.
   a. Getting the job done
   b. Working with others
   c. Imagination
   d. Bravery
   e. Knowledge of geography
   f. Self-confidence
3. Assume that Columbus sees your report card. What will he say about the grades you gave him?
4. Write a headline that might have appeared in Spanish newspapers to announce Columbus's discoveries if newspapers had existed at the time.

2 Magellan: The World Is Round

The land masses of North and South America stood in the way of Columbus's plan to sail in a direct line from Europe to Asia. But Columbus never realized he had come upon the New World. He died thinking he had reached the coast of Asia. Other explorers later determined that Columbus had not sailed to Asia at all. This discovery soon set off a new search for a passageway to Asia through the Americas.

Ferdinand Magellan thought he could find a way through or around South America. Born in Portugal, Magellan had made voyages around Africa to India and Malaya in the service of the king of Portugal. He became unhappy about the rewards he had received and decided to go to Spain. The Spanish king was persuaded to let Magellan sail to the Spice Islands (the Moluccas, now part of Indonesia). Magellan knew the islands could be reached by going around the tip of South Africa and across the Indian Ocean. But it was a long, difficult journey. There had to be a shorter route, he thought. Possibly he could sail through the Americas to the Pacific Ocean and avoid Africa and the Portuguese. If so, he would then be on his way to the Spice Islands by a faster, safer route. Fame and fortune would surely be his.

Magellan did not find an easy route through the Americas. But in 1520 he did find a way *around* them, through a passageway at the southern tip of South America (now called the Strait of Magellan). It took him 38 days to sail through it to the Pacific. For 99 more days, the ships he led sailed across the Pacific Ocean without finding a place to rest and get food and water. Finally, the sick, starving crew arrived at what is now the island of Guam. Magellan then knew that a voyage around the world was possible.

In our imaginary story, the survivors of Magellan's voyage (the ones who lived) have finally returned to Spain. Two of them are talking about their experiences. One is Juan Sebastian del Cano, captain of the ship *Victoria*. The other is Don Antonio Pigafetta, an Italian traveler who took part in the voyage. The two men stand shakily on the deck of the ragged and weather-beaten ship.

Ask yourself why Captain del Cano and Don Antonio have different opinions about Magellan? Why does Don Antonio feel that Magellan deserves more credit than Captain del Cano for making the round-the-world voyage?

31

Off the coast of Spain, September 7, 1522

DON ANTONIO. Captain, Captain, is that really Spain I see?

DEL CANO. Yes, Don Antonio, we will be landing in Seville tomorrow.

DON ANTONIO. I can't believe my eyes. After three years at sea! And your ship, the *Victoria*, is the only one of the five that left Spain to return, Captain del Cano. Our voyage has shown all of Europe that it is possible to sail around the earth.

DEL CANO. I wish I could be as excited as you. But I am so weak from sickness and lack of food that I can hardly stand. Thank God that even a few of us are still alive.

DON ANTONIO. Just 18 men are with us. If only Magellan could have been one of them! How the sight of Spain would have thrilled him! Remember how hard he worked to make this voyage possible?

DEL CANO. Why did you have to mention Magellan's name?

DON ANTONIO. Because the voyage was his idea. His planning, imagination, and leadership made it come true.

DEL CANO. And what about the rest of us? There were five ships with five captains. Magellan was just one of the captains. He had his ship; the others belonged to their captains.

DON ANTONIO. I must differ with you, Captain del Cano. Magellan was the captain general. Remember how jealous you were that he was in command? Remember how you tried and failed to get him to turn back two years ago? How quickly you forget!

Both men were silent as they recalled the events of early 1520. Magellan's fleet had sailed as far as the southern part of South America. Each day Magellan expected to find a passage or an opening from the Atlantic Ocean to the Pacific Ocean. He felt that he could not fail. The ships came to what is now called the Rio de la Plata, but it turned out to be a river, not an opening to the Pacific.

Farther and farther south the ships sailed. Magellan would not stop even though the officers and crews of the four other ships did not want to go on. The men insisted that they vote whether or not to continue the voyage. This was not a mutiny. It was a vote that Spanish crews were permitted to take at that time. Magellan saw that the crews would no longer follow his orders to continue sailing farther south. He decided to talk to them to try to convince them that he, Magellan, was right.

On February 2, 1520, Magellan spoke to the crews of the five ships. (Because the seasons in the Southern Hemisphere are the reverse of those in the Northern Hemisphere, autumn was approaching. Most of South America is in the Southern Hemisphere. Spain is in the Northern Hemisphere.)

Magellan argued that they must sail farther south to avoid being caught in territory belonging to the Portuguese enemies of their king. The freezing weather of the Antarctic winter would not cause them problems, he assured them, because the passageway to the Pacific was sure to be near. Once they sailed through it, they would soon find warmth and wealth in the Spice Islands. The crews voted to continue south.

DEL CANO. Magellan was quite a talker. He convinced the men that we were close to the passageway, but he was a dreamer. Remember, we sailed south for 60 more days—1,000 miles down the coast of South America. Some days we pushed forward for a few miles; other days we were moved backward by the headwinds.

DON ANTONIO. And what of Magellan? You forget that he was the leader, with responsibility for all of us. I watched him during those 60 days. He never rested and never wore dry clothes. The winds tore at the ships and brought hail and sleet. Ice covered the rigging. Still, Magellan carried on. What a man! What a leader!

DEL CANO. Yes, what a leader! We couldn't light any fires because of the winds and storms. We had no warm food for 60 days. For a meal we ate a piece of dried fish or salt pork or perhaps a soggy biscuit and a handful of raisins. We had sores on our skin, and waterlogged shoes rubbed our feet raw. The palms of our hands and our fingers cracked. Icicles formed on our beards, and the tips of our noses, ears, and toes were frostbitten.

DON ANTONIO. Of course we suffered, but he suffered along with us. He knew that we had gone as far as we could, so on March 31, 1520, we anchored at Port San Julian. There we were sheltered from the harshness of the winter.

DEL CANO. The men could take no more punishment.

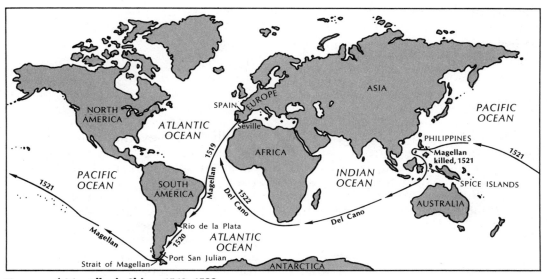

Voyage of Magellan's Ships, 1519–1522

DON ANTONIO. Magellan asked for the loyalty and support of the men. He told them of his promises to King Charles of Spain that he would not turn back until he got to the Spice Islands. They agreed to follow him.

DEL CANO. The men were easily fooled by Magellan's fancy words. But the officers were not.

DON ANTONIO. Right, the officers mutinied. You tried to take over the fleet, but you failed. Magellan was too clever and too brave for you!

DEL CANO. We failed because we were weak. We had our chance to take over the fleet, but we could not do it. The leaders of the mutiny, myself included, were sentenced to die.

DON ANTONIO. But Magellan did not kill you.

DEL CANO. No, we were put to hard labor. In chains, up to my waist in water, and in the freezing weather, I repaired the ships' hulls. I worked the pumps and cut wood.

DON ANTONIO. Better than death, eh, Captain?

DEL CANO. Perhaps, but we were almost dead. Magellan gave us just enough food to keep us alive.

DON ANTONIO. After three months, he restored you to duty.

DEL CANO. It was not kindness. He needed us for the voyage to the Pacific.

DON ANTONIO. If only Captain General Magellan could be with us today. It is too bad he was killed in the useless battle with natives in the Philippine Islands.

DEL CANO. Too bad, indeed! But he isn't here—and he will never be here. I am the one who brought back this load of spices. The credit of the journey around the world will always be mine. I am the one who sailed around the globe.

DON ANTONIO. No, Captain del Cano, this is a ship from Magellan's fleet. It is Magellan's voyage around the world—even if he cannot be with us. People will always remember his name. Yours will be forgotten.

POSTSCRIPT

King Charles of Spain welcomed Captain del Cano as a hero who had sailed around the earth. He gave Del Cano a fancy coat of arms and a large pension. But the king refused to make him a knight of Santiago, as Magellan had been, and rejected Captain del Cano's pleas for other favors.

Del Cano was appointed chief pilot of the second armada (fleet) to the Moluccas. When he tried to duplicate Magellan's achievements in the passage through the Strait of Magellan, he suffered huge losses. Later he died at sea.

Don Antonio wrote and talked about his experiences with Magellan. He became popular and successful. He always insisted that Magellan be given full credit for leading the first voyage around the globe.

Homework Questions

1. How did Magellan's route differ from that of Columbus?
2. Why did Del Cano and Don Antonio have different opinions about Magellan?
3. How did Magellan persuade his men to sail farther south?
4. What was life on board ship like for Magellan's men as they sailed south along the coast of South America?
5. Why did Don Antonio say that people will remember Magellan's name?

Understanding the Story

A. Write *F* for each statement that is a fact and *O* for each statement that is an opinion.
   1. Magellan was the greatest navigator who ever lived.
   2. One of Magellan's ships sailed around the world.
   3. Magellan found a passageway in South America between the Atlantic and Pacific oceans.
   4. Magellan should not have fought against the natives in the Philippines.
   5. Juan Sebastian del Cano was captain of the *Victoria*.
   6. Magellan should have killed the leaders of the mutiny against him.
   7. Del Cano wanted credit for sailing around the world.
   8. Don Antonio was as good a sailor as Del Cano.

B. List the numbers of the statements Don Antonio made or might have made.
   1. Magellan was not much of a leader.
   2. If only Magellan were here.
   3. Magellan's planning made the voyage possible.
   4. Magellan should have turned back.
   5. Magellan deserved to be killed.
   6. Magellan must be given full credit for the first voyage around the globe.
   7. The men were fooled by Magellan's fancy words.
   8. Magellan was the captain general of the fleet.

C. Imagine that you are the king of Spain. You need a leader for a trip to explore the west coast of the Americas. Will you choose Captain del Cano? Why or why not?

Activities and Inquiries

1. Study the map of Magellan's voyage around the world on page 33. Then answer the following questions.
   a. Which continents did Magellan's ships visit? Which islands?
   b. List the oceans Magellan's men crossed.
   c. Which continents were *not* visited?
   d. Trace Magellan's voyage on a globe. Then explain how it proved that the earth is round.
2. Write an outline for a motion picture about the voyage of Magellan.
3. Imagine that Magellan returned to Spain. Write a speech that he might have made before the king.
4. Suppose that you are a reporter and that Magellan is holding a press conference. What questions would you like to ask him?
5. What will Magellan say in response to your questions?

3 Montezuma Meets Cortez

When Magellan started his round-the-world voyage in 1519, Europeans knew nothing about the Aztec peoples of Mexico. But by the time Magellan's ship, the *Victoria*, returned to Spain in 1522, Europeans had heard about the treasures of the Aztecs.

The highly developed culture of the Aztecs became well known in Europe because of the adventures of Hernando Cortez. He was given the job of setting up a trading post on the coast of Mexico. In February, 1519, Cortez left Cuba with 11 ships, about 600 men, and perhaps most important, guns and horses.

Although greatly outnumbered by the Aztecs, Cortez won many victories and conquered the Aztec Empire for Spain. His conquest led to a gold rush. Adventurers from Spain poured into Mexico and what is now the U.S. Southwest. For the first time, people in Europe became really interested in the New World because they wanted gold for themselves.

In this chapter we find Montezuma, the emperor of the Aztecs, in his palace in Tenochtitlán (now Mexico City). The emperor is disturbed by many problems—especially the coming of Cortez.

Ask yourself why Montezuma is afraid. Is his fear justified? Should he have fought Cortez?

Tenochtitlán, Mexico, 1519

I am Montezuma, Emperor of the Aztecs. I am a rich and powerful man who has everything a person can want. In my palace at Tenochtitlán, I have 3,000 servants and the greatest jewels and works of art made by my people. Everyone worships me. Even though I have their love and respect, my people are afraid of me. No one dares to look at my face. When I come near, all turn away. In the streets my nobles walk before me. They sweep the ground and place cloaks down for me as I walk because my feet must not touch the earth.

I have a guard of 200 chiefs. When they are with me, they must wear cloaks of little value and walk with bare feet. They must never turn their backs on me. No one may speak to me when I eat or make a noise above a whisper. No one may eat until I have completed my meal. Then, and only then, are a thousand dishes served to my guards and servants.

If all this wealth and power is mine, why am I afraid?

My future and that of my people worry me because the omens for the future are all bad. When the wise men of the nearby town of Texcoco predicted the fall of my empire, I challenged their ruler to play a game. I made a ridiculous bet of three turkeys against his kingdom.

I lost because I was too sure of myself. I looked like a fool. The gods spoke out against me, Montezuma, Emperor of the Aztecs.

Now another challenge faces me. I hear stories about four-legged monsters with human bodies on their backs landing on our shores. These strangers use weapons we have never seen. With a great noise, the weapons shoot fire and smoke. We outnumber the strangers, but they are able to kill our people easily.

I have a right to be afraid.

Are these invaders gods? Or are they messengers of the gods? Are they here to tell us that our empire is soon to fall?

What shall I do? Shall I fight the invaders? Would it be better for me to die bravely in battle? The strangers have won battle after battle. It seems they cannot lose. No, I will not fight the invaders yet. I will wait and see what happens.

Cortez, the strangers' leader, has been assured of my friendship. I sent him gold and jewels and invited him to visit my capital of Tenochtitlán. For now, I will watch the invaders to discover their weaknesses. Let them come deeper and deeper into my empire until my warriors can surround and crush them.

Indeed, why should I worry? Perhaps these strangers have come here only to get gold, silver, and precious stones. If we give them what they want, will they not leave? Let them look around. We will treat them kindly, and they will leave us in peace. Ah, if only I could be sure of that!

Cortez is coming closer every day. What shall I do? Where shall I hide? No, I cannot hide. I am the emperor.

Montezuma (*seated left*) and Cortez holding a meeting.
(*Courtesy of The American Museum of Natural History*)

I know what I will do. I will send more gold to him. I will tell him that we have no food and that the roads are bad. The city can be entered only by canoe. Ah, it is hopeless. He does not believe us; he continues his march to Tenochtitlán.

I have decided what to do. I will stay and meet the gods. Whatever happens to me will happen. Yes, I am afraid. All Aztecs are afraid. We know that we may not win the struggle against the gods and the weapons of the gods.

POSTSCRIPT

On November 8, 1519, Cortez and his 400 remaining men finally met Montezuma. Cortez said to Montezuma, "Is it you? Are you truly Montezuma?" Montezuma replied, "I am Montezuma. You have arrived in your city of Tenochtitlán. The throne and the people are yours. You have come through the clouds and the snow. You have come down to earth to live in your palaces. Rest now. Welcome to your kingdom, lords!"

Cortez answered, "Fear nothing, Montezuma. We love you very much. We are happy to see you and speak with you and to reach your house in Tenochtitlán."

Montezuma, Cortez, and their followers embraced. Yet Cortez was afraid. He was outnumbered and surrounded by many thousands of Aztecs. He did not trust the Aztecs, and he thought they did not trust him. Six days later Cortez and his men felt powerful enough to imprison Montezuma. The Aztec leader gave in to his fears that he could not win against the "gods" and did what the Spaniards told him to do.

In time, the Aztecs forced Montezuma to give up his power and turned on the Spaniards. Cortez brought Montezuma to the roof of the palace to speak to his Aztec warriors, but they refused to listen. According to the Spanish story, three stones hit Montezuma, and he died from the wounds. According to the Aztecs, the Spanish killed Montezuma.

Cortez's horses were an important reason for his success against the Aztecs. The Aztecs were frightened when they saw the four-legged monsters because the horse was unlike any animal they had seen before. More important, Spanish horsemen killed and wounded many Aztecs with the accurate fire of their crossbows and guns.

Homework Questions

1. Why did Spanish officials send Cortez to Mexico?
2. How did the Aztecs show their respect for Montezuma?
3. Why was Montezuma afraid of Cortez?
4. How did Montezuma plan to encourage Cortez to leave Mexico?
5. Why was Cortez afraid after he had captured Montezuma?

Understanding the Story

A. Complete each of the following sentences by filling in the missing word or words.
   1. The Aztecs became well known in Europe because of the adventures of _____.
   2. Cortez was given the job of setting up a trading post on the coast of _____.
   3. _____ was the emperor of the Aztecs.

4. Montezuma thought the Spanish might be _____.
5. Even nobles dared not look at Montezuma's _____.
6. No one could eat until Montezuma _____.
7. Montezuma thought that horses were _____.
8. Cortez was outnumbered and surrounded by _____.

B. Write *A* for each statement that Montezuma would agree with and *N* for each statement that he would not agree with.
1. I wish I had more jewels and works of art.
2. Everyone loves and respects me.
3. I have a right to be afraid.
4. I will never give gold and jewels to Cortez.
5. Cortez is just like any other man.
6. I will stay and meet Cortez.
7. I will kill Cortez when I meet him.
8. Monsters are landing on our shores.

C. Imagine that you are a ruler like Montezuma. You face an enemy you believe to be far more powerful than you. Will you fight? Give reasons for and against fighting, and tell what you would do.

Activities and Inquiries

1. Montezuma tells the story in this chapter. Retell the story from the point of view of Cortez.
2. You are Montezuma's adviser. Tell him how to save his kingdom.
3. Use references in your library to find out how Aztec life was changed by the coming of the Spaniards. Report on your findings.
4. Look at the picture on page 37 and answer the following questions.
   a. Why has Montezuma given these gifts to Cortez?
   b. What does Cortez want?
   c. What should Montezuma say to Cortez?

4 Cartier Finds the St. Lawrence River

While Spain was exploring and conquering parts of the New World, other countries were not idle. England sent out John Cabot in 1497. He landed somewhere on or near the northeastern coast of America—probably in Newfoundland. He took possession of the land in the name of the English king. Cabot was sure he had found the northern part of Asia. If he could sail a little farther on his next voyage, he felt sure he would reach Japan. But John Cabot died at sea on that next voyage.

In 1508 Sebastian Cabot, John's son, also sailed to North America to search for a way to Asia. England later based its claims to land in North America on the voyages of the Cabots.

France did not want to be left out of

the search for treasure in Asia. So King Francis I hired Giovanni da Verrazano, another seaman from Genoa, to look for a passage through the New World to the Indies. The silk merchants of the French city of Lyons paid for Verrazano's voyage. They wanted to shorten the sea route to China, where they could buy silk cloth.

In 1524 Verrazano entered New York Bay and then Narragansett Bay (Rhode Island). From there he sailed northeast as far as Nova Scotia. When none of the waterways he saw turned out to be a shortcut to China, the merchants of Lyons felt they had wasted their money.

Sailing from France in 1533, Jacques Cartier also dreamed of finding a northwest passage to Asia. He traveled west along the coast of Newfoundland to the Gulf of St. Lawrence. Cartier met Indians for the first time on Prince Edward Island and the Gaspé Peninsula. Polar bears and walruses impressed him greatly, and so did the huge trees on Prince Edward Island. In fact, he landed four times just to examine the trees, which were several hundred years old. No passage to the Pacific Ocean could be found, so he took two Indians aboard ship and returned to France to plan his next voyage.

The second trip started in 1535. When Cartier returned to his home port of St. Malo, on the northwest coast of France, he immediately reported to the king of France. The following imaginary letter tells about this second voyage, on which he discovered the St. Lawrence River. (He called it the River of Canada.)

Ask yourself whether Cartier was justified in thinking that his voyage had been successful. Why was King Francis I interested in the discovery of a northwest passage?

St. Malo, France, 1536

Special Dispatch to: King Francis I, Ruler of France

Your Royal Majesty:

I landed in St. Malo today. I have so much to tell you about my voyage to the New World that I simply cannot wait until I see you in Paris. I want you to hear my good news at once.

Your Majesty, I hope you will agree that this was the most successful voyage ever made for our beloved France. I saw and heard things that are impossible for Europeans to imagine.

I am bringing Chief Donnaconna of the Huron Indian nation to see you. He will talk to you about the Kingdom of Saguenay and describe the mines of gold, silver, and rubies there. Even spices grow in the region of the Saguenay, he says. There is great wealth in what we have called Canada, Your Majesty. We will find it on my next voyage. Because France will then have more gold and silver than are in all of Mexico, we can challenge Spain.

But there is even more exciting news. We are very close to discovering the northwest passage to the Indies and China.

Although I failed to find the shortcut through America on my voyage last year, this time I was fortunate. I sailed along the northern coast of the Gulf of St. Lawrence, and suddenly there it was—the mouth of a great river, the River of Canada. Feeling sure that this must be the northwest passage to the Pacific Ocean, I turned the ships into that river to sail into the unknown.

We moved very slowly because we had no idea where we might find rocks and shallows. I knew that if we hit rocks, the ships could be damaged beyond repair. Often we left our ships and rowed our small boats close to shore on both sides of the river. Danger seemed to be everywhere.

We saw many whales and great beasts like oxen. These oxen [walruses] have two tusks in their jaws and swim in the water.

At last we came to a large Indian village called Stadacona [Quebec]. The Indians were frightened when they saw us and ran away. However, our two Indian interpreters called them back, and they swarmed around us. It was a blessing to have our two Indians who could speak both French and Huron.

Next day, the Huron chief, Donnaconna, came to see us. Our two Indians told him how well Your Majesty had treated them in France. But Donnaconna did not trust us and refused to give us permission to continue up the river. He tried to frighten us by sending three Indians dressed like devils downriver in a canoe. They made terrible noises, but they could not change my mind. I took one ship and two rowboats and moved upstream to the Indian village of Hochelaga [Montreal].

Outside Hochelaga, we saw fields planted with Indian corn. Each ear is covered with grains about the size of a pea. Indians live on corn as we in Europe live on wheat.

I should also tell you about tobacco. The Indians grind tobacco leaves into a powder and put it into pipes, which they place in their mouths. They lay a small piece of burning wood on top of each pipe

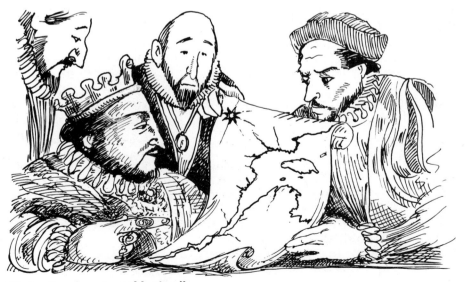

"But a river is not a gold mine."

to set fire to the tobacco. The smoke then pours out of their mouths and noses. I tried smoking but did not like it because the tobacco tasted like powdered pepper. The Indians say that tobacco keeps them warm and healthy. It must be true because many of them walk naked through the winter snow. We French froze, but the Indians looked comfortable!

Near Hochelaga is a high mountain. I named it Mount Royal in Your Majesty's honor. I climbed it one day and saw mile after mile of land I wanted to explore. As far as the eye could see, the River of Canada stretched out—long and wide.

After I climbed back down the mountain and returned to my ship, I moved upriver beyond Hochelaga. Then I could go no farther because of the rapids. Indians told me that there was clear sailing beyond the rapids if only I could somehow get around them. I could not do it this time, but on my next voyage I will be prepared. We will carry small boats and supplies on our backs over the Indian trails around the rapids until we reach smooth water.

I know this river will be the way to the Kingdom of the Saguenay and to the Pacific Ocean. Soon the wealth of China and the Indies will be ours, and our glorious French nation will be the leader of the world in trade.

Your Majesty, I will be in Paris in two weeks. I cannot wait to describe every detail of what I have seen and done on this voyage. Afterward, I hope to discuss plans for my return to the New World.

I hope and pray that Your Majesty is in his usual excellent health.

Your obedient mariner,

Jacques Cartier

POSTSCRIPT

King Francis believed the stories of Chief Donnaconna and Cartier. He thought that the precious metals of the Saguenay would make France rich and powerful. In 1541 Cartier returned to the New World with ten ships. But he failed to find a shortcut to China or discover the Kingdom of the Saguenay. Its wealth seemed always beyond the next rapid or around the next bend of the river. Cartier sailed back to France with iron pyrites (fool's gold) that he thought were gold and with quartz crystals that he hoped were diamonds. They were all worthless. "Canadian diamonds" became a joking phrase in France to describe something of no value.

Cartier's voyages did not make France rich. But his explorations of the St. Lawrence River opened Canada to French settlements. Cartier has been called the Christopher Columbus of France.

Homework Questions

1. Why did the merchants of Lyons feel that they had wasted the money given to Verrazano?
2. Why did Cartier want to reach the Kingdom of Saguenay?
3. What dangers did Cartier face in taking his ships up the St. Lawrence River?
4. How did Chief Donnaconna try to discourage Cartier?
5. What did Cartier report about corn and tobacco?
6. Why is Cartier called the Christopher Columbus of France?

Understanding the Story

A. Write *T* for each statement that is true, *F* for each statement that is false, and *N* for each statement that is not mentioned in this chapter.
  1. Verrazano found the northwest passage to India.
  2. Cartier's discoveries made France rich and powerful.
  3. Cartier thought that the St. Lawrence River would lead to the Pacific Ocean.
  4. Sailing up the St. Lawrence was the most dangerous voyage of all.
  5. Cartier saw whales and walruses.
  6. Indian corn is a better food than wheat.
  7. Indians said that tobacco made them warm and healthy.
  8. Cartier has been called the Cortez of France.

B. Choose the term or phrase that best completes each statement.
  1. One result of Cartier's voyages was that (*a*) Canada was opened to French settlers   (*b*) he found a northwest passage   (*c*) New England was opened to French settlers.
  2. In Canada Cartier hoped to find (*a*) gold   (*b*) tall buildings   (*c*) large cities.
  3. Cartier returned to France with (*a*) gold and diamonds   (*b*) an Indian chief   (*c*) animals of North America.
  4. The mountain Cartier named in honor of the king of France was (*a*) Mount Francis   (*b*) Mount Royal   (*c*) Mount Washington.
  5. King Francis I thought that Cartier's voyages (*a*) would lead to war with England   (*b*) were a waste of time   (*c*) would make France rich and powerful.
  6. On his next trip, Cartier planned to get past the rapids by (*a*) carrying small boats around them   (*b*) sailing the large ships through them   (*c*) looking for another route.
  7. Chief Donnaconna (*a*) told Cartier that he could sail as far as he wished up the river   (*b*) refused to give Cartier permission to sail up the river   (*c*) helped Cartier to move around the rapids.
  8. During the cold winter, the Indians (*a*) suffered more than the Europeans   (*b*) stayed indoors   (*c*) walked naked through the ice and snow.

C. Imagine that you are Jacques Cartier. How will you treat the Indians you meet in Canada? Write a memo to your helpers explaining how they should act toward Indians, and the reasons why.

Activities and Inquiries

1. Look at the cartoon on page 41 and answer the following questions.
   a. Why is the king disappointed?
   b. How would Cartier answer the king?
   c. How would you have answered the king?
   d. How would the people of Canada and the United States answer the king?
2. Imagine that you are Cartier and that you must prepare a summary of your second trip for the king. Write the summary.
3. Assume that you are the king of France. You read Cartier's summary. What parts please you?
4. Using library references, prepare an outline map of North America. On it trace Cartier's voyages.
5. Copy the following chart headings into your notebook. *Explorer / Nation / Discovery or Accomplishment / Goal or Purpose.* Then fill in information about the explorers described in Unit Two.

Who Built America?

JUAN. Hey, Mr. Miller, this is a pretty good unit.

MR. MILLER. Thanks, Juan. What do you like most about it?

JUAN. The names, Mr. Miller. I like the sound of the Spanish names.

ROSA. Just one minute. Sure, Columbus and others sailed for Spain. But he was Italian. An Italian discovered America.

MR. MILLER. You both have a right to be proud.

CARLA. Yes, we're proud. For one unit we've heard names like ours. Now we'll be back to names like Washington and Jefferson and, and—

CASIMIR. Adams and Madison and Jackson and Lee.

MR. MILLER. You're right. You will read about people with English-sounding names. But there will also be many names like your own.

SAM. Yeah, yeah. You'd think that no Jewish people helped build America.

MR. MILLER. No. I promise that this course will be different. We'll talk about all the people who made our country great.

CASIMIR. What about the Polish people?

HEINRICH. And the Germans?

TOM. And the Irish?

HANS. And the Dutch?

JOSEPHINE. What about black people? Sure, you'll talk about slaves. I want to know what free blacks did.

RICARDO. And what about my group? Mexicans didn't just fight a war against the United States. They did plenty for this country.

ROBERT. So did the French.

JANET. Let's hear more about women in the United States.

MR. MILLER. All right, class. I'm telling you that no group will be overlooked.

VOICES. How can we learn about all of them?

MR. MILLER. Easy. We'll plan individual reports about Americans of many ethnic backgrounds, people you are really interested in.

VOICES. Okay, let's do it. When do we start?

MR. MILLER. How about right now?

"You were right, Mr. Miller. I did learn something new about the explorers."

"Yes, Jack?"

"Well, Columbus, Cortez, Cartier, and Magellan were a lot alike."

"In what way?"

"They all knew exactly what they wanted to do. Nothing could stop them from reaching their goals. They built their lives around those goals."

"Isn't that necessary for success in many things?" asked Mr. Miller.

"I suppose so," replied Jack. "But they all had unusual dreams. Columbus thought he could find the passage to the Indies by sailing west. That was his goal in life. Magellan had to prove that the earth was round by sailing around it. He didn't live to finish the voyage, but one of his ships made it."

"Very good, Jack."

"And that Cartier," continued Jack, "he dreamed that the northwest passage was just around the next bend of the St. Lawrence River. It's interesting that Columbus, Cartier, and Magellan all did great things, but none of them saw his dreams come true."

"But some people do see their dreams come true," said Mr. Miller. "Look at Cortez."

"Oh, he was unusual. He and a few men took on Montezuma and the Aztec Empire and won. He was an adventurer—a real soldier of fortune! By the way, Mr. Miller, which explorer do we read about next?"

"Explorers find new lands, but they don't build them up. Let's find out how people from Europe came to America and stayed here. Let's find out about the people who started the colonies."

Colonizing America

"Explorers are exciting people," said Jack. "But who cares about settlers?"

"The settlers had their adventures too, Jack. They took many risks in America and often lived dangerous lives. You'll see."

"I hope so, Mr. Miller, because the colonists all sound dull to me. I remember that they were mostly people running away from their problems. Because they were unhappy in Europe, they got out. America must have seemed like the best place to go."

"True, Jack, but do you think that every unhappy person wanted to come to the New World?"

"No, I guess it wasn't that simple," said Jack. "Maybe a person had to be a little braver than most to make the voyage. But even people who weren't so brave might want to be colonists in some cases. If I were in jail because I owed a person money, I'd take a chance on America. Anything would be better than staying in jail!"

"Some of the first settlers would have agreed with you. But not many of them had to choose between jail and America."

"All right, Mr. Miller. Let's say that some colonists were looking for adventure, a new life, or just a change of scene."

"Exactly. Can you imagine what life must have been like for a poor person in 17th-century England?"

"Well, they didn't eat or live too well. With no voice in the government, they had to do as they were told. And their future was probably more of the same. Why not try life in America?"

"You're beginning to see the light," Mr. Miller said with a smile. "Now, let's say that the government disapproves of your religion."

"So the authorities make it tough for me? Then I'd leave. But wasn't life difficult in America, too? How did they live?"

"Slow down, Jack. You'll get your answers in this unit on the settlement of the colonies."

1 Life in Jamestown

England had little success in its efforts to colonize the New World in the 1500's. One English adventurer, Sir Humphrey Gilbert, tried to start a colony on the coast of Newfoundland. When his ship sank in a storm in 1583, he lost his gamble and his life.

In 1585 and again in 1587, Sir Walter Raleigh, Gilbert's half-brother, sent settlers to colonize Roanoke Island, off the coast of North Carolina. The first group returned to England. The second disappeared, possibly the victims of disease. (One of the lost settlers was Virginia Dare, the first English child born in the New World.) As the 16th century ended, the English had still not managed to start a colony in North America.

One reason was that England was pouring much of its energy into competing with Spain for control of the seas. In 1588 England defeated the Spanish Armada (fleet) in a famous sea battle near the English coast. In 1604 the English ruler, James I, finally signed a peace treaty with the Spanish. By this time the English had less to fear from Spanish seapower. Money, men, and ships could now go to colonizing the New World.

A number of English businessmen formed the Virginia Company of London in order to profit from the settlement of colonies in North America. In 1607 the company's first settlers landed in what is now Virginia. They founded the colony of Jamestown, or James Towne, as it was first called. Some newcomers were free people, guaranteed the same rights they enjoyed in England. Others were like the young man in our story. He was one of many English subjects in their late teens and early twenties who secured passage to the New World by becoming indentured servants.

Such servants agreed to work for and be ruled by a colonial master for four to seven years. Then they would become free. In return, the master paid their passage and provided food, clothing, and shelter. Indentured servants came from many walks of life. Among them were convicts, political prisoners, poor people, adventure seekers, and people who were trying to escape from religious persecution.

Ask yourself whether you would have been willing to become an indentured servant.

James Towne, Virginia, December, 1618

Dear Mother and Father,

Please, please, I beg you to get me out of James Towne. I live only to get home to England again.

Why did I listen to that man from the Virginia Company? Why did I trust him? I can hear him saying, "We will pay your passage to America. It will not cost you one penny. All you have to do is work for seven years at whatever jobs we ask of you. After that you will be free and can work at anything you choose. We will give you a share of Virginia Company stock and part of the profits. We'll even give you a piece of land. You may never be rich, but you will have more than if you stay in England."

You know I was not happy at home. I did not want to be a tailor like you, Father. I wanted to see far-off places, have adventure and excitement. I wanted to make something of myself, too. This sounded like my best opportunity.

The title page of a pamphlet advertising America to the English. It was printed in 1609.

(*The Bettmann Archive, Inc.*)

I asked the man if there weren't other things I'd have to do.

"No," he said. "Just whatever tasks are set out for you. No hidden obligations, no debts."

He made James Towne sound wonderful, too. Green fields, good farmland, trees hundreds of feet high. More food than I could eat and ships from England every week. The woods full of animals for meat, streams overflowing with fish. My own room and a comfortable bed.

Ah, dear Mother and Father, how that man could talk! I signed the paper. Now I am an indentured servant without rights. I am virtually a slave for seven years. I must do everything they tell me. They beat me; they starve me. I dream constantly of running away, but I know what will happen if they find me. You remember Tom, I am sure. He ran away. They caught him a few days later and beat him to death!

The Virginia Company man said I would be a free landowner after seven years. I'm sure I will never live to see that day. Each day people die of the shaking disease [malaria], spotted fever [typhoid fever], or starvation, or they freeze to death. Each day bodies are buried in our small cemetery. Burial must be done very soon after death. Otherwise, it is feared that people may eat the corpses. Starving people eat anything: rats, cats, dogs, or other horrible things.

Mother and Father, I am freezing. I have one pair of stockings, one pair of shoes, and one hat. I do not have a shirt on my back. Two rags cover my body. I had a coat, but a young fellow stole it. I cannot prove it, but I think he traded my coat for some meat from a ship that recently arrived. Why did he not at least share the meat with me? I would willingly have given my coat for any decent food!

I am starving. Every day I grow weaker. I ate more in one day at home than I eat here in James Towne in a week. My food allowance is eight ounces of cornmeal and half a pint of peas for an entire day!

Do you have any idea of the kind of work I do? Last week I unloaded a ship. I was on and off that ship for two full days, working in the soaking rain. Then the wind blew so hard we thought that we would all be smashed to bits. It was nasty, dirty work.

What did they feed us on that ship? One loaf of bread for two men for the two days. After the two days, I got a plate of pea soup. I suppose I should be grateful that it was thick and not watery!

I am lucky to have a place to rest my tired body. No, I do not have my own room. With five other men, I share the space of one of your closets. There is scarcely enough air to breathe!

Mother and Father, I cannot stand it here any longer. Please, please pay my debt to the Virginia Company. If you love me, buy back my indenture. Otherwise, my life is over. Please act fast and rescue me. I will spend the rest of my life repaying you.

Your loving son,

Richard

POSTSCRIPT

In April, 1618, there were 400 settlers in Jamestown; by the end of the year there were 1,000. Between 1618 and 1624, about 4,000 more settlers arrived. Despite such heavy immigration, the population in 1624 was only 1,275. Many probably returned to England, but many more died in the colony.

In 1624 King James ordered an investigation of conditions in Jamestown. The report concluded that the settlers were being shockingly neglected by the Virginia Company of London. The king decided to do away with the Virginia Company and rule the colony himself.

In spite of the many hardships it had to suffer through, the community of Jamestown survived. As the years passed, settlers moved beyond Jamestown to start other communities and turn more land into farms.

Jamestown was much more than the first permanent English settlement in America. It was also the site of the first elected legislative assembly in the New World. This assembly, called the House of Burgesses, was set up in July, 1619. Jamestown served as the center of government for the Virginia colony until 1699, when the capital was moved to Williamsburg.

Homework Questions

1. Why did England fail to colonize the New World in the 1500's?
2. How did the man from the Virginia Company persuade Richard that he would be happy in Jamestown?
3. How were the company man's promises different from Richard's actual working conditions in Jamestown?
4. For what purpose was the House of Burgesses set up?

Understanding the Story

A. Write *F* for each statement that is a fact and *O* for each statement that is an opinion.
   1. Virginia Dare was the first English child born in America.
   2. The English should have had more American colonies by the end of the 16th century.
   3. England defeated the Spanish Armada.
   4. Richard should not return to England.

   1. I wanted to see far-off places.
   2. I can do nothing and go nowhere on my own.
   3. I enjoy living in James Towne because I am free.
   4. Each day people die of sickness or starvation.
   5. I am stronger than I was in England.
   6. The work is easy here.
   7. I am lucky that I have a place to rest my tired body.
   8. Indentured service is the life for me.

C. Imagine that you are living in the early 1600's. Would you be willing to indenture yourself, as Richard did, to settle in a new land? Why or why not?

Activities and Inquiries

1. On page 49 is the title page of a pamphlet that was used to try to convince English people to settle in Virginia. Guess what is written in the pamphlet. Would Richard say that the pamphlet is telling the truth? Explain your answer.
2. Write an advertisement for an indentured servant that might have appeared on a 17th-century English poster. Include a description of working conditions and benefits.
3. Suppose you could meet with Richard. What questions would you ask him?
4. What answers would Richard give to your questions?
5. Suppose Richard's parents take his letter to a director of the Virginia Company. How might the director react?

2 Blacks Come to the Colonies

Not every indentured servant who came to America was a white European. Nor could everyone ask parents for help. In 1619, one year after Richard wrote his letter, the first black people arrived in Jamestown from Africa. These individuals were considered to be indentured servants. The Dutch ship captain who brought them sold their indentures to people in the Virginia colony. Many, possibly all, of this group of blacks became free after they had served their time of indenture. Some may have been given land of their own.

As the years passed, the number of blacks in the Virginia colony and in the other English colonies along the Atlantic Coast of North America increased. Most were brought against their will. By 1660 about 1,000 blacks lived in Virginia and about 2,000 in the other colonies. The white population numbered about 26,000 in Virginia and 50,000 in the rest of the colonies.

At this time, few blacks were looked upon as slaves even if their period of service was for a lifetime.

Among the blacks who arrived in 1619 were two named Antony and Isabella. Their son William was the first black child born on the mainland of English North America, in 1624. Because not much is known of Antony and Isabella's real life, our story is imaginary. Experiences such as those described here were common to many blacks of this period and later years.

Antony and Isabella are landowners. By now they have an indentured servant of their own. They are sitting on the porch of their small farmhouse, not far from Jamestown. It is a hot, dry day. The sun has wilted the tobacco in their fields.

Ask yourself whether there were any differences between the white and black indentured servants. Why do you suppose William wants to know about his African past?

Near James Towne, Virginia, 1634

"No sign of rain," sighed Antony. "The fields sure could use some water."

William, helping his mother pat out corn cakes, looked up. "Father," he said, "tell me again about the old country. About the hyenas and the leopards and the village where you used to live."

Antony smiled. "That's the part I like to tell. You know it as well as I do, William. I was part of a poor family, but we were happy together. We lived in grasslands not far from the Gambia River in northwestern Africa. My father—your grandfather—used to take me hunting with him. There were antelopes, lions, and many kinds of birds. We always had enough to eat, even in the dry times like now, when crops wouldn't grow."

"What has happened to your father and the rest of your family?"

A frown clouded Antony's face. "I'm afraid we'll never know, William. We have no way of getting word from back home."

"But John and Roger and my other white friends still hear from *their* kin in England. Why don't we hear from Africa?" William wanted to know.

Antony sighed. "We came to America in quite a different manner from your friends' families, William. We came against our will—and we have no means of getting in touch with our loved ones."

William moved nearer and looked up at the older man. "Father, tell me again how you came here. I want to know all about Africa and all about coming to America. Someday maybe I will go back and see our relatives."

"It's not a pretty story, William. It begins with a raid on our village by warriors from a nearby village. They caught us by surprise, when my father and many other men were out hunting. Two men burst into our home and carried me away. They tied my hands tightly so I couldn't fight back. I was barely in my teens at the time, and they were stronger than I was."

"These were black men like you, weren't they, Father? Why did they want to capture you?"

"They wanted slaves, Son."

"But why? Did they have such large fields that they couldn't work them all themselves?"

"No, they didn't want slaves for themselves. They wanted slaves to sell. Oh, in the old days a village might have wanted slaves for itself. It would take people captured in a war and make them haul water and do many unpleasant tasks. Slavery like that is known all over the world. In recent times, however, a new kind of slave taking has begun. Some villages make a practice of grabbing as many slaves as they can and selling them to slave traders from Europe. That's what happened to me."

"Where did the black men take you?"

"They chained me to other young men they had grabbed, and made us walk for five days until we got to the seacoast. If one of us fell, they would beat him and make him keep walking."

"Then what?"

"The village sold us to a sea captain—a Spanish captain. When I saw what was happening, my heart sank. I had no idea where I was going or what I would be forced to do. But I knew I would never see my home or my dear parents again. I began to kick and struggle, trying to break free, but white sailors clubbed me and dragged me on board their ship."

"Is that when you first saw Mother?"

"Yes, your mother was on the ship already. She was in a cage with other women from her village."

Isabella spoke up for the first time. "You were limp and bleeding, Antony. You and many of the others."

Antony went on, "The women were allowed on the deck for part of the time. We men were led down to the cargo hold, where we had to lie on our backs and be chained to a platform. I'm six feet tall but the space they gave me was only five and a half feet long and about 16 inches wide. There was no way I could straighten my body. I couldn't have stood even if I hadn't been chained, because the ceiling was only three feet above my head."

"It must have been awful," said William.

"The smells and the noises made me sick. I could barely turn my head to look around. I wanted to die. How I prayed for release from that dismal hole."

"What else do you remember about the trip?" William asked.

"One day I felt sick. The sailors came with the slop they called food. I couldn't eat, and they became very angry. They took off my chains, dragged me to the deck above, and beat me with knotted ropes. Finally, they dragged me below again. How can men be so cruel to one another?"

"I will never forget those terrible days," said Isabella. "In dreams I still see two strong men jumping overboard. No one knows how they got on deck. They shouted that they would rather die than live that way. Only one was lucky enough to drown. He escaped from the cruel world of the living. Sailors rescued the other one and put him back in chains."

"I lost track of time," continued Antony. "I have no idea how many weeks I lay there on my back. One day I tried to talk to my chained companion. There was no answer. He was one of the lucky ones; he had died. He lay there rotting and smelling for three days before sailors took his body away. How I wished I was the one they were throwing overboard!"

"Did you have any idea where the ship was headed?" William asked.

"No. To me the ocean was a mysterious place. I had never even seen the ocean before, and I didn't know what lay on the other side.

Since then, I've learned that the ship was headed for the West Indies, where Spanish colonists grow sugar with the labor of African slaves. But we never got there. A Dutch ship attacked the one we were on and captured it. Many sailors and some of the blacks lost their lives. Those of us who lived were taken on board the Dutch ship and brought to James Towne."

"I guess you're lucky you didn't end up on a sugar plantation," said William.

"Very lucky. But it wasn't too pleasant here in Virginia at first, either. The ship captain sold us as servants. For seven years we had to work like slaves and be treated like slaves."

"It wasn't all bad," Isabella remarked. "We got married. We had our happy moments. We knew the harshness and cruelty would not last forever. And now we are free. We have our own farm and our own indentured servant. We mingle with the whites. They're a little standoffish at times, but they seem to accept us as neighbors."

"I wonder," said Antony thoughtfully. "I wonder how long we will be accepted. I wonder what life will be like for our son and his children."

"Why are you worried, Antony?" asked Isabella. "More Africans are arriving as indentured servants. I feel perfectly safe in Virginia."

"Well, I can't say that I do," Antony replied. "What's to stop the whites from keeping Africans under contract for 10 years or 14 years or 20 years or, heaven help us, for life?"

"Let's hope that never happens in Virginia," said Isabella.

William looked wistful. "I wonder what my grandparents would say if I showed up back in Africa someday. Do you think I'll ever get to see Father's old village?"

"Why are you worried, Antony?"

POSTSCRIPT

Antony was right to be worried. In the 1660's Virginia and Maryland changed their laws about servants. From this time on, Africans brought into these colonies were indentured servants for *life*. They were slaves. Some free blacks continued to live in the colonies, but their rights were restricted by many laws.

Homework Questions

1. Why does William want to know about his relatives?
2. According to Antony, how had slave taking in Africa changed in recent times?
3. What was life aboard the slave ship like for Antony and Isabella?
4. What were Antony and Isabella's lives like as indentured servants?

Understanding the Story

A.   List the numbers of the statements that are true.
   1. All indentured servants were white Europeans.
   2. Antony and Isabella were brought from Africa.
   3. William wanted to know more about his relatives.
   4. Antony did not object to going with the slave traders.
   5. Antony was chained below deck on the slave ship.
   6. Antony tried to jump from the slave ship.
   7. Antony and Isabella landed in James Towne.
   8. Antony and Isabella enjoyed being indentured servants.

B.   List the numbers of the statements Antony made or might have made.
   1. Life in Africa was bitter and hard.
   2. My family was poor, but we were happy.
   3. Black Africans never take slaves.
   4. I was sold to a Dutch sea captain.
   5. I wanted to die.
   6. How can men be so cruel to one another?
   7. We had an easy life as indentured servants.
   8. I don't feel safe in Virginia.

C.   Find out how your family originally came to the United States. How did their experiences compare with those of Antony and Isabella?

Activities and Inquiries

1. Study the drawing on page 55. Then answer the following questions: Why was Antony worried? What probably happened to William?
2. Imagine that Antony and Isabella are now slaves, and you are interviewing them. You ask them how they would compare the life of an indentured servant with that of a slave. How do they answer?
3. Write an outline for a television film about the lives of Antony, Isabella, and other black indentured servants.
4. Antony and Isabella meet Richard, the white indentured servant in Chapter 1. They all discuss how they came to the Virginia colony. How were Antony and Isabella's experiences different from Richard's? How do you account for the differences?

3 The Pilgrims Sign an Agreement

Now we turn from Virginia in the south to New England in the north. Our story starts at a time of religious troubles in England. That nation had an official state church—the Church of England (also called the Anglican Church). This was a Protestant church tightly controlled by the king and supported by taxes. No other church was allowed to hold services in England. Roman Catholics, in particular, were persecuted (treated badly).

A group of English Protestants, known as Puritans, opposed the king's strict control over the Anglican Church. They wanted to "purify" the church by changing certain rituals, or ceremonies, that they thought were "too Catholic." They also wanted to end central control of the church. While most Puritans wanted to reform the Church of England from within, a few wanted to break away and start a new church. This group was known as Separatist Puritans or just Separatists.

Like Catholics, Separatists were persecuted in England, and in 1608 one group of them moved to Leiden in Holland. Although they were accepted in Leiden, life was not easy for them. The Separatists were foreigners in a strange land. They thought of moving on to America, but they had little money. The Virginia Company provided the answer to their problem. The English merchants of the Virginia Company agreed to provide a ship, a crew, and supplies. In return, the colonists would work in Virginia for seven years. Then the profits from their work would be divided between the colonists and the merchants.

In September, 1620, a ship called the *Mayflower* sailed for the New World. Most of the 102 people aboard as passengers were Separatists, 35 of them from Leiden and others from England. Those who were not Separatists were known as Strangers. Nine of the passengers were indentured servants. The majority of the passengers thought of themselves as pilgrims to a new land. Today we call these people the "Pilgrims."

Toward the middle of November, 1620, land was sighted. As our story opens, the adult freemen are standing on the deck of the *Mayflower*. All look pale and tired. The cold, gray day contributes to the feelings of hostility and tension.

Ask yourself why the Pilgrims came to America. Why is the Mayflower Compact so important?

Cape Cod, Massachusetts, November, 1620

WILLIAM BRADFORD. Captain Jones, where are we? What land is this?

CAPTAIN CHRISTOPHER JONES. This is Cape Cod, in what our map calls "New England." We are in shallow water, and we risk being shipwrecked. We are anchoring here.

JOHN CARVER. Cape Cod? What are you talking about? We're supposed to land in Virginia. In heaven's name, get us out of here. Pull up the anchor, and get on to the Hudson's River.

[The island of Manhattan, at the outlet of the Hudson River, was at the northern edge of the Virginia Company's territory.]

JONES. I am sorry, Mr. Carver, but this looks like a safe harbor. We have been at sea for many weeks. My men are sick and tired and need a rest. The sea is stormy, and winter is near. You are going to have to forget about Virginia. This is where the *Mayflower* stays.

THOMAS TINKER. The charter says we land in Virginia. I say let's go on to Virginia.

OTHER VOICES. On to Virginia. Let's get away from this cold, dreary place.

PETER BROWNE. Look at that shore. There's nothing on it. It doesn't look fit to grow anything. Is this where we're supposed to live? Who among you wants to die in this wilderness?

VOICES. Not I! Not I! Let's go on to Virginia!

BRADFORD. Captain Jones says we are staying here. We have no choice. We cannot sail the *Mayflower* without a captain and crew.

CARVER. We must be thankful to be in America. We will make our homes here.

VOICES. [*Murmurs of discontent.*]

WILLIAM BREWSTER. Let us not forget how good God has been to us. He brought us to America. He protected us; only one of us died at sea. We will prosper here and be happy.

BROWNE. We're not listening to you.

TINKER. Wait. It may not be such a bad idea to land here.

RICHARD GARDINER. What do you mean?

TINKER. We have a charter for land in Virginia—not in New England. If we land here, outside Virginia, our contract with those greedy merchants in London will not matter. You all know how unhappy we were when they insisted that all profits be shared in common for the first seven years.

GARDINER. That's true. They refused to let us work two days a week for ourselves or even to keep a private garden. It would serve them right if we stop here!

VOICES. We'll show them. Let's stay here!

BRADFORD. It would appear that we have little choice in any event. But this is a harsh land, and we face many dangers. Surely there are savages nearby. For our own protection, we must set up a system of government to take the place of our patent, our grant, from the company.

VOICES. Why bother? Who needs government? Every man for himself!

TINKER. You Pilgrims are in a majority. You can dominate any government we set up. I don't think that's fair.

BRADFORD. We're all in the same boat, Pilgrims and Strangers together. Surely as children of God we can work this out. If we don't stand together, the savages may well wipe us out.

CAPTAIN MYLES STANDISH (*in the booming voice of military command*) Quiet, men. Listen to Bradford and Carver. They know what they are talking about. You know me; I'm not a Pilgrim. I'm a soldier. Let them explain what they want to do.

[*John Carver holds up a paper.*]

TINKER. What's that?

BRADFORD. We have thought a great deal about what is the fair thing to do for all here. We have written a document for all men to sign. We will agree to set up our own government, with equal laws for everyone. And all must pledge to obey the laws that we shall make.

BROWNE. Why do we need laws? We've come here to escape bad laws.

CARVER. Exactly. But we must make good laws to take their place. A community cannot exist without laws. Laws will help us make sure that everyone lives safely, happily, and peacefully together.

TINKER. You say "we" must do this and laws will help "us." I suppose by that you mean only the Pilgrims.

CARVER. No, no. We mean every adult male in the colony.

GARDINER. Sounds fair to me. I think we have a new charter that we can all live with. I will sign it.

STANDISH. Men, let Mr. Carver and Mr. Bradford sign first.

[*A majority of the men—41—sign the compact.*]

BROWNE. We've forgotten something. We need a leader. Who will lead us?

GARDINER. Here's our first chance to vote. Let's decide among ourselves who will be our first governor.

VOICE. I nominate John Carver as the first governor.

VOICES. I second the nomination.

[*John Carver is overwhelmingly elected the first governor.*]

STANDISH. Volunteers for the first landing party over here! Let's see what this Cape Cod looks like!

POSTSCRIPT

The Mayflower Compact is important to us today because it established an idea we still believe in. This idea is that free people can decide how to rule themselves.

The colonists concluded that Cape Cod was not suitable for a colony. On December 26, 1620, the passengers of the *Mayflower* landed west of Cape Cod to begin the community of Plymouth. The first winter there was very difficult for them. The settlers were weak from constant work and could not fight off disease. Almost half the group died from tuberculosis, pneumonia, or scurvy (a disease caused by lack of vitamin C). Governor John Carver was among those who died. William Bradford replaced him as governor.

In spite of all the hardships it faced, the Plymouth colony lived on. It never grew very large. Eventually, in 1691, it became part of the larger Massachusetts Bay colony.

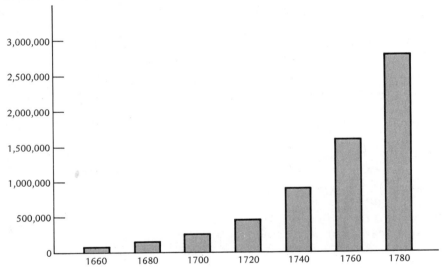

Estimated Population of the English Colonies in America, 1660–1780

Homework Questions

1. Why did the Pilgrims come to America?
2. Why did the *Mayflower* first stop at Cape Cod?
3. What was the difference between Pilgrims and Strangers?
4. How did Thomas Tinker react to Bradford's proposal to set up a government?
5. What is the significance of the Mayflower Compact to us today?

Understanding the Story

A. Write *T* for each statement that is true, *F* for each statement that is false, and *N* for each statement that is not mentioned in the story.
   1. The Separatists were persecuted in England.
   2. The Separatists were happy in Holland.
   3. After the Pilgrims came to America, persecution of Separatists ended in England.

4. Most of those on the *Mayflower* were Pilgrims.
5. The Pilgrims came to America for religious reasons.
6. The Pilgrims first landed at Cape Cod.
7. All Pilgrims decided to be farmers.
8. Myles Standish was a Pilgrim soldier.

B. Number the following events in the order in which they took place.
1. The *Mayflower* reached Cape Cod.
2. Separatists were persecuted in England.
3. Pilgrims and Strangers signed the Mayflower Compact.
4. Separatists moved to Leiden, Holland.
5. The men elected John Carver governor.
6. Separatists landed in Plymouth.
7. Separatists left England on the *Mayflower*.
8. William Bradford was chosen governor.

C. Imagine you are a passenger on the *Mayflower*. What do you think of the compact proposed by Carver and Bradford? Will you sign? Why or why not?

Activities and Inquiries

1. In an interview with William Bradford, you ask why he and the Pilgrims believed that the Mayflower Compact was needed. How does he answer?

2. Now you interview a woman who was aboard the *Mayflower* when the compact was signed. You ask how she feels about what is written in the document. How does she answer?

3. Imagine that you are a Pilgrim leader. You are thinking about what must be done in order to make the settlement in the new land a success. Prepare a list of all the things you want your group to do when they go ashore.

4. You interview a Pilgrim who has barely survived the first cruel winter in Plymouth and ask if the person would have left home if the hardships to follow had been known beforehand. Explain the answer.

5. Study the graph on page 60. Then choose the term or phrase that best answers each question.
   a. How much greater was the colonial population in 1760 than it was in 1660? (*1*) about 3 million (*2*) about 1½ million (*3*) about 2 million
   b. Which period saw the greatest growth in population? (*1*) 1660–1700 (*2*) 1700–1740 (*3*) 1740–1780
   c. The population reached 3 million just about the year (*1*) 1740 (*2*) 1760 (*3*) 1780.
   d. The period of slowest population growth was (*1*) 1660–1700 (*2*) 1700–1740 (*3*) 1740–1780.
   e. What reasons can you give for the fact that the population in 1780 was almost 40 times what it was in 1660?

4 Roger Williams Flees to Providence

Most Puritans, unlike the Separatists, did not want a separate church. The Puritans wanted to change the way people worshiped in the Church of England. They preferred simpler services and a different form of church government. But they realized that these changes would not happen right away. So, some of them, too, decided to come to America.

Puritan settlers tended to be farmers, trades people, and people with special skills. Many were members of the middle class. Some were university graduates. A group of them came to Massachusetts Bay in 1630 in 11 ships that carried more than 1,000 settlers. By 1634, 10,000 people made their homes in New England.

Puritan settlers came to America because they wanted freedom of worship for themselves. Colonists went to the one church in each town and followed the rules of their religious leaders. Those who complained were asked to leave the colony.

In a letter to his daughter, Roger Williams describes what happened to a person who did not follow the Puritan leaders' rules. Roger Williams was a man who said and wrote what he thought and felt.

Ask yourself why Roger Williams had to leave the Massachusetts Bay colony. Should he have kept his opinions to himself? Why or why not?

Providence Plantations, 1647

Dear Mary,

Last week you asked whether I was happy in Providence. I laughed and said that I would not live here if I did not like it. I am sure that my answer did not satisfy you. Let me tell you more about how I feel.

Perhaps you think I had no choice—that I was forced to come to Providence. That is not so. I did have choices. I might, for example, have stayed in England and become an official of the Church of England. It would have been a much easier way of life for all of us. But I could not stay in the Church of England. There were too many things I did not like. I wanted to worship in a church that followed the Word of God as revealed in the Bible. Anglicans may think their church meets this test, but I do not.

Because it is not possible to have my kind of church in England, I came to America to look for a church without faults. I am a Puritan.

Was I wrong to want a pure church? I am a person. I have ideas of my own about religion. Should I have kept my thoughts about religion to myself? No, each person must say what he thinks and be given the chance to share his point of view.

The religious leaders of Massachusetts preferred that I keep my ideas to myself. But you know me; I had to speak out. At this point, I had another choice. I could have stopped complaining and criticizing. I could have accepted the decisions of the elders of the Puritan church and stayed in Salem. But was this the way of Roger Williams?

No, I could not keep quiet. I had to tell people that religion should be kept in its place, separate from government. I know this is a strange idea to many people. But religion should concern itself with God and worship, not with government. What right do government officials have to force people to attend church? True worship cannot be forced. To compel people to worship is an insult to God.

The colonial governors did not like me to spread my ideas about church and state. They said I was causing divisions and stirring up trouble. They said I had no right to speak out so freely.

Another thing bothered me. I said that the king of England could not parcel out land to settlers—because it was not his to give. The land belongs to the Indians and is theirs to keep or to give. I said that we should buy the land from the Indians at a fair price. The colonial leaders refused even to talk about it.

The leaders rejected my ideas, but the people of the Salem church loved my sermons. We did not all agree, but does everyone in a community have to think and act alike? Why could I not preach what I believed? Was I harming anyone? Yet the leaders called me before the General Court of Massachusetts Bay.

The General Court ruled that I was a dangerous person. My sermons and letters, they said, were full of errors. By this they simply meant that I disagreed with them—that's all. They have their understanding of the Bible. I have mine.

Was freedom of speech a crime? They thought so. The court said I must leave Massachusetts the next spring.

I refused to keep quiet. I could not preach in the Salem church, but they could not stop me from preaching in my home and making plans to start a new colony in America. The court heard what I was up to and ordered me back to England at once. At the time, I was sick with fever and worry. I feared this was the end of my life in America.

Mary, I still had a choice. They could not send me back to England if they could not find me. So I decided to escape into the wilderness. How well I remember that day in January of 1636, when you were only two years old. Your mother crammed a knapsack with food. She was crying softly. I was shaky from my illness and could barely stand. "Don't worry, I will seek shelter with my Indian friends. The servant lad, Thomas Angell, will go with me. He will carry supplies and paddle our canoe. I'll send for you and the girls as soon as I am settled."

We left Salem on foot, heading south and west. The weather was terribly cold; snow covered the ground. Luckily I knew the trails because I had been over them before. For 14 weeks Thomas and I struggled to survive. We stayed in Indians' smoky homes. We borrowed an Indian canoe and paddled down the Seekonk River. Near the place where we would settle, a Narragansett Indian greeted us. We landed our canoe at a place called Slate Rock and spoke to the Indians. I wanted to assure the chiefs that I was here to live in peace with them.

I offered the chiefs what little I had for the land. But it was not money that bought the land—it was love. The Indians knew I loved them, and they returned my feelings. They knew that I would always be fair with them, that my house would always be open to them. They may not believe as we do, but they are creatures of God!

I started this settlement called Providence. Your mother came and you children. That first year (1636–1637), we were joined by 32 people, living in 13 homes. It was a small town, with few comforts, full of mosquitoes. There were no other English people nearby. Except for the Indians, we were alone. But, Mary, there was freedom in this place. In this town, all Christians could pray as they wished. Providence has become a refuge for religious dissenters. I am proud of what we have done here.

Now perhaps you will understand why I chose to live in Providence and why I am happy here.

> Affectionately,
>
> Your father, Roger Williams

POSTSCRIPT

Providence was one of two mainland settlements in the colony of Providence Plantations, for which Williams got an English patent in 1644. Two other settlements were on an offshore island called Rhode Island. In later years, the entire colony—a mainland area and several islands—took the name Rhode Island.

The colony continued to be noted for its relative religious tolerance. It became home to one of the earliest congregations of Jews in America, at Newport.

Religious differences continued in Massachusetts Bay colony. Several groups of dissatisfied colonists left to start their own settlements. By 1650 new colonies had sprung up in what are now Connecticut, New Hampshire, and Maine.

Homework Questions

1. How were the Pilgrims and Puritans different and alike with regard to: (*a*) religious beliefs (*b*) why they came to America?
2. Why did Roger Williams object to Puritan practices in Massachusetts?
3. Why did the General Court feel that Williams was a dangerous person?
4. Why did Williams flee to the wilderness?
5. How did Williams treat the Indians?

Understanding the Story

A. Write *T* for each statement that is true and *F* for each statement that is false.
1. Many Puritans were from the lower class.
2. The Puritans wanted freedom of worship for themselves.
3. Roger Williams said and wrote what he thought.
4. Williams was told he could stay in Massachusetts as long as he wanted.
5. Williams believed that religion must be separate from government.
6. Williams refused to leave his Massachusetts home.
7. The General Court ruled that Williams was a dangerous person.
8. Williams agreed to return to England.

B. Write *A* for each statement Roger Williams would agree with and *N* for each statement that he would not agree with.
1. I was looking for a church without faults.
2. Pay nothing to the Indians for their land.
3. The king had no right to grant land to settlers in America.
4. I refused to keep quiet.
5. Indians are not my friends.
6. I'll send for you as soon as I am settled.
7. Providence in 1636 was a comfortable place in which to live.
8. I knew the trails because I had been over them before.

C. What reasons might the leaders of Massachusetts Bay colony have had for wanting a single church? What arguments did Roger Williams make against the colony's practices? Do you think Williams was right? Why or why not?

Activities and Inquiries

1. Imagine that Roger Williams asks you to leave Massachusetts Bay and go with him to Providence. Would you go? Explain your decision.
2. Roger Williams is placed on trial for breaking the laws of Massachusetts Bay colony. Prepare his defense.
3. Prepare the case against Roger Williams.
4. You are a member of the jury. What is your decision? Why?

5 A New England Town Meeting

Democracy means that people share equally in their government. We saw how the Pilgrims agreed to share in the government of Plymouth and obey its laws. A few years later (1639), the colonists of Connecticut went a step further. They agreed to a more detailed outline of government. This was called the Fundamental Orders of Connecticut, the first constitution written in the New World.

How are laws passed under a compact or a constitution? The simplest way is for voters to get together to make their own laws. This is *direct democracy*. Obviously it works best where there are few voters or where distances are short enough so that the voters can come together easily.

For larger communities, another way may be used—a way called *representative democracy*. This was introduced in Virginia in 1619. Voters elected delegates, or representatives, to the Virginia House of Burgesses, the first elected colonial legislature in America. The delegates met each year in Jamestown (later in Williamsburg) and made the laws for the entire colony. Voters in other colonies also began to choose men to represent them in legislatures. (Women did not have the right to vote or to hold an elective office.)

People in the New England colonies continued to pass their own local laws through direct democracy. Each town had its meetinghouse in the center of the settlement. This building was used for church services on Sundays and for meetings and social events during the week. In the 17th century, meetings to discuss town problems were held as often as once each week. Today such meetings are held about once each year.

The scene of our story is the meetinghouse in Dorchester, Massachusetts, now part of Boston. Freemen who are members of the town's Puritan church fill the building. No women are present. The men greet each other in a friendly fashion.

Ask yourself why the town meeting is an example of direct democracy. Why do most parts of the United States today use representative democracy?

Dorchester, Massachusetts, 1643

MODERATOR (*Chairman*). This meeting of the town of Dorchester is called to order. What business would you like to talk about first?

JOHN. I say we should get rid of the town ducking stool. It's a cruel punishment!

CHARLES. Look who's talking! It's Mr. Ducked-in-the-Stool himself!

JOHN. It isn't a joke, Charles! You should get ducked. You'd see.

CHARLES. I go to church every Sunday. Why should anyone want to punish me?

SAMUEL. We have the stocks and the pillory for punishment. People mend their ways quickly after having their heads and feet locked in those wooden frames. Why have a ducking stool as well?

CHARLES. I think we should keep the ducking stool. Let the clear water wash the devil, that filthy Satan, out of John's body. Then, he'll go to church.

JOHN. How will ducking get me to church?

MODERATOR. John, you are out of order! You have no right to speak at this meeting.

JOHN (*angrily*). No right? What are you saying? I'm a freeman. I have lived in Dorchester as long as anyone in this room.

MODERATOR (*reads from town laws*). "A man who is not a member of the Dorchester church cannot take part in town meetings."

JOHN. I am a member of the church. You don't have to go to church to be a member.

REVEREND THOMAS. No, John, you are wrong. Because you do not attend church services, I say you are not part of the church.

[*Mixed murmurs of approval and disagreement.*]

VOICE. I say let us vote!

MODERATOR. You are all out of order. How can we vote on a motion by a man who is not a member of our church?

SAMUEL. All right. I am a voter and a member of the church. I move that we throw away the ducking stool.

VOICES. Vote! Vote!

MODERATOR (*wearily gives in*). Those in favor of keeping the ducking stool say "aye."

[*Strong chorus of ayes.*]

"You can say what you want, as long as you follow our rules."

MODERATOR. Those against the ducking stool say "nay."

[*Weak chorus of nays.*]

MODERATOR. The ducking stool stays. What's our next business?

JAMES. I have a problem. My children are not learning to read and write.

MODERATOR. The laws of the Massachusetts Bay colony say that parents are responsible for teaching their children to read and write. You must do it.

JAMES. No matter what the law says, I can't do it. I want my children to learn, but I read poorly myself. I can't teach them.

VOICES. Neither can I. My children can't read either.

MODERATOR. One at a time. Quiet down.

REVEREND THOMAS. Remember, a good Christian must be able to read and write. Above all, he must be able to read the Bible. We want our children to learn the Word of God, do we not?

EDWARD. Yes, but how shall we teach our children? I say that we parents can't do the job. And I say that this town must hire a schoolmaster.

JAMES. Yes, we need a person in Dorchester who knows how to teach children.

MODERATOR. Hiring a schoolmaster means we would have to raise taxes, or else charge each child a fee. Are you prepared to pay more money?

VOICES. No! No!

JAMES. I have a suggestion. Why not appoint a committee to look into the whole thing? How badly are our children doing? Can they learn to read and write at home?

EDWARD. And how much would the cost of keeping a *good* schoolmaster add to our taxes?

ROGER. Don't forget to find out where we can get a good schoolmaster.

MODERATOR. Excellent suggestions. I appoint James, Robert, Edward, and myself to a committee to look into the schoolmaster question. We'll try to get the facts and report back to the town meeting in one month.

ROBERT (*grumbles*). I'll do it, but I know it will cost me more money.

MODERATOR. It's getting late. I declare this meeting is over. We will meet again one week from today.

POSTSCRIPT

The Puritans thought education was most important. In 1647 the Massachusetts Bay government passed a law requiring towns with 50 or more families to hire a schoolmaster to teach reading and writing. A town with 100 or more families had to have a grammar school (high school) to teach Latin grammar to boys.

Homework Questions

1. Why is it now impossible for voters in most places to pass their own laws?
2. How did the New England colonists pass their own local laws?
3. Why was there a question about John's right to speak in the town meeting?
4. Why did some colonists argue against getting a schoolmaster?
5. How did the town meeting deal with the schoolmaster question?

Understanding the Story

A. Write *F* for each statement that is a fact and *O* for each statement that is an opinion.
   1. The Fundamental Orders of Connecticut was the first written constitution in America.
   2. The New England town meeting is more democratic than any other kind of meeting.
   3. The first elected colonial legislature in America was in Virginia.
   4. New England town meetings were held as often as once each week.
   5. Women should have taken part in the town meetings.
   6. The ducking stool was used to punish wrongdoers.
   7. Puritan punishments were too harsh.
   8. Parents were responsible for teaching their children to read and write.

B. List the numbers of the statements that describe a part of the Puritan way of life.
   1. All Puritans had to attend church services.
   2. Puritan children went to schools in large cities.
   3. Men could make suggestions at town meetings.
   4. Puritan men and women had equal rights.
   5. Every Puritan man over 21 could vote at the town meeting.
   6. Each town made its own local laws.
   7. Puritans had no respect for education.
   8. There were harsh punishments for wrongdoers.

C. Imagine that your community is holding a town meeting. What matters do you want to talk about? Compare these with the matters discussed in the story.

Activities and Inquiries

1. Look at the cartoon on page 67 and answer the following questions.
   a. What does the moderator mean?
   b. What is democratic about the scene?
   c. What is undemocratic about the scene?
   d. How would you make the scene more democratic?
2. These issues were discussed at the town meeting: (*a*) the ducking stool and other punishments (*b*) the right to talk and vote at meetings (*c*) education of the young. What position would you have taken on each of these issues? Explain.
3. You have given your opinions on the issues in question 2. Will most others at the Dorchester meeting agree or disagree with you? Explain.
4. Many of the Puritans' laws were different from our laws today. Visit your library and look up some of the Puritan laws. Make a list of them.

6 A Religious Refuge in Pennsylvania

The English colonies we have read about thus far were sponsored by businessmen (Jamestown and Plymouth) or by the settlers themselves (Massachusetts Bay and Rhode Island). There was another way of starting a colony. Suppose that a man was a good friend of the king of England or of the king's brother. He might be granted a charter to colonize land in America. This person would be given complete control of the colony. In fact, he would be called the owner of the colony, or its proprietor.

George Calvert (Lord Baltimore), a Roman Catholic, was given 10 million acres, and his son began the colony of Maryland. Both Catholics and Protestants settled there. The Maryland Toleration Act of 1649 protected the right of most Christians to worship freely. Later laws, however, took many rights away from Catholics. This was a time when Catholics and Protestants in England were engaged in bitter feuds over religion.

General James Oglethorpe and 19 of his friends were given control of the colony of Georgia. As proprietors for 21 years, they provided a refuge for English people who had been jailed for not paying their debts. These trustees chose certain debtors to go to Georgia to start a new life.

New Amsterdam, a Dutch colony, was captured in 1664 by English forces sent by the Duke of York. The colony was renamed New York. The duke's brother, King Charles II, granted him an area that included what are now New York, New Jersey, and part of Connecticut. The duke, in turn, gave New Jersey to his friends Lord Berkeley and Sir George Carteret.

The royal family was also very kind to the subject of our story, William Penn. Penn's father had lent the king large sums of money. Charles II repaid the loans in 1681 by making William Penn the proprietor of a large forested region in North America. This became the colony of Pennsylvania (Penn's Woods).

Penn made Pennsylvania into a refuge for thousands of persecuted Quakers (members of the Society of Friends). The Quakers faced trouble because they would not worship in the same way the Anglicans or Puritans did. Quakers spoke plainly and wore simple clothes. They refused to bow to another person or to fight or make war. They asserted that all people—even women—were equal.

Ask yourself why the Quakers were persecuted. How did William Penn encourage others as well as Quakers to settle in Pennsylvania?

Philadelphia, Pennsylvania, 1701

"I am greatly troubled," said William Penn with a sigh. "Perhaps it was not the best idea to start this colony. My debts are enormous, and the colonists have been so troublesome."

Andrew Hamilton, the deputy governor of Pennsylvania, shook his head. He was concerned for Penn's health. The portly Quaker had not looked well on this second visit to his colony. And no wonder. The colony had problems, as always. Its legislature seemed constantly to be making new demands on Penn and his representatives.

"Let us take a stroll, Mr. Penn. Perhaps a walk and some talk will take your mind off your troubles," said Hamilton.

For some time the men wandered through the gardens of Penn's estate. "I call this colony my 'holy experiment,'" Penn said. "But just now it seems anything but holy. People can be so quarrelsome!"

"It is a worthy experiment indeed, Mr. Penn. But perhaps you have trusted too far in the goodness of human nature. Perhaps you have given your colonists too much self-government for their own good."

"At times it does seem so," Penn replied. "And yet, what else could I do? Run my colony as a feudal kingdom, with myself an absolute ruler? My grant from the king would not allow that. Besides, who would want to settle in such a place? I want settlers to come to Pennsylvania—many settlers. Pennsylvania will prosper when it has many settlers and a thriving trade."

"You are certainly attracting many settlers," remarked Hamilton. "There are Germans, Dutch, Swedes, Finns, and many others besides English people."

"Yes," sighed Penn. "If only they would keep up payments on their lands. As you know, even settlers who lack money can acquire land here for a small rent. Yet so many have fallen behind in their payments. And now the legislature wants me to put a 20-year limit on rents, so that renters would own their land outright after that time. I cannot agree to that. The income from Pennsylvania is small enough, heavens knows, and my debts are so large. Oh, those debts!"

"Yet you did not start Pennsylvania as a money-making venture, Mr. Penn. You had grander ideas."

"Oh, much grander, Mr. Hamilton. I saw—I still see—my colony as a Christian commonwealth, where men can put into practice the ideals that are discouraged in other lands. Self-government, for instance. And religious liberty."

"I can see that religious liberty means much to you, Mr. Penn. You offer freedom of worship to Catholics as well as Anglicans and other Christians."

"Yes I do—and not only for Christians, Mr. Hamilton. As a Quaker I believe that all people should be free to respond to God's inner light. That is why in Pennsylvania all are allowed to worship, or not to worship, as they see fit. Only in certain matters, such as holding public office, do we require that a man be a Christian."

"You seem to place great emphasis on religion, Mr. Penn. That is an admirable quality," Hamilton said.

"I was not always so admirable, Mr. Hamilton. In my youth I was rather happy-go-lucky—something of a dandy, even. I was an excellent swordsman and even fought a duel once."

"Not unusual for a man of your background, Mr. Penn. Your father was a great admiral in the English Navy. Your family had great wealth and vast estates in Ireland."

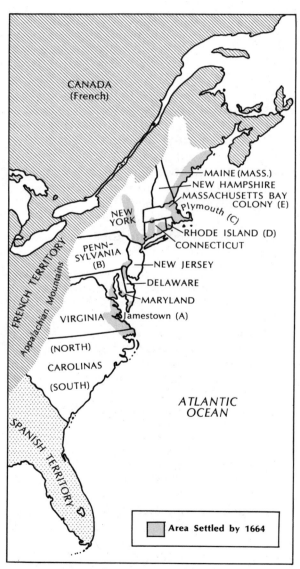

The American Colonies, 1607–1690

"Yes. It was a great shock to my father when I became a Quaker. For a time I believe he wanted to disinherit me."

"Your beliefs certainly caused you a lot of trouble. Weren't you shut up in the Tower of London for a time?"

"Yes, like many Quakers I was put in prison for my beliefs. The English government has not often been tolerant of religious dissenters. Religious quarrels, especially between Catholics and Anglicans, have been too much a part of English history. Many people feel that there can be peace only when all people worship in the same church. But I believe that is wrong. Forced religion leads to persecution and only makes civil war *more* likely."

"Well, civil war does not seem to be a danger in Pennsylvania," Hamilton said thoughtfully. "But we do have our quarrels. It's not necessarily Quaker against Anglican but sometimes Quaker against Quaker or town against country."

"People will always disagree, Mr. Hamilton, as long as their interests are different. The job of government is to create a balance among different groups, so that no one group can get control. In framing a constitution for my colony, I made sure that neither I nor the settlers alone had the full power. My constitution may have some rough edges, but it has worked so far. And, if God is willing and the English government leaves us alone, it will continue to work for many years to come."

POSTSCRIPT

Pennsylvania did continue to grow—although not under Penn's original constitution. That constitution was changed later in 1701 to give more power to the settlers' representatives.

Penn, like many thinkers of his day, believed that a good government should be a "mixed" one. It should have neither too much monarchy nor too much democracy. Thus, Penn's original plan of government provided for power to be shared by an elected assembly (representing ordinary people) and council (representing the wealthy) and Penn's representatives (in place of a king). Voters were adult male Christians who owned land.

For its time, Penn's system was considered quite advanced. Most of the countries in Europe and most of the American colonies had laws that placed far more restrictions on the rights of various groups. Changes introduced in 1701 (mainly putting an end to the aristocratic council) made the system somewhat more democratic.

Penn expressed great concern for the rights of all—including Indians. He signed a treaty of peace with Indians in his colony and bought land from them instead of just taking it. He tried to assure that trade with Indians was carried on fairly so that no one was cheated.

Penn went back to England at the end of 1701 and never returned to Pennsylvania. But the colony remained under his family's ownership up to the American Revolution.

Homework Questions

1. Why did Quakers face troubles in England?
2. Why did Penn consider the Pennsylvania colonists troublesome?
3. Were people of all religions equal in Pennsylvania? Explain.
4. How did Penn seek to provide a "mixed" government for Pennsylvania?
5. What was Penn's attitude toward the Indians in his colony?

Understanding the Story

A. List the numbers of the statements that are true.
1. The Maryland Toleration Act permitted all Christians to worship freely.
2. James Oglethorpe was a proprietor of the colony of Pennsylvania.
3. George Calvert was the proprietor of what is now Maryland.
4. Quakers wore simple clothing and refused to fight.
5. William Penn was born a Quaker.
6. Penn went to jail for his beliefs.
7. The Quakers in Pennsylvania all agreed with one another.
8. Penn wrote Pennsylvania's first constitution.

B. List the numbers of the statements William Penn made or might have made.
1. I never carried a sword in my life.
2. My family was poor but honest.
3. God guides people through an inner light.
4. Quakers sometimes quarrel with one another.
5. Absolute monarchy is the best form of government.
6. Men in public office should be Christians.
7. Neither the settlers nor I should have full power.
8. Everyone in Pennsylvania must worship as I do.

C. American Indians today are demanding certain rights and the return of lands that they say have been stolen from them. If William Penn were alive, what might he say about this issue? How would you respond to such Indian claims? Why?

Activities and Inquiries

1. Study the map on page 72. Then choose the letter that shows where each event occurred.
   a. The Pilgrims first settled here. *(1)* A *(2)* C *(3)* E
   b. The story about William Penn takes place here. *(1)* D *(2)* B *(3)* C
   c. Richard, the white indentured servant, complained about life in this place. *(1)* C *(2)* D *(3)* A
   d. The town meeting was held here. *(1)* B *(2)* C *(3)* E
   e. Roger Williams founded his own colony here. *(1)* D *(2)* A *(3)* B
2. Ask William Penn the following question: "Why are you willing to go to jail or even die for your beliefs?" How will Penn answer? Do you agree with him? Why or why not?
3. Assume that you live in Massachusetts in the 17th century. William Penn invites you to move to Pennsylvania, and you decide to go. How is the government in Pennsylvania different from the government in Massachusetts? Which do you prefer? Why?
4. Pretend that you live in England and are planning to go to America. Which colony would you settle in? Why?

Who Built America?

Anne Hutchinson

JANET. Just my luck! Why do I have to give the first report?

MR. MILLER. Don't be upset, Janet. You're setting the standard for all future reports. How can you make a mistake?

JANET. Okay, here goes. I'm reporting on Anne Hutchinson. Anne lived in the Massachusetts Bay colony in the 1630's. She didn't like most of the sermons the ministers preached in the churches. She wasn't afraid to tell others what she thought.

JUAN. Big deal! I'll complain about my priest's sermons. See if I get into the history books.

JANET. You forget, Juan, that Puritans weren't supposed to complain or criticize. But Anne went further and called meetings of her own. Can you imagine a person with no formal education doing that?

RICARDO. What happened at her meetings?

JANET. She explained what the ministers were saying—or should have been saying. There would be 80 to 90 Puritans at her meetings—mostly women. But some men came, too.

HEINRICH. How did she get away with it? The ministers must have been angry.

JANET. All the Puritan authorities were angry. They told her to keep quiet, but she refused.

JOSEPHINE. How could Anne Hutchinson talk about God and religion? You said she had no education.

JANET. She said she could feel what was right or wrong. Truth was in her heart—as well as in the Bible. And she didn't need a minister to tell her what to do because God spoke to her directly.

CARLA. Wow! The Puritans didn't stand for that, did they?

JANET. They certainly did not. They put her on trial for heresy—for expressing opinions different from those of her church. In the end, they forced her to leave Massachusetts Bay.

ROBERT. She sounds more like a tough, stubborn woman to me. I'll bet she hated all men—not just ministers.

JANET. No, Robert, you're wrong. She was happily married, and she had 14 children. She was a very brave woman who was willing to stand up for her beliefs.

HANS. What happened to her?

JANET. She and her family were killed in an Indian uprising on Long Island.

SAM. What a shame!

MR. MILLER. Would you call Anne Hutchinson a woman's rights supporter, Janet?

JANET. Not exactly, but I think that she was a real hero. She did something no other Puritan woman had the nerve to do. She refused to go to church and keep quiet. She was the first American woman to insist that she had the right to think for herself.

MR. MILLER. Very good report, Janet. You captured the true spirit of Anne Hutchinson.

MR. MILLER'S OFFICE

"I get your point, Mr. Miller. There was a lot more to being a colonist than I thought."

"Do you see the difference between colonists and explorers?"

"Sure," answered Jack. "Explorers keep moving, trying to find new things. Colonists get to a new place and settle there. I admit that it's not an easy life."

"Very good," said Mr. Miller.

"Colonists had to be strong and brave. America was no place for weaklings."

"Did anything about the colonists surprise you?" asked Mr. Miller.

"Yes. I didn't know that both blacks and whites were indentured servants in the 17th century. It was a tough life for them all. At least the whites had a choice. They didn't have to come here. But the blacks were captured and shipped over here. That was horrible!"

"Right," said Mr. Miller. "Do you understand the difference between a slave and an indentured servant?"

"That's easy!" replied Jack. "An indentured servant could see some light in the future. One day the time of serving would be over, and freedom would come. But a slave had nothing to look forward to. He or she would always belong to someone."

"Did you notice how many settlers came here for religious reasons?"

"Yes. I was surprised by that. So many different groups came: the Pilgrims, the Puritans, the Quakers, and, I guess, many others. But, Mr. Miller, something bothers me about the first two."

"What's that, Jack?"

"They came here to escape religious persecution in England. Why didn't they let people worship as they pleased in their colony? Look what the Puritans did to Roger Williams and Anne Hutchinson!"

"Well, you must remember, Jack, at that time most countries of the world had official religions. They wanted everyone to worship in one way. Can you say something good about the New England colonies?"

"Well, I did notice a desire for democracy. The Mayflower Compact was a good beginning. Then, those town meetings gave the colonists a chance to voice their opinions about almost every subject. One thing wasn't so good about those meetings, Mr. Miller."

"What's that, Jack?"

"You had to be a man and a church member to take part."

"Anyway, it was a start," said Mr. Miller.

"It's too bad that we can't get together and solve our problems as easily today," said Jack thoughtfully.

"I'm afraid that there are just too many of us now," replied Mr. Miller.

"When will we learn about our problems with Great Britain?" asked Jack. "I can't wait to get to our American Revolution!"

"Patience, Jack. That's our very next unit."

The American Revolution

"At last we're coming to a part of American history that really interests me," said Jack. "I can't wait to read about the Americans beating the English. Let's get to those battles!"

"Not so fast, Jack. There's a lot more to the American Revolution than fighting battles."

"I was afraid of that."

"First, we have to find out why we fought the British. You know, of course, that the official name of England in the mid-1700's was Great Britain. The people were known as the British."

"British or English, we fought them because we wanted to be free and because we didn't like having another country push us around," said Jack.

"That's close," said Mr. Miller. "The Declaration of Independence will tell you how the revolutionists felt."

"Come on, Mr. Miller. I know all about the Declaration. All men are created equal. Freedom and liberty and all that stuff."

"Yes, and do you know the meaning of equality?"

"Sure, everyone's as good as everyone else," replied Jack.

"That's not a bad beginning, but it means a lot more."

"I'm willing to learn all that," said Jack. "But will we ever get to the fighting?"

"Soon, Jack. This unit should give you the answers about the Revolution. And see if you can figure out how 13 American colonies were able to beat the mighty British Empire."

1 Freedom of the Press

By the middle of the 1700's, ownership of many of the colonies had changed. No longer did business groups or individuals control them. The king had gained direct rule over the 13 colonies. He appointed the governors as well as the governors' advisers to carry out his orders.

In most of the colonies, qualified voters elected assemblies to make their laws. The men in these bodies often refused to accept the commands of the governors. As a result, a power struggle developed between the appointed governors and the elected assemblies. In several colonies the governor lost the right to introduce laws. He could only approve or veto (disapprove) laws sent to him by the assembly. The assemblies began to tell the governors how much money they could spend and to appoint many colonial officials.

Individual colonists also felt that they had the right to criticize their governors. They said that they should be free to speak and publish both facts and opinions, even if high officials objected.

Our story tells of the struggle of one man to print the truth as he saw it. John Peter Zenger, a newspaper publisher, was jailed for criticizing the royal governor of New York. He spent more than nine months in prison while waiting for his trial to begin. Zenger was accused of *libel*. In those days one meaning of libel was printing remarks harmful to the crown (the king and his government). Today, largely because of the Zenger case, a remark must be false before it can be considered a libel.

Ask yourself whether Zenger should have had the right to criticize the governor. Why is freedom of the press (the right to print both facts and opinions) so important?

New York City, July, 1735

The scene is the noisy, crowded dining room of an inn. Three men sit at a rear table eating dinner. They are uneasy and look around constantly. At last a fourth man walks slowly toward their table. The three rise to greet him.

JAMES ALEXANDER. Mr. Hamilton, what a pleasure to see you! I cannot tell you how much we appreciate your coming all the way from Philadelphia. First, let me introduce my friends. This is William Smith. He and I *were* Zenger's lawyers. And this is John Chambers. He is Zenger's lawyer now.

ANDREW HAMILTON [*exchanges greetings with the two men*]. Yes, Mr. Alexander, it was a long, bouncy trip. But I wouldn't miss this case for all the tea in India! I read your letters with great interest. I will do all I can to get Zenger out of jail.

WILLIAM SMITH. We hope you won't be sorry. You know, of course, that James and I were disbarred. We can no longer practice law in New York.

HAMILTON. Yes, I know. How did it happen?

SMITH. James and I told Chief Justice James Delancey that he should not be the judge at Zenger's trial. We reminded him that Zenger's newspaper had criticized his appointment as chief justice. How could he be fair?

ALEXANDER. Delancey was enraged. He lost his temper, started shouting that we would never practice law again, and ordered us out of the courtroom. We want you to know that your law career may be in danger if you take this case.

HAMILTON. I know the risks. But I am not in New York because I am afraid. I am an old Philadelphia lawyer, a former attorney general of Pennsylvania and lawmaker. Chief Justice Delancey would not dare disbar me!

SMITH. Mr. Hamilton, you must be careful. The representatives of the king will not stand for any criticism. We cannot write or say publicly what we think about the colonial government. Freedom of expression is strictly limited.

HAMILTON. Please don't worry, gentlemen. I will be careful. I will not criticize the chief justice. But I will do whatever I think is necessary to defend Zenger. They will not stop me!

SMITH. At last, I think we have a chance to win this case.

HAMILTON. You must fill me in on the facts of the case. First, tell me how Zenger is being treated.

SMITH. At first, it was as though he were a common thief or murderer. He could talk to no one. They would not even let him have paper and pen.

HAMILTON. And then?

SMITH. Zenger appealed to Chief Justice Delancey, who agreed to let him speak to his wife and lawyer. Now Zenger even writes articles for his newspaper, the *New York Weekly Journal.*

HAMILTON. Good, good! Now, tell me how Zenger got himself into this mess.

ALEXANDER. Governor William Cosby dismissed Chief Justice Lewis Morris for no earthly reason. Morris is a good man with an excellent record. He is fair, and he knows the law.

HAMILTON. Yes, go on!

ALEXANDER. Cosby then appointed Delancey to the position of chief justice. I tell you, Mr. Hamilton, Delancey knows nothing of law— nothing at all. He is a stupid, ignorant man, the governor's puppet. Delancey does what he is told to do.

HAMILTON. Please, Mr. Alexander, tell me why Zenger was put into jail.

ALEXANDER. Zenger is a printer. Morris and I hired him to print the truth about Governor Cosby. Zenger and I wrote the articles, but he was responsible for everything in the paper.

HAMILTON. Why was Zenger responsible?

ALEXANDER. We never signed our articles, but Zenger's name was in the newspaper as the publisher.

HAMILTON. Does Zenger admit that he was responsible for the articles criticizing the governor?

ALEXANDER. Yes, but every word in them is based on truth.

HAMILTON. I believe you. It won't be easy, but I will defend Zenger.

CHAMBERS. How do we work this out, Mr. Hamilton? I am supposed to be Zenger's lawyer. Shall we tell the court that you are taking over the case?

HAMILTON. No. Tell them nothing! On the morning of the trial I will sit in the back of the courtroom. At the proper moment I will step forward, introduce myself, and speak for the defense.

SMITH. Excellent! That will take the prosecution by surprise. They will have no time to think of reasons for removing you from the courtroom. I can't wait to see their faces!

The scene shifts to a courtroom. It is August 4, 1735. Chief Justice Delancey is on the bench. The attorney general of New York sits at a small table on one side of the room. Zenger and his attorney, John Chambers, are seated at another table.

ATTORNEY GENERAL. Your honor and gentlemen of the jury, this case is very simple. Mr. Zenger has confessed to printing libels about His Excellency, Governor Cosby. He admits publishing these remarks in the *New York Weekly Journal.* We need know nothing more! The government of the colony of New York cannot allow these libels to be printed. Criticism excites the people and can lead to the overthrow of our government, of our very way of life. I tell you that Zenger broke the law. He must be punished!

Andrew Hamilton steps forward from the rear of the courtroom. He introduces himself to the court. The attorney general and the chief justice are surprised and shocked.

HAMILTON. The attorney general is mistaken. Mr. Zenger has done nothing wrong. He did not libel Governor Cosby. He merely wrote the truth. Gentlemen of the jury, you cannot punish a man for telling the truth!

CHIEF JUSTICE DELANCEY. A libel is a libel. Even if it is true, it is still a crime. Mr. Zenger criticized the governor. That is a libel! The law is clear.

HAMILTON. Gentlemen of the jury, I must appeal to you. Truth *is* the issue in this case. I am not permitted to prove that Mr. Zenger's articles were true. Therefore, I must ask you to decide on your own whether Mr. Zenger printed false and dangerous material.

I say that truth is never dangerous. And I am sure you will decide that his articles were true. Gentlemen of the jury, I am here in this

"Next time, Zenger, keep the truth to yourself!"

courtroom because I cannot be silent. I must speak out against a government that does not permit criticism. We must have the right to criticize and the right to tell the truth.

This is an important case. It is not just the case of a poor printer, nor a case for New York alone. No! It affects every free person in British America.

Gentlemen of the jury, I ask you to speak out against tyranny, against the unjust use of power. Take a step for liberty by finding John Peter Zenger not guilty!

Chief Justice Delancey repeats his explanation of the libel law to the jury. The men of the jury leave the courtroom to make a decision. One hour later they return.

COURT CLERK. Gentlemen of the jury, have you agreed on a verdict? Is John Peter Zenger guilty of printing libels?

JURY FOREMAN. Your honor, we have agreed on a verdict. We find the defendant, John Peter Zenger, not guilty!

ALEXANDER [*walks over to Zenger, Hamilton, and Chambers*]. Congratulations, Mr. Hamilton. You won the day for our friend Zenger.

ZENGER. Correction, Mr. Alexander. Mr. Hamilton won the day for all colonists and for the rights of free people.

POSTSCRIPT

The Zenger case paved the way for the freedom of the press, later guaranteed by the First Amendment to the United States Constitution. Some 40 years after the Zenger trial, the words of Andrew Hamilton would be on the lips of many people. Free people in British North America would be speaking out against "tyranny," against "the unjust use of power." In the 1770's, these words would be directed against the British king, not an appointed governor.

Homework Questions

1. Why do you suppose elected assemblies and appointed governors often clashed?
2. Why did John Peter Zenger go to jail?
3. What danger did the attorney general see in allowing newspapers to criticize officials?
4. For what were James Alexander and William Smith disbarred? Why was Andrew Hamilton not afraid of being disbarred?
5. How did Andrew Hamilton's idea of libel differ from Delancey's?

Understanding the Story

A. Write *F* for each statement that is a fact and *O* for each statement that is an opinion.
  1. Zenger should have had the right to criticize the governor.
  2. The elected assemblies struggled with the appointed governors.
  3. People should never criticize their rulers.
  4. Zenger was jailed because he criticized the governor.
  5. John Chambers was one of Zenger's lawyers.
  6. Chief Justice James Delancey was unfair.
  7. Andrew Hamilton was the best lawyer in the colonies.
  8. Andrew Hamilton was not allowed to prove that Zenger's articles were true.

B. List the numbers of the statements that give the outcomes of the Zenger case.
  1. The governor of New York resigned.
  2. A jury found Zenger not guilty.
  3. Zenger spent another six months in jail.
  4. Andrew Hamilton could no longer practice law.
  5. The case paved the way for freedom of the press, which is guaranteed by the First Amendment.
  6. Zenger was freed but could not write for newspapers in New York.
  7. A jury went against a judge's advice about the law.
  8. The Zenger case marked a step for liberty.

C. In your opinion, why is freedom of the press important? Do you think there should be any limits on this freedom? Explain.

Activities and Inquiries

1. Imagine that you have attended Zenger's trial. Now report on it for your school newspaper. Your article should include: (*a*) the charge against Zenger (*b*) the case for the prosecution (*c*) Zenger's defense.

2. Suppose you have the job of defending Zenger. What arguments will you use to persuade the jury that Zenger is innocent?
3. Suppose you are the prosecuting attorney. State the case against Zenger.
4. Look at the cartoon on page 83 and answer the following questions.

a. Explain the meaning of the cartoon caption.
b. What might Zenger say to the judge?
c. How would you answer the judge? Justify your answer.
d. How would the judge defend himself?

2 Washington Fights on the British Side

For more than a hundred years, the British and the French had engaged in a worldwide struggle for control of an empire. In the mid-18th century, they fought a major war in Europe, India, and North America. In Europe, it was called the Seven Years' War; in America, it was called the French and Indian War.

During this conflict, both France and Britain had allies among the American Indians. France and its Indian allies fought Britain, its Indian allies, and the American colonists for control of the middle part of North America. Both sides wanted the furs, fish, lumber, and land of the rich Ohio Valley. Many Indian groups sided with the French, fearing that English-speaking settlers would drive them from their lands. (French colonists usually did not farm the land. They moved about, trapping animals for their furs and trading with the Indians.)

The war began after the French claimed the area west and north of the Ohio River. The French protected their claim by building a number of forts along the Allegheny and Ohio rivers.

The British and the colonists had their own dreams of Indian trade and Western land settlement. The governor of Virginia decided to challenge the French claim. In 1754 he sent Lieutenant Colonel George Washington with 150 men to build a fort at what is now Pittsburgh, where the Allegheny and Monongahela rivers meet to form the Ohio River. The French had gotten there first, and they defended their Fort Duquesne. Washington lost the battle for the fort and had to return to Virginia.

The individual colonies were no match for the French. But many leaders saw a chance to win if they could work together. Representatives from 8 of the 13 colonies met in 1754 in Albany, New

North America in 1713

York, under the leadership of Benjamin Franklin. The group worked out a plan to unite the colonies to fight the common enemy, the French.

But the colonies did not yet have the will to join together. They did not approve the Albany Plan and neither did Great Britain.

Great Britain sent General Edward Braddock to lead an army against the French forts in the Ohio Valley. We shall see what happened to General Braddock, his army, and one of his officers, Lieutenant Colonel Washington. Ask yourself whether Franklin and Washington were correct in their opinions of Braddock.

Fredericksburg, Maryland, May 1, 1755

The Honorable Benjamin Franklin
Deputy Postmaster General, His Majesty's Colonies

My dear Mr. Franklin:

I will soon lead my army into Pennsylvania. We plan to attack and capture Fort Duquesne. That should take three to four days of actual fighting. Then I shall push on to Fort Niagara and Fort Frontenac.

Before I go, I must thank you again for your wonderful service. My soldiers would be helpless without the 150 wagons and 259 horses you found for us. We would not be able to march against the French and Indian enemy and make North America safe for English people. Our glorious victory in days to come would not be possible.

Mr. Franklin, I do indeed appreciate your concern about my army's battle plans. You feel very strongly that my men must fight differently in North America. This is not Europe, but men are men and bullets are bullets! Let me assure you that it is not necessary to change battle-tested English ways of fighting wars. My men are brave and strong. They are well-trained veterans of many battles. They will destroy the French and the Indians with their accurate musket fire. No enemy is a match for British soldiers. We cannot lose.

Your kindness and help will never be forgotten.

Yours very sincerely,

Major General Edward Braddock
Commander-in-Chief
His Majesty's Armies in North America

Philadelphia, Pennsylvania, July 16, 1755

Lieutenant Colonel George Washington
Fort Cumberland, Maryland

Dear Colonel Washington:

News of the defeat of General Braddock's army has reached Philadelphia. What a shock! What a disappointment! Braddock was so sure of easy victory—and now this! We shall never see General Braddock and most of his men again.

What can I say about this terrible loss? Of course, I am sorry that so many British and colonial soldiers were killed by a small French and Indian force. But thank God, Colonel Washington, you were not hurt. Your bravery under fire has excited all the colonies. People talk of little else.

I am not a military man, nor do I pretend to know much about fighting a war. Nevertheless, I did speak to General Braddock about the differences of fighting in Europe and in America. I must say that his remarks disappointed me. He told me again and again how successful he had been in leading British soldiers on European battlefields. I pointed out that the backwoods of Pennsylvania are far different from the fields of Europe. He refused to listen. How could I, a Pennsylvania colonist, know more than a great British general?

I would not stop. "Beware of an ambush," I warned him. "Unless you are very careful, the enemy will surround you and cut you down!"

Braddock laughed. "You colonials think that the Indians are a powerful enemy. Mr. Franklin, you forget that I command the king's soldiers. Indians are no match for my men!"

I tried to warn him that the French soldiers in America had learned from the Indians. Although trained in Europe, they had changed their plans to fit the forests and rocks of our uncleared land.

Now, the battle is over, but we must still win a war. It is my fondest hope that the other British generals will learn how war in America must be fought.

I hope and pray that you have recovered from your ordeal of battle. Until we meet again, I am

Your devoted friend,

Benjamin Franklin

Williamsburg, Virginia, August 20, 1755

The Honorable Benjamin Franklin
Deputy Postmaster General
Philadelphia, Pennsylvania

Dear Mr. Franklin:

Thank you for your very kind letter. Yes, I am recovering from the shock and sorrow of the battle of Fort Duquesne. But I will never forget the death and destruction as long as I live.

You were right about General Braddock. He had a closed mind and refused to listen to any of us in the colonies. What foolish stubbornness! How could a British general who had never been in America know how to fight in the forests of western Pennsylvania? He insisted that a battle was a battle no matter where you fought.

Braddock could not see that his army would have to fight in small groups. He said that his army must stay together, draw the enemy's fire, and push him back. British soldiers were not trained to hide behind trees and bushes, he declared. What nonsense!

Perhaps you would like to know how the battle was lost. We crossed the Monongahela River in good order. We were on level ground, only about nine miles from the fort. We moved easily through the thick forest until we came to an open clearing. Then I heard a shot followed by Indian war whoops. Shot followed shot. Our advance guard had been attacked. I was riding beside Braddock. He led the main group of soldiers forward to help the advance guard. I could not wait to get into the thick of battle.

As we rode up, I could see that the clearing was now filled with red-coated soldiers running away from their attackers. Terrified, they ran into us. We could not move. Fear and panic gripped the men. Then I realized that we had been surrounded. The unseen enemy, hiding behind trees and bushes, shot down our men in bloody heaps. I hate to write this, but the British soldiers behaved like cowards.

I was very lucky. Two horses in succession were shot from under me. Bullets tore my coat and knocked off my hat. Somehow I was not wounded. General Braddock was wounded badly. Bravely he continued to give orders, which I tried to carry out. But it was a lost cause.

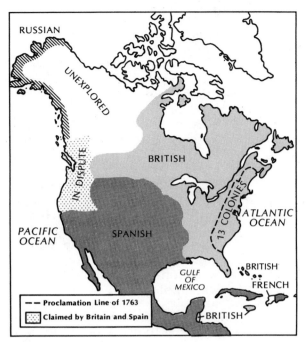

North America in 1763

The men would not listen, or they could not hear me. Unable to see the enemy, they continued shooting aimlessly. Often they shot one another! Dead and dying lay all around us.

The officers tried to rally the men. The officers behaved bravely even though they were perfect targets. Officer after officer fell. Finally, the survivors simply ran away. Even the wagon drivers took horses from their teams and galloped off, leaving behind wagons, cannons, and supplies. Our 1,850 men had been defeated by 900 Frenchmen and Indians!

Yes, Mr. Franklin, July 9, 1755, is a day I shall never forget. It will be known as the worst day in the history of British America. Braddock failed to take Fort Duquesne, and he lost his life because he would not listen to you and me. Just before he died, Braddock said, "We shall know better how to deal with those Indians another time." There will be no other time for him.

Please give my best wishes to your family.

Your devoted friend,

George Washington

Homework Questions

1. How did the governor of Virginia seek to challenge the French claim?
2. How did Benjamin Franklin help General Braddock?
3. What advice did Franklin give Braddock about fighting the French?
4. Why were the British defeated so easily by the French?
5. Why did George Washington say that July 9, 1755, would be known as the worst day in the history of British America?

Understanding the Story

A. List the numbers of the statements that are true.
1. The colonists worried about the French threat in the Boston area.
2. The French claimed the land west and north of the Ohio River.
3. Washington lost a battle at Fort Duquesne.
4. General Braddock brought the colonists together at Albany.
5. Colonel Washington served under Braddock.
6. Braddock won a major victory in America against the French.
7. Franklin wrote to Washington.
8. Braddock never agreed that he needed new battle plans for fighting in North America.

B. Choose the term or phrase that best completes each statement.
1. General Braddock wrote to thank Benjamin Franklin for (a) his advice on military strategy (b) his congratulations (c) the wagons and horses he had provided.
2. Franklin thought that the British should change their way of fighting because (a) Indians were better fighters than Europeans (b) Indians used bows and arrows (c) conditions in backwoods America were different from conditions in Europe.
3. Braddock ordered his men to (a) stay together (b) ambush the French and Indians (c) hide behind trees.
4. Washington felt that the British soldiers, except for officers, behaved like (a) cowards (b) savages (c) heroes.
5. The British troops (a) outnumbered (b) evenly matched (c) were outnumbered by the French and Indian forces.
6. The French and Indian War is sometimes called the (a) War of Secession (b) Seven Years' War (c) Napoleonic War.

C. Imagine that Braddock and Washington are living today and war threatens to break out in Europe. Which one would you prefer as the leader of your army? Why?

Activities and Inquiries

1. Study the maps on pages 86 and 89. Then choose the term or phrase that best completes each statement.
   a. Between 1713 and 1763, British control of land in North America (1) increased (2) decreased (3) stayed the same.
   b. Between 1713 and 1763, French control of land in North America (1) increased (2) decreased (3) stayed the same.
   c. In 1763 Spain (1) was pushed completely out of North America (2) gained a great deal of land from France (3) neither gained nor lost land.
   d. Between 1713 and 1763, the amount of unexplored land (1) did not change (2) increased (3) decreased.

e. In 1763 the British controlled (*1*) what is now Mexico and Central America   (*2*) the Pacific Coast (or western part of North America) (*3*) the Atlantic Coast (or eastern part of North America) and much of Canada.

2. Imagine that you are a historian and have just read the letters written by Braddock, Franklin, and Washington. Use the information in these letters to write an account of how the British felt about the colonists. Quote sections of each letter to prove your points.

3. Benjamin Franklin asks for your help in persuading the colonists to approve the Albany Plan of Union. How would you do this?

4. Just before he dies, Braddock says that he now knows how to deal with the French and Indians. Describe how you think he would change his battle plans.

5. You are a reporter. You ask Franklin and Washington what they think of British military tactics. What do they tell you?

3 Who Pays for Protecting the Colonies?

The struggle between France and Britain continued for seven years, from 1756 to 1763. Finally France was defeated. Britain became the master of North America and of India, where France had had colonies. The British Navy controlled the seas.

The British colonists in America were happy with the results of the war. Now they no longer had to worry about French and Indian attacks. But the war had been costly, and the British treasury was empty. British leaders thought the colonists should pay their "fair" share for their own defense.

Parliament, the British lawmaking body, had passed tax laws in the past. For instance, it set duties (taxes) on goods brought into the American colonies. However, little money had been collected from such taxes, which could be evaded by smuggling (secretly bringing goods into the colonies). The British had not tried very hard to collect taxes or to end smuggling.

Now all this was to be changed. Britain needed money, and the colonies would have to pay. There were new taxes, and they would be collected.

In our story about an imaginary dinner party, several individuals from different sections of the colonies and a Frenchman talk about Great Britain and the new taxes.

Ask yourself what a country should expect of its colonies. What should a colony expect of the country controlling it?

Williamsburg, Virginia, 1765

The scene is a wealthy planter's house. The planter, his wife, and their guests have just finished dinner.

ROGER LaTOURETTE. What a marvelous dinner! And how kind you were, Mr. Sampson, to ask me to your house. Even though I fought on the French side in the French and Indian War, you treat me as a friend.

REBECCA SAMPSON. The war is over. We are all friends in this house. Besides, you are going to stay in the colonies. Soon you will be an American just like the rest of us.

LaTOURETTE. Yes, I will stay in America. People here live so much better than they do in Europe. I don't see the great differences between the rich and the poor that I see there. The poor are not so poor, and the rich are not so rich. Though you are certainly rich enough!

JAMES SAMPSON. We are well off, but we have our problems. It hasn't been easy—and now those taxes!

LaTOURETTE. Everyone should pay taxes. Do you have any idea what taxes are like in France or in Great Britain?

WILLIAM BLAINE. I don't think you understand our position in the colonies, Mr. LaTourette. My grandparents came to Virginia to escape the harsh life in England. They worked very hard in those early days. Life in the colonies was brutal. They were lucky to survive.

LaTOURETTE. I understand that, but you are not suffering!

MATTHEW WILSON. You still do not understand! We built these colonies in the wilderness, fought the Indians, and suffered through sickness and starvation. We've earned what we have. And we're going to keep it!

REBECCA SAMPSON. Don't forget that we did all this on our own, cut off from our friends and relatives in Britain. We have made new lives for ourselves.

JOHN SMITHSON. Aren't you forgetting something? Yes, we struggled. Yes, we are far from our families. But we cannot turn our backs on Britain. It needs money now. We should pay our fair share.

LaTOURETTE. Ah, Mr. Smithson, you are saying that the colonists should be grateful for all that Britain has done.

SMITHSON. Right! These colonial lands belonged to the British king. He permitted the colonists to come here, to own their land, and to work at whatever they wanted. You all admit that you live far better here than you would in Britain. Don't you think that you owe your home country something for your good lives here?

BLAINE. Owe Britain? You don't know what you are talking about! Without our work, these colonies would be a dangerous wilderness.

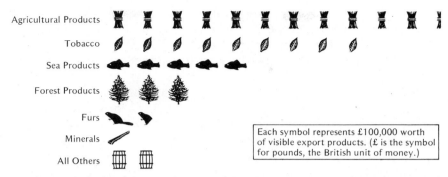

Major Exports From the American Colonies to Great Britain in 1770

We provide the things Britain wants. I grow tobacco. Can I sell to the highest bidder? No sir! I can sell only to those places the British government says I can.

JAMES SAMPSON. Why should I pay taxes to Britain? I pay my colonial taxes. That's enough!

SMITHSON. Look, William, I'm a newspaper owner and I pay taxes. It isn't easy, but it must be done. Besides, taxes in America are less than half of those in Britain. And why are you complaining, Mr. Wilson? Parliament lowered taxes on molasses for the rum you make up there in Massachusetts.

WILSON. The difference now is not between higher and lower taxes. It is between taxes and no taxes. Before the French and Indian War, Britain left us alone. We enjoyed being neglected. We were happy to be forgotten. Let the British government forget about our taxes once again—and we'll all be happy.

SMITHSON. The French and Indian War changed all that. Britain spent a lot of money fighting for us. Now we have to pay for the war and the 10,000 soldiers who protect us.

REBECCA SAMPSON. Who decides how much we should be taxed? Are there any colonial representatives in Parliament? Not a one! Those who seek to tax the colonies are the very people who want to use us and wring us dry!

SMITHSON. Wrong again! We colonists are represented in Parliament. Each member of Parliament represents every citizen of the British Empire.

BLAINE. It's not enough, and it's too much!

LATOURETTE. That I do not understand.

BLAINE. We do not have real representation, and we pay too much in taxes.

WILSON. We alone should decide whether we want to pay to support the British Empire.

LATOURETTE. The British think the colonies should help the colonial power, the homeland. You Americans, except for Mr. Smithson, feel that the colonies exist for you alone.

BLAINE. No, it is not that simple. There is a middle ground. We want to be part of the British Empire. But we will not let ourselves be pushed around. We want to be treated fairly. We will trade. We will provide things that the British can use. Then, as we profit, so will the people in Britain.

JAMES SAMPSON. We are British subjects and proud to admit it, but we are colonists first. After that we will think of the Empire.

SMITHSON. This is our first point of agreement. We will always be British. I just think we should pay our import taxes. Mr. Blaine, Mr. Wilson, and Mr. and Mrs. Sampson have other ideas.

LATOURETTE. Mr. Smithson, you said that you own a newspaper. You do not object to any of the taxes that Mr. Blaine and Mr. Sampson must pay. That is very decent of you. But what do you think of the Stamp Act passed earlier this year?

SMITHSON. Young man, you are talking now of a very nasty tax. This is something that everyone in the colonies is against.

LATOURETTE. Yes, I have heard a lot of talk against the Stamp Act. But you believe that Britain needs money. Why do you object to a stamp tax?

SMITHSON. It would force me to print my news on special paper. I would have to get these sheets of paper from the tax office and pay for them. I can't afford to print a newspaper or a book if I have to do it that way.

LATOURETTE. Aha, this sounds like self-interest to me. You publish a newspaper; you pay a tax.

JAMES SAMPSON. Oh, he wouldn't really pay those taxes. He'd pass them on to his readers.

WILSON. Even so, it would be a nuisance. And don't forget all the little taxes on every single document written in the colonies.

REBECCA SAMPSON. And playing cards and diplomas and wills.

LATOURETTE. Mrs. Sampson and gentlemen, you complain and complain. Yet you know that you are going to have to pay these taxes, or are you revolutionists?

JAMES SAMPSON. Careful, LaTourette. There is a limit to our hospitality!

WILSON. Don't be so sure about Britain's ability to collect these taxes. We are planning some interesting times for His Majesty's tax collectors. The colonies will not stand for these taxes!

POSTSCRIPT

The colonists disliked the new taxes and the stepped-up efforts of the British government to collect them. Many looked upon these actions of the British government as unnecessary meddling in colonial affairs.

Another law passed by Parliament that troubled the colonists was the Proclamation of 1763. It forbade American colonists to settle west of the Appalachian Mountains. By this rule, the British hoped to keep peace with the

Indians. The colonists felt that good farmland was being set out of their reach.

The Quartering Acts of 1765 and 1766 also angered the colonists. These laws required the towns in which Brit-ish troops were located to provide housing and supplies for the troops. Now that the French and the Indian tribes in the East had been defeated, the colonists wondered why Britain needed to keep troops in the colonies.

Homework Questions

1. How were France and Britain affected by the French and Indian War?
2. Why did Roger LaTourette choose to stay in America?
3. How were the colonists affected by the change in Britain's colonial tax policy?
4. Why did James Sampson object to the colonial taxes passed by the British Parliament?
5. Why did the colonists object to the Stamp Act?

Understanding the Story

A. Write *T* for each statement that is true, *F* for each statement that is false, and *N* for each statement that is not mentioned in the story.
   1. Great Britain defeated France in North America.
   2. France lost no territory in Europe after the French and Indian War.
   3. The French navy controlled the seas in 1763.
   4. The colonies taxed Britain heavily to pay for the war.
   5. LaTourette was the son of a French nobleman.
   6. Taxes in America were much lower than those in Britain.
   7. The French and Indian War cost the British a great deal of money.
   8. No one objected to paying the stamp tax.

B. Match each name in Column *A* with the description in Column *B*.

Column A

1. Roger LaTourette
2. Rebecca Sampson
3. James Sampson
4. William Blaine
5. Matthew Wilson
6. John Smithson

Column B

a. wealthy planter
b. tobacco grower
c. newspaper owner
d. visitor from France
e. wife of a planter
f. maker of rum

C. Some of the colonists argued that British taxes were unfair because colonists could not elect their own representatives to Parliament. If they could have elected such representatives, do you think they would have been more willing to pay taxes? Why or why not?

Activities and Inquiries

1. Study the graph on page 93. Then choose the term or phrase that best completes each statement.
   a. The export that had the greatest value was (*1*) tobacco (*2*) minerals (*3*) agricultural (farm) products.
   b. The total value of sea products and forest products is (*1*) less

than that of tobacco (2) more than that of tobacco (3) the same as that of tobacco.

c. The British imported mostly (1) manufactured goods (2) raw materials (unfinished products) (3) precious jewels and metals.

d. The value of agricultural products was (1) almost half the total of the other exports (2) twice the total of the other exports (3) equal to the value of the other products.

e. From the graph you can find out (1) that the British liked American tobacco better than any other kind (2) that the American colonies imported more British manufactured goods in 1770 than in 1750 (3) the value of the furs and minerals exported from America to Great Britain in 1770.

2. What do you think Roger LaTourette thought of the Americans he met at dinner?

3. Imagine that you live in Great Britain. Select one of the people in the story and write a letter to that person explaining why taxes are necessary.

4. Imagine that you are one of the people in the story. Answer the letter from the person in Britain about taxes.

5. The earliest colonists thought of themselves as English people. By 1765, the colonists were calling the English foreigners and were thinking of themselves as Americans. List the arguments in the story that help explain why this change came about.

4 The Boston Massacre

In the last chapter you saw that many colonists objected to the new taxes, especially the stamp tax. They showed their unhappiness in a number of ways. In major towns, citizens joined together as the "Sons of Liberty." These "liberty boys" burned stamps and attacked tax collectors and distributors of the stamps. In 1765, just before the tax was to go into effect, nine colonies sent delegates to a Stamp Act Congress in New York City. The delegates agreed that Parliament did not have the right to tax the American colonies without the consent of the colonial assemblies. The Stamp Act Congress organized an effective boycott of British goods. Not buying British goods hurt British businesses. Many people in Britain also began to urge the repeal of the Stamp Act.

Parliament studied the situation and voted to repeal the hated Stamp Act in March, 1766. A year later, Parliament placed new taxes on colonial imports of tea, paper, glass, lead, and paint. These new taxes, called the Townshend duties, were collected more efficiently than earlier taxes. Smuggling became more difficult because of the use of writs of assistance. These were court orders allowing officials to enter any building at any time to search for smuggled goods. The colonists complained bitterly, but payments and tax collections increased.

In Boston in 1768, protesting colonists treated the tax collectors from Great Britain very roughly. As a result, British soldiers were sent to the city to protect officials. During the next two years, many small brushes occurred between Bostonians and soldiers. But there were too many soldiers for the colonists to challenge openly. Then, in 1770, a number of the British forces left the city. Now the remaining soldiers did not seem so fearsome.

In our story we find ourselves in the midst of a mob attack on British soldiers. Ask yourselves what right the British had to station troops in Boston. Why did Bostonians object so strongly to having British troops in their city?

Boston, Massachusetts, March 5, 1770

Donald excitedly knocked on the door of Margaret's house, located on a quiet street in Boston. Waiting for Margaret, he could hear church bells ringing all over the city.

"Hurry, Meg," called Donald. "What's taking you so long?"

"Why are you in such a hurry? Why are all those bells ringing? What's happening?" asked Margaret.

"Haven't you heard? The crowd is supposed to go after the Lobster Backs again."

"I don't want to see anyone get hurt. And why can't you call them British soldiers instead of those silly names?" said Margaret.

"Redcoats, Lobster Backs, Bloody Backs, British soldiers—what's the difference?" asked Donald. "Anyway, let's get started. I don't want to miss the excitement."

"All right," said Margaret, "I'll go. But promise me that we'll stay far away from any fighting."

"Sure, sure. Let's get started."

The two walked rapidly toward the customshouse on King Street. The noise of the crowd grew louder. They could hear shouts and screams, whistling, and Indian war whoops. Above the noise of the mob were the constantly ringing church bells.

"Why don't they leave the soldiers alone?" asked Margaret breathlessly, as she tried to keep pace with Donald. "Why do people throw things at them?"

"Oh, those Redcoats are going to get it now!" shouted Donald, paying no attention to what Margaret was saying.

"Donald, you're not answering me. Slow down and talk to *me*!"

"Calm down, Meg. It's very simple. Those Redcoats are foreign soldiers—King George's men. They stand for everything we colonists hate. They represent taxes we can't afford to pay. I look at them, and I don't feel free. Let's get them out of Boston!"

"Very brave, Donald. But where were you strong men when the soldiers came here two years ago? Where were you when they said the soldiers were here to protect their tax collectors? Did you say anything? Did you do anything?"

"You're right, Meg, you're right. That was two years ago. We let the soldiers land in Boston. Now this is our chance to get them out of town. Perhaps we made a mistake, but this is 1770. We can still win!"

"We can win," repeated Margaret hollowly. "How? By picking fights with a few British soldiers? You throw rocks at them and surround them in narrow alleys. Are they going to stand for that abuse forever?"

"Oh, stop worrying, Meg. They have orders not to shoot. They'll threaten us and point their bayonets at us. Their guns will be ready to shoot. But they dare not fire at us."

Margaret and Donald reached the customshouse. A single soldier was on guard duty. Surrounding him was a shouting crowd of more than 200 people.

"What's all the yelling about?" asked Margaret.

"You'll see; you'll see," shouted Donald. "Get that Lobster Back. Kill him! Send him back to Britain where he belongs!"

"Look, they're throwing snowballs at the poor fellow. They'll hurt him," said Margaret. "Stop, stop, stop!"

"You'd better keep out of this, Meg."

Moments later, 20 British soldiers marched up to protect the guard. Their captain, Thomas Preston, tried to talk to the crowd. He asked people to leave. The people in the mob shouted back and refused to move. The soldiers drew their bayonets. Then chunks of ice, rocks, sticks, and clubs filled the air.

"Back away or we will fire!" shouted Captain Preston.

"Come on, you rascals, you Bloody Backs, you Lobster scoundrels. Fire if you dare!" screamed the mob.

"We know you dare not fire."

"Don't force me to do it!" pleaded Captain Preston.

"We know you dare not fire. You don't scare us!"

Captain Preston stood between the mob and his soldiers. He watched as the mob pushed forward. Now they were at the points of the bayonets. The colonists hit some of the bayonets with their sticks and tried to push the muskets aside.

"Look, Meg, our people are attacking! Give it to them! Drive them out! Show the world who owns America!"

"A soldier is down," said Margaret. "They're going to fire!"

Somewhere a voice shouted, "Fire!" The soldiers emptied their guns into the mob. The colonists backed away. Five men lay dead or dying. The soldiers prepared to fire again, but Captain Preston stopped them.

Margaret turned on her heels and hurried away.

"Where are you going, Meg? Now comes the real fighting. We'll show those Redcoats!"

"I don't want to see any more," said Margaret.

"Mark my words. This is only the beginning. We won't stop until all Redcoats are out of America!"

POSTSCRIPT

The five men killed that night were treated as martyrs (dead heroes) by the Sons of Liberty and by others trying to stir up the colonists against the British. One of the dead men was Crispus Attucks, a black seaman who may have been a runaway slave. A Crispus Attucks Monument was later put up in memory of the event that became known as the Boston Massacre.

Preston and eight other soldiers were arrested and tried for murder. Their defense attorney was John Adams, a Massachusetts lawyer who later became a leader of the American Revolution. All but two of the soldiers were found not guilty. Those two were let off with minor punishment.

For a time, until July 4 became a national holiday, the Sons of Liberty staged a parade and made speeches on March 5. The purpose was to remind everyone of the Boston Massacre.

Homework Questions

1. How did the colonists react to the Townshend duties?
2. Why did Donald feel it was proper to attack the British soldiers?
3. Why did Margaret object to Donald's reaction to the British?
4. What were Donald's reasons for thinking that the British soldiers would not shoot?

Understanding the Story

A. Write *T* for each statement that is true and *F* for each statement that is false.
   1. The Sons of Liberty did not object to the stamp tax.
   2. The Stamp Act Congress met in New York City.
   3. Smuggling increased after passage of the Townshend duties.

4. A writ of assistance allowed colonists to search British officials' houses.
5. The British sent soldiers to Boston to protect British officials.
6. Some colonists called the British soldiers "Lobster Backs."
7. No colonial lawyer would defend the British soldiers.
8. The colonists thought the British soldiers would not shoot at them.

B. Write *A* for each statement Margaret would agree with and *N* for each statement that she would not agree with.
1. I don't want to see anyone get hurt.
2. Let's kill the Redcoats.
3. People should leave the British soldiers alone.
4. I get upset every time I see a Redcoat.
5. Someday there will be bloodshed.
6. I can't wait to see the fighting.
7. Let me throw some rocks at the British soldiers.
8. Stop, they'll hurt him.

C. Donald looked upon the British troops as "foreign soldiers." Would you agree with that description? Why or why not?

Activities and Inquiries

1. What will Margaret tell her grandchildren about the Boston Massacre?
2. The grandchildren ask Donald to tell them the story of the Boston Massacre. What will he tell them? Will his story be the same as Margaret's? Explain.
3. You interview a British soldier who took part in the Boston Massacre. How does he defend his actions? Do you agree with him? Why or why not?
4. Look at the drawing on page 98 and answer the following questions.
   a. Why are the colonists saying this to the British?
   b. What did the British do? Why?
   c. Does violence solve problems? Why or why not?
   d. Did the British have a right to protect their officials? Why or why not?
   e. How would you have acted in this situation?

5 Samuel Adams, Revolutionary

Many colonists resented the new taxes, the soldiers in their cities, and other restrictions. They felt that Great Britain was treating them harshly, so they complained, held meetings, and stopped buying British products. At times, they became violent and mistreated British officials and Americans who supported the British.

How far would the colonists go? Would protest be enough for them? Or would Americans break away from Britain? Would a revolution occur?

Many colonists preferred to stay under British rule. Some of these colonists were people of considerable wealth who enjoyed close connections with British officials. Others were backwoods settlers who distrusted the city folk who took the lead in criticizing the British. Still others were common people of many kinds who looked upon critics of the British as hotheaded radicals and troublemakers.

But leaders of the anti-British movement were determined to have their way. Leaders like Samuel Adams felt that revolution and independence were the answers to the colonists' problems. Adams strongly believed that America must be free. He devoted his life to accomplishing that goal.

Samuel Adams was an outstanding leader of the revolutionary movement. He became expert at changing people's minds, at getting them to think his way. He was not a great speaker, so he left the speeches to James Otis and Joseph Warren. Instead, Sam Adams wrote, plotted, and planned. We shall see how he helped many Americans make up their minds.

Ask yourself how a revolutionary leader gets people to agree with his or her point of view. How does such a leader control the thoughts and actions of the people?

Boston, 1774

I am Sam Adams, a middle-aged man of simple tastes. My clothing is plain and worn from long use. I am proud of being poor. I am a revolutionist!

I love people and they know it. I am at ease with the rich and the poor alike. Business people respect me because of my family name and my strong religious beliefs. But I spend much of my time with the working people of Boston. I speak to them. They listen to me.

I am at home in a meetinghouse or a tavern. I have made the Green Dragon Inn on Union Street the headquarters of the revolutionary movement. Here the Sons of Liberty meet to hear me speak out against British tyranny and Tory injustice.

I warned that the Stamp Act would ruin the colonies. Any action that takes away our rights I call tyranny. Any colonist who supports the British point of view is a Tory and should be silenced. I was the first to say that members of Parliament had no right to tax Americans. First, they would tax our trade, next, our lands and all we grow on them. Soon, there would be nothing left for us from the sweat of our work. Over and over again, I said that we must tax and govern ourselves. Taxation without representation is tyranny!

I have long believed that America must be free. We must throw off the chains of British rule and make our own decisions in our own government. I am doing everything I can to guide our people to independence. We have set up Committees of Correspondence to link all the colonies by an exchange of letters. One purpose is to keep everyone informed about our plans. The people are starting to work together.

I have learned how to make people act. I have discovered many ways of getting their attention. Fireworks are often more interesting than words. A parade excites both rich and poor. Bonfires heat up American opposition to the British. I pass cartoons of evil Tories and English officials from hand to hand. Often, I add explanations of why these people are so bad.

I have every newspaper on our side carrying news to every corner of Massachusetts. Fire up the people. Get them to act. Never lie, but perhaps make things sound a little worse than they really are.

I have known for a long time that we will have to fight the British. How? We do not have an army, but we have hundreds of men who learned to fight in the French and Indian War. These men are eager for action. When I go into the taverns, I find many men willing to take their chances in a fight.

My enemies say that Boston is controlled by a trained mob. How right they are! I am the keeper and the leader of that mob. I tell them when and how to attack the king's soldiers. They move when I tell them to move. For now they do not use guns. Their weapons are rocks and sticks and fists.

I have found that we do not have to riot to annoy the British. All we need do is surround a commissioner's home, beat drums, blow horns, and howl like attacking Indians. The British know they are sitting on the edge of a volcano. When will Sam Adams turn his mob loose? Will he allow the officials to collect their taxes?

I did everything I could think of to drive the British soldiers out of Boston. I wrote articles about their beating small boys, harming young girls, hitting old people. I made the colonists resent them. I made the British responsible every time a soldier answered insults or responded to rock throwing. All I needed was a spark. The Boston Massacre on March 5, 1770, was a day all America will never forget. Five men gave their lives for the cause of freedom in our country. However, I was not happy when most of the British were found not guilty.

Something had to be done to cause an open break with Britain. What could we do to upset the British government? In 1773 I got the answer: TEA. Huge amounts of Dutch tea were being smuggled into the colonies. The British decided to remove most of the tax on tea sold by the East India Company of Great Britain. The British thought the colonists would buy the East India tea because it would be so much cheaper. American business people would suffer, and the East India Company would have complete control of the tea trade.

This was our chance to anger Britain and stir up the colonists! Other colonies took action. In Charleston the tea was landed but left to rot in warehouses. In Philadelphia and New York the tea ships were not allowed to land. Boston had to show the other colonies that it was still the leader in the fight against Britain.

Three tea ships sailed into Boston harbor. "Turn them around," we said. "Don't try to land your tea in our port. Sail back to Britain."

They did not listen to us. The ships landed. Then we showed them what Boston thought of East India tea!

When I gave the signal, a group of men dressed as Mohawk Indians broke away from the crowd. They headed for Griffin's pier, followed by the rest of the mob. The "Indians" boarded the ships and quickly threw 342 chests of excellent tea into the water.

We had done it! Boston was leading the colonists! Our Boston Tea Party upset the British government. It took strong steps to punish Boston. The other colonies rallied behind us. The revolution had begun! There would be no turning back now!

I am Sam Adams. I helped start a revolution.

POSTSCRIPT

Samuel Adams continued his work as a revolutionary. He served as a delegate from Massachusetts to the Continental Congress from 1774 to 1781. After the Revolutionary War, he became lieutenant governor and governor of his state.

Homework Questions

1. Give three reasons why Samuel Adams is considered to be a great revolutionary leader.
2. Why did Sam Adams object to Britain's taxation of the American colonies?
3. In what ways did Adams work for an independent America?
4. Why did Adams want to upset the British with his Boston Tea Party?

Understanding the Story

A. Write *F* for each statement that is a fact and *O* for each statement that is an opinion.
    1. Many colonists preferred British rule.
    2. The colonies were better off under British rule.
    3. Samuel Adams devoted his life to making America free.
    4. Samuel Adams was a bully.

5. Samuel Adams said that Parliament had no right to tax Americans.
6. Samuel Adams worked with the Committees of Correspondence.
7. Samuel Adams should have had more parades.
8. Samuel Adams helped plan the Boston Tea Party.

B. List the numbers of the statements that Samuel Adams made or might have made.
1. Let's keep the British in America.
2. Taxation without representation is tyranny!
3. It's only fair that colonists pay British taxes.
4. America must be free.
5. Get the people to act.
6. We must never fight the British.
7. I am the leader of the Boston mob.
8. I made the colonists oppose the British.

C. Sam Adams wanted to silence colonists who supported the British point of view. In your opinion, was this right or wrong? Explain.

Activities and Inquiries

1. You are planning a television film on the life of Samuel Adams. What will you call the film? Why?
2. What scenes will you include in your film? Describe them.
3. In your last scene there is a closeup of Adams's tombstone. It reads, "Here lies Samuel Adams _____." Fill in the blank.
4. Imagine that the British have posted a sign that reads: "Wanted: Sam Adams for _____." Complete the sign.

6 Opening Battles of the Revolution

The Boston Tea Party made King George III furious. He insisted that the colonists, particularly those in Boston, be punished. And they were punished by a number of laws called the Coercive Acts. To coerce means to use force or threats to make someone do something. The port of Boston was closed off. The king took control of the government of Massachusetts. Town meetings could be held only when the governor permitted them. A large number of British troops were to be quartered (sheltered) in colonists' homes. These were serious punishments indeed.

About the same time that it passed the Coercive Acts, Parliament passed the Quebec Act. This law set up the government of Canada. Since the end of the French and Indian War, what was once French North America had been ruled by the British military. Now Canada was to have an appointed governor and council but no elected lawmaking body. The act gave special rights to the Roman Catholic Church, the leading church group among French settlers. The act also added the Ohio River Valley to Canada.

The Quebec Act alarmed many in the colonies south of Canada. Would Parliament take away their elected assemblies? Would the Catholics become powerful enough to interfere in the rights of Protestants? Losing the Ohio Valley also troubled the colonists. They wanted that good farmland for themselves. Many colonists lumped the Coercive Acts and the Quebec Act together and referred to them as the Intolerable Acts.

Those who were working for separation between Britain and the colonies saw the Intolerable Acts as an attack on colonists' rights. They vowed to resist. To help Massachusetts, other colonies sent food and money. In May, 1774, the Virginia legislature called the closing of Boston's port a hostile (enemy) invasion. It set aside June 1, 1774, as a day of fasting and prayer.

Committees of Correspondence throughout the colonies agreed that an attack on one colony should be considered an attack on all. They decided to call together people from all the colonies. Delegates from 12 colonies, all but Georgia, met at Philadelphia on September 5, 1774, to begin the First Continental Congress.

What should Britain's position be in North America? Many suggestions were made. For example, some colonial delegates agreed that the king might control foreign affairs and trade. But they said Parliament must quit making laws for the colonies.

Others hoped the king would send a commission to America to find out what the colonists wanted. Remove the troops from Boston, said some. End the Coercive Acts, said still others. The king would accept none of these ideas.

The First Continental Congress tried to force the king's hand by stopping all trade with Britain until the Coercive Acts were repealed. Pressures on both sides increased.

Redcoats could be seen everywhere in Boston. British ships sent to enforce the blockade filled Boston harbor. All winter long, a group called the Massachusetts Committee of Safety collected guns and ammunition. Each day the colonial militia, or Minutemen, drilled to be ready for instant action. The royal governor could not safely travel anywhere in the colony outside of Boston. An intelligence network was set up to keep the colonists informed of any movement of British troops.

In our story, we see that the colonists were not surprised when General Thomas Gage moved his British troops into Lexington and Concord. Shots are fired by both sides, and many men fall. The stage is set for the American Revolution.

Ask yourself whether the American Revolution could have been prevented. Is Katherine Barker a traitor because she is against bloodshed?

Lexington, Massachusetts, April 20, 1775

The scene is the home of Roger and Evelyn Clark. Several women are seated at a long table, busily stitching sections of a large quilt. An air of excitement fills the room.

Harriet Smith has just sat down. "I'm sorry I'm late. With so much happening around here, I can't keep my mind on my work. Have you spoken to Sam Adams or John Hancock yet?"

"No," said Evelyn. "They would never dare come back here so quickly."

"You mean they are still in danger?" asked Harriet.

"I don't think so," answered Abigail Thompson. "Sam and John were alerted by Paul Revere and William Dawes at about midnight on the 18th. They rode off toward Woburn. I'm sure they're all right."

"But why did it have to happen in Lexington? I am so upset!" said Harriet.

"Sam and John were here, and the British wanted to capture them," answered Evelyn.

"Then the British thought they would push on to Concord and capture our guns and ammunition," added Anna Ward.

"But our Minutemen had other ideas," declared Abigail.

"Our brave men marched to the common in the center of town," said Anna. "Captain Parker told me that he warned his men not to

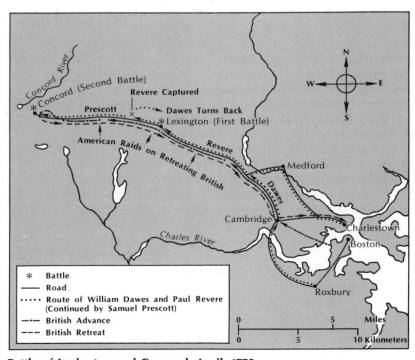

Battle of Lexington and Concord, April, 1775

fire unless the British fired first. The British officer told our men to get out of there. Imagine telling our own Minutemen to go home!"

"Somebody fired a pistol or a musket or whatever—and the battle was on!" said Abigail.

"I don't want a war," said Evelyn, raising her voice. "But we must fight for our freedom. What better place for our Revolution to start than our own town of Lexington!"

"A great place to start a revolution and a great place to be killed!" said Katherine Barker, who had been silent up to this point. "What in heaven's name did those Minutemen do? They fired a few shots and got themselves killed. Who needs that?"

"You don't know what the Minutemen did," replied Anna angrily. "Yes, eight were killed. No, the British were not stopped. But now everyone in America and Europe will know about our struggle for freedom. They will find out about the tyranny and cruelty of the British."

"American patriots can stand up to British Lobster-Back soldiers!" added Evelyn.

"Yes, and Lexington will always be famous," said Harriet.

"Let's stop fooling ourselves," said Katherine. "It's true they didn't capture John and Sam. I am grateful for that—if it was true that the soldiers really were looking for them. But there's something more important. Did the Minutemen save our supplies at Concord? No, they did not!"

"What will we do about guns and ammunition now?" said Harriet.

"Never mind that!" Abigail said sharply. "We proved that we're not afraid of British soldiers. They took our guns, but we are not weaklings!"

"And our men shot at the British soldiers all the way back to Boston. Everywhere those Redcoats marched, American bullets knocked them down," added Anna.

"They will think twice before they attack Americans again," said Harriet.

"You know, you're all wrong!" said Katherine firmly. "This isn't a show. It's a life-and-death matter, and you're babbling on about bravery and strength—and revolution. We're not playing a game now. This is war. This is a fight against our own British Empire."

"Then you are not with us in this fight?" asked Evelyn sternly.

"I am with you, but I don't want my husband and sons to die."

"You are not with us, Katherine," said Anna, "if you are afraid."

"Why do you have to talk this way? We've been friends all our lives. Can't we have differences of opinions?"

"You know, Katherine, John and Sam might have been hanged if they had been caught," said Anna.

"Don't forget that we would have been punished for sheltering them," said Evelyn. "We are risking everything! What's wrong with you?"

"You just don't see that it does not have to be war and revolution!"

Katherine said in firm tones. "There is another way. King George might forgive us and take us back into the British Empire."

"Take us back!" said Evelyn, raising her voice. "We don't want to be taken back. We are Americans, and we are going to go our own way. We will be free! Ask King George anything? Nonsense!"

"Now, don't get so excited," said Katherine, trying to calm everyone. "I feel differently about our king. He will understand our problems if we explain everything clearly once again. We could send him a list of our grievances, what we think is wrong. But it must go directly to him, not to his advisers. The king would quickly turn matters around, I'm sure."

"You can't be serious," said Anna. "You mean you think the king would stop asking us to pay unfair taxes or stop quartering British soldiers in our homes? He'd call all his soldiers back to Great Britain and let us pass our own laws? He'd forget that we shot at his men and that they shot back?"

"He'd stop the use of those vicious writs of assistance?"

"He would not fight a war against us?"

"Why wouldn't he understand?" asked Katherine hesitantly. "Are we not his children, his sisters and his brothers? Forgive and forget, I say."

"Absolutely not," said Abigail.

"We have not come this far to beg forgiveness," said Evelyn. "We cannot turn back!"

Homework Questions

1. List three ways Massachusetts was punished for the Boston Tea Party.
2. How did the colonies respond to the punishment of Massachusetts?
3. How did the colonists prepare for the fighting of the revolution?
4. Why were the battles of Concord and Lexington important to the colonists?
5. How would Katherine Barker overcome the differences between the colonies and Britain? How did the others answer her?

Understanding the Story

A. List the numbers of the statements that are true.
   1. The British closed off the port of Boston.
   2. British troops were not quartered in colonists' homes.
   3. The First Continental Congress met in Philadelphia.
   4. Paul Revere warned Sam Adams and John Hancock that the British soldiers were near.
   5. Most British soldiers were called Minutemen.
   6. Americans and British soldiers fought at Lexington.
   7. The Americans defeated the British at Lexington.
   8. Some colonists wanted to remain loyal to the king.

B. List the numbers of the statements that describe results of the Battle of Lexington.
   1. The American Revolutionary War began.
   2. American fighting men showed no fear of the British army.

3. The British soldiers captured Sam Adams and John Hancock.
4. People in Europe learned about the colonists' fight for freedom.
5. The British were afraid to fight against Americans.
6. The Minutemen saved the supply of guns and ammunition at Concord.
7. American fighting men were killed and wounded.
8. Every colonist hoped the British would lose.

C. Imagine that you are a delegate to the Continental Congress. You have just heard about the fighting at Lexington and Concord. What do you think the Congress should do? Why?

Activities and Inquiries

1. Evelyn Clark keeps a diary. What will she write about Katherine Barker?
2. Katherine Barker also keeps a diary. What will she write about Evelyn Clark?
3. A British spy overhears the women's conversation. What good news would the spy report back to a commanding officer?
4. What bad news would the spy report back to a commander?
5. You interview a colonist who is against the revolution. How does the person try to convince you that the anti-revolution side is right? Do you agree with the arguments? Why or why not?

7 Declaring Independence

The Revolutionary War had begun with the firing of shots at Lexington and Concord. After this battle, a Second Continental Congress met. It created an army and navy and appointed George Washington commander in chief of a continental army. Washington then began the job of turning 15,000 mostly untrained militiamen into soldiers.

Even though actual fighting had taken place, most members of Congress hoped that a final break with Britain could somehow be avoided. In July, 1775, a final petition (request), signed by almost every leader of the revolution, was sent to King George III. In it Congress urged the king to stop the war, repeal the Coercive Acts, and restore friendly relations.

The king refused to pay attention to this petition. He said he would not be satisfied until the colonial rebellion was crushed and its leaders punished. The American leaders now decided to declare complete independence from Great Britain. They saw no other way.

In our story Congress is about to take this fateful step. It has formed a committee to write a declaration of independence. The committee has five members—John Adams, Thomas Jefferson, Benjamin Franklin, Roger Sherman, and Robert Livingston. Though our story is fiction, it is based on real events. Ask yourself why declaring independence was such a difficult step to take.

Philadelphia, June, 1776

John Adams was speaking to the committee. "Gentlemen, I propose that we ask Thomas Jefferson to do our work for us. Thomas, how about it? Will you write a draft declaration? Afterwards, we'll all go over it together. This will be a historic document, and we want it to be the best we can possibly make it."

"John, you know I'm perfectly willing to do whatever needs to be done," said Jefferson. "But why me? Why not you or one of the others?"

Adams smiled. "Because you write with better style than any of us, Thomas. Besides, people like myself have made too many enemies by speaking out bluntly on political matters. Everyone likes you, so the delegates will not be tempted to pick your work apart out of jealousy."

Now Benjamin Franklin spoke up. "John's right. Thomas Jefferson is the one to write the draft."

"Hear, hear," chimed in Roger Sherman.

"I agree," said Robert Livingston.

"It's settled then," said Adams. "Thomas will write a draft. God be with you, Thomas."

Later, alone in his study, Jefferson stared at the ceiling. Writing the declaration would not be easy. Its phrasing and arguments would have to capture the imagination of Congress and the American people. Too many people still held back. Loyalty to the king was strong—as well it might be! Didn't the Bible tell people to obey their rulers? Hadn't obedience to the laws been one of the first rules taught in almost every colonial home? Declaring independence was an act that would be viewed as treason under British law. Those who supported the declaration would be placing in danger their property, their liberty, their very lives. Jefferson's work was cut out for him!

Jefferson wanted to tell Americans not to be afraid to break away from Great Britain. He knew there were powerful arguments on his side. Many thinkers agreed that a king and his subjects were bound together by an unwritten compact (agreement). If the king broke that compact, he no longer had a right to claim obedience. Jefferson must put the argument as plainly and forcefully as possible. He must stress the rights that belong to all people—rights that no king could take away.

Excitedly, Jefferson began to write. He started with a statement announcing the breaking of ties between the colonies and Great Britain. Then he set down certain basic political rights the colonists held to be important. (In the quoted passages, most of the words are as Jefferson wrote them. Some phrases were changed by other members of the committee, however, and others were changed by Congress. The words are as they appeared in the final version.)

"When in the course of human events, it becomes necessary for one people to dissolve the political bands which have connected them with another, . . . they should declare the causes which impel them to the separation.

"We hold these truths to be self-evident, that all men are created equal, that they are endowed by their Creator with certain unalienable rights, that among these are life, liberty, and the pursuit of happiness."

Next the document told why governments are created, where they get their powers, and when governments should be changed or done away with.

"That to secure these rights, governments are instituted among men, deriving their just powers from the consent of the governed. That whenever any form of government becomes destructive of these ends, it is the right of the people to alter or to abolish it, and to institute new government. . . ."

To convince everyone of the rightness of the colonies' decision to be independent, Jefferson listed some 30 complaints against King George. He accused the king of preventing colonial legislatures from passing laws, of controlling judges and courts, and of sending troops to the colonies. He also accused the king of cutting off trade, waging war against the colonies, and burning towns. In harsh words he blamed the king for killing people and stirring up the Indians.

Jefferson and Adams wanted to include one more criticism of the king:

"He has waged cruel war against human nature itself, violating its most sacred rights of life and liberty in the persons of a distant people who never offended him, captivating and carrying them into slavery . . . or to incur miserable death in their transportation. . . ."

Southern slave owners and Northern slave traders banded together in the Congress to strike out this passage on slavery.

Jefferson and the other members of the Congress gave careful attention to the closing words of the declaration. Each knew that if Great Britain defeated the colonial forces, he might be hanged for treason. The delegates wanted to emphasize the seriousness of their cause and their loyalty to it.

"And for the support of this declaration, with a firm reliance on the protection of Divine Providence, we mutually pledge to each other our lives, our fortunes, and our sacred honor."

POSTSCRIPT

On Thursday, the fourth of July, 1776, Congress voted to adopt the Declaration of Independence. All the 13 colonies approved it except New York, which did not vote. When the declaration was read to the public four days later, the crowd cheered and tore off the king's coat of arms from the front of the statehouse. The Declaration of Independence was now a fact. It would serve as a beacon to guide many generations of Americans and as an inspiration to later revolutionaries in other countries around the world.

Homework Questions

1. Why did Congress send a petition to King George III in 1775? What was his reply?
2. Why was the Declaration of Independence written?
3. Which criticism of the king did the Congress strike out?
4. According to the Declaration of Independence, when do people have the right to set up a new government?
5. How many colonies voted for the Declaration of Independence?

Understanding the Story

A. Write *T* for each true statement, *F* for each false statement, and *N* for each statement that is not mentioned in the story.
   1. George Washington was born in Virginia.
   2. George Washington was commander in chief of the continental army.
   3. King George was happy to receive the colonists' petitions.
   4. Thomas Jefferson wrote the Declaration of Independence.
   5. The Declaration of Independence explained why the colonies broke away from Great Britain.

6. The Declaration of Independence was published in British newspapers.
7. According to the declaration, a government gets its powers from the king.
8. There are about 30 complaints, or grievances, against the king in the Declaration.

B. Write *A* for each statement that Thomas Jefferson would agree with and *N* for each statement that he would not agree with.
   1. Fighting the war against Britain is a great mistake.
   2. I must write something about slavery in the Declaration.
   3. A king always has the right to claim obedience.
   4. Writing the Declaration will not be easy.
   5. We Americans should cut ourselves loose from Great Britain.
   6. I'm glad there is nothing in the Declaration about slavery.
   7. It may be dangerous to be the author of the Declaration.
   8. I know exactly how the war is going to turn out.

C. Imagine that you are Thomas Jefferson and are writing a Declaration of Independence today. What would you add? What would you subtract? Does the Declaration of Independence still have meaning for us? Explain.

Activities and Inquiries

1. Imagine that Thomas Jefferson is on trial for treason in Great Britain for having written the Declaration of Independence. Prepare the case for the British government.
2. Prepare the case for Jefferson's defense.
3. You are a member of the Second Continental Congress. Will you sign the Declaration of Independence? Why or why not?
4. You are an American newspaper editor in 1776. Write an editorial about the Declaration of Independence, which has just been approved by Congress.
5. Now write an editorial about the Declaration that might appear in a British newspaper.

8 Victory at Yorktown

The Declaration of Independence gave new meaning to the American Revolution. Before, the colonists had been fighting against British taxation. Afterwards, they fought for their freedom from Great Britain.

The war brought tremendous hardships and, at first, few victories. Somehow General Washington kept the colonial army together as a fighting force. Finally, at Yorktown, Virginia, in 1781, Washington's patience and determination paid off. American troops, ably assisted by French soldiers and a large French navy, soundly defeated a British army led by Lord Charles Cornwallis. Great Britain no longer had the will to continue the fight. At long last, the Revolutionary War was over.

Our story takes place at about noon in the Yorktown battlefield. Cornwallis and his army will officially surrender in two hours. The French and American armies are drawn up in two lines extending for more than a mile. The Americans are on one side of the road with General Washington in the lead. The French are on the other side with Count Rochambeau at the head of their column.

Ask yourself why the American victory at Yorktown was so important to the colonists. Why was this victory important to General Washington?

Yorktown, Virginia, October 19, 1781

General George Washington is thinking about many things as he waits.

This was to be the greatest moment of my life. It's the end of six years of struggle against the British. We proved that an untrained army with a cause is more than a match for King George's trained regulars and hired soldiers. They fought for money; we fought for freedom. And now Cornwallis will surrender his army to me!

Alas, the British were not my only foes. I could understand having to fight on the battlefield, but worrying about Congress was too much. Would I have become commander in chief of the American armies if I had known the troubles I would face? I wonder.

Congress never gave us enough money. We were always short of uniforms, blankets, guns, and ammunition. And where were the men to fight the British? How can you fight a war without enough soldiers? How can you win when men leave their posts in the middle of battle? My officers tried to stop them. The men would wave their enlistment papers and shout, "My time is up!" They were right. They had signed up for a year—for six months—even for three months! Congress should have insisted that soldiers fight for the entire war.

No, I am not sorry I took the job. It was a great challenge. Thirteen tiny colonies against the strength and resources of the most powerful nation on earth.

Victory was a long time coming. There were six years of fighting and retreating. There were some great moments, too. I shall never forget how we surprised them at Trenton, New Jersey, in 1776. Then in 1777 the turning point came at the Battle of Saratoga, New York. That battle made the French realize that we could win. Seeing their chance to get back at the British, they gave us money, soldiers, and ships. Thousands of French troops helped us win here at Yorktown. The French fleet would not let the British retreat. They cut them off completely. What a blessing!

Ah, but victories did not come often to our small colonial army. We faced a hard struggle just to survive through the dark months and years of British control. New York, Philadelphia, Boston—all were held by the enemy. What hope could we have? But I never gave up and kept the army together as best I could. The winters were impossible. How my soldiers suffered through the snow and ice of Valley Forge in 1777 and early 1778. They had so little food and clothing that many starved or froze. Yet most remained loyal to me and the Revolution.

My faith and determination gave my men the will to keep fighting against impossible odds. I do not know how I succeeded, but I did. Now we are here, the winners. The British are surrendering!

Will I ever forget how my enemies in Congress and in New England tried to take my command from me? They said they were tired of my retreating from the British. They wanted me to stand and fight. I would have liked to do as they wished. But how? With what? Could anyone have done any more? I think not. The fighting is over now. I must not think of those men any longer. I showed my critics that the American army could stand and fight—when we had the men and the guns.

It's almost two o'clock. I'll be glad when Cornwallis has handed me his sword and these ceremonies are over.

A group of high-ranking British officers approaches Washington.

"I don't see Cornwallis," declares General Benjamin Lincoln. "Something's wrong! Where is he?"

"Don't get excited," says Washington. "We'll soon find out what's wrong."

"I am General Charles O'Hara, second in command to Lord Cornwallis," says the British officer. "I am very sorry but Lord Cornwallis is sick. It is impossible for him to be here today. He asked me to surrender for him."

"Very well, this is my second in command. General Lincoln, you will accept General O'Hara's sword!"

Earlier, Lord Cornwallis had also been thinking about many things.

How could I, Charles Cornwallis, have been such a fool? I never wanted to come to America. I was against taxing the colonies in the first place. Why did the government have to pick me? I protested and complained, but it was not enough.

Perhaps Yorktown was the wrong place to make my stand. But how could I know that the French would send such a large fleet and cut us off? There was no way we could escape. I had to surrender!

Surrender to that so-called general, George Washington? What else could I do? Trained British troops, the flower of our army, had to give up. Soon they will surrender their guns, their swords, and their honor.

Oh, I suppose I could have fought on to the death. What would have been the sense of it? From now on, I will live in the past. I'll think back to my great victories in Europe and a few here.

I could have won this battle if only I had been in supreme command. Why did they have to put General Henry Clinton in charge? He's a weak, stupid fool. I tried to explain to him that we must capture Virginia to end this revolutionary war. But he stayed safely in New York. Where were the troops, the reinforcements, that would have rescued my army? He wanted me to send 3,000 soldiers back to New York! The battle was here in Virginia, but Clinton would not believe me.

Why did I pick Yorktown? Clinton told me to take over a spot and hold it—with my whole army if necessary. Yorktown looked easy to defend. And I could have won if only that man had sent those extra troops.

North America in 1783

At two o'clock I must give my sword to Washington. It is my duty as a British officer and a gentleman. I agreed to Washington's terms.

I feel sick when I think of the shame, the dishonor, the pain. I can't do it. I can't give my sword to Washington in front of all those colonial and French soldiers. Let them call me "coward." I don't care.

"General O'Hara, take over the surrender. The job is yours."

POSTSCRIPT

The British troops marched sullenly between the French and Americans and threw their guns into a pile. The British officers bit their lips. Some cried. Others could not hide their anger and disgust.

All during this time, the British band played the tune "The World Turned Upside Down."

The Battle of Yorktown was the last important battle of the American War for Independence. But the fighting lasted, off and on, for another two years. Then in 1783, Great Britain and America signed a peace agreement, the Treaty of Paris. It gave the new country all the territory from Canada to the northern border of Florida and from the Atlantic Ocean to the Mississippi River. More important, the treaty recognized the independence of the United States.

Homework Questions

1. Why was the Battle of Yorktown so important to the Americans?
2. According to George Washington, for what cause did the American army fight?
3. How could the American army win the war if it had so few victories?
4. What were some major differences between Washington and Congress?
5. According to Lord Cornwallis, why did the British lose?

Understanding the Story

A. Write *T* for each statement that is true and *F* for each statement that is false.
1. Commander-in-Chief George Washington kept the American army together.
2. Yorktown was the first battle of the American Revolution.
3. Lord Charles Cornwallis won the Battle of Yorktown.
4. During the Revolution, the American army was short of men and materials.
5. The American army won victories at Trenton and Saratoga.
6. The British army lost every battle of the Revolutionary War.
7. Cornwallis disliked General Henry Clinton.
8. Cornwallis would not surrender to Washington in person.

B. Complete each of the following sentences by filling in the missing word or words.
1. The British surrendered their army after the Battle of _____ in 1781.
2. Washington worried about _____ as well as about the British.
3. Washington did not have enough _____ and _____.
4. The Revolutionary War lasted _____ years.
5. The _____ fleet helped the Americans win the war.
6. The American army suffered through the winter of 1777–1778 at _____.
7. As a symbol of surrender, a British general handed over his _____.
8. The commander of the British forces in America in 1781 was _____.

C. Great Britain, a powerful nation, was defeated by the infant United States. What advantages did the U.S. have in the war? What advantages did Britain have? Would a small nation today have similar advantages against a big and powerful nation? Why or why not?

Activities and Inquiries

1. The map on page 89 shows North America in 1763. The map on page 116 shows the same area in 1783. Study both maps. Then choose the term or phrase that best completes each statement.
   a. In 1783 the area belonging to the United States was (1) exactly the same as that of the original 13 colonies (2) smaller than the 13 colonies (3) much larger than the 13 colonies.
   b. In 1783 Florida belonged to (1) Spain (2) the United States (3) Great Britain.
   c. In 1783 the United States extended from (1) the Mississippi River to the Pacific Ocean (2) the Atlantic Ocean to the Mississippi River (3) the Atlantic Ocean to the Pacific Ocean.

   d. The maps show that between 1763 and 1783 the amount of unexplored land (*1*) increased (*2*) decreased (*3*) stayed the same.

   e. In 1783 Russia claimed (*1*) Alaska (*2*) Mexico and Central America (*3*) New York.

2. You interview a French diplomat and ask why his country wanted to help America break away from Great Britain. What does he tell you?

3. You ask Cornwallis if he thinks Britain made a mistake in trying to hold the American colonies. What does he say?

4. Write an account for an American newspaper of the surrender of Cornwallis's army.

5. Write an account of the surrender for a British newspaper.

Who Built America?

Casimir Pulaski

MR. MILLER. It's your turn to report, Cass.

CASIMIR. I was named after a hero of the American Revolution. I'm going to talk about my namesake, the Polish count, Casimir Pulaski.

CARLA. How can a Polish noble be an American hero?

CASIMIR. Pulaski was a freedom fighter. He fought for the independence of Poland, but that struggle failed. Then the American Revolution broke out. It gave him another chance to fight for freedom. He came here and asked General Washington for a commission in the United States Army.

RICARDO. What happened?

CASIMIR. After a long time, he got his commission as a brigadier general.

JACK. How do you come over here from Europe and get a job as a general?

CASIMIR. Everyone was aware of Pulaski's ability. He knew a great deal about horses, was a trained fighter, and was a respected leader. He had won battles in Poland. Benjamin Franklin, who was a representative of the United States in France, knew what Pulaski could do for America. He and others wrote to Washington. Believe me, Washington was glad to have Pulaski on his side! He needed experienced military men to help train the soldiers.

HEINRICH. All right, Pulaski is here. What does he do for us?

CASIMIR. First of all, he was put in charge of all American cavalry, the part of the army that fights on horseback. His job was to train and mold the cavalry into a strong military unit. Then, he had the infantry, the foot soldiers, working with his horsemen. Before long, the British learned what Pulaski and his men could do! His raids confused and upset the enemy.

HEINRICH. Did he win any battles?

CASIMIR. Oh, yes! Picture this: The governor of South Carolina and his council are ready to surrender Charleston to the British. Pulaski angrily walks into the room. "I forbid you to surrender!" he says. "What right do you have to tell us what to do?" asks the governor. "I am an officer of the Continental Army," replies General Pulaski. "I will fight with you or without you!"

ROSA. Wow! What a forceful person!

CASIMIR. Right. The governor and his council listened to Pulaski. He rallied the troops and encouraged them to fight. He helped Americans see that the British could be beaten.

ROSA. He does sound heroic.

CASIMIR. At Savannah, Georgia, he was helping the French capture the city from the British. As usual, he was absolutely fearless on the battlefield. Bullets barely missed him as he led the charge against enemy guns. Victory was in sight. Suddenly he was hit. He would never see another battlefield.

ROBERT. Too bad! He could have lived in a free America!

CASIMIR. True, but he helped us win our freedom. And he gave his life for us!

MR. MILLER. You can learn something else from Pulaski's part in America's battles.

CASIMIR. I know, Mr. Miller! People from many countries helped fight our American Revolution. We might have lost without them.

MR. MILLER. Excellent, Cass. That's exactly right.

"Say, Mr. Miller, what was the British government trying to do to its American colonies?"

"What do you mean, Jack?"

"Well, first, in the Zenger case the British wouldn't let Americans criticize colonial officials. No one is perfect. You have to tell it like it is!"

"That's true," said Mr. Miller. "But the British government wasn't treating the colonists any differently from the way it treated people back in Britain. The idea of a free press took a long time to develop. Americans like Zenger played an important part."

"Oh, I see. Well, later the British tried to make the colonies pay for the French and Indian War," added Jack.

"What was so wrong about that? Weren't the French and Indians a danger to the colonists?"

"Yes," replied Jack. "But the British had never taxed the colonists before."

"Are you sure about that?"

Jack thought for a moment. "I remember. There were taxes, but the British didn't collect—or couldn't collect! This time, the British were going to pull money out of the colonists' pockets. They meant business!"

"Very good. Now, can you see how dissatisfaction with these policies could turn into a revolution?"

"Sure, Mr. Miller. We wanted to pass our own tax laws, or at least we wanted to be represented in the British Parliament. Who wants to be bossed around by a faraway king?"

"Is that a revolution?"

"It's a beginning," answered Jack. "They wouldn't give us a share in governing ourselves. We moved from being a colony to being a nation, from being a monarchy to being a republic. That's a full turn of the wheel—a revolution!"

"Was it really that simple?"

"No, Mr. Miller. People like Sam Adams had to do a lot of plotting and planning and organizing. And don't forget the skirmishes with British troops, like the Boston Massacre. It was a long, hard road from colonial dependence to independence!"

"And what else?" Mr. Miller asked.

"There were a lot of battles," continued Jack. "I guess that we didn't win too many. But Saratoga and Yorktown were our big winners. We won when the chips were down!"

"Have you figured out how we managed to beat the British Empire?"

"Foreigners like Pulaski joined our army. More important, we had the help of the French—after Saratoga. Also, we won because we knew why we were fighting."

"And why was that, Jack?"

"It's all in the Declaration of Independence. Americans were unhappy with British rule. King George had been harsh and unfair to us. So we felt we had the right to break away and govern ourselves in our own democratic way. The revolutionists wanted freedom and decided they could never get that under British rule. We had to be independent to be free."

"Excellent, Jack. Freedom certainly was worth fighting for."

"Can we go on to our government under George Washington now?" asked Jack.

"Not yet," replied Mr. Miller. "First, let's look at the Constitution of these United States."

The Government of the United States

"I know what you're going to say, Mr. Miller. Every American should know about the Constitution and the government."

"Don't you agree, Jack?" asked Mr. Miller.

"Sure, but I know all that stuff."

"Fine," said Mr. Miller. "What do you remember about the Articles of Confederation?"

"No fair. That's not our government today."

"True, but you should know what was wrong with our government under the Articles. Otherwise, you can't understand why we needed a new Constitution."

"Come on, Mr. Miller. I understand enough about our government. There's a President and a Congress and—a—a Supreme Court."

"All right, Jack. What are the President's powers?"

"Well, he vetoes bills and makes a lot of speeches. I guess I'm a little fuzzy on the other things he does."

"Try again," Mr. Miller said with a smile. "Do you know how the President is elected?"

"There's a college of some sort," replied Jack.

"It's the Electoral College, Jack. I admit that our way of electing the President is somewhat complicated. But don't you think you should know how it happens?"

"Okay, I don't know much about the President. But I know what Congress does. It passes laws."

"That's a start," said Mr. Miller. "But how does it go about passing a law? And what do you know about the Bill of Rights? And—"

"Mr. Miller, I give up. Bring on the government unit."

1 A Rebellion of Farmers

The new United States was only one third the size of our country today. But the area was much larger than most European nations.

How would this large nation govern itself? How much power would the individual states (the former colonies) keep? How much would the states give up to a central government? The Continental Congress tried to answer these questions.

During the war, Congress had created a government called a confederation. The constitution, or Articles of Confederation, established a central government with limited powers. Americans could not easily forget the tyranny of the king and Parliament. So they made sure that the individual states remained all-important, or sovereign, and continued to hold most of the real governing power.

Under the Articles, the Continental Congress became the Congress of the Confederation. It had all powers connected with war and peace but not the power to raise money. Congress could not tax imports (goods coming into the country) nor control trade among the states. The central government could coin money but so could the states.

It was difficult for Congress to use its limited powers because 9 of the 13 states had to approve important laws. What is more, all 13 states had to approve any change in the Articles. Twice, 12 states voted to allow a tariff (a tax on imports). Because Rhode Island voted against it, no tariff could be set.

The central government consisted almost entirely of the Congress. There was no executive, or president, to carry out the laws. There was no central court system—only state courts.

Despite its limitations, the Confederation accomplished many things. It carried the nation through the Revolution and brought the war to a favorable end. It worked to resolve the confusion resulting from war debts. Two laws passed by Congress had a great influence on the future development of the United States.

One, the Land Ordinance of 1785, set up a system to make the sale of public lands easier and fairer. The second, the Northwest Ordinance of 1787, set up a government in a region that was beyond the boundaries of existing states. This region was called a *territory*—the Northwest Territory. The law provided a way for this territory to become a state with all the rights and privileges of the original states. The Northwest Ordinance set the pattern of government for later territories and states.

In spite of the accomplishments, many problems developed during these years of confederation. Much later the years from 1781 to 1788 came to be called the Critical Period. The colonies were now the United States, but they were weak. They could not force the British to respect the peace treaty and remove their troops from the Northwest Territory. They could not stop the Indians from attacking settlers going west toward the Mississippi. They could not protect Americans from the Indians, the Spanish, and the British in the Mississippi Valley. Many Americans were unhappy with government—with their state governments and with their central government. In Massachusetts, the discontent turned into rebellion.

In our story, Massachusetts farmers face financial ruin. Who will help them? Certainly not the central government. The story takes place in the town hall in Springfield. A meeting has been called to discuss the farmers' complaints. About 200 people are in the room. They want to appeal to their state government for help.

Ask yourself why the farmers were so upset. Was the meeting a waste of time? Should the farmers of Massachusetts have rebelled against their state government?

Springfield, Massachusetts, July, 1786

CHAIRMAN. The meeting will come to order.

JAMES JOHNSON. Mr. Chairman, we farmers are desperate. We can't sell our crops—nobody has any money to buy them. We can't pay our taxes—*we* haven't got any money either. What will we do?

RICHARD BEDFORD. Even worse—we can't pay our debts. I had to borrow money from the bank to buy seeds the last few years. But I've made so little on my crops that I haven't been able to pay the money back. I'm in debt up to my neck.

DAN STRONG. You're not the only one, Richard. Lots of farmers have debts they can't pay. Some have even been sent to debtors' prison.

JOSEPH WILLIAMS. It's so unfair. It's not our fault we can't pay.

STRONG. Maybe not, but that's how the law works. If you can't pay the bank, the bank goes to court. The court orders you to pay. You can't, so either you sell your farm or the court does it for you. You and your family are out in the cold, and you can't do a thing about it.

THOMAS READ. Well, I say we can do something about it. We can send a list of things we want changed to the state legislature. We can ask that taxes be postponed for six months. That will give us time to earn some money.

BEDFORD. Tell the legislature to put off debt payments for six months, too.

JOHNSON. It would help us more if the legislature would approve the use of paper money. The way I see it, the root of our problem is that there's not enough money to go around. People can't buy our goods if they don't have enough money.

BEN MARTIN. You're right. Coins are fine, but the number of coins depends on how much gold and silver is mined. Paper money makes more sense because the government can just print enough to go around. Let's ask the legislature to make paper money legal for paying taxes and paying off debts.

BEDFORD. Don't expect the legislature to vote for paper money. Why, that's the last thing that bankers and other rich men want. It would help people like us—people who owe money—but it would hurt people who have lent money out. Don't you see, a paper dollar would never be worth as much as a gold or silver dollar, even if the law said it was. We'd be paying off our debts with "funny money"—after they'd lent us good solid gold or silver.

JOHNSON. But isn't paper money better than what we have now? If people had money to spend, we could sell our crops. Merchants could sell their goods. Everybody would be more prosperous. Even bankers, I'll bet.

LUKE DAY. Pipe dreams, just pipe dreams! Don't you know who controls the legislature? The rich, that's who! Sure, we voters elect the Assembly—and it passes some good laws. But only the rich elect the state Senate, and a bill has to pass both houses before it becomes a law.

READ. We need to change the legislature itself, then. The Senate should be abolished!

WILLIAMS. And the legislature should move out of Boston. Get the government away from those greedy merchants and shipowners.

BEDFORD. Springfield would be the perfect spot for the capital. If the legislature were moved here, farmers would have more influence.

CHAIRMAN. Shall we add a move of the capital to our list?

VOICES. Yes, yes.

DAY. You're wasting your time. Nothing will come of your requests. Nothing!

Shays and his followers taking possession of a court house

ELI PARSONS. Luke is right. If we want to change things, we'll have to take more drastic steps.

DAY. We've sent lists of requests to the legislature before. Nothing happened.

PARSONS. If we want help, we'll have to help ourselves. Let's stop the courts from collecting debts! Let's throw out the judges!

STRONG. Not so fast! How do you expect to do that?

PARSONS. We've talked to Captain Daniel Shays. He will be our leader. We'll fight if we have to!

JOHNSON. Stop! This is rebellion—treason!

DAY. This is not rebellion. We only want to protect what we own.

CHAIRMAN. We've heard enough today. Meeting adjourned. Let's go home.

PARSONS. Don't go home! You men who want to save your farms, meet me outside!

POSTSCRIPT

In the fall of 1786, farmers did prevent the courts from sitting in the western counties of Massachusetts and in the area around Concord. The state appealed to Congress for help, but Congress could not do much. Finally, the state militia was called out to break up the farmers' groups. A battle took place at Springfield between the militia and 1,100 men under Shays, Day, and Parsons. The farmers lost. The militia took many prisoners, but Shays escaped to Vermont. The court sentenced 14 of the farmers to death. Eventually, all received pardons or short prison terms.

The people of Massachusetts elected a new state legislature in which the majority favored the farmers. The legislature approved a few of the farmers' requests, over the protests of bankers and the well-to-do. Prosperity (good times) helped the farmers forget their remaining demands.

Nevertheless, many Americans saw the Massachusetts events as a warning of trouble to come. George Washington thought that another rebellion could break out in any state at any time. Many well-to-do people feared that farmers and debtors were gaining too much power in many states. Washington and many other Americans feared that the government under the Articles of Confederation was too weak to solve the nation's problems. They thought something would have to be done—and soon.

Homework Questions

1. Why was the central government given only limited powers under the Articles of Confederation?
2. How did the limitations of the Articles make the confederation difficult to govern?
3. Why did the Massachusetts farmers think that paper money would help them pay their debts?
4. Why was it suggested that the state capital be moved from Boston to another city?
5. How did Shays's Rebellion affect the thinking of leaders such as George Washington?

Understanding the Story

A. Write *F* for each statement that is a fact and *O* for each statement that is an opinion.
   1. In 1783 the United States was much larger than most European nations.
   2. In 1783 the western boundary of the United States should have been the Pacific Ocean.
   3. The Articles of Confederation provided for a central government with limited powers.
   4. Congress can never have too many powers.
   5. Congress under the Articles could not tax imports.
   6. Under the Articles there was no executive to carry out the laws.
   7. The years 1781 to 1788 need not have been called the Critical Period.
   8. The Articles of Confederation carried us through the Revolutionary War.

B. Choose the term or phrase that best completes each statement.
   1. Massachusetts farmers complained about (*a*) high profits (*b*) high taxes (*c*) not enough rain.
   2. Farmers worried about (*a*) how to pay their debts (*b*) high prices for their crops (*c*) too much help from the state government.
   3. Farmers who could not pay their debts might be (*a*) given financial help (*b*) given extra bushels of wheat (*c*) thrown into jail.
   4. Farmers were afraid they might (*a*) be drafted into the state militia (*b*) not have enough help at harvest time (*c*) lose their farms.
   5. Farmers believed paper money would (*a*) help them pay their debts (*b*) cause prices to go down (*c*) cause shipowners to get rich.
   6. Some farmers suggested that the state capital be moved to (*a*) Boston (*b*) Springfield (*c*) New York City.
   7. Creditors and business people wanted to be paid in (*a*) cheap money (*b*) solid money (*c*) corn.
   8. The leader of the farmers who rebelled was (*a*) Daniel Shays (*b*) John Adams (*c*) Ben Martin.

C. Do you think the Massachusetts farmers had a right to rebel in 1786? Do you think the 13 colonies had a right to rebel in 1776? Do you think the two cases are similar or different? Explain.

Activities and Inquiries

1. Assume you have just interviewed James Johnson. What does he think of the ideas of Parsons and Day? What do you think of their ideas?
2. Draw a poster that Day and Parsons can use to get farmers to join Shays's army.
3. A group of farmers is listening to Parsons and Johnson. Which speaker will the group agree with more? Why?
4. Study the drawing on page 126. Imagine that you are on the courthouse steps with Daniel Shays.
   a. What do you think Shays is saying?
   b. What thoughts are going through your mind as he makes his speech?
   c. Will you follow Shays? Why or why not?
5. Imagine that you are a banker in 1786 and have lent money to farmers. Do you want farmers to pay you back in paper money? Why or why not?

2 The Constitutional Convention

Shays's Rebellion worried many Americans, especially the well-to-do. They feared that mobs might get out of hand and bring radical changes to government in state after state. This worry and other problems helped convince many people of the need for a stronger central government. In May, 1787, delegates from 12 states met in Philadelphia. Their purpose was to change the Articles of Confederation in order to strengthen the central government.

Some of the leading men in the country attended the Constitutional Convention. Many of the key figures of the Revolution took part. Most of the delegates were leaders in their states. Of the 55 members, 31 were college graduates at a time when very few Americans finished grade school.

Three quarters of the delegates had been members of Congress. Most of the men were themselves well-to-do. Only one was a typical farmer. The most common profession among them was law. The average age was 42. Absent from the convention were women, blacks, and Indians.

In our story we sit in on the debates of the convention. The men who speak are stating positions they took in real life, although not in exactly the same words. We see that the convention goes far beyond its original purpose of amending (changing) the Articles of Confederation.

Ask yourself why the convention decided to write a new constitution. How did the Virginia Plan propose to create a strong central government?

Philadelphia, May, 1787

The convention delegates agreed that George Washington should be the chairman, or president. They also agreed to keep secret what they said and decided until the convention ended. At first they had trouble agreeing on the purpose of the convention.

WILLIAM PATERSON (*New Jersey*). We are here to change the Articles of Confederation.

ALEXANDER HAMILTON (*New York*). Change is not enough. We must write a completely new set of articles. Our central government has failed.

PATERSON. Give it a chance!

HAMILTON. How many chances do you want? Farmers rebelled in Massachusetts last year. Where will the troubles be next time? Our central government cannot maintain order. It can do little to defend the rights of property owners.

GEORGE MASON (*Virginia*). Shays's Rebellion was serious. I'm not saying that it wasn't. Farmers—debtors—made a little noise. But a state army crushed them. There is no problem that the states cannot handle.

JAMES WILSON (*Pennsylvania*). A rebellion is not a state concern. It is an attack against the government of the nation. We must have a stronger central government. What we need is a united country, not 13 separate countries going off in 13 different directions. We must work together—or this is the end of us!

LUTHER MARTIN (*Maryland*). I disagree completely. This is a government of states. They must be supreme. The national government exists only for them. Perhaps the states could give more power to the national government—but only a little more. You talk as if you want the states to be swallowed up. I say that a strong central government will make slaves of us all!

GOUVERNEUR MORRIS (*Pennsylvania*). The government we have now does not work. We must be willing to make great changes. If necessary, we must start all over.

MARTIN. That is revolution! I oppose it.

HAMILTON. Gentlemen, the time has come for this convention to take strong steps to save our nation. A weak national government is for a weak people. Believe me, we will be British colonies once again unless we build a strong central government.

EDMUND RANDOLPH (*Virginia*). Virginia has a plan. We believe it will answer all complaints about our government.

WASHINGTON (*Virginia*). Please read your plan.

RANDOLPH. Thank you, Mr. President. Before I read our plan, may I say a few words about the Articles of Confederation? The writers of those Articles did a fine job. They wrote under the pressure of a revolution and had no other constitution to serve as a model. How could they know how it would work in practice?

How could anyone know that our government would face a rebellion? How could they know what fierce arguments would arise between states? But a government that cannot control trade or raise money cannot last. We have learned that we need a strong national government.

HAMILTON. Hear, hear!

RANDOLPH. According to our plan, a national legislature of two houses should be formed. This legislature, or Congress, would have the power to pass all laws needed by the whole country.

JOHN LANSING (*New York*). And what does that mean?

RANDOLPH. Congress would have the power to pass laws in the national interest, even if one or more states objected.

LANSING. What kinds of laws?

RANDOLPH. Laws concerning interstate and foreign commerce, for example. Laws to raise taxes and coin money. Laws to help put down rebellions and settle arguments between the states.

MORRIS. Good, but suppose the states pass their own laws about these things?

RANDOLPH. A law passed by Congress would have the power to set aside any law passed by a state.

MARTIN. That's monstrous! We might as well still be governed by King George!

WASHINGTON. You are out of order, Mr. Martin. Let Mr. Randolph finish!

RANDOLPH. We should also have a national executive—a president—to carry out the laws. And a national judiciary—courts—to decide whether the laws are just or unjust.

PATERSON. You go too far, Mr. Randolph. You are proposing a new constitution entirely. I say make some changes but keep the Articles of Confederation. There's nothing wrong with our one-house Congress with each state having one vote. We should, however, increase the powers of Congress. Let it tax imports. Give it the power to get money from the states. In fact, we could even allow Congress to regulate trade among the states.

HAMILTON. That's not enough, sir. Congress would still be too weak. It must have all the powers it needs to make it strong. It must be able to control the flow of trade and money. It must be strong enough to prevent any attacks on it. It must win the respect of our friends and enemies in Europe. Our central government must be a true government, Mr. Paterson!

PATERSON. Not so fast! I haven't finished. We could add an executive branch. Three people would share the executive duties. These men would be appointed by Congress. We could also have federal courts, but I would limit their powers.

WILSON. You haven't learned from experience, Mr. Paterson. Can't you see that we must have a central government with real strength?

LANSING. Mr. Randolph's plan destroys the power and life of the states. Mr. Paterson would have the states remain sovereign. Isn't that what our American Revolution was all about?

ROGER SHERMAN (*Connecticut*). Gentlemen, gentlemen, there must be a way to solve this problem to everyone's satisfaction.

OLIVER ELLSWORTH (*Connecticut*). Why can't we work out a compromise between Randolph's ideas and Paterson's ideas?

POSTSCRIPT

A compromise was indeed worked out. It blended features of Randolph's ideas (the Virginia Plan) and Paterson's ideas (the New Jersey Plan). The result was called the Connecticut Compromise, or the Great Compromise, and it required a completely new constitution.

From the Virginia Plan, the compromise took the idea of a strong central government. It provided for a two-house Congress. From the New Jersey Plan came the idea that each state should be equal in at least one house of Congress. The lower house, or House of Representatives, would be chosen on the basis of population. States with large populations would have many representatives; states with small populations would have few. The upper house, or Senate, would have two members from each state. All states would be equal in the Senate.

The suggestion that the national government be allowed to set aside the laws of the states was dropped. It was replaced by this statement in the new constitution: "This Constitution, and the laws of the United States, . . . shall be the supreme law of the land . . ." (Article VI, Clause 2).

Homework Questions

1. Why did James Wilson feel that the central government must be stronger?
2. How did Luther Martin reply to Wilson's arguments?
3. In what way did Edmund Randolph's Virginia Plan propose to strengthen the central government?
4. What were the differences between William Paterson's New Jersey Plan and Randolph's Virginia Plan?
5. How did the Connecticut Compromise overcome these differences?

Understanding the Story

A. Write *T* for each statement that is true, *F* for each statement that is false, and *N* for each statement that is not mentioned in the story.
   1. Rhode Island did not send a delegate to the Constitutional Convention.
   2. Delegates from 12 states met in Philadelphia in 1787.
   3. Thomas Jefferson and John Adams were not among the delegates at Philadelphia.
   4. Some of the delegates were less than 30 years old.
   5. The majority of the delegates had been members of Congress.
   6. The original purpose of the convention was to write a new constitution.
   7. The convention met in secret.
   8. George Washington was chosen to be the president of the convention.

B. In this story the delegates disagree about an important issue. Instead of simply arguing with each other, however, they negotiate. *Negotiation* means working out differences through reasonable discussion. It also involves *compromise*, or give and take in which everybody wins a little and nobody loses everything.

The following statements reflect positions taken by the delegates in the story. Write *S* for a statement favoring a strong central government, *W* for one favoring a weak central government, and *C* for one favoring a compromise.
   1. We cannot have 13 separate countries.
   2. The states must be supreme.
   3. Our present central government cannot maintain order.
   4. There is no problem the states can't handle.
   5. There must be a way to solve this problem to everyone's satisfaction.
   6. We fought a revolution so that our states would be sovereign.
   7. Our central government must be a true government.
   8. The new plan of government blended features of the Virginia Plan and the New Jersey Plan.

C. Suppose that the United States was still governed under the Articles of Confederation. Do you think the nation could thrive under such a constitution today? Why or why not?

Activities and Inquiries

1. Imagine that William Paterson has written a letter home. He has mentioned Edmund Randolph. What has he said about Randolph's ideas?

2. Now, suppose that Randolph has written a letter home. What has he said about Paterson's ideas?

3. Assume that Paterson and Randolph want to leave the convention. It is your job to persuade them to stay in Philadelphia. What will you say to them?

4. Imagine that you are a delegate to a convention being held today to amend the Constitution of the United States. What changes will you recommend? Explain your recommendations.

3 Slavery and the Constitution

The delegates had made their most important decision. They had decided to create a new constitution rather than revise the Articles of Confederation. The new constitution would set up a strong central government consisting of three parts: a legislature (Congress), an executive (President), and a judiciary (court system).

The new Congress would have two houses, or divisions. It would have the power to pass whatever laws were necessary to take care of the business of the country. In fact, congressional laws would be the supreme law of the land. The national government would be more important than the state governments.

Many questions remained to be answered: How many legislators should represent each state? The number would be determined by each state's population, but should slaves be counted in the same way as free people? Should states permitting slavery ("slave states") be allowed to import more slaves? Is trade in human beings acceptable at all in a society that treasures freedom? The debates continued.

Are you surprised that George Mason, a Virginia slave owner, took such a strong antislavery position at the Convention? Why do you think some of the Northern delegates felt that slavery would disappear before long?

Philadelphia, July, 1787

WASHINGTON. Gentlemen, at last the problem of representation in the Congress has been solved. We will have two houses. Each state will have two members in the Senate. The number of members in the House of Representatives will be based on how many people live in each state.

BENJAMIN FRANKLIN (*Pennsylvania*). Exactly. Equal representation in the Senate should make the small states happy. Yet the larger states will have more members in the House of Representatives. An excellent compromise.

LUTHER MARTIN (*Maryland*). Just a minute! How many representatives will each state have in the House?

GOUVERNEUR MORRIS (*Pennsylvania*). Why not one representative for every 40,000 people?

MARTIN. Ah, but what do you mean by people? Does that include slaves?

CHARLES PINCKNEY (*South Carolina*). Of course slaves will be counted. They are people.

MORRIS. I will never agree to that. It would give slave states too many representatives. It would be unfair to free states like Pennsylvania.

PINCKNEY. Sir, South Carolina will not stay in the union unless all slaves are counted.

MORRIS (*trying to control himself*). Only free people should be counted for representation in the House. There is just no need for slavery in this country. It is a curse!

PINCKNEY. Then curse the world, Mr. Morris. Slavery exists in more than half the world.

MORRIS. That is not the point. How can you count slaves for representation? If they are people, then make them citizens and let them vote. If they are property, then include all other property. No, Mr. Pinckney, slaves are people; they must be free!

PINCKNEY. Now you go too far!

MORRIS. I will go further. The houses in my city of Philadelphia are worth more than all your poor slaves. I say let's count our houses to decide each state's representation.

FRANKLIN. Gentlemen, we must control ourselves. It's a very hot day, but we cannot let the temperature heat up our words. We must compromise. There is a simple way to end this argument. Let us count each slave as three fifths of a free person.

WASHINGTON. That sounds fair. Let us vote.

[*The vote is taken. The Three-Fifths Compromise is approved.*]

WASHINGTON. Now, for the question of importing slaves.

MARTIN. Not one slave should be shipped into this country. We should not allow human beings to be brought to our shores in filthy ships. It would be a disgrace to allow the slave trade under our new constitution.

PINCKNEY. South Carolina needs more slaves. Yes, we Southerners will profit from the labor of these slaves. But they are brought here in Northern ships. This means more profits for the North as well.

MARTIN. How can you speak this way? Making a profit from selling human beings is disgraceful!

ROGER SHERMAN (*Connecticut*). I, too, am against the slave trade. But the states are the best judges of what they should do. States now have the right to import slaves. Let them continue to have it. Before long, slavery will disappear, and the whole problem will solve itself.

GEORGE MASON (*Virginia*). I'm not so sure that slavery will disappear. But I do know that slavery discourages free people from coming here. Slavery discourages art and manufacturing. Every slave master becomes a tyrant. We cannot abolish slavery today, but we must not encourage more of it. Otherwise, gentlemen, this country will one day be punished for the sin of slavery. Something terrible will happen to us!

PINCKNEY. South Carolina will never approve this constitution if we cannot import slaves!

SHERMAN. I am not a slave owner, and I have no idea about what owning a slave does to a master. Slavery is wrong, but I would not interfere with it. Our Southern neighbors say that they must import slaves to survive. I accept that. We must not be unfair to those states. Anyway, there will soon be so many free laborers that slaves will no longer be needed!

PINCKNEY. I have a suggestion. Congress has been given the power to tax imports. Why not also give it the power to tax the importation of slaves?

MARTIN. You mean that slaves would be imported forever?

PINCKNEY. No, we will agree that imported slaves will be taxed at no more than $10 each for 20 years. Then, after 1808 Congress can decide whether to continue to permit the importation of slaves.

FRANKLIN. Sounds like a fair compromise. It would allow a way to bring an end to the slave trade in the future.

MARTIN. I wish I could share your rosy outlook, Mr. Franklin. I believe that slaves will be bought and sold within this nation for many years to come.

Homework Questions

1. Why were the delegates concerned about the number of members in each house of Congress?
2. How did Benjamin Franklin feel about a two-house Congress?
3. For what reason did Southern delegates want to count each slave as one person? Why were Northern delegates opposed to this idea?
4. How did Benjamin Franklin's compromise overcome these differences?
5. How did the convention deal with the question of the slave trade?

Understanding the Story

A. List the numbers of the statements that describe decisions of the Constitutional Convention.
 1. The laws of Congress will be the supreme laws of the land.
 2. Each state will send only one person to the Senate.
 3. The number of representatives a state has will depend on how many people live in that state.
 4. Slaves and free people will be counted in the same way.
 5. Slavery will be ended in every state.
 6. Each slave will be counted as three fifths of a free person.
 7. Imported slaves are not to be taxed.
 8. The importing of slaves can be made illegal after 1808.

B. Charles Pinckney, a Southerner, and Gouverneur Morris, a Northerner, have different ideas about slavery. Write *P* for each statement that Pinckney made or might have made and *M* for each statement that Morris made or might have made.
 1. I will never agree to count slaves as equal to free people.
 2. I want slaves counted as equal to free people.
 3. Counting slaves as free people would be unfair to my state.
 4. Slavery is a curse.
 5. Slavery brings profits to both South and North.
 6. My state needs more slaves.
 7. Let's count houses as people.
 8. Slavery exists in more than half the world.

C. The Constitutional Convention did not seriously consider requiring an end to slavery in all 13 states. In your opinion, why was this so?

Activities and Inquiries

1. Imagine that you are at the Constitutional Convention. You have heard many different ideas expressed about slavery. List those you agree with. Give reasons why.
2. List the ideas you do not agree with. Explain.
3. A black civil rights leader today decides that one person in the story deserves a special award for excellence. Which person would it be? Explain the reasons for the choice.
4. Which person in the story would the civil rights leader like the least? Why?
5. Imagine that you are George Mason of Virginia, a slave owner. Write a diary entry explaining why you spoke out so strongly against slavery.

4 What Kind of Executive Shall We Have?

The delegates decided that the new government must have an executive. The central government under the Articles of Confederation had been leaderless. There had been no executive—no president—to make decisions and carry out the laws passed by Congress.

An important question for the delegates was what kind of executive to create. As the debate continues, ask yourself why some delegates preferred a plural executive (more than one serving together). Is it possible for a plural executive to be a strong executive?

Philadelphia, August, 1787

Inside Independence Hall the delegates pressed on grimly.

EDMUND RANDOLPH (*Virginia*). There should be a national executive body chosen by Congress for a single term of seven years. Its job would be to carry out the laws passed by Congress.

JAMES WILSON (*Pennsylvania*). I don't understand what you mean by an executive body.

RANDOLPH. The executive body should be a committee of three men.

WILSON. A committee? Three men? What are you saying, Mr. Randolph? You're not proposing an executive—you're talking about a group. Why not have 5 or 10 or even 20? The result would be the same. There would be no single authority, no chief executive. Your executive would be weak, weak, weak!

RANDOLPH. You are right, Mr. Wilson. The executive would be weak—because that is the way we want it. A single chief would be like a king, not an executive. Have you forgotten that we are a republic? Haven't you had enough of kings?

JOHN RUTLEDGE (*South Carolina*). I disagree, Mr. Randolph. We need a one-man executive who can be responsible for making decisions. We need a man who knows what to do and will do it. That way we'll know who's to blame if things go wrong.

ROGER SHERMAN (*Connecticut*). I am afraid of your one-man executive making all those decisions by himself. You concentrate power in one person's hands and what have you got? A tyrant! I would

"I disagree, Mr. Randolph. We need a one-man executive who can be responsible for making decisions."

not trust one man to do the job. He would do whatever he pleased!

WILSON. That's impossible! He could not be a tyrant because he would be checked every step of the way by Congress and the courts. On the other hand, he could do things speedily—and with energy. He would get things done!

SHERMAN. Never mind the speed and the energy. First things first. You simply don't understand why we need an executive. The three-man executive should have exactly one thing to do—carry out the wishes of Congress. No more and no less! Congress should have the power in this government—not the executive! I agree completely with Mr. Randolph. We want an executive of three men—with limited power.

WILSON. Mr. Sherman, you shock me. Have you forgotten why we are here? Are the Articles of Confederation good enough for you? No, sir, we must create a government that is strong enough to last. To me the Articles of Confederation represent a failure. And certainly one reason for their failure is the lack of an executive. Our new government must have strong leadership.

RANDOLPH. You are wrong, Mr. Wilson, all wrong! Government can be strong without a strong executive. Mr. Sherman is right. We do not want a tyrant!

JAMES MADISON (*Virginia*). Mr. President, I think we have had enough of this debate. Both sides know where they stand on this issue. Let us vote.

   [*A vote was taken, and the single executive was approved.*]

MADISON. Now we can be sure that we will have an executive strong enough to lead this country.

Homework Questions

1. Why did Edmund Randolph want a three-man executive committee?
2. How did John Rutledge answer Randolph's arguments?
3. Why were some delegates afraid that a one-man executive might be a tyrant?
4. How was the argument settled?

Understanding the Story

A. Write *T* for each statement that is true and *F* for each statement that is false.
   1. Edmund Randolph said a strong executive would be like a king.
   2. James Wilson said Congress could keep a single executive from getting too much power.
   3. Randolph favored a one-man executive.
   4. The Articles of Confederation had a strong executive.
   5. Randolph wanted the executive to have a seven-year term.
   6. Roger Sherman thought Congress should carry out the executive's wishes.
   7. Wilson was afraid of a strong executive.
   8. The delegates voted for a single executive.

B. Edmund Randolph and James Wilson had different ideas about the executive. Write *R* for each statement that Randolph made or might have made and *W* for each statement that Wilson made or might have made.

1. The executive should be chosen by Congress for a seven-year term.
2. A three-man executive would be too weak.
3. The executive should be a committee of three men.
4. We have had enough of kings.
5. This nation cannot survive with a weak government.
6. Our new government must have a strong executive.
7. We can have a strong government without a strong executive.
8. The Articles of Confederation have been a failure.

C. Edmund Randolph argued that a three-man executive would be better than a single President. Would you agree or disagree? Explain.

Activities and Inquiries

1. A colony will soon become independent. Which person in the story would have the best advice for the new nation? Explain your choice.
2. Which person would have the worst advice? Explain your choice.
3. Conduct your own public-opinion poll. Ask your friends and neighbors if they are happy with a single President. List reasons they give.
4. In your poll ask the people how they would feel about being governed by three presidents.
5. What would the President of the United States say to convince people that a single executive is best?

5 Electing the President

The delegates now knew what kind of an executive the United States was going to have. But they had difficulty deciding how to elect this executive. The suggestions and the debates continued all through the convention.

Ask yourself why it was so difficult to decide how to elect the President. Which of the suggested methods do you prefer? What is the Electoral College?

Philadelphia, August, 1787

GEORGE WASHINGTON. Now let's turn to the question of choosing our President. There is some objection to having Congress choose him.

JAMES WILSON (*Pennsylvania*). Yes, General Washington. There certainly is objection. If Congress were to choose the President, the election would be open to corruption and intrigue—to plots and schemes. The President must be independent of Congress. He must not have to curry favor with its members. Why not have the people choose the President?

JAMES MADISON (*Virginia*). Why not, indeed?

ELBRIDGE GERRY (*Massachusetts*). Mr. Wilson, your idea is unwise. The people of this nation are poorly informed. They know the leading men of their own states but few of the leaders of other states. They would end up voting only for men from their own state. Besides, in a national election the people might easily be fooled. I tell you, Mr. Wilson, a few clever and designing men can lead the voters astray.

GEORGE MASON (*Virginia*). Mr. Gerry is right. The country is too big for the voters possibly to know all of the leading men well enough to choose among them. I would not trust the people to choose the President. I would sooner depend on a blind man to tell me the colors of my clothes.

GERRY. I suggest that the governors of the states elect the President.

EDMUND RANDOLPH (*Virginia*). If the governors were to make the choice, smaller states would have too big a voice. They could insist that the President come from a small state.

WILSON. All right, I have another idea. Why not have the people in each state choose leading men to make the choice of a President? These men would serve as electors. They could meet together, discuss the candidates, and make an informed choice.

GOUVERNEUR MORRIS (*Pennsylvania*). Yes, yes. At least that way the people could have a voice in the President's election.

MADISON. I agree. That would be a wise decision.

RANDOLPH. I'm sorry to disagree with you gentlemen, but I believe Congress should choose the President. We will limit the President to one term, so he would not have to worry about staying on friendly terms with a majority of the members of Congress. That way the President could be elected by Congress and still stay independent.

WILSON. We have already rejected that idea. Most of us agree that the executive should not be picked by Congress.

WASHINGTON. We are moving further and further from a decision. There are too many suggestions. We must make up our minds.

GERRY. Gentlemen, why not let the state legislatures vote for the President?

VOICES. No, not that!

WILLIAM PATERSON (*New Jersey*). Many of us object to giving the people a voice in choosing the President. There is a simple solution. Let the legislature in each state choose electors, who in turn will pick the President.

OLIVER ELLSWORTH (*Connecticut*). Good idea! But why not allow each state to decide for itself how to choose its electors? Some states might have the voters make the choice; other states, the legislators.

WASHINGTON. Gentlemen, gentlemen. We are still drifting.

MADISON. Why don't we call for a report from the Committee of Detail? Then we can see how far we have gone on the selection of a President.

WASHINGTON. Mr. Rutledge, what do you have for us?

JOHN RUTLEDGE (*South Carolina*). We have agreed that the executive power of the United States shall be given to a single person. His title shall be the President of the United States of America. He shall be elected for seven years but shall not be elected again.

MORRIS. What do you mean that he cannot be elected again? You are taking away any hope the man might have of being rewarded by another term. If he knows he is in office for only a short time, what is to stop him from trying to accumulate wealth and taking care of his friends?

RUFUS KING (*Massachusetts*). Suppose a man proves to be a good President. What right do we have to keep him out of office?

WASHINGTON. It is obvious that we cannot settle this matter now. The more we discuss the election of the President, the more confused we sound. He cannot be chosen by five different methods. I am turning this problem over to a special committee. We will eagerly await its report.

September, 1787

WASHINGTON. Mr. Morris, do you have the committee report on the election of the President?

MORRIS. Yes, Mr. President. We have agreed that he will be elected for a term of four years, not seven. And he will be able to serve for more than one term. He will be elected by electors chosen by each state. The legislature in each state will decide how to select the electors from that state.

BENJAMIN FRANKLIN (*Pennsylvania*). How many electors will there be?

MORRIS. The number of electors in each state will equal the number of its representatives in the House plus its two Senators.

FRANKLIN. What do you call this plan for electing our President?

MORRIS. The Electoral College.

FRANKLIN. Let us hope our labors have been worthwhile and that the Electoral College will choose the best person for the job.

POSTSCRIPT

In practice, members of the Electoral College (*presidential electors*) have come to be chosen by the voters in all states. The voters choose among presidential candidates in an election held in November of every fourth year. But voters do not vote for the candidates directly. Instead, they vote for a group of electors who promise to vote in the Electoral College for a certain presidential (and vice presidential) candidate. In each state, each political party puts up its own list of electors. The party that gets the most votes wins. Its electors get to cast all of their state's votes in the Electoral College.

About a month after the election, presidential electors meet in each state capital to cast their votes for President. (The Electoral College is thus many separate gatherings—not one gathering of all electors in one place.) Although electors are not le-

gally bound to keep their promise to vote for a specific candidate, all but a handful of them normally do so. Thus, the people do choose the President, although indirectly.

The votes from each state are sent to the U.S. Senate. There the votes are counted, and the winner is formally announced in January. In fact, however, the winner is known long before, when the popular votes (the people's votes) are counted in November.

The delegates to the Constitutional Convention provided for the case in which *no* candidate wins more than half of the electoral votes. In such a case, they decided, the President would be chosen by members of the House of Representatives. The House would choose from the top three candidates, with each state having a single vote. This method has been used only twice, in 1801 and in 1825.

Homework Questions

1. Why did some delegates feel that the people should not be permitted to elect the President?
2. Why was George Washington so annoyed by the debate over the election of the President?
3. What argument did Gouverneur Morris make against one seven-year term for the President?
4. What system did the convention set up for choosing the President?

Understanding the Story

A. Write *F* for each statement that is a fact and *O* for each statement that is an opinion.
  1. Too much time was spent debating how the President should be chosen.
  2. Washington felt there were too many suggestions on how to select the President.
  3. One suggestion was to have the people elect the President.
  4. The President should be chosen by Congress.
  5. Until September, the delegates could not agree on how the President should be chosen.
  6. Washington turned the problem of how to choose the President over to a committee.
  7. The President should be elected for a seven-year term.
  8. The Convention decided to have the President chosen by electors in each state.

B. Write *D* for each statement or question favoring direct election of the President by the people. Write *I* for each statement or question favoring indirect election of the President.
  1. Why not have the people choose the President?
  2. In a national election, the people might be easily fooled.
  3. The governors of the states should elect the President.
  4. Let the voters make the decision.
  5. Why not have the people in each state choose leading men to make the choice of a President?
  6. The state legislatures should vote for the President.
  7. Let the legislature in each state choose electors, who in turn will pick the President.
  8. Some states might have the voters choose the electors.

C. Do you think the Electoral College is a good way of choosing the President today? Why or why not?

Activities and Inquiries

1. Make a chart showing the methods proposed for choosing a President.
2. Add to your chart the main arguments for and against each proposed method.
3. Which method or methods do you think would appeal most to a delegate to the Constitutional Convention from a state with a small population?
4. Which method or methods would appeal most to a delegate from a state with a large population?
5. Imagine that a delegate to the Constitutional Convention shows up in the present. He asks you to explain how the American people elect a President today. Do you think your explanation will surprise the delegate? Explain.

6 Checks and Balances

The delegates created a strong executive to be elected by the Electoral College. But how was the Executive to be prevented from becoming too strong? How was Congress to be kept from going too far? And how could the power of the courts be limited?

The answers are found in a system of checks and balances built into the Constitution. The three branches of the United States government are separate. Each one checks and balances the other two in many different ways.

In our story James Madison and Thomas Jefferson exchange opinions about the Constitution. Jefferson, you will remember, was the leading author of the Declaration of Independence. In 1787 he was in Paris as the U.S. ambassador, the official representative, to the government of France.

Ask yourself why Madison felt that the Constitution was a good one. Why did Jefferson have doubts about it?

Philadelphia, October, 1787

Thomas Jefferson
American Embassy
Paris, France

Dear Tom,

Glorious news! The Convention is over. The United States of America has a new constitution. And it's a good one, Tom. It may not be all that we wanted it to be. Many, many compromises had to be made during those hot months. No matter. Now we can be sure that our nation will survive and our government will be strong.

You know better than I what the European nations think of the United States. They look down on us and expect every month will be our last. Well, they can think what they wish. The Articles of Confederation will disappear, but our new Constitution will last forever!

Soon Europeans will know that only our national government can make treaties, tax imports, and coin money. We will have a solid currency; we will pay our debts. We will raise money with national taxes instead of begging the states for charity. Foreigners will trade with us and lend us money. We will gain their respect.

Let me tell you how our new Constitution provides the leadership and organization we lacked under the Articles of Confederation.

You have often said that the central government must be able to enforce its authority. We have brought this about by making the national government more powerful than the state governments. No longer will we have to tolerate the weaknesses that showed up at the time of Shays's Rebellion last year. State governments can no longer blot out private debts with worthless paper money. The central government now controls the money supply.

You suggested that the government be organized into three separate parts. This we have done. The Congress, or legislature, will make the laws. The executive, or President, will carry out the laws passed by Congress. And the judiciary, the Supreme Court and other federal courts, will hear cases involving laws passed by Congress and treaties made by the executive.

I know you worry about tyrants. We must guard against a ruler who goes against the wishes of the people. But we must also guard against the tyranny of the people themselves. We must not allow a majority of the people to take away the rights of a minority, as can so easily happen in a democracy. That is exactly the purpose of having the three branches of government. No one of them can become too strong. One branch cannot control the other two.

Let us suppose that a bill is passed by the House of Representatives. The bill must also be approved by the Senate. Then it is sent to the President who may sign (approve) the bill, making it a law. Or he may veto (disapprove) it.

Perhaps this seems to tip the balance of power in favor of the President. But we are not finished with the bill. The Congress has one more chance to act on a vetoed bill. Two thirds of the membership of both houses of Congress can pass the bill over the President's veto. This tips the balance a trifle in favor of Congress—if it can put together enough votes. The President must execute, or carry out, that law—whether he likes the law or not.

Of course, there are many other checks and balances. For example, the President and U.S. judges can be impeached (charged with wrongdoing) by the House. They can then be tried, and if found guilty, they can be removed from office by the Senate. Two thirds of the senators must vote for the removal to make it happen.

Notice the many double checks. The President appoints federal judges for life, but the Senate must approve his choices. The President has the power to make a treaty with a foreign nation. To make the treaty binding on our country, the Senate must approve it. Then, if a dispute arises about its terms, the Supreme Court may interpret the meaning of the terms.

You can see how the new Constitution protects our republican ideals. It creates a strong central government, but checks and balances prevent the government from being too strong.

Now we face the challenge of convincing at least 9 of the 13 states to approve the Constitution. We will have to work very hard, but I assure you that this Constitution will be ratified. It must be—or the United States cannot remain independent!

I hope to have good news in my next letter. Until then, I remain your devoted friend.

James Madison

Paris, December, 1787

James Madison
Richmond, Virginia

Dear James,

Your letter describing the Constitution was very helpful. I approve of the checks and balances. However, I still think the government will be too strong. I am afraid that a powerful government can crush our people. We must be very careful.

You wrote once again of Shays's Rebellion. I feel that this uprising frightened you unnecessarily. Think about it, James. There was one rebellion in 13 states during a period of 11 years. This is one for each state in 150 years! No country should be so long without a rebellion! What if a few lives were lost? The tree of liberty must be refreshed from time to time with the blood of patriots and tyrants!

Let me tell you what I do not like about the new Constitution. First, why does it have no bill of rights? I see nothing about protecting people from standing armies. And where are the guarantees of freedom of religion and freedom of the press? Most states provide such guarantees. If the national government is to be more powerful, the Constitution should have a bill of rights.

Oh, yes, there is one other part of the Constitution I do not like. I am not happy that the President can be elected more than once. I am terribly afraid that once a man is elected President he will be elected over and over again. He might become President for life—a tyrant or a king. We must be careful not to let this happen in America. We must make sure that no man stays in office for too long.

I am sorry if I have annoyed you with my complaints. However, it is my opinion that the will of the majority must always be followed.

Jefferson replying to Madison

Therefore, if a majority of the states approve the Constitution, I will agree with their decision cheerfully. I also hope that the people will amend the Constitution if they find that it does not work properly.

I shall be awaiting further news. Until then I remain, Dear Sir, your affectionate friend.

Thomas Jefferson

POSTSCRIPT

The Constitution does not clearly state that the Supreme Court has the right to interpret laws passed by Congress. Some of the men who wrote the Constitution assumed that the Court had this right. Then in 1803 the Court established for itself the right to determine whether laws passed by Congress agreed with the Constitution (see Unit Six, Chapter 9). After this time, the Court became a stronger force in the checks-and-balances system.

Homework Questions

1. How did Madison think the new Constitution would help gain the respect of European nations?
2. Why is our national government based on a system of checks and balances?
3. How does the President check Congress and Congress check the President?
4. Why did Jefferson feel that a bill of rights was necessary?

Understanding the Story

A. Write *T* for each statement that is true, *F* for each statement that is false, and *N* for each statement that is not mentioned in the story.
  1. The branches of the government check one another.
  2. Most European governments in 1787 had no system of checks and balances.
  3. Madison did not support the Constitution.
  4. Thomas Jefferson was the U.S. ambassador to France in 1787.
  5. Jefferson was happy with everything in the Constitution.
  6. The national government can coin money.
  7. The Constitution said the salaries of federal judges could not be reduced.
  8. The 1787 Constitution had a bill of rights.

B. Match each of the items in Column *A* with one of the items in Column *B*. Some letters will be used more than once.

Column A

1. Passes laws
2. Approves presidential appointment of judges
3. Signs or vetoes bills
4. Decides certain court cases
5. Impeaches federal officials
6. Carries out the laws
7. Makes treaties
8. Approves treaties

Column B

a. President
b. Congress
c. U.S. Supreme Court
d. House of Representatives
e. Senate

C. What do you think Thomas Jefferson meant when he wrote, "The tree of liberty must be refreshed from time to time with the blood of patriots and tyrants"? Do you agree with Jefferson's statement? Why or why not?

Activities and Inquiries

1. Imagine that you are a delegate to a state convention to ratify the Constitution. Prepare a short speech to tell why you support ratification.
2. Prepare a speech opposing the Constitution and supporting the Articles of Confederation.
3. Why does Jefferson think it is important to limit a President to one term of office?
4. Prepare a chart or diagram showing how a bill becomes a law.

7 The Bill of Rights

The Constitutional Convention had finished its work. Now at least nine states would have to ratify the document before it could take effect. In each state the voters elected delegates to special state conventions. These delegates had one job: to decide for or against the new Constitution.

People were sharply divided over the Constitution. Those who wanted a strong national government tended to like the document. They were called Federalists because they favored the new, federal form of government. Those who wanted to keep the states strong and the central government limited were called Antifederalists.

Antifederalists thought the Convention had gone too far beyond its original purpose of revising the Articles. Many feared that the new federal system gave the central government too much power over the states. Others argued that the basic rights of the people and the states needed to be spelled out more clearly.

Federalists were better organized than the opposition. James Madison of Virginia and Alexander Hamilton and John Jay of New York argued effectively in favor of ratification. They wrote a series of newspaper articles, later called *The Federalist*, to persuade people to support the Constitution. Their writings helped swing many people to the Federalist side. In addition, promises to add a bill of rights won the votes of many possible opponents.

By the end of July, 1788, all but North Carolina and Rhode Island had approved. This was more than the nine states needed. Congress acted immediately. National elections for the new government occurred in January, 1789. In March the members of the first

Congress took their seats. The following month, George Washington took the oath of office as the first President. The new government was on its way.

Federalists did not forget the promise to add a bill of rights. Congress quickly approved a series of amendments to the Constitution. These passed by a two-thirds majority in September, 1789. By December, 1791, ten amendments had been ratified by three fourths of the states, as the Constitution required.

In our story Margaret Rutherford is reading a newspaper in her sitting room. Daniel, her husband, enters the room.

Ask yourself why Margaret is so excited about the passage of the Bill of Rights. Do you think these ten amendments satisfied Thomas Jefferson?

Philadelphia, December, 1791

"I told you they would do it," said Margaret.

"Do what?" asked Daniel.

"Enact a bill of rights. I told you that a bill of rights would be added to the Constitution."

Daniel looked at the newspaper. "You're right, Meg. I thought it would be a long time before our leaders changed the Constitution."

"But why?"

"Well, I don't know. The Constitution somehow looked so, so—complete," Daniel replied. "There were the three branches of the government with all the checks and balances. We had a strong central government at last. Yet there were protections against anyone obtaining too much power."

"True, we had protection from tyrants such as George III," answered Margaret. "But the Constitution said little about the rights of the people."

"I don't understand."

"Our Declaration of Independence said that people have a right to life, liberty, and the pursuit of happiness. Just try to find *that* in the Constitution."

"Next I suppose you'll tell me that ten amendments will guarantee us those rights."

"I think the amendments will help," said Margaret.

At this point, 13-year-old Ellen Rutherford entered the room.

"We're talking about the Bill of Rights," said Daniel.

"Oh, yes," Ellen replied. "I hear that ten amendments have been added to the Constitution. Can they do all the things they're supposed to do?"

"What do you mean?" asked her mother. "What are they supposed to do? Have you read them?"

"I've read *about* them," Ellen said.

"Let's take a look at the Bill of Rights," Margaret said, looking down at her newspaper. She passed the paper to Ellen. "Here. Read this aloud."

Ellen began slowly. "'First Amendment: Congress shall make no law respecting an establishment of religion, or prohibiting the free exercise thereof; or abridging the freedom of speech, or of the press; or the right of the people peaceably to assemble, and to petition the government for redress of grievances.'"

She paused, and then her face lit up. "Oh, I understand," she said. "I can go where I want and say what I please. No one can stop me."

"Not so, young lady," snapped her father. "The First Amendment doesn't say anything of the sort."

"The First Amendment does give us the right to express ourselves," said Margaret in a tone of patient explanation. "It also means that people can say and print things in public. But I don't think it means that a person can say anything he or she pleases at all times. There have to be limits."

"All people live by rules, and so do we," said Daniel. "Our rules are part of the law. I don't think the First Amendment means you can tell or write lies, for instance. If you did, you could be sued. Your rights and other people's rights go hand in hand."

"Can I meet with my friends wherever and whenever I want to?" Ellen asked. "That's what assemble means, isn't it?"

"I suppose you may—so long as your meetings don't interfere with other people's rights," said Daniel. "I think the Amendment probably means *political* meetings. For example, a meeting to protest a law you don't like."

"And of course, you can draw up a letter or a petition and send it to your government," Margaret added. "That's another way to let the government know how you feel about important matters."

"And freedom of religion—does that mean I can worship any way I want?" asked Ellen.

"Yes," answered Margaret, "and it means that our government can't choose one religion and favor it. Church and government must be kept apart. We can't have an official religion."

"So that's the Bill of Rights," said Ellen.

"No, that's only the First Amendment," said her father with a smile. "There are nine more."

"The Second is much briefer," said Margaret. "It simply gives people the right to bear arms so their states can have a militia for the purpose of opposing tyranny."

"We needed arms during the recent Revolution, Ellen," Daniel added. "We haven't forgotten that now."

"Nor have we forgotten how much it angered us to house British troops in our homes," said Margaret. "The Third Amendment says that no homeowner can be forced to house troops during peacetime."

Ellen was reading over her mother's shoulder. "Hmmm. The Fourth Amendment looks complicated. What does it mean?"

"Our homes cannot be searched without a kind of court order known as a warrant," said Margaret. "That is meant to insure that some tyrant doesn't try to conduct searches and arrests without a good reason."

"And the Fifth?"

"The Fifth Amendment protects our rights when we are accused of having committed a crime, such as murder," said Margaret. "It says that we cannot be put in jail for that crime unless we are formally accused by a grand jury. It also says that we cannot be tried twice for the same offense and that we cannot be forced to say anything against ourselves in a court of law."

"Trials, punishment, criminals!" said Ellen. "We're not criminals. Who cares what happens to them?"

"Ah, but how do you know someone won't someday accuse you of a crime?" said Margaret. "Even innocent people are sometimes accused. Our system of laws provides that a person is innocent until proven guilty. The Sixth and Seventh Amendments also deal with the rights of people accused of crimes. They give us the right to a speedy and public trial, to a lawyer to defend us, and to a trial by jury. They allow us to obtain witnesses in our defense. And the Eighth Amendment says there aren't supposed to be any cruel or unusual punishments."

"Well, I guess I understand that," said Ellen. "The amendments I really don't understand are the last two—the Ninth and Tenth. What do they mean?"

Margaret read Amendment Nine: " 'The enumeration in the Constitution, of certain rights, shall not be construed to deny or disparage others retained by the people.' I believe it means that we, the people, have more rights than those listed in the Constitution or in the other amendments. These unlisted rights are also important and cannot be taken away from us."

Daniel picked up the newspaper and read Amendment Ten aloud. " 'The powers not delegated to the United States by the Constitution, nor prohibited by it to the states, are reserved to the states respectively, or to the people.' As I understand it, state governments are worried that the national government will have total control. This is a way of saying that the state governments still have power."

"But how do the state and national governments divide their powers?" Ellen asked.

"National powers are listed in the Constitution and in many cases are powers forbidden to the states," replied Daniel. "All the other powers belong to the states."

"Now I see," said Ellen. "The rights of the states are also protected. By the way, what are some of the powers left to the states?"

"The Tenth Amendment doesn't say. But the list might include the regulation of businesses that operate only within a state, control over education, and marriage and divorce," said Daniel.

"I'm glad we have a written Bill of Rights," declared Margaret. "Now the American people and the states know what their rights are, and no one can ever take them from us."

"Perhaps you're right, Margaret," said Daniel. "The Bill of Rights does look good on paper. Now we'll have to see how it works in practice."

Homework Questions

1. How were the supporters of the Constitution able to get it ratified?
2. In what ways are the people protected by the First Amendment?
3. How are the people protected by each of the following   (a) search warrant   (b) trial by jury   (c) speedy and public trial?
4. Why is the Tenth Amendment important to the states?

Understanding the Story

A.   List the numbers of the statements that are true.
   1. There was no opposition to the Constitution.
   2. Hamilton, Madison, and Jay argued for the ratification of the Constitution.
   3. *The Federalist* opposed the Constitution.
   4. The Bill of Rights guarantees Americans many freedoms.
   5. Freedom of speech means that a person can say whatever he or she wants at any time.
   6. Church and government are separated in the United States.
   7. People accused of crimes are not protected by the Bill of Rights.
   8. The states keep powers not given to the national government and not forbidden to them by the Constitution.

B.   List the numbers of the statements that give results of the Bill of Rights.
   1. The rights of the American people are protected.
   2. Congress can impose taxes.
   3. People can assemble peaceably.
   4. Homes can never be searched by the police.
   5. Cruel and unusual punishments are not permitted.
   6. Accused people are guilty until proven innocent.
   7. Some powers are reserved for the states.
   8. Americans can petition, or complain to, their government.

C.   In a democracy, the people rule. If that is the case, why do you think a bill of rights might still be necessary? Can it protect people against themselves? Explain.

Activities and Inquiries

1. Imagine that you are a European visiting the United States in 1791. What questions will you ask Margaret and Daniel about the Bill of Rights?
2. How will they answer your questions?
3. Will both Margaret and Daniel give you the same answers about everything? Why or why not?
4. Read the Bill of Rights. Which right impresses you the most? Why?
5. What other rights do you think are especially important? Why?

8 The Growth of the Constitution: Mr. Miller's Class Looks at the Constitution

ROBERT. I know that we have a great government, but I wish our Constitution were easier to understand.

JANET. I agree.

MR. MILLER. We have to read the Constitution. Otherwise, we can't appreciate how our government works.

ROSA. We'll have to look up the meanings of all the hard words.

MR. MILLER. Why don't you rewrite the Constitution in your own words?

SAM. Sounds impossible!

CARLA. How should we begin?

MR. MILLER. With the Preamble, of course.

HEINRICH. What's the Preamble?

MR. MILLER. It's the introduction to the Constitution. It tells why the Constitution was written.

Constitution of the United States

Preamble

We, the people of the United States, in order to form a more perfect union, establish justice, insure domestic tranquility, provide for the common defense, promote the general welfare, and secure the blessings of liberty to ourselves and our posterity, do ordain and establish this Constitution for the United States of America.

The Constitution as seen by the class:

The people of the United States have set up a strong government to provide for peace, liberty, and justice for all.

ARTICLE I. Legislative Department*

Section 1. Congress*

All legislative powers herein granted shall be vested in a Congress of the United States, which shall consist of a Senate and House of Representatives.

Making laws is the job of Congress. Congress is made up of the House of Representatives and the Senate.

Section 2. House of Representatives

1. The House of Representatives shall be composed of members chosen every second year by the people of the several states, and the electors in each state shall have the qualifications requisite for electors of the most numerous branch of the State legislature.

Representatives are elected for two years.

2. No person shall be a Representative who shall not have attained to the age of twenty-five years, and been seven years a citizen of the United States, and who shall not, when elected, be an inhabitant of that State in which he shall be chosen.

They must be at least 25 years of age, citizens for 7 years, and residents of their states.

3. Representatives and direct taxes shall be apportioned among the several States which may be included within this Union, according to their respective numbers, which shall be determined by adding to the whole number of free persons, including those bound to service for a term of years, and excluding Indians not taxed, three fifths of all other persons. The actual enumeration shall be made within three years after the first meeting of the Congress of the United States, and within every subsequent term of ten years, in such manner as they shall by law direct. The number of Representatives shall not exceed one for every thirty thousand, but each State shall have at least one Representative; and until such enumeration shall be made, the State of New Hampshire shall be entitled to choose three, Massachusetts eight, Rhode Island and Providence Plantations one, Connecticut five, New York six, New Jersey four, Pennsylvania eight, Delaware one, Maryland six, Virginia ten, North Carolina five, South Carolina five, and Georgia three.

The number of representatives depends on the total number of people in each state. Every ten years a new count is made. At first a slave only counted as three fifths of a person. Slavery was abolished by the 13th Amendment in 1865. Now all people are counted equally.

4. When vacancies happen in the representation from any State, the executive authority thereof shall issue writs of election to fill such vacancies.

Sometimes representatives die or resign. Then the governor of the representative's state calls an election to fill the vacancy (opening).

*Headings and paragraph numbers have been inserted to assist the reader. The original Constitution contains only article and section numbers. Modern capitalization and punctuation have been used.

5. The House of Representatives shall choose their Speaker and other officers; and shall have the sole power of impeachment.

The House elects its own officers. The speaker directs its debates. The House also has the job of bringing charges against federal officeholders who may have broken the law. If the House decides that an official has done wrong, it impeaches (brings formal charges against) that official, who must then go on trial.

Section 3. The Senate

1. The Senate of the United States shall be composed of two Senators from each State, chosen by the legislature thereof, for six years; and each Senator shall have one vote.

There are two senators from each state. Senators are elected for six years.

2. Immediately after they shall be assembled in consequence of the first election, they shall be divided as equally as may be into three classes. The seats of the Senators of the first class shall be vacated at the expiration of the second year, of the second class at the expiration of the fourth year, and of the third class at the expiration of the sixth year, so that one third may be chosen every second year; and if vacancies happen by resignation, or otherwise, during the recess of the legislature of any State, the executive thereof may make temporary appointments until the next meeting of the legislature, which shall then fill such vacancies.

One third of the senators are elected in each even-numbered year.

At first, all senators were picked by state legislatures. Since the 17th Amendment (1913) they are chosen directly by the voters.

3. No person shall be a Senator who shall not have attained to the age of thirty years, and been nine years a citizen of the United States, and who shall not, when elected, be an inhabitant of that State for which he shall be chosen.

Senators must be at least 30 years of age, citizens for 9 years, and residents of their states.

4. The Vice President of the United States shall be President of the Senate, but shall have no vote, unless they be equally divided.

The Vice President directs Senate debates.

5. The Senate shall choose their other officers, and also a President *pro tempore*, in the absence of the Vice President or when he shall exercise the office of President of the United States.

The Senate elects its other officers.

6. The Senate shall have the sole power to try all impeachments. When sitting for that purpose, they shall be on oath or affirmation. When the President of the United States is tried, the Chief Justice shall preside: And no person shall be convicted without the concurrence of two thirds of the members present.

After the House impeaches an official, the Senate conducts the official's trial. A two-thirds vote is necessary for conviction.

7. Judgment in cases of impeachment shall not extend further than to removal from office, and disqualification to hold and enjoy any office of honor, trust or profit under the United States: but the party convicted shall nevertheless be liable and subject to indictment, trial, judgment and punishment, according to law.

Section 4. Election of Senators and Representatives; Meetings of Congress

1. The times, places, and manner of holding elections for Senators and Representatives, shall be prescribed in each State by the legislature thereof; but the Congress may at any time by law make or alter such regulations, except as to the places of choosing Senators.

Each state sets its own election laws. But Congress must set a uniform law for the whole nation. It has set the first Tuesday after the first Monday in November of even-numbered years as the date for electing representatives and senators.

2. The Congress shall assemble at least once in every year, and such meeting shall be on the first Monday in December, unless they shall by law appoint a different day.

Congress meets each year. Since the 20th Amendment (1933), sessions start on January 3.

Section 5. Powers and Duties of Each House of Congress

1. Each House shall be the judge of the elections, returns, and qualifications of its own members, and a majority of each shall constitute a quorum to do business; but a smaller number may adjourn from day to day, and may be authorized to compel the attendance of absent members, in such manner, and under such penalties, as each House may provide.

Each house decides for itself if a member has been properly elected. For business to be done, at least half of all members must be present. This minimum number is called a quorum.

2. Each House may determine the rules of its proceedings, punish its members for disorderly behavior, and, with the concurrence of two thirds, expel a member.

Each house can expel (remove) a member by a two-thirds majority.

3. Each House shall keep a journal of its proceedings, and from time to time publish the same, excepting such parts as may in their judgment require secrecy; and the yeas and nays of the members of either House on any question shall, at the desire of one fifth of those present, be entered on the journal.

Each house keeps a record of its doings. But the record may be incomplete. For example, unless one fifth of the members request it, the house is not required to write down how each member voted on a question.

4. Neither House, during the session of Congress, shall, without the consent of the other, adjourn for more than three days, nor to any other place than that in which the two Houses shall be sitting.

Both houses must meet in the same place.

Section 6. *Compensation, Privileges, and Disability of Senators and Representatives*

1. The Senators and Representatives shall receive a compensation for their services, to be ascertained by law, and paid out of the Treasury of the United States. They shall in all cases, except treason, felony, and breach of the peace, be privileged from arrest during their attendance at the session of their respective Houses, and in going to and returning from the same; and for any speech or debate in either House, they shall not be questioned in any other place.

Members of Congress are paid for their service. They cannot be arrested or sued for anything they say in Congress. Except for serious crimes, they cannot be arrested at all while Congress is in session.

2. No Senator or Representative shall, during the time for which he was elected, be appointed to any civil office under the authority of the United States, which shall have been created, or the emoluments whereof shall have been increased during such time; and no person holding any office under the United States shall be a member of either House during his continuance in office.

Members of Congress cannot hold any other federal job.

Section 7. *Passing Laws*

1. All bills for raising revenue shall originate in the House of Representatives; but the Senate may propose or concur with amendments as on other bills.

Bills to set taxes must begin in the House. Like other bills they must be approved by the Senate, which can make changes in the House bill.

2. Every bill which shall have passed the House of Representatives and the Senate, shall, before it becomes a law, be presented to the President of the United States; if he approves he shall sign it, but if not he shall return it, with his objections, to that House in which it shall have originated, who shall enter the objections at large on their journal, and proceed to reconsider it. If after such reconsideration two thirds of that House shall agree to pass the bill, it shall be sent, together with the objections, to the other House, by which it shall likewise be reconsidered, and if approved by two thirds of that House, it shall become a law. But in all such cases the votes of both Houses shall be determined by yeas and nays, and the names of the persons voting for and against the bill shall be entered on the journal of each House respectively. If any bill shall not be returned by the President within ten days (Sundays excepted) after it shall have been presented to him, the same shall be a law, in like manner as if he had signed it, un-

A bill must pass both houses of Congress. Then, it is sent to the President. He or she has ten days to think about it. If he or she signs (approves) it, the bill becomes a law. If the President does not like the bill, he or she may veto (disapprove) it. However, a vetoed bill can still become a law by a two-thirds vote of each house. What happens if the Presi-

less the Congress by their adjournment prevent its return, in which case it shall not be a law.

3. Every order, resolution, or vote to which the concurrence of the Senate and House of Representatives may be necessary (except on a question of adjournment) shall be presented to the President of the United States; and before the same shall take effect, shall be approved by him, or being disapproved by him, shall be repassed by two thirds of the Senate and House of Representatives, according to the rules and limitations prescribed in the case of a bill.

dent neither signs nor vetoes the bill in ten days? If Congress is still in session, the bill becomes a law. If Congress has adjourned (gone home), the bill dies. (This is called a pocket veto.)

Section 8. Powers Granted to Congress

The Congress shall have power:

1. To lay and collect taxes, duties, imposts, and excises, to pay the debts and provide for the common defense and general welfare of the United States; but all duties, imposts, and excises shall be uniform throughout the United States;

Congress has the power to
—tax the people, notably through tariffs (duties) and excise taxes (taxes on making, selling, or using goods); tariffs and excise taxes must be equal in all parts of the country

2. To borrow money on the credit of the United States;

—borrow money

3. To regulate commerce with foreign nations, and among the several States, and with the Indian tribes;

—control foreign trade and interstate (among-the-states) trade

4. To establish a uniform rule of naturalization, and uniform laws on the subject of bankruptcies throughout the United States;

—decide how foreigners can become citizens

5. To coin money, regulate the value thereof, and of foreign coin, and fix the standard of weights and measures;

—coin money and set a national system of weights and measures

6. To provide for the punishment of counterfeiting the securities and current coin of the United States;

—punish people who make counterfeit money or fake government bonds

7. To establish post offices and post roads;

—set up a mail system and a highway system

8. To promote the progress of science and useful arts, by securing for limited times to authors and inventors the exclusive right to their respective writings and discoveries;

—set up a system of patents and copyrights

9. To constitute tribunals inferior to the Supreme Court;

—set up a system of federal courts

10. To define and punish piracies and felonies committed on the high seas, and offenses against the law of nations;

—set rules about crime at sea

11. To declare war, grant letters of marque and reprisal, and make rules concerning captures on land and water;

—declare war

12. To raise and support armies, but no appropriation of money to that use shall be for a longer term than two years;

—maintain an army

13. To provide and maintain a navy;

—maintain a navy

14. To make rules for the government and regulation of the land and naval forces;

—set rules to organize and control the armed forces

15. To provide for calling forth the militia to execute the laws of the Union, suppress insurrections, and repel invasions;

—call out state militias

16. To provide for organizing, arming, and disciplining the militia, and for governing such part of them as may be employed in the service of the United States, reserving to the States respectively the appointment of the officers, and the authority of training the militia according to the discipline prescribed by Congress;

—set rules for state militias, although the running of the militias is left to the states

17. To exercise exclusive legislation in all cases whatsoever, over such district (not exceeding ten miles square) as may, by cession of particular States, and the acceptance of Congress, become the seat of the government of the United States, and to exercise like authority over all places purchased by the consent of the legislature of the State in which the same shall be, for the erection of forts, magazines, arsenals, dockyards, and other needful buildings;—And

—pass laws for the nation's capital city and for lands sold by states to the federal government

18. To make all laws which shall be necessary and proper for carrying into execution the foregoing powers, and all other powers vested by this Constitution in the Government of the United States, or in any department or officer thereof.

Perhaps the most important power of Congress is the right to pass any law necessary to carry out its powers. This is called the Elastic Clause because it can stretch to cover new situations.

Section 9. Limitations on Powers Granted to the United States

1. The migration or importation of such persons as any of the States now existing shall think proper to admit, shall not be prohibited by the Congress prior to the year one thousand eight hundred and eight, but a tax or duty may be imposed on such importation, not exceeding ten dollars for each person.

Congress is not allowed to
—stop the bringing of slaves into the United States before 1808

2. The privilege of the writ of habeas corpus shall not be suspended, unless when in cases of rebellion or invasion the public safety may require it.

—stop the courts from issuing orders that require jailers to bring a prisoner to court; these orders, called *writs of habeas corpus,* are to protect people from being jailed unjustly; only in time of rebellion or invasion can Congress suspend the right of habeas corpus

3. No bill of attainder or ex post facto law shall be passed.

—pass laws to punish people without a trial or to punish people for acts that were not crimes when they were committed

4. No capitation, or other direct, tax shall be laid, unless in proportion to the census or enumeration hereinbefore directed to be taken.

—set any "head tax" (that is, a tax on each person) unless that tax applies equally to all people; other direct taxes must apply to each state according to that state's population; since the 16th Amendment (1913), income taxes do not come under this rule

5. No tax or duty shall be laid on articles exported from any State.

—put a tax (tariff) on exports

6. No preference shall be given by any regulation of commerce or revenue to the ports of one State over those of another; nor shall vessels bound to, or from, one State, be obliged to enter, clear, or pay duties in another.

—pass laws about trade that give one state or city an advantage over other states or cities

7. No money shall be drawn from the Treasury, but in consequence of appropriations made by law; and a regular statement and account of the receipts and expenditures of all public money shall be published from time to time.

—spend money without first passing a law giving proper authority

8. No title of nobility shall be granted by the United States; and no person holding any office of profit or trust under them shall, without the consent of the Congress, accept of any present, emolument, office, or title, of any kind whatever, from any king, prince, or foreign state.

—award titles such as earl, duke, or lord

Section 10. *Powers Prohibited to the States*

1. No State shall enter into any treaty, alliance, or confederation; grant letters of marque and reprisal; coin money; emit bills of credit; make anything but gold and silver coin a tender in payment of debts; pass any bill of attainder, ex post facto law, or law impairing the obligation of contracts, or grant any title of nobility.

The states cannot
—make treaties
—issue money or allow materials other than gold and silver to be used as money
—pass laws to punish people without trial or to punish people for acts that were not crimes when they were committed
—award titles such as earl, duke, or lord

2. No State shall, without the consent of the Congress, lay any imposts or duties on imports or exports, except what may be absolutely necessary for executing its inspection laws; and the net produce of all duties and imposts, laid by any State on imports or exports, shall be for the use of the Treasury of the United States; and all such laws shall be subject to the revision and control of the Congress.

—establish a tariff (tax on imports or exports), unless Congress approves

3. No State shall, without the consent of Congress, lay any duty of tonnage, keep troops, or ships of war in time of peace, enter into any agreement or compact with another State, or with a foreign power, or engage in war, unless actually invaded, or in such imminent danger as will not admit of delay.

—maintain a permanent army or navy, unless Congress approves

—make alliances with states or nations

—fight a war, unless the state is invaded or is about to be invaded

ARTICLE II. Executive Department

Section 1. The President

1. The executive power shall be vested in a President of the United States of America. He shall hold his office during the term of four years, and together with the Vice President, chosen for the same term, be elected as follows:

2. Each State shall appoint, in such manner as the legislature thereof may direct, a number of Electors, equal to the whole number of Senators and Representatives to which the State may be entitled in the Congress; but no Senator or Representative, or person holding an office of trust or profit under the United States, shall be appointed an Elector.

3. The Electors shall meet in their respective States, and vote by ballot for two persons, of whom one at least shall not be an inhabitant of the same State with themselves. And they shall make a list of all the persons voted for, and of the number of votes for each; which list they shall sign and certify, and transmit sealed to the seat of the Government of the United States, directed to the President of the Senate. The President of the Senate shall, in the presence of the Senate and House of Representatives, open all the certificates, and the votes shall then be counted. The person having the greatest number of votes shall be the President, if such number be a majority of the whole number of Electors appointed; and if there be more than one who have such majority, and have an equal number of votes, then the House of Representatives shall immediately choose by ballot one of them for President; and if no person have a majority, then from the five highest on the list the said House shall in like manner choose the President. But in choosing the President, the vote shall be taken by States, the representation from each State having one vote; a quorum for this purpose shall consist of a member or members from two thirds of the States, and a majority of all the States shall be necessary to a choice. In every case, after the choice of the President, the person having the greatest number of votes of the Electors shall be the Vice President. But if there should remain two or more who have equal votes, the Senate shall choose from them by ballot the Vice President.

The President is the chief executive of the United States. The President and Vice President are elected for four years.

The people do not vote directly for the President. Instead they choose electors, who vote for the President. The meeting of the electors in each state is called the Electoral College. The method of voting was changed by the 12th Amendment (1804).

4. The Congress may determine the time of choosing the Electors and the day on which they shall give their votes; which day shall be the same throughout the United States.

Congress sets a date for the presidential election, when voters choose the presidential electors. That date is the first Tuesday after the first Monday in November of every fourth year.

5. No person except a natural-born citizen, or a citizen of the United States at the time of the adoption of this Constitution, shall be eligible to the office of President; neither shall any person be eligible to that office who shall not have attained to the age of thirty-five years, and been fourteen years a resident within the United Staes.

The President and Vice President must be natural-born citizens, at least 35 years of age, and residents of the country for at least 14 years.

6. In case of the removal of the President from office, or of his death, resignation, or inability to discharge the powers and duties of the said office, the same shall devolve on the Vice President, and the Congress may by law provide for the case of removal, death, resignation, or inability, both of the President and Vice President, declaring what officer shall then act as President, and such officer shall act accordingly, until the disability be removed, or a President shall be elected.

If the President can no longer act, the Vice President takes over. New procedures were set up by the 25th Amendment (1967).

7. The President shall, at stated times, receive for his services, a compensation, which shall neither be increased nor diminished during the period for which he shall have been elected, and he shall not receive within that period any other emolument from the United States, or any of them.

The President is paid a salary. The amount the President receives may not be raised or lowered during the President's term of office.

8. Before he enter on the execution of his office, he shall take the following oath or affirmation:—"I do solemnly swear (or affirm) that I will faithfully execute the office of President of the United States, and will to the best of my ability, preserve, protect, and defend the Constitution of the United States."

The President must take an oath of office, promising to support the Constitution.

Section 2. *Powers of the President*

1. The President shall be commander-in-chief of the Army and Navy of the United States, and of the militia of the several States, when called into the actual service of the United States; he may require the opinion, in writing, of the principal officer in each of the executive departments, upon any subject relating to the duties of their respective offices, and he shall have power to grant reprieves and pardons for offenses against the United States, except in cases of impeachment.

The President has many powers and duties. He or she
—commands the armed forces
—may ask for reports from leading officials, such as cabinet members

2. He shall have power, by and with the advice and consent of the Senate, to make treaties, provided two thirds of the Senators present concur; and he shall nominate, and by and with the advice and consent of the Senate, shall appoint ambassadors, other public ministers, and consuls, Judges of the Supreme Court, and all other officers of the United States, whose appointments are not herein otherwise provided for, and which shall be established by law; but the Congress may by law vest the appointment of such inferior officers, as they think proper, in the President alone, in the courts of law, or in the heads of departments.

—may pardon people accused of crimes
—may make treaties (with the approval of two thirds of the Senate)
—appoints department heads, judges, ambassadors, and others (with the approval of a majority of the Senate)

3. The President shall have power to fill up all vacancies that may happen during the recess of the Senate, by granting commissions which shall expire at the end of their next session.

If a job is vacant and the Senate is not in session, the President may appoint someone without Senate approval to serve until the next meeting of the Senate ends

Section 3. Duties of the President

He shall from time to time give to the Congress information of the state of the Union, and recommend to their consideration such measures as he shall judge necessary and expedient; he may, on extraordinary occasions, convene both Houses, or either of them, and in case of disagreement between them, with respect to the time of adjournment, he may adjourn them to such time as he shall think proper; he shall receive ambassadors and other public ministers; he shall take care that the laws be faithfully executed, and shall commission all the officers of the United States.

—sends a State of the Union message to Congress, as well as other messages suggesting bills to be passed
—calls special sessions of Congress
—may set an end to a session of Congress if the two houses cannot agree on a date
—carries out (executes) all the laws passed by Congress

Section 4. Impeachment

The President, Vice President, and all civil officers of the United States, shall be removed from office on impeachment for, and conviction of, treason, bribery, or other high crimes and misdemeanors.

The President and other federal officials (but not members of Congress or people in the armed forces) may be impeached and tried for treason, bribery, and other crimes. If found guilty, an official must give up his or her job. Impeachment is by a simple majority of the House. Trial is by the Senate. A two-thirds vote of the Senate is necessary for conviction.

ARTICLE III. Judicial Department

Section 1. Judicial Powers Vested in Federal Courts

The judicial power of the United States shall be vested in one Supreme Court, and in such inferior courts as the Congress may from time to time ordain and establish. The judges, both of the Supreme and inferior courts, shall hold their offices during good behavior, and shall, at stated times, receive for their services a compensation, which shall not be diminished during their continuance in office.

The Supreme Court is the highest court in the nation. Congress sets up lower federal courts (such as district courts and appeals courts). Judges hold office for life or until they are convicted of wrongdoing.

Section 2. Jurisdiction of the United States Courts

1. The judicial power shall extend to all cases, in laws and equity, arising under this Constitution, the laws of the United States, and treaties made, or which shall be made, under their authority; to all cases affecting ambassadors, other public ministers and consuls; to all cases of admiralty and maritime jurisdiction; to controversies to which the United States shall be a party; to controversies between two or more States; between a State and citizens of another State; between citizens of different States; between citizens of the same State claiming lands under grants of different States, and between a State, or the citizens thereof, and foreign States, citizens or subjects.

The power of the federal courts is very broad. It covers all cases having to do with the Constitution, laws passed by Congress, treaties, shipping, and diplomats. It also covers disagreements between states, between people living in different states, and between Americans and foreigners. Since the 11th Amendment (1798), federal courts can no longer settle disputes between a state and someone living in another state.

2. In all cases affecting ambassadors, other public ministers and consuls, and those in which a State shall be party, the Supreme Court shall have original jurisdiction. In all the other cases before mentioned, the Supreme Court shall have appellate jurisdiction, both as to law and fact, with such exceptions, and under such regulations as the Congress shall make.

Cases involving state governments and diplomats may begin in the Supreme Court. In other cases, a lower federal court must hear the case first.

3. The trial of all crimes, except in cases of impeachment, shall be by jury; and such trial shall be held in the State where the said crimes shall have been committed; but when not committed within any State, the trial shall be at such place or places as the Congress may by law have directed.

Except for federal officials who are impeached, all people accused of crimes are tried by a jury. The trial is held in the state where the crime took place.

Section 3. Treason

1. Treason against the United States, shall consist only in levying war against them, or in adhering to their enemies, giving them aid and comfort.

Treason is the most serious crime against the nation. Only a citizen who fights against the United States or helps an enemy can be found guilty of treason. (Such a person is called a *traitor*).

2. No person shall be convicted of treason unless on the testimony of two witnesses to the same overt act, or on confession in open court.

3. The Congress shall have power to declare the punishment of treason, but no attainder of treason shall work corruption of blood, or forfeiture except during the life of the person attainted.

Congress sets the punishment for treason. It may not punish a traitor's family.

ARTICLE IV. The States and the Federal Government

Section 1. Full Faith and Credit

Full faith and credit shall be given in each State to the public acts, records, and judicial proceedings of every other State. And the Congress may by general laws prescribe the manner in which such acts, records, and proceedings shall be proved, and the effect thereof.

The states must remember that they are equal parts of our nation. Americans must respect the laws of all states.

Section 2. Citizens of the States

1. The citizens of each State shall be entitled to all privileges and immunities of citizens in the several States.

A citizen must receive fair treatment in every state of the Union.

2. A person charged in any State with treason, felony, or other crime, who shall flee from justice, and be found in another State, shall on demand of the executive authority of the State from which he fled, be delivered up, to be removed to the State having jurisdiction of the crime.

States must send runaway criminals and people accused of crimes but not yet tried back to the states where the crime occurred.

3. No person held to service or labor in one State, under the laws thereof, escaping into another, shall, in consequence of any law or regulation therein, be discharged from such service or labor, but shall be delivered up on claim of the party to whom such service or labor may be due.

Before the ending of slavery, states had to send runaway slaves back to their masters.

Section 3. New States and Territories

1. New States may be admitted by the Congress into this Union; but no new State shall be formed or erected within the jurisdiction of any other State; nor any State be formed by the junction of two or more States, or parts of States, without the consent of the legislatures of the States concerned as well as of the Congress.

Congress may admit new states to the Union. It may not, however, carve a new state out of an old state or join two states together, unless those states agree.

2. The Congress shall have power to dispose of and make all needful rules and regulations respecting the territory or other property belonging to the United States; and nothing in this Constitution shall be so construed as to prejudice any claims of the United States, or of any particular State.

Congress may make rules about federal lands. It may decide how to run territories that are not parts of states.

Section 4. Protection of States Guaranteed

The United States shall guarantee to every State in this Union a republican form of government, and shall protect each of them against invasion; and on application of the legislature, or of the executive (when the legislature cannot be convened), against domestic violence.

The United States must make sure that the government of each state is one in which the people rule. No state may have a king. The national government must protect each state against outside invasion. If requested, it must also help states to put down riots.

ARTICLE V. Amendments

The Congress, whenever two thirds of both Houses shall deem it necessary, shall propose amendments to this Constitution, or, on the application of the legislature of two thirds of the several States, shall call a convention for proposing amendments, which, in either case, shall be valid to all intents and purposes, as part of this Constitution, when ratified by the legislatures of three fourths of the several States, or by conventions in three fourths thereof, as the one or the other mode of ratification may be proposed by the Congress; provided that no amendment which may be made prior to the year one thousand eight hundred and eight shall in any manner affect the first and fourth clauses in the ninth section of the first article; and that no State, without its consent, shall be deprived of its equal suffrage in the Senate.

These are the ways the people can change the Constitution.

First, an amendment must be *proposed.* This is done by a two-thirds vote in each house of Congress. Or it may be done by a special convention, which must be set up if two thirds of the state legislatures ask for it.

Second, the proposed amendment must be *ratified.* This may be done by a majority vote in three fourths of the state legislatures. Or it may be done by conventions in three fourths of the states. Congress decides which method of ratification is to be used.

ARTICLE VI. General Provisions

1. All debts contracted and engagements entered into, before the adoption of this Constitution, shall be as valid against the United States under this Constitution, as under the Confederation.

The debts of the government under the Articles of Confederation will be paid by the new national government.

2. This Constitution, and the laws of the United States which shall be made in pursuance thereof, and all treaties made, or which shall be made, under the authority of the United States, shall be the supreme law of the land; and the judges in every State shall be bound thereby, anything in the Constitution of laws of any State to the contrary notwithstanding.

The Constitution, laws passed by Congress, and treaties made by the United States are the highest law in the land. If state constitutions or state laws go against the federal Constitution, state judges must obey the federal Constitution.

3. The Senators and Representatives before mentioned, and the members of the several State legislatures, and all executive and judicial officers, both of the United States and of the several States, shall be bound by oath or affirmation, to support this Constitution; but no religious test shall ever be required as a qualification to any office or public trust under the United States.

A person does not have to promise to support any religion in order to hold public office. But state and federal officials must agree to support the U.S. Constitution.

ARTICLE VII. Ratification of the Constitution

The ratification of the conventions of nine States, shall be sufficient for the establishment of this Constitution between the States so ratifying the same.

Done in convention by the unanimous consent of the States present the seventeenth day of September in the year of our Lord one thousand seven hundred and eighty-seven, and of the Independence of the United States of America the twelfth. In witness whereof we have hereunto subscribed our names.

Signed by George Washington as President of the Convention and deputy from Virginia and by the thirty-eight other representatives of twelve states.

Nine states had to approve (ratify) the Constitution before it could take effect.

Amendments

Amendment 1 (1791) Congress shall make no law respecting an establishment of religion, or prohibiting the free exercise thereof; or abridging the freedom of speech, or of the press; or the right of the people peaceably to assemble, and to petition the Government for a redress of grievances.

Amendments 1–10 are known as the Bill of Rights.
No federal law may limit freedom of speech, press, religion, assembly (group meetings), and petition (asking the government to right a wrong).

Amendment 2 (1791)   A well-regulated militia being necessary to the security of a free State, the right of the people to keep and bear arms shall not be infringed.

People may own arms (guns, weapons) so that states may have militias.

Amendment 3 (1791)   No soldier shall, in time of peace, be quartered in any house, without the consent of the owner, nor in time of war, but in a manner to be prescribed by law.

In peacetime, soldiers are not to be quartered (housed) in a building without the owner's approval. In wartime, quartering of soldiers must be done according to law.

Amendment 4 (1791)   The right of the people to be secure in their persons, houses, papers, and effects, against unreasonable searches and seizures, shall not be violated, and no warrants shall issue, but upon probable cause, supported by oath or affirmation, and particularly describing the place to be searched, and the persons or things to be seized.

A person's dwelling place (house or apartment) cannot be searched without a warrant (court order). Warrants are also required to search a person's clothes, papers, and other possessions.

Amendment 5 (1791)   No person shall be held to answer for a capital, or otherwise infamous, crime, unless on a presentation or indictment of a grand jury, except in cases arising in the land or naval forces, or in the militia, when in actual service in time of war or public danger; nor shall any person be subject for the same offense to be twice put in jeopardy of life or limb; nor shall be compelled, in any criminal case, to be a witness against himself; nor be deprived of life, liberty, or property, without due process of law; nor shall private property be taken for public use, without just compensation.

People accused of serious crimes
—must be indicted (charged) by a grand jury
—cannot be tried twice for the same crime; two trials would amount to double jeopardy
—need not testify (give evidence) against themselves
—must be given all the protections the law offers
People must be fairly paid when their property is taken over by the government.

Amendment 6 (1791)   In all criminal prosecutions, the accused shall enjoy the right to a speedy and public trial, by an impartial jury of the State and district wherein the crime shall have been committed, which district shall have been previously ascertained by law, and to be informed of the nature and cause of the accusation; to be confronted with the witnesses against him; to have compulsory process for obtaining witnesses in his favor, and to have the assistance of counsel for his defense.

People accused of crimes
—must be given a speedy, public trial by a jury of local people
—must be able to require witnesses to appear
—must be able to get a lawyer

Amendment 7 (1791) In suits at common law, where the value in controversy shall exceed twenty dollars, the right of trial by jury shall be preserved, and no fact tried by a jury shall be otherwise re-examined in any court of the United States, than according to the rules of the common law.

People who sue or are sued for more than $20 may ask for a jury trial.

Amendment 8 (1791) Excessive bail shall not be required, nor excessive fines imposed, nor cruel and unusual punishments inflicted.

In criminal cases —bail or fines should not be too high —punishment should not be cruel or unusual

Amendment 9 (1791) The enumeration in the Constitution, of certain rights, shall not be construed to deny or disparage others retained by the people.

It is understood that the people have other rights even though they may not be listed in the Constitution and its amendments.

Amendment 10 (1791) The powers not delegated to the United States by the Constitution, nor prohibited by it to the States, are reserved to the States respectively, or to the people.

The people or the states have all the powers not given to the national government and not denied to the states in the Constitution.

Amendment 11 (1798) The judicial power of the United States shall not be construed to extend to any suit in law or equity, commenced or prosecuted against one of the United States by citizens of another State, or by citizens or subjects of any foreign State.

A person cannot sue a state in the federal courts.

Amendment 12 (1804) The Electors shall meet in their respective States and vote by ballot for President and Vice President, one of whom, at least, shall not be an inhabitant of the same State with themselves; they shall name in their ballots the person voted for as President, and in distinct ballots the person voted for as Vice President, and they shall make distinct lists of all persons voted for as President, and of all persons voted for as Vice President, and of the number of votes for each, which lists they shall sign and certify, and transmit sealed to the seat of the government of the United States, directed to the President of the Senate; the President of the Senate shall, in the presence of the Senate and House of Representatives, open all the certificates and the votes shall then be counted; the person having the greatest number of votes for

Electors vote for the President and Vice President on separate ballots. If no candidate gets a majority of the electoral votes, the House of Representatives picks a President from the top three candidates. In this vote, each state has a single ballot, cast by the representatives of that state.

President shall be the President, if such number be a majority of the whole number of Electors appointed; and if no person have such majority, then from the persons having the highest numbers not exceeding three on the list of those voted for as President, the House of Representatives shall choose immediately, by ballot, the President. But in choosing the President, the votes shall be taken by States, the representation from each State having one vote; a quorum for this purpose shall consist of a member or members from two thirds of the States, and a majority of all the States shall be necessary to a choice. And if the House of Representatives shall not choose a President whenever the right of choice shall devolve upon them, before the fourth day of March next following, then the Vice President shall act as President, as in the case of the death or other constitutional disability of the President. The person having the greatest number of votes as Vice President, shall be the Vice President, if such number be a majority of the whole number of Electors appointed, and if no person have a majority, then, from the two highest numbers on the list, the Senate shall choose the Vice President; a quorum for the purpose shall consist of two thirds of the whole number of Senators, and a majority of the whole number shall be necessary to a choice. But no person constitutionally ineligible to the office of President shall be eligible to that of Vice President of the United States.

Amendment 13 (1865)   *Section 1.* Neither slavery nor involuntary servitude, except as a punishment for crime whereof the party shall have been duly convicted, shall exist within the United States, or any place subject to their jurisdiction.

Section 2. Congress shall have power to enforce this article by appropriate legislation.

Amendment 14 (1868)   *Section 1.* All persons born or naturalized in the United States, and subject to the jurisdiction thereof, are citizens of the United States and of the State wherein they reside. No State shall make or enforce any law which shall abridge the privileges or immunities of citizens of the United States; nor shall any State deprive any person of life, liberty, or property, without due process of law; nor deny to any person within its jurisdiction the equal protection of the laws.

Section 2. Representatives shall be apportioned among the several States according to their respective numbers, counting the whole number of persons in each State, excluding Indians not taxed. But when the right to vote at any election for the choice of Electors for President and Vice President of the United States, Representatives in Congress, the executive and judicial officers of a State, or the members of the legislature thereof, is denied to any of the male inhabitants of such State, being twenty-one years of age, and citizens of the United States,

To be elected by the House, a presidential candidate must have the votes of a majority of the states. If the House fails to elect a President by the time for a President to take office, the Vice President acts as President.

If no candidate for Vice President has a majority of the electoral votes, the Senate picks a Vice President from the top two candidates. To win, a vice presidential candidate must get the votes of a majority of all the senators (not just of the senators voting).

Slavery is not allowed. People may not be forced to work, except as part of a criminal sentence handed down by a court.

Freed slaves and all other people born or naturalized in this country are citizens. Such people must be given all the protections offered by our laws. No person shall lose life, liberty, or property without going through every legal step.

To determine how many representatives a state will have in the House of Representatives, all residents of

or in any way abridged, except for participation in rebellion, or other crime, the basis of representation therein shall be reduced in the proportion which the number of such male citizens shall bear to the whole number of male citizens twenty-one years of age in such State.

Section 3. No person shall be a Senator or Representative in Congress, or Elector of President and Vice President, or hold any office, civil or military, under the United States, or under any State, who, having previously taken an oath, as a member of Congress, or as an officer of the United States, or as a member of any State legislature, or as an executive or judicial officer of any State, to support the Constitution of the United States, shall have engaged in insurrection or rebellion against the same, or given aid or comfort to the enemies thereof. But Congress may, by a vote of two thirds of each House, remove such disability.

Section 4. The validity of the public debt of the United States, authorized by law, including debts incurred for payment of pensions and bounties for services in suppressing insurrection or rebellion, shall not be questioned. But neither the United States nor any State shall assume or pay any debt or obligation incurred in aid of insurrection or rebellion against the United States, or any claim for the loss or emancipation of any slave; but all such debts, obligations, and claims shall be held illegal and void.

Section 5. The Congress shall have power to enforce, by appropriate legislation, the provisions of this article.

Amendment 15 (1870) *Section 1.* The right of citizens of the United States to vote shall not be denied or abridged by the United States or by any State on account of race, color, or previous condition of servitude.

Section 2. The Congress shall have power to enforce this article by appropriate legislation.

Amendment 16 (1913) The Congress shall have power to lay and collect taxes on incomes, from whatever source derived, without apportionment among the several States, and without regard to any census or enumeration.

a state except untaxed Indians are counted as whole people. This section ended the "three-fifths clause." (Article I, Section 2, Paragraph 3) All states must give equal voting rights to all males over the age of 21. A state that does not do this can be punished by having its voting rights in the House reduced.

Certain former leaders of the Confederate states cannot vote. But Congress may give voting rights back to such people.

The U.S. government will not pay back the debts of the Confederacy. State governments cannot pay those debts, either. On the other hand, the United States promises to honor the Civil War debts of the Union side.

People of all races and colors have equal voting rights. Former slaves can vote, too.

Congress can pass income tax laws.

Amendment 17 (1913)   *Section 1.* The Senate of the United States shall be composed of two Senators from each State, elected by the people thereof, for six years; and each Senator shall have one vote. The electors in each State shall have the qualifications requisite for electors of the most numerous branch of the State Legislatures.

Section 2. When vacancies happen in the representation of any State in the Senate, the executive authority of such State shall issue writs of election to fill such vacancies: *Provided*, That the legislature of any State may empower the executive thereof to make temporary appointments until the people fill the vacancies by election as the legislature may direct.

Section 3. This amendment shall not be so construed as to affect the election or term of any Senator chosen before it becomes valid as part of the Constitution.

Senators are to be elected directly by the people, rather than by the state legislatures. If a senator dies or leaves office, a new election shall be called by the governor. Until that election is held, a governor may appoint a temporary senator.

Amendment 18 (1920) *Section 1.* After one year from the ratification of this article the manufacture, sale, or transportation of intoxicating liquors within, the importation thereof into, or the exportation thereof from the United States and all territory subject to the jurisdiction thereof for beverage purposes is hereby prohibited.

Section 2. The Congress and the several States shall have concurrent power to enforce this article by appropriate legislation.

Section 3. This article shall be inoperative unless it shall have been ratified as an amendment to the Constitution by the legislatures of the several States, as provided in the Constitution, within seven years from the date of the submission hereof to the States by the Congress.

Alcoholic drinks cannot be made or sold. (See Amendment 21)

Amendment 19 (1920)   *Section 1.* The right of the citizens of the United States to vote shall not be denied or abridged by the United States or by any State on account of sex.

Section 2. Congress shall have power to enforce this article by appropriate legislation.

Women and men have equal voting rights.

Amendment 20 (1933)   *Section 1.* The terms of the President and Vice President shall end at noon on the 20th day of January, and the terms of Senators and Representatives at noon on the 3d day of January, of the years in which such terms would have ended if this article had not been ratified; and the terms of their successors shall then begin.

Section 2. The Congress shall assemble at least once in every year, and such meeting shall begin at noon on the 3d day of January, unless they shall by law appoint a different day.

Section 3. If at the time fixed for the beginning of the term of the President, the President-elect shall have died, the Vice-

The period between election and taking office is shortened. The President is sworn in on January 20 rather than on March 4. The new Congress starts in January, two months after election, rather than in December, 13 months after election.

President-elect shall become President. If a President shall not have been chosen before the time fixed for the beginning of his term, or if the President-elect shall have failed to qualify then the Vice-President-elect shall act as President until a President shall have qualified; and the Congress may by law provide for the case wherein neither a President-elect nor a Vice-President-elect shall have qualified, declaring who shall then act as President, or the manner in which one who is to act shall be elected, and such person shall act accordingly until a President or Vice President shall have qualified.

Section 4. The Congress may by law provide for the case of the death of any of the persons from whom the House of Representatives may choose a President whenever the right of choice shall have devolved upon them, and for the case of the death of any of the persons from whom the Senate may choose a Vice President whenever the right of choice shall have devolved upon them.

Section 5. Sections 1 and 2 shall take effect on the 15th day of October following the ratification of this article.

Section 6. The article shall be inoperative unless it shall have been ratified as an amendment to the Constitution by the legislatures of three fourths of the several States within seven years from the date of its submission.

Amendment 21 (1933) *Section 1.* The eighteenth article of amendment to the Constitution of the United States is hereby repealed.

Section 2. The transportation or importation into any State, Territory, or possession of the United States for delivery or use therein of intoxicating liquors, in violation of the laws thereof, is hereby prohibited.

Section 3. This article shall be inoperative unless it shall have been ratified as an amendment to the Constitution by conventions in the several States, as provided in the Constitution, within seven years from the date of the submission hereof to the States by the Congress.

Amendment 22 (1951) *Section 1.* No person shall be elected to the office of the President more than twice, and no person who has held the office of President, or acted as President, for more than two years of a term to which some other person was elected President shall be elected to the office of the President more than once. But this article shall not apply to any person holding the office of President when this article was proposed by the Congress, and shall not prevent any person who may be holding the office of President, or acting as President, during the term within which this article becomes operative from holding the office of President or acting as President during the remainder of such term.

If the person elected President dies before taking office, the person elected to be Vice President will become President.

If no candidate for President gets a majority, either in the Electoral College or in the House, the person elected to be Vice President will act as President temporarily, until a President is chosen.

Congress may pass a law telling the House and Senate what to do in case they must choose a President or Vice President and one of the candidates has died.

The 18th Amendment is removed from the Constitution. However, a state may make it illegal to bring alcoholic drinks across its borders. In such a case, it becomes a federal as well as a state crime to take alcoholic drinks into the state.

A President may not serve more than two terms. If a President serves more than two years of a term, he or she may serve only one more term. If the President serves less than two years of the first term, he or she may serve two more terms.

Section 2. This article shall be inoperative unless it shall have been ratified as an amendment to the Constitution by the legislatures of three fourths of the several States within seven years from the date of its submission to the States by the Congress.

Amendment 23 (1961)   *Section 1.* The District constituting the seat of Government of the United States shall appoint in such manner as the Congress may direct:

A number of Electors of President and Vice President equal to the whole number of Senators and Representatives in Congress to which the District would be entitled if it were a State, but in no event more than the least populous State; they shall be in addition to those appointed by the States, but they shall be considered, for the purposes of the election of President and Vice President, to be Electors appointed by a State; and they shall meet in the District and perform such duties as provided by the twelfth article of amendment.

Section 2. The Congress shall have power to enforce this article by appropriate legislation.

Citizens of Washington, D.C., may vote for President and Vice President. The number of electors will be set as if the district were a state. But the district may have no more electors than the smallest state.

Amendment 24 (1964)   *Section 1.* The right of citizens of the United States to vote in any primary or other election for President or Vice President, for Electors for President or Vice President, or for Senator or Representative in Congress, shall not be denied or abridged by the United States or any State by reason of failure to pay any poll tax or other tax.

Section 2. The Congress shall have power to enforce this article by appropriate legislation.

A citizen cannot be asked to pay a poll tax to vote in a national election. A poll tax is a special tax on voting.

Amendment 25 (1967)   *Section 1.* In case of the removal of the President from office or of his death or resignation, the Vice President shall become President.

Section 2. Whenever there is a vacancy in the office of the Vice President, the President shall nominate a Vice President who shall take office upon confirmation by a majority vote of both Houses of Congress.

Section 3. Whenever the President transmits to the President *pro tempore* of the Senate and the Speaker of the House of Representatives his written declaration that he is unable to discharge the powers and duties of his office, and until he transmits to them a written declaration to the contrary, such powers and duties shall be discharged by the Vice President as Acting President.

Section 4. Whenever the Vice President and a majority of either the principal officers of the executive departments or of such other body as Congress may by law provide, transmit to the President *pro tempore* of the Senate and the Speaker of the House of Representatives their written declaration that

If the chief executive dies, resigns, or is removed from office, the Vice President becomes President.

If there is no Vice President, the President names a person to this office with the approval of a majority in each house of Congress.

The Vice President becomes acting President if the chief executive says, in writing, that he or she is too sick to do the job. The Vice President remains the acting

the President is unable to discharge the powers and duties of his office, the Vice President shall immediately assume the powers and duties of the office as Acting President.

Thereafter, when the President transmits to the President *pro tempore* of the Senate and the Speaker of the House of Representatives his written declaration that no inability exists, he shall resume the powers and duties of his office unless the Vice President and a majority of either the principal officers of the executive department or of such other body as Congress may by law provide, transmit within four days to the President *pro tempore* of the Senate and the Speaker of the House of Representatives their written declaration that the President is unable to discharge the powers and duties of his office. Thereupon Congress shall decide the issue, assembling within forty-eight hours for that purpose if not in session. If the Congress, within twenty-one days after receipt of the latter written declaration, or, if Congress is not in session, within twenty-one days after Congress is required to assemble, determines by two-thirds vote of both Houses that the President is unable to discharge the powers and duties of his office, the Vice President shall continue to discharge the same as Acting President; otherwise, the President shall resume the powers and duties of his office.

President until the elected President recovers.
What if leading officials think the President is too sick to hold office, but the President is either unable or unwilling to say so? Then the Vice President and a majority of the cabinet may declare, in writing, that the President is unfit to stay in office. The Vice President then takes over the President's powers until the President is well. Congress is to decide any dispute over whether or not the President has recovered. The President may take over again unless two thirds of each house of Congress decides the President is still too sick.

Amendment 26 (1971)   *Section 1.* The right of citizens of the United States, who are eighteen years of age or older, to vote shall not be denied or abridged by the United States or by any State on account of age.

The minimum voting age is set at 18 years.

Section 2. The Congress shall have power to enforce this article by appropriate legislation.

Amendment 27 (1992)   No law varying the compensation for the services of senators and representatives shall take effect, until an election of representatives shall have intervened.

Members of Congress are prevented from passing immediate salary increases for themselves. Salary changes cannot take effect until after the next Congressional election.

Homework Questions

1. How are the jobs of the House and Senate different?
2. In what way is the President chosen if no candidate gets a majority of Electoral College votes?
3. What sorts of cases are handled by the federal courts?
4. Which amendments gave new voting rights to the American people? Explain.
5. How can new amendments be added to the Constitution?

Understanding the Story

A. Write *T* for each statement that is true and *F* for each statement that is false.
   1. The minimum age is the same for representatives and senators.
   2. All senators are elected at the same time.
   3. The Senate tries officials who have been impeached by the House.
   4. Tax bills must begin in the House.
   5. No bill may become a law unless the President signs it.
   6. Federal judges hold office for life or until they are convicted of wrongdoing.
   7. All the rights guaranteed by the Constitution may be found in the Bill of Rights.

8. The system of electing a President has changed since the Constitution was first adopted.

B. Write *G* for each power given to to the national government in the Constitution. Write *D* for each power denied to the national government.
   1. Coin money.
   2. Punish a traitor's family.
   3. Put a tax on exports.
   4. Set an income tax.
   5. Pass laws to punish people without a trial.
   6. Maintain a navy.
   7. Set up a system of patents and copyrights.
   8. Establish an official religion.

C. The Constitution has been amended 27 times. Have the amendments made our Constitution more democratic? Why or why not?

Activities and Inquiries

1. Imagine that you are a member of Congress. What is your most important job under the Constitution?
2. Imagine that you are the President. What is your most important job under the Constitution?
3. Look at all of the amendments passed since the Bill of Rights. Which seems most important to you? Why?
4. Imagine that you can propose just one further amendment to the Constitution. What would that amendment be? Explain.

"You looked surprised, Jack."

"Yes, I didn't know that the revolutionists wanted the Articles of Confederation to be so weak. Yet that government held the colonies together during the Revolution and the Critical Period."

"That's true, Jack. But you can't really blame the revolutionists. Think of their experiences with King George III and a strong British government."

"Well, Mr. Miller, our leaders certainly learned a lot from the Critical Period."

"What do you mean?"

"A weak government with few powers just couldn't survive," replied Jack. "That's why the new Constitution gave the central government many powers."

"What happened to the states?"

"The states had lots of power, too—all the powers the central government didn't have. These powers weren't listed, but they let the states keep control of their local affairs."

"Very good, Jack. Now you have a strong central, or federal, government. How are you going to make it run effectively?"

"Easy, Mr. Miller. The central government is separated into three parts. Each one does its special job and watches the other two. The legislature, or Congress, makes the laws. The executive, or President, carries out the laws. And the judiciary, or courts, explains or interprets them."

"Right on target!" Mr. Miller said, smiling. "But weren't some of the delegates worried about the danger of a tyrant taking over?"

"I suppose so," answered Jack. "Because each branch checks and balances the other two, no one can get too powerful. It reminds me of the balance scale in my science class. Imagine that the President puts too much weight or power on one side of the scale. Congress pops right back with a power of its own. Presto, the President is checked. The scale is back in balance. The same thing happens if Congress tries to take too much power. And the courts check the other two."

"Let's go back to the President. Do you remember how he's elected?"

"Yes. The people don't vote directly for the President. They vote in November for electors. The electors then meet in their own state capitals. These people are the ones who finally choose the President."

"Why do you think that it was set up in that roundabout way?"

"I don't think the delegates at the Constitutional Convention trusted the people," said Jack. "Besides, the delegates had a very difficult time trying to decide how to elect the President. The

Electoral College is really a compromise that arose from all sorts of suggestions."

"That's true, Jack. But doesn't this method sound undemocratic?"

"It wasn't meant to be democratic," replied Jack. "But the electors usually vote the way the people want them to."

"What would you say is the most democratic part of our Constitution?" asked Mr. Miller.

"It certainly wasn't the part that allowed the slave trade to continue. That would be the opposite of democratic! It was the Bill of Rights, added later as the first ten amendments. The Bill of Rights protects us and lets us enjoy the rights, pleasures, and responsibilities of American democracy."

"Fine, Jack! We're ready to launch the government under the new Constitution."

A Half Century of Independence

"Say, Mr. Miller, how did our leaders launch the nation? I bet they had never launched anything before—except maybe a ship."

"Well, Jack, why not think of the United States as a new ship? Let's imagine that the ship's hull, or body, is finished."

"Yes, I can see that the Constitution is like the hull. What do we do next?"

"Why not see whether the hull floats?"

"Right! Into the water it goes!"

"What's your next move, Jack?"

"I guess to add the cabins, masts, and sails."

"Don't forget the rudder and the steering wheel," added Mr. Miller.

"And a captain and a crew—plus a few guns for protection."

"Yes, it will have to be strong, Jack. But we're not really shipbuilders. What does all this mean?"

"The Constitution gave the nation a framework. But Americans had to build it up."

"We are going to watch the way they did that," said Mr. Miller. "They had some bad times. Sometimes it looked as if the ship might sink. Let's find out why it didn't. We'll begin with our first 'captain,' George Washington."

1 The United States Must Pay Its Debts

George Washington, the hero of the Revolutionary War, was unanimously chosen to be the first President of the United States. (All the presidential electors voted for him.) Naturally, he faced many problems in getting the new government under way.

Washington had to build a government from the ground up. In fact, all he inherited from the government under the Articles of Confederation was a dozen clerks. Money had to be raised, the national defense provided for, and territories organized. A system of courts had to be established, executive departments created, trade regulated, foreign and Indian nations dealt with. Above all, Washington had to win respect for the office of the President.

In addition, the government still owed a huge war debt of more than $54 million. This money had been borrowed from foreign governments and from individuals. Could the federal government afford to repay 100 cents on the dollar? Should the states be repaid for the money they had borrowed to help win the war?

Alexander Hamilton of New York, the first secretary of the treasury, prepared a complete plan to repay these debts and to raise money for the operation of the government. The major opponent of the plan was Representative James Madison of Virginia.

In our story, Hamilton meets with Madison to persuade him to support the new financial program in Congress. See if you can understand why they disagree so strongly. Which one do you think is right? Why?

New York City, 1790

"Madison, why can't you understand what I'm trying to do?" asked Alexander Hamilton angrily. "My program will save our country."

"My dear Hamilton, I beg to disagree," answered James Madison. "I fear your plan will wreck the United States!"

"You are just being contrary, Madison. You'll never understand."

"Do you deny that your plan will help some people more than others?"

"Ah, I see what you mean," answered Hamilton. "Some people sold their bonds because they refused to wait until our government paid them in full. Is it my fault that they were afraid to keep them?

Those who hold our bonds now deserve 100 cents on the dollar. They have faith and courage."

"Bondholders are not the only Americans with faith and courage. Many loyal, patriotic Americans gave almost every penny they had to fight the war against Great Britain. When the war was over, they had very little left. There was small hope that the government under the Articles of Confederation could pay its debts. Do you blame the original bondholders for selling their bonds? Some received as little as ten cents on the dollar. That's only 10 percent of the value of the bond."

"Madison, you don't know the first thing about money!" (Hamilton banged his fist on the table.) "It is not important who holds our bonds today. We *must* pay every dollar to the present holders. Everyone must know that the United States of America will pay what it owes. If this happens, people and nations will trust us. They will have faith in us."

"Do you really care about the credit of the United States?" asked Madison. "Aren't you mainly interested in helping your friends who bought the bonds from the Patriots? Don't you really want to help those speculators, those risk takers, make large profits and get rich?"

"Not at all," said Hamilton. "I think that even you will agree that every nation must have a good name. We are young and lack credit and reputation. We must show the world that we will keep our promises."

"I agree on the importance of our credit," said Madison. "And I agree that we should pay our foreign debts in full. But pay those speculators in full? I think it is more important to show support for the widows and orphans they cheated."

"Madison, you don't know the first thing about money!"

Madison started to get up from the table, but Hamilton stopped him. "Wait, let me make one more point. I think the government of the United States should pay the war debts of the states. The states borrowed money to pay for freeing our great nation from British rule. It is only right that our nation pay for the sacrifices the states made. It would be unfair to make the individual states carry this heavy load."

"You know very well that the New England states have large war debts. Others, like Virginia, have repaid most of their debts. Why should we in Virginia pay New England's debts plus our own? Why should we have to suffer because we manage our money carefully? Each must pay its own debts."

"Suppose," continued Hamilton, "the Revolutionary War had been fought entirely in one state. Imagine that it had not spread over all the states. And suppose that one state had borrowed more than $21 million to fight the war for all of us. Would it be fair to let that state pay the entire amount? Would you then call this a state debt? No, state debts are national debts."

"You know the war was fought in more than one state. Your example is a poor one; your reasoning is false."

"It is you who will not listen to reason, Madison. You forget that we fought a revolution to free the nation. Virginia, sir, is only one of 13 states making up that nation."

"All right, I will support full payment of our foreign and national debts—even though the wrong people may profit. However, I cannot support the payment of the state debts because it would give the national government too much power. I assure you that Congress will never pass such a law."

POSTSCRIPT

Madison was right—at first. Congress voted to pay off the foreign debt in full. But the House of Representatives defeated the bill for the assumption of state debts by two votes.

Then Madison had a change of heart. Working with Thomas Jefferson, a fellow Virginian, Madison made a deal with Hamilton. Madison agreed to win Southern votes to put through Hamilton's plan for assumption of state debts. In return, Hamilton would seek Northern support for a plan to move the nation's capital farther south. The deal went through, and Congress finally agreed to pay off the state debts.

What did Madison get in return? First, from 1790 to 1800, the nation's capital was moved from New York to Philadelphia. During this time work began on a new capital city along the Potomac River, on land given up by Maryland and Virginia. In 1800 the capital was moved to the still-unfinished city, where roads ran over and around tree stumps that had not yet been cleared. The new capital was named Washington, D.C. (The "D.C." stands for District of Columbia.)

Congress's decision on paying off the war debts strengthened the powers of the national (federal) government. This caused many people to worry that the states were losing too much power. During the years ahead, much more would be said about the division of power between the states and the national government.

As Madison and Hamilton argued about policies, people took sides. Rival groups eventually developed into political parties. On the one side were Hamilton and Washington; their sup-porters were called Federalists. The Federalists wanted to strengthen the national government. On the other side were Jefferson, Madison, and their supporters. These people became known as Democratic-Republicans or just plain Republicans. The Republicans wanted to keep the states strong.

Homework Questions

1. What reasons did Alexander Hamilton have for wanting to repay national bondholders in full?
2. Why did James Madison object to their repayment in full?
3. How did Hamilton plan to establish the credit of the United States?
4. On what grounds did Madison at first object to the payment of state debts by the national government?
5. Why did Madison later work to convince Southern lawmakers to vote in favor of the payment of state debts?

Understanding the Story

A. Write *T* for each statement that is true and *F* for each statement that is false.
   1. George Washington won the presidency in a very close election.
   2. Alexander Hamilton was the first secretary of the treasury.
   3. Hamilton and James Madison agreed completely on ways to solve the nation's money problems.
   4. Americans bought bonds to raise money to pay the expenses of the Revolutionary War.
   5. Hamilton prepared a financial program for the United States.
   6. Madison agreed from the first that all bondholders must be repaid fully.
   7. Hamilton favored payment of the states' war debts.
   8. Congress never approved Hamilton's plan to pay off war debts.

B. Write *H* for each statement that Hamilton made or might have made and *M* for each statement that Madison made or might have made.
   1. My program will save our country.
   2. Those who hold our bonds deserve 100 cents on the dollar.
   3. You can't blame the original bondholders for selling their bonds.
   4. Aren't you mainly interested in helping your friends?
   5. Speculators want to make large profits and get rich.
   6. Every nation must have a good name.
   7. State debts are national debts.
   8. The payment of state debts would give the national government too much power.

C. In politics, back-room deals are frequent—"you vote for my bill and I'll vote for yours." Do you think Madison did the right thing when he and Jefferson worked out a deal with Hamilton? Why or why not?

Activities and Inquiries

1. Imagine that Madison is writing a friend before Congress's first vote on the state debt-assumption bill. What will he say about Hamilton and his financial plan?
2. Suppose that Hamilton is writing a friend *after* the first vote in Congress. What will he say about Madison?
3. Imagine that it is 1790. At one time you owned a United States government bond worth $100, but you had sold it for $10. What action do you want Congress to take on the national debt? Give arguments to support your position.
4. Imagine that it is 1790. You have bought many United States government bonds from individuals who were willing to sell at bargain rates. What action do you want Congress to take? Give arguments to support your position.
5. Find information in your school or public library to help you prepare a report or chart on the difference between the national debt in 1789 and the debt today. One reference you might consult is *Historical Statistics of the United States*.

2 The Hero of the Revolutionary War Retires

In 1789 France was rocked by a revolution even more sweeping than the one that had freed the American colonies a few years earlier. Before the French Revolution ended, warfare had spread across all of Europe. The fighting lasted more than 20 years. In the United States, the French Revolution was regarded with a mixture of joy and fright. Americans simply could not agree on whether to support the French.

Secretary of State Thomas Jefferson and his followers were greatly excited by the start of the French Revolution. They saw it as a struggle for liberty, a continuation of the revolution in the United States. Washington, Hamilton, and their followers had a different re-

action. They were shocked when French revolutionists beheaded the king and queen in 1793. Perhaps even more shocking to them was the wave of arrests and executions that followed, sweeping away many of the original leaders of the French Revolution.

In an attempt to spread their revolution to other lands, the French declared war on European monarchies, including Britain. This put the United States in a very awkward position. In 1778 the United States had signed a treaty of alliance promising to help France defend its colonies in the West Indies. What if the British now decided to attack the French West Indies? If the United States honored its treaty with France, it could be forced into another war against Great Britain. If it did not honor the treaty, its word would seem to be worthless.

Washington was determined to avoid war. He thought the nation too young and weak to become involved in Europe's quarrels. In order to keep the nation out of war, he issued a Proclamation of Neutrality declaring that the United States would not take sides. The proclamation angered Jefferson and his followers, who were openly favoring the French.

Washington had hoped to retire at the end of his first term. He was well liked and admired, but four years of the Presidency were enough for him. However, his friends urged him to stay on—and he did.

Many people turned against Washington during his second term. A major reason was his refusal to help France. His enemies called him "the stepfather of his country" and "the American caesar" (dictator). He was accused of being unfriendly and acting like a king. His critics claimed he was more concerned with the success of the wealthy than with the welfare of the ordinary citizen. Washington was tired of these attacks, and he was exhausted physically by his two terms as President. He decided to return home, and nobody could change his mind.

In 1796 he announced his decision to retire in a Farewell Address, which was printed in a newspaper. He also included some "fatherly" advice about the future conduct of the nation.

In our story Ellen Rutherford is visiting her friend Lillian Bliss in Boston. The two young women have been writing letters back and forth. Four years have passed since they last saw each other.

See if you understand why Lillian and Ellen feel so differently about President Washington. Was Washington a great leader?

Boston, 1796

"It's wonderful to see you again, Lillian," said Ellen.

"Yes, it's been almost four years," said Lillian. "Remember, Washington had just been elected President for the second time."

"How could I forget? Now I see that he is retiring and going back home to Virginia. He says that eight years as President are more than enough for him. How right he is!"

"What do you mean?" asked Lillian.

"One term would have been enough for him. It's really too bad he didn't retire in 1792. Why did he have to stay in office so long?"

"How can you talk this way, Ellen? Washington is the greatest living American. I wish he would be President as long as he lives!"

"You can't mean that. Washington has served this country for too many years. He has worked hard and earned a rest."

"You've changed so much," said Lillian. "Last time you agreed that Washington was a marvelous man."

"That was four years ago, Lil. I was young. So much has happened since then. True, Washington led our soldiers during the Revolution. Everyone admired and respected what he did for the United States through those difficult years. And he was a good choice to be our first President. But people's feelings about him have changed."

"He's been good for our country. Don't forget he got our government started," said Lillian. "Look at the problems he solved: What a President is supposed to do. How he can carry out the laws of the Congress. What he should say to members of the House and Senate. What advisers he should have."

"I agree."

"Then, why—how—can you criticize Washington?" asked Lillian.

"You left out one thing, foreign policy. That's where he went wrong!"

"That's where you're wrong, Ellen," answered Lillian. "He has a strong foreign policy."

"Yes, strong with the wrong people. He'll do anything to isolate America, to keep it apart from other nations."

"What's wrong with that?" snapped Lillian. "Look what he did with the British. Through the Jay Treaty he persuaded them to give up their military forts in the Northwest. That got them out of our country."

"Oh, come on, Lil. You know that the British didn't move out of the forts very fast. Also, they are still forcing American seamen to join the British Navy. Don't be too easy on them."

"And don't forget the Spanish," continued Lillian. "Through the Pinckney Treaty the United States has the right to bring goods to the Spanish port at New Orleans and reship them from there."

"I agree," said Ellen. "It's a big help for farmers. They can float their crops down the Mississippi River to New Orleans."

"Yes, then the cargo can be put on big ships and sent off to our Atlantic ports," added Lillian. "You see, you agree with me most of the time. I'm sure that you'll admit that the ending of the Indian danger in the Northwest by the Battle of Fallen Timbers in 1794 was a good thing."

"Certainly," said Ellen. "But would we have had to fight the Indians if the British hadn't stirred them up? No, the British are our enemies in every way. How can you forget so quickly? It's 13 years since the end of our revolution. Yet King George still thinks we will become his colonies once again!"

"I'm sorry, Ellen, but we have too much in common with the British to be enemies. We speak the same language, and we think the way they do. Remember, our great-grandparents came from England. No, our enemy is France. There is so much violence in France—so much killing."

"Violence or no violence, we can't forget our ties to France," said Ellen. "The French helped us win our revolution. Now we must help them win theirs. Where do you think they got their ideas about freedom and equality? We have a Declaration of Independence. They have their Declaration of the Rights of Man. The British stood in our way, so we sent them packing. Now the British stand in the way of the French Revolution. We must help France in order to save their revolution from their British enemies."

"They killed their king," said Lillian. "How many more people must die before their revolution is over?"

"As many as necessary to assure freedom and equality for all!"

"You sound just like Jefferson and his friends. You must be a Republican!" said Lillian.

"And you're a Federalist like Hamilton. The Federalists no longer believe in freedom. They are friends of the rich and enemies of the poor. I think Washington sides with the British king against the people's government of France."

"But, Ellen, that's not at all what Washington says in his Farewell Address. He says that Europe's interests have little or nothing to do with us. He says that Europe's disagreements are for European nations to settle. Therefore, we must not involve ourselves in European politics. In fact, we must not join in permanent alliances with any other nation. Washington doesn't ask us to help the British. His advice is to stay out of European affairs and alliances. Isn't that the best path for a new nation?"

"No, no, he isn't saying that at all," replied Ellen. "He says turn our backs on our French friends. Don't help the people who helped us win our freedom. Forget about our treaty with France. Alliances should not be permanent anyway."

"I don't care what you say," answered Lillian. "Washington knows what's best for this country. He and his Federalist supporters will lead us down the right path. We will be strong, and the world will respect us."

"Or the Federalists will lead us into a fight with our beloved France."

Homework Questions

1. Why was George Washington a good choice to be the first President?
2. What was the purpose of Washington's Proclamation of Neutrality?
3. For what reasons did many people turn against Washington during his second term?
4. How did Washington try to isolate the United States through his foreign policy?
5. How did Washington's Farewell Address emphasize his policy of isolation?

Understanding the Story

A. Write T for each statement that is true, F for each statement that is false, and O for each statement that is an opinion.
1. George Washington was happy to serve a second term as President.
2. Washington was the best President the United States ever had.
3. Washington was called "the American caesar."
4. Washington's foreign policy was just right for a new country.

5. The British agreed to give up their military forts in the Northwest.
6. An agreement with Spain gave the United States the right to re-ship goods from New Orleans.
7. British sailors were forced to join the United States Navy.
8. Hamilton was a Federalist.

B. Write *A* for each statement that Ellen would agree with and *N* for each statement that she would not agree with.
1. Washington should have retired in 1792.
2. Washington was a good choice to be our first President.
3. Washington was too hard on the British.
4. Washington will do anything to isolate the United States.
5. The British are our enemies in every way.
6. Our real enemy is France.
7. I support the French Revolution.
8. The best thing we can do is stay out of European affairs.

C. When he retired, Washington gave advice that later Presidents remembered. Is the President following that advice today? Explain why you think he is or is not.

Activities and Inquiries

1. Using what you have learned about George Washington, grade him *A* to *F* in the following areas and justify your grades.
   a. Military leadership
   b. Setting up the new government
   c. Foreign policy
   d. Money matters
2. Imagine that you are a newspaper editor. Write an editorial criticizing Washington.
3. Now write an editorial praising Washington.
4. Washington reads the editorial criticizing him. How will he answer the editorial?
5. Why do you suppose that most historians still rank Washington as one of the nation's best Presidents?

3 How Free Should the Press Be?

Washington's retirement gave Vice President John Adams his chance to become President. Actually, Adams, a Federalist, barely won the electoral vote in 1796. Jefferson, a Republican, was the runner-up and so became Vice President. This created an unusual situation in American history: a President and Vice President of opposing political parties. (The 12th Amendment to the Constitution, ratified in 1804, prevented such a situation from occurring again.)

A growing crisis in the United States's relations with France faced President Adams. French warships, trying to block trade with Britain, were capturing more and more U.S. merchant ships on the high seas. Diplomatic efforts to end these French raids failed. In truth, the United States was in a war—an undeclared war on the ocean.

Adams also faced troubles on the home front. At least 25,000 French refugees (people who leave home to escape danger) had come to the United States. In addition, a large number of refugees from a 1798 Irish rebellion against British rule found shelter here. Many of the Federalist politicians were suspicious of the foreigners and worried about what these people might do.

Congress tried to solve the problem by passing several laws. One, the Alien Act, gave the President the power to expel foreigners suspected of illegal activities in this country. Another law, the Naturalization Act, increased the residency requirement for citizenship. Previously, a foreigner could become a citizen after 5 years in this country. This waiting period was raised to 14 years. Was it not true, the Federalists

reasoned, that most naturalized foreigners (those who had become citizens) voted for the Republicans? Why not then make it harder for the Republicans to win new voters?

Republican politicians and editors attacked Adams and his policies fiercely and endlessly. The Federalists answered by accusing the Republicans of sedition (stirring up resistance to the government's authority). Influenced by the Federalists, Congress passed the Sedition Act. It set penalties for such activities.

There follows an exchange of letters between John Adams and Abigail Adams, his wife. The letters have been adapted from the originals. As you read them, notice how strongly both felt about a Republican writer. Ask yourself why the Adamses believed that this person was guilty of sedition. Did the Sedition Act violate the rights of freedom of the press guaranteed in the First Amendment?

Philadelphia, 1798

Dear Abigail,

I wish I had good news to tell you, but everything bothers me. I feel old—very old. I know that I shall never feel very well while I am President. The drudgery, the work, of this job is too much for me. If only I were a little stronger.

Why do I feel this way? I simply cannot stand the pressures of those Jacobin writers. [The Jacobins were a radical political group in the French Revolution. Adams used the term for Americans he thought too radical.]

You know that we are almost at war with the French. And you know how hard I work to protect our country. Yet what is my reward? Not a word of praise comes from the pens of those radical writers. All they do is attack, attack! Why can't they leave me alone? Why can't they understand that I am strengthening and defending the United States?

I am sure that you will agree that the worst of these writers is Benjamin Franklin's grandson, Benjamin Franklin Bache. His pen drips with acid. His words are disgraceful lies, and his sentences are twisted attacks against me, the nation—and all Federalists. I cannot stand that man!

Remember what Bache did with the 1794 treaty with Britain, the Jay Treaty? He stole a copy and printed it in his newspaper, the *Aurora*. How that wretched man worked to stir up the people against the treaty and against England! It was all a waste of energy because the Senate approved the treaty.

I could forgive his publishing the treaty before it was approved. It was dirty business, but perhaps he was merely expressing his opinion. The one thing I cannot forgive, Abigail, is his personal and unreasoned attack on President Washington. The greatest man in this nation was retiring to a well-earned rest. Did Bache bid him a pleasant farewell and Godspeed? Of course not! He blamed Washington for all the problems of our nation. He wrote that people should be happy because the name of Washington would no longer be connected with the government.

Bache went even further. He said that the nation had been deceived by Washington. He wrote that our beloved first President had been a false idol, a false leader. Unbelievable! I wrote to you then that Bache was dangerous and pointed out that he (like other Republican editors) was guilty of sedition. I knew that one day he would go too far.

Can this nation live with men like Bache? I think not! Our government cannot survive these attacks. Republican editors arouse and inflame the masses of the people. They encourage the overthrow of our federal system. Jefferson and his friends insist that a man may write anything he pleases. True, the First Amendment guarantees freedom of press and speech. But I say that a person cannot write lies. He must tell the truth! He cannot libel the government.

My enemies say that these are not attacks on the government. These are attacks on me, on my honesty, on my very honor. Dear Abigail, these are not merely libels about my person. Remember, I am the President of the United States, the First Citizen of this young nation. Therefore, an attack on me is the same as an attack on our government. And these attacks may very well lead to rebellion.

Yes, I am very worried. I fear for this nation. Listen to some of the things Bache has been writing about me. He says that I will do anything to fight a war against the French. I am accused of being a tool of the British. I am undemocratic and a tyrant. How can anyone say these things about John Adams? People forget so quickly how I struggled for freedom during the Revolution!

Ah, Abigail, I honestly think that these attacks will soon stop. Congress has passed the Sedition Law. Now, a person who prints, writes, or speaks evil things about the President, the Congress, or the government itself, will be sent to prison! At last, I can breathe easily. Possibly I will even be able to sleep at night. I can't wait until that B. F. Bache is behind bars!

I do hope that you are feeling much, much better. I miss you very much, my dear. I cannot wait until I can leave Philadelphia to return to our home in Quincy.

Your affectionate husband,

John

Quincy, Massachusetts, 1798

Dear John,

Thank you, I am feeling better. My illness left me rather weak, but in a few weeks I should be myself again.

I am concerned about your health. The last time you were here, you looked so pale. You had lost weight; you definitely did not seem well. No doubt you need some good country air—away from the cares of Philadelphia and the presidency. I do hope you will be able to get back to Quincy very soon.

That is wonderful news indeed about the passage of the Sedition Law. I agree absolutely that Bache is all you say and more. I think, John, that he is the worst person I have ever seen on this earth. He is the devil himself come to roost in Philadelphia. Woe upon us that Ben Franklin had such a grandson! I, too, cannot wait until he is found guilty of printing his filth. The worst prison is too good for him!

I will never forget his personal attacks on you. The nerve of that nasty man calling you old, bald, blind, crippled, and toothless! And you, John, a mere 63, in the flower of your handsome manhood! You and Bache are both wrong; you are *not* old!

You and the Congress have been very patient. You have withstood Bache's attacks in good spirit. But the time has come to put a stop to this nonsense. Punish all the Republican editors. Let those Jacobins understand that they cannot try to pull down the government of these United States without penalty. Their lies must be ended—or we will find ourselves in a civil war!

I know how strongly you believe in freedom of the press. But, surely, freedom should not include deliberate lies and the spitting forth of vicious attacks upon our persons. Never fear, John, our republic will survive. The Sedition Act will protect the United States.

Please return to Quincy. The soft, sea breezes will be a marvelous tonic for you.

Affectionately,

Abigail

POSTSCRIPT

Bache was arrested for sedition and released on bail. But he died of yellow fever before his trial.

Under the provisions of the Sedition Act, 25 men were arrested and 10 convicted of sedition. This number included one congressman (Matthew Lyon of Vermont) and several Republican editors. The longest sentence of four years was given to a man who had set up a political symbol in a Massachusetts village.

Homework Questions

1. Why were the Federalists worried about the refugees who came here from Europe?
2. How did Congress deal with the refugees?
3. Why did Adams feel so strongly about Republican newspaper editors?
4. What was the aim of the Sedition Act?
5. Why did Abigail Adams feel that Bache's imprisonment would not violate freedom of the press?

Understanding the Story

A. Write *F* for each statement that is a fact and *O* for each statement that is an opinion.
   1. Jefferson and Adams were supporters of opposing political parties.
   2. The United States should have declared war against France.
   3. Adams should not have disliked foreigners.
   4. Adams was given the power to expel certain foreigners from the United States.
   5. Sedition is really a more serious crime than murder.
   6. Benjamin Franklin Bache attacked Adams's policies.
   7. Encouraging people to resist their government is sedition.
   8. The Alien and Sedition Acts were good for the United States.

B. Match each item in Column *A* with its description in Column *B*.

   Column A

   1. freedom of the press
   2. naturalization
   3. refugee
   4. sedition
   5. alien
   6. Federalist
   7. libel
   8. Republican

   Column B

   a. Person who is not a citizen
   b. Untrue and hurtful printed remarks
   c. The party of Jefferson
   d. A guarantee of the First Amendment
   e. Process by which a foreigner becomes a citizen
   f. Encouragement of resistance to government authority
   g. Person who flees to another country to escape danger at home
   h. The party of Adams and Hamilton

C. Americans freely criticize policies of the U.S. government today. Select one group that is currently opposing a government program and describe its activities and statements. Do you think the group is involved in sedition? Why or why not?

Activities and Inquiries

1. Imagine that you have been charged with sedition for criticizing Adams. Write your defense.
2. You are the prosecuting attorney in the case about criticizing Adams. Prepare the arguments for the prosecution.
3. Suppose that you are a member of the jury in the Adams criticism case. How will you vote? Explain your reasoning.
4. John Adams agrees to testify at the trial. What testimony will he give?
5. Reread the chapter on John Peter Zenger (see pages 80–84). Do you think his writings might have been illegal under the Sedition Act? Why? How might Andrew Hamilton have defended those who were arrested for **sedition during Adams's Presidency?**

4 Jefferson Stretches the Constitution

The Alien and Sedition Acts alarmed the Republicans. They argued that these laws went against the Constitution, especially the First Amendment. The people being jailed for disobeying these laws seemed to be mainly Republicans who criticized Adams and the Federalists. Jefferson and Madison insisted that the laws were unconstitutional. But Federalist judges did not agree.

What could the Republicans do to get rid of the laws? Jefferson and Madison drew up resolutions for two state legislatures to pass. The resolutions said that states could nullify (wipe out) federal laws. Virginia and Kentucky passed the resolutions, but no other state followed their lead. The Alien and Sedition Acts remained in effect.

Republicans made the Alien and Sedition Acts a major issue in the presidential election of 1800. Jefferson defeated Adams by only eight electoral votes. After this, the Federalists lost strength and would never again elect a President of the United States.

Jefferson began his first term as President by stressing his goodwill toward the Federalists. He cut government costs in many areas, but he made no startling changes. The government remained basically the same, although criticism was possible once again. People fined or imprisoned under the Sedition Act were pardoned. The Alien and Sedition Acts were allowed to expire (end) in 1801.

Washington and Adams had been deeply concerned about the power struggles of France and England. Now Jefferson also became caught up in European politics. In our story he is meeting with his cabinet about a very serious issue facing the United States. A decision must be made.

Ask yourself why New Orleans was so important to Western farmers. What constitutional power was used to buy Louisiana?

Washington, D.C., 1802

JEFFERSON. Gentlemen, I have very important news. New Orleans will soon be in the hands of the French! Napoleon, the ruler of France, has forced Spain to give up that city.

SECRETARY OF STATE JAMES MADISON. This is terrible! The farmers must have the right to land their goods in New Orleans. What if the French close the port to them?

SECRETARY OF THE TREASURY ALBERT GALLATIN. Who knows what Napoleon will do? Why would he want New Orleans?

JEFFERSON. Very good questions, Mr. Gallatin. That is exactly why I am so worried. The port of New Orleans must be kept open for United States trade. Almost half of all our farm products go down the Mississippi River and pass through that city. This nation cannot survive if New Orleans is in the hands of an enemy.

ATTORNEY GENERAL LEVI LINCOLN. But couldn't we be friendly with the French?

JEFFERSON. This has nothing to do with friendship. It is all a matter of power among nations. Spain is weak. France under Napoleon is strong and becoming more powerful and ambitious. France *was* our friend. You know how much I admired the French people and their revolution. But that is all in the past.

MADISON. Are you saying, Mr. President, that the United States must try to prevent France from taking over New Orleans? What can we do?

SECRETARY OF WAR HENRY DEARBORN. We need a friendly nation in New Orleans. But we are in no condition to fight a war. In fact, our army has been cut from 4,000 to 2,500 men. We are in bad military shape.

SECRETARY OF THE NAVY ROBERT SMITH. And the navy! We have only a handful of ships. We'd better let Napoleon do what he wants. Pretend he doesn't exist because we can't stop him.

JEFFERSON. Of course we will not fight a war to take New Orleans. The United States will buy the city from France.

GALLATIN. It will take a lot of money to satisfy Napoleon, but it is a good idea.

MADISON. Mr. President, suppose Napoleon refuses to sell?

JEFFERSON. Then we must make an alliance with the British against the French.

Jefferson wrote to Robert Livingston, the American ambassador to France, and told him to offer Napoleon up to $10,000,000 for New Orleans and West Florida. The President sent James Monroe to Paris to assist Livingston. Napoleon eventually offered the whole vast territory of Louisiana for $15,000,000. Monroe and Livingston hesitated briefly, then accepted.

Washington, D.C., 1803

JEFFERSON. Mr. Monroe has come to this meeting directly from Paris. He will give us up-to-date information on the talks about New Orleans.

MONROE. Gentlemen, I have good news. I have a better treaty than any one of us dreamed possible. We will have all of Louisiana for $15,000,000. Our troubles with France are over!

GALLATIN. $15,000,000!

DEARBORN. Where is Louisiana? I thought we were buying New Orleans.

JEFFERSON. Please let Mr. Monroe continue.

MONROE. We have no idea how large Louisiana is. (*Unrolls a map.*) You can see how incomplete this map is. All we know is that Louisiana includes much of the land west of the Mississippi River. Adding this land will double the size of the United States.

SMITH. Who needs it all? Why spend all that money on some worthless land? I've heard that most of the area is desert. You can't live there, and if you could, you would not be able to grow a thing!

MONROE. True, we have no idea what much of the land is like. But it's a great bargain. We were offering $10,000,000 for New Orleans and as much of West Florida as we could get. An extra $5,000,000 gives the United States control of New Orleans and a huge piece of land.

GALLATIN. We will never have to worry about a foreign nation blocking our shipping on the Mississippi. The Western farmers will be very happy about this!

LINCOLN. Haven't we forgotten something? We're talking about whether we should buy Louisiana. But do we have the power to do that? Where in the Constitution does it say that the President can buy land? Where in the Constitution does it say that the United States can be made larger?

JEFFERSON. True, the Constitution does not give the President the power to buy land. Therefore, I will ask Congress and the states to pass a constitutional amendment.

MONROE. Mr. President, we cannot take the time to pass an amendment. We must act now to get France out of North America. I recommend that you sign the treaty and send it to the Senate at once for its approval.

JEFFERSON. But what will our rivals, the Federalists, say?

LINCOLN. You know they will say that it is unconstitutional. They will argue that the President cannot enlarge the United States single-handedly.

MADISON. Correct. This power is not listed or written in the Constitution. But surely the President has an implied power, an understood power, to buy land for the good of the nation. I agree with Mr. Monroe. Sign the treaty and rush it to the Senate.

GALLATIN. Wait! Everything is a bit confused. Do you remember how we Republicans argued against Hamilton's Bank of the United States? We said Congress was not specifically given the power to charter a bank. Therefore, a bank was not constitutional. Now aren't we saying that Hamilton was right about the Constitution in 1791? Congress has power over money. A bank handles money. Therefore, stretch the Constitution a bit, and a bank is perfectly legal. The President has the power to make a treaty. Stretch that power, and you have a treaty buying Louisiana.

LINCOLN. Mr. President, please don't rush into this. There is nothing in the Constitution about buying land. Take a little more time. Add a constitutional amendment.

JEFFERSON. I would like to agree with you, Mr. Lincoln, because I prefer to follow the Constitution word for word. In normal times I would support an amendment. But the purchase of Louisiana is important for the survival of the nation. Therefore, I must take sides with Mr. Monroe. We must act fast before Napoleon changes his mind.

LINCOLN. We're acting exactly like the Federalists.

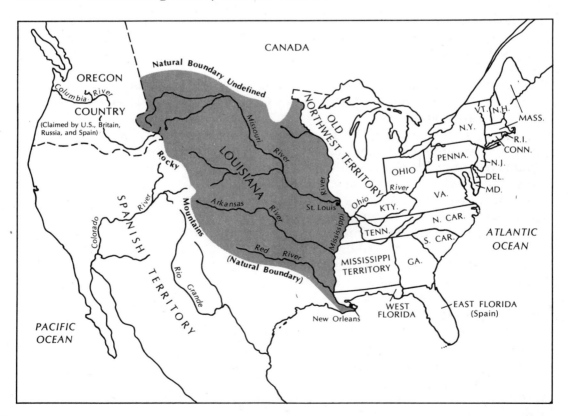

The Louisiana Purchase, 1803

JEFFERSON. No, we are not Federalists. The people elected us because they trust us and know that we will not take advantage of our power. Unlike the creation of the Bank, the purchase of Louisiana will benefit all the people. Let the Federalists criticize. The right to criticize and the right to change governments are what our republican form of government is all about.

MADISON. Sign the treaty. You will never regret adding Louisiana to the territory of the United States.

POSTSCRIPT

The Senate approved the treaty by a vote of 24 to 7.

By purchasing the Louisiana Territory, the United States added 828,000 square miles to its territory. Within this territory lay millions of acres of rich land and vast natural resources. The area extended from the Mississippi River west to the Rocky Mountains. It stretched from New Orleans to an unexplored part of Canada in the north.

In 1803 Jefferson sent Meriwether Lewis and William Clark to explore and map the Louisiana Territory. For two years, they followed the Missouri River north and west to its source. They crossed the Rocky Mountains and traced the Snake and Columbia rivers until they reached the Pacific Ocean. Their journey strengthened the United States's claim to the Oregon Territory. When Lewis and Clark returned, Jefferson and his advisers gained a better understanding of the vast size and resources of Louisiana.

Homework Questions

1. What did the Virginia and Kentucky Resolutions say about the Alien and Sedition Acts?
2. On taking over as President, how did Thomas Jefferson change the government?
3. Why was Jefferson concerned about Napoleon's taking over New Orleans?
4. Why did the purchase of Louisiana involve a constitutional question?
5. How did Jefferson's followers answer the constitutional objections to the purchase?

Understanding the Story

A. Write *T* for each statement that is true and *F* for each statement that is false.
1. The legislatures of Virginia and Kentucky tried to nullify the Alien and Sedition Acts.
2. Jefferson won the presidential election of 1800.
3. The Federalists elected Washington, Adams, and many other Presidents.
4. Jefferson did not allow criticism of the government.
5. Napoleon forced Spain to give up New Orleans.

6. Jefferson suggested that the United States fight Napoleon for New Orleans.
7. Napoleon offered the United States all of Louisiana for $15,000,000.
8. Most Western farmers were unhappy about the purchase of Louisiana.

B. List the numbers of the true statements about the U.S. purchase of Louisiana.
1. France sold Louisiana to the United States.
2. The purchase made it more difficult for Western farmers to ship their goods.
3. The western boundary of the United States moved from the Mississippi River to the Rocky Mountains.
4. The United States in 1803 became smaller in size.
5. The United States spent $50,000,000 for Louisiana.
6. New Orleans became a part of the United States.
7. Jefferson refused to sign the Louisiana Treaty.
8. The United States gained control of the entire Mississippi River.

C. The Louisiana Purchase raised a serious question about the meaning of the Constitution. Do you think it was a good thing to interpret the Constitution in such a way as to expand the powers of the federal government? Why or why not?

Activities and Inquiries

1. Study the map on page 196. Then choose the term or phrase that best completes each statement.
   a. In 1803 the United States extended from (1) the Pacific Ocean to the Atlantic Ocean (2) the Pacific Ocean to the Rocky Mountains (3) the Rocky Mountains to the Atlantic Ocean.
   b. The Louisiana Purchase (1) doubled the size of the United States (2) had no effect on the size of the United States (3) turned all of North America into the property of the United States.
   c. To the north of the Louisiana Territory is (1) Canada (2) Oregon (3) Maine.
   d. The Old Northwest Territory was (1) east of the Mississippi River and north of the Ohio River (2) west of the Mississippi River and north of the Ohio River (3) between the Mississippi and the Missouri rivers.
   e. A river that flows through the Louisiana Territory is the (1) Ohio (2) Red (3) Rio Grande.
2. Imagine that you are the editor of a Federalist newspaper. Write an editorial criticizing the Louisiana Purchase.
3. How might Jefferson answer your editorial?
4. Describe what the United States might be like today if Jefferson had *not* bought the Louisiana Territory.

5 War Divides a Nation

President Jefferson solved the problem of possible French control of New Orleans by buying Louisiana. But he could not solve the problems faced by U.S. seamen as they sailed to and from European ports.

During the wars that kept Europe in turmoil in the early 1800's, United States ships carried goods to both sides. Neither Britain, on one side, nor France, on the other, liked this. Each tried to keep the United States from trading with the other side. They did so by seizing U.S. ships. The British held more ships than the French did. United States shipowners and the U.S. government protested vigorously against this practice. But complaints had little effect, and the practice continued.

Just as upsetting to the people of the United States was the British practice of taking seamen from American ships. The British Navy was often short of men. To fill its crews, it used a practice known as impressment. In effect, men were kidnapped and forced to serve in the navy.

The British claimed that the men they impressed were deserters from the British Navy. But they took British-born sailors who had become U.S. citizens as well as actual deserters. Under British law, a person could not change citizenship. British officers might impress any sailor with a British or an Irish accent.

In 1807 a crisis developed when the British warship *Leopard* demanded to search the American warship *Chesapeake* about ten miles off the Virginia coast. The U.S. commander refused.

The British then fired on the *Chesapeake*, killing 3, wounding 18, and badly damaging the ship. The Americans could fire only one shot. Four sailors were seized by the British.

Americans were outraged, and many called for war. Jefferson decided to apply economic pressure instead. The idea was to do enough damage to Britain's businesses to make the British government change its policies. For good measure, Jefferson applied his pressure to France as well. He wanted to stop interference with U.S. rights at sea.

Jefferson tried a variety of different measures. James Madison, who replaced Jefferson as President in 1809, kept on trying. But none of the measures was a great success. The United States suffered more than either Britain or France.

What kinds of economic pressure were used? First, in 1807, came an *embargo*—a total cutoff of U.S. trade with the rest of the world. U.S. ships sat idle in port; shipowners lost money; sailors had no work. Farmers and planters could not ship their wheat, cotton, and tobacco to buyers abroad. Americans began to complain. Republicans feared they were making the voters angry.

So in 1809 the United States gave up the embargo and restored trade with all nations. Then the U.S. offered a deal. If either Britain or France stop seizing U.S. ships, the U.S. would cut off trade with the other of the two nations. This deal was set forth in 1810 in an act of Congress called Macon's Bill Number Two.

France reacted first. It promised to stop seizing U.S. ships. In fact, the French did not keep their promise. But in 1811 the U.S. again cut off trade with Britain.

Once again U.S. business dipped. Especially hard hit was New England, which depended heavily on trade with Britain. The Federalist Party was still strong in New England, and its leaders denounced the Republicans for their policies.

Meanwhile, Westerners were voicing their own complaints. They were upset by Indian attacks and accused British agents in Canada of stirring up the Indians. A major clash between Indians and U.S. soldiers occurred at Tippecanoe in Indiana Territory in November, 1811. Troops led by Indiana's governor, William Henry Harrison, took heavy losses but defeated Indians armed by the British.

A group in Congress known as the War Hawks demanded war with Britain. These men were mainly from the South and West. They wanted the United States to take over Canada so that region could no longer be used as a base for arming the Indians. They also wanted the U.S. to take Florida, then owned by Britain's ally, Spain. Besides, they felt that British actions on the high seas had insulted the American national honor. "On to Canada" was their slogan.

The War Hawks, mainly Republicans, dominated Congress in the session of 1811–1812. President Madison, giving in to their pressure, asked Congress to declare war on Britain. This Congress did on June 18, 1812. Woefully unprepared, the United States was now at war with the world's greatest naval power.

In our story, two New Englanders, one a Federalist and the other a Republican, discuss the War of 1812. Ask yourself why so many New Englanders opposed the war. Were those who opposed the war traitors?

Boston, August, 1814

"The British have burned down Washington," said Dennis, holding up a copy of a Boston newspaper.

"I don't believe a word in that Federalist, anti-war newspaper," replied Lissa. "Its writers twist and turn the news to make Madison and the Republicans look bad."

"They report the news as they see it," answered Dennis. "Madison makes mistakes; they publish them. Listen to the headlines: 'WASHINGTON IN FLAMES. PRESIDENT AND MRS. MADISON FLEE AS BRITISH BURN WHITE HOUSE, CAPITOL, AND OTHER PUBLIC BUILDINGS.'"

"Why, that's terrible. Our nation is in danger, and you're smiling."

"Don't get excited, Lissa. I don't want the British burning our cities any more than you do. Baltimore could be next and someday even Boston. But I can't help feeling that Madison deserves to be punished for forcing us into this war."

"Why on earth do you say that?"

"All I'm saying is that we New England Federalists saw no reason for going to war against Britain. The United States has no navy worthy of the name, and our army hardly has enough equipment and trained men for a parade."

"Think about the United States rather than New England for a moment, Dennis. Our nation's honor is at stake. That's why we're fighting. Remember, the British dragged United States citizens from our ships to force Americans into their navy. Those were American ships that were captured and sunk by the British—ships built and owned by your friends. And surely you can't excuse the British for stirring up their Indian allies and killing Americans in the West."

"Slow down, Lissa. Impressment has been going on for at least 20 years. We've lived with it. Of course, we're unhappy about losing our ships, but the greater the risk, the greater the profit. Besides, the French captured our ships, too. Why aren't we fighting the French?"

"The French weren't impressing our sailors and arming the Indians," said Lissa. "Nor do they have a base in North America. Madison's plan was to capture Canada and end the Indian attacks that the British were stirring up."

"I don't believe these stories about the British provoking the Indians," said Dennis. "Besides, the United States doesn't need any more territory. Add Canada and before long there will be new states sending more Republicans to Congress. As for Madison's plans, they're ridiculous. That was some planning in 1812. Why, our General William Hull surrendered Detroit to British General Isaac Brock without firing a shot. Hull couldn't invade Canada, and two other attempts were no more successful—even though our men did burn many public buildings in York, the capital of Upper Canada."

"You're right about Canada. We failed in our attempts to take it over. On the other hand, we're doing well at sea, even with our few ships. Who could fail to be inspired by Oliver Hazard Perry's victories on Lake Erie in 1813? And don't forget the victories of the *Constitution* and the *United States*. Their crews have sunk many British men-of-war on the high seas."

"That's good, but not good enough," replied Dennis. "How are we going to win this war and push the British off our soil? New England's shipping industry is being crippled. The region's whole economy is shattered. We should never have fought the British; it's too damaging to trade. Our fight should have been against that French tyrant Napoleon."

"What are you saying, Dennis? The British threatened our rights and our lives. Besides, the war has cut off imports of British goods. Now dozens of new factories are thriving because they face no competition from British goods. Americans are buying American products."

"Perhaps the war has helped our factories, but other businesses are suffering."

"Nonsense," said Lissa angrily. "New England farmers are selling foodstuffs and cattle across the Canadian border. Banks are lending gold to the British. And if doing business with the enemy isn't bad enough, New England states won't allow their militias to serve outside state borders. You can call it opposition to the war. I call it Federalist treason to the government of the United States!"

"I am a Federalist, and I am as loyal as you Republicans," answered Dennis grimly. "I say that something must be done to prevent our nation from fighting unnecessary wars."

POSTSCRIPT

Wanting to show opposition to the war, five New England states sent delegates to a convention at Hartford, Connecticut, in December, 1814. All who attended were Federalists. Although some Federalists wanted New England to secede (withdraw) from the United States, the Hartford Convention favored less extreme measures.

The convention proposed a series of amendments to the Constitution. For example, it proposed that the Constitution require a two-thirds vote in both houses of Congress for imposing an embargo, admitting new states, or declaring war (unless an enemy invaded). It suggested limiting Presidents to one term. And it sought to prohibit the election of two Presidents in a row from the same state.

The convention also spoke up for states' rights. It adopted a report that said the states had the right to block federal actions they considered to be unconstitutional. This was the doctrine of nullification, stated in 1798 by opponents of the Alien and Sedition Acts (see page 189).

But the Hartford resolution had little effect. Early in 1815 came news that General Andrew Jackson had won a major victory over the British at New Orleans. Soon after came word that the War of 1812 was over. A peace treaty had been signed at Ghent, Belgium, on December 24, 1814—two weeks before the Battle of New Orleans.

The U.S. had not won any of its war aims. It had not seized Canada. It had not conquered Florida. It had not gotten Britain to give up impressment. In fact, the war ended in a draw. But many Americans, delighted by Jackson's victory at New Orleans, concluded that the United States had won the war. Many made fun of the Federalists for their opposition to the war.

The war had one unexpected benefit: It furnished the United States with a national anthem. An American named Francis Scott Key watched a night-long British bombardment of Fort McHenry, in the harbor of Baltimore, Maryland. Thrilled to see the U.S. flag still waving "by dawn's early light," Key wrote the words to "The Star-Spangled Banner." Congress made the song the national anthem in 1931.

Homework Questions

1. What reasons did the British give for impressing United States sailors?
2. Why did many Americans object to the embargo of 1807?
3. What other measure did the U.S. take to put economic pressure on Britain and France?
4. Why did the War Hawks want to take over Canada?
5. How did New Englanders feel about the War of 1812? Why?

Understanding the Story

A. Write *T* for each statement that is true and *F* for each statement that is false.

1. Both Britain and France captured American ships.
2. Both the French and British impressed large numbers of U.S. sailors.
3. The *Chesapeake* was attacked near the coast of Virginia.
4. The embargo of 1807 hurt many U.S. business interests.
5. U.S. forces were defeated by Indians at Tippecanoe.
6. The War Hawks were generally from the South and West.
7. The Federalists supported Madison's war plans.
8. The British set fire to the city of Washington.

B. Choose the term or phrase that best completes each statement.

1. Attacks on United States ships were a result of (*a*) war in Europe (*b*) a British plot to seize Canada (*c*) French efforts to defend colonies in the West Indies.
2. Impressment was the British policy of (*a*) seizing U.S. ships (*b*) denying British subjects a right to change citizenship (*c*) taking men forcibly for the British Navy.
3. Thomas Jefferson sought to put pressure on Britain by (*a*) declaring war (*b*) making an alliance with France (*c*) using economic pressure.
4. Jefferson's policy failed because (*a*) it hurt Americans more than others (*b*) Americans refused to carry it out (*c*) the War Hawks were against it.
5. The area hurt most by Jefferson's and Madison's embargo policies was (*a*) the West (*b*) New England (*c*) the South.
6. Dennis was a (*a*) Federalist (*b*) Republican (*c*) traitor.
7. Lissa thought one good result of the war was that (*a*) the U.S. had captured Canada (*b*) American factories were thriving (*c*) American unity had been strengthened.
8. The Hartford Convention proposed that (*a*) New England secede from the union (*b*) the President resign (*c*) the Constitution be amended.

C. What did New Englanders do that caused Lissa to accuse them of "Federalist treason"? Do you think Lissa's harsh words were justified? Why or why not?

Activities and Inquiries

1. Prepare a report on the life of James Madison. Emphasize: (*a*) accomplishments at the Constitutional Convention (*b*) role in ratification of the Constitution (*c*) work as secretary of state under Jefferson (*d*) success and failure as President.
2. Compare the American Revolution and the War of 1812 with regard to: (*a*) causes (*b*) battle plans and military campaigns (*c*) effectiveness of military leaders (*d*) life on the home front (*e*) results.
3. Suppose that you are an American soldier invading Canada in the War of 1812. Using library sources and your imagination, write a letter home describing your experiences.
4. If you had been a delegate to the Hartford Convention, how would you have reacted to the news from Ghent and New Orleans? Why?

6 Keeping Europe Out of the Americas

On the home front after the War of 1812, the divided country pulled itself together. Differences among the various areas of the nation were patched up. The people began to think of themselves as Americans rather than as residents of particular states. This was the only time in history when the United States had only one major political party—the Republican Party. The Federalist Party was disappearing from the national scene. A Boston newspaper referred to this period of unity between 1816 and 1824 as an "Era of Good Feelings." That is how historians remember it today.

The Treaty of Ghent brought peace to the United States but not to Great Britain. The British continued to wage war against Napoleon and his armies. A group of European nations finally defeated Napoleon in 1815. In countries that Napoleon had conquered, kings once more took charge.

The rulers of Russia, Austria, and Prussia soon formed an alliance. One purpose was to stop revolutionary changes in European nations and their colonies. Another was to keep the monarchs of Europe on their thrones. This alliance among three Christian rulers was popularly known as the Holy Alliance. Eventually a fourth nation, France, became associated with the other three.

The Holy Alliance successfully crushed revolutions in different parts of Italy. Americans did not worry much about these actions. But they watched with concern as the alliance turned its attention to Spain, where a revolution had broken out in 1820.

Would the Holy Alliance first put down the Spanish revolution and then go on to put down the revolutions that had been sweeping Spain's Latin American colonies? That is what worried Americans. Latin American revolutionaries had been setting up republics in the lands south of the United States. These new republics were independent—no longer tied to the apron strings of a European nation. Americans wanted to encourage this trend.

In our story, President James Monroe and Secretary of State John Quincy Adams react to newspaper headlines about developments in Europe and the Americas. What did they think the United States should do to help the new American republics? Why did Britain want to join with the United States to take a stand against the Holy Alliance?

As you read, keep in mind the distinction between a republic and a monarchy. A *republic* is a country that has no king—a country where the people rule themselves. A *monarchy* is a country that has a monarch such as a king, queen, or emperor. In the early 19th century, all of the leading European nations were monarchies.

August 1, 1821

REVOLUTIONS CONTINUE IN SPAIN AND IN LATIN AMERICA; WILL THE HOLY ALLIANCE ACT?

"Well, Mr. Adams, what do you think of the news?" asked President James Monroe.

"It's good for Latin America, and it's good for us," replied Secretary of State John Quincy Adams.

"What do you mean?"

"How many republics are there in the world besides the United States?"

"Precious few."

"Naturally we are happy to see more republican governments—especially in this hemisphere," said Adams. "The Latin Americans are winning their freedom. No longer will they be ruled by that tyrant, King Ferdinand VII of Spain. The Spanish, too, have made great gains. Ferdinand has been forced to accept a constitution and to allow the election of a national assembly."

"Excellent," said the President. "Anything that weakens Ferdinand is to our advantage. While Spain is in turmoil, its armies are not likely to reconquer Latin America."

"Just so," said Adams. "We do not want any European nation to have much influence in this part of the world."

Thinking out loud, President Monroe said, "What I would like to see is for American soil to exist for American nations only."

"That is a distant dream, I fear, Mr. President. The British are well established in Canada. The Portuguese still rule Brazil. And Russia is claiming land along the northwest coast of North America."

"Well, each step counts," said Monroe. "The Latin American revolutions must succeed! If only Spain remains weak and the Holy Alliance keeps its nose out of the Americas."

December 29, 1821

CZAR CLAIMS MORE LAND FOR RUSSIANS, ORDERS SHIPS TO KEEP AWAY FROM COAST

"Mr. President, the Russian czar, the emperor, is claiming more land in North America. Now he says foreign ships must stay out of coastal waters in the Pacific everywhere north of the 51st parallel."

"The 51st parallel!" exclaimed Monroe. "That's way too far south. Why, that's right in the middle of the Oregon country."

"Exactly," replied Adams. "And the Russians are claiming control of waters as far as 100 miles offshore. That's well out on the high seas."

"Well, we can't stand for that," said Monroe. "You tell the Russian minister that the czar has no right to tell us where our ships can sail."

"I'll do that. And I'll make clear that the Russians have no valid claim to land in North America. We must keep European nations from setting up any new colonies on this continent."

November 1, 1823

FRENCH TROOPS WIN VICTORY IN SPAIN; ABSOLUTE POWER OF KING IS RESTORED; NEXT—JOINT ACTION IN AMERICAS?

"Oh, my," said a distressed President Monroe. "I was afraid of this. The Holy Alliance asked France to do its dirty work. French armies moved into Spain, and now King Ferdinand is an absolute monarch again. What will this mean for the Americas?"

"It may mean trouble to our south," replied Adams. "The Spanish may feel strong enough now to put down the revolutions in Latin America. There is talk of a joint French-Spanish expedition backed by the Holy Alliance."

"It would be a terrible blow to liberty if the revolutions should be crushed. Would Britain stand by and let such a thing happen, do you suppose?"

"That's hard to say," Adams replied. "The British have an interest in seeing the Latin American republics survive. British trade with that part of the world is booming, now that Spain is no longer in control. If the revolutions were put down, Spain would probably cut off that trade, and British merchants would suffer severely."

"Does that mean the British might want to take strong action to defend the American republics?" the President asked.

"It might," Adams answered. "But we must remember that Britain too is a monarchy. There is strong feeling in Britain against the idea of republican government. Up to now, the British have refused to grant diplomatic recognition to the new republics."

"Very confusing," commented Monroe. "I'd like to hear more from the British about what they will do."

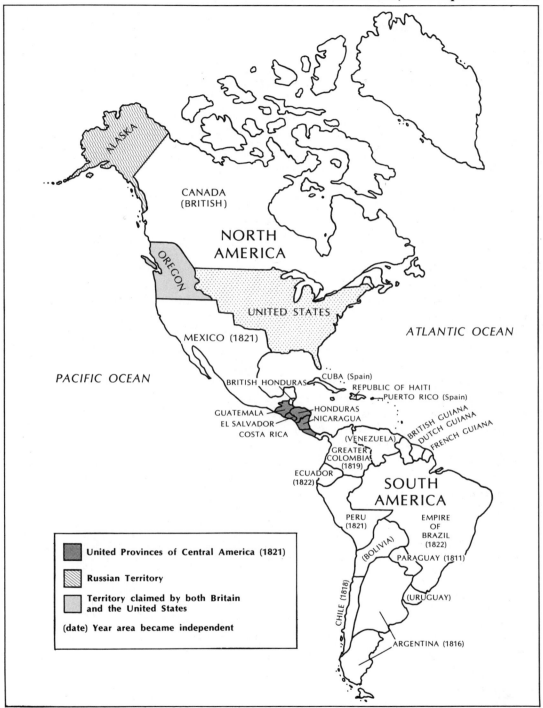

North and South America, 1823

November 7, 1823

BRITAIN BACKS INDEPENDENCE
OF LATIN AMERICAN NATIONS

"Mr. Adams, we must discuss our reply to the proposal from the British," said President Monroe.

"Yes, Mr. President. The British foreign secretary, George Canning, has made a most interesting suggestion. He wants our two nations to issue a joint declaration to let the Holy Alliance know how we feel about Latin America."

"The terms of his proposal sound rather good," Monroe said.

"Yes, the British want pretty much what we want. They want the former Spanish colonies to stay free. They oppose any return of these American lands to the control of Spain or any other country."

"Do you think we should agree to Canning's proposal?"

"It is tempting," Adams replied. "But there are problems. For one thing, Canning wants both of us to pledge not to take any part of Spanish America for ourselves. I don't think the United States should tie its hands for all time. Cuba is so close to our shores that eventually it cannot help but come under our influence."

Adams paused and then continued. "There is also the question of our national pride. The United States is a small nation with a small navy. Britain is a great power with a mighty navy. If we went along with Canning, we would be like a rowboat towed along in the wake

"We must not look like a rowboat being towed behind a British man-o-war."

of a British man-of-war. I believe it would be more dignified for us to make our own declaration to the Holy Alliance."

"That does sound more dignified," the President said. "But what if the Holy Alliance ignores our declaration? Is there a danger we might have to fight to defend the new American republics to our south?"

"Not much danger," Adams replied. "Even if we don't agree to Canning's declaration, the British would probably stand beside us."

"In that case," said Monroe, "I approve of your idea. Let's work out the details."

POSTSCRIPT

On December 2, 1823, President Monroe delivered his annual message to Congress. Almost hidden in that message was a declaration that would play a major role in United States foreign policy in the years to come. We know it as the Monroe Doctrine. The major points are these:

1. The Americas are not to be considered as areas for future colonization by European nations.

2. The United States will not interfere with the existing colonies of European nations in the Americas.

3. The United States would consider it an unfriendly act for a European nation to interfere in the affairs of the newly independent nations of the Americas or to set up monarchies in this hemisphere.

4. The United States will not interfere in the internal affairs of European nations.

Monroe's words had little impact at the time, although they annoyed the nations of the Holy Alliance. Britain, applying pressure to France, extracted a promise that the French would not join Spain in putting down the revolutions in Latin America. Spain alone proved too weak to act effectively. Thus, as Adams expected, the danger of intervention withered away. That was fortunate for the United States, for in 1823 the United States was too weak to enforce the Monroe Doctrine by itself.

The doctrine of "America for Americans" became a frequent theme in U.S. diplomacy. In later years, the United States would have the power to back up Monroe's words.

The Monroe Doctrine applied not only to Latin America but also to areas farther north. In 1824 Russia abandoned its claim to the Oregon Country. But Monroe and Adams did not succeed in evicting the Russians completely from North America. It was much later, in 1867, that the United States bought Alaska from Russia.

Homework Questions

1. Why were the years after the War of 1812 called the "Era of Good Feelings"?
2. What were the main goals of the Holy Alliance?
3. How did Russia manage to annoy President James Monroe and Secretary of State John Quincy Adams?
4. What joint action did the British propose to the United States?
5. Why did Adams and Monroe decide the United States should act on its own?

Understanding the Story

A. Match each item in Column *A* with its description in Column *B*.

Column A

1. Ferdinand VII
2. James Monroe
3. John Quincy Adams
4. Alaska
5. Holy Alliance
6. Czar
7. George Canning
8. Monroe Doctrine

Column B

a. Once a Russian colony in North America
b. Group of European nations
c. United States secretary of state in 1823
d. Policy aimed at closing the Americas to future European colonization
e. King of Spain in the 1820's
f. President of the United States in 1823
g. British foreign secretary
h. Ruler in Russia in the 1820's

B. Write *F* for each statement that is a fact and *O* for each statement that is an opinion.

1. Americans grew more united after the War of 1812.
2. The defeat of Napoleon was good for Europe.
3. People in the United States welcomed the revolutions in Spain's American colonies.
4. The period between 1816 and 1824 is called the "Era of Good Feelings."
5. Russia had a colony in North America in the early 1800's.
6. Ferdinand VII of Spain was a kindly king.
7. The Holy Alliance had no business meddling in the affairs of the Latin American republics.

8. The French were wrong to invade Spain in 1823.

C. Do you think the Monroe Doctrine was a good policy for the United States in 1823? Why or why not? Do you think it is a good policy for the United States today? Explain.

Activities and Inquiries

1. Study the map on page 207. Then choose the term or phrase that best completes each statement.
   a. European nations claiming colonies in the Americas after the Monroe Doctrine included (*1*) Germany and Russia (*2*) Portugal and Austria (*3*) Great Britain and Spain.
   b. An independent country in South America in 1823 was (*1*) Oregon (*2*) Uruguay (*3*) Ecuador.
   c. Areas in North America controlled by European nations in 1823 were (*1*) Mexico and Canada (*2*) Canada and Alaska (*3*) Alaska and Brazil.
   d. Two Spanish colonies were (*1*) Jamaica and Colombia (*2*) Haiti and Brazil (*3*) Cuba and Puerto Rico.
   e. A part of South America controlled by three European nations was (*1*) Honduras (*2*) Guiana (*3*) Peru.
   f. According to the Monroe Doctrine, European nations should *not* interfere in the affairs of (*1*) Mexico (*2*) Canada (*3*) British Honduras.
   g. According to the Monroe Doctrine, the United States would permit European interference in the affairs of (*1*) Peru (*2*) Dutch Guiana (*3*) Argentina.
2. Look at the cartoon on page 208 and answer the following questions.
   a. Explain the meaning of the cartoon.

b. How would the Americans change the cartoon?

c. What would the British say about the cartoon?

3. Assume that you are George Canning, the British foreign secretary. Convince U.S. Secretary of State John Quincy Adams that the United States and Great Britain should issue a joint declaration supporting the independence of the new Latin American republics.

4. Assume that you are John Quincy Adams. Write a newspaper article explaining why you turned down Canning's suggestion.

7 Jackson and the Common Man

The period from the 1820's to the 1840's is often called the Age of Jackson, or the Age of the Common Man (the ordinary person). The period was dominated by one man—Andrew Jackson, who served as President from 1829 to 1837. It was a time of change, when many voting barriers were dropped and the common people had a greater voice in United States affairs than ever before. Who was Andrew Jackson? Why were common people making such gains?

Jackson was a war hero and a Southerner. He had led U.S. troops in the Battle of New Orleans—the greatest U.S. land victory of the War of 1812. By the 1820's, Jackson was a Tennessee planter of considerable wealth. But he remembered his own humble birth and saw himself as a representative of the common people. Many thousands of voters came to agree with him. Jackson was one of the most popular public figures since George Washington.

The United States was going through a spurt of growth. New factories appeared, population grew, new states entered the Union. The new states, near the frontier, gave the right to vote to almost all white males over the age of 21. This posed a problem for the older states, which had tended to restrict voting to men who owned property. Older states feared they might lose population to the newer states because of the differences in voting rights. So older states too began to allow more and more people to vote. There were two exceptions to this trend. Women still did not have the vote. And free blacks, who had long been able to vote in many Northern states, saw that right taken away in such states as Ohio (1818), Rhode Island (1822), and Pennsylvania (1838).

The Age of Jackson was a period of reform (change that improves). Organizations sprang up to alter American life. Efforts were made to improve working conditions, win equal rights for women, and abolish (do away with) slavery, war, and the sale of alcoholic drinks. Some people struggled for better conditions for prisoners and the insane. Americans felt sure they could build a better world for themselves and their children and grandchildren. It was an exciting time to be alive.

Jackson first sought the Presidency in 1824. He was one of five major candidates—all members of the Republican Party. The race was a bitter one. It split the party and put an end to the Era of Good Feelings.

The Electoral College divided four ways. Jackson had a plurality (more votes than any rival), but he was not the winner. To win he needed a majority (more than half the votes). For the second time in U.S. history, the House of Representatives had to pick the President. In the House, two of Jackson's opponents joined forces to defeat him. John Quincy Adams became President, with the support of Henry Clay.

Jackson felt that Clay's support of Adams had cheated him of his victory. He resolved to run again in 1828. He did, and in a two-man race he easily beat Adams.

By 1828 the original Republican Party had fallen apart. Jackson's supporters called themselves the Democratic Republicans. The Adams-Clay side took the name National Republicans. Within a few years, these groups had evolved into two new parties, which dominated U.S. politics up to the 1850's. Jackson's party came to be called the Democratic Party. The Adams-Clay forces became the Whig Party.

Jackson spoke out against many of the policies the national government had been following. The government, he said, had sided with special interests against the people. Also, the government had taken on too many tasks and should be cut back. Jackson fired many federal workers and replaced them with new men. He said government jobs should not be held too long by one group of men. They should be passed around among ordinary people.

To his supporters, Jackson was a hero. "Old Hickory," as they called him, represented all that was good about democracy. To his critics, Jackson was a demagogue (someone who stirs up the common people to advance his or her own interests). He represented all that was dangerous about democracy.

In our story, note how two men react to Jackson and his party. Ask yourself why people felt so strongly about Jackson.

Jefferson City, Missouri, 1836

"George, I just don't believe what is happening," said Joe. "Do you know what that Andrew Jackson has done now? He's got me fired from my job registering deeds at the land office. Of course, he didn't fire me personally, but he's to blame with all his 'common man' talk. They told me four years was enough for one man to hold a job. Gave my place to some young upstart who hardly knows a deed from a donkey."

"I'm sorry you lost your job, Joe," George replied. "But remember, you didn't know much about deeds yourself when you first got that job."

"Maybe not, but I know a lot now. I'm the best man for the job. Have you heard what some of Jackson's men say? They say: "To the victors belong the spoils.' Well, public jobs aren't 'spoils,' like booty in a war. They should be held by men with skills—not by party hacks.''

"Your pride is hurt, Joe. You'd like to think you needed some special skill to do your job. But Jackson says any honest man can do the public's work. He says we should shift people around every few years—rotate the jobs. That way more people get a chance at each job.''

"It's just not fair,'' Joe declared.

"Don't brood so,'' George replied with a grin. "The world hasn't come to an end. Business is booming with all the new people moving in lately. You've got property. You'll find another job.''

"It's not just that, George. Sure I can get a job. But it makes my blood boil the way that Jackson has shaken things up so. I tell you, he's carrying democracy too far. Remember how a mob of Jackson supporters charged through the White House the day he took over? *That's* what Jackson is for—mob rule!''

"Why, Joe, that's just nonsense.'' George's voice rose. "Sure, the crowd got a little carried away that day. Why not? We common people finally had our kind of man in the White House. Old Hickory wasn't born to wealth, like that snob John Quincy Adams. Every penny Jackson's got, he earned. Some day I'll have what he has—a fancy house, land, servants. This is a land of opportunity!''

"You'd better hope you don't get rich, George. The way things are going you wouldn't get to enjoy your wealth. Why, last election day you could see every sort of rabble coming to vote. I stood there and listened. Do you know, before long I could tell how a man would vote just by the way he looked.''

"The rabble, as you call it, is mostly honest workingmen like you and me,'' George declared.

"Well, I call it rabble,'' said Joe. "Democracy can't be carried to such extremes. Only people with property should be allowed to vote. After all, they're the people with the biggest stake in a community. They won't vote for foolish spending schemes, because it's *their* tax money that would have to pay for the projects.''

"Hold on now, Joe. You talk as if it was the plain people, the Democracy, who wanted more public spending. If you'll remember, it's Clay and his supporters who want the federal government to spend money to build roads and canals. Jackson is against such projects. He says they should be left to the states. Didn't Jackson veto that Maysville Road Bill, the one to use federal funds for a road that was entirely inside the state of Kentucky?''

"Well, yes, I guess he did,'' Joe said. "That just shows how short-sighted Jackson is. We need *more* roads and canals to move goods and people around the United States. How can farmers and manufacturers get their goods to market? Only the federal government can build a truly *American* system.''

George smiled. "Sounds as if you're the big spender now, Joe.

Listen, Clay and his sort are only out to line their own pockets. They want roads and canals so there'll be contracts to pass out to friends. And what about the Bank of the United States that Clay and his friends in the East want to keep going? Jackson's out to bust the Bank, and it looks as if he's succeeding."

"It's a pity, George," Joe replied. "That Bank has been around for almost 20 years. It's helped keep our dollar sound. It's made loans to businesses that want to expand. Jackson made a mistake in '32 when he vetoed the bill to give the Bank a new charter."

"You're wrong, Joe. The Bank's no good. Sure, it lent money to businesses—but just to its friends. Do you think a little guy like you or me could get a loan from the Bank? Don't kid yourself! Clay talks about keeping the dollar sound, but what that means is keeping money scarce so the bankers get high interest and we common people suffer."

"Well, I think Clay's a darn sight better than that Jackson." Joe's eyes flashed. "When Jackson vetoed the Bank bill he acted so high and mighty—just like a king. 'King Andrew the First.'"

George pounded a fist against his palm. "Don't you talk that way about our President! You call him King Andrew, but the people sure love him. Why, in the '32 election Jackson whipped Clay so badly Clay *still* doesn't know what hit him."

"Don't count Clay out," answered Joe. "That new party of ours will put up a fight come election day. Do you know why we're calling ourselves the Whigs? Because we're fighting King Andrew—just as the British Whigs fought to cut down the power of *their* king. The Whigs will save America from the Democracy!"

"Well, I'm part of the Democracy," George exclaimed, "and your Whigs can just go back to Britain for all I care. This is America. I have rights, and I can vote. I can even run for political office if I want to. My children can go to school and make something of themselves. They'll go places!"

"They'll go to the poorhouse if business fails because of King Andrew's foolish policies," Joe said.

"We Democrats are working to make sure they *don't* go to the poorhouse, Joe. We'll see that state legislatures pass laws to help the workingman. We'll cut the working day down to 10 hours. We'll get laws passed to make sure that workers get the wages they're owed. Why, sometimes a boss just doesn't pay his workers. Claims his other debts don't leave him any money. As it is now, there's nothing a simple mechanic, or worker, can do in such a case. Once a legislature passes a mechanics lien law, though, a mechanic can go to court to get help. We Democrats are going to make sure everyone gets a fair shake!" George was panting, almost out of breath.

"Well," said Joe, "we all want everyone to get a fair shake, George. That's what free elections are for. You work for your man, and I'll work for mine—and may the best man win."

POSTSCRIPT

The Democrats won the election of 1836 and put Jackson's friend Martin Van Buren in the White House. But the Whigs were building up their strength. The Whigs were especially popular among business people in the North, wealthy planters in the South, and farmers in the West who were eager for roads to get their crops to market. The Democrats drew their greatest support from workingmen in cities of all sections of the country and from people who wanted a weak federal government and strong state governments.

Joe and George didn't know it, but hard times were ahead—for Democrats and for the nation. During 1835 and 1836 business was good. The U.S. government paid off all its debts. Jackson took government money out of the Bank of the United States and put it into smaller banks in various states. The Bank finally closed its doors. The state banks were less strict with their loans. They put more money into circulation, and people had more money to spend. Sales of federal land reached dizzying heights. Worried, Jackson finally ordered that anyone buying federal land must pay in gold or silver. No more paper money would be accepted. This ended the boom in land sales.

Soon, other kinds of business dropped off too. Many banks failed. The paper money they had printed became worthless. (At the time, only private banks issued "bank notes." The U.S. government did not print paper money.) Panic spread as business dried up. Many firms shut down. People went without work, and sometimes without food. This was the Panic of 1837, and it was the worst depression (time of business troubles) the United States had yet seen. Nowadays, most people believe that the Panic of 1837 was part of a worldwide depression, caused by many different things. But the Whigs blamed the Panic on the Democrats alone. Whigs rode the issue to victory in the presidential election of 1840.

Homework Questions

1. Why was the election of 1824 decided by the House of Representatives?
2. What did people often call the period of the 1820's to the 1840's?
3. How did many people think that education and the right to vote would help them achieve equality?
4. Why did many people admire Jackson? Why did others call him a demagogue?
5. For what reason did Jackson favor rotation in office?

Understanding the Story

A. Write *T* for each statement that is true and *F* for each statement that is false.
   1. Andrew Jackson got more electoral votes than any of his rivals in the election of 1824.
   2. Jackson won the election of 1824.
   3. Henry Clay supported Jackson in 1824.
   4. The 1820's and the 1830's are called the Age of the Common Man.
   5. No one tried to reform American society in the 1820's and the 1830's.

6. The National Republicans, or Whigs, and the Democrats, or Democratic Republicans, were the two political parties of the period.
7. Jackson was called King Andrew by his enemies.
8. Jackson was not popular with the working people.

B. Write *J* for each statement that Joe made or might have made and *G* for each statement that George made or might have made.
1. Andrew Jackson got me fired.
2. We common people finally have our kind of man in the White House.
3. Every penny Jackson has, he earned.
4. Jackson's men say, "To the victors belong the spoils."
5. The Bank of the United States is no good.
6. Only people with property should be allowed to vote.

7. The people love Andrew Jackson.
8. Jackson should be called "King Andrew the First."

C. Would you say, as Andrew Jackson's supporters did, that rotating government jobs is a good thing? Explain your answer.

Activities and Inquiries

1. Imagine that you are a reporter. What questions will you ask Andrew Jackson about using federal money to build roads and canals?
2. What will he say in answer to your questions?
3. Draw or describe a cartoon about Andrew Jackson.
4. Write a paragraph telling Jackson's reactions to your cartoon.

8 Webster and Hayne Debate

Congress has seen some important debates over the years, but one of the most memorable took place in 1830. The two chief debaters were Daniel Webster, a senator from Massachusetts, and Robert Hayne, a senator from South Carolina.

The Webster-Hayne debate had many layers of meaning. On the surface, the debate concerned a bill being considered by the Senate. That bill, opposed by Hayne, called for a halt in the sale of Western land belonging to the United States govern-ment. But this issue was of minor importance. A second issue concerned tariffs. Even more important was the issue of national power against state power.

Because the tariff issue was central to the debate, it must be examined in some depth. Tariffs, as we have seen, are taxes on imports. Such taxes tend to help American manufacturers by making foreign goods more expensive. At the same time, they can hurt consumers by causing prices to rise.

In 1816 Congress passed a tariff that

had support in all sections of the United States, including the South. At the time, leading Southerners hoped to make their region a center of manufacturing. But such hopes soon faded. Cotton and tobacco were profitable crops, and slave labor made them cheap to grow. The South specialized in agriculture and made little effort to start up industries.

The Northeast, on the other hand, became a center of industry. Factories there produced cloth (textiles), shoes, and other goods. Manufacturers in the Northeast sought still higher tariffs so that their products would face less competition from European imports.

By 1820, when Congress considered another tariff bill, Southern leaders had turned against tariffs. In their opinion, high tariffs took money out of Southern pockets for the benefit of Northern manufacturers. Southerners managed to defeat the tariff bill of 1820. But in 1824 and again in 1828, Congress passed bills that raised tariffs to new heights. The Tariff of 1828 was so high that Southerners called it the Tariff of Abominations. (An abomination is something that is thoroughly disgusting.)

Southerners protested strongly against the Tariff of 1828. The most important protest came from Vice President John C. Calhoun, a native of South Carolina. In an essay called *The South Carolina Exposition and Protest*, Calhoun argued that such high tariffs were unconstitutional because they taxed one part of the nation for the benefit of another. He also declared that a state could decide for itself whether or not to obey a federal law it considered unconstitutional. In other words, a state could *nullify* (cancel) a federal law.

In our story, we see that Webster and Hayne have strikingly different ways of understanding the nullification issue and the Constitution. Do you agree more with Webster or with Hayne? What reasons did each man have for believing as he did?

Washington, D.C., January, 1830

David, a newspaper reporter, is having dinner at Mary's house.

"Mary, how would you like to join me at the Senate tomorrow? Webster and Hayne will be debating."

"Why should that appeal to me?"

"You know that Daniel Webster is the greatest orator in the United States," said David, "and Robert Hayne isn't far behind. Come along. I know you'll find it interesting."

"First, tell me what the debate is about," said Mary.

"It all started when Webster spoke in favor of a bill to end the sale of Western land. Naturally, Hayne spoke out against the bill.

"Why 'naturally'?"

"The South is backing the West on the land deal," replied David. "In return, the South hopes that the West will vote for its pet projects."

"Which ones are they?"

"One is killing the tariff that Hayne and Webster are now arguing about," answered David. "Southerners hate the Tariff of 1828 because it raises the prices of manufactured goods they must buy."

"I can see that," said Mary. "But doesn't it also raise prices for Northerners?"

"Not so much," continued David. "There are many factories in the North and very few in the South. The tariff keeps out competing British goods because it raises the prices of the imports, making them cost more than goods produced here. The Northern factory owners are happy because their goods are protected."

"Then Southerners should be just as happy," replied Mary. "They must be buying their goods from the North."

"No, Mary, that's the strange part. The South buys most of its manufactured goods from Britain."

"I see. The South then pays higher prices for British goods. But wouldn't Southerners be better off trading with the North—instead of with a European country?"

"Perhaps," answered David, "but the South sells much more cotton to Britain than to the North. I guess that Britain is a more natural trading partner."

"That's why people in South Carolina feel that their money is supporting Northern manufacturers," said Mary. "No wonder they hate the tariff."

"Exactly," added David. "I've heard that tomorrow Webster and Hayne will talk about much more than the tariff. They're going to discuss what our whole federal system is all about. Won't you change your mind? I think it will be worth your time."

"You've convinced me," replied Mary. "I'll go with you."

The next day: Forty-eight senators are seated at their desks. Every bit of floor space behind the senators is filled with people, and the Senate gallery is packed. Vice President Calhoun, the presiding officer, watches the speakers. Senator Hayne from South Carolina starts talking.

HAYNE. Gentlemen, South Carolina cannot live with the Tariff of 1828. It is ruining our state, and soon it will ruin the entire South.

WEBSTER. I cannot agree with the Senator. The tariff will not harm, much less ruin, the South. However, Senator Hayne knows how a law of this great country can be changed. Let the people change it. Let the people elect anti-tariff congressmen to repeal it.

HAYNE. Impossible, Senator Webster. You know that we in the South are a minority in Congress. I tell you, sir, South Carolina must take steps to protect itself from such unfair laws!

[*Cheers from the audience.*]

CALHOUN. The gallery must remain silent. Proceed, Senator Webster.

WEBSTER. The tariff is an act of Congress and can be changed by Congress alone. There is no way that a state can change a national law by itself. That kind of action, Senator Hayne, would bring about the end of our beloved federal Union!

[*Mixed cheers and boos. Vice President Calhoun stares the crowd into silence.*]

HAYNE. We are not interested in changing a law. We want to nullify a law. The state of South Carolina, sir, will refuse to obey a law that is harmful. And may I point out, Senator, that the idea of nullification has drawn support from New Englanders as well as from Southerners. You will recall the Hartford Convention of 1814. At that meeting Federalists refused to support the war against Great Britain. They spoke out in favor of the doctrine of nullification. And let's not forget the Virginia and Kentucky Resolutions drawn up by Thomas Jefferson and James Madison in response to the Alien and Sedition Laws of 1798. They, too, backed the doctrine of nullification.

[Applause.]

WEBSTER. This is a nation of people. The people—not the states— formed this federal Union. The Union cannot exist if a part of it can set aside laws of the Congress. If each of the 24 states can defy the national government, there will be no Union. All we will have left will be a rope of sand!

[Extended cheers and applause.]

CALHOUN. Please continue, Senator Webster.

WEBSTER. The laws of Congress must be obeyed by every person in the United States. Only the Supreme Court can decide whether or not a federal act is constitutional. Unless the Court throws out an act, it is the law of the land.

HAYNE. Is it fair to have a *federal* court decide whether a *federal* law is satisfactory? Congress passed the law, and the President signed it. Now the Supreme Court will make the final decision. Who is affected by this law? We know the answer—the states. And what have the states to say about the law? Again we know the answer—nothing! Absolutely nothing! (*Some applause.*) This is not liberty; this is tyranny. We are talking about a federal government with unlimited power. We will not allow the federal government to enslave us. We will take whatever steps are necessary to preserve our freedom. We in South Carolina love our country, Senator. But we love liberty above all else! (*Some cheers.*)

WEBSTER. We all love liberty. But we cannot preserve our liberty if the ties that bind our Union are broken. I could not imagine a future without our beloved Union. (*Cheers.*)

God grant that my eyes never see the torn and broken pieces of this nation. May I never see this land covered with the blood of our people! May our flag always wave over us—every stripe and every star clear and bright! And with our flag let our motto be clear for all to see. Not "What is all this worth?" Not "Liberty first and Union afterward." But "Liberty *and* Union, now and forever, one and inseparable!"

[Tremendous cheers and continuing applause.]

CALHOUN. This session is ended.

[He walks out slowly while the cheering continues.]

POSTSCRIPT

A few weeks later at a dinner, President Jackson rose, looked at Vice President Calhoun, and proposed a toast: "Our Federal Union—it must be preserved." As Calhoun raised his glass, some thought his hand shook so that he spilled his wine. He hesitated and then answered: "The Union, next to our liberty, most dear."

Jackson's words were the ones people remembered. Soon his words were tested when South Carolina passed a nullification law stating that it would not obey the Tariff of 1828. Jackson responded swiftly. He got Congress to grant him authority to use troops to make sure federal laws were enforced. Privately, Jackson threatened to lead troops himself into South Carolina and to have Calhoun hanged for treason.

South Carolina, unable to win support from other Southern states, had to back down and repeal its nullification law. Congress helped South Carolina to save face. In 1833 it passed a compromise measure that lowered tariff rates one step at a time.

Nevertheless, the basic issue of national power against state power had yet to be settled. It continued to lie beneath the surface.

Homework Questions

1. Why did the South change its position on tariffs after 1816?
2. How did *The South Carolina Exposition and Protest* express the idea of nullification?
3. Why were Southerners angered by the passage of the Tariff of 1828?
4. What arguments did Hayne use in favor of nullification and states' rights?
5. How did Webster answer Hayne's arguments?

Understanding the Story

A. List the numbers of the statements that are true.
   1. John C. Calhoun was against the Tariff of 1828.
   2. The South became an important manufacturing region after the War of 1812.
   3. Calhoun wrote *The South Carolina Exposition and Protest*.
   4. Senators Daniel Webster and Robert Hayne agreed that the central government must be more powerful than the states.
   5. Webster was considered the greatest orator of his day.
   6. A tariff tends to raise the prices of imported manufactured goods.
   7. Most Southerners backed the Tariff of 1828.
   8. The South bought most of its goods from the North.

B. Write *A* for each statement that Webster would agree with and *N* for each statement that he would not agree with.
   1. The Tariff of 1828 will hurt the South.
   2. Let the people change any law they don't like.
   3. This is a nation of people, not of states.
   4. A state can change a national law.
   5. Only the Supreme Court can decide whether or not a law is constitutional.

6. We must limit the power of the national government.
7. I must think first of the prosperity of Massachusetts.
8. Liberty and Union, now and forever.

C. What was the doctrine of nullification, and why did it cause such a heated debate in the 1830's? Do you think an issue other than a tariff could have touched off this debate? If so, what issue? If not, why not?

Activities and Inquiries

1. Imagine that you are David, the newspaper reporter. How will you begin your story about the Webster-Hayne debate?
2. Assume that you are a Southern planter. How do you feel about the Webster-Hayne debate? Explain.
3. Assume that you are a Northern manufacturer. How do you feel about the Webster-Hayne debate? Explain.
4. Imagine that you are a senator from your region in 1830. Whom will you support, Hayne or Webster? Why?

9 The Growth of the Constitution: The Supreme Law of the Land

Both Webster and Hayne spoke about the role of the Supreme Court in the government. Webster insisted that the Court alone could decide whether or not a law of Congress was unconstitutional. According to Hayne, the states had this responsibility.

The Constitution does not tell how a law can be declared unconstitutional. It neither gives nor denies this great power to the Supreme Court. How then could the Supreme Court obtain the right to review laws passed by Congress?

The answer is in our story about a decision made by the Court under Chief Justice John Marshall. President John Adams appointed Marshall to the Supreme Court in 1801. For the next 34 years, Marshall's opinions strengthened the power of the national government and of the Court.

In our story, Marshall is considering a case known as Marbury v. Madison. The "v." stands for versus, or against. The first name, Marbury, is that of the person who filed the lawsuit. The second name, Madison, is the name of the person against whom it was filed. One might also call this simply "the Marbury Case."

As you read, ask yourself whether you agree with Marshall's decision. Would Marshall support the position of Webster or of Hayne? Why do you think so?

Washington, D.C., 1803

I am John Marshall, the Chief Justice of the United States and the head of the judicial branch of our government. My job is to interpret, or explain, the laws passed by Congress. More important, I must protect our Constitution, strengthen it, and make it work more effectively. While I am deciding cases that come before the Court, I must remember what the creators of the Constitution said: "This Constitution shall be the supreme law of the land."

The case I am considering now seems of minor importance, but perhaps looks are deceiving. President John Adams appointed William Marbury to be a justice of the peace. Adams did this on his last day in office—March 3, 1801. James Madison is secretary of state in the new administration. He refuses to turn over to Marbury the papers giving Marbury his commission. So Marbury has asked the Supreme Court for a writ, a court order, to make Madison pass along the commission.

The case involves politics, of course. Adams and Marbury are Federalists, and so am I. Madison, on the other hand, is a Republican, like the current President, Thomas Jefferson. But party politics do not interest me. The laws and the Constitution are what my job is about.

What does the law say on the matter? It seems clear that Marbury does have a right to his commission. But does the Supreme Court have any authority to issue the writ that Marbury wants? According to the Judiciary Act of 1789, passed by Congress, the Court does have such authority.

But there is more here than meets the eye. Did Congress act properly in passing such a law? I have read the Constitution, and it spells out the powers of the Supreme Court. The power to issue such a writ is not to be found in the Constitution. Does Congress have a right to change the terms of the Constitution by adding to the Court's powers? I think not.

It seems to me that I have two choices. I can follow the Judiciary Act of 1789 and grant Marbury his writ. If I do that, I will be issuing a challenge to the Jefferson administration. People will think I am acting as a Federalist, for party purposes. And in my own mind I will be going against the Constitution—the supreme law of the land.

On the other hand, I can refuse to issue the writ. I can declare that the Constitution gives the Supreme Court no such power. The Judiciary Act of 1789 cannot change the Constitution. It is an unconstitutional act and does not have to be obeyed.

I have made up my mind. I will take the second choice. That way I will avoid a direct challenge to the Jefferson administration. And I will be asserting an important power—the power of the federal courts to review acts of Congress. Perhaps more important, I will be defending the supremacy of the Constitution.

If the Constitution is the supreme law of the land, then it is more important than a mere law of Congress. The Constitution is a yardstick by which to measure the laws passed by Congress. Indeed, it is a yardstick by which all acts of the federal government must be measured. A law that goes against the Constitution is not law! It is null and void—as if it had never been passed.

Marbury will not have his commission. Congress was wrong to pass the Judiciary Act of 1789, and that evil is greater than the evil of Marbury's not receiving his commission.

POSTSCRIPT

Like other Federalists, John Marshall believed that the federal government should be strong. During his years as Chief Justice, Marshall influenced the Supreme Court to make many decisions that increased federal powers and gave the Supreme Court a major voice in national affairs. The Marbury Case established the power of the Supreme Court to declare acts of Congress unconstitutional. This decision strengthened the power of the judicial branch at the expense of the legislative branch.

Some other important Marshall decisions and the principles they established are:

1810—*Fletcher* v. *Peck:* The Supreme Court can nullify state laws that go against the Constitution.

1816—*Martin* v. *Hunter's Lessee:* The Supreme Court can review the decisions of state courts.

1819—*Dartmouth College* v. *Woodward:* A state cannot change the terms of a corporation's charter. To do so would be to change the obligations of a contract.

1819—*McCulloch* v. *Maryland:* The powers of Congress listed in the Constitution are not the only powers of Congress. Congress has other, implied powers. Also, a state government may not tax an agency of the federal government.

1824—*Gibbons* v. *Ogden:* Congress has broad powers to regulate commerce among the states.

Homework Questions

1. What did John Marshall think his job was?
2. Why did Marshall refuse to issue a writ to order that William Marbury be given his job as justice of the peace?
3. Why did Marshall declare the Judiciary Act of 1789 unconstitutional?
4. How did Marshall's decisions help to increase federal powers?
5. Do you think Marshall's decisions strengthened the Constitution? Why or why not?

Understanding the Story

A. Write *T* for each statement that is true, *F* for each statement that is false, and *O* for each statement that is an opinion.

1. The Constitution gave the U.S. Supreme Court the power to declare laws unconstitutional.
2. The Supreme Court is too powerful.
3. John Marshall was Chief Justice of the United States for 34 years.
4. Marshall was a follower of the Republican Party.
5. Justices of the U.S. Supreme Court should serve for fixed terms.
6. Marshall had more power than President Thomas Jefferson.
7. In the case of *Marbury* v. *Madison*, a federal law was declared unconstitutional.
8. The U.S. Constitution is the supreme law of the land.

B. Complete each of the following sentences by filling in the missing word or words.

1. John Marshall was the _____ of the United States.
2. John Marshall was a follower of the _____ Party.
3. John Marshall interpreted the nation's _____.
4. William Marbury was appointed by President _____.
5. Secretary of State _____ refused to give Marbury his commission.
6. A law contrary to the Constitution is _____.
7. The Supreme Court ruled that the Judiciary Act of 1789 was _____.
8. This was the _____ time the Supreme Court had overturned an act of Congress.

C. In your opinion, why is the power of the Supreme Court to review federal laws and cases from lower courts an important power?

Activities and Inquiries

1. The Senate is considering John Marshall's appointment. He is questioned by members of the Senate Judiciary Committee. What questions will the committee ask him?
2. How will he answer the committee's questions?
3. Imagine that you are a senator who opposes Marshall's appointment. Why are you opposed?
4. You are a senator who favors Marshall. Why will you vote for him?
5. In an almanac, a newspaper, or an encyclopedia yearbook, read about a case recently decided by the U.S. Supreme Court. Would Marshall have agreed with the decision? Explain your answer.

Who Built America?

Benjamin Banneker

MR. MILLER. All right, Josephine. You can start now.

JOSEPHINE. I'm going to talk about Benjamin Banneker.

JACK. Who? Never heard of him!

JOSEPHINE. Give me a chance, and you'll hear plenty. Benjamin Banneker was a black American—a free black born in 1731. He became a mathematician and an astronomer—a person who studies stars and planets. When he was only a little older than we are now, he built his own clock. He later helped to plan the city of Washington, D.C.

CASIMIR. How did he learn enough to do all those things?

JOSEPHINE. Banneker had to teach himself much of what he knew about mathematics and astronomy. Once he became old enough to help his father in the tobacco fields, he could no longer go to school. A friend lent him books and a few instruments. But he got no instructions, no directions. He worked everything out for himself.

ROBERT. How did Banneker happen to help plan Washington?

JOSEPHINE. He became known to one of the nation's foremost scientists, a white man named Andrew Ellicott. In 1791 President George Washington chose Ellicott to help draw up plans for the new federal city. Ellicott then invited Banneker to be his assistant. Banneker considered it a great opportunity to work with such a well-known scientist. Banneker could not pass up the chance.

HANS. Were Ellicott and Banneker the city's only designers?

JOSEPHINE. By no means. The main designer was an engineer who had been born in France, Pierre L'Enfant. L'Enfant decided where to put the White House, the Capitol, and some other public buildings. Banneker and Ellicott seem to have been more involved in determining the borders of the district.

TOM. What did Banneker do after finishing his job in Washington?

JOSEPHINE. Well, he had figured out astronomical information in advance for every day of 1792. You know—what time the moon rises, what time the sun sets. That sort of thing. Why not publish it in an almanac? he asked himself. He did publish an almanac, and it became very popular. Even Thomas Jefferson took notice of Banneker's work.

CARLA. How did Jefferson notice him?

JOSEPHINE. Banneker sent a copy of his almanac to Jefferson, who was then the secretary of state. Jefferson was impressed. After all, this was the first scientific writing by a black American. Jefferson sent the almanac to a French scientist. We know that Banneker published at least five more almanacs before he died in 1806.

RICARDO. There's one thing I don't understand, Josephine. Jefferson was a slave owner; Banneker was a free black. How could Banneker have been friendly with him?

JOSEPHINE. Banneker told Jefferson very bluntly that slavery had no place in a nation that claimed all men were created equal. Jefferson replied by saying that he hoped for an improvement in the conditions of black Americans. But that was the end of it. Slavery continued.

MR. MILLER. Thank you, Josephine. You've helped us to know one of the first black Americans to gain public acclaim.

MR. MILLER'S OFFICE

"What do you think of our first 50 years, Jack?"

"Our ship had plenty of ups and downs, and it changed direction, too."

"What do you mean?"

"Well, George Washington got the nation started on a Federalist course. He and Hamilton solved our money problems. Washington even tried to work out our disagreements with Spain and England."

"Sounds very good," said Mr. Miller.

"Wait, it's not all that good. The French asked for help in fighting the British. Washington said, 'Absolutely not!' and that ended his popularity with the American people."

"No one can be a hero forever," said Mr. Miller.

"Adams had more trouble with France. And at home he forgot that people in a republic should be free to criticize their leaders."

"Excellent start, Jack. Where did the ship go then?"

"Then our ship shifted to a Republican course. Jefferson started off believing in a strict interpretation of the Constitution. But that didn't last long. He had the chance to buy Louisiana and double the country's size. There was nothing in the Constitution about adding new territory, but he bought Louisiana anyway."

"How do you explain Jefferson's change of heart?"

Jack thought for a long time. "I guess you look at things differently when you're the one making the decisions."

"Anyway, Jefferson must have been happy about Louisiana."

"Sure, but the war in Europe was a big headache. He and Madison tried to avoid war, but they failed. Less than 30 years after the Revolution, we were fighting the British again. The War of 1812 was one that many Americans didn't want."

"That war could have been the finish of the United States," said Mr. Miller.

"Well, we didn't win many battles, but we didn't lose the war. Anyway, the Europeans finally agreed that the United States was here to stay."

"Which direction did we take after the war?" asked Mr. Miller.

"I think Monroe steered between the Federalist and Republican lanes."

"What do you mean, Jack?"

"The country came together, and there was only one political party for a while after 1816. It was a time of nationalism and good feeling. Too bad it couldn't last."

"People do have differences. They had to surface again," said Mr. Miller.

"Sure, there were splits between rich and poor, workers and bosses."

"Ah, yes," said Mr. Miller. "The 1820's and the 1830's were the time of Andrew Jackson and the common man."

"And woman," said Jack, "although women had little part in public life at the time."

"True. Now, don't forget the differences between the sections of the country. Our ship is beginning to move in several different ways."

"Right," said Jack. "There's a split starting between North and South—the free and the slave areas. Looks like our ship is heading for trouble."

"Well said, Jack. You're ready for the background of the Civil War."

The Background of the Civil War

"That's enough background, Mr. Miller. I'm ready to study the Civil War!"

"I'm sorry, Jack. But I don't agree with you."

"Why not? I know all about slavery and sectionalism, the differences between North and South."

"Do you know what it was like to live as a slave? Do you know why the South was willing to fight to defend slavery?"

"Not exactly," replied Jack.

"Do you have any idea how hotly Congress debated the questions relating to slavery? Or what happened each time a new territory, or area of the country, wanted to become a state?"

"Well, no, Mr. Miller. I think my knowledge is a bit fuzzy on these points."

"Wouldn't you like to be able to answer such questions?"

"I suppose so. I can see that we're talking about more than a system of labor. Slavery must have influenced the whole way of life in the South."

"Precisely, Jack. And life in the South was very different from life in the North."

"Southerners must have felt threatened by the efforts to end slavery," said Jack thoughtfully. "Otherwise, why would they have fought a war?"

"In this unit, we'll find out more about the feelings of the North and the South before the Civil War."

1 The Runaway Slave

What made Southerners like John Calhoun and Robert Hayne feel different from other Americans? Slavery, of course. Only in the South was slaveholding a way of life.

During colonial times slavery had existed in both North and South. But Northern states abolished (did away with) slavery during or soon after the Revolutionary War. Slave labor did not suit the needs of Northerners, most of whom farmed small plots that a single family could work alone.

Many of the men who wrote the Constitution opposed slavery. Yet the Constitution allowed for slavery as a fact of life in the South. In three places, the Constitution took note of the slave system. First, in discussing representation in Congress, it said that each slave counted as three fifths of a free person (Article One, Section Two). Second, it allowed the slave trade to continue at least until 1808 (Article One, Section Nine). Third, it provided that runaway slaves had to be returned to their owners (Article Four, Section Two).

Early leaders of the federal government thought that slavery would die out in a few decades. But they were wrong. Rather than disappear, slavery became stronger. One reason was the invention in 1793 of a simple machine, the cotton gin. It removed seeds from cotton so the cotton could be used to make cloth. The new machine cleaned cotton easier, faster, and cheaper than

workers could clean it by hand. Thus the gin helped to lower the cost of cotton cloth. As the price dropped, people bought more cotton cloth. The market for cotton grew rapidly, and Southern farmers grew more and more cotton to meet the demand. Plantations (large farms) worked by slave labor were especially profitable. Slaves were much in demand.

A few figures tell the story. In 1793 there were fewer than one million slaves in the South. By 1850 there were more than three million. During the same period, the price, or value, of a field hand rose from about $200 to about $2,000. Slavery was certainly not dying!

Yet only about one out of four Southern families owned slaves. Two thirds of these families owned fewer than ten slaves. In fact, of all slaveholders, only 1,700 families owned more than 100 slaves. However, the majority of Southern whites supported the slave system, even if they did not own slaves themselves. There was always the hope of buying a slave or two and starting on the way to becoming a planter (plantation owner). Also, the slave system gave the poorest whites a feeling of superiority over a group even lower on the social scale—the blacks.

By law, slaves were the property of their masters much as the masters' furniture and animals were. Despite laws against undue cruelty, the treatment

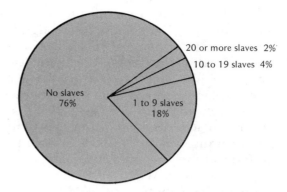

Percentage of Southerners Who Owned Slaves in 1860

of slaves depended largely on their owners' wishes. Some slaves suffered great harshness and cruelty. Others knew more kindly treatment. Cruelty, however, was a necessary part of the slave system. As we see in our story, physical punishment was used as a form of discipline or control. Fear haunted the slaves through every moment of their lives.

Southern whites paid a price for living with slavery. They became used to exploiting other human beings. Many whites also came to consider physical labor to be degrading (beneath them). After all, that sort of work was for slaves! Ever on whites' minds was the fear of slave uprisings. And despite all its seeming advantages, slavery made life harder for some whites. Many small planters and farmers found they could not compete with the large plantation owners and their many slaves. Some whites left to seek a better life in the North or West.

As you read the runaway slave's story, watch for clues about the differences between the lives of free persons and the lives of slaves. Was the slave in the story right to run away? What risks was he taking?

Near Louisville, Kentucky, 1830

A man is moving cautiously through a forest of pine trees on a hot, cloudy summer night. He talks to himself to quiet his fears.

Where am I? Which way shall I go? It's no use. I'm lost and running in circles. I'll never escape. If I rest until daylight, I'll be able to see where I'm going.

No, I must keep moving so I won't get caught. They'll kill me if they capture me. Or else that overseer will beat me until he's too tired to swing the whip. I can just imagine the pain. It will be so bad I'll want to die!

I'm so tired. Why don't I rest for a few minutes to catch my breath? (He sits down under a tree.) Maybe I can figure out an escape route. I've got to get farther away from the plantation. I'll close my eyes, but I won't sleep.

Am I dreaming? I see our tiny, one-room cabin. There are no windows; the only light comes in through the door and a few holes in the log walls. In winter the cold wind whistles through the holes. The naked earth is the floor of our home. Home? What's a home without beds? We just wrap up in thin blankets and lie on the floor close to the fireplace so we can keep warm. I never want to see that place again!

Am I awake? I'm not sure. Now I see myself in the cotton field. There's a wild-looking white man with a huge whip in his hand. He's coming toward me, but he won't beat me—I'm picking cotton as fast as I can. He must be looking at someone else. Oh, no he's beating me anyway. What have I done? "Pick faster!" he shouts. "Pick more of that cotton every day! Or you'll feel this lash every time I see you!" Every inch of my back is on fire. I can hardly stand the pain.

I must learn to pick cotton faster. Look at the others. How fast their hands move among the cotton bolls! What's this? The pace is slowing. What's happening? Oh, of course, the overseer has moved to another part of the field. When he's not near, the work slows down. I'll have to keep an eye out, though. When he comes back, he'll give me another crack if he thinks I'm loafing. I live in a world of hatred and fear where one wrong move can cause terrible pain.

I'm always tired. There's never time to rest. At dawn we go to the cotton fields and it's work, work, work. At noon, a short break—10 or 15 minutes. Just time to swallow a little bacon. Then back to work until it's too dark to see. If there's a moon, we keep working until the overseer says stop.

This past Christmas, the master gave us a three-day vacation! Three whole days with no work to do! But last year we got five days, and the year before, seven. Why must the only days we have for ourselves all year be cut back? I still see the disappointed looks on the faces of the others. Just a flicker, and then their expressions change. We must act happy, pretend we're grateful, keep our complaints to ourselves. The master won't stand for a surly slave.

What if I can't get out of these woods? Maybe plantation life is better than being all alone and lost in the forest. No! Nothing is worse than that plantation!

Now I think I see my wife and two little boys. Oh, my miserable family! It's for them that I've run away. The master sold my wife and boys to other slave owners. What could I do? I begged—please, don't sell them without me! I cried. I threw myself at the master's feet. But his heart was like stone. Men dragged my dear ones away. I started to run after them. Strong white hands stopped me, and someone started beating me. That was last week, and even today I am numb with shock and grief. I must find my dear family.

The man wakes up suddenly and pushes himself to his feet. The sky has cleared, and the moon casts a dim light through the trees. He starts running, knowing that he must not stop again. Much later,

"Please, please, help me."

panting, he sees a small house in a clearing. Tired and hungry, he has gone as far as his strength will take him.

Fear grips him. He wonders, shall I knock? Will they treat me as a fellow human being? Or will they send me back to the plantation? Perhaps there's a reward for my capture. Well, I must take the risk. I just can't go on!

He knocks on the door.

"Who is it?" shouts a sleepy voice. The weary man knocks again. He hears shuffling behind the door. When it opens, the light from a lantern blinds him for a moment. Then he sees two white faces—a man's and a woman's.

"Please, please, help me," whispers the runaway.

"You've come to the right place!" says the woman, motioning for him to enter. "We'll get you to safety."

POSTSCRIPT

The lucky runaway had come to a "station" of the Underground Railroad. This was not a real railroad, but an informal network of people who helped slaves escape to Northern states and to Canada.

"Trains" were large farm wagons that could hide and carry the runaways. They moved along "tracks"—back country roads. They stopped at "stations"—homes where people cared for and fed the runaway slaves. "Conductors" were the men and women, white and black, who defied state and federal laws to lead the slaves to freedom. The "passengers," or "parcels," were the slaves. Passengers paid no fare, and conductors got no wages.

During the day, the runaways were hidden in cellars, attics, barns, haylofts, or haystacks. At night, they were moved toward freedom. Their goal was to cross the boundary that divided the South from the North. Between Maryland and Pennsylvania, that boundary was called the Mason-Dixon Line. Farther west, it was the Ohio River.

Even in the North the runaways often stayed out of sight. Under the Constitution they were still considered someone's property, and if caught they might be sent back to their owners. In some states, however, runaways breathed more freely. These Northern states had "personal liberty laws" aimed at helping runaway slaves. Such laws told police officers and courts not to help return runaways to the South.

One of the most famous conductors was Harriet Tubman, an escaped slave. Called Moses, she returned to the South 19 times to bring out some 300 slaves. She was wanted dead or alive in the South but was never captured and never lost a passenger.

Whites also worked effectively as conductors. Thomas Garrett, a white Quaker, and Samuel Burris, a free black, ran a station in the slave state of Delaware. Garrett paid a fortune in court fines for their work. Once Burris was captured and sold as a slave. The buyer was Garrett—who returned him to freedom.

In 1826, Levi Coffin, a Quaker, moved from North Carolina to Newport, Indiana, where his home became a center of "Railroad" activities. Because of his success in getting many slaves to freedom, he came to be known as the "president" of the Underground Railroad. Two blacks, David Ruggles and William Still, maintained key stations in New York and Philadelphia. From the 1830's to the 1860's, hundreds of people helped thousands of slaves to freedom by way of the Underground Railroad.

Homework Questions

1. Why did the number of slaves grow so rapidly in the South during the 19th century?
2. How did the Constitution recognize the existence of slavery?
3. Describe how slaves lived and worked on plantations in the South.
4. Why did the slave in the story run away?
5. How did the Underground Railroad help slaves escape from the South?

Understanding the Story

A. Write *T* for each statement that is true and *F* for each statement that is false.
   1. Slavery never existed in the North.
   2. The Constitution provided that runaway slaves be returned to their owners.
   3. The cotton gin was a machine for getting the juice out of cotton.
   4. Cruelty was a part of the slave system.
   5. The slave in the story is running away from his plantation.
   6. The slave's house was large and comfortable.
   7. Slave owners and overseers were not allowed to beat their slaves.
   8. The runaway slave's wife and children had been sold to other slave owners.

B. List the numbers of the statements that the runaway slave made or might have made about his life.
   1. My owner must never catch me.
   2. They'll treat me with kindness if I return.
   3. The forest is more comfortable than my cabin.
   4. I must learn to pick cotton faster.
   5. I'm not worried; the overseer is my friend.

6. We work only eight hours a day in the cotton field.
7. Nothing is worse than the plantation.
8. I love my family.

C. Imagine that you are a slave forced to work for someone else. Do you think you would try to run away? List reasons for and against an attempt to escape.

Activities and Inquiries

1. Study the graph on page 231. Then choose the term or phrase that best completes each statement.
   a. Most Southerners (1) owned slaves (2) did not own slaves (3) sold their slaves between 1820 and 1860.
   b. In 1860 (1) every Southerner owned at least one slave (2) there were more slaveholders with 20 or more slaves than those with 1 to 9 slaves (3) the number of Southerners with 1 to 9 slaves was greater than the total number who owned more than 10 slaves.
   c. Which choice is true, according to the graph? (1) Every slaveholder owned a large plantation. (2) Every Southerner lived or worked on a plantation. (3) Slavery existed in the South in 1860.
   d. Which information can you find on the graph? (1) the percentage of white Southerners who owned no slaves (2) the number of slaves in the South (3) the number of freedmen (freed slaves) in the South
   e. The percentage of Southerners who did not own slaves was about (1) four times greater than the percentage of those who owned 1 to 9 slaves (2) the same as the total percentage of all the slaveholders (3) twice the percentage of those who owned 10 to 19 slaves.

2. Assume that you are going to film the story you have just read. What scenes will you include?
3. Write a newspaper advertisement for your motion picture.
4. Look at the drawing on page 233 and answer the following questions.
   a. Why is the black man asking for help?
   b. Will the white couple help him? Why or why not?
   c. How would most people react? Why?
5. In the library read about the life of Frederick Douglass or another slave who escaped to the North. Then write a story describing the kind of life the runaway in this chapter might lead as a free man.

2 The "Wage Slave"

Samuel Slater built the first successful American cotton-spinning mill (factory) in Pawtucket, Rhode Island, in 1790. Born in England, Slater had memorized the plans of an English factory before coming to the United States. He copied the English factory with great accuracy. Slater has been called the "Father of the Factory System" in America.

Soon machines in Northern factories were spinning Southern cotton into thread. At first the thread was woven into cloth by women and men working at their own looms at home. Not until 1814 did a manufacturer in Waltham, Massachusetts, combine the spinning and weaving operations in a textile factory. (*Textile* is another word for cloth or fabric.)

It was a good time to start such a factory. The War of 1812 had cut off imports from Europe, and Americans needed their own textile mills. Throughout New England and the Middle States business people set up textile factories. Wherever a river or stream was available to turn the wheels that powered the machines, factories were built. The demand for Southern cotton went up.

Manufacturing shifted from the home or small shop to the factory. It took little skill to operate the machines. Workers learned on the job. Women and children who had few opportunities to get other jobs, gladly took factory jobs—despite long hours and low wages.

The factory in our story stands beside the Charles River in Massachusetts. Although it is a steaming hot day, all windows are tightly shut. Inside, the clatter of 500 looms makes it almost impossible to hear a person talk. Lint from the cotton fills the moist air and sticks to the workers' bodies. A few male supervisors oversee 150 women workers. The women rush back and forth tending three (or sometimes four) looms. They watch carefully for breaks in the threads and see that the threads feed properly into each machine. There are no rest periods, and no talking is permitted.

Ask yourself if it is fair to compare factory workers with slaves. Do the workers in the story have freedom of choice?

Waltham, Massachusetts, August, 1832

It is exactly 7 P.M. Bells ring loudly, the machines stop, and the women walk wearily to the exit.

"We're wage slaves," said Sarah angrily.

"Quiet down," said Lucy. "You don't want the foremen to hear you say that. Besides, you don't know what you're talking about."

"I know that we work 13 hours a day," said Sarah more calmly.

"The hours are shorter in the winter," replied Lucy. "Days are shorter then, and we only work from dawn to dusk."

"They'd make us work just as long in winter if there were some light in the building. Roast in the summer, freeze in the winter. Always hungry. And for what? Pennies! Wage slaves, that's what we are!"

"I don't like conditions any more than you," said Lucy. "But I don't feel like a wage slave."

"Up at 4:30, in the factory at 5 o'clock and 30 minutes for lunch at noon. There's scarcely a moment to eat. By the time I get to the boardinghouse, all I can do is gulp down some food and run back to the factory. Is a slave treated more cruelly?"

"I'm not sure, but I think I can stand the pace for three years. I'll save some money. Perhaps I'll be able to help my family pay the mortgage on our farm. Then I'll be free to do as I please."

"Free? You'll never be free if you stay here that long, Lucy. You'll always be a slave to this job. You breathe that filthy factory air, never get enough fresh air, and tend twice as many looms as a human being should. In three years you'll be a tired, worn-out, old woman. You may leave the factory, but you will never escape from what it did to you."

"Look, Sarah, I'm just as tired as you. But this is a job, and I need the money. My friends tell me that all their factory jobs are like this."

"That's just my point," smiled Sarah. "A slave woman on a plantation is better off than we are. She's well fed. She's looked after. A slave is well clothed and is never without a job."

"I have a job," said Lucy.

"Only for as long as the boss wants to keep you. Come in late a few times or make a few mistakes, and you'll see how long you keep this job!"

"Slaves are treated cruelly, Sarah. They're beaten terribly. They have no rights or lives of their own. They're bought and sold like cattle. No, there's no way that a slave has a better life than I do."

"Don't tell me you're not afraid of the foreman's whip," sneered Sarah. "Have you forgotten what happened when you tried to say a few words to me?"

"The whip scarcely hurt me. I'm not afraid of him or his whip. Yes, I can be punished for mistakes on the job, but I'm here because I choose to be. And no slave captured in Africa and sold in America can say that."

"You have a short memory, Lucy. Remember the day we met? We were riding in that long, low, black wagon, the one called a 'slaver.' We sat close together on those narrow, uncomfortable seats and listened to the driver tell us about the wonderful jobs he would find for us. We believed him when he said we would be able to dress well, save money, and have lots of spare time to read books."

"It was the driver's job to go around the state and find girls to work in factories. I guess he lied a little."

"He lied a lot!" said Sarah. "He said we'd tend one or two looms; we tend four. He said we could go home on Sunday, our day off. He never told us that the farther from our homes he drove us, the more he got paid. Now we're so far from home that we have to spend Sundays in that miserable boardinghouse. We sleep six to a room, and the food—"

"Speaking of the boardinghouse, here it is," said Lucy. "By the way, unlike a slave, you do have a choice. If you hate this job so much, why don't you quit?"

"You're right, I am a free woman. Tomorrow, I'll tell the foreman I want to leave. I'll be out of here in two weeks. I'm going home to freedom."

"I've made my decision," added Lucy. "I'm staying."

POSTSCRIPT

From the 1830's to the 1860's, workers were eager to reduce their working day from 13 to 10 hours and improve their pay. For the unskilled factory worker, complaining did little good. A manager could easily replace a "troublemaker" with a farm woman or an immigrant. Conditions were different for artisans (skilled workers) whose jobs required training and experience. They could and did complain.

Almost all adult white men now had the right to vote, and many male workers tried to improve working conditions through political parties. Some formed workingmen's parties and ran for public office. Some men and women organized labor unions, although courts often held that such groups were illegal. During the 1830's and the 1840's, there were dozens of strikes. Most ended in failure, with workers in jail.

In 1842 came a major breakthrough for labor unions. The Massachusetts Supreme Court ruled that labor unions were legal after all and peaceful strikes were legal too—in Massachusetts. Strikes did not immediately become legal throughout the nation. But gradually other states began to follow the Massachusetts lead. Labor unions began to grow.

Homework Questions

1. Why was the shift in manufacturing from the home to the factory important?
2. What reasons did Sarah have for feeling like a slave?
3. How did Lucy respond to Sarah's statements?
4. How did the lives of factory workers differ from those of plantation slaves?
5. Why did unskilled workers find it hard to protest against their working conditions?

Understanding the Story

A. List the numbers of the statements that are true.
  1. Samuel Slater built the first successful American cotton-spinning mill.
  2. Martin Van Buren is called the "Father of the Factory System" in America.
  3. In 1814 a factory combined spinning and weaving operations.
  4. The women in the factory worked a ten-hour day.
  5. The working day in the factory started at 7 A.M.

6. The factory workers were not permitted to talk to one another.
7. Wagons called "slavers" brought girls to work in factories.
8. Unions were generally legal in the United States in 1830.

B. Complete the following sentences by filling in the missing word or words.

1. Samuel Slater brought the ideas for his spinning mill from _____.
2. The product made by a spinning mill is _____.
3. The machines on which Sarah and Lucy worked were called _____.
4. Hours at the factory were _____ in winter.
5. Sarah and Lucy lived in a _____.
6. If Sarah and Lucy talk on the job, the foreman may strike them with a _____.
7. From the 1830's to the 1860's, workers were seeking a _____- hour day.
8. A Massachusetts court ruled in 1842 that labor unions were _____.

C. Imagine that Lucy and Sarah had been able to join a labor union. What changes might such a union have worked for? Do you think a union of textile-factory workers would have been effective in 1832? Why or why not?

Activities and Inquiries

1. Imagine that you are preparing a report card on the working conditions in Lucy's and Sarah's factory. Grade each of the items listed—excellent, pass, or fail. Write a sentence explaining the reasons for each grade. How can the failing grades be raised to passing grades? How can the passing grades be raised to excellent grades?
   a. wages
   b. hours of work
   c. light and air
   d. living quarters
   e. air pollution
   f. treatment by foremen
   g. time for relaxation
   h. time for meals
2. Pretend that it is 1832 and you are the owner of the factory where Lucy and Sarah work. What response would you make if they asked you to improve their working conditions? Explain.
3. Write a diary covering one week in the life of a factory worker such as Sarah or Lucy.
4. Prepare a library report on the development of labor associations and unions before 1860.
5. Do you agree that Sarah was a wage slave? Why or why not?

3 Free the Slaves—Now!

For a long time, many Americans protested the existence of slavery. As early as the mid-1700's, Quakers such as Anthony Benezet and John Woolman attacked slavery as cruel and un-Christian. Even some slave owners, such as Thomas Jefferson, spoke of slavery as wrong. In a draft of the Declaration of Independence, Jefferson called the slave trade evil and blamed it on the king. But these words were taken out of the final version. Although Jefferson continued to speak of slavery's evils, he never freed his own slaves.

The first national antislavery society was organized in the South in 1774. It supported the gradual abolition (ending) of slavery. In fact, most antislavery societies started in the South. (In 1826, there were 103 such societies in the South and only 40 in the North.)

Northerners held many opinions about slavery. Some people were indifferent—neither for nor against. Some, such as Abraham Lincoln, considered slavery an evil but were willing to let it exist in the South. But they did not want it spread into the territories (areas not yet organized into states). Some people, known as moderates, wanted to end slavery gradually, step by step. Others, known as radical abolitionists (or just abolitionists), wanted to abolish slavery at once, without paying slave owners for their losses.

Most white Southerners, and many Northerners, considered abolitionists to be wild-eyed extremists. In their view, abolitionists threatened not only the property rights of slave owners but also the survival of the Union. The Constitution, after all, had been based in part on a trade-off between Southern and Northern interests. It had left slavery as a matter for each state to decide for itself.

A turning point in the antislavery movement came in 1833. That year all slaves within the British Empire were freed. If the British could take such a step, why couldn't the Americans?

Within a short time, religious societies in the United States flooded the country with pamphlets. Men such as Arthur and Lewis Tappan (New York merchants), Gerrit Smith (a New York landowner), and Benjamin Lundy (a New Jersey Quaker) worked to broaden the antislavery crusade. More than 30 antislavery newspapers preached abolition. From lecture and church platforms throughout the North, dozens of speakers called for an end to slavery.

Hinton Helper, a North Carolina writer, attacked slavery as being harmful to the South's economy. His book, *The Impending Crisis of the South*, published in 1857, was addressed to Southerners who owned no slaves. In it he argued that only the large plantation owners profited from the slave system. All other Southerners were losers, he said, because slavery held back economic progress. The book was banned in the South, but thousands of copies were distributed in the North.

An increasingly popular form of antislavery writing was the novel. *Uncle Tom's Cabin*, written by Harriet Beecher Stowe and published in 1852, was the most widely read of the novels describing the cruelties of slavery. The book had a tremendous sale in the United States and overseas and convinced thousands that plantations were run by brutal overseers like Simon Legree. Readers could not forget the description of a beaten and dying Uncle Tom or of Eliza crossing a frozen river to get away from the dogs of the slave catchers. This story made many decide that slavery had to end.

In 1837 a number of regional female antislavery societies joined together to become the Anti-Slavery Convention of American Women. The members distributed petitions, collected signatures, lectured, wrote essays, and did whatever they could to further the abolitionist cause. Among the leaders in the fight were the Grimké sisters, born to a wealthy slave-owning family in Charleston, South Carolina. Angelina and Sarah Grimké were Quakers who pursued both women's rights and abolitionist causes. They were the first women to speak to audiences in the North that included both men and women.

Many blacks played leading roles in the struggle against slavery. William Wells Brown, an escaped slave, became one of the best-known abolitionist speakers here and in Europe. He was America's first black novelist and playwright. Frederick Douglass, also a former slave, was an effective writer and speaker for the abolitionist cause. He also spoke for Irish freedom, world

peace, and political rights for all. In his own newspaper, the North Star, he called for an end to capital punishment. He supported fairer treatment of Chinese immigrants and American Indians and improved education for the poor. His home in Rochester, New York, was a station on the Underground Railroad. His sons became conductors for slaves escaping to Canada.

The most outspoken antislavery reformer was William Lloyd Garrison. He was an abolitionist who refused compromise and called for the immediate emancipation (freeing) of slaves. For 35 years through his newspaper, The Liberator, and through public speeches, he called for change. Northern moderates as well as slave owners hated him.

Most Northerners had a deep respect for private property—even if the property was human. A disruption of the Southern plantation system might cut cotton shipments to the North, slash production of cloth, turn profit to loss, and cause unemployment. What's more, freed slaves might move North and compete for Northerners' jobs.

As you read the story, ask yourself what, if anything, you admire about Garrison. Would you call him an extremist? Why or why not?

Boston, 1835

I am William Lloyd Garrison, an abolitionist. I believe that America must free its slaves now—not tomorrow, not next week.

Slavery is a crime against black people and a curse that corrupts all who are part of it. We are all guilty of continuing this national sin because we support the Constitution, which approves slavery. Such a constitution is a contract with death and an agreement with the Devil! Slavery must go! Burn the Constitution!

The Declaration of Independence says that all men are created equal. No one has the right to enslave his brother or treat another human being like furniture. Every man has a right to the wages of his own labor, and each deserves the equal protection of the law. Every man should have the vote—yes, even slaves!

We should not pay slave owners for freeing their slaves. Because no person may own another, slave masters have never owned and do not now own human beings. You cannot lose something you never had. So freeing slaves would not deprive the slave owners of their property. It would only return control of the slaves' lives to their rightful owners—the freed slaves themselves.

Only they should receive payment for their suffering. The masters who abused and tortured them deserve nothing. NOTHING!

We are all guilty! North as well as South. Can we ever forget that New England money is spent for human flesh? That New England ships carried the slaves from Africa? That New England workers forged the chains that bind the slaves?

I will never forget.

New Englanders talk of freeing the slaves in some imaginary tomorrow. But they forget that slaves are people suffering today. The bodies of New Englanders are not the ones being crushed and beaten now, so they can easily speak about future freedom.

How people hate men of action and abolitionists like me! They will kill me if they can. I do not want to die, but I am not afraid.

I will never forget what that mob did to me just as I was going to speak to the Boston Female Anti-Slavery Society in October of this year. It was nothing unusual, just one more of hundreds of speeches I have made. What could go wrong? It was daylight, and I was in Boston, the Cradle of Liberty.

Something seemed strange as I pushed my way into the meeting hall through a crowd of more than 100 men. What were they doing in a meeting for women? Although some 20 women waited in the front of the hall for me to speak, I did not want to begin because that mob of men looked ugly and threatening. To escape them, I ran out of the hall into a small office, locked the door, and waited.

Suddenly, the men were smashing down the door. Through the noise I heard their cries, "Garrison is in there! Garrison! Garrison! We must have Garrison! Out with him! Lynch him!"

It was no time to be brave, so I squeezed through the back window and dropped to the ground. At first, I was able to hide, but soon the crowd saw me. Several men grabbed me, shouting, "Kill him! Kill him!" One coiled a rope around my body and led me through the mob. Another called out, "Let's not kill him right away!" Fortunately, three strong men protected me, shouting, "Don't hurt him! You shouldn't hurt him! He's an American."

They dragged me through the city over ground stained with the blood of the heroes of the Boston Massacre of 1770. The thousands in the jeering, vicious mob screamed, cursed, and threw rubbish at me. Worst of all, they ripped off most of my clothes—in front of thousands of people.

Finally, the mayor ordered them to carry me to his office in the city hall. I was afraid, but I was prepared to die. Somehow, the three men protected me from the worst of the mob. I was given some clothes.

The mayor then came to a great decision: I must be moved because the city hall was in danger! It might be destroyed by the mob as long as I was in it. The officials would protect me (and the building) by sending me to jail for disturbing the peace!

I was pushed into a coach. At first, the mob did not recognize me. I thought I would be safe, but suddenly the people saw me. Dozens of hands tried to drag me out of the coach. They held the wheels, smashed the doors, grabbed the horses, and even tried to upset the coach. The police pushed them back, and the driver whipped the shouting mob as well as the horses. We finally escaped to the safety of a jail cell.

On my cell walls I wrote:

"William Lloyd Garrison was put into this cell to save him from a mob of respectable men. They were going to kill him because he preached that 'all men are created equal.'

"Jail me as a prisoner—but don't tie me up like a slave.

"Punish me as a criminal—but don't treat me like property.

"Torture me as a man—but don't drive me like an animal."

I will not retreat a single inch. I will not stop my fight until every slave is free! I will be heard!

POSTSCRIPT

Garrison was not the only antislavery leader to be attacked. Mobs in many cities roughed up critics of slavery or destroyed their property.

One such mob tore through the New York home of Lewis Tappan in 1834. It smashed his furniture. Two years later, a mob in Cincinnati, Ohio, sacked the offices of an abolitionist journal called *The Philanthropist*, published by James Birney. The next year another abolitionist editor, Elijah Lovejoy, was killed. He was trying to defend his presses against a mob in Alton, Illinois. Mobs had already destroyed Lovejoy's presses three times.

The abolitionists aimed to stir up the conscience of the North against slavery, and in many ways they succeeded. But they also aroused harsh opposition. There seemed to be no room for compromise between the opposing sides. The radical abolitionists were on one side. The bitter-end defenders of slavery and the Constitution were on the other. In the end, the issue would be settled by war.

Homework Questions

1. How was the position of the abolitionists different from that of moderates who opposed slavery?
2. What did abolitionists other than Garrison do in the fight against slavery?
3. How did abolitionists suffer because of their antislavery position?
4. Why did many in the North dislike William Lloyd Garrison?
5. What part did women take in the antislavery struggle?

Understanding the Story

A. Write *T* for each statement that is true, *F* for each statement that is false, and *O* for each statement that is an opinion.
   1. Abolitionists were the bravest people in America.
   2. Abolitionists said that slavery should be ended immediately.
   3. Northern moderates admired William Lloyd Garrison.
   4. Garrison should have been more moderate about slavery.
   5. Garrison said that blacks should vote.
   6. Garrison agreed that slave owners should be paid for freeing their slaves.
   7. Garrison should have known better than to criticize the Constitution so harshly.
   8. The attack on Garrison took place in Boston.

B. Write *A* for each statement that Garrison would agree with and *N* for each statement that he would not agree with.
   1. Slavery is a curse.
   2. Slavery cannot be bad because the Constitution allows it.
   3. Slaves should be paid for their suffering.
   4. North and South are both guilty.
   5. Most people approve of abolitionists.
   6. New England ships carried the slaves from Africa.
   7. The mayor of Boston was kind to put me in jail and save me from the mob.
   8. Slaves are people.

C. The abolitionists painted the world in terms of good against evil. Their cause was good; slavery was evil. Name a modern political cause that takes a similar approach. Do you support the cause you have named? Why or why not?

Activities and Inquiries

1. Assume that Garrison is put on trial in Boston for disturbing the peace and you are his defense lawyer. Prepare his defense.
2. You are the prosecuting attorney. State the case against Garrison.
3. Garrison insists on addressing the jury. What will he tell them?
4. You are a member of the jury. Decide whether Garrison is innocent or guilty. Explain your verdict.

4 Women Have Rights

Many of the abolitionists were women. They formed discussion groups in which to express their feelings about slavery and other issues. In most of the reform movements, opposition by males prevented women from holding positions of power. Women could talk among themselves, but their ideas were not usually welcomed by men. Very simply, most men refused to accept women as equals and told them to stay at home.

America in the first half of the 19th century was a man's world. Most high schools and colleges were closed to females. Women were barred from most professions, from speaking in public places, and even from offering prayers at religious services. They could not vote or hold public office.

Within the family, the husband was lord and master—he had to be obeyed. Laws recognized the husband as head of the family. If a woman brought property into a marriage, her husband took full control of it. If a married woman held a job, her wages legally belonged to her husband. Laws even allowed a husband to beat a wife who disobeyed. In the eyes of some, such laws gave women a legal position comparable to that of a slave.

Of course, the way women were treated and the rights they had varied from family to family and from place to place. On the frontier, especially, women tended to come closer to equality with men.

Two women whom men learned to listen to were Elizabeth Cady Stanton and Lucretia Mott. Both were active in the Underground Railroad and helped many slaves escape to freedom. They came to believe that women were caught in a slavery of their own. This condition would not change until women gained equal rights with men.

These women and others felt that they were being treated like children or outsiders. They were tired of it! Their goal was equality of the sexes, and they would accept nothing less.

Our scene is Seneca Falls, a small town in northern New York State. Lucretia Mott has come from Philadelphia to visit her friend Elizabeth Cady Stanton.

See if you can understand why the two chose the framework of the Declaration of Independence to express their grievances. Which of the goals of their declaration have since been achieved?

Seneca Falls, New York, 1848

"Lucretia, I'm so glad you could come to Seneca Falls," said Elizabeth Cady Stanton.

"I'm happy to see you again," replied Lucretia Mott. "Your letter was so exciting. I've dreamed about a women's rights convention ever since our experience in London in 1840."

"I'll never forget that World Anti-Slavery Convention and the horrible way those men treated us. Why, they wouldn't even admit us to the convention floor. They made us sit in a balcony, behind a curtain, and not say a word—just like little children. They didn't want us women to bother the men!''

"Only one man understood how we felt," recalled Mrs. Mott. "The greatest abolitionist of them all, William Lloyd Garrison, rose from his seat and said: 'I have battled for many years for the freedom of African slaves. Now I can take no part in a convention that strikes down the most sacred rights of all women. Not all of the slaves are men!' That wonderful man then joined us in the balcony."

"Yes, Lucretia, our eyes were opened. We finally understood that slaves were not the only people who deserved to be freed. We women too must be free."

"Right! At our convention we women will talk about our problems and tell the nation what we want and what we expect. Women must be equal to men."

"Now, let's plan the convention," said Mrs. Stanton with great excitement. "I am not going to ask organizations to send delegates because there aren't many women's groups. We'll just have individuals come on their own. My feeling is that we should meet for two days. On the first day, the meeting will be for women only. On the second, men can take part too."

"That sounds fine," said Mrs. Mott. "We must invite men—we need all the help we can get. We mustn't forget that men control the political machinery. We have to win over enough of them to change state and national laws."

Mrs. Stanton went on: "We must tell the world what the women's rights movement stands for. What do you think about taking the

"The right to vote is the first step toward equality in politics."

Declaration of Independence as a model? We can start with 'When, in the course of human events,' and go on to list some 'self-evident' truths.''

"Fine," said Mrs. Mott. "People should understand that all men *and women* are created equal. That women have *inalienable* rights, just like men. That women should not be forced to obey laws they have no part in passing.''

"Don't forget the tax argument, Lucretia. Like the colonists in 1776, women today are subject to taxation without representation. And we have little opportunity to earn money. Men control the better jobs. Women's pay is usually a pittance.''

Mrs. Mott nodded in agreement. "Let's not forget to point out that most colleges are closed to women. How can we compete with men, Elizabeth, when we are blocked from getting a proper education?''

While the women were talking, Henry Stanton had entered the room. He listened quietly and approvingly to the women's complaints.

"You two make it sound as though women have very few rights in our society," said Mr. Stanton. "I'm beginning to think that's so!''

"Thank you, Henry," replied Mrs. Stanton. "I think we have taken a giant step toward the organization of a successful women's rights convention. Now we have to think about the resolutions we should offer at the convention. Of course, several recommendations will be about equal rights. The right to vote will be the most important one.''

"Elizabeth, I can't agree with you on that," said Mrs. Mott. "I don't think that women are ready for the vote. We must go slowly—otherwise, we will look ridiculous.''

"Not ready for the vote? What do you mean? Of course, women must have the right to vote, because it is the first step toward equality in politics. Without the vote, there is little we can do. Women must be able to influence the politicians who make the laws, and the politicians must know it!''

"I agree with Mrs. Mott," said Henry Stanton. "We must fight for equality in marriage and the home. Later we can turn to politics. You will look like fools if you insist on votes for women. Don't you realize how long it took to get the right to vote for most men? Demanding votes for women now is insane! If you insist on doing this, I will not attend your convention!'' (Henry Stanton left the room hurriedly.)

"Women will have the vote," insisted Mrs. Stanton quietly.

The convention was held as scheduled. Men who asked to be admitted the first day were seated with the women and joined in the discussion.

The Declaration of Sentiments and Resolutions put forward by the women was approved unanimously. Then came a long, heated debate about votes for women. Some were afraid that supporting such an idea would draw people's attention away from the other resolutions. Others said that it would turn people away from the entire women's rights movement. Many felt that Mrs. Stanton had gone too far.

Then Frederick Douglass, an abolitionist leader and a former slave, spoke. He talked about the importance and power of the ballot. Every oppressed group must win the right to vote before it can hope for equality, he insisted. The resolution calling for voting rights for women passed by a narrow margin. It was added to the declaration.

The convention's work stirred much debate. Many newspapers carried bitter attacks on the declaration. As a result, many of the men and women who had signed the declaration withdrew their names. They now thought that women might be seeking too much, too soon.

POSTSCRIPT

The Seneca Falls Convention helped to spark a women's rights movement in the United States. By the time of the Civil War, the legal standing of women was beginning to change.

Although women still did not have the right to vote, a few states gave married women the right to own property. New York allowed married women to sue in court.

New opportunities continued to open up in education. More and more women gained jobs as elementary school teachers. A few high schools and teacher-training schools opened their doors to women. A few colleges also began to admit them. Oberlin College in Ohio was the first coeducational college—that is, the first college for both men and women. It had opened in 1833. Three years later Mount Holyoke Female Seminary (now known as Mount Holyoke College) opened as the first permanent college for women.

The women in our story were among many women who became important in U.S. life. Some took active roles in promoting public causes. For example, Lucy Stone, an Oberlin graduate, and the Grimké sisters (see page 241) lectured and wrote about women's rights and abolition. And Sojourner Truth, a former slave, stirred antislavery and women's rights meetings with vivid stories about wrongs against black women. But perhaps the leading figure in the fight for women's rights was Susan B. Anthony (see pages 379–382). From the 1850's until her death in 1906, she worked untiringly to win new rights for women—especially the right to vote.

Dorothea Dix worked to improve the treatment of the insane. Margaret Fuller edited a literary magazine, *The Dial*, then became the literary editor of a daily newspaper, the *New York Tribune*. Emma Willard developed new methods of educating girls. In 1821 she founded the first college-level school for women in this country, the Troy (New York) Female Seminary. Dr. Elizabeth Blackwell, the first woman to graduate from medical school, became a well-known physician.

Women also became inventors. One 19th-century women's rights leader, Matilda Joslyn Gage, gave women credit for some inventions generally thought to have been created by men. She claimed that Catherine Greene actually invented the cotton gin because Greene suggested a key feature of the machine made by Eli Whitney. Whitney took out a patent on his cotton gin and has usually been called the gin's inventor.

Homework Questions

1. In what ways was the United States a man's world in the first half of the 19th century?
2. Why did female abolitionists decide to start their own reform groups separate from men's groups?
3. What was the purpose of the Seneca Falls convention?
4. How did other women besides Lucretia Mott and Elizabeth Cady Stanton help in the movement for equal rights?
5. Why did many people feel that women were asking for too many reforms too quickly?

Understanding the Story

A. Which of these statements might be included in a list of results of the Seneca Falls convention?
   1. Women received the right to vote in 1848.
   2. A Declaration of Sentiments and Resolutions was made public.
   3. People now knew that many women were unhappy about how they were treated.
   4. A women's rights movement began.
   5. Women began to be known as inventors.
   6. Women were given half of all the top jobs in the nation.
   7. For the first time a U.S. college opened its doors to women.
   8. Some men publicly showed their support for women's rights.

B. Write *F* for each statement that is a fact and *O* for each statement that is an opinion.
   1. Lucretia Mott opposed slavery.
   2. Elizabeth Cady Stanton and Lucretia Mott should have been pleased with their treatment as women.
   3. The two women planned a meeting to be held in Seneca Falls, New York.
   4. The women's convention should have been held in Chicago.
   5. Mrs. Stanton and Mrs. Mott felt they had been treated badly at an abolitionist convention in London.
   6. Men should not attend a women's rights convention.
   7. The Declaration of Independence served as a model for the statement on women's rights at Seneca Falls.
   8. Mrs. Stanton felt that women should have the right to vote.

C. Do you think American women have now gained most of the goals discussed by Lucretia Mott and Elizabeth Cady Stanton? Explain your answer.

Activities and Inquiries

1. You have a choice. You may interview Elizabeth Cady Stanton or Lucretia Mott. Which one will you choose? Why? What questions will you ask her? What answers do you expect?
2. If you were planning a women's rights convention today, what issues would you bring up? Why?
3. Go to the library and write a report on the rights women have gained since 1848.
4. Report on the life and accomplishments of a woman who became well known in the 1800's. Choose from among Dorothea Dix, Elizabeth Blackwell, Margaret Fuller, and Sojourner Truth. Tell why you think the woman was able to do what she did in spite of male prejudice against achievements outside the home.

5 It's Mr. Polk's War

While reformers were working to change the social order, the United States continued to expand. The United States had purchased the Louisiana Territory in 1803 and East Florida in 1819. For a time, this satisfied the American hunger for land. But then settlers began to spill over the U.S. boundaries. They went south into Texas and (later) west into Upper California—both belonging to Mexico. They went northwest into the Oregon Territory—claimed jointly by Britain and the United States but officially part of neither.

The new lands were only thinly settled. Indians lived there, of course, and there were scattered Mexican ranches and British and American fur-trading posts. But to many Americans, the lands seemed empty, ripe for the taking. Writers and speakers began to promote the idea that the United States had a God-given right to fill in the empty spaces and make the lands prosper. By 1845 a term had been coined to describe this notion. The United States, it was said, had a Manifest Destiny—an obvious mission—to spread over the whole continent from the Atlantic to the Pacific.

What was "obvious" to some Americans was anything but obvious to the leaders of Britain and Mexico. The stage was set for some very heated quarrels.

Britain and the United States had agreed in 1818 to put off any settlement of their dispute over the Oregon Territory. They approved what they called "joint occupation" of this enormous region. Oregon was much bigger than the present-day state. It reached from Upper California on the south to Russian-owned Alaska on the north. West to east, it stretched from the Pacific Coast to the Rocky Mountains.

Britain's claim to Oregon dated to 1579, when Sir Francis Drake sailed along the Pacific Coast. Britain could also base its claim on visits to Oregon in the 18th century by James Cook and George Vancouver. In addition, the British-owned Hudson's Bay Company had fur-trading posts in the area.

The United States had its own claim to Oregon. It could point out that Captain Robert Gray had sailed into the mouth of the Columbia River in 1792. Lewis and Clark had explored the region between 1805 and 1806. It could also note that John Jacob Astor had founded Astoria as a fur-trading center on the Columbia River in 1811.

While the Oregon question festered, Texas burst into the news. Trouble began between U.S. settlers and Mexican officials. The Mexicans had opened up Texas to American settlement in the years after 1820. Thousands of Americans moved in, and many brought slaves, although Mexico's laws did not allow slavery. By 1830 some 20,000 free Americans and 1,000 slaves lived in Texas. Then Mexico suddenly shut the door to future settlement by Americans. It also ordered an end to the bringing in of slaves and collected heavy taxes on imports of U.S. goods.

American settlers were outraged. They began to revolt against Mexican rule, and on March 2, 1836, declared Texas to be independent under the Lone Star flag. The Mexican dictator, General Antonio López de Santa Anna, led troops into Texas to put down the rebellion. Santa Anna trapped a band of 200 Texans inside the Alamo mission at San Antonio. All were killed, including two famous frontiersmen, Jim Bowie and Davy Crockett. With war cries of "Remember the Alamo," other Texans kept fighting. On April 21, 1836, a Texan army led by General Sam Houston defeated the Mexicans and captured Santa Anna. The war was over. Texas was free.

The Texas government legalized slavery and applied to the United States to be admitted as a new state. But slavery was a hot issue in American politics. The U.S. Senate did not want to stir up controversy by adding a new slave state. For several years, Texas existed as an independent country.

Then in 1844 the issue of Texas statehood revived. James Polk, a Democrat, raised the issue in his campaign for President. He proposed that the United States should add territory in two regions—Texas and Oregon. It was generally agreed that Oregon was not suited to slavery, so the proposal appealed to both proslavery and antislavery forces. Polk's appeal for more land carried him to victory. But what would happen next? Mexico still claimed Texas, and Britain had its own claim to Oregon.

Actually, Mexico's claim to *all* of Texas was unrealistic, and Mexico knew it. The real point of dispute was the location of the border between Texas and Mexico. When Texas was part of Mexico, its southern border had been the Nueces River. When Texas became independent, it had Santa Anna sign a paper mentioning another river farther south as a boundary. This was the Rio Grande. But Santa Anna was a prisoner at the time, and Mexico continued to claim the land north to the Nueces.

Polk forced the issue of the boundaries. He sent U.S. troops under General Zachary Taylor across the Nueces River almost to the Rio Grande. The troops were fired upon, and American blood was spilled. Insisting that America's honor was now at stake, Polk asked Congress to recognize that war existed between Mexico and the United States. Congress quickly did so.

In our story, we learn the opinions of two people about the war with Mexico. See if you can understand why their feelings about the war were different.

St. Louis, Missouri, May, 1846

"Why are you here so early?" asked Ruth.

"I have something important to tell you," replied Paul. "I'm going to enlist."

"Enlist—are you crazy?" asked Ruth, with obvious alarm.

"You know we're at war with Mexico, and President Polk is asking for 50,000 volunteers. I want to be one of them."

"You want to shoot defenseless Mexicans? You should be ashamed!"

"What are you talking about?" said Paul. "Haven't you heard what the Mexicans did? They shot American soldiers in cold blood—for no reason."

"No reason!" exclaimed Ruth. "The Americans had no right to be near the Rio Grande. They were invading Mexico. If I were Mexican, I'd have shot them too."

"Wrong, Ruth! Our soldiers were on American soil. That land is part of Texas, and Texas is a state now. I don't think those foreigners should get away with murdering our soldiers."

"Go, Paul, fight Mr. Polk's War to take land away from the Mexicans. Turn Mexico into one big plantation for slave masters. But don't tell me about it!"

"You're all mixed up, Ruth. This is not Mr. Polk's War. It's America's war, and I'm an American! I must fight to defend my country."

"What are you defending? Is Mexico attacking New York or New England or Virginia or Missouri? Did Mexican soldiers try to stop you from entering my house? Of course not."

"Look, Ruth, this is a war against the United States," replied Paul. "I know the fighting isn't here in Missouri. But I also know that all of America is very dear to me, and I believe our nation is a very special one with a special purpose."

"Of course we're special," Ruth exclaimed. "We have a wonderful way of life, and we have government by the people. I love America too. But what's our special purpose?"

"Don't you see?" asked Paul. "We have a duty to spread our way of life—to spread our freedom. Our way of life and our form of government will benefit people everywhere. It is our duty, even our God-given destiny, to take control of our continent—all the way to the the Pacific."

"Destiny, you say," Ruth replied. "I guess you're talking about Manifest Destiny again."

The Mexican War, 1846–1848

"Exactly. We must fill in all the empty spaces and make the land give forth its riches. We must spread industry, culture, and freedom and serve as an example to all the world."

Ruth looked scornful. "What about the Mexicans and Indians who already live in those 'empty spaces'? Suppose they don't want our 'culture'? Suppose they would rather rule themselves?"

"Come on, Ruth. We're talking about vast spaces and only a handful of people. What have they done to improve the land, anyway? Hardly a thing! Believe me, they'd be better off if they'd let us show them how to really put the land to good use. Besides, America is growing; we need more room."

"Listen, Paul," said Ruth, "if we're going to expand our country we must do it the right way. We should try to get Mexico to agree to a border we both can accept and to sell us any land it doesn't need."

"We've tried—you know that as well as I. President Polk offered a fair price for California, and the Mexicans turned him down. If we don't get California soon, the British will grab it, and then what chance will we have to hold Oregon?"

"So," Ruth exclaimed, "you admit that the United States is fighting this war to grab more land—not just to defend a scrubby patch of land along the Rio Grande!"

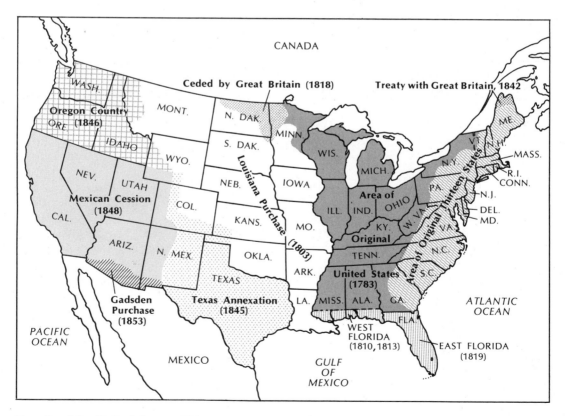

Growth of the United States, 1853

"Oh, Ruth, it's not that simple. First, Mexico attacked our soldiers—you can't forget that. And second, Mexico has such a shaky government that there seems to be no one in charge to deal with. We're at war now, and we have a chance to knock some sense into those Mexicans."

"Well, I just wish someone would knock some sense into you. You're going to try to spread 'freedom' with guns and cannon. That sounds to me like the wrong way to go about it!"

POSTSCRIPT

United States forces led by generals Zachary Taylor and Winfield Scott won victories in Mexico. On February 2, 1848, Mexico agreed to the peace treaty of Guadalupe Hidalgo. Mexico gave up all claim to Texas north of the Rio Grande and turned over New Mexico and California to the United States. In return the United States paid Mexico $15 million. In 1853, the United States bought more land from Mexico in what was called the Gadsden Purchase.

Through the years, four states (New Mexico, Utah, Arizona, and Nevada) were carved from New Mexico Territory. Other sections of the territory became parts of other states.

Just after the war with Mexico began, the United States and Britain settled the Oregon dispute. The U.S. gave up its claim to lands as far north as the border of Alaska at latitude 54°40′. This point was accepted even though some Americans had earlier shouted the slogan "54-40 or Fight." The United States and Britain agreed to extend the U.S.-Canadian border due west from the Rocky Mountains to the Pacific. Thus, the Oregon Territory was divided along the 49th parallel. Eventually most of the U.S. part of the Oregon Territory was divided into the states of Washington, Oregon, and Idaho. The rest became parts of Wyoming and Montana.

Homework Questions

1. Why did Texans revolt against Mexican rule?
2. How did President Polk's orders to General Taylor lead to the start of the Mexican War?
3. On what deeds did Britain and the United States base their claims to the Oregon Territory?
4. How did Paul explain the meaning of America's "Manifest Destiny"?
5. What did the United States gain from the war with Mexico?

Understanding the Story

A. Write *T* for each statement that is true and *F* for each statement that is false.
   1. The United States and Great Britain quarreled over the ownership of Oregon.
   2. In the years after 1820, Mexico refused to admit Americans into Texas.
   3. American settlers in Texas were happy to have Texas remain a part of Mexico.
   4. James Polk was elected President in 1844.
   5. Polk sent General Zachary Taylor to Oregon.

6. Many felt that the United States had a Manifest Destiny to expand from the Atlantic to the Pacific.
7. Mexico and the United States agreed on the boundary of Texas in 1844.
8. The United States won the war with Mexico.

B. Choose the term or phrase that best completes each statement.
1. The Oregon Territory was (a) smaller than (b) bigger than (c) the same size as the present-day state of Oregon.
2. The term Manifest Destiny came into use (a) by 1776 (b) by 1818 (c) by 1845.
3. Britain's claim to Oregon dated to a visit by (a) John Jacob Astor (b) Lewis and Clark (c) Sir Francis Drake.
4. Texas became independent in (a) 1836 (b) 1844 (c) 1845.
5. Sam Houston was a general in the army of (a) the United States (b) Texas (c) Mexico.
6. Paul thought American soldiers had been shot (a) on U.S. soil (b) on Mexican soil (c) by mistake.
7. Ruth thought the United States should (a) invade weaker nations (b) spread democracy (c) let the Mexicans alone.
8. The word "manifest" in Manifest Destiny means (a) biblical (b) obvious (c) democratic.

C. Warfare tends to arouse strong emotions, as our story shows. Imagine that the United States has just become involved in a war. Are there any circumstances in which you might take Ruth's position? Are there any circumstances in which you might take Paul's position? Explain.

Activities and Inquiries

1. Study the map on page 252. Then choose the term or phrase that best completes each statement.
   a. The distance from San Francisco to San Antonio is about (1) 600 miles (2) 1,200 miles (3) 1,500 miles.
   b. The distance from Los Angeles to Mexico City is (1) 900 kilometers (2) 2,400 kilometers (3) 5,000 kilometers.
   c. The land disputed by Mexico and the United States was between the (1) Nueces River and the Rio Grande (2) Nueces and Missouri rivers (3) Rio Grande and the Pacific Ocean.
   d. The Alamo is in (1) Mexico City (2) San Antonio (3) Vera Cruz.
   e. The Mexican War pushed the boundary of the United States farther (1) east (2) west and south (3) northeast.
2. Imagine that Paul captures a Mexican soldier during the fighting. What might the Mexican soldier tell Paul about his reasons for fighting?
3. Go to the library and find a biography of Abraham Lincoln. Read what it says about Lincoln's opposition to the Mexican War. Compare his arguments with Ruth's.
4. One reason given for declaring war on Mexico was to defend America's honor. What does that mean to you? In your opinion, is defending a nation's honor reason enough to fight a war? Why or why not?
5. How might the United States be different today if there had been no war with Mexico?

6 Compromise Saves the Union

Back in 1819 the proposed admission of Missouri as a state had threatened to break the balance between slave and free states in the Union. The Missouri Compromise of 1820, prepared by Representative Henry Clay of Kentucky, had solved the problem. Missouri came into the Union as a slave state, while Maine was admitted as a free state. In addition, all future slavery in the Louisiana Territory was barred north of latitude 36°30′—the southern boundary of Missouri.

During the Mexican War, the public and Congress discussed the question of whether lands gained from Mexico should be slave or free. Representative David Wilmot from Pennsylvania had one answer: Slavery should be barred from these territories forever. His bitterly debated Wilmot Proviso passed the House twice but failed in the Senate.

Senator John Calhoun of South Carolina expressed another view. He insisted that all the new territories should permit slavery. His proposal was also defeated. Congress could not decide whether or not to allow slavery in New Mexico and California.

Gold was found in California in 1848, and by the next year tens of thousands of settlers had arrived. They wanted the area to become a state. Other settlers were going to New Mexico. Something had to be done. Governments had to be organized, and the question of slavery had to be faced.

Senators Lewis Cass of Michigan and Stephen Douglas of Illinois promoted a solution called popular sovereignty. As they saw it, people living in each territory should decide for or against slavery. This was a democratic way, they said, and Congress would not have to make the choice.

The new President was Zachary Taylor, the winning general in the war with Mexico. Taylor, a slave owner, agreed in late 1849 that popular sovereignty was indeed the answer. He suggested that California and New Mexico write constitutions and apply for admission as states. California did this at once and banned slavery. New Mexico acted more slowly, but in 1850 it too banned slavery.

The problem seemed to have been easily solved. All Congress had to do was to admit California as a free state right away and New Mexico when it was ready. But this was not to be. Some Southern leaders thought that popular sovereignty went too far. The balance of slave and nonslave states in the Senate would be broken. Also, a wider principle was involved. Southern leaders thought that holding slaves was a basic right. Neither Congress nor the government of a territory should interfere with this right. They feared that efforts to regulate slavery might spread, and soon Congress might try to end slavery in the South itself. Abolitionists, on the other hand, protested that popular sovereignty did not go far enough. They wanted slavery to be banned right away in every area.

What could Congress do now? Obviously another approach was needed. In our story we see how Henry Clay of Kentucky, now a U.S. Senator, worked to end the national crisis over slavery. His answer was to compromise—to give something to each side so that both would be happy.

Ask yourself why the South felt so strongly about efforts to bar slavery from the territories. Who gained more from Clay's compromise, the North or the South? Why?

Washington, D.C., 1850

Several days before introducing a bill containing compromises, Henry Clay knocked on the door of the home of Senator Daniel Webster of Massachusetts. Clay knew he had to have Webster's help in getting his bill passed by the Senate.

"This is a surprise," said Webster. "What can I do for you?"

"We have had our differences," replied Clay, wearily sliding into a chair. "But I know we agree that the Union must be saved."

"You are absolutely right," said Webster. "The problem of slavery is tearing our nation apart. We must do everything possible to keep the split from becoming wider."

"I think my compromise bill is the answer."

"Mr. Clay, how can you possibly satisfy both proslavery and anti-slavery people in this argument over the new territories we gained in the Mexican War? Now I wonder whether we would have been better off without those new lands. We must not let the North and South fight a war over those Mexican acres!"

"Don't worry, Mr. Webster. There will be no war if people listen to me. I propose that California be admitted as a free state and the New Mexico territories be organized with no limit on slavery. How does that balance strike you?"

"Isn't that going too far with the proslavery people?"

"No," said Clay. "We know that slavery won't be profitable in the Southwest because the geography and climate make plantations impossible. I tell you, Mr. Webster, slavery will not exist in New Mexico."

"Then why not be honest and say that?"

"By not barring slavery from the Southwest we will please the Southerners and make them feel as if they have won something."

"I see," replied Webster. "Go on."

"We will put an end to the slave trade in the city of Washington but will allow slavery to continue here."

"I wish we could do away with slavery here in the capital of the United States," said Webster. "It makes such a bad impression on visitors."

"One more thing we can offer the South, Mr. Webster, is a stronger fugitive slave law. The federal government can do more to return runaway slaves to their owners."

"Will people like our colleague from New York, William Seward, agree? You know how violent some Northerners can get. And the abolitionists get even more violent than most!"

"Perhaps they won't like it," said Clay, "but after all, the abolitionists are a small minority."

"Small, perhaps, but certainly vocal," said Webster. "Is that your whole package?"

"We'll offer to pay Texas to give up its claim to New Mexican lands, which should quiet both sides in that dispute. Well, what do you think, Mr. Webster?"

"I need more time to think about your plan, Mr. Clay, because I am not sure about every one of your suggestions. But I promise you this: I will support the general idea of your compromise."

The scene shifts to the tense Senate chamber in early March, 1850. A historic debate was under way. Well-known senators from different parts of the country and with different points of view took part. Senator Calhoun was so old and ill that he wrote out his remarks and had a colleague deliver them. Calhoun sat and listened.

WEBSTER. I speak today not as a Massachusetts man, nor as a Northern man, but as an American. I speak for the preservation of the Union.

CALHOUN. How can this Union be saved? Not by crying Union, Union, this glorious Union. You Northerners, you attackers of the South, are always talking about the Union. If you loved the Union, you would not be destroying the Constitution. Never forget that the Constitution was written for both the North and the South. Our property in slaves deserves as much protection as your property in land and factories.

WEBSTER. I don't completely disagree with Senator Calhoun. True, many in the North feel that slavery is wrong, but all should respect the Southern way of life and Southern property. Fugitives should be returned quickly, and Northern legislatures should mind their own business and let the South pass its own laws about its slaves.

CALHOUN. Too many Northerners do not want to mind their own business. The abolitionists are out to destroy the Southern way of life. If they keep up their agitation, they will force the South out of the Union. They will drive us to secession.

WEBSTER. I never want to hear that word secession! The very sound of it fills me with pain and sadness. This Union must never be dissolved—never!

CALHOUN. Then how can the Union be saved? Give the South simple justice without compromises because we have nothing left to surrender. What do we want? We want to take our slaves into the territories, reduce the tariffs that destroy our economy, and preserve the sovereign powers of each state. Is that too much to ask?

SEWARD. Senator Calhoun does not want a compromise, and neither do I. Free Americans must not surrender one foot of land to the slave masters. Gentlemen, examine our Constitution carefully. Nowhere does it say that land in the territories must be held open to slavery. Even if the Constitution said such a thing, we would be duty bound to ignore it. There is a higher law than the Constitution—the law of God. Slavery is an abomination before the Lord!

CLAY. We need not call upon God to make our territories free. All the land taken from Mexico will be free because slavery cannot exist in the geography and climate of that area. Why then should we hurt Southern pride and talk about slavery in New Mexico? Silence about slavery will not hurt the North.

SEWARD. The Senator is wrong. He should go back and study his history books! Slavery can exist anywhere!

CALHOUN. The key point is that we must provide for equal rights in the territories. We must protect the rights of the South. I propose a constitutional amendment to provide for a balance of power between two equal sections, North and South. Each will have a president with a veto. Only when such a division is made will the South be protected from the growing power of the North.

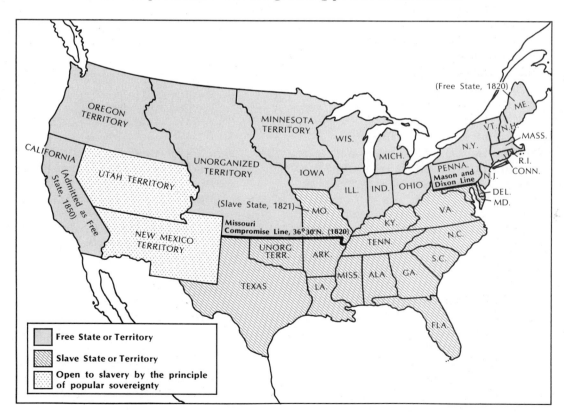

The Compromise of 1850

WEBSTER. The North will never agree to such an amendment.

CALHOUN. We will not submit to tyranny. If you in the North refuse to grant the South its just rights, then the states should separate and go their own ways in a peaceful manner.

WEBSTER. Peaceful secession? Sir, we will never see that miracle. It is impossible for our Constitution and government to disappear quietly. If secession occurs, I see, as plainly as I see the sun in heaven, a war that I cannot describe. No matter how hard we try, we cannot separate peaceably. Our duty is to work to keep our nation together and to preserve the Constitution and all the links that make up the golden chain of our United States of America.

CLAY. Please, gentlemen, we *must* compromise our differences.

POSTSCRIPT

Calhoun died within weeks, but the debate raged for eight months. Finally, the Compromise of 1850 was passed by Congress and signed by the President. It included the following: California was admitted as a free state; the territories of New Mexico and Utah were created with no restrictions on slavery; the Texas boundary was fixed as it exists today; Texas was given $10 million for yielding claims to New Mexico east of the Rio Grande; slave trading was barred from the District of Columbia; the return of runaway slaves was aided by a strict fugitive slave law. For the time being, secession had been avoided. But the tragedy of slavery remained.

Homework Questions

1. How did David Wilmot and John Calhoun differ in their proposals to settle the problem of slavery in the territories?
2. In what way did Clay's Compromise of 1850 try to solve the slavery problem?
3. Why were Clay and Webster willing to place no limit on slavery in the territories?
4. How did Seward and Webster differ about slavery?
5. How did Calhoun and Webster differ about the nature of our Union?

Understanding the Story

A. Write *T* for each statement that is true and *F* for each statement that is false.
   1. The Wilmot Proviso became a law.
   2. Calhoun said that slavery must be permitted in all territories.
   3. Popular sovereignty meant that the people of a territory would decide whether to permit slavery or not.
   4. Almost all Southerners supported the idea of popular sovereignty.
   5. Abolitionists felt that popular sovereignty did not go far enough in blocking slavery.

6. Henry Clay suggested a compromise to solve the problem of slavery in the territories.
7. Daniel Webster refused to support Clay's compromise.
8. Slavery and the slave trade were to be barred from Washington, D.C., by Clay's compromise.

B. Which of these statements might be included in a list of results of the Compromise of 1850?
1. Slavery was abolished in all the territories of the United States.
2. California was admitted as a slave state.
3. New Mexico would make its own decision on slavery.
4. The Fugitive Slave Law was made stronger.
5. Slavery was abolished in the nation's capital.
6. Texas was paid to give up its claim to certain land.
7. The North and South settled all of their differences.
8. Henry Clay's reputation as a compromiser was strengthened.

C. Compromise is often necessary in public and private life. Give an example of a compromise that you made recently or that you know about. Did it prevent a conflict or settle an issue or a question? Explain.

Activities and Inquiries

1. Study the map on page 259. Then choose the term or phrase that best completes each statement.
   a. California was admitted to the Union as a (1) slave state (2) free state (3) both free and slave state.
   b. Utah and New Mexico territories were to be (1) free (2) slave (3) open to slavery by popular vote.
   c. The Missouri Compromise Line of 36° 30′ extended as far west as (1) New Mexico Territory (2) the Pacific Ocean (3) Oregon Territory.
   d. The Mason-Dixon Line forms the border between (1) Pennsylvania and Maryland (2) Kentucky and Indiana (3) Missouri and Iowa.
   e. Oregon and Minnesota territories were (1) open to slavery (2) slave (3) free.
2. Read the story again. Write down Webster's strongest argument. Why does this argument impress you?
3. Now write down Calhoun's strongest argument. Why does this argument impress you?
4. How would Calhoun answer Webster's argument?
5. How would Webster answer Calhoun's argument?
6. Would you say Henry Clay's ideas were closer to Calhoun's or to Webster's? Explain.

7 A Southerner Defends His Honor

The Compromise of 1850 brought about a truce between North and South that lasted for four years. The truce broke down during debate over the organization of the Nebraska Territory in 1854. Because the area was north of the Missouri Compromise line of 36°30', many expected it to be free. But most Southerners objected strongly. Congress, led by Senator Stephen A. Douglas of Illinois, decided to divide the area into two sections, Nebraska and Kansas. Whether slavery should exist there was to be left up to the people to decide for themselves through popular sovereignty. By passing the Kansas-Nebraska Act, Congress in effect repealed the Missouri Compromise.

Because Nebraska bordered on free territory, it was not expected to allow slavery. Kansas, however, bordered on the slave state of Missouri. As both anti- and proslavery people pushed into the territory, debate over slavery turned violent. The territory soon became known as "Bleeding Kansas."

Since 1850 feelings in Congress about slavery had grown stronger. Members of Congress traded insults and accusations and lost their tempers more often. A number of lawmakers carried guns.

Our story deals with an act of violence in Congress sparked by a speech about the struggle in Kansas. Words seemed to be giving way to direct action.

Ask yourself who was the "hero" of the story and who was the "villain." Why did Charles Sumner use such strong language? Why did Preston Brooks attack him?

Washington, D.C., 1856

I am Preston Brooks, a congressman from the state of South Carolina. A quiet man, I do my job and mind my own business. Of course, I speak for the slave owners because slavery is part of the Southern way of life.

I do not aim to upset my colleagues in Congress. I want our Union to prosper. I believe in following a middle road.

I've never considered myself a fancy talker. I suppose that many congressmen think I am just plain dull. Once, I thought I would change my image and do something to rattle their brains. I proposed that congressmen check their guns before entering the House. They laughed but did not act on my suggestion.

Only a very few things really upset me. I love my family and state. I will do almost anything to protect their honor. And, yes, I hate abolitionists! Those fanatics must be stopped, or they will destroy the Union.

It was Senator Charles Sumner from Massachusetts who drove me to forceful action. I had to act to avenge his insults against my family and my state. That Sumner, that wretched abolitionist—his words are foul and coarse. Every syllable is used to slap and smear. He insults everyone who does not agree with him.

How did it all happen? One day I heard that Sumner was going to make a speech about "Bleeding Kansas." I walked to the Senate chamber to hear what he had to say. Of course, Kansas was "bleeding." Those evil abolitionists were killing slave owners, but that was all right with Sumner. He wanted Kansas to be free—no matter what the cost.

Sumner spoke again and again of "The Crime Against Kansas." He said it would be a crime to admit Kansas to the Union as a slave state. I say it would be a crime to throw slave owners out of Kansas!

Thinking Sumner's speech was almost finished, I was ready to leave when I heard the name of my Uncle Andrew (Andrew Butler, U.S. Senator from South Carolina). Sumner said:

"Senator Butler is a fanatic and a zealot. He is so confused that no one understands what he is saying! A foul-mouthed liar, Butler will say anything to prove a point. He repeats every lie he hears about Kansas! In fact, every time he opens his mouth, a lie flies out. . . . He is a lover of slavery and will do anything to protect his love!"

I was shocked. I had never heard such insults about anyone—much less my old Uncle Andrew, who was back home in South Carolina. Then Sumner brought up South Carolina.

"Do you know that Butler once dared to compare his slave state of South Carolina to the free territory of Kansas? How can you compare a tyranny with a free land? Everyone knows what South Carolina is like. If we erased the history of South Carolina from its beginnings, what would we lose? Nothing, absolutely nothing!"

As I walked slowly out of the Senate chamber, I knew I would have to act to avenge the insults to my family and my state. Two days later, I waited for Sumner outside the Senate door. Then, thinking I might have missed him, I walked into the Senate chamber. There was the villain, seated at his desk. I waited until the other senators had gone. Only Senator Sumner was left in the room. This was my chance to do what I had to do.

He was writing at his desk with his head bent very low, near the paper. He did not know I was in the room until I walked over and spoke to him. "Mr. Sumner." He raised his head. I said, "I heard your speech, and I read it twice. You have insulted South Carolina and Senator Butler!"

"Senator Sumner, you've insulted South Carolina and Senator Butler."

Thinking he was going to stand up, I tapped him lightly with my cane. He threw out his arms to protect his head. Then I let him have it! I hit him again and again, even after the head of my cane broke off. He was battered and bleeding before other senators came in and made me stop.

POSTSCRIPT

Public meetings were held in almost every Northern city to protest the attack. Brooks was called a coward because he had beaten a defenseless man. His action was called a crime against freedom of speech as well as against Sumner. What can you expect? Northerners asked. After all, they said, Brooks was a product of the slave system. He is an animal, playing with deadly weapons!

In his own way, Sumner had shed his blood for Kansas. Almost one million copies of his speech on "The Crime Against Kansas" were given out.

In the South, Brooks was treated as a hero. His followers gave him a new cane with a gold head. Most Southern newspapers applauded the beating, although a few criticized Brooks for hitting a man seated at his desk.

In the House of Representatives, an attempt to expel Brooks failed. A federal court fined him $300 for the assault.

Sumner stayed away from the Senate for three and a half years. His empty desk was a constant reminder of the attack and his views. Where would it all end? people kept asking. Was violence going to be the only way to solve the problems between the North and the South?

Homework Questions

1. What did Congress do about slavery in the Nebraska Territory in 1854?
2. Why did people say that Kansas was "bleeding"?
3. Why did Sumner's speech anger Brooks?
4. How did Brooks justify his attack on Sumner?
5. Why was Brooks considered a hero in the South and a villain in the North?

Understanding the Story

A. Match each item in Column *A* with its description in Column *B*.

Column A

1. Preston Brooks
2. Bleeding Kansas
3. Charles Sumner
4. "The Crime Against Kansas"
5. Andrew Butler
6. Abolitionist

Column B

a. Representative from South Carolina
b. Senator from South Carolina
c. Title of Sumner's speech
d. Abolitionist Northern senator
e. Common term for one territory
f. Person who strongly opposed slavery

B. Write *T* for each statement that is true, *F* for each statement that is false, and *N* for each statement that is not mentioned in the chapter.
1. Nebraska Territory was north of the Missouri Compromise line.
2. Congress appointed governors for Kansas and Nebraska.
3. Under the Kansas-Nebraska Act, Nebraska was to be a slave state while Kansas was to be free.
4. Speeches in the Senate were printed in newspapers.
5. Some senators and representatives carried guns.
6. Brooks wanted to defend the honor of his state.
7. Sumner supported slavery.
8. President Pierce was upset about the beating of Sumner.

C. People in public life usually keep in mind some code of honor. In what ways might today's code of honor differ from that followed in the 1850's? Who do you think violated the code: Sumner? Brooks? Both? How might a violation of the code of honor be punished today?

Activities and Inquiries

1. Look at the drawing on page 264 and answer the following questions.
   a. How have South Carolina and Senator Butler been insulted?
   b. In what other way could Brooks have shown his anger toward Sumner?
   c. What effect will the attack have on North-South relations?
2. Why did the issue of slavery arouse such violent feelings?
3. Brooks called himself a gentleman. How should a gentleman act? Why, in your opinion, did the House fail to expel Brooks?
4. Assume that you are a Southerner. Write a letter to the editor of a Northern newspaper about the way it handled the account of the attack.
5. Assume that you are a Northerner. Write a letter to the editor of a Southern newspaper about the way it handled the account of the attack.

8 John Brown: God's Angry Man

For years many Southerners had feared the possibility of slave uprisings. To prevent any from occurring, strict rules known as Black Codes regulated slave actions. Slaves could not travel from place to place without special permission or get together for any meetings except Sunday church services. Teaching slaves to read and write was a crime.

Two revolts, one in 1822 and one in 1831, sent a shudder of fear through Southern whites. Each of the uprisings involved more than a hundred blacks. The first, planned and led by Denmark Vesey of Charleston, South Carolina, was betrayed before it gathered strength. The second took place in Virginia. Nat Turner and his followers killed some 60 whites before armed whites stopped the uprising.

After these revolts, any hint that slaves might act against whites caused great anxiety. This was one reason why Southerners opposed the abolitionists so strongly.

One man in particular caused Southerners to shudder. That person was John Brown. He and several of his sons first attracted public attention when they murdered a number of proslavery people in Kansas in 1856.

Willing to kill and be killed for the antislavery cause, John Brown felt that he had to do something for all the slaves. He was certain that slavery was against God's will. He had no hesitation about trying to end slavery through violence, and a few prominent abolitionists gave him support. As his point of attack, he chose the town of Harpers Ferry, Virginia (now Harpers Ferry, West Virginia). Located on a narrow neck of land between the Shenandoah and Potomac rivers, it was less than 60 miles from Washington, D.C. It also contained a federal arsenal (storehouse of weapons).

In our story, John Brown is ready to carry out his plan to capture Harpers Ferry, get weapons, and free slaves. When this was done, he planned to capture other Southern towns and free more slaves—until all slaves were freed.

See if you understand why Brown attacked Harpers Ferry rather than some other town. What kind of a person was John Brown? Why did he think his plan would succeed?

October 16, 1859

Our story begins in a broken-down farmhouse about seven miles from Harpers Ferry, on the Maryland side of the Potomac River. Brown is talking with his sons and other followers.

JOHN BROWN. Men, we march tonight. At last our time has come!

OLIVER BROWN. Do you still think that 18 of us can capture and hold Harpers Ferry?

JOHN BROWN. Absolutely! There are no federal troops in Harpers Ferry, so it will take the government days to bring in soldiers.

JOHN COOK. While checking out the town, I found that the weapons storehouse and the rifle works are not guarded. We can just walk in and take them over!

WATSON BROWN. What happens when the militia and the army start to attack us? Eighteen men against thousands. What chance will we have, even if God is on our side?

JOHN KAGI. Let's not worry about the soldiers. They can't shoot straight!

OWEN BROWN. They have guns, haven't they? They'll shoot and they'll kill!

JOHN BROWN. Now listen to me. You have nothing to worry about. If we capture the two bridges into town, the troops will never get into Harpers Ferry.

G. P. TIDD. We won't be able to hold them off for long. There will be too many for us.

JOHN BROWN. I've thought of that, too. We'll take prisoners. The troops won't shoot for fear of killing our captives.

OLIVER BROWN. Suppose they do fire? And, Father, you know they will. We're dead!

JOHN BROWN. Oliver, don't be afraid. We won't have to hold off the troops for very long. Thousands of slaves and white men will soon rush to our side, and we'll have more help than we need. After we use our guns to free all the other slaves in the area, we'll hide in the hills. The soldiers will never find us!

Men, you have a chance to strike a blow for freedom in this slave-cursed land! Kill if you must, but do not shed blood needlessly. Now get your guns—we are moving to the Ferry. This will be the end of slavery!

John Brown climbed into the wagon that carried the weapons and tools. The others, thirteen whites and five blacks, walked behind. East and west of Harpers Ferry, they cut the telegraph lines and guarded the bridges according to plan. In town, Brown's small army captured the watchman at the government buildings. The road to the weapons storehouses and rifle works was now open.

John Brown soon controlled a great quantity of federal guns and ammunition. The prisoners his men took included a great-grand-nephew of George Washington. Shots awakened the town, and soon the outside world knew that something very unusual was taking place in Harpers Ferry.

October 17, 1859

News of the events at Harpers Ferry quickly spread throughout the country. Newspaper headlines told a threatening story: *NEGRO REVOLT AT HARPERS FERRY; VIOLENCE ON THE VIRGINIA BORDER.*

Farmers and soldiers rushed toward the town, trapping the raiders in the rifle works and the weapons storehouse. President Buchanan ordered three artillery companies and one Marine company to Harpers Ferry under the command of Lt. Col. Robert E. Lee. Shocked by the fast reaction to his raid, Brown could not make the decision to escape. Now it was too late. He was surrounded, and his men were being picked off one by one. Retreat became impossible.

JOHN BROWN. I can't understand what went wrong. Thousands should have joined us. What's keeping the freed slaves? Don't they realize that this is their big chance? Where are the white men who hate slavery?

JEREMIAH ANDERSON. They're all afraid, Captain Brown, and unwilling to face enemy bullets. We are all alone.

JOHN BROWN. All right, men, we have plenty of ammunition. Sell your lives dearly!

ANDERSON. There's a soldier coming with a white flag.

JOHN BROWN. Stop firing!

LT. J.E.B. STUART. Open the door! I have a letter from Colonel Lee.

[*John Brown opens the door and aims his rifle at Stuart's head. He takes the letter and reads it.*]

JOHN BROWN. Lee wants me to surrender. He says that no harm will come to me. (*laughs*)

STUART. You will be protected and turned over to the proper authorities.

JOHN BROWN. Thank you very much, Lieutenant. I'm no fool. You know very well that the government will hang me!

STUART. Then you refuse to surrender?

JOHN BROWN. I will surrender this building. But you must allow my men and me to go free.

STUART. Impossible! Colonel Lee will not change his terms.

JOHN BROWN. Then, I would rather die here!

[*Suddenly Stuart moves away from the door and waves his hat. The Marines attack, tear down the door, and bayonet two of the raiders.*]

PRISONER. That's John Brown. Grab him! Kill him!

LT. ISRAEL GREEN. I'll take care of him.

[*Slashes at Brown with his sword, then beats him about the head with the sword handle until Brown falls to the floor. The fighting is over.*]

COL. LEE. Green, call the doctor to look at Brown's wounds. He will be put on trial. He must be punished as a lesson to others who might try to pit race against race and destroy our way of life.

POSTSCRIPT

Many in both South and North looked upon John Brown and his followers as part of a treasonous plot to overthrow slavery. Leaders of all major political parties condemned Brown's actions. But great numbers of Northern abolitionists thought that Brown was a hero because he was willing to die for the cause of black freedom.

John Brown's conduct during his trial impressed many people, including some who did not sympathize with his ideas. Brown refused to plead insanity because he thought he knew what he was doing. Insisting that the raid was entirely his idea, he would not name the people who had helped him. He maintained that he, alone, was responsible for the events at Harpers Ferry.

On December 2, 1859, Brown was hanged for slave rebellion, murder, and treason against the state of Virginia. Six of his little band were also hanged. Only two of the 18 raiders escaped death. During the fighting, seven townspeople had been killed and ten wounded. Not one of Brown's prisoners had been harmed.

John Brown and his attack on Harpers Ferry would not be forgotten. During the Civil War, Northern troops marched into battle singing about him: "John Brown's body lies a-mouldering in the grave, his soul is marching on."

Homework Questions

1. Why do you suppose John Brown selected Harpers Ferry as the place for his attack on slavery?
2. What caused John Brown to think his plan would succeed?
3. How did the nation and government react to John Brown's raid?
4. Why was John Brown disappointed with the response of slaves and abolitionists?
5. Do you think John Brown should be looked upon as a hero or as a villain? Why?

Understanding the Story

A. Write *F* for each statement that is a fact and *O* for each statement that is an opinion.
   1. John Brown went too far.
   2. John Brown planned to capture Harpers Ferry.
   3. John Brown should not have tried to free the slaves.
   4. John Brown was willing to die for his cause.
   5. John Brown thought that thousands of slaves would join him.
   6. President Buchanan should not have sent troops to Harpers Ferry.

7. Brown and his men could not escape from Harpers Ferry.
8. Many Northern abolitionists thought that Brown was a hero.

B. List the numbers of the statements that John Brown made or might have made.
1. The troops will never get to Harpers Ferry.
2. We can't defeat the federal troops.
3. Thousands of slaves and whites will help us.
4. This will be the end of slavery.
5. We will free no more than 100 slaves.
6. We must not kill anyone.
7. I can't understand what went wrong.
8. The government will not harm me if I surrender.

C. John Brown did not hesitate to break laws he thought were evil. Name someone in recent times who has broken laws to promote a cause. Do you think such an approach can be justified? Why or why not?

Activities and Inquiries

1. You want to produce a television film about John Brown. What scenes will you include in the picture?
2. You are an abolitionist who supports John Brown's raid. Write a letter telling a friend about your opinions.
3. You are Lt. Col. Robert E. Lee. Write a letter to a friend telling your opinion of John Brown.
4. If you had been the judge at John Brown's trial, would you have ordered him hanged? Why or why not?
5. Find in the library the poem *John Brown's Body* by Stephen Vincent Benét. After reading it, write a short report describing Benét's feelings about Brown.

9 Can a Civil War Be Avoided?

John Brown's raid came at a dangerous time. North and South had been drifting apart. Political moods were shifting, and an important presidential election was coming up in 1860.

A new political party had appeared on the scene and was gathering strength in the North. This was the Republican Party, organized in 1854. It brought together groups that opposed the spread of slavery beyond the area where it already existed. The party also supported tariffs and the use of federal money to build roads, waterways, and railroads.

Unlike the abolitionists, the Republicans did not favor immediate abolition of slavery in the South. The party's leaders felt that such a step would go against the Constitution and might cause the Union to split in two. Still, most white Southerners saw little difference between Republicans and abolitionists.

A rising figure in the Republican Party was Abraham Lincoln of Illinois. Born in a log cabin on the Kentucky frontier, Lincoln was a lawyer and a self-educated man. He had belonged to the Whig Party and served a term in Congress during the Mexican War. Later he had narrowly missed election to the Senate. In 1856 he became a Republican and was considered as a possible Republican candidate for Vice President.

Lincoln was an outspoken critic of slavery, but he was no abolitionist. He had gained wide attention in 1858 when Republicans chose him to run for U.S. Senator from Illinois. Lincoln's opponent was Stephen A. Douglas, a nationally known leader of the Democratic Party. Lincoln challenged Douglas to a series of debates. In the debates, Lincoln argued that slavery was a moral evil. He believed that it would die a natural death if it could be stopped from spreading into new territories and states. Douglas answered, saying that slavery was not a moral issue at all but a question of practical politics. It was more important to preserve the Union, said Douglas, than to end slavery. In the end, Douglas won the election.

Both Lincoln and Douglas were widely hated in the South. Lincoln had condemned John Brown's raids in 1859 and called Brown a criminal. Even so, most white Southerners saw Lincoln as an abolitionist in disguise. Douglas had tried to please moderate Southern leaders by supporting the doctrine of popular sovereignty. But he made enemies in the South by suggesting that the doctrine might be a way to block the spread of slavery.

Douglas hoped that the Democrats would nominate him for the Presidency in 1860. But his views caused such disagreement that the party split in two. Northern Democrats chose Douglas, while Southern Democrats chose John C. Breckenridge of Kentucky to be their candidate. The Republicans, meanwhile, picked Lincoln. A fourth group, the Constitutional Union Party, unhappy with the other three, chose John Bell of Tennessee as its candidate.

The election campaign showed how deeply the nation was divided. Lincoln's support came almost entirely from the North. Many Southerners vowed that if Lincoln won, their section would secede (withdraw) from the Union. They were afraid that the South would have little influence in a Lincoln government and that Northern interests alone would count.

Although Lincoln received only 40 percent of the popular vote, he won the election by getting a majority of the electoral votes. Within weeks after the November, 1860, election, Southern states began to secede. By March 4, 1861, when Lincoln was inaugurated (took office) as President, seven states had left the Union.

By that time, the seceding states had joined to form the Confederate States of America. They had held a convention, written a constitution, and elected Jefferson Davis of Mississippi to be their president. The Confederate states began taking control of federal property within their borders—post offices, customs offices, even forts.

In our story, President Lincoln thinks about how he should handle such Southern takeovers. In particular he is concerned about Fort Sumter, which guarded the harbor of Charleston, South Carolina. Leaders of South Carolina and the Confederacy argued that the island fort was now state property and that U.S. soldiers must leave. Lincoln disagreed. But would he fight to defend the fort?

Ask yourself what questions Lincoln had to take into account in deciding what to do. Did he make the right decision? If he had acted differently, could the Civil War have been avoided?

Washington, D.C., March, 1861

John Hay, President Abraham Lincoln's secretary, approached the President, who was reading at his desk.

"Mr. Lincoln, it's almost 11 o'clock. You've had a long day. Perhaps you could leave those papers for tomorrow."

"You're right, John. But I get so little time to be alone during the day. I'm finding that a President's work is never done."

"We should keep those office seekers away from you. Why do you have to waste your days with those people?"

Lincoln sighed. "They are members of our party, John. I suppose every Republican thinks he deserves a government job. Each one tells me how hard he worked for my election."

"Then there are all those people with advice about the South. I don't see how you can live through a day with all these interruptions."

"You're young, John. You must learn to be more patient. Sometimes problems have a way of solving themselves. I listen to everyone. Who knows? One may have the answer!"

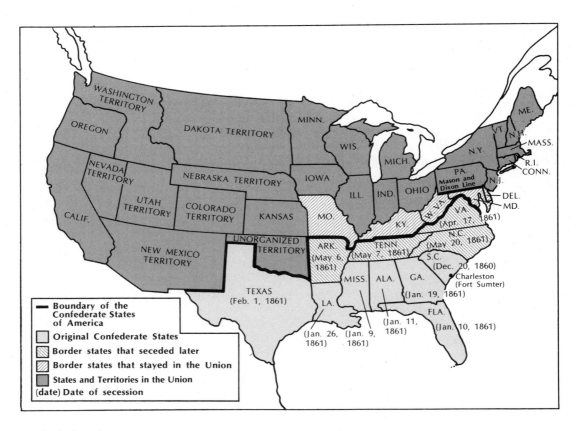

A Divided Nation, 1861

"But what can you do?" asked John Hay. "Seven states have seceded from the Union. Can you stop the other eight slave states from joining them? And what will you do about Fort Sumter?"

"Hold on, John, one question at a time," said President Lincoln with a chuckle. "You skipped the first question. How do we get the seven seceding states back into the Union?"

"Have you thought of a way?"

"Not yet, but I haven't stopped trying. You remember what I told them about slavery in my inaugural address a few weeks ago?"

"Yes, sir. You told them you would not interfere with slavery in the slave states. They know you are not an abolitionist, so why are they afraid of you? Why did they leave the Union as soon as you were elected?"

"Well," said Lincoln thoughtfully, "I've said that slavery must go no farther. I don't care whether new territories are north or south of the Missouri Compromise line. They must be free! Southern slave owners think slavery will die if it can't expand. And I think they are right."

"I see. So you think they fear for slavery's survival."

"I am the first President of the United States who does not believe that slavery belongs everywhere in this nation," said Lincoln. "Seven states did not accept me as their President, so they picked themselves up and left the other 27 states."

"But what right do they have to do that?"

"None, John, none. They have no right to secede. They claim that the Union is nothing more than a voluntary compact among independent states. Each state joined of its own accord, they say, and each can leave whenever it wishes. But the Union is a whole and must remain whole. Federal laws and the Constitution make no provision for secession. What the slave states are doing is illegal and must be resisted or else the laws of our nation will count as nothing."

"But how can the seceding states be stopped? If you use military force against them, the other eight slave states may join them and we shall have war. Surely a civil war would be a disaster for us all."

"Absolutely, John. I pray with all my heart that war may be avoided. The best way to avoid war, I believe, is to keep any more states from joining the seven that have seceded. Those fire-eaters, the rebels in the seceding states, must see that their example will not be followed. Perhaps then they will realize the folly of their ways."

"That is easier said than done, Mr. President. Soon you must make a decision about Fort Sumter."

"I know, John," the President sighed. "If only I had more time."

A few days later, the President holds a meeting with his cabinet.

"Gentlemen, Fort Sumter is surrounded by Southern ships and guns," said President Lincoln. "Our troops in the fort are cut off and soon will run out of food. What shall we do? We must not seem to be the ones to begin an attack, lest we drive the rest of the slave states into secession. Yet we must show the people that we mean to keep the Union together. We cannot give up such an important federal fort."

General Winfield Scott, the chief of staff, spoke up. "Mr. President, we no longer have a choice. The South has had too much time to add to its forces around Fort Sumter. I say withdraw the men. We must face the facts. It would take at least 25,000 men to batter our way through to the fort, and thousands would die in a bloody battle."

"Then you don't think we can hold the fort?" asked the President.

"No, sir," replied Scott. "We cannot."

President Lincoln frowned. "There must be a way. When I took office a few short weeks ago, I promised to hold on to federal property in the South. If we yield the fort, I will have gone back on my word."

Gideon Welles, the secretary of the navy, spoke up. "Mr. President, Southern defenses are indeed strong. But small boats might be able to slip by them under cover of darkness. If all goes well, we could reinforce Fort Sumter before the South knew what was happening."

Lincoln shook his head. "We've already considered that plan. It's risky—very risky. If the boats are fired on, our men will be hopelessly outnumbered. Many lives will be lost."

After a few moments of thought, a firm resolve settled over the President's face. "I believe there may be a way, after all," he said. "I will send an unarmed supply ship to the fort. And I will notify the governor of South Carolina in advance. If we must fight, we will do so, but we will not fire the first shots. If the South fires on our unarmed ship, all will know that an unwanted war has been forced upon us."

POSTSCRIPT

Lincoln's plan was carried out. But the Southern leaders did not sit idly by. In their eyes, the North had forced the issue and was attacking. As they saw it, the South wanted only to be allowed to go its own way in peace. It had a perfect right to take possession of federal property that lay within its borders.

The South demanded that the troops in Fort Sumter surrender at once, before the supply ship arrived. Major Robert Anderson, the fort's commander, refused. Anderson said, "Do not batter the fort to pieces around us. We will be starved out in a few days."

But the South did not wait. At 4:30 A.M., April 12, 1861, its guns went into action against the fort. The Civil War had begun. Although the fort was badly damaged, no one was killed. The next day, Major Anderson and his men surrendered. They had lived through the ordeal of shot and flame, but what would happen to the Union?

Homework Questions

1. Why might Lincoln be called the "President of the North"?
2. Why did seven Southern states secede after Lincoln was elected?
3. How did Lincoln respond to the South's claim to a right of secession?
4. Why did Lincoln spend so much time with office seekers?
5. What made Fort Sumter a focus of tension?
6. Why did Lincoln think that Fort Sumter had to be supplied?

Understanding the Story

A. Write T for each statement that is true and F for each statement that is false.
   1. The Southern Democrats ran Stephen A. Douglas for President in 1860.
   2. Lincoln had only one opponent in the 1860 presidential election.
   3. Lincoln was elected President in 1860.
   4. Most Southerners voted for Lincoln.
   5. All Southern states stayed in the Union after Lincoln's election.
   6. John Hay thought office seekers wasted Lincoln's time.
   7. Lincoln was an abolitionist.
   8. Lincoln was unwilling to surrender Fort Sumter without a fight.

B. Number the following events in the order in which they took place.
   1. Lincoln is elected President.
   2. Southern troops attack Fort Sumter.
   3. John Brown attacks Harpers Ferry.
   4. Lincoln sends a supply ship to Fort Sumter.
   5. John Brown is hanged.
   6. Fort Sumter is surrendered.
   7. Lincoln is inaugurated.
   8. Seven Southern states secede.

C. Imagine you are Jefferson Davis, president of the Confederacy. Would you allow federal forces to resupply Fort Sumter? Why or why not?

Activities and Inquiries

1. Study the map on page 272. Then choose the term or phrase that best completes each statement.
   a. Two free states were (1) Pennsylvania (Pa.) and Ohio (2) Arkansas (Ark.) and Virginia (Va.) (3) Texas and Florida (Fla.).
   b. Two border states that did not secede were (1) Maryland (Md.) and Tennessee (Tenn.) (2) West Virginia (W. Va.) and Virginia (Va.) (3) Maryland (Md.) and Missouri (Mo.).
   c. Two border states that did secede from the union were (1) Tennessee (Tenn.) and Kentucky (Ky.) (2) Tennessee (Tenn.) and Arkansas (Ark.) (3) Kentucky (Ky.) and Virginia (Va.).
   d. An original Confederate state was (1) Georgia (Ga.) (2) Kansas (3) Missouri (Mo.).
   e. By June, 1861, the number of states in the Confederacy was (1) sixteen (2) seven (3) eleven.
2. Imagine that you are a Northern member of Congress. What arguments would you use to persuade Lincoln to take action against the South?
3. Imagine that you are a Southern member of Congress. What arguments would you use to persuade Lincoln to give in to the South?
4. Lincoln has decided to ask Congress for a declaration of war. Suppose you are writing speeches for Lincoln. Prepare the speech that Lincoln will make to Congress and the American people.
5. What do you think might have happened if the South had been allowed to secede peacefully?

10 The Growth of the Constitution: The Dred Scott Case

As the strains on the Union grew during the 1850's, an explosive case reached the U.S. Supreme Court. It concerned a black man named Dred Scott—born a slave and now claiming his freedom.

The issues in the case went far beyond the liberty of a single man. They touched on many of the points that Congress had been debating for decades. By its ruling, the Court might settle once and for all some of the most troubling problems concerning slavery. Many people hoped that a solution could be found so easily.

In our story, Chief Justice Roger Taney is discussing the case with Justice Benjamin Curtis. Taney was a Maryland Democrat who had had a distinguished career of more than 20 years as Chief Justice. Curtis was a Massachusetts Whig who was appointed to the Supreme Court in 1851.

Do you agree with Taney or Curtis? Why did the Dred Scott decision please some people and anger others?

Washington, D.C., February, 1857

"Come now," said Taney with annoyance, "this is a very simple case. Why can't you understand my thinking? You and I have argued about this Dred Scott case long enough."

"Let's review the facts once again," said Curtis. "Perhaps we'll find something we can agree on."

"All right," replied Taney. "Here they are: Scott is a slave. His master took him from a slave state to a free state. Later, Scott was taken to what is now Minnesota Territory. And, finally, he was returned to the slave state of Missouri."

"You're right," said Curtis. "It *is* very simple. Scott was taken to Minnesota—which is a *free territory*. Because Congress barred slavery in that area, Scott was free under federal law the moment he crossed the border. That's it! He's free! Case closed."

"You're forgetting that slaves are property," replied Taney. "A man can take his property with him wherever he goes. He doesn't lose his property because he enters a so-called free territory. Surely, you can see, Curtis, that would be unfair."

"Unfair?" snapped Curtis. "Unfair to whom? You're talking about a human being—not a horse and wagon. No matter what you say, slaves are people with rights and feelings. I repeat, Taney, in 1820 Congress barred slavery from the northern parts of the Louisiana Purchase, and free territory makes free people."

"There is no such thing as 'free' territory," said Taney.

"Now, you're going too far. Do you deny that Congress has the power to make laws for our territories? The Constitution says—"

"The Constitution says a lot of things, Curtis. More important, look at the Fifth Amendment: 'no person shall be . . . deprived of . . . property. . . .' I don't know what it means to you. To me, it means that Dred Scott, or any other property, belongs to his owner unless the owner sells or gives the property away. Congress can't take it away from the owner."

"Not so," answered Curtis. "You're saying that the Congress cannot bar slavery anywhere in this nation. Therefore, there will be no free states or free territories. You're turning the United States into one big slave state!"

"Not so fast, Curtis. You know very well that each state may decide for itself whether it will have slavery. But a territory is not a state—a territory belongs to all Americans. It should be clear to you that Congress cannot bar slavery from the territories."

"But Congress has barred slavery from the territories at least eight times—starting with the very first Congress. Now you're saying that the Missouri Compromise and all these laws were mistakes!"

"Since you mention the Missouri Compromise in particular, let's limit our discussion to that one law of Congress. It goes against the Constitution. Therefore, the Missouri Compromise of 1820 must be erased from the law books!"

"The Missouri Compromise has already been repealed by the Kansas-Nebraska Act of 1854. The Missouri Compromise is no longer on the books."

"No matter!" said Taney. "I say it's unconstitutional."

"Then what happens to Dred Scott?" asked Curtis.

"Forget about Scott," answered Taney. "Slaves are not citizens and never can be—even if they are freed. They have no rights in the courts, so Scott shouldn't have been allowed to sue in the first place. The case should have been thrown out."

POSTSCRIPT

On March 6, 1857, the Court made its decision public. Chief Justice Taney's ideas carried the day. The Missouri Compromise was unconstitutional. Slaves (and former slaves and their descendants) were not citizens and could not sue. Dred Scott must remain a slave.

Southern whites were happy with the decision. In their view, the Court had settled once and for all a key issue—Congress *could not* block slavery in the territories. Even popular sovereignty, in this view, was now unconstitutional.

But blacks and many Northern whites were outraged. Abolitionists resolved to work harder to end slavery, and members of the Underground Railroad increased their efforts to help more slaves escape. Abolitionists posted notices describing the slave catchers who came to Northern cities looking for runaway slaves. Some abolitionists pointed out these Southerners in streetcars and stores, making it difficult for the slave catchers to operate.

Prominent lawyers were hired to defend fugitives. Abolitionist leader Wendell Phillips told a cheering Boston audience, "Law or no law, Constitution or no Constitution, humanity shall be paramount."

Homework Questions

1. What were the key issues in the Dred Scott case?
2. Why did Justice Benjamin Curtis believe that Dred Scott should be free?
3. Why did Chief Justice Roger Taney maintain that there could not be a "free" territory?
4. What did Taney think of the Missouri Compromise?
5. Would you say the Dred Scott decision settled the issue of slavery? Why or why not?

Understanding the Story

A. List the numbers of the statements that are true.
   1. Dred Scott was a slave.
   2. Dred Scott asked to be set free.
   3. The Missouri Compromise was declared unconstitutional in 1850.
   4. Scott had been taken by his master to the Minnesota Territory.
   5. A territory is a state.
   6. Taney said that slavery cannot be barred from United States territories.
   7. The majority of the Supreme Court agreed with Justice Curtis.
   8. The Court decided that Dred Scott had the right to sue for his freedom.

B. Write *T* for each statement that Taney made or might have made and *C* for each statement that Curtis made or might have made.
   1. Dred Scott should be free.
   2. Slaves are property.
   3. People in a free territory are free.
   4. There is no such thing as free territory.
   5. Slaves have no rights in the courts.
   6. Slaves are people with rights and feelings.
   7. The Missouri Compromise is unconstitutional.
   8. The Missouri Compromise has already been repealed.

C. Assume that the majority of the Supreme Court had agreed with Justice Curtis's opinion that Dred Scott was a free man. In your opinion, would this decision have solved the problems between the North and South and prevented the Civil War? Explain.

Activities and Inquiries

1. Imagine that you are Dred Scott's lawyer and that the Supreme Court is still hearing arguments on the case. List the main points you will present to the Supreme Court.
2. Imagine that you are a lawyer arguing against Dred Scott. What points will you make?
3. Imagine that you are able to ask Dred Scott how he feels about being treated like property. Write down what you think he will tell you.
4. Imagine that you are able to ask Dred Scott's owner about Scott's court suit. What do you think the owner's feelings will be?
5. Assume that you are an abolitionist who has just heard about the decision in the Dred Scott case. Prepare a talk to an audience describing what you (and they) should do to overcome the effects of the decision.

Who Built America?

Henry David Thoreau

MR. MILLER. Robert, you've made an interesting choice for your report.

ROBERT. Yes, I'm going to talk about Henry David Thoreau, a 19th-century writer, born in New England, of French descent. I think he would be popular if he were alive today.

RICARDO. How is that possible?

ROBERT. Thoreau was a free spirit. He believed that you should do what you want to do—as long as you don't hurt anyone else. Be different from others, he said, but more important, be yourself. He wouldn't do something merely because others were doing it or because it was required.

HANS. Give us some examples of what he did.

ROBERT. Okay. The rules in the Harvard University Chapel called for wearing a black coat. Thoreau wore a green coat.

HANS. I see; he didn't like uniforms.

ROBERT. Exactly. Why should everyone look alike? Another time, while he was a teacher, the school authorities wanted him to whip pupils who wouldn't obey. He refused, but the school officials insisted. One day, he flogged a dozen students for no apparent reason. Then he walked out of the classroom, resigned his job, and never went back to teaching school!

CARLA. Why did he do that?

ROBERT. He was trying to show how stupid it was to whip schoolchildren.

CASIMIR. Sounds silly. It didn't end flogging in that school, did it?

ROBERT. No, but Thoreau made his protest against something that he disliked.

TOM. How did he get along with other people?

ROBERT. He had a few friends. But he did like to be alone a good deal. In fact, he lived alone for two years in a cabin he built himself on the shore of Walden Pond near Concord, Massachusetts.

Being alone gave him time to think and write. You might want to read all about his experiences in his book *Walden*. Thoreau's writings and actions tell us a lot about America before the Civil War. He disliked some of the things our country was doing and wasn't afraid to express himself. Thoreau supported the abolition of slavery and did everything he could to end the horror. He hid runaway slaves, was part of the Underground Railroad, and openly supported John Brown's raid.

JUAN. Did he have anything to say about war?

ROBERT. He thought of himself as a man of peace. He opposed the Mexican War and went to jail rather than pay a tax to his state of Massachusetts because it supported the war. He wrote about this experience in an essay titled "Civil Disobedience."

SAM. How would Thoreau's going to jail end the war?

ROBERT. It wouldn't, but it was his way of protesting something he hated.

ROSA. What a waste!

ROBERT. Thoreau's going to jail for his beliefs and his ideas about nonviolent protest have never been forgotten. Mahatma Gandhi, a leader of the independence movement in India, said he got his ideas for protesting British rule from Thoreau. In our country, Thoreau's ideas had a great influence on Martin Luther King, Jr., and the civil rights movement in the 1960's.

JOSEPHINE. I learned something from Thoreau.

ROBERT. What's that?

JOSEPHINE. It's important to be an individual and to stand up for what you believe.

MR. MILLER. Isn't that what America is all about? To make our democracy work, we must make our opinions known.

RICARDO. I wonder how Thoreau would react to that idea?

ROBERT. I think he'd say that we don't speak out enough and that we let others do our thinking for us.

"You know, Mr. Miller, I didn't expect to see so much conflict in this unit."

"What do you mean?"

"Slaves, abolitionists, members of Congress, and women who wanted to vote were being pushed around and hurt. Look at that business with Bleeding Kansas. And let's not forget John Brown at Harpers Ferry!"

"You've raised a good point, Jack. What was the one thing that seemed to upset people the most in both North and South?"

Jack thought for a while. "I guess inequality upset people as much as anything. Activist women were searching for equal rights with men. Abolitionists were fighting for freedom and equality for blacks. And white Southerners felt outnumbered by Northerners. They no longer felt equal within the Union, and they thought Northerners looked down on them."

"Why would people in the North do that?"

"Well, the South had a slave society," answered Jack. "Some Northerners felt that the Southern way of life was built with the work of the slaves."

"Excellent, Jack. What do you mean when you say Southerners felt outnumbered?"

"For many years, North and South had an equal number of U.S. Senators. The problem was how to keep it that way."

"How did they try to solve that problem?" asked Mr. Miller.

"They compromised. Each side gave a little. Every time a free state was admitted to the Union, a slave state would be let in. But it became hard to keep a balance. Soon there was more free than slave territory."

"Then a clash could be avoided only if they continued to compromise?" asked Mr. Miller.

"That's right, Mr. Miller. But compromises never seemed to last. They solved today's problem but not tomorrow's. Each crisis required a new agreement. For instance, when the United States went to war with Mexico, it picked up a lot of territory and a big headache. Should the land be free or slave? The Compromise of 1850 might have been the answer, but it lasted for only four years."

"Wasn't popular sovereignty a solution?" asked Mr. Miller.

"Stephen Douglas thought it was," replied Jack. "But the Dred Scott decision put an end to that idea by ruling that slavery could not be kept out of a territory!"

"Slavery was pulling North and South further and further apart."

"With the shelling of Fort Sumter, the bonds between the two sections snapped apart."

"Yes, they did," Mr. Miller agreed. "Now let's look at the war that almost destroyed our nation."

The Civil War and Reconstruction

"I'm almost afraid to read this unit, Mr. Miller."

"I thought you couldn't wait to get to the Civil War, Jack."

"That's true, then I started thinking what it must have meant to be in a civil war."

"Go on. Explain what you mean."

"Well, all wars are horrible, but a war between people of the same country is especially terrible. The person a soldier might be shooting at could be a relative or a friend. The land on which battles are fought might belong to you or someone you know. It's a personal kind of fight with deep feelings of hate on both sides. What could the North and South have hoped to gain from all of the killings?"

"This unit should answer your questions," answered Mr. Miller.

"And what happens to the losing side?"

"We'll find out. We'll take a look at plans for the Reconstruction, the rebuilding, of the South."

1 Save the Union or Free the Slaves?

Upon the fall of Fort Sumter, President Lincoln declared the Confederate states to be in rebellion. He asked for 75,000 volunteers, enlarged the regular army, and ordered the navy to blockade Southern ports. Most Northerners, upset by the South's firing on the United States flag, backed the President. On the other hand, most white Southerners saw the Confederacy's struggle as a fight for states' rights, not as a rebellion. Some 100,000 Southerners answered President Jefferson Davis's call for volunteers. Four more states joined the Confederacy.

The Union of 23 states included the four border slave states of Missouri, Kentucky, Maryland, and Delaware. It seemed to have many advantages over the considerably smaller Confederacy of 11 states. The population of the seceded states of 9 million (including 3.5 million slaves) compared with 22 million in the North. Over the four years of the war, the South brought 900,000 men into its armies; the North, 2 million men. The Confederacy was a country of farms and plantations with few large cities, little industry, and very few skilled workers. Nearly 80 percent of the nation's factories were in the North, as were most of the minerals, grain, meat, shipping, and banks.

Even though the South had many handicaps, it did have some advantages over the more powerful North. It would fight a defensive war, forcing the Northern enemy to attack Southern territory. The defender's lines of supply would be short compared with those of the invader. Furthermore, Southerners believed that their men were better soldiers than any Yankees could ever be. Indeed, many of the best officers in the U.S. Army, including Robert E. Lee, switched to the Confederate forces. Perhaps the greatest asset Southerners had was the strong belief that their cause was right. They were willing to die for that belief.

Confederate leaders were sure that the textile mills of Britain and France would close if the shipments of Southern cotton were cut off. To prevent this, they thought, Britain and France would feel it necessary to support the South. In part, this reasoning was correct. As the war cut off Southern cotton, many mills in Europe did have to shut down. But new sources of cotton in India and Egypt kept other mills going. In fact, the South got only limited support from Europe. As the war continued, grain from the Northern states became more important to Britain than cotton from the South.

On the battlefront, President Lincoln decided that the Union armies must attack and destroy the Confederate government. His object was to force the seceded states to return to the Union. Lincoln's long-range plan called for blockading the Southern coast in order to keep ships from going into or out of Southern ports. He also planned to win control of the Mississippi River, opening it to Northern shipping and cutting the South in two. Meanwhile, several Northern armies would march south to crush the Confederacy.

Many in the North insisted on immediate action, so Lincoln agreed to an attack on the Southern capital of Richmond, Virginia. In July, 1861, 30 miles southwest of Washington, General Irvin McDowell's Union army was badly defeated in the First Battle of Bull Run (also called the Battle of Manassas). Northerners now knew that the road to Richmond would be long and hard. The war would not be over quickly.

Meanwhile, other Northern efforts were more successful. In Kentucky and Tennessee, Ulysses S. Grant and other Union generals won a series of victories and captured forts Henry and Donelson. In April, 1862, Grant won a bloody battle at Shiloh (Tennessee). Flag Officer (later Admiral) David Farragut occupied New Orleans, and a Union army took Baton Rouge (Louisiana). In May, 1862, the Union had control of all but a small part of the Mississippi River. The Union blockade had closed off most Southern ports along the Atlantic coast. Few supplies were getting through to the South from Europe.

Fortunately for the South, Confederate armies led by General Lee stopped a new Northern attempt to capture Richmond. Lee's success offered the Confederacy some hope for winning the war. Suddenly Northern forces were on the defensive, and General Lee boldly crossed the Potomac River and moved into Union territory in Maryland.

Ask yourself why Lee invaded Maryland. How did this mark a change in Southern strategy?

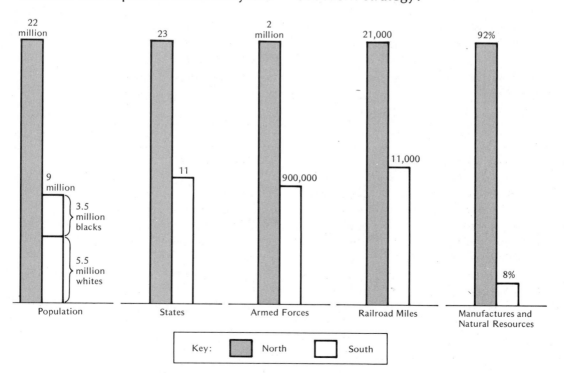

A Comparison of North and South in the Civil War

Baltimore, Maryland, October, 1862

"Philip!" exclaimed Estelle as she opened the door. "What are you doing here?"

"Is that all you can say to your only brother, after not seeing him for months?"

"Oh, I am happy to see you. Come in, come in," answered Estelle. "But I didn't know you were coming, and you look terrible. Your uniform's torn, and you haven't shaved in days. You're so thin."

"Never mind how I look," snapped Philip. "I'm here and alive. Be thankful. Do you have any food? I'm hungry."

"What happened, Phil? Tell me while I fix you a meal."

"Let me wash up and change my clothes. Then I'll try to tell you everything that has happened in the last few months."

Phil bathed and dressed. About an hour later, the two were seated at a table. Philip's mood had brightened.

"During the fighting at Antietam in September, I never thought I'd see you and this old house again," smiled Philip. "Lee had us worried for a bit."

"Thank goodness you didn't get hurt. Tell me—what in heaven's name was Lee doing in Maryland?"

"We wondered about that for a while," said Philip. "Then we understood. Lee wanted to fight the Union Army on Union soil and take the fighting away from the South."

"Why would he do that?" asked Estelle.

"His men could live off the Northern countryside for a change. Also, by forcing the fight he could choose the battlefield and the time. If he could win a major victory in Maryland, then he might cut Washington off from the rest of the Union. And after that, who knows?"

"Are you telling me that if Lee had won—?"

"Exactly. We might have lost the war," said Philip.

"But you stopped him. Lee had to return to Virginia."

"Yes, we stopped him," sighed Philip. "But it cost us much suffering. I'll never forget that cornfield. We knew the enemy was there hiding in the acres and acres of corn. Suddenly, our cannons started blasting. The shells screamed over us without letup. It was horrible!"

"And, then?"

"Then the guns had cut down the corn and I saw everything. Nothing was left growing in that field. Instead, I saw death everywhere. Northern and Southern bodies lay in heaps, and the wounded shrieked in pain, begging for help. I was too afraid to move."

"You're home now and safe. Try to forget."

"I can't forget that day," continued Philip. "The next thing I knew I was in another field. The enemy in gray was out in the open, close enough for me to see their faces. Estelle, I knew some of them!"

"That's impossible, Phil. You only thought you knew them."

"It was no dream, I tell you. Through the smoke I saw Bob and Tom, my dearest friends. I was firing at them. When bullets hit them, I could see their shock and pain. I killed them. I killed my friends." He buried his head in his hands.

"You helped save the Union, Phil."

"But was it worth the slaughter?" asked Philip. "We lost 13,000; Lee lost 10,000, a fourth of his army. Why did so many have to die?"

"Perhaps we are having to pay for the great wrongs we have done—such as holding people in slavery. Oh, Phil, at last our nation seems to be taking a new course, and now the North has something important to fight for—freedom—freedom for the slaves. After Antietam, President Lincoln ordered slaves behind enemy lines to be freed as of January 1, 1863."

"Why should Union troops rally behind an order like that?" asked Philip. "I wish the President had forgotten about slavery. This is a war to save the Union. What do I care if those people are free?"

"You have always been against slavery. How can you talk this way?"

"Sure, I think slavery is wrong," replied Philip. "But I'm not willing to fight and die to end it. Besides, some of our relatives are slave owners."

"That's true, but the slaves in Maryland and the three other border states have not been freed."

"When will they be?"

"Not until this Civil War is over," said Estelle. "Don't you see what Lincoln is trying to do? He's trying to punish the states on the Confederate side. Taking away slave labor will make it harder for the South to produce food and guns."

"I don't see how. Lincoln can't really free any slaves in the South unless we win the war."

"Well, at least now the world will know that the Union is against slavery. That should gain sympathy for our cause from Europeans, and it might even keep the British from supporting the South."

"All right, an emancipation proclamation may help us win the war. But when the war is over, how are we going to deal with the freed slaves? There aren't going to be any easy answers—I can tell you that!"

POSTSCRIPT

On January 1, 1863, blacks and white abolitionists crowded into churches and halls throughout the North and parts of the South held by Union troops. They waited together to hear what Lincoln's Emancipation Proclamation would say.

Finally, the words came over the telegraph wires and were read aloud to the crowds. Cheers and shouts came from the people. For the first time the former slaves, the new freedmen, heard the words "forever free." (The term "freedmen" includes men, women, and children.)

In fact, few slaves were actually freed by the Emancipation Proclamation. But the Union was now committed to a policy of freedom for slaves. In a broad sense, the North was now fighting for freedom as well as for preserving the Union.

The Union victory at Antietam was also important to United States relations with Britain. British opinion about the Civil War was divided. People from the upper classes tended to support the Confederacy. However, most English people, even unemployed workers in the cotton goods industry, were on the side of the Union. At the start of the war, the British government had hoped for a Southern victory. It helped the Confederacy by building ships to break the Northern blockade. At one point the British prime minister was ready to recognize the Confederacy officially as an independent country. But he decided to wait for a major Southern victory.

After Lee failed at Antietam, the British position changed. The government never again officially considered recognizing the Confederacy as one of the nations of the world. The Emancipation Proclamation produced much sympathy for the North in Britain. It showed the British people that the Civil War was a fight to end slavery— not merely a war to save the Union.

Homework Questions

1. Why did many think that the North would defeat the South?
2. What reason did Southerners have to think that Britain and France would support them?
3. How did Lincoln plan to defeat the Confederacy?
4. Why did Lee invade Union territory?
5. Why was the Battle of Antietam so important for both North and South?
6. How did the Emancipation Proclamation serve the cause of the Union?

Understanding the Story

A. Write *T* for each statement that is true and *F* for each statement that is false.
1. Almost 80 percent of the nation's factories were in the North.
2. All slave states joined the Confederacy.
3. The Confederacy was a country of many large cities and few plantations.
4. The North had more than twice as many people as the South.
5. Northern armies were successful in the West in 1862.
6. A Confederate army, under General Lee, invaded Union territory.
7. Lee wanted his army to live off the Union countryside.
8. Lee lost half of his army at Antietam.

B. Choose the term or phrase that best completes each statement.
1. There were (*a*) 7 (*b*) 11 (*c*) 23   states in the Confederacy.
2. One Southern asset was the strong belief that (*a*) the Confederate cause was right (*b*) Northerners were abolitionists (*c*) Britain and France needed Southern cotton.
3. The North suffered a defeat at (*a*) New Orleans (*b*) Antietam (*c*) Bull Run.

4. A major Northern goal was the capture of (*a*) Maryland (*b*) Richmond (*c*) Fort Donelson.
5. The First Battle of Bull Run showed that (*a*) the South could be beaten (*b*) the war would be a long one (*c*) the North had the best leaders.
6. The Emancipation Proclamation was issued after the fighting at (*a*) Fort Sumter (*b*) Bull Run (*c*) Antietam.
7. The Emancipation Proclamation was aimed at freeing slaves in (*a*) the border states (*b*) Maryland (*c*) the seceded states.
8. Southern trade with Europe was cut down by (*a*) a blockade of Southern ports (*b*) an increase in the amount of cotton grown in India and Egypt (*c*) European support for the Union.

C. Imagine that you are an adviser to President Lincoln in September, 1862. You are asked to list reasons for and against issuing the Emancipation Proclamation. What reasons will you list on each side? Do you think Lincoln made a wise decision?

Activities and Inquiries

1. Study the graph on page 285. Then choose the term or phrase that best completes each statement.
   a. The North had (*1*) more than twice as many states as the South (*2*) the same number of troops as the South (*3*) resources about equal to those of the South.
   b. In the area of manufactures and natural resources, (*1*) the North had a very small advantage (*2*) the North had a major advantage

(*3*) the South had a major advantage.
   c. In the South, the number of slaves was (*1*) a small part of the population (*2*) a major part of the population (*3*) about the same as the number of whites.
   d. The population of the North was (*1*) about the same as that of the South, if we include the slaves (*2*) smaller than that of the South (*3*) more than twice as large as that of the South.
   e. From this graph we can learn (*1*) that the North had many advantages over the South (*2*) why the South should have won the war (*3*) why the South won many of the early battles of the war.
2. Antietam is often called the turning point of the Civil War (a battle that changed the direction of the war). Go to the library and look for information about other battles that might be called turning points. Describe one. Two from the Civil War are Vicksburg and Gettysburg. One from the Revolutionary War is Saratoga.
3. Imagine that you are a reporter at the Battle of Antietam. Write a description of how the battle looks through a soldier's eyes.
4. Write the headlines for the Battle of Antietam as they might have appeared in a Southern newspaper. Then write the headlines for the Battle of Antietam as they might have appeared in a Northern newspaper.
5. Describe how you think Phil's experience might affect his life. Is it important to have a cause to fight for? Why or why not?
6. Describe how each of the following might have felt about the Emancipation Proclamation: Southern planters, abolitionists, Northern factory workers.

2 To Punish or Forgive?

By the end of 1862, General Grant was attacking the Southern fortress of Vicksburg, Mississippi. President Davis and General Lee had to decide whether to aid the Confederates in the West or make a new attempt to invade the North. They agreed that a victory in Pennsylvania would threaten Washington and Philadelphia and might weaken Grant by forcing him to send some of his army east. Southern troops marched north. From July 1 to 3, 1863, Lee's army faced that of General George Meade at Gettysburg, Pennsylvania, in one of the most important battles of the war.

The Confederate forces almost won, but they lacked the manpower to overcome the larger Union army. Huge losses forced Lee to retreat. A Confederate invasion of the North had failed for the second and last time. The cost was high. More than 25 percent of the men on both sides were killed or wounded.

The next day (July 4, 1863) Grant won a major victory by capturing Vicksburg. The Mississippi River was now under Union control. The Confederate states west of the river were cut off from the rest of the South. The losses at Gettysburg and Vicksburg ended the South's ability to take the offensive. Grant's victories continued at Lookout Mountain and Missionary Ridge (near Chattanooga, Tennessee), where Union troops drove the Confederate army into Georgia.

In 1864 Grant was promoted by Lincoln and brought east to become commander in chief of all Union armies.

Lincoln had at last found a winning general.

At first both Union and Confederate armies had consisted of volunteers. But as the war continued, it became more difficult to fill the ranks. In 1863 Congress passed a conscription, or draft, law to build up the Union army. It allowed drafted men to hire a substitute or buy an exemption for $300. The draft was resented by poor people, who could not afford an exemption. In New York City, mobs burned and robbed for several days, shouting, "Down with the draft!" White rioters attacked and killed blacks, blaming them for the "war to free the slaves."

The Confederate draft started earlier (1862) and was greeted with remarks that the war was a "rich man's war but a poor man's fight." There were no large-scale draft riots in the South.

Inflation (rising prices) became a problem in the North, but prices in the South rose even higher. By the end of the war, the Confederate paper dollar was worth only 1.6 cents. Too, the Confederacy suffered from the Northern blockade, which caused shortages of many goods. By contrast, Northern industry boomed, sheltered by a high protective tariff passed by the Republicans.

Now that the Union forces were close to victory, Lincoln felt it was necessary to decide the future of the seceded states. He insisted that these states had not left the Union, and he referred to Southerners as "disloyal" or "rebels" or "insurgents." He said they should not be punished severely as traitors. Rather, he thought that they should be accepted back into the Union as wayward brothers and sisters who had strayed or made mistakes.

On the other hand, Congressman Thaddeus Stevens of Pennsylvania and other leaders of Congress viewed Southern leaders as traitors. They argued that the South had indeed left the Union and should now be treated as a conquered nation or province. Congress and not the President, they said, should decide how to punish the South and its leaders.

The two opinions were sharply at odds. The President and Congress squared off in a battle for control of Reconstruction—the rebuilding of the Union to include once again the seceded states. At issue were two points: Who should set Reconstruction policy? Should that policy be "soft" or "hard"?

Issues of both principle and politics were at stake. What was the best way to restore harmony to the Union? What was the best way to protect the interests of the freed slaves? How would Reconstruction affect the political future of the Republican Party? President Lincoln put emphasis on rebuilding a strong Union, while Congressman Stevens stressed the needs of the former slaves. Yet neither was indifferent to politics. Both were Republicans, and both were keenly aware of how much white Southerners had hated Republicans before the war. Would a "soft" policy win support for the Republicans among leading whites, as Lincoln hoped? Or would it, as Stevens feared, turn control of the South back to Democrats—the same people who had led the South into secession?

President Lincoln made the first move. In December, 1863, he offered a group pardon, or amnesty, to Southerners who agreed to pledge loyalty to the federal government. Such a pledge would imply acceptance of an end to slavery. As soon as 10 percent of a seceded state's voters took the pledge, a new state government could be set up. In the meantime, conquered parts of the South were placed under martial law—that is, military control. Lincoln's chief concern was to restore the Union as quickly as possible.

In our story, President Lincoln and Congressman Stevens talk about their views of Reconstruction. What are the major differences between their points of view? With which view do you agree? Why?

Washington, D.C., 1864

Very slowly Thaddeus Stevens walked into President Lincoln's office, where the President was seated at his desk. The President nodded at the congressman and pointed to a chair.

"Mr. President," Stevens declared, "I strongly dislike your plan for Reconstruction."

"I was afraid you would, Congressman Stevens," the President replied. "Please consider my motives. My plan is a simple method of bringing the South back into the Union. Surely you don't expect this war to last forever. Let's get the fighting over as quickly as possible, heal our wounds, and make a fresh start."

"What do you mean 'make a fresh start'? You're going to pardon the rebels. How can you pretend that the war never took place? What is the punishment for rebellion and murder? Kind words?"

"The people of the South have suffered enough," said Lincoln. "Yes, there has been a rebellion, but it caused a terrible loss of life and property on both sides. Hasn't there been enough suffering and cruelty? Isn't this the time to say to our Southern sisters and brothers, 'Return to the Union, we need each other'?"

"The slave owners almost wrecked our nation. You're not punishing them; you're rewarding the rebels. All they have to do is swear an oath of loyalty to the Union. Do you truly believe that a rebel could possibly tell the truth? He'll swear to anything. I wouldn't believe a one because they're all liars."

"You're not being fair, Congressman Stevens. You're leaving out the other parts of my plan. Ten percent of those who voted in 1860 can organize a new state government. There can be no slavery; the rights of blacks and whites must be protected."

"I suppose, Mr. President, that you think this is enough punishment. Well, it does not satisfy me. Ten percent—I will not be satisfied with 100 percent. Let them all swear for the next ten years that they are sorry. It's not enough. Those rebels will not be equal citizens until they pay for their sins!"

"You are too hard on the people of the South," said Lincoln. "Let me ask you two questions. Why are we fighting this horrible Civil War? Will our nation be stronger if we are cruel to our defeated brothers and sisters?"

"You want me to say that we are fighting to save our nation," said Stevens grimly. "But there's more, much more. We are fighting to end the slavery of human beings, to assure black people equality, and to defend ourselves against rebel attacks. No, Mr. President, never again do I want to see this nation controlled by the South and King Cotton. Welcome the rebels? Never! They could not destroy our government with bullets, and they must not poison the halls of Congress!"

"I see that your mind is made up," said the President.

"You're right, Mr. President, I will never change. You have to hit those rebels hard. Never let them forget the pain our nation is suffering. Take away their slaves! And take away their land!"

"Are you still talking about breaking up the Southern plantations? You know that I'm opposed to anything like that."

"It's a good idea," continued Stevens. "Aren't you the one who's always talking about charity and fairness? Well, what could be fairer? Slaves worked for their masters year after year. What were they paid? Nothing! What did they get? Pain and torture! I say we should give the planters' land to the freed slaves. Lord knows they've earned it!"

"Impossible!" shot back Lincoln. "That's unfair to the landowners."

"You don't fool me," replied Stevens. "You're just protecting those landowners."

"No one would dream of trying to fool you," said Lincoln, smiling for the first time.

"Why can't you agree with me, Mr. President? Why can't we give each freedman's family 40 acres, a home, and a pension? The freed slaves have nothing to show for centuries of work. It is our duty to help them get started as free people."

"Even though I would like your support, Mr. Stevens, I cannot give other people's property to the freed slaves. That would go too far. It would completely overthrow the social order."

"Perhaps so, Mr. President, but by ending slavery we are already overthrowing the old order. Unless we provide a way for the freedmen to become self-supporting, they will remain dependent on their former masters. Sooner or later we will have slavery in fact, if not in name."

"Mr. Stevens," said the President, "I pray that you are wrong. We have made our vow—slavery must end. And it will end—in fact as well as in name!"

Stevens turned, as though to leave, then turned again to face the President. "There is one thing you can do, Mr. President. Insist that the freedmen be given the right to vote."

"I agree," replied Lincoln. "They should have the vote. But I honestly don't think they are ready. Most of them, after all, can neither read nor write. Perhaps a way could be found to let the educated among them vote."

"That's not good enough," said Stevens. "All black men must be able to vote in order to protect themselves from their former masters. Besides, you know they will all vote for the Republican Party!"

"Mr. Stevens, I think we really want the same thing for our country. We want to win the war and bring North and South together. You are worried about Reconstruction in the South. So am I. But there is a difference; you and the army would force the Southern whites to act your way. I would rather encourage them to do their own rebuilding."

"I'm sorry, Mr. Lincoln, but I don't trust traitors. And I don't have as much time as you. I'm an old man with only a few years left, so I must move fast. This is a revolution, my chance to change the South completely. Plantations and slavery are dead, and I plan to see that they stay dead!"

"Reconstruction means to build anew. Why don't we build new lives and hope? Forget destruction! Forget your revenge!"

POSTSCRIPT

Several Southern states took advantage of Lincoln's plan and reorganized their governments by the end of 1864. But Congress refused to admit the newly elected congressmen and senators.

Thaddeus Stevens died in August, 1868. Although he was white, he was buried in a cemetery for blacks in Lancaster, Pennsylvania. His gravestone explained why he had chosen this spot:

". . . finding other cemeteries limited as to race by their rules,
I have chosen this that I might illustrate in my death
The Principles which I followed
Through a long life:
EQUALITY OF MAN BEFORE HIS CREATOR."

Homework Questions

1. Why were the battles of Gettysburg and Vicksburg so important?
2. How did economic conditions during the war differ in the North and South?
3. Describe the differences between Lincoln's and Stevens's plans for the treatment of the defeated South.
4. Why was Lincoln's plan so mild and Stevens's so harsh?

Understanding the Story

A. Write *T* for each statement that is true, *F* for each statement that is false, and *N* for each statement that is not mentioned in the chapter.
   1. Lincoln was eager to bring the South back into the Union.
   2. Stevens agreed with Lincoln's plan of Reconstruction.
   3. Jefferson Davis sent Lincoln a plan of his own.
   4. Lincoln said that ten percent of those who had voted in 1860 could organize a new state government.
   5. Stevens did not trust the Southern rebels.
   6. The women of the South refused to support any plan.
   7. Stevens wanted to punish the rebels severely.
   8. Stevens felt that Congress would welcome rebel congressmen.

B. Write *S* for each statement that Stevens made or might have made and *L* for each statement that Lincoln made or might have made.
   1. Let's make a fresh start.
   2. You're rewarding the slave owners.
   3. All rebels are liars.
   4. The rights of blacks and whites will be protected.
   5. Make them pay for what they have done.
   6. The rebels must not poison the halls of Congress.
   7. I cannot give other people's property to the freed slaves.
   8. We might let the educated Negroes vote.

C. Imagine that you are a member of Congress in 1865. Describe what sort of Reconstruction you would favor. Do you think the newly freed blacks should have special help to begin their freedom? Why or why not?

Activities and Inquiries

1. Imagine that you are a member of a debating team. Your assignment is to prove that Lincoln's plans for the South were better than those of Stevens. Prepare your arguments.
2. Now imagine that your assignment is to prove that Stevens's plans were better than Lincoln's. Prepare your arguments.
3. What will be the strongest argument for Lincoln's plan? What will be the weakest argument?
4. What will be the strongest argument for Stevens's plan? What will be the weakest argument?

3 Lee Surrenders

In mid-1864 Union General William T. Sherman led a force of 100,000 men from the Tennessee border southeast through Georgia to Atlanta. After burning Atlanta, he and 60,000 men continued to Savannah, some 300 miles away. They destroyed everything of value in a 60-mile-wide path. Sherman's March to the Sea broke the spirit of the South. If such destruction could take place without serious interference, what chance did the Southerners have? By January, 1865, the Confederacy held only the Carolinas and the southern half of Virginia. The small Southern armies that remained beyond the Mississippi River and in Alabama could not affect the outcome of the war.

Meanwhile, 115,000 Union soldiers under General Ulysses S. Grant faced 54,000 Confederate soldiers under General Robert E. Lee in trenches at Petersburg, Virginia. Lee had to hold Petersburg to protect the Confederate capital at Richmond, just to the north. For nine months the lines held steady. Then, in April, 1865, Union troops managed to cut through Confederate lines. Rather than let himself be surrounded, Lee pulled his troops back. Union troops captured Richmond, and Union General Philip Sheridan moved to cut off Lee's escape routes to the west and to the south. What should Lee do?

In our story, Lee faces the most important decision of his military career. Ask yourself whether he chose wisely. Were Grant's terms for surrender fair? Why or why not?

Amelia Court House, Virginia, April 6, 1865

Grant's Federal troops outnumbered Lee's Army of Northern Virginia by more than two to one. The Union troops seemed to be everywhere, attacking from the flanks, pressing close to the rear, even cutting in front of the fleeing Confederates. Retreat was all but impossible. Most of the Southerners had no shoes; their clothes were in rags; they had not eaten a full meal in days. How long could they last?

General William Pendleton said what was on the minds of many Southern officers. "General Lee, the time has come for surrender. I hate to speak to you like this, but there's no way that we can win now."

"General Pendleton," said Lee, "our men must fight on. True, they're tired, but they have spirit and the desire to beat the enemy. We must not give up!"

"They need more than spirit, sir. They're hungry, surrounded, outnumbered, and outgunned. They haven't a chance!"

"We will not surrender," Lee said firmly.

"Why waste lives?" asked Pendleton. "We've lost. The war is over, General, and we must swallow our bitter fate."

Of course, he's right, thought Lee to himself. But he could not agree openly. Instead he said, "Suppose I tell Grant that I'm ready to surrender? He'll think that we're weak and take advantage of our weakness by insisting that we surrender unconditionally. I must not let him know how bad things are, or he will offer us nothing."

General Grant knew what was happening to General Lee and his army and decided to send a letter to Lee from nearby Farmville, Virginia:

April 7, 1865

General R. E. Lee
Commanding, Confederate States Army

General:

I am sure that you see that your army is in a hopeless position. Your forces are shattered, your food supply is low, and your men are starving.

There is no point to further resistance by your Army of Northern Virginia. Stop the bloodshed and save your men by surrendering your army.

Very respectfully,

U.S. Grant, Lt. General, U.S. Army

The Civil War, 1861–1865

Lee replied at once:

April 7, 1865

General U.S. Grant
  Commanding, United States Army

General:

Thank you for your note. However, I do not agree that our situation is hopeless. We can continue to fight.

Yet we should stop this useless shedding of blood, because too many have died already.

Suppose I were thinking of surrender. What terms, or conditions, would you offer me?

Very respectfully,

R. E. Lee, General

The following evening Lee received Grant's answer:

April 8, 1865

General R. E. Lee
  Commanding, Confederate States Army

General:

What I want above all is peace. There is only one condition I insist on now. Your men and officers must give up their arms. They must stop fighting against the government of the United States.

I will meet you at any place you name. At that time I will tell you the specific terms for the surrender of the Army of Northern Virginia.

Very respectfully, your obedient servant,

U. S. Grant, Lt. General, U.S. Army

Lee then wrote:

April 8, 1865

General U.S. Grant
  Commanding, United States Army

General:

I am sorry that I did not explain myself clearly. I did not agree to surrender my army at this time. I merely wanted to know your conditions of peace IF I agree to surrender. Our emergency is not great enough for surrender.

I will be happy to meet you tomorrow at 10 A.M. on the Old Stage Road to Richmond between the two armies.

Very respectfully,

R. E. Lee, General

Lee met with his officers. They knew there was little or no chance for success, but still some said, "Fight on!" Two of his units would try to cut through Grant's lines at daybreak. Perhaps Lee would not have to meet with Grant after all. Or would he be wasting more lives by continuing the fight?

On the morning of April 9, Lee arose before 3 A.M. He dressed very carefully, putting on his new gray uniform, a silk sash, gold-colored spurs, and a handsome sword. As he mounted his horse and rode toward the Federal lines, he could hear the harsh sounds of battle.

A horseman rode up with a message from two officers closer to the battle lines.

"Our men have gone as far as they can. They've fought themselves out. They broke through the cavalry, but there are just too many Federal infantry. We need more men."

Lee smiled grimly. "We have only 8,000 men left to fight all of Grant's army. There's nothing more I can do. I will see General Grant because we can fight no more."

When General Pendleton saw Lee, he asked, "Why the fancy dress on the battlefield?"

"I may be General Grant's prisoner today. I wanted to be sure to look my best," answered Lee. Lee had made up his mind: this WAS the time for surrender.

Suddenly Colonel John Haskell, who had only one arm, came riding up at full gallop. He saw Lee and tried to stop his horse, but couldn't for another hundred yards. "We've found a new road!" he called breathlessly. "Our army can escape! We'll fight those Feds another day!"

"Never mind the road. It's too late for that," replied Lee wearily.

Later, they found that there was no other road.

POSTSCRIPT

General Grant would not meet until Lee agreed to surrender. After he did, the meeting was held in the home of Wilmer McLean in the village of Appomattox Court House on the afternoon of April 9.

Lee, 15 years older than Grant and five inches taller, wore his full dress uniform. Grant was dressed in his rough traveling outfit: the uniform of a private with the straps of a lieutenant general. His dark blue coat was unbuttoned and coated with mud. He wore riding boots, but no belt, sword, or spurs.

The men talked of happier times in the army. Finally, they came to the terms of the surrender:

- Confederate soldiers were to give up rifles and other equipment.
- Officers could keep their side arms (pistols, swords).
- All could keep their horses and mules.
- The soldiers must promise not to take up arms against the government of the United States.
- The Confederates would be issued food for 25,000 men by the Union forces.

The Civil War came to a sudden end without a formal peace treaty. Southern soldiers simply quit and went home. Both North and South were happy that the fighting and bloodshed were over. Of course, many problems remained to be solved.

Returning Southern soldiers found it difficult to continue their prewar lives. Many areas of the South had been destroyed. Major cities such as Charleston, Atlanta, and Richmond had been shelled and burned. Schools and churches had been destroyed; many plantations had been abandoned. Southern farmers were not thriving, and the plantation economy built on slave labor was dead. The slaves (valued at $2 billion) had been freed. Banks, businesses, and factories were closed. Northern armies had torn up most of the railroad tracks in the South.

In the North, business had prospered during the war. Now the factories had to shift from producing military orders to re-tooling for civilian production. The national debt had climbed from $65 million in 1860 to $3 billion in 1865.

Some Southerners could not accept defeat. They still insisted that they had fought a just war and that secession had been right. In spite of all their suffering, they insisted that they had won a moral victory. Northerners, on the other hand, thought of themselves as the true victors, in spirit and in fact. Most expected the South to be punished for seceding from the Union.

Homework Questions

1. What was Sherman's March to the Sea, and what were its main results?
2. Why was Lee unwilling to tell Grant that he was ready to surrender?
3. Describe Grant's terms for surrender.
4. Why did some Southerners refuse to accept defeat?
5. What problems did Northern industries have to face at the end of the war?

Understanding the Story

A. List the numbers of the statements that are true.
   1. General Sherman's march helped Georgia.
   2. Lee was afraid that his army would be surrounded.
   3. Lee's troops outnumbered Grant's.
   4. General Pendleton felt that the South could win.
   5. General Grant knew the weaknesses of Lee's army.
   6. Grant asked Lee to surrender his army.
   7. Colonel Haskell found a way to defeat Grant's army.
   8. At the surrender, Lee wore his dress uniform.

B. Write *A* for each statement that Lee would agree with and *N* for each statement that he would not agree with.
   1. Pendleton is right—the war is lost.
   2. I must tell Grant how desperate we are.
   3. I need to know Grant's terms for surrender.
   4. I may be a prisoner of General Grant.
   5. Our army will escape.
   6. There's nothing more I can do.
   7. Too many have died in this war already.
   8. The Confederate army is in excellent shape.

C. Assume that you are the President of the United States in 1865. What terms will you grant to or demand from the Confederate army? Explain.

Activities and Inquiries

1. Pretend that you are General Pendleton. Write a letter to Lee telling him why he should surrender.
2. Now pretend that you are Colonel Haskell. Write a letter to Lee telling him why he should not surrender.
3. Imagine that you are Grant during Lee's surrender. What are your thoughts?
4. Now imagine that you are Lee. What are your thoughts as you surrender your army?

4 A President Is Impeached and Tried

At last the war was over, and Abraham Lincoln could turn his thoughts to peace and Reconstruction. But he was not able to be peacemaker for long. Five days after Lee's surrender, a Southern sympathizer shot Lincoln while the President was attending a play in a Washington theater. Lincoln died the next morning.

Vice President Andrew Johnson, a Democrat, took Lincoln's place. Although a Southerner from Tennessee, he had remained loyal to the Union. Johnson was the only senator from a Confederate state who had stayed in the Senate at the start of the war.

As President, Johnson adopted Lincoln's Reconstruction plan (see page 291) with only a few changes. Southern whites were to reorganize their state governments. Special state conventions were to repeal succession laws. The Confederate debts were to be canceled. And the 13th Amendment (freeing the slaves) was to be approved.

In the second half of 1865, Southern states organized new governments and held elections for Congress. In December, 1865, the newly elected Southern congressmen and senators went to Washington to take their seats. The group included 58 former members of the Confederate Congress and former Confederate Vice President Alexander Stephens.

Radical Republicans, who were in the majority in Congress, refused to seat the Southerners. The Radical Republicans believed that the South should be severely punished and that freedmen (males only) should be given the right to vote. They viewed President Johnson's plan as an outrage.

Under the leadership of Thaddeus Stevens and Charles Sumner, Congress set up a Joint Committee on Reconstruction. It was made up of 15 members from the House and Senate. This committee would attempt to decide the fate of the South, bypassing President Johnson.

Early in 1866 Congress acted to protect freedmen from new Southern laws known as Black Codes. These laws attempted to regulate relations between blacks and whites. Some parts of the codes gave blacks rights they had never before had in the South. For example, they could now own property and sue in court. Other parts called for harsh penalties for freedmen who broke labor contracts. Also affected were vagrants (those who did not have specific jobs or who wandered about the countryside) and blacks who committed minor crimes. Freedmen without jobs or homes could be bound (apprenticed) to white employers under conditions that were like slavery.

In February, 1866, Congress passed a bill extending the life of the Freedmen's Bureau, which protected and assisted the former slaves in the Southern states. Johnson vetoed the bill. He felt that the bill was unfair because the South had no part in passing it. Congress later passed the bill over the President's veto.

In April, 1866, Congress passed the Civil Rights Act, giving blacks the same rights of citizenship as whites had. (The law did not include the right to vote.) Congress expected that this federal law would take the place of state laws that regulated the rights of blacks.

President Johnson vetoed the Civil Rights Act, saying it took away the rights of the states. But the act became law when Congress passed it over the President's veto. Later the ideas in the Civil Rights Bill were added to the U.S. Constitution as the 14th Amendment. This amendment went into effect in 1868. It provided citizenship for freed slaves.

In 1867 tension increased between the President and Congress when the Radical Republicans passed the Tenure of Office Act over Johnson's veto. The act required the President to obtain the Senate's consent before dismissing any officeholders previously approved by the Senate.

In our story we see what happened to Johnson. The newspaper headlines and his thoughts tell of the growing conflict between the President and Congress. Note that impeachment means being accused of wrongdoing. Under constitutional procedure, impeachment is a first step, performed by the House of Representatives. The next step is a trial by the Senate.

Ask yourself why Johnson and Congress disagreed about Reconstruction. Was Johnson wrong in dismissing Secretary of War Edwin Stanton? Why did Congress impeach and try the President?

Washington, April 15, 1865

LINCOLN ASSASSINATED BY COWARDLY KILLER; CAN JOHNSON FILL LINCOLN'S SHOES?

I am Andrew Johnson, the President of the United States. No, I am not the great Lincoln, but I will work hard and try my best to be a good President. Although I cannot and will not try to fill Lincoln's shoes, I will follow in his footsteps.

I grew up as a poor orphan, so I always had to work hard. For a time I was a tailor's apprentice. It's an honorable trade, but the rich people looked down on me and laughed at my poor speech, my clumsy ways, and my poverty. I never forgot their sneers. Someday, I said, I would show them.

I taught myself to read, and my wife taught me to write when I was 20. I vowed that I would be the best speaker in the whole state of Tennessee. Before long, they came from miles away to listen to me.

I went into politics, speaking, shaking hands, making promises. People believed in me—well, many poor people did, anyway. They chose me, Andrew Johnson, to be city councilman, mayor, state representative, congressman, governor, senator. I climbed the ladder, and now I am at the very top: the Presidency of the United States.

May, 1865

JOHNSON STARTS RECONSTRUCTION —FOLLOWS LINCOLN'S PLAN

The war is over. Let's try to erase the memories of hatred and slaughter. I want to bring the former Confederate states back into the Union as quickly as possible. The South needs no more punishment. Southerners have suffered enough.

Put the blame for the war where it belongs: on the upper-class Southerners who pushed the people into the war. The poor were misled. They thought they were fighting for the honor of the South. Instead, they died trying to save the property of the rich slave owners!

I'll pardon most rebels if they swear loyalty to the United States government and approve the 13th Amendment, ending slavery. We should get Federal troops out of the South so the states can hold elections and send senators and representatives back to Washington. The sooner we get back to normal, the sooner we can forget the Civil War and be a whole nation again.

Only rich Southerners will have trouble getting a pardon. Any rebel who owns property worth more than $20,000 will have to ask me personally for forgiveness.

March, 1867

CONGRESSMEN SAY TREAT CONFEDERATE STATES LIKE CONQUERED PROVINCES! RECONSTRUCTION BILLS PASSED OVER VETO; LINCOLN-JOHNSON PLAN IS DEAD!

The Radical Republicans don't agree with me about Reconstruction. My plan would have created new state governments in the South and brought the South back into the mainstream of our national life. But the Radical Republicans say there are no legal governments in the Southern states. Instead, they have divided the South into five military districts, policed by thousands of soldiers. Worst of all, Congress has taken the command of these soldiers from my hands. All military orders must come through General Grant, the general of the army. This is unconstitutional because I am the commander in chief!

The Radical Republicans are traitors! Unless they are stopped, they will destroy our country. I won't let them tear our nation apart. I fought treason in the South during the Civil War, and I can fight it in Congress now that the war is over. How? By vetoing their bills and speaking out against their treason.

The Radicals may pass their bills over my veto. But someday they will see that they have gone too far and that I am right. Then we will return to the moderate Lincoln-Johnson Plan for the South.

March, 1867

TENURE OF OFFICE ACT PASSED; SENATE APPROVAL NEEDED TO FIRE JOBHOLDERS

February, 1868

JOHNSON FIRES SECRETARY OF WAR STANTON—DEFIES SENATE

Once again the Radical Republicans have gone too far. How could Congress pass a law like the Tenure of Office Act? Why, it's downright unconstitutional—can't they see that? The Constitution plainly states that the Senate must approve certain appointments when they are made by the President. But it says nothing about Senate approval for dismissing an official. No President has ever had to ask permission to fire an official—and I won't be the first! As President, I have the duty of carrying out the nation's laws, and I must have helpers I can count on.

Sure, Stanton served the nation well during the late war, but he's an impossible man for me to work with. He makes no bones about his disapproval of my plan for Reconstruction. Why, he openly sides with the Radicals in Congress. That's why they passed this cursed law in the first place—to keep me from firing Stanton and choosing a man more to my liking. Oh, I know, Stanton spoke out against the Tenure of Office Act. He even said he supported my veto of it—my useless veto. But he's the wrong man for the job he's in. And when I asked him to resign, he flatly refused. As long as Stanton stays on as secretary of war, the Radicals will have a spy within my cabinet.

The only way I can assert my own authority—my constitutional authority—is to fire Stanton. Let the Radicals take me to court! I know I'm in the right. Congress has its proper duties, and I as President have mine—and the proper balance must be preserved. The courts *must* stand behind me!

February, 1868

HOUSE IMPEACHES JOHNSON; PRESIDENT TO BE TRIED BY SENATE

The Radical Republicans did not submit their dispute with President Johnson to the normal courts of the nation. Rather, they turned to the method of impeachment—never before used against a President. The Senate itself served as a court to try the President for "high crimes" and "misdemeanors" (lesser crimes) against the United States.

Of the 11 charges of wrongdoing against Johnson, eight dealt with supposed violations of the Tenure of Office Act. The ninth article charged Johnson with communicating with an army officer directly rather than through the general of the army. Articles ten and eleven accused the President of criticizing Congress and of using language and threats unbecoming to a President.

Johnson's trial opened in March, 1868. Present were Chief Justice Salmon Chase, the presiding judge; the 54 members of the Senate, acting as the jury; leading women and men of Washington society; and the lawyers who defended the President. In fact, it seemed as though everyone was there except the accused: the President himself.

No, sir, I will not let my enemies make a fool of me. I'm not going to stand in front of that bloodthirsty audience. Besides, I can't govern this country from the Senate. I have a job to do; my place is right here in the White House.

There is no reason why I should waste my time at the trial. I can't lose. My lawyers tell me that my enemies don't have a chance because everything I've done is strictly legal. Can they take the presidency away from me for firing Stanton? Of course not!

Johnson was right—but barely. The trial dragged on for two months. Johnson's lawyers argued that the Tenure of Office Act didn't even apply to the case because Stanton had been appointed by Lincoln and not by Johnson. Finally, late in May, the trial came to a close.

May 26, 1868

SENATE VOTES 35 TO 19 FOR REMOVAL, ONE VOTE SHORT OF TWO-THIRDS MAJORITY; JOHNSON IS STILL PRESIDENT

POSTSCRIPT

Johnson served the nine months remaining in his term, but he was little more than a figurehead (a leader without power). The executive branch had been weakened by the trial. Congress, on the other hand, had shown its power to check the President—even though he kept his position.

Johnson's impeachment was a major test of the system of checks and balances set up in the Constitution. Neither the President nor Congress won a clear victory—and in that sense, the checks and balances worked. But no one was entirely happy with the outcome. In the North, Radical Republicans grumbled that the President had had his way. In the South, military rule continued, and Southern whites grumbled against the harshness of Reconstruction.

Edwin Stanton, his health shattered, resigned soon after the impeachment trial ended. In 1869 he was appointed to the U.S. Supreme Court, but four days after the Senate confirmed him, he died. Years later, the Supreme Court ruled that the Tenure of Office Act was indeed unconstitutional, just as Johnson had argued.

Homework Questions

1. How did Johnson propose to reconstruct the South?
2. Why did the Radical Republicans reject the Lincoln-Johnson Plan?
3. How did the President and the Congress differ over the Freedmen's Bureau Act, the Civil Rights Act, and the Tenure of Office Act?
4. Why was Johnson impeached?
5. Which side was the winner in the struggle between Johnson and the Radical Republicans in Congress? Explain.

Understanding the Story

A. Write *F* for each statement that is a fact, and *O* for each statement that is an opinion.
1. Vice President Johnson replaced President Lincoln.
2. Johnson was the only senator from a Confederate state who stayed in the Senate at the start of the Civil War.
3. Johnson had been an orphan.
4. Johnson was the best choice to be Lincoln's Vice President.
5. Johnson had been a governor.
6. Johnson should have tried to get along with Congress.
7. Johnson was impeached but not removed from office.
8. Johnson should have resigned.

B. List the numbers of the statements Andrew Johnson made or might have made.
1. I will try my best to be a good President.
2. I taught myself to read.
3. Keep the rebels out of the Union as long as possible.
4. The Radical Republicans agree with me about Reconstruction.

5. I will veto the Radicals' bills.
6. Stanton is my best friend in the cabinet.
7. The Radicals have a spy within my cabinet.
8. Everything I've done is strictly legal.

C. Under the Constitution, removal of a federal officer by Congress involves two steps—first impeachment by the House, then trial and conviction by the Senate. What, in your opinion, is the reason for this two-step requirement?

Activities and Inquiries

1. Pretend that you are one of Johnson's lawyers. Prepare his defense.
2. Imagine that you are a lawyer for the prosecution. Prepare your case against Johnson.
3. You are a member of the Senate. How will you vote? Explain.
4. Do you think it would have been good for the nation if Johnson had been convicted by the Senate and removed from office? Why or why not?
5. Find in the Constitution the parts relating to impeachment proceedings. What, in your opinion, would be "high crimes and misdemeanors"?

5 What Are You Doing to the South?

Among those who supported Radical Republican policies in the South was a group of white Northerners who had gone south after the war. These people were known as "carpetbaggers" because many of them carried suitcases made of carpet material. Most went looking for a better life. They bought land, built factories and railroads, and engaged in trade and business. A large percentage were Union veterans who liked the Southern climate and saw a way of improving their chances for success. Others went as teachers, clergy, officials of the Freedmen's Bureau, or agents of Northern Negro aid societies. They set up schools and churches and distributed clothing and medical supplies. A few were corrupt adventurers interested only in political power and financial profit. Most Southern whites hated carpetbaggers as intruders and meddlers.

A second group, the "scalawags" (scamps or rascals), were the minority of white Southerners who worked with the Radical Republicans. Some had favored the Union cause during the war and had been persecuted by their neighbors. Others were poor whites and small farmers whose hatred of the planters drove them to the radical side. Southern business people who, like the Republicans, supported a high tariff and a national banking system, were also called scalawags.

After the war, freed slaves faced a difficult adjustment. Without preparation, they had to begin lives in a society that had been closed to them. They had experience in farming, cleaning house, cooking, or woodworking. But most were without land or property. To support themselves, they had to find paying jobs.

Slave codes had prevented blacks from learning to read and write. Only a few had taught themselves without their masters' knowledge. Slaves had been discouraged from thinking for themselves and from being self-reliant. They had been encouraged to follow orders and feel inferior to whites. As far as many Radical Republicans were concerned, this had to be changed.

Most slaves fled from their plantation homes as quickly as they could. Their flight caused the collapse of the Southern labor system. Happy that they could now move about without the approval of white masters, blacks searched for relatives and went to cities to look for jobs or an education.

In March, 1865, Congress created the Freedmen's Bureau to help former slaves adjust to their new lives. The Bureau provided food, clothing, and medical care, settled blacks on abandoned lands, found jobs for them, and built schools. Private organizations provided teachers and books for the schools. These were the first public schools for blacks in the Southern states. In addition, the Bureau helped establish four colleges for blacks: Howard University in the District of Columbia, Hampton Institute in Virginia, Atlanta University in Georgia, and Fisk University in Tennessee.

The Bureau tried to prevent landowners from taking advantage of the freedmen. Labor contracts involving freedmen were supervised, and the civil rights of blacks were protected. Special freedmen courts were created, or observers were sent to regular courts to make sure that freed slaves got fair trials.

Our story takes place on election day. A new constitution had been put in effect in South Carolina. Blacks could now vote. They looked to the Freedmen's Bureau and other organizations for advice about how to vote. Many also needed help in marking their ballots. Most tended to vote for the Republican Party.

Charleston, South Carolina, November, 1869

A long line of men stood outside a small store on a narrow street. A sign in the store window said, VOTE HERE. The line moved slowly, and many of the men were restless. (At this time, only men were allowed to vote.)

"Joe, what are you doing here?" asked Sam Garner in great surprise.

"Same as you, Mr. Garner," replied Joe Rainey. "I'm here to vote."

"That's right. You can vote now," said Garner with obvious distaste. "But do you know what you're doing?"

"Sure, Mr. Garner, I have a good idea of what's going on. I've tried to find out as much as I could about the candidates, and I'm going to vote for the best man for each job."

"That's not exactly what I mean. After all, Joe, until a couple of years ago you people never voted. Because you've been slaves most of your lives, you've never had to make decisions. Why start now? We know what's best for you."

"Oh, I see," Rainey said with a smile. "You'd like to continue to make decisions for us. Well, let me tell you, Mr. Garner, times have changed. We're on our own now. You're not my master anymore. I'm here to vote as a free man."

The men behind them murmured: "Come on, move along. Close up those gaps in the lines."

"I'm not stopping you from voting," said Garner hastily. "But with the new constitution for South Carolina, you're turning everything upside down. What are you doing to the South?"

"Not upside down, but right-side up," answered Rainey. "Look at it from our point of view. You had a good place to live. We had nothing! Blacks had no rights because you whites controlled everything. Well, that's finished! Now everyone—black and white, rich and poor—can have a chance."

"Do you blacks intend to take over South Carolina?"

"I don't think that will happen even though there are many more blacks than whites in this state. We don't intend to push you out. Everyone should have a fair chance to share in the state government. First, though, we'll do a few things to make life easier for the poor."

"What do you plan to do?" asked Garner.

"We'll lower taxes for the poor. We won't put people who haven't paid their debts into jail. We'll build more hospitals and schools. You see, Mr. Garner, we want everyone in South Carolina to be equal."

Other men shouted: "Come on, get in there and vote! Don't waste time!" Garner and Rainey finally entered the store and voted. As they left, Garner looked glum, while Rainey's face bore a smile.

"I think voting is exciting," said Rainey. "We were choosing people to run our government."

"*You* were choosing," Garner replied. "Voting doesn't mean much to me anymore. Not when I know my side can't win. You people and your carpetbagger friends control the state legislature. What chance do we whites have to win anything?"

"Why can't blacks and whites share control of the state? Why can't we work together?"

"Do you think I'm a scalawag? Now, tell the truth, Joe. Don't you have a feeling of power? Don't you want to grab your share of the money that's being thrown around?"

"What are you talking about, Mr. Garner? There's no money in that election booth!"

"Oh, you know what I mean," Garner replied. "There's a lot of easy money around. And lawmakers make the green stuff stick to their fingers. Don't tell me you haven't heard about the gold spitoons for the state legislature. Or the votes to pay off lawmakers' gambling losses!"

"There will always be a few who will take money," said Rainey.

"And look at all the whiskey and cigars bought at public expense," Garner continued. "Fancy horses and carriages suddenly replace worn-out nags and buggies. Where does the money come from? From the public treasury—from my pocket!"

"But who's corrupting the lawmakers? Some people, black and white, can't resist money. Do I have to tell you that there's graft everywhere?"

"But when it happens right here in South Carolina, it hurts. You people had better fight against corruption. All of us—white and black alike—will have to pay in the end."

"Thanks for the advice, Mr. Garner. See you around," said Joe as he turned and walked away.

POSTSCRIPT

Black voters played an important role in the South during Reconstruction. For a time, blacks made up a majority of the voters in five states—Alabama, Florida, South Carolina, Mississippi, and Louisiana. Many blacks were elected to public office. Two served in the U.S. Senate and 15 in the House of Representatives. Blacks served in many state and local offices as well, up to the rank of lieutenant governor.

Homework Questions

1. Why did carpetbaggers move to the South after the Civil War?
2. Why were scalawags willing to work with the Northerners?
3. How did the Freedmen's Bureau help the freed slaves?
4. Why was the right to vote so important to Joe Rainey and other blacks of the Reconstruction Era?

Understanding the Story

A. Write *T* for each statement that is true and *F* for each statement that is false.
   1. Scalawags were white Southerners who favored the Union cause.
2. Most freed slaves could read and write.
3. The Freedmen's Bureau provided food and jobs for former slaves.
4. Most Northern carpetbaggers were adventurers.
5. Blacks voted in South Carolina in 1869.
6. Joe Rainey could not vote when he was a slave.
7. Sam Garner was happy that Joe Rainey was voting.
8. Sam Garner had been a slave.

B. Write *R* for each statement that Rainey made or might have made and *G* for each statement that Garner made or might have made.
   1. Why do you want to vote anyway?
   2. You're not my master.

3. What are you doing to the South?
4. Everyone will be equal.
5. We'll build more hospitals and schools.
6. My side can't win.
7. We don't intend to push you out.
8. Why can't we work together?

C. What, in your opinion, are the issues that divided Joe Rainey and Sam Garner the most? Explain.

Activities and Inquiries

1. Imagine you are a reporter interviewing Sam Garner. What questions will you ask? How will he respond?
2. Now imagine you are interviewing Joe Rainey. What questions will you ask? How will he respond?
3. Imagine it is 1869. Write an editorial about carpetbaggers for a South Carolina newspaper.
4. Do you think the Freedmen's Bureau was a good idea? Why or why not?
5. Imagine you are setting up a school for freed blacks in 1869. What subjects do you consider to be most important to teach? Why?

6 Trial by Fire

The right to vote was only one demand that Radical Republicans made on behalf of the freed slaves. Another was for land. Some Radicals believed the freedmen should be given land so they could become independent farmers.

Most Southern—and many Northern—whites disagreed. They argued that it was unfair to white landowners to take their land. It was also unfair to poor whites to give special treatment to the freedmen. According to this view, freed slaves should be left to take care of themselves as best they could—like everyone else.

For some whites, there was a very practical reason to take such a view. Blacks who had no land of their own would have to seek paying jobs. White planters needed laborers to work their fields. Black Codes (see pages 301–302) tended to push blacks into becoming farm laborers. In some states, blacks were barred from most jobs *except* farm work. Some Black Codes kept blacks from owning or renting land outside of towns.

Radical Republicans like Thaddeus Stevens wanted the federal government to give each family of freed slaves "40 acres and a mule." No such plan ever became law. Instead, blacks who wanted land of their own had to get it in other ways. A few were able to buy land. Some settled on lands that had been abandoned or confiscated (taken from former owners by legal action). The Freedmen's Bureau sometimes helped freed slaves to get land in such ways.

The Bureau's activities ended in 1869, and the situation for blacks became worse. Many whites sought to restore "the Southern way of life." Some did so by peaceful means, such as working to elect Democrats in place of Republicans. Others turned to violence and terror. They formed secret societies like the Ku Klux Klan to frighten blacks and force them back into a slave-like existence. Former slaves (and a few whites) were beaten, whipped, and even murdered. In some areas, Klan raids followed no pattern. In others, the cabins of blacks were raided night after night—on a regular schedule.

In our story, we see the Ku Klux Klan at work. A black farmer has received a warning note and must decide what to do. Ask yourself why the Klan did not want Elias Hunter to own his farm. Do you agree with Hunter or with his wife about facing the Klansmen? Why?

Spartacus, Georgia, 1870

Elias Hunter, a black farmer, was reading a note when his wife, Marcelle, walked into the small room.

"Let's see that note, Elias," said Marcelle.

"It's nothing," he replied. "Forget it."

"Why hide it if it's nothing?" questioned Marcelle.

He handed her the dirty piece of paper. "It's from the Klan," she gasped. "'Get out of town or die!' They mean business. What are we going to do?"

"I'll tell the Negro Militia. They'll protect us."

"You can't count on them," objected Marcelle. "They'll never get here in time. We've got to get out of here."

"No, Marcelle, we can't leave. Everything that matters to us is right here. These few acres and our house belong to us. Our child was born here. No one is going to force me to leave my property."

"Don't be a fool, Elias. You know what the Klan has been doing in this county. How many of us have they beaten, whipped, or killed? How many houses, churches, and schools have they torn down or burned? I don't want us to be next!"

"Sit down, Marcelle." He held her hands affectionately. "Don't you see it's more than just the farm. It's more than just you and me. All of us are free now. If we keep running from the Klan, we will lose our freedom. We'll be the slaves of their terror!"

"I'm sorry," said Marcelle, crying softly. "I can't agree that it's freedom or slavery. I think it's life or death."

Two days later a black horseman galloped up to the house. "The Klansmen are riding this way! They'll be here in less than an hour! Get out or they'll whip you. They'll kill you!" He rode off to warn others.

"Well, what are you going to do now?" said Marcelle.

"I'm not leaving." He picked up a shotgun. "This is my land, and I'm going to defend my property!"

"No!" she screamed. "Do you want to be a dead hero? Don't your wife and child count for anything?"

"Marcelle, you don't understand."

"I understand. You want to prove that you're not afraid. You'll fire a few shots, and then they'll kill you. People will say that Elias Hunter died fighting. Is that what you want?"

"No, no!" insisted Elias. "You're wrong. If I fire a few shots, they'll be frightened off."

"You always were a dreamer. Six or eight or ten of the Klansmen will come after us. Your one gun won't frighten them. You haven't a chance—and you know it! Get out of here and save your life. I'm packing now." She walked out.

Elias stood in the room alone. To.himself he said, "A few years ago I was freed from a life of slavery. For what? For this? Shall I stay here and fight? And possibly die? Or shall I run?" His face twisted by sorrow, Elias threw up his hands. "Oh, I know that Marcelle is right. I can fight back—only if I live."

Marcelle stood watching from the doorway. "Don't worry," she said, "this is just the beginning for us. Someday we will overcome."

Later that evening eight hooded members of the Ku Klux Klan rode up to the house. They carried guns, whips, and lighted torches.

"Elias," the leader shouted, "come out here and take your medicine!"

There was no answer.

"Will we ever be free?"

"I know you're in there. You can't hide from us! Get out here now!"

Again, silence.

The leader signaled to the other Klansmen, and they fired shot after shot through the windows. Finally, at a motion from the leader's torch, several of the men dismounted and set the house afire. The riders admired their work and slowly turned away.

POSTSCRIPT

State and local governments were not strong enough to deal with violence in the South. They called on Congress to act. The Force Act of 1870 provided severe penalties for anyone using force, bribery, or intimidation (threats of violence) to prevent any citizen from voting. It also placed congressional elections under federal supervision. A second Force Act in 1871 strengthened the penalties of the first.

At the same time Congress passed the Ku Klux Klan Acts of 1870 and 1871. They authorized the President to act against organizations such as the Klan. The activities of these armed bands were compared with outright rebellion against the United States. President Ulysses S. Grant ordered federal troops into the most unruly areas of the South. Appointed commissioners made hundreds of arrests on charges of conspiracy. The power of the Klan was broken in 1872, although violence in the South did not end.

As the years passed, Northerners became less and less interested in the problems of the South. More and more Southern governments were returned to the control of white Southern Democrats. In 1877 the last of the federal troops were withdrawn from the South. Reconstruction had come to an end. In later years, whites in the South barred most blacks from voting. Many of the advances made by blacks during Reconstruction were lost.

In the North, blacks concentrated on winning the right to vote. At the end of the Civil War, only six states (Maine, New Hampshire, Vermont, Massachusetts, Rhode Island, and New York) permitted blacks to vote. Radical Republicans supported the campaign for black voting rights. Three more states (Iowa, Minnesota, Wisconsin) gave blacks the vote. Then, in 1870, the 15th Amendment became part of the Constitution. This amendment forbade a state to keep a person from voting because of race, color, or having been a slave.

Northern blacks generally lived in cities and were limited to working at unskilled trades or as servants. They were waiters, shoe shiners, washerwomen, maids, butlers, manual laborers, and so on. Wages were low. Efforts by blacks to join labor unions were unsuccessful.

In both North and South, blacks were free, but they continued to be treated as third-class citizens. The dream of equality for all remained just that: a dream. It would not become an important national issue again for almost a century.

Homework Questions

1. How did the Black Codes affect job opportunities for freedmen?
2. How did the Ku Klux Klan attempt to keep black people from achieving equality?
3. Why was it important to the freed-men to own land...

#7 Q1 + 2

...never hurt anyone.

3. The Klan was active in New York State.
4. The Klan raided homes of blacks.
5. The Klan encouraged blacks to own farms.
6. The Klan did not destroy churches and schools.
7. Klan members mainly lived in cities.
8. In 1877 the last Federal troops were withdrawn from the South.

B. Write *A* for each statement that Elias Hunter would agree with and *N* for each statement that he would not agree with.
1. I'll call in the Negro Militia.
2. Let's not argue with the Klan.
3. If we keep running, we will lose our freedom.
4. Our farm is small, but it's ours.
5. Being a slave wasn't so bad after all.
6. Perhaps they'll be frightened off.
7. Marcelle is right.
8. I don't want to fight back.

C. Terrorism remains a force in today's world. Can you think of a recent example? If so, how would you compare the terrorists of your example with the Ku Klux Klan as to goals and methods used?

Activities and Inquiries

1. Look at the drawing on page 313 and answer the following questions.
   a. Explain the caption of the cartoon.
   b. Why was this farm being destroyed?
   c. What steps should have been taken to prevent this from happening?
   d. Today what answer would you give to the question in the caption?
2. You have decided to prepare a television movie about this story. What scenes might you add?
3. What do you think was the goal of the Ku Klux Klan during Reconstruction? Would you say the Klan achieved its goal? Explain.
4. If you had been Elias or Marcelle Hunter, what would you have done about the note from the Klan? Explain why.

7 The Growth of the Constitution: The 13th Amendment

The Emancipation Proclamation changed the Civil War by making it broader than a fight to save the Union. The conflict also became a war against slavery. One result was the opening of the armed forces to blacks.

Actually, slaves had begun coming into Union army camps from the first month of the war. At first they had been turned away. Later they were permitted to help and eventually to enlist. By the end of the war, black men made up 10 percent of the Union army.

Would the Emancipation Proclamation alone be enough to destroy slavery? Many thought not, because the proclamation was a wartime order. Once peace came, the order would be disregarded. Even a law passed by Congress would have little effect on the slave system. Only an amendment to the Constitution would be strong enough to change American society.

In our story, a black war correspondent and a Union soldier (a former slave) talk about freedom and slavery. It is a happy moment for both, but the fears of slavery are still there.

Ask yourself why Chester believes that a constitutional amendment is necessary. How did the Civil War change Private Smith's life? Why did he join the Union army?

Charleston, South Carolina, February 18, 1865

Confederate troops fled from Charleston on February 17, 1865. The next day Union soldiers marched into the city. They were led by the 55th Massachusetts Regiment, a black unit with white officers.

T. Morris Chester, the only black war correspondent for a major Northern newspaper (the *Philadelphia Press*), walked around speaking to the men of the 55th. They were all extremely happy, excited, and tired. One soldier seemed even more excited than the others.

"Well, soldier, why are you so happy today?"

"I don't think I could put it into words," replied Private Godfrey Smith.

"Try," said Chester encouragingly.

"You see, the last time I was in Charleston I was a slave. I came here because my master needed my muscle, and I worked hard because I was afraid. Now I'm back in Charleston as a Union soldier.

There's such a difference. I'm somebody now—not just some thing. I'm free!"

"I think I understand—though I was never a slave myself," said Chester. "How did you become a soldier?"

"It was easy. I knew that the Union camp was only a few miles away from my master's farm, and I hated being a slave. The army was there to make me free, so one night I just ran as fast as I could to the Union lines."

"Weren't you afraid?" asked Chester.

"No, I knew they wouldn't hurt me," said Smith. "Besides, it was my chance to be free."

"And then they made you a soldier?"

"Not right away," said Private Smith. "At first they had me helping out. I loaded and unloaded supplies, dug ditches and trenches, and carried food and ammunition to the front lines. It was hard work, but I liked it better than working as a slave."

"Weren't you disappointed?" asked Chester. "Didn't you want to be a soldier?"

"Sure I was disappointed. But I can't say that I was surprised. After all, I had just been a slave. I—and the army—still had a lot of questions about me. Was I ready to be a soldier? Could I learn to shoot? Would I be afraid when I saw the enemy? Would I stand my ground? Then one day, a hundred of us were given blue uniforms and rifles."

"At last you were in the army," said Chester.

"Right. I couldn't wait to fire my rifle at those slave masters. Now I know slavery is finished, and I can never be a slave again."

"How can you be so sure?"

"I've seen it with my own eyes," said Private Smith. "This army puts an end to slavery wherever it goes. That's what this war is all about. Didn't President Lincoln order slavery abolished in the rebel states?"

"What you say is true, but we have to be sure that slavery stays abolished. Two border states, Delaware and Kentucky, still allow it."

"Don't tell me that I could be a slave again. That can't be true!"

"No, no, you have nothing to worry about. I'm sure that slavery will soon disappear from this country. But each state can still decide whether it wants to be free or slave. We have to take away that right."

"You mean that many years from now a state could go back to slavery?" asked Smith. "We can't let that happen."

"Don't worry. It won't happen. The Constitution will be amended. The 13th Amendment to finish slavery forever has already been approved by two thirds of both houses of Congress."

"Good. You had me worried there for a minute, Mr. Chester. At long last the Constitution will protect me."

"Here," said Chester, "let me read the amendment to you: 'Neither slavery nor involuntary servitude except as a punishment for crime . . . shall exist within the United States . . .'"

"It's short enough," said Smith thoughtfully. "But what's involuntary servitude?"

"It would mean that you could be forced to work without pay. The amendment makes sure you can choose your job and get paid for it," replied Chester.

"You're right; my worries are over."

"The amendment will help me, too," added Chester. "I've been a free black all my life. But I've always lived in the shadow of slavery. White people looked at me strangely because I was different from them. They wondered whether I was an escaped slave. Was I a criminal? How could I possibly do a white man's work? Now this 13th Amendment will end all those doubts, and everyone will know that I am a free man. At last, I have a chance to be equal."

"Freedom," shouted Private Smith, "freedom, it's wonderful!"

"Yes, it is wonderful. But you need a few other things, like a job, the right to vote, and the chance for an education."

POSTSCRIPT

On December 18, 1865, the 13th Amendment was declared ratified (approved) by three fourths of the states. It became part of the Constitution, and slavery ("involuntary servitude") became illegal in all parts of the United States. But even today charges of involuntary servitude come up from time to time. Recent examples have had to do with farm workers, professional athletes, and draftees.

For instance, migrant farm workers (those who move from farm to farm) have sometimes had trouble leaving a farm where they have been working. An employer might claim that the workers owe money for food or shelter and try to force them to stay and "work it off." Courts have held such actions to be unconstitutional. Under the 13th Amendment, no one may be held in peonage—that is, be forced to work to pay off a debt.

In the sports world, baseball players and others at one time accused pro teams of making virtual "slaves" of players. The criticism had to do with the so-called reserve clause, which binds a player to a specific team. Under the reserve clause, a team owner can sell a player to another team, but the player cannot switch teams without permission. In recent years, under pressure from players' unions, owners have made changes in the reserve clause to give athletes greater freedom of action. A modified reserve clause is still in use.

The military draft has also been challenged as a form of involuntary servitude. The U.S. Supreme Court ruled in 1918 that the draft does not violate the 13th Amendment. As you have read, imprisonment for a crime is also allowed under the 13th Amendment.

Homework Questions

1. Why couldn't the Emancipation Proclamation alone destroy slavery?
2. How did Smith become a Union soldier?
3. What did Chester mean by saying that he had always lived in the shadow of slavery?
4. How has the 13th Amendment been used to protect workers in recent times?

Understanding the Story

A. Match each item in Column *A* with its description in Column *B*.

Column A

1. T. Morris Chester
2. Slavery
3. Godfrey Smith
4. Kentucky
5. Emancipation Proclamation
6. 13th Amendment
7. 55th Massachusetts Regiment
8. New Jersey

Column B

a. Slave state
b. Black soldier
c. Free state
d. Involuntary servitude
e. Black war correspondent
f. Order freeing slaves behind enemy lines
g. Constitutional change ending slavery
h. Black military unit

B. List the numbers of the statements that are true.
1. Former slaves did not join the Union army.
2. Ten percent of the Union army was made up of black soldiers.
3. Private Smith had been a slave.
4. Private Smith became a Confederate soldier.
5. T. Morris Chester had been a slave.
6. Kentucky and Delaware were slave states in 1865.
7. The 13th Amendment abolished slavery in all states.
8. Chester was not happy with the 13th Amendment.

C. "Freedom is wonderful," said Private Smith. Describe what freedom means to you.

Activities and Inquiries

1. Assume that Congress is debating the 13th Amendment. Chester is called to give his views. What will he say?
2. Another black American is asked to give her opinions. She says that the 13th amendment does not go far enough. What do you suppose she means?
3. Imagine that you are a member of a Senate committee. Rewrite the 13th Amendment to meet the complaints referred to in question 2.
4. Suppose that a Ku Klux Klansman was interviewed about the 13th Amendment during the Reconstruction Era. What would he say?
5. How would you answer the arguments of the Klansman?

"Did this unit answer your questions about the Civil War and Reconstruction?" asked Mr. Miller.

"Yes," replied Jack. "I could see that the South would fight to protect the slave system and the rights of Southern states. But I wasn't sure about what would cause the North to fight."

"What did you discover, Jack?"

"The North felt that the South was breaking up the nation. Northerners would fight and die to save the Union, the United States of America."

"Very good, Jack. But aren't you overlooking the Northern attitude toward slavery?"

"Not really, Mr. Miller. Slavery wasn't too important to most of the North until Lincoln's Emancipation Proclamation. And even that didn't free the slaves in areas under Union control. It took the 13th Amendment to free them all."

"That's true," said Mr. Miller. "Of course, you remember that thousands of slaves ran off to join the Union armies. They were lost to the Confederacy."

"Right," said Jack.

"After the war was over, what happened to the states that left the Union?"

"Well," replied Jack, "Lincoln wanted to make it easy for them to return, and Johnson tried to follow Lincoln's plan. But the Radical Republicans in Congress wouldn't stand for it. Punish the rebels! they said."

"Who won?" asked Mr. Miller.

"Congress. Johnson was impeached. He was tried by the Senate and almost lost his job!"

"Which plan of Reconstruction would have been the best for the rebel states?" asked Mr. Miller.

"I think I would have gone along with Lincoln. Too bad he was shot."

"What happened in the South under the Reconstruction plan Congress set up?"

"Federal troops were sent in to regulate voting and keep order. Many white Southerners didn't want to see blacks get ahead, so they formed terrorist groups like the Ku Klux Klan. Some blacks were elected to Congress and to the new state legislatures, but the reforms blacks wanted turned out to be temporary."

"All true, Jack. The Reconstruction period was a difficult time for both the North and the South."

"Where do we go from here?" asked Jack.

"Let's look at business and labor after the Civil War."

The Industrial Revolution Comes of Age

"Mr. Miller, I know why the Civil War began and how it ended. But what happened to the country afterwards?"

"As you know, Jack, Americans fought the Civil War to right certain wrongs. But the war did more than that. It created a new America."

"A new America? What do you mean?"

Mr. Miller continued. "An America where everything suddenly grew larger—business, labor, government."

"How did this make a difference?"

"Growth created new conflicts. We Americans had to deal with them if ours was to become a great country."

"Were the problems solved?" Jack asked.

"Not entirely. We are still trying to solve some."

"What were some of the problems we faced?"

"Let's turn to the unit to find out."

1 John D. Rockefeller, Oil Tycoon

In 1861, as the Civil War began, the United States was not primarily an industrial nation. It lagged far behind Britain, France, and Germany in industry. A country of small towns and small businesses, the United States concerned itself mainly with agriculture and westward expansion.

But by 1890, just 30 years later, production in the United States almost equaled the industrial output of Britain, France, and Germany combined. How did this change happen so fast?

The Civil War provides some answers to this question. Northern armies needed quantities of guns, ammunition, uniforms, and food. New industries began and old ones expanded to fill these needs. After the South seceded from the Union, Congress could easily pass whatever legislation it wanted to benefit the North and West. As a result, Congress set up high protective tariffs to keep out foreign goods and provide money for railroad building. Railroads made it easier to get raw materials to factories, food to consumers, and homesteaders (settlers) to unsettled land. New inventions and manufacturing processes used more of the country's large supplies of natural resources. A growing population, boosted by more and more immigrants, provided workers to build the railroads, mine the resources, and run the machines.

Of course, business expansion required huge sums of money. To meet this need, business people formed *corporations*. A corporation is a type of business especially suited to large-scale operation. It can raise money by selling shares of stock (portions of the business). The buyers of stock, called stockholders, become joint owners of the corporation.

Business firms began to grow large, and competition in many industries became fierce. Sometimes a strong firm would try to drive one that made a similar product out of business. It would do this by cutting prices. Sometimes several companies joined together to destroy competitors. A few groups of companies were so successful that they drove out all their competition. Then they were free to charge higher prices. They might also join together into one giant corporation.

A firm or group of firms that has no effective competitors is called a *monopoly*. Many monopolies developed in the United States in the decades after the Civil War. Such businesses as oil, steel, sugar, and railroads were controlled by monopolies.

The men who ran monopolies and other large corporations became extremely wealthy. And with wealth came political power. Leading businessmen and corporations tried to use their power to influence government in ways that would advance their interests.

One of the wealthiest business leaders was John D. Rockefeller, head of the Standard Oil Company. How did Rockefeller become rich? How did he make his company one of the largest and most important in the nation?

Florida, May, 1937

You are John D. Rockefeller, and you believe that one should allow nothing to stand in the way of success.

At age seven you raised turkeys, sold them, and made a profit. Your mother taught you to give part of your profit to charity. You never forgot this lesson.

At 16 you were a clerk in a food company. You worked hard, listened, learned, saved your money, and invested it. By the time you were 20 you owned a food company.

When you made a profit, you put most of that money back into your food business. You also borrowed money and put that into the business. As the business grew, you became rich. But you wanted more money. Your food business was not enough for you. So in the 1860's, during the Civil War, you invested in a business that was still brand new in America—oil. You saw that oil could be used instead of candles for light and that it could be used for fuel.

You bought crude oil as it came from the ground. Then you refined (processed) the oil to turn it into such products as lamp oil (kerosene). Crude oil was cheap, but lamp oil was expensive, so you made a good profit. You wasted nothing. The best parts of the crude oil you turned into kerosene. The rest you turned into products such as paraffin (wax) and petroleum jelly.

In 1870 you started the Standard Oil Company. The firm grew rapidly. You wanted to control all parts of your oil business, so you built your own wagons and oil barrels. You began to build pipelines. You made deals with railroads to get special rates for shipping your oil.

Your deals made it harder for other refiners to get railroad cars and send their products to market. That was just what you wanted. You told rivals that you would buy their oil and handle it for them. Of course, you offered to pay a low price. You wanted to make sure that you—not they—made the most profit.

In time many refining companies were losing money and found themselves in deep trouble. You bought many firms, including some of your largest competitors. You hired their top men. If firms would not sell out to you, you cut your prices so low that you took away their customers and drove them out of business. You would not take "no" for an answer.

In 1879 you organized the Standard Oil Trust. The trust gave you control of more than 90 percent of the oil refined in the entire country. Under your trust agreement, the stockholders of competing oil companies turned over their shares of stock to you. This gave you control of their companies. In return, you gave the stockholders a share of the profits of the new giant trust. Other industries, such as steel, sugar, and tobacco, followed your lead and formed trusts.

But your efforts to get rid of competitors ran into problems with the government and the courts. For years some Americans had argued that Congress should pass laws against trusts and monopolies. Owners of smaller businesses were among those seeking such laws. They said the laws were needed to protect free competition. Others— like you—disagreed. You argued that government should keep its hands off business. Such a hands-off policy is sometimes called *laissez-faire* (pronounced LESS say FARE), from French words meaning "let alone."

Congress tended to favor laissez-faire policies. But pressure for change built up, and in 1890 Congress passed the Sherman Anti-Trust Act. The act said it was illegal to form trusts or monopolies that interfered with trade that crossed state boundaries. The act didn't worry you at the time. The wording was vague, and you figured the government and the courts would do little to enforce the act. For several years it appeared that you were right.

Then in 1911 came a blow. The U.S. Supreme Court decided that your main firm, known by then as the Standard Oil Company of New Jersey, was acting against the Sherman Anti-Trust Act. The Court said your firm was competing with other oil companies in an illegal way. Standard Oil had to be split up into 34 separate companies.

It would take more than one court decision to undo your business empire. You were already the richest man in the United States. After 1911 you retired from active direction of your companies. But the companies went right on making money for you. You were proud of what you had accomplished. As you saw it, you had brought order to the oil industry by doing away with wild competition.

You continued to live in an expensive house and own fine horses. But you dressed simply, ate little, and took care not to spoil your four children. (When they were young, they had to share one bicycle).

What interested you most was your business. Long after you had earned more money than you could ever hope to spend, you continued to be at your desk by six every morning. Even at home, you talked of little else except business.

After you retired, you spent your days raising roses, playing golf, and giving away a great deal of money. You gave more than $750 million to charities. Many people began to think of you as a kindhearted old man. But many others remembered less pleasant things about you. They thought of you as a ruthless man, driven by greed.

Now, at the age of 97, you are known as one of the geniuses of the modern business world. And that is no surprise. You have rarely allowed anything to stand in the way of your success.

Homework Questions

1. How did the Civil War pave the way for the industrial growth of the North?
2. How did John D. Rockefeller gain control of his competitors' businesses?
3. Why did Rockefeller form the Standard Oil Trust?
4. Which other industries formed trusts like the one formed by Standard Oil?
5. What effect did the Sherman Anti-Trust Act have on the Standard Oil Company?

Understanding the Story

A. Write *T* for each statement that is true and *F* for each statement that is false.
   1. In 1861 Britain was ahead of the United States in industrial production.
   2. In 1890 Germany was in first place in industrial production.
   3. Rockefeller became the richest man in the United States.
   4. Rockefeller became an oil refiner.
   5. Rockefeller wanted everyone in the oil business to make a large profit.
   6. Rockefeller could not control the oil refining industry.
   7. Because of a ruling by the Supreme Court, the Standard Oil Company had to be broken up.
   8. Rockefeller retired early because he was a failure in business.

B. List the numbers of the statements that apply to John D. Rockefeller.
   1. He became very rich.
   2. He organized the Standard Oil Company.
   3. He invested most of his money in coal mines.
   4. He sold refined oil at a great profit.
   5. He lived in a simple house.
   6. He refused to give money to charities.
   7. He was mainly interested in his business.
   8. He was penniless in his last years.

C. Two views of John D. Rockefeller are presented in this chapter. One is of a ruthless and greedy man. The other is of a kindhearted and generous man. With which view do you agree? Why?

Activities and Inquiries

1. List the personal qualities and economic conditions you feel are necessary for success in business.
2. Visit your library and do research to find out how another American became very rich. Some suggestions are: Andrew Carnegie, J. P. Morgan, Cornelius Vanderbilt, E. H. Harriman, or George Eastman.
3. Re-read the story. Make a list of the things Rockefeller did that you liked. List things you did not like.

2 Railroad Workers Strike

American business went through periods of boom and bust in the years after the Civil War. The economy was growing fast but not steadily. Periods of hard times struck in the mid-1870's, the mid-1880's, and the mid-1890's. Many people lost their jobs in those hard times, and many investors lost their money.

The wages of workers were generally improving. By 1890 the average wage was $486 a year—roughly $9.30 a week. To get this the worker toiled ten hours a day, six days a week.

As you have read, this was a period when businesses were growing larger and more powerful. In earlier times, manufacturing had been done on a small scale. Most shops or factories had few workers. The boss could know each worker by name. Now some large companies employed thousands of workers. Dealings between workers and employers become more and more impersonal.

To protect their interests, some workers organized labor unions. They hoped to bargain with employers for higher wages and better working conditions. Most employers were hostile to unions. They thought they had enough problems struggling to compete with other companies. They wanted to keep their costs as low as possible. Much of the public sided with the employers.

By the 1870's there were 20 to 30 national trade unions. Most represented skilled workers in a specific trade. One major union, the Knights of Labor, hoped to organize all working people—not just those with special skills. It encouraged its members to take an interest in politics. The Knights of Labor supported a movement for laws to shorten the workday to eight hours. It also favored laws to end child labor.

The struggle between employers and unions was a bitter one. Employers had many ways to put pressure on unions. They could fire troublesome workers, cut wages, and generally make things difficult for union members. Unions, in turn, had a major weapon against management. They could call workers out on strike.

A number of bitter strikes took place in the 1870's. Bloodshed marked a particularly explosive strike in 1877. In the midst of a business slump, the Baltimore & Ohio Railroad cut wages by 10 percent without warning. Workers walked off the job. The strike spread to other railroads. Strikers blocked trains, disrupting rail traffic from Baltimore to St. Louis. The Pennsylvania state militia, sent to Pittsburgh to clear the tracks, fired on a mob and killed 26 people. This touched off a riot that destroyed $5 million in railroad property. In the end, federal troops were sent to get the trains running, and the strike collapsed. The violence had alarmed many people and tended to make labor unions more unpopular with much of the public.

One businessman, George W. Pullman, thought he had the answer to labor-management problems. Pullman had developed the first railroad sleeping car in 1864. He formed a company to produce such cars. Pullman hired thousands of workers and built them a town near Chicago. He called the town Pullman. Besides homes the town contained churches, schools, playgrounds, parks, a bank, and a library. Pullman boasted that he treated his workers very well and in return expected their complete loyalty.

But Pullman was in for a surprise. In 1894 his workers voted to strike. Their leader was Eugene Debs, the head of the American Railway Union.

The dispute grew ugly and soon halted most railroad traffic in the United States.

In our story, we have brought together George Pullman and Eugene Debs for a joint interview. In real life, such an interview could never have taken place, for the two men were bitter foes. Ask yourself what the key issues are between Pullman and Debs. Who won the strike? How?

Pullman, Illinois, July 3, 1894

REPORTER. Mr. Debs, why is this strike taking place?

EUGENE DEBS. To defend the rights of workers. The Pullman Palace Car Company caused the strike by cutting workers' wages by as much as 25 percent. The workers have a right to a decent wage. That's what this strike is about.

GEORGE PULLMAN. Hold on there! Of course the workers have a right to a decent wage. But times are hard. Business is in a bad slump—perhaps the worst this country has ever seen. The company has to cut its costs, and part of the burden must be borne by the workers.

DEBS. *All* of the burden, you mean. I don't see you taking a cut in profits! You have just paid out the usual dividend of $2.5 million to your stockholders.

PULLMAN. Mr. Debs, no man treats his workers better than I. Remember, I built a town for my workers. I put them into clean houses—much better houses than they could rent elsewhere. I give my workers good jobs, and I pay them well.

DEBS. The houses may be clean, but they are small and cheaply built. The rooms are dark and airless. Besides, the rents you charge are higher than rents in nearby places. The prices in your company store are higher than elsewhere. And you did not cut the rents when you cut the workers' wages.

PULLMAN. How could I cut the rents? The costs of that housing are fixed costs. I must spend just as much to keep up the town in bad times as in good times.

DEBS. Well, the workers can't afford such rents on the wages you pay. I've spoken to some of your workers. When they've paid the rent, they have just $5 to live on for the two weeks until the next payday. How are they supposed to survive? Food alone for a family of five people costs $6 a week. And what about clothes? You're a greedy man, Mr. Pullman. You're demanding that your workers give up their bodies and souls to your heartless corporation.

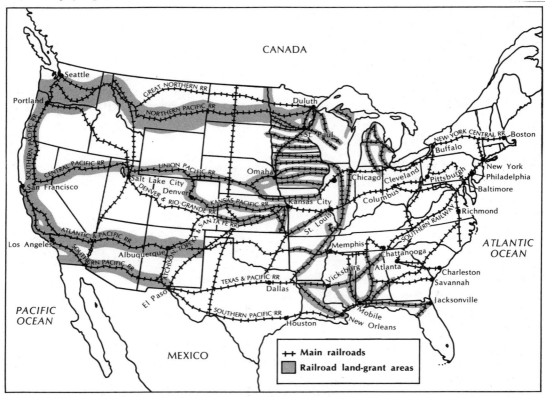

Major Railroad Lines, 1850–1900

PULLMAN. And you, Mr. Debs, are a revolutionary. You are the most dangerous man in America.

REPORTER. Gentlemen, let's focus on issues—not personalities. Mr. Pullman, perhaps you would explain why you have refused to bargain with union leaders. Just what is your position?

PULLMAN. Sir, we live in a nation that has been made great by the spirit of free enterprise. It is men with capital—men like myself—who have invested the money that has created our industrial progress. The decisions about how to run my business must remain in my hands. I must be able to set wages at a level that allows the company to earn a reasonable profit. If I could not earn a profit, this company would die—and all my workers would be without jobs.

DEBS. Of course the company has a right to earn a profit, Mr. Pullman. But workers have a right to a fair wage, too. Obviously you will not listen to reason, so the union has been forced to resort to its ultimate weapon—the strike. If workers cannot talk to you with words, they will talk with power.

PULLMAN. Mr. Debs, you have come in here and stirred up the workers. You tell them to follow you if they want better wages or better working conditions. I think all you really want is power for your-self—at my expense!

DEBS. Your workers were stirred up long before I ever came to Pull-man. You'll recall that a committee of your workers met with you to ask that you reduce rents to match your wage cuts. Not only did you refuse, but you fired three members of the committee. You—not I—stirred up your workers.

PULLMAN. And you, Mr. Debs, have made this strike into a nation-wide crisis. You have spread the strike to include workers for the railroad companies. Your workers are boycotting—refusing to handle—any train that includes a Pullman car. Rail lines are tied up from coast to coast. Not even the mail can get through!

DEBS. The lines can quickly be untied, Mr. Pullman. All the rail-road companies have to do is to take the Pullman cars out of their trains until our strike against you is settled. The American Rail-way Union will happily run the mail trains—so long as they do not include any Pullman cars. It is the railroad companies that are blocking the mails. They refuse to remove Pullman cars. And they are firing our members who refuse to work. You and the railroad companies are out to destroy the union.

PULLMAN. Indeed we are, Mr. Debs. We cannot stand for such black-mail tactics as yours. Your union is a gang of lawless men. The courts have ruled as much.

REPORTER. Mr. Pullman has a point, Mr. Debs. Yesterday a court ordered the boycott of Pullman cars to stop. It said you were vio-lating the Sherman Anti-Trust Act by blocking trade between the states.

DEBS. The laws are being twisted to support the rich owners against the rights of the poor workers. It is the owners—not the workers—who are blocking trade. It is the courts that are lawless. I will not obey the court. Instead, I will ask labor unions all over the coun-try to stage a general strike. Workers must stick together if they hope to get their rights.

POSTSCRIPT

On July 4, President Grover Cleve-land ordered federal troops to step in. He said: "If it takes every dollar in the treasury and every soldier in the United States Army to deliver a postal card to Chicago, that postal card shall be de-livered." In a violent clash between troops and demonstrators on July 7, twelve people died.

Other unions refused to heed Debs's call for a general strike. Debs spent six months in jail for contempt of court. The Pullman workers went back to work on Pullman's terms, their strike broken.

Richard Olney, the United States attorney general, declared that the government had tried to be fair. Union leaders saw things in a different light. They accused the government of breaking the strike by siding with the companies against the workers. Debs said he was fed up with Republicans and Democrats alike. After serving his prison term, Debs traveled about speaking on behalf of a working-people's party. Five times he ran for President on a Socialist ticket. In 1920 he received more than 900,000 votes, even though he was again in prison.

George Pullman died three years after the strike. His town, Pullman, is now part of Chicago.

Homework Questions

1. Why did workers form labor unions?
2. How did the Knights of Labor try to improve working conditions?
3. How did the railroad strike of 1877 help turn many people against labor?
4. What did George Pullman mean by accusing Eugene Debs and his union of blackmail?
5. What reason did the court give for ordering the union to end its boycott?

Understanding the Story

A. Write *T* for each statement that is true, *F* for each statement that is false, and *O* for each statement that is an opinion.
  1. George Pullman built railroad engines.
  2. Pullman built a town for his workers.
  3. Pullman was the best friend the workers ever had.
  4. The Pullman strike in 1894 was led by Eugene Debs.
  5. Pullman agreed that his workers had good reasons for striking.
  6. Pullman and Debs were friends.
  7. The President had no choice but to send in federal troops.
  8. Debs thought the government sided with the companies.

B. Write *P* for each statement that Pullman made or might have made and *D* for each statement that Debs made or might have made.
  1. The company caused the strike.
  2. No one treats workers better than I.
  3. I must earn a reasonable profit.
  4. All you really want is power for yourself.
  5. The workers were stirred up before I came.
  6. You are using blackmail.
  7. The railroad companies are blocking the mails.
  8. The laws are being twisted.

C. If you had lived in the 1890's, would you have agreed to work for an employer who had views like those of George Pullman? Why or why not?

Activities and Inquiries

1. Assume that you are a reporter covering the strike. What questions would you ask a Pullman worker?
2. How would the worker answer your questions?
3. How would George Pullman reply to the worker?
4. Write a letter to Attorney General Olney telling him your views on the use of troops to break up the Pullman strike.
5. Now write Olney's reply to your letter.

3 A Matter of Conscience

Business people were making lots of money in the years from 1860 to 1890. They had a slogan: "To make money, you have to spend money." While many business people were honest, some found that it paid to spend money for a shady purpose—buying favors from politicians. They found more than a few government officials "on the take."

What could unscrupulous people buy for their money? They could buy railroad charters, land grants, government contracts, high tariffs on special goods—all sorts of favors. Of course, buying favors was against the law. But the risks of being caught were small compared to the promise of financial gain.

Nonetheless, many examples of corruption came to light:

• A "whiskey ring" cheated the federal treasury out of several million dollars. By paying off federal officials, a group of whiskey makers avoided paying large amounts of taxes. This happened during the administration of President Ulysses S. Grant (1869–1877). Although Grant himself was not involved, some of his close friends were.

• Directors of the Union Pacific Railroad cheated the railroad's stockholders and the federal government out of millions of dollars. They set up a separate company (known as Crédit Mobilier) to lay tracks and had this company charge the railroad far more than the work was worth. (The government lost too because it was giving land and aid to the Union Pacific and other railroads.) To avoid investigation, company officials offered stock in Crédit Mobilier to high government officials. The scandal hit the newspapers in 1872. Critics said similar practices were common at other railroads.

• Over a seven-year period, a politician named William ("Boss") Tweed swindled New York City out of $200 million. He demanded money from contractors and permitted them to overcharge the city. For example, the city paid almost $2 million to a builder for plastering one city building. Much of this money went back to Tweed and his followers.

Fortunately for the country, some politicians were *not* for sale. A leading example was John Peter Altgeld. For refusing to betray the public trust, he paid a terrible price. What set him apart from many other politicians of the late 1800's?

Chicago, Illinois, 1900

My name is John Peter Altgeld. Born in Germany to poor farmers, I came to America when I was very young. America treated me well, and I became wealthy. Today, however, I am poor again. Being poor doesn't bother me because I learned all about poverty and hard work as a boy.

I left my family's farm in Ohio to fight for the Union in the Civil War. Afterwards, the farm seemed too small, so I set out to find my own way.

Because I wanted to see every part of the country, I moved around a great deal. Whatever jobs I could find, I took. Mainly I worked on farms and on railroads. Often I was lonely, cold, and hungry. But learning about life, people, and places gave me great satisfaction.

Once I took a job teaching children. Many of their parents became my friends. A few parents suggested that I study law. The idea appealed to me, so I taught in the morning, worked on a farm in the afternoon, and studied law at night. Once again, hard work paid off, and I became a lawyer in Missouri.

My clients were hard-working farmers. I respected them and opposed anyone who tried to hurt them. At 27 years of age, I was afraid of nothing. But Savannah, Missouri, was becoming too small for me. The time had come to move on again.

I went to Chicago in 1875. Most of the city's houses had burned in the Great Fire of 1871, and new houses were going up everywhere. I designed and built six of the finest business blocks in the city. I bought and sold real estate, too. In ten years I was a rich man.

Now everyone looked up to me. Even though the wealthy liked me and the poor respected me, I was still restless. Politics attracted me.

At this time, a great conflict was going on between working people and the owners of giant businesses. The public was taking sides. My friends who were newspaper owners and politicians lined up on the side of business. But poverty had left scars on my soul, and I could not turn my back on the poor. I hoped I would never have to choose between my poor friends and my rich ones.

My career skyrocketed. I became a judge and, in 1893, the governor of Illinois. I set my sights on becoming a United States Senator. From there, who knows? A poor person could go a long way in this great country.

Little did I know how an event that had occurred seven years before I became governor would affect my future. This event was the Haymarket Riot of 1886. Police had moved into a labor protest rally in Haymarket Square, Chicago, intending to break up the meeting. Someone had thrown a bomb, killing one police officer and six civilians. In the riot that followed, seven policemen and four civilians had been killed.

Newspapers all over the country had screamed for revenge. Emotions had run high. The Chicago police had arrested 31 people on the basis of weak evidence. Authorities should have dropped the charges, but the public demanded victims.

Finally, eight men came to trial. A jury found them guilty, and the judge gave one a long prison term and sentenced seven to death. A year passed while lawyers for the eight appealed to higher courts. Two had their death sentences reduced to life imprisonment. One committed suicide. Four were hanged. Three men I considered to be innocent were left behind bars.

I was now the governor of Illinois with a long political career ahead of me. I felt sorry for the Haymarket Three, but wealthy and powerful people wanted them in jail. Only a fool would risk a political career for them. Let someone else speak out, I reasoned. I had worked too hard and too long to risk my future for them.

But I could not sleep nights. I began to like myself less and less. Although I was very ambitious, the price for success was becoming too high. I made a long and careful study of the case. As I did, I became convinced that the three men had not received a fair trial. Having convinced myself of this, I had only one course. On June 26, 1893, I pardoned the three men.

The storm broke. Now the poor and defenseless considered me their champion, but wealthy critics cut me to pieces. In the eyes of many citizens, I was revolutionary. They said that I was using my powers as governor to destroy "the American way." My dream of success began to fade.

I tried to ride out the storm and ran again for governor in 1896. I lost. Then I ran for mayor of Chicago. Again, I lost. I could no longer fool myself. My political career was finished. Many people hated me. But I had been true to myself. Perhaps someone would remember that.

POSTSCRIPT

When Altgeld left office, his once large fortune was all but gone. He had neglected his business affairs during his four years as governor. Also a severe business recession had resulted in the loss of all of his property except for a small home. But Altgeld was not beaten. He continued to speak out for law and justice right up to the time he died in 1902. Although disliked by many, he remained a hero to large numbers of working people. They admired his determination to stand by his beliefs, no matter what the cost.

Homework Questions

1. Why are the years from 1860 to 1900 called a period of corruption in government?
✦ 2. How was Altgeld different from many other politicians of his time?
3. Why were the Haymarket rioters tried in spite of the weak evidence against them?
4. How was Altgeld's career affected by his pardon of three men connected with the Haymarket Riot?
✦ 5. Why did many workers admire Altgeld?

Understanding the Story

A. Write *F* for each statement that is a fact and *O* for each statement that is an opinion.
  1. As a boy, John Altgeld was poor and hardworking.
  2. Altgeld worked on farms and railroads.
  3. Altgeld should have stayed on his father's farm.
  4. Much of Chicago was destroyed in the Great Fire.
  5. Altgeld was better as a lawyer than as a politician.
  6. Altgeld became governor of Illinois.
  7. Altgeld should not have pardoned the Haymarket Three.
  8. The Haymarket Riot led to the destruction of Altgeld's political career.

B. Write *A* for each statement that Altgeld would agree with and *N* for each statement that he would not agree with.
  1. I was eager to see my country.
  2. Hard work never agreed with me.
  3. A smart lawyer could earn a lot of money.
  4. I could not turn my back on the poor.
  5. I knew the eight Haymarket men were guilty.
  6. The price of success was never too high for me to pay.
  7. The poor and defenseless considered me their champion.
  8. In 1896 my political career was reborn.

C. How would you compare John Altgeld with William ("Boss") Tweed? Explain.

Activities and Inquiries

1. Altgeld became a wealthy man. What was his formula for success? Would it work today? Explain.
2. Imagine that Altgeld and Eugene Debs meet. Would they become friends? Why or why not?
3. Suppose that Altgeld cannot decide whether to pardon the Haymarket Three. He asks for your advice. What will you tell him?
4. You have been called upon to speak at Altgeld's funeral. What will you say about him?

4 An Immigrant Discovers America

During the late 1800's, industrial America needed many laborers to build railroads, mine minerals, and work in factories. It needed people willing to do hard and dirty work. America needed immigrants.

Between 1860 and 1900, some 14 million immigrants poured into the United States. The nation's population more than doubled, reaching 76 million. Immigrants contributed greatly to that growth. Most of the newcomers were Europeans, but a number came from China and Japan. Chinese workers helped to build the transcontinental railroads. Japanese labor harvested fruits and vegetables on the West Coast.

Immigrants who came before 1870 were called "old immigrants." They were usually from Northern European countries, and many could read and write. But after 1870, most immigrants came from Southern and Eastern Europe. These "new immigrants" were often unskilled and illiterate. They crowded into slum sections of cities. Many Americans looked down upon these newcomers. They blamed "new immigrants" for high crime rates, filthy streets, and even political corruption. It wasn't long before laws were passed to keep "unwelcome" newcomers out.

In 1882 Congress passed a Chinese Exclusion Act halting immigration from China for ten years. In 1907 the Japanese government agreed to prevent its laborers from going to America. The Emergency Quota Act of 1921 and the Immigration Act of 1924 stopped almost all immigration from Southern and Eastern Europe.

Why did immigrants come to America? What were they looking for? What did America mean to them?

New York City, 1896

Benjamin tossed restlessly in his bed. In a few hours he would be reunited with his wife and children. He had not seen them for five years.

Thinking about his family brought back memories of the old country, of Russian Poland. He remembered the poverty, hunger, and illness. He thought about the people who said awful things to him and sometimes struck him with their fists just because he didn't believe in their religion. It hadn't been easy being a Jew in the old country. No matter how hard he had worked, he still had not been able to feed and clothe his family properly. He thought back to the many nights he and his wife went to bed hungry so that the little ones could have a bit more to eat.

Life in the old country became so difficult that Benjamin decided to leave. He borrowed money from his family and friends and set out for America. He had to leave his family behind until he was settled in the new country.

Benjamin arrived in America with very little money. He knew little about the country. He could neither speak nor write the English language. All he possessed was a willingness to work hard—that and a dream. His dream was that his children would grow strong in this new country. Here, he hoped, they would at least have a chance to make something of their lives.

Benjamin rented the cheapest room he could find in a neighborhood that housed others of the Jewish faith. With the guidance of some of his neighbors, he was able to find work right away. He did not care what sort of work he did. He swept floors, washed dishes, emptied trash cans, and did anything else that was asked of him. Benjamin also toiled at a sewing machine in a factory.

He took jobs other people did not want because the work was hard and the pay low. There were immigrants like him all over America. They were building railroads, digging canals, drilling for oil, planting and farming, working in mines and factories.

As in the old country, Benjamin worked long hours for little pay. For working 10 to 14 hours a day, 6 days a week, he earned $8 or $9. Saving money was difficult, but Benjamin was determined to save enough to bring his family over. He took a cheap room in a tenement in a slum. His room had no window and no heat, so he roasted in the summer and froze in the winter. On summer nights he escaped to the roof or to the streets for some fresh air. Often Benjamin ate no more than a buttered roll for his main meal. His nights were lonely. He missed his family terribly.

America was different from the old country, Benjamin felt. Here a person could improve his life. Benjamin enrolled in night school and learned to speak, read, and write English. He began to make

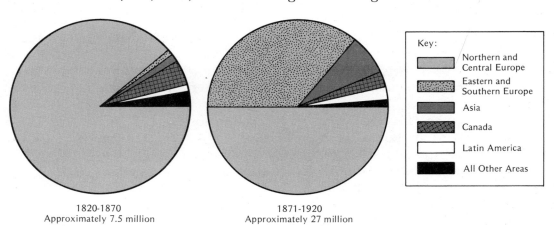

1820-1870
Approximately 7.5 million

1871-1920
Approximately 27 million

Key:

Northern and Central Europe

Eastern and Southern Europe

Asia

Canada

Latin America

All Other Areas

Immigration to the United States, 1820–1920

plans for himself. Even after his family came to America, he would continue to save money. With these savings he would buy a little shop. He wanted to earn enough money so that he would never have to work for someone else again. In America, even a poor immigrant like Benjamin could have dreams like this.

Still Benjamin thought that in some ways America was like the old country. There were people here who snubbed him because he was not of their faith or because he looked "different." Others worried that he would take their jobs. Some said that immigrants like Benjamin were criminals who made the streets unsafe.

Benjamin was puzzled by people like this. Didn't they see that most of the "Benjamins" of America worked hard and went to school to learn how to become good citizens in their adopted country? That they respected America's laws and taught their children these same values?

Benjamin had great plans for his children. He wanted them to get a good education. He believed that in America, a person could become whatever he or she wanted to be. His children would have good jobs. They might become doctors, lawyers, teachers, engineers, or business people. He, Benjamin, would help them succeed.

America had given Benjamin a new home and an opportunity to succeed. Benjamin would repay his adopted land by giving it his loyalty, his children, and the sweat of his brow.

With a feeling of joy, Benjamin leaped out of bed. He would put on his best suit. Today his family was starting a new life with him in America.

POSTSCRIPT

Immigrants have brought much with them to America, and America is richer because of them. They have brought their music, dance, customs, foods, and ideas. Immigrants have also made great contributions in science, medicine, mathematics, literature, and art. Without their contributions, it is unlikely that the United States would be the great country it is today.

There are still oppressed people in the world. Most nourish the dream that their children will grow up in a free society. For many such people, America continues to be a haven and a land of opportunity.

Homework Questions

1. In what ways did immigrants contribute to the growth of America?
2. Why were "new immigrants" not accepted as easily as "old immigrants"?
3. How was immigration from China restricted by Congress?
4. Why do people from other countries still want to come to the United States?
5. How would you describe Benjamin's life in America? *and in what way did that other immigrants contribute to the growth of America*

Understanding the Story

A. Write *T* for each statement that is true and *F* for each statement that is false.

1. Immigrants always came here to get rich and then leave.
2. Immigrants dreamed of a better life for their children.
3. Immigrants would not work with their hands.
4. Immigrants took jobs that no no one else wanted.
5. Immigrants often lived in slum tenements.
6. Americans never snubbed people who looked different.
7. "New immigrants" came mainly from Northern Europe.
8. People no longer seek to immigrate to the United States.

B. Choose the term or phrase that best completes each statement.

1. Between 1860 and 1900 (*a*) 2 million (*b*) 14 million (*c*) 76 million immigrants came to the United States.
2. "Old immigrants" came mainly from (*a*) China and Japan (*b*) Poland (*c*) Northern Europe.
3. The "new immigrants" came mainly from (*a*) Northern Europe (*b*) Southern and Eastern Europe (*c*) Africa.
4. Congress acted in the 1920's to block the arrival of (*a*) "new immigrants" (*b*) "old immigrants" (*c*) all immigrants.
5. Benjamin thought the United States was (*a*) completely different from the old country (*b*) just like the old country (*c*) like the old country in some ways and different in other ways.

C. Immigration has been described as one of the great themes of American history. After reading this chapter, why do you suppose this might be so?

Activities and Inquiries

1. Study the graph on page 336. Then choose the term or phrase that best completes each statement.
   a. Between 1820 and 1870 most immigrants came from (*1*) Canada (*2*) Eastern and Southern Europe (*3*) Northern and Central Europe.
   b. A very noticeable difference between the two circles is the great increase in immigration from 1871 to 1920 in the group from (*1*) Eastern and Southern Europe (*2*) Northern and Central Europe (*3*) Canada.
   c. Compared with immigration from Latin America, immigration from Asia between 1871 and 1920 was (*1*) much less (*2*) more than double (*3*) about the same.
   d. The total number of immigrants between 1871 and 1920 was (*1*) less than half the number between 1820 and 1870 (*2*) more than three times the number between 1820 and 1870 (*3*) at least ten times the number between 1820 and 1870.
   e. Which of the following can you learn from the graphs? (*1*) the sources of immigration to the United States during the years 1820 to 1920 (*2*) the reasons for increases in immigration from certain areas (*3*) how native Americans felt about the immigrants.
2. Imagine that you are an immigrant in America. Write a letter home describing the good things that have happened to you here.
3. Now write about the things you do not like.
4. Assume that you live in a foreign country. You receive the second letter. Would you come to America? Explain.
5. Imagine that you are Benjamin's great-grandchild. Describe how your life compares with Benjamin's.

5 More Brings Less

Between 1860 and 1900, the number of farms in the United States more than doubled. Farm acreage jumped from 407 million to 839 million. Farmers also invested heavily in machinery so that they could produce more. From 1870 to 1900, the total value of farm machinery increased from $246 million to $750 million.

Among these farm machines was the horse-drawn mowing machine, used to cut hay. Horse-drawn harrows prepared the ground after plowing. Cultivators kept down weeds and loosened the soil so that crops could grow strong and tall. Farmers still used the hand scythe, but only for cutting weeds. For cutting wheat, the mechanical harvester, or reaper, was faster. There was even an improvement on the harvester—an automatic knotter that tied grain into bundles to dry before it was threshed.

The new machines made work easier and helped a farmer produce more crops and raise more animals. But they did not make farmers more prosperous. Indeed, farm prices began to drop as farmers turned out more food than people needed. From 1866 to 1886, wheat dropped from $2.06 to 69 cents a bushel. Corn dropped from 66 to 36 cents a bushel. Cotton dropped from 31 to 9 cents a pound.

Farmers desperately needed money. Many were deeply in debt. They had borrowed to buy land, machinery, seeds, or livestock. Now it was a struggle just to keep up interest payments. As a rule farmers paid higher interest than other people because bankers considered them poor risks. (They might not be able to pay back the loans.)

Many farmers were in fact unable to pay back loans and lost their land to banks. In 1865, almost all cultivated land in the United States was worked by a farm owner. By 1900, more than a third of U.S. farms were worked by tenants, who rented their land.

During the 1870's, farmers sought ways to increase their earnings. In many places they joined together to start farmer-owned businesses such as gristmills, dairies, grocery stores, and even factories. Such businesses were known as *cooperatives*. Many failed, however, either because of opposition from other business people or because they were poorly run.

As hard times got worse, farmers were at first puzzled. Why can't we seem to get ahead? they wondered. Then they became angry. Who or what is causing our troubles? they asked. They placed special blame on "greedy bankers" and on the railroads. Farmers accused railroads of charging unfair prices to store farm products and to ship them to distant markets.

In our story, a farmer by the name of Martha Duff talks with a politician, a banker, and a railroad owner. Duff is angry about practices she thinks are hurting her interests. The men are angry because they think her views are one-sided. In Duff's opinion, who is responsible for the farmers' problems? How does Duff think farmers can solve their problems?

Kansas, 1874

MARTHA DUFF. Yes, sir. We farmers are slaves, and you gentlemen are our masters.

POLITICIAN. Mrs. Duff, aren't you exaggerating? This country fought a bloody war to put an end to slavery. There are no slaves in America today.

DUFF. Oh, no? Well, we farmers certainly feel like slaves. And unless we're set free, this country just might fight another bloody war!

RAILROAD OWNER. Mrs. Duff, just who do you think is holding you in slavery?

DUFF. The railroads for a start. You're nothing but robbers. You force us to store our products in your warehouses, and you charge us a healthy price for this service. Then you charge us as much as you like to ship our goods. We don't work for ourselves. We work for you.

RAILROAD OWNER. Without us, you couldn't get your crops to market.

DUFF. We both know that. You've got us over a barrel.

RAILROAD OWNER. Look, Mrs. Duff. It's true that we charge farmers higher rates to ship goods than we charge other customers. But we send empty cars out west to pick up your farm products. This is very expensive for us.

DUFF. I understand. You come here with empty cars, and you leave with full pockets.

BANKER. Now, Mrs. Duff. Don't be so hard on these fellows. Without railroads, you farmers would be out of business. They make it possible for you to keep your farms. And we bankers do our share, too.

DUFF. Don't you mean you *take* your share?

BANKER. How can you talk that way? Without our loans, you couldn't live another day on your farms.

DUFF. You talk as if loans were some charity you give farmers. Well, they're not. They're a hard-nosed business deal. God help those who can't pay the bank on time. You swoop down on them like a vulture and take away farms that have been irrigated by their sweat and tears. Yes, it's true that you lend us money. But we put our lives in your hands. You are well paid for your loans. Too well paid!

BANKER. But farmers are poor risks. We have to charge high interest rates. One month of dry weather, one hailstorm, one insect attack can ruin your crops for an entire season. It's a wonder that we gamble by lending you any money at all.

DUFF. You gamble with your money, and we gamble with our sweat and hard work. We risk everything we have to feed the world and to make you rich. Your gamble is small compared with ours.

POLITICIAN. Please, Mrs. Duff, be reasonable. Railroad owners and bankers are in business to make money, just like farmers. They take risks, just as you do. Aren't they entitled to a profit?

DUFF. Just as I would expect—you're defending the money interests. It would seem that we farmers are not important enough for you to pay attention to us.

POLITICIAN. That's not so, Mrs. Duff. The government listens to farmers. Why, there are many policies aimed at helping people like you. Didn't you get your land as a free homestead from the government?

DUFF. As a matter of fact, my family did. The government lured us out west with its promise of 160 acres of free land. Big deal! By the time most of us homesteaders arrived here, the railroads had taken the best lands. We had to settle for leftovers. You can't fool me. The government serves bankers, railroad owners, and big business—not farmers.

POLITICIAN. What sort of things do you think government could do for farmers? Surely you're not arguing that farmers should get special favors from government?

DUFF. Not special favors—just a fair chance. Why not start by setting rules that would keep railroads from gouging every penny they can get from farmers? Or by coining more money so people can afford to pay higher prices for our farm products?

RAILROAD OWNER. Whoa! Government can't set rules for railroads. That would be unconstitutional! It would interfere with free enterprise!

BANKER. And government can't go turning out too much money. Sound business depends on sound money.

POLITICIAN. As you can see, Mrs. Duff, your ideas can stir up a powerful lot of argument. But I'm sure that we politicians are willing to listen to your views. We must of course consider them in the light of the Constitution and of sound business principles—

DUFF (*interrupting*). And of getting elected next time around! I might remind you, Mr. Politician, that the railroads and bankers may have plenty of money to pour into your next election campaign, but we farmers have plenty of votes. You'll be hearing from us!

POSTSCRIPT

Indeed the nation did hear from its farmers. The final decades of the 19th century were a time of unrest in many rural areas. And the unrest had political consequences.

Farmers formed a number of organizations to advance their interests. One such group, started in 1867, was the Grange. It set up many cooperatives to buy and sell products. It also worked for state laws to put the railroads under government regulation. Many states, especially in the Midwest, passed such "Granger laws" in the 1870's. Railroad rates were forced down.

Railroads went to court to challenge the laws. They said the laws were unconstitutional. But in 1877, in the case of *Munn* v. *Illinois*, the U.S. Supreme Court rejected this argument. The Court ruled that states had the right to regulate railroad rates.

The railroads did not give up. They kept filing suits against the laws. New justices joined the Supreme Court, and in 1886 the Court made a new ruling, in the case of *Wabash, St. Louis, and Pacific Railway Co. v. Illinois*. It noted that railroads crossed state lines and thus took part in interstate commerce, or trade. Under the Constitution, said the Court, Congress alone has the right to regulate trade among the states.

Now the farmers put pressure on Congress. They got Congress to pass the Interstate Commerce Act of 1887. The act said that interstate railroad rates had to be the same for everyone. It did not make the rates any lower, however.

Many farmers felt that Congress had not gone far enough. Since Congress alone could control the main railroads, the farmers would have to have greater influence in Congress. But many felt that farmers could not get enough influence in the two parties that controlled Congress—the Republican and Democratic parties. So the farmers decided to develop a political party of their own. You will read about that party in the next chapter.

Homework Questions

1. Why did farm prices drop between 1866 and 1886?
2. How did farm machinery increase production?
3. Why were so many farmers in debt?
4. Why were farmers especially angry at the railroads?
5. How did the Grange seek to help farmers?

Understanding the Story

A. Write *T* for each statement that is true, *F* for each statement that is false, and *N* for each statement that is not mentioned in the story.
1. Most farmers were happier without machinery.
2. Martha Duff thought farmers were like slaves.
3. The three men refused even to talk to Duff.
4. Farmers were charged higher rates to ship goods than other customers were.
5. The banker felt that farmers were good risks for loans.
6. The banker had lost money on a large loan to one of Duff's neighbors.
7. Farmers often borrowed money to buy machinery.
8. Duff thought the politician was a friend to farmers.

B. List the numbers of the statements Martha Duff made or might have made.

1. There are no slaves in America today.
2. We don't work for ourselves.
3. Railroads steal from the farmers.
4. The government helps the farmers.
5. Bankers swoop down like vultures on farmers who don't pay their debts.
6. We risk everything we have to feed the world and make bankers rich.
7. Railroads left the best land for the farmers.
8. I am earning more money each year.

C. If you were Martha Duff, would you try to produce and sell as much as possible? Why or why not?

Activities and Inquiries

1. Using your library, write a report on the activities of the Grangers in the 1870's.
2. Also using your library, compare the activities of the Grangers of the 1870's with those of present-day Grangers.
3. Imagine that you are a factory worker in the late 19th century. You visit a farm relative and attend a farm protest meeting. Which of the farmers' arguments might also be applied to factory workers?
4. Why did farmers feel that railroads and banks were their major enemies?
5. What would you say is Martha Duff's strongest argument? What is her critics' strongest argument? Give reasons.

6 "The Great Commoner"

In 1892 the angry farmers (with some help from the Knights of Labor) formed a new party that they called the Populist, or people's, Party. It demanded an income tax—a tax based on a person's ability to pay. It called for secret ballots for voters. And it sought the election of United States Senators by the people instead of by state legislatures. The party also wanted the federal government to take over ownership of the railroad, telephone, and telegraph systems.

Above all, the Populists sought aid for the debt-ridden farmers. They wanted to help such farmers by putting more money in circulation. At that time the U.S. money supply was linked to the gold supply. Before a coin could be issued, the government had to have gold of equal worth. The Populists wanted the nation to use both gold and silver to back up its currency. That way, the government could coin more money. This would lower the value of the dollar, cause inflation, and lead to higher farm prices. With higher incomes, farmers thought they could repay their debts more easily. Populists argued that their proposal would improve business and benefit the nation.

The Populists sought the support of city people by calling for additional reforms that would appeal to factory workers. One such reform was an eight-hour workday. A second was a limit on immigration. The purpose of setting limits was to keep out people who would compete with American-born workers for jobs.

Now the Populists looked for someone who could win the Presidency for them. General James B. Weaver, their choice in 1892, received more than a million votes out of 12 million cast. He won 22 of the 444 electoral votes. That was not good enough, so the Populists looked for another candidate. Four years later, they found a man they could support—William Jennings Bryan.

Both the Populists and the Democrats nominated Bryan. Besides sharing a candidate, the two parties made many of the same proposals. The focus of Bryan's campaign was his call for the free, or unlimited, coinage of silver.

Why did the Populists think that William Jennings Bryan could win the Presidency? How did Bryan try to get elected? Did he succeed?

November, 1896

The eyes of the nation are on you, William Jennings Bryan. You have come a long way from your boyhood in a small Illinois town. You became a lawyer, moved to Nebraska, and twice won election to the U.S. House of Representatives. Young and handsome, you see yourself as voicing the hopes and fears of farmers and working people—those who fit your picture of "the common man." At the age of 36 you have a chance to be elected President of the United States.

Your booming voice can arouse crowds to a frenzy of excitement. You have a "voice of silver," people say. You are called the greatest orator (speaker) of your day.

You have used your voice to try to persuade people that the farmer represents all that is best in America. "Burn down your cities and leave our farms," you said, "and your cities will spring up again as if by magic; but destroy our farms and the grass will grow in the streets of every city in the country."

At the Democratic convention in July you brought the delegates to their feet with a rousing speech. You made clear that you were for silver and against the gold interests. You closed with a warning to the backers of gold: "You shall not crucify mankind upon a cross of gold." The crowd went wild. You were saying exactly what your listeners wanted to hear.

But not all Americans wanted to hear those words. Your appeal is strongest in the West, where silver is mined. The rural areas of the South, where farmers are deeply in debt, also give you strong support. People with debts want cheaper money. But people who have lent money want "sound money." They prefer gold.

The backers of gold include some of the most powerful interests in the country, especially in the North and East. They include bankers, owners of industry, shopkeepers, and owners of newspapers. They also include many farmers who are not in debt—especially farmers in the more prosperous Midwest. Many such people are backing the Republican Party and its candidate, William McKinley, the governor of Ohio.

McKinley's supporters have given him millions of dollars to help his campaign. You, meanwhile, have struggled to get contributions. Only the owners of silver mines seemed to take much interest in donating to your campaign.

You needed money to pay for your travels. More than any previous candidate, you "went to the people." You traveled by train from town to town, making speeches with that silver voice of yours.

All the while McKinley stayed at home, talking to reporters on his front porch. He promised the voters that the Republicans would bring prosperity to the country. Prosperity is a popular theme in these difficult times. Business has been in a slump for the past three years. It would be better for you if the Presidency had not been held by a Democrat, Grover Cleveland, during that time. (Presidents are often blamed for slumps or depressions.)

You have used strong words to condemn your opponents, and they have used strong words against you. They call you a dangerous radical whose ideas could set the country on an untried path.

"You shall not press down upon the brow of labor this crown of thorns. You shall not crucify mankind upon a cross of gold."

Besides gold and silver, one major issue divides you and McKinley. That is the tariff. McKinley backs the high tariff that Congress put into effect with the support of industries in the North and East. The tariff tends to keep out foreign goods by making their prices higher. You, like the Populists and like many (but not all) Democrats, want the tariff reduced. You say it hurts "the common man" by making goods more expensive.

On election day, 1896, it looks as if a record number of people will vote. Will they support you—"the Great Commoner," as your backers call you? Or will they support McKinley and his promise of prosperity?

POSTSCRIPT

The voters backed McKinley. Bryan received 6,468,000 votes—more than any other presidential candidate up to that time. But McKinley won even more votes, 7,036,000, and took 271 electoral votes to Bryan's 176. Twice more Bryan ran for the Presidency, in 1900 and 1908, but he never again received that many votes.

By 1900 European countries were buying twice as much American wheat as in earlier years. As a result, wheat prices began to rise. Also, Americans discovered new sources of gold. This increased the money supply, caused inflation, and made it easier for farmers to get credit and repay loans. Happy with their new prosperity, many farmers lost interest in political protest. This spelled the end of the Populist Party.

But Bryan's campaign left its mark. The great numbers of people who voted for Bryan impressed both Democratic and Republican leaders. Because they wanted the support of those voters, the major parties tried in later years to find answers to their complaints. Such proposals as the secret ballot, popular election of U.S. Senators, and a federal income tax began to get closer attention.

Homework Questions

1. How did the Populists propose to help farmers?
2. How did the Populists appeal to city people for support?
3. What groups did Bryan claim to represent?
4. Why did Bryan's opponents argue that he was a dangerous radical?
5. Why was Bryan's defeat in 1896 not a total defeat for his ideas?

Understanding the Story

A. List the numbers of the statements that are true.
   1. Bryan was the Democratic candidate for President in 1896.
   2. Bryan was not popular with farmers.
   3. Bryan did not like the gold interests.
   4. McKinley was the Republican candidate for President in 1896.
   5. Bryan spoke poorly.
   6. McKinley got more campaign donations than Bryan.

7. In 1896 Bryan got more votes than any presidential candidate before him.
8. Bryan wanted the money supply to be based on gold.

B. Which statements were goals of William Jennings Bryan?
1. The American people must listen to the advice of big business people.
2. The common people should control the country.
3. American money should be backed by silver.
4. Tariffs on foreign goods should be raised.
5. Government policies should do more to help the farmer.
6. The Republican Party should nominate me.
7. The people must have cheaper money.
8. The defeat of silver interests is essential.

C. Imagine that it is 1896 and you are a factory worker in the Northeast. What reasons might you have to vote for Bryan? For McKinley? Explain.

Activities and Inquiries

1. Read the following lines from a poem by Vachel Lindsay about William Jennings Bryan, then answer the questions. (Look up in a dictionary any words you don't understand.)

"The bard and the prophet of them all.
Prairie avenger, mountain lion.
Bryan, Bryan, Bryan, Bryan.
Gigantic troubadour speaking like a siege gun
Smashing Plymouth Rock with Boulders from the West."

a. What kind of man is described in this poem?
b. What do the last two lines mean? (Remember that Plymouth Rock is the spot where the Pilgrims landed in New England.)
2. Write a newspaper article attacking Bryan and his ideas.
3. Write a newspaper article praising Bryan and his ideas.
4. Would you have voted for Bryan or McKinley? Give the reasons for your choice.

7 The Last Dance

Between 1870 and 1890, about 10 million settlers moved west of the Mississippi River. Many went to claim free land. Congress, responding to pressure from Westerners, passed the Homestead Act in 1862. It provided that any adult male citizen could acquire a 160-acre farm on public land simply by paying a registration fee and staying on the farm for five years. To get title more quickly, a homesteader could buy the land for $1.25 an acre.

In addition, the federal government gave 131 million acres to the railroads and 140 million acres to the states during the period from 1870 to 1890. Most of this land was sold or given away to land-hungry settlers. In this way the railroads were assured new customers and the states acquired new settlers.

The new settlers faced many hardships. On the great, flat grasslands, the prairies of the West, there were few trees to cut into lumber for houses and fences. Settlers often built houses of sod, the top layer of the ground. They cut the sod into chunks, like bricks, and plastered the sod chunks together with straw, dirt, and water. Plain dirt formed the floors of the houses. Because the sod houses had few windows, they were dark inside.

The settlers suffered through brutally cold winters, sweltering summers, wind and dust storms, and swarms of grasshoppers and locusts. They fought against cattle and sheep ranchers whose animals trampled their crops. They also fought the Indians who believed that the land was theirs. Finally, they fought loneliness and despair. Many lost the battle and went back to their home states.

Some practices in the West later spread and helped the United States to become more democratic. As early as 1869, women voted in state elections in parts of the West. Some Western states allowed citizens to help make laws. In a process called a *referendum*, voters could make known their opinions on certain issues being considered by lawmakers. In some states, the people also had the right to remove unpopular officials from office through a process known as *recall*. Some Western states gave citizens the right to initiate, or recommend, laws. This is called the *initiative*.

Democratic rights were not given to the oldest settlers of the region—the Indians. The West that made the United States more democratic also destroyed the Indian way of life.

The federal government had settled the tribes on reservations. It built schools to educate the children and teach skills to the adults. In 1887 Congress passed the Dawes Act, which granted citizenship and 160 acres of land to every Indian family that gave up tribal life for farming. But most Indians did not want to farm.

The Plains Indians watched the settlers make homes on Indian lands. They saw the newcomers kill the buffalo, the main source of food, clothing, and shelter for the Indians. They remembered the promises of the United States government that certain lands would remain "forever Indian." When these promises continued to be broken, the Indians prepared to battle for their way of life.

In 1874, prospectors discovered gold in the Black Hills of North Dakota. Gold hunters soon moved into places used by the Dakota and Sioux Indians. Some of the areas were sacred; they had religious importance to the Indians. The miners ignored the claims of the tribes, and the government did little to keep the miners out. To protect their land, the Indians decided to fight. Led by Sitting Bull, the Sioux met General George Custer's troops in 1876 at Little Big Horn, Montana. They defeated and killed Custer and his men. But more troops kept coming, and by the late 1880's, all the tribes had surrendered.

In our story, a group of Sioux is performing a dance as part of a religious ceremony. They hope the dance will bring back the old days, when they were safe from outsiders. An Indian couple watches the dance and talks about life before so many settlers came. What do they say about life on the reservation? How do they account for the death of their old ways?

Wounded Knee, South Dakota, 1890

"Why don't you join the others?" asked Sun Bird of her husband, Yellow Bull.

Yellow Bull was silent for a moment. "I don't believe it will do any good."

Sun Bird moaned, "If you have lost your belief, then surely all is lost."

"All was lost years ago," said Yellow Bull. "Even today we dance in the shadow of white people."

"Yellow Bull, you mustn't lose heart. The Sioux will be great once again."

"You're wrong," said Yellow Bull firmly. "We will never again return to the land of our fathers. We dance the dance of death."

Sun Bird spoke with an angry voice. "I have always respected you, my husband. But today you bring shame upon yourself. Each day we die a slow death in this reservation prison. We do not get enough food or clothing. We are cheated by the government agents, who call us savages. And you would have us do nothing?"

"How will your Ghost Dance help?"

Sun Bird thought for a moment and said, "If we dance this dance in our hour of need, perhaps the spirits of our fathers will hear us. What better time for the spirits to rescue us than when we stand at the foot of the grave?"

"Bah! You don't understand," muttered Yellow Bull. "This is no time for the Ghost Dance. Let us fight like warriors instead. Let us ride and fight and die if we have to, rather than live a life without freedom."

"We have fought that fight many times," said Sun Bird. "We have fought from our horses and shot down enemy soldiers. And still settlers have come and driven us from our lands and killed our buffalo. No, Yellow Bull, fighting is the dance of death."

"But we are already dead," protested Yellow Bull. "We died when we signed treaties with the whites—treaties they never kept. We died when we moved from our ancient lands and agreed to live on reservations. We died when we gave up the hunt and became farmers. We died when the railroads came and the white hunters killed our buffalo. We died when we accepted the white people's food and tried to learn their ways. We are no longer Sioux, and we will never be whites. We are doomed to be strangers in our own country. We are dead."

Sun Bird interrupted. "Those who dance the Ghost Dance don't agree with you. They dance even though it is forbidden by the whites. They dance to remember the way it once was for our people. Perhaps if we dance long enough, the spirits will drive the whites from our lands and bring back the buffalo."

Unknown to Yellow Bull, Sun Bird, and the other Sioux, government troops were riding toward the reservation. They were coming to stop the forbidden dance.

Soon the troops surrounded the band of Indians. Soldiers started taking away the Indians' rifles. One young man refused to do as the soldiers asked. A shot was fired and a soldier knocked down. The troops turned on the Indians and fired at close range.

Men, women, and children ran for their lives, pursued by government troops with rapid-fire rifles. The troops gained on the Sioux and fired at them. The Sioux could not protect themselves. Soon some 200 men, women, and children lay dead. The dance of hope had ended.

POSTSCRIPT

Many people were upset over the Battle of Wounded Knee, the last major military action against the Indians. These people protested against the government's treatment of the Indians. Even so, life did not improve for most Indians. They could not find a way of life they wanted to follow, one that would provide as great a sense of well being as the old ways.

In 1924 the United States granted full citizenship to all adult American Indians within its borders. Adult Indians gained the right to vote. Ten years later, the Wheeler-Howard Act encouraged the Indians to preserve their tribal cultures and skills and to handle their own affairs.

According to the 1980 census, 1,362,000 Native Americans live in the United States. About 500,000 live on reservations. To a large extent, they manage their own affairs through their councils and court systems. Some of the tribes have become wealthy from the oil and other valuable minerals discovered on their property. But most Indians live in poverty. Those who choose to leave the reservations also continue to face serious problems. Unemployment for them is three times the national average.

Some tribes have sued the federal and state governments to recover their lands or the cash value of the lands. In some cases the courts have decided in the Indians' favor and awarded tribes land and money. The courts have ordered the government to live up to treaties it signed many years ago.

Homework Questions

1. In what ways did the Homestead Act help farmers?
2. How did the settlers live on the prairies?
3. What government practices in the West encouraged Americans to become more democratic?
4. What did the settlers in the West do to the Indians?
5. Why did the Battle of Wounded Knee upset many people?
6. What did the federal government do for the Indians?

Understanding the

A. Write *F* for each a fact and *O* that is an opin

1. The Sioux forming a r
2. The Sioux time by dancing.
3. Sun Bird felt that whites treated the Indians badly.
4. Indians do not belong on reservations.
5. Sun Bird hoped that the Ghost Dance would be heard by the spirits.
6. Yellow Bull should not have given up hope.
7. The Sioux were forbidden to dance the Ghost Dance.
8. The Sioux had signed treaties with the government of the United States.

B. Write *S* for each statement that Sun Bird made or might have made and *Y* for each statement that Yellow Bull made or might have made.

1. The Ghost Dance will do no good.
2. The Sioux will be great once again.
3. We died when the white hunters killed the buffalo.
4. Government agents cheat us.
5. Perhaps the spirits will hear us.
6. We will never be free.
7. We are no longer Sioux, and we will never be whites.
8. Indians should stand up and

he would rather live a life with- uld you agree or view? Explain.

iries

are going to produce a motion picture based on the story you have just read. What scenes will you include?
2. How are Indians usually portrayed in the movies and in television programs? Give examples.
3. Which view of Indians comes closer to the truth: yours or those you have seen in movie theaters or on television? Explain your answer.
4. An Indian asks for your advice. Should he give up his Indian ways and live like other Americans? What will you say to him? Give reasons for your answer.

8 The Growth of the Constitution: The 14th Amendment

The 14th Amendment to the Constitution was proposed in 1866 for the purpose of guaranteeing the rights and privileges of citizenship to the former slaves. It went into effect in 1868. The most important parts of the amendment can be stated as follows:

"All persons born or naturalized in the United States . . . are citizens of the United States and of the state where they live. No state may make any law that limits the rights of United States citizens. No state may take life, liberty, or property from any person without due process of law. No state may deny to any person the equal protection of the laws."

Armed with the 14th Amendment, black people laid claims to their rights as citizens. Ask yourself what was the original purpose of the amendment. Did the amendment achieve that purpose?

The scene is the lobby of a hotel near the railroad station in a city in the 1890's. Two couples have just gotten off a train and are looking for a place to spend the night.

BLACK PERSON. I'd like a room for two, please.

DESK CLERK. I'm sorry. We have no accommodations for you. You'll have to go to the rooming house across town. Next, please.

BLACK PERSON. Wait just a minute. You tell me that there are no rooms. Yet you call "next." What's going on?

DESK CLERK. Don't you understand? For you this hotel will never have rooms. If you want a place to stay, go over to the section of town where you'll be with your kind of people.

WHITE PERSON. A room for two, please.

DESK CLERK. Yes, sir. We have a nice quiet one on the second floor.

Blacks were free, but they were usually not treated as equals. Many whites, in the North and South, had *prejudices* (bad feelings) against blacks. They did not want to mix with blacks on an equal basis. Blacks were turned away from many hotels, theaters, and restaurants. They were sent to separate schools. In the South, especially after the 1890's, blacks were forced to travel in separate railroad cars and in separate sections of streetcars or buses. Blacks faced many kinds of *discrimination* (unequal treatment).

In the 1880's, a number of blacks sought help from the courts. They were largely disappointed. The U.S. Supreme Court ruled in 1883, in the Civil Rights Cases, that the 14th Amendment banned racial discrimination by states but not by private individuals or companies. Thus, a hotel owner or a restaurant manager, for example, had the right to refuse service to blacks. Government could not meddle in what the Court considered a "private" matter.

In 1896, in the case of *Plessy* v. *Ferguson*, the Supreme Court spelled out further limits on the 14th Amendment. A man of mixed race sued the state of Louisiana over a law that required separate railroad cars for blacks and whites. The Court upheld the law, even though it involved discrimination by state action. The Court said separate facilities for the two races were legal as long as they were equal. In 1899 the Court approved "separate-but-equal" schools, too. Blacks argued that blacks-only schools and other facilities were rarely "equal," but the argument fell on deaf ears.

While blacks found the 14th Amendment of limited use, the owners of businesses found it an unexpected help. Look again at the summary of the amendment on page 352. You will note the words "due process of law." The 14th Amendment requires the states to follow "due process"; the Fifth Amendment requires the federal government to do the same. But what does "due process" mean?

The most obvious meaning has to do with procedures. If you are accused of a crime, you can't be thrown in jail and kept there. You have a right to a trial. Jury trials are part of the "due process of law." Similarly, the government cannot just go out and take someone's property. It must follow the procedures set out by law and the Constitution.

In the following scene, a lawyer is speaking before a court:

LAWYER. Gentlemen, my client's rights have been violated. I must insist on the constitutional right to due process.

FIRST JUDGE. But your client is a railroad company—a corporation. Constitutional rights are for persons, not for companies.

LAWYER. The word "person" is a very broad one. If you will look at the record, I believe you will see that the members of Congress meant the word to apply to corporations as well as to flesh-and-blood persons.

SECOND JUDGE. The gentleman's point is well taken. What are corporations but "fictitious persons" created by law? They have a right to enter into contracts, just as individuals do. Why shouldn't they have other rights that individuals have?

The U.S. Supreme Court accepted such reasoning in an important case in 1886. It declared that corporations were persons in the eyes of the law. Now railroad companies and others could argue that their property rights were protected by the 14th Amendment. The railroads had another tool in their fight against state regulation. They used the tool vigorously. One railroad challenged a Minnesota law that provided no way for a railroad to appeal a decision that went against it. In 1890 the Supreme Court threw out the law. Many other state laws met a similar fate in the years that followed. Those who favored regulation of business decided it would have to be done by Congress, not by the states.

Much later, in the middle of the 20th century, the courts took a new look at the 14th Amendment. The amendment would play an important part in winning broader rights for blacks and others (see Unit Thirteen, Chapter 10).

Homework Questions

1. How are U.S. citizens protected by the 14th Amendment?
2. In what ways did black people face discrimination in the 1890's?
3. What did *Plessy* v. *Ferguson* mean for blacks?
4. How did the 14th Amendment help corporations?

Understanding the Story

A. Write *T* for each statement that is true and *F* for each statement that is false.
   1. The 14th Amendment was meant to guarantee the rights of former slaves.
   2. Equality for blacks came quickly and easily.
   3. The Supreme Court ruled in 1883 that the 14th Amendment does not bar discrimination by individuals.
   4. State legislatures tried to regulate railroads in the 19th century.
   5. The U.S. Supreme Court ruled in 1896 that facilities for blacks and whites could never be separate.

6. Big business was not helped by the 14th Amendment.
7. A corporation is a person in the eyes of the law.
8. Some U.S. Supreme Court decisions in the 1890's favored the railroads.

B. Complete each of the following sentences by filling in the missing word or words.
   1. According to the 14th Amendment, all persons _____ or _____ in the United States are citizens.
   2. Blacks faced many kinds of _____.
   3. Blacks brought their complaints to the _____ Court.
   4. The *Plessy* v. *Ferguson* decision said the practice of providing _____ but _____ facilities for blacks and whites was constitutional.
   5. In 1886 the Supreme Court declared that corporations were _____ in the eyes of the law.
   6. Railroads used the 14th Amendment to challenge state laws that sought to _____ them.
   7. The Supreme Court decided that some state laws took away corporations' property without _____ of law.

8. Many people thought businesses would have to be regulated by _____ rather than by the _____ .

C. Re-read the 14th Amendment. Do all Americans today have all of the rights mentioned in this amendment? Explain. Are blacks and other groups given equal rights under the law? Explain.

Activities and Inquiries

1. Imagine that you are interviewing a black person in the 1870's. You ask if freedom has brought equality. How will the person answer? Explain the answer.
2. Imagine that you are arguing the case for equality under the law before the Supreme Court. What will you say about the "separate-but-equal" rulings?
3. Now, a lawyer is defending "separate-but-equal" laws. What will the lawyer say?

Who Built America?

Charles Steinmetz

HEINRICH. My report is on Charles Steinmetz, who was born in Germany in 1865 and came to the United States in 1889.

CASIMIR. Why did he leave Germany?

HEINRICH. As a college student, he wrote an article for a socialist newspaper. The German government didn't like the article and tried to stop the publication of the paper. Steinmetz left Germany before the police could arrest him.

SAM. Sounds like another Zenger case. [See Unit Four, Chapter 1.]

MR. MILLER. That's very good, Sam. Zenger also came here from Germany, but there is a difference. Zenger got into trouble for writing in America.

HEINRICH. But Steinmetz was more than a newspaper writer. He gained fame as an electrical engineer. His work and ideas improved electric motors and the education of engineers. In the 1890's he was one of the people who made possible the widespread use of electricity. He helped move the United States out of the era of gaslight and steam into the age of electric power.

JUAN. What about Thomas Edison? I thought *he* was the one who gave us all kinds of electrical equipment.

HEINRICH. He did. Edison developed a usable electric light bulb. He improved the telegraph, telephone, and motion picture projector. He also invented the phonograph and set up the first industrial research laboratory. Edison's contributions were practical and useful in our daily lives. Steinmetz, on the other hand, worked with theories. He developed broad principles about the workings of electric motors and alternating current.

ROBERT. What's alternating current?

HEINRICH. That's the kind of electrical current we use in the United States today. Steinmetz's theories made it possible to know how certain motors and electrical systems would perform before they were built. Problems could be solved in the design stage rather than after the systems and motors were actually created. Two of his most important theories had been developed by the time he was only 27 years old.

CARLA. Wow! He must have been very intelligent. Did he become famous for anything else?

HEINRICH. Yes, he developed a lightning arrester to protect power transmission lines. Steinmetz was also interested in education. As an elected government official in Schenectady, New York, he worked to get more money for the schools. He set up classes for young people who had long-term diseases or mental or physical handicaps. Steinmetz knew what it was like to have a handicap himself. He had been a hunchback from early childhood.

TOM. Did he take an interest in colleges, too?

HEINRICH. You bet. Steinmetz taught engineers at Union College in Schenectady and continued to write about history, mathematics, and the future. He urged the use of more electricity so that the costs of producing it would go down. The burning of coal should be stopped, he said, in order to reduce air pollution. He was also concerned about water pollution from sewage. He said wastes should be carried into unpopulated areas and used to fertilize soil.

JOSEPHINE. It sounds as though Steinmetz was ahead of his time.

HEINRICH. In some ways he was. He died in 1923, long before air pollution became the issue it is today.

MR. MILLER. Well done, Heinrich.

"Well, Mr. Miller, you've done it again. Studying about business and labor and the Indians was very interesting."

"What did you like in particular?"

"Well, there were some things I didn't like," said Jack. "I didn't like the way large corporations were growing more powerful, sometimes at the public's expense. I didn't like the violence of the Pullman strike. I especially didn't like the way the Indians and blacks were treated."

"Why do you think these things were happening in the United States at that time?

"I think we were suffering from growing pains. The Union experienced a business boom during and after the Civil War. Many people believed that big business would make this country rich and powerful, and the government agreed. I guess that's why it stood behind big business on just about everything."

"Do you think the government made a mistake?" asked Mr. Miller.

"Not really. Big business was good for this country. It gave people work, and it provided them with goods and services. It's just that—"

"Yes," prodded Mr. Miller.

"Well, maybe big business became *too* powerful. Some of its actions were against the public interest. Much of the time, the government was right to support big business. But the government should also have insisted that big business behave itself."

"Anything else, Jack?"

"Maybe I did like a few things after all. I admired Steinmetz. I also respected Altgeld and Bryan. They all contributed a great deal to the United States. And now, Mr. Miller, I have a question for you."

"Okay," replied Mr. Miller.

"What's next?"

Mr. Miller smiled. "The Americans who built up this country after the Civil War left many questions unanswered. We are going to study how other Americans tried to answer these questions."

Imperialism, Progressivism, and World War I

"Mr. Miller, you said that we are going to study about how Americans tried to answer some unanswered questions. I think I know what you meant."

"Okay, Jack, let's hear it."

"I think we're going to learn how Americans tried to change things they didn't like."

"That's right, Jack. Some Americans wanted the United States to play a bigger role in the world outside. Others wanted to change things here at home."

"What do you mean by 'a bigger role in the world outside'?"

"Well, Jack, other powerful nations—Great Britain, France, Germany, among them—had taken control over weaker nations around the world. They had created empires."

"Isn't that called imperialism?" asked Jack.

"That's what it's called, all right. Some Americans were disturbed by imperialism and thought it was wrong. But others thought that if the United States wanted to be a big power, it should get colonies of its own."

"I'll bet that caused lots of arguments," said Jack.

"You can be sure of that. Americans seemed to be of two minds about imperialism. Almost everyone agreed that *other* nations' imperialism was wrong. For instance, Americans were especially critical of the way Spain dealt with its colony of Cuba, not far off the coast of Florida. In the end, we fought a war against Spain. And we ended up taking over Spain's Asian colony of the Philippines."

"Did the U.S. then become an imperialist power?" asked Jack.

"In a way, yes. But we never built as large an empire as other nations did. And many Americans continued to argue that imperialism was wrong."

"Well, I think it's wrong for one nation to control another," said Jack.

"So do most people today, Jack. In this unit we'll see how World War I helped give imperialism a bad name. The war began between imperialist powers in Europe—Britain and France on one side, Germany on the other. Later the United States entered the war on the side of Britain and France. Our President, Woodrow Wilson, thought imperialism had been a major cause of the war. He fought for a League of Nations to put an end to imperialism and guarantee future peace."

"I see," said Jack. "And what about conditions in the United States? You said some people wanted to change things at home."

"Ah, yes. Those people were called Progressives. They had ideas about how to improve life in America."

"What sort of ideas?"

"They wanted to put an end to graft and corruption. They wanted to help the poor. And they wanted to give common people a greater voice in public affairs."

"Did they succeed?" asked Jack.

"Suppose we look at the unit. Let's find out about imperialism, progressivism, and World War I."

1 The United States Discovers Imperialism

For many years after the Civil War, the reunited country concentrated on building up its industries and farms. People were busy learning new skills to work in the new and expanding factories or settling the recently opened areas of the West. Few showed interest in events in the rest of the world. Building up their country seemed more important to Americans than becoming involved elsewhere.

The late 19th century was a time of great change in the world. Several European nations that did not already have colonies were eager to acquire some. European nations that already controlled distant lands wanted *more* colonies. A scramble for territory began, particularly in Africa and Asia.

As time passed, the urge to develop an empire was felt in the United States as well. Some Americans argued that the U.S. needed colonies of its own if it hoped to be a truly powerful nation. They said colonies could provide the United States with raw materials and serve as an outlet for U.S. goods. They wanted the United States to become a world power with a strong navy to protect its trade and its colonies. A navy that sailed to faraway places needed bases for refueling and taking on supplies, they pointed out.

Other Americans thought differently. Some argued that it was wrong for one nation to control another. Hadn't the United States fought a rev-

olution to free itself from British rule? they asked. Others argued that it was just not necessary for the U.S. to have colonies. They said the U.S. could become strong through peaceful trade rather than through conquest.

The practice of extending a nation's control over peoples outside its borders is called *imperialism*. The late 19th century became known as an age of imperialism. It was a difficult time for people who opposed imperialism. Wouldn't the U.S. be left behind if it didn't get its own colonies? Didn't the U.S. have a duty to bring civilization to "lesser peoples"? Hadn't the U.S. better build up its strength so that other nations wouldn't seize colonies in the Americas? Questions such as these were asked by many Americans, and they helped swing U.S. policy in the direction of imperialism.

In the years before 1898, the United States had added some territory. In 1867 it bought Alaska from Russia for $7.2 million. In 1872 it took control of part of the Samoan Islands in the South Pacific.

Ever since the early 1800's, Americans had been sailing to Hawaii. As the years went by, Americans gained more and more power over the government and economy of Hawaii. Finally, in 1893, U.S.-backed interests overthrew Hawaii's Queen Liliuokalani. The islands then came under the protection of the United States.

361

Within five years, the United States formally declared Hawaii to be one of its possessions.

Another island captured the attention of Americans in 1898. It was Cuba, located only 90 miles off the coast of Florida. Caught up in a bitter war for independence from Spain, the Cubans hoped for help from the United States. Americans sympathized with the Cubans' wish to govern themselves. Many strongly objected to the way Cubans were being treated by the Spanish. Newspapers in the United States reported stories, often about the horrible conditions in prison camps in Cuba. Such stories sold more papers and encouraged U.S. support for a war to help the Cubans drive out the Spanish. Business people in the United States also supported the move to make war on Spain. For one thing, the revolution hurt U.S. trade with Cuba. For another, business prospects might be brighter in an independent Cuba.

In early 1898, the United States sent the battleship *Maine* to the harbor of Havana, Cuba, to protect American lives and property. On the night of February 15, the *Maine* exploded. Two hundred sixty Americans were killed. The Spanish were blamed, although they denied having anything to do with the explosion. "Remember the *Maine!*" became a rallying cry for war. Pressure for U.S. action built up. At the end of April, 1898, Congress declared war against Spain. At the same time, Congress passed the Teller Resolution, which promised that the Cuban people would control their own country following Spain's defeat.

As soon as the war with Spain started, Commodore George Dewey, commander of U.S. Navy ships then in Hong Kong, was ordered to the Philippines. He destroyed the Spanish ships in Manila Bay on May 1. Reinforced with troops from the United States, Dewey took Manila, the capital city.

In our story, Dewey and Emilio Aguinaldo, a rebel leader in the Philippines, are trying to reach an understanding. What does each want from the other?

The Spanish-American War

In the Caribbean

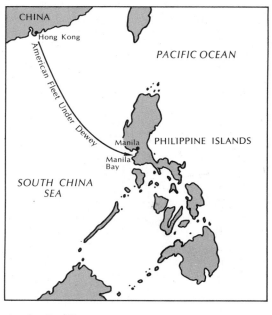

In the Pacific

Manila, Philippines, August, 1898

"I have brought you back to your country for a very important reason," said Commodore Dewey.

Aguinaldo tensed. "Commodore Dewey, I am here for one reason only—to help drive the Spanish from my country."

"That is exactly what I want you to do."

"Commodore Dewey," Aguinaldo continued, "right now we are friends because we both fight the same enemy. But will we still be friends after the Spanish have been defeated?"

Dewey asked, "What can possibly interfere with our friendship?"

"Only this," Aguinaldo warned. "A decision by your country to follow in Spain's footsteps."

"Are you saying that you would not welcome help from the United States after this war is over?" Dewey asked.

"The only way that your country can help my people is to leave us alone. Allow us to rule ourselves, and you will win our undying friendship and loyalty. But if you do otherwise, our hatred for the Spanish will be turned against you. You will face a war to the death."

Dewey protested, "We are not like the Spanish. The United States has no interest in conquering people, only in helping them."

"Then deliver this message to your government. Leave us in peace, and let us follow our way of life as we see fit. Your people should understand this message. They once fought for the same things for themselves."

Dewey smiled but said nothing.

The United States government did not understand Aguinaldo's message. President McKinley and his supporters wanted the Philippines to become a base for American trade in East Asia. They also believed that the Filipinos (the people of the Philippines) were not able to rule themselves and would welcome U.S. help. Other Americans wanted the Filipinos to have their independence. They felt that a United States takeover of the Philippines would be against the principles of the Declaration of Independence. The United States Senate had to decide the issue.

In February, 1899, the Senate, by a vote of 57 to 27, approved a U.S. takeover of the Philippines. A band of Filipino rebels, led by Aguinaldo, immediately took up arms against the United States.

The war was bitter and ugly. The Filipino fighters used hit-and-run methods, attacking mostly by night. By day, they returned to their villages and blended into the population. American troops became frustrated and attacked villages, killing many innocent Filipino men, women, and children. Both sides used torture. When the American people began to learn about how the war was being fought, many were shocked.

United States forces captured Aguinaldo in March, 1901. To save his men, the Filipino leader took an oath of allegiance to the United States. The war was over. It had cost the Filipinos 20,000 lives; the Americans, 5,000 lives.

POSTSCRIPT

The Spanish-American War lasted only four months. U.S. forces defeated Spain in August, 1898. In the peace treaty signed in December, Spain agreed to set Cuba free. It also transferred control of Puerto Rico (in the Caribbean) and Guam (in the South Pacific) to the United States. In addition, Spain agreed to sell the Philippine Islands to the United States for $20 million. Now the United States controlled a small empire and was firmly committed to a policy of imperialism.

For a time the United States took control over Cuba. It helped Cuba to build itself up and to form a new government. In 1902, the United States, acting according to the principles of the Teller Resolution, withdrew its troops from Cuba.

But the United States continued to exert strong influence over Cuba. It pressured the country to accept the Platt Amendment. This allowed the United States to decide Cuba's foreign policy. It also permitted the United States to use troops to restore order and to protect American life and property if the need should arise. Four times over the next 30 years, U.S. troops were sent to Cuba. Many Cubans resented the Platt Amendment and wanted to see an end to American involvement in Cuban affairs. In 1934, President Franklin D. Roosevelt, as part of his Good Neighbor Policy toward Latin America, abolished the Platt Amendment.

Along with business investments, Americans brought to the Philippines education and better health care. In time the United States gave Filipinos the opportunity to govern themselves. In the Jones Act of 1916 and the Tydings-McDuffie Act of 1934, the United States promised the Filipinos future independence. This promise was made good in 1946. The Philippines became an independent nation with close economic and military ties to the United States.

Homework Questions

1. What arguments were made by those who wanted a United States empire? By those opposed to such an empire?
2. Why did the United States become interested in Cuba?
3. List the possessions the United States acquired between 1865 and 1900.
4. How did the U.S. government and Aguinaldo differ about the future of the Philippine Islands?
5. Why did many Cubans oppose the Platt Amendment?

Understanding the Story

A.   Write *T* for each statement that is true and *F* for each statement that is false.
   1. Between 1867 and 1898 the United States acquired Alaska, part of the Samoan Islands, and Hawaii.
   2. The Cuban people revolted against the Filipinos.
   3. Congress declared in the Teller Resolution that the United States should rule Cuba.

4. Spain was happy to sell the Philippine Islands to the United States.
5. Aguinaldo did not want the United States to follow in Spain's footsteps.
6. Aguinaldo hoped that Americans would stay and teach the Filipinos how to govern themselves.
7. Dewey claimed that the United States had no interest in conquering other people.
8. Americans disagreed about the question of taking over the Philippines.

B. Study the maps on page 362. Then choose the term or phrase that best completes each statement or answers each question.
1. Cuba is in which direction from Florida? (*a*) North (*b*) East (*c*) South
2. The closest Spanish city to Key West is (*a*) Havana (*b*) Santiago (*c*) Manila Bay.
3. The Philippine Islands are bordered by which ocean? (*a*) Pacific (*b*) Atlantic (*c*) Indian
4. The United States is closer to Cuba than China is to the Philippines. (*a*) True (*b*) False (*c*) Not enough information given

5. The American fleet landed in which of the following places? (*a*) Havana and Manila (*b*) Santiago and Hong Kong (*c*) Santiago and Manila Bay

C. If you had been living in 1898, would you have wanted the United States to take over the Philippines? Why or why not?

Activities and Inquiries

1. Imagine that you are visiting a Cuban classroom. The teacher says that the United States declared war on Spain for selfish reasons only. What will you say in reply?
2. Imagine that you are a U.S. newspaper writer living in 1898. Write a story that will gain U.S. sympathy for the Cuban people.
3. Imagine that you are a writer for a Spanish newspaper in 1898. Write a story that warns the United States to mind its own business.
4. Write a letter to Aguinaldo to convince him that Americans do not mean to harm his people.
5. Write Aguinaldo's answer to your letter.

2 "Fire! Fire!"

By 1900, there were 76 million Americans. Ten years later there were 92 million. The nation seemed to be growing more prosperous with almost every passing year. Many people—factory owners, shopkeepers, bankers, even clerks—lived a life of relative ease. In fashionable sections of the American cities, almost every home had servants to help out.

But not all Americans shared in the good life. Poverty lurked in the slums of every city and in many farming regions. Wages were low, especially for the unskilled. Working conditions were often grim.

Of some 38 million jobholders, about 8 million were women. Some workers had special skills. Many skilled workers belonged to labor unions such as the American Federation of Labor (started in 1886). These unions tried hard to improve wages and job conditions. But most workers were unskilled, belonged to no union, and worked for very low wages indeed.

In many factories, working conditions were unsafe. Accidents were common—especially toward the end of a 10-hour day when workers were weary. Laws to ensure worker safety were few and rarely enforced. In most states there was no such thing as social insurance to guard workers against illness, old age, or unemployment.

Poorly paid workers often lived in run-down tenement buildings. Whole families might share a single airless room. Drunkenness and disease were widespread.

Such conditions troubled many people of the middle and upper classes. Between 1900 and 1910 these people began a movement to bring about reforms. The reformers were called Progressives.

Unlike the earlier Populists, Progressives tended to be city folk rather than farmers. Among them were Republicans, Democrats, and Socialists, as well as people who joined a party called the Progressive Party. What they had in common was a desire to advance three main goals. These were "less monopoly" in business, "more democracy" in government, and "social justice" for the poor. Many Progressives also pushed for other goals—laws against the sale of alcohol, voting rights for women, restrictions on immigration, and so on. As you can see, the Progressive movement had many points of view. Progressives often differed with one another about what goals to work toward.

Monopoly control of business was a key concern of Progressives. By 1909, a few large companies (1 percent of all United States businesses) turned out 44 percent of the nation's manufactured goods. Progressives felt this was unfair to small business people, who often could not compete effectively against big business. Progressives argued that monopolies hurt the common people by raising prices. They proposed new government regulations as a way to fight monopolies and called for stricter enforcement of existing antitrust laws.

Progressives also worked for changes in city, state, and national government. They voiced alarm about corruption in government—the buying and selling of favors. Certain Progressives made a career of exposing misdoings by public officials and business people. Lincoln Steffens, in his book, *The Shame of the Cities*, described shady dealings between bribe-taking officials and such businesses as streetcar companies. Ida Tarbell, in a series of magazine articles called "History of the Standard Oil Company," described John D. Rockefeller's ruthless business methods. Frank Norris, in his novel *The Octopus*, portrayed California railroads as evil forces taking advantage of farmers. President Theodore Roosevelt (himself a Progressive) coined a term to describe such writers. He called them "muckrakers," because of their vivid descriptions of the muck, or filth, in American life.

"Social justice" was the concern of other muckrakers such as Jacob Riis. An immigrant from Denmark, Riis became a newspaper reporter and an author. His articles and books called attention to crime, drunkenness, and despair in New York's poorer districts. Among other things, he told of foul-smelling cellars in which humans, pigs, goats, and horses lived side by side.

Progressives such as the muckrakers hoped to arouse indignation and move people to demand changes in business, government, and social conditions. As you read the following story, ask yourself how it might have affected a reader of the early 20th century. How does it affect you? Does it make you want to change things?

The scene is a building in New York City, where the Triangle Shirtwaist Company factory occupies the eighth, ninth, and tenth floors. Two sewing machine operators, Marie and Bella, are waiting impatiently for their workday to end. It is a Saturday. Both young women are looking forward to Sunday, their one day off. They are complaining about their jobs.

New York City, March 25, 1911

"Bella, what time is it?"

"Patience, Marie, it's almost quitting time."

"Thank goodness. I feel as if I've been working for days."

"You're right," said Bella, "the work here makes it seem as if every day is a week. And working long hours is not the worst of it. The company crowds hundreds of us in here and locks us in to make sure we won't steal from it or take a break. The supervisors even check our pocketbooks when we leave. They work us like animals and pay us what they please."

"Well, we can always try again to join a union," said Marie.

"What for?" asked Bella. "Have you forgotten what happened the last time we joined a union and went on strike? The police were called, and we were beaten and arrested. The leaders of the strike were fined. No, thank you. I'm through with joining unions."

Many of the workers were beginning to finish up for the day. The two women rose and stretched. They walked to the ninth-floor washroom.

Meanwhile, on the eighth floor, a woman screamed, "Fire! Fire!" Flames licked up from beneath a worktable. Other women came running. They grabbed pails of water and tried to put the fire out, but it began to spread. The room filled with smoke. A foreman yelled for the workers to leave the building. There were more than 500 of them on the eighth, ninth, and tenth floors.

Some workers on the eighth floor tried to leave by the freight elevators. Others rushed to the outside fire escape. Most tried to go down the narrow winding stairway inside the building. The people on the tenth floor ran up to the roof and climbed over to the roof of the next building to safety.

But the 260 workers on the ninth floor had few choices. Bella and Marie went from the washroom into a smoke-filled room. People were running everywhere. Marie shrieked and pointed to the windows. The fire was burning through the wooden frames.

Marie and Bella joined others running toward the stairway. A door blocked their way. The workers pulled and pushed, but it did not open. They were trapped.

Some workers sank to their knees and began to pray. Others collapsed. Coughing, their eyes and lungs filled with smoke, Bella and Marie held hands and ran about trying to find a new way to escape. Bella turned to Marie and whispered, "The elevators!"

The two rushed to the freight elevators, looked down, and shrank back in horror. The elevators were stuck in the shafts many floors below. People were climbing down ropes, desperately trying to get to the lower floors. As Bella and Marie watched, some of the women lost their grip and fell to their death. More fell. Dismayed, the two turned from the elevator shafts and ran toward the fire escape.

Many others were there already. By now the fire escape was filled with people. Amidst the panic and the screams, a great noise was heard. It was the sound of the fire escape pulling away from the building. Many fell to their deaths.

Bella and Marie had one last hope: the windows.

Others were huddled around the windows, jumping to and fro to avoid the flames. Some had crept out on the ledge and were looking down on the crowd that had gathered in the street. Bella and Marie prayed for a miracle, for rescue.

From the distance, the sound of fire bells could be heard. New hope stirred in the hearts of the women. The horse-drawn fire engines stopped in front of the building. Quickly the firemen raised a ladder. From the ninth-floor window, the women watched as the ladder came closer and closer. Then their hearts sank. The ladder could reach no higher than the sixth floor.

Now the flames began to touch clothing and flesh. Women screamed and jumped toward the street. Their bodies landed with such force that they made holes in the pavement.

The last to climb out on the ledge, the two young women held each other tightly, tears streaming down their faces. The firemen offered one last hope. They held a 14-foot rope net and called for Bella and Marie to jump.

Trembling with fear, Bella hugged Marie even tighter. Both were afraid to jump. If the flames had not blocked their way, they would have climbed back into the room.

"I can't jump," said Bella, "I'm too scared."

"Me too," said Marie. "Jumping scares me just as much as the fire."

"But we have no choice. Let's jump together," said Bella.

Marie nodded. With a last look back at the flames, holding one another, they jumped. The firemen tensed and gripped the net tightly. The women were headed in the right direction and were going to land squarely in the middle of the net. The crowd began to cheer.

Bella and Marie struck the net and ripped right through it. Their bodies thudded on the hard pavement. Like so many others that day, the two women were killed. All in all, 146 workers died in the Triangle fire. Most of them were young women like Bella and Marie.

POSTSCRIPT

The Triangle fire outraged many people, and not only Progressives. Investigations were held, building codes strengthened, fire-safety laws passed. New laws forced factory owners to take more care to prevent accidents on the job. By 1914, three years after the Triangle fire, 36 new labor laws had been put into effect in the state of New York.

Progressives wholeheartedly supported reforms such as these. But many of them felt that further reforms would be slow in coming. Something had to be done to cut the corrupt ties between government leaders and business people. Also the control of "party bosses" over the masses of uneducated immigrants had to be loosened.

To make it easier to get reform laws passed, Progressives sought to give "the common people" a greater say in government. By "common people," they usually meant the middle class. Progressives worked to extend such practices as the initiative, the recall, and the referendum at the state level (see page 348). They sought to take political power away from "party bosses" by requiring that each party choose its candidates in a public vote. Between 1902 and 1915, every state adopted some form of direct primary election. Progressives also fought to end the practice of having state legislatures choose members of the United States Senate. The 17th Amendment, which went into effect in 1913, provided for voters to elect all U.S. Senators.

The Progressive movement remained strong up to the time of World War I, and even after that in the Midwest. The movement had a lasting effect on the nation. Progressives were largely responsible for a number of federal reform laws. The Hepburn Act (1906) barred rebates (kickbacks) by railroads. The Clayton Antitrust Act (1914) strengthened federal antitrust laws. Progressives also introduced such new forms of local government as the city manager plan. Under this plan, a hired expert rather than an elected mayor runs city affairs.

The Progressive movement did relatively little for one group of "the common people"—black Americans. Progressives were mainly middle-class whites who had little social contact with black Americans. Whites tended to overlook the complaints of blacks that they had been left out of the American dream.

Homework Questions

1. Why did people say that not all Americans shared in the good life at this time?
2. How did the Progressives propose to improve the lot of small business owners and "the common people"?
3. In what ways did the muckrakers call the attention of the public to corruption and poverty? Why did the muckrakers think their efforts would help end these problems?
4. How did the Triangle fire affect factory working conditions?
5. What sorts of measures did Progressives back in pursuing their goal of "more democracy"?

Understanding the Story

A. List the numbers of the statements that are true.
1. Muckrakers were satisfied with the way things were.
2. Some politicians took bribes in this period.
3. The Triangle Shirtwaist factory was overcrowded.
4. Bella wanted to join a union.
5. Fire trapped Bella and Marie in the building.
6. Some workers tried to walk down the fire escape to safety.
7. Fire ladders could not reach the ninth floor.
8. Progressives felt the tragedy of the Triangle fire was unavoidable.

B. Complete each of the following sentences by filling in the missing word or words.
1. The fire took place in the _____ factory.
2. Supervisors checked pocketbooks to prevent _____.
3. A foreman told the workers to leave _____.
4. Some workers on the eighth floor tried to leave by the _____.
5. Those on the tenth floor climbed over to the _____ _____.
6. The _____ pulled away from the building.
7. Firemen told Bella and Marie to jump into a _____.
8. After the Triangle factory burned, laws were passed that made factories _____ places in which to work.

C. Do you think Bella was right to be against joining a labor union? Why or why not?

Activities and Inquiries

1. Pretend that you are a building inspector. List every violation you find on the floors occupied by the Triangle factory.
2. You are a reporter looking over the ruins of the Triangle fire. Write an article describing what you see.
3. You write a follow-up article. What recommendations do you make to prevent a future Triangle fire?
4. Compare the goals of the Progressives with those of the Populists.

3 Theodore Roosevelt and the Politicians

Progressives were unhappy with many elected government officials. They felt that too many national leaders spoke only for big business. They felt that too many city leaders used the immigrant vote to keep their "machines" in power. Progressives wanted to elect politicians who shared their own point of view.

President William McKinley, who had been elected over William Jennings Bryan in 1896, was no Progressive. He was a traditional Republican with strong backing from party bosses and business leaders. In 1900, Republican Party leaders backed McKinley for re-election. The country was in the middle of a business boom. The prices of iron, steel, and cotton were high. Factories were operating at full production and hiring more workers. Even farmers were doing better. Republican leaders believed the voters would give McKinley credit for the nation's prosperity and elect him by a landslide.

McKinley's vice-presidential running mate was Theodore Roosevelt, a Republican who shared many of the Progressives' goals. Roosevelt had become popular by fighting for social reforms and decent government in New York State. Traditional Republican leaders worried that this young politician, just past 40 years old, might one day run for the Presidency. This

would be dangerous, they thought, because he would be his own man and not listen to them. By nominating him for the Vice Presidency, a powerless job, they hoped to keep Roosevelt from doing much to call attention to himself. Traditional Republican leaders wanted the public to forget Theodore Roosevelt.

The McKinley-Roosevelt ticket won the election of 1900 easily. Republican leaders congratulated themselves on their double triumph—McKinley's victory and Roosevelt's political burial.

Then came a shocking event. On September 6, 1901, at a reception in Buffalo, New York, a young man approached McKinley, appearing to want to shake his hand. Instead, the man pulled a gun and fired two shots into the President's body. Eight days later, McKinley was dead. For the Republican bosses, the worst had happened. Theodore Roosevelt had become President.

Many, of course, were happy that a man with Roosevelt's energy and interests had risen to the nation's highest office. Many Progressives felt he represented a new kind of politician with fresh ideas. How did Roosevelt behave as President? How did he act toward business interests? What did he do about the problems affecting the poor?

Washington, D.C., 1912

You are Theodore Roosevelt, the man some politicians hoped the public would forget. But an assassin's bullet ruined these politicians' plans, and you became President of the United States.

Millions of Americans are under your spell. They have followed your career from the start. Rancher, mountain climber, big-game hunter, author, state legislator, police commissioner, civil service commissioner, assistant secretary of the navy, war hero, governor, Vice President, and President. You had reached the top at the young age of 42.

As a child you suffered from asthma, poor eyesight, and many illnesses. But you refused to be handicapped by your weak body, so you lifted weights, exercised, took boxing lessons, and learned to ride and shoot. You became strong, powerful, and healthy.

You had inherited enough money to buy horses, tennis courts, and yachts for your large family. You could have had an easy life. Instead you chose to enter politics. You had made over your body, and you now wanted to make over America.

As President, you believed that you had the power to do anything for the good of the country. You promised to give all Americans a "square deal," especially the farmers, workers, and small business people. So you rolled up your sleeves and went to work. You searched the government for signs of corruption and stopped wrongdoing when you found it. You supported union demands for better wages and shorter hours.

Like many Progressives, you were undecided about how to deal with monopolies. At first you described all monopolies as evil. You became a "trust-buster." Later you decided that times had changed and that bigger businesses might be necessary in some industries. You argued that it was wrong to try to turn the clock back to earlier, simpler times. There were "good" big businesses and "bad" ones, you said. Only the "bad" ones, like Standard Oil, should be broken up. "Good" ones should be allowed to continue—but under government regulation to protect the public interest. Business growth was natural, you felt, and government must grow bigger too.

Congress answered your call and passed a series of laws with teeth in them. The Meat Inspection Act (1906) helped to protect people from diseased and rotten meats. (It was inspired by a book, *The Jungle*, by the muckraker Upton Sinclair.) The Pure Food and Drug Act (1906) helped to protect people from dangerous medicines and drugs. Especially important to you, Congress passed a number of conservation laws. These aimed to protect public lands and the nation's forests for years to come.

Most Progressives praised your actions. But along with your admirers, there were many who did not like you or what you were doing. Some said that *all* monopolies should be broken up. Others said that you were more interested in publicity than in getting things done. Still others frowned when they read about how you, the President, boxed and wrestled in the White House.

Although you easily won the 1904 election and continued to have strong support, you made a public promise not to run again in 1908. And you kept that promise. As the election of 1908 drew near, you decided that your good friend Secretary of War William Howard Taft should run in your place. Taft happily agreed.

You pitched in and helped Taft win the Republican nomination and the election. But in your heart you knew that you really wanted to keep on being President. You were barely 50 years old, and you wondered what you would do with the rest of your life. So you went big-game hunting in Africa and waited and hoped for someone to call you back to the game of politics in America.

Meanwhile, your friend Taft was trying to follow your policies, but he displeased you and your supporters. He had promised to help pass a low tariff bill. Some of your Republican opponents, including party leaders, had called for a high tariff instead. Taft found it hard to stand up to them and finally signed a high tariff bill.

On other issues, Taft came closer to your way of thinking. Politicians who wanted reforms got Congress to pass a batch of new bills for Taft to sign. He signed a bill creating a Department of Labor within the federal government. He also approved a bill regulating railroad rates. In four years, Taft tried to break up more than twice as many giant companies as you had in seven. You did not like the comparison.

When Taft appeared to undo some of your conservation work, you became angry. You argued that traditional Republicans were blocking the path to further reform. The time had come for you to get back into politics. You decided to run for the Presidency in 1912.

To win, you hoped for the Republican Party's nomination. Taft also wanted that nomination, so you would have to see that he didn't get it. How? By telling the American people that Taft had not carried out your policies. Why should the voters settle for Taft, you asked, when they could have you back in the White House?

The Republican bosses said no to you. Traditional leaders preferred to work with Taft, so the Republican nomination went to him.

As a result, you and your supporters formed a new party, called the Progressive Party and nicknamed the Bull Moose Party. Some people warned that this would only split the Republican vote and that neither you nor Taft would win. You refused to believe them.

You and Taft campaigned throughout the country. Your Democratic opponent was the governor of New Jersey, Woodrow Wilson. Many voters were confused because all three of you seemed to be talking like Progressives. You knew you had a tough fight on your hands, and so you campaigned hard. You had to beat the money and the organizations of the two major parties in the United States.

After the votes were counted, you were delighted to learn that you had beaten Taft by more than a half million votes. But your dream of retaking the Presidency had failed anyway. Wilson beat you by more than two million votes. You would never run for public office again.

Homework Questions

1. Why were Republican Party leaders sure that President McKinley would be re-elected to a second term in 1900?
2. Why did Republican leaders choose Theodore Roosevelt as McKinley's Vice President?
3. In what ways did Roosevelt capture the imagination of the American people?
4. How did Roosevelt propose to deal with monopolies?
5. Why did Roosevelt change his mind and run for another term as President in 1912?

Understanding the Story

A. Write *T* for each statement that is true, *F* for each statement that is false, and *N* for each statement that is not mentioned in the story.
  1. Theodore Roosevelt was popular with traditional leaders of the Republican Party.
  2. All Progressives spoke well of Roosevelt.
  3. Roosevelt was sickly as a child.
  4. Roosevelt was the youngest President yet.
  5. Roosevelt broke up large business combinations.
  6. Roosevelt made peace between Russia and Japan.
  7. Taft followed Roosevelt as President.
  8. After the election of Taft, Roosevelt never wanted to return to the White House.

B. Which statements describe events or activities in the life of Theodore Roosevelt?
  1. Roosevelt became President after McKinley died.
  2. Roosevelt became a fire marshal.
  3. Roosevelt was a state governor.
  4. Roosevelt went big-game hunting in Africa.
  5. Roosevelt forced Japan to pay its debts.
  6. Roosevelt got more votes than Taft in the election of 1912.
  7. Roosevelt vetoed the Meat Inspection Act.
  8. Roosevelt wrote books.

C. In your opinion, what was the most important goal that Theodore Roosevelt fought for? Do you think Roosevelt made a good President? Why or why not?

Activities and Inquiries

1. Prepare a report card for Theodore Roosevelt. Grade him in the following areas and justify each grade:
  a. Leadership
  b. Training
  c. Point of view
  d. Accomplishments while President
  e. Maturity
2. Imagine that you are a reporter assigned to interview Roosevelt. What questions will you ask him?
3. What answers will Roosevelt give to your questions?
4. You have to decide to vote for either Taft or Roosevelt. How will you vote? Why?

4 Big-Stick Diplomacy

Theodore Roosevelt liked to say that the United States should speak softly and carry a big stick. By this he meant that the U.S. must have military strength if it wanted to command respect. Under Roosevelt, the United States built a strong modern navy. Roosevelt was not shy about using force or the threat of force to carry out his foreign-policy goals. Because of this, his methods were called "Big-Stick" diplomacy.

One area that felt the Big Stick more often than most was Latin America. Like earlier Presidents, Roosevelt looked on Latin America as a special area of interest for the United States. You will recall that the Monroe Doctrine, dating back to 1823, warned the European nations not to acquire new territory in the Americas. Roosevelt gave new life to the Monroe Doctrine.

Some Latin American countries had borrowed money from European bankers and had not been able to pay it back. At first Roosevelt seemed willing to let European nations send warships to collect the debts. He wrote: "If any South-American country misbehaves toward any European country, let the European country spank it." But he began to worry. What if European countries ended up in control of the countries they "spanked"?

In 1902 Britain, Germany, and Italy sent warships to Venezuela in order to collect debts. Roosevelt waved his big stick gently at the Europeans and asked them to send their ships home. In the meantime, Venezuela agreed to settle its debts.

Two years later, the Dominican Republic could not pay its debts. This time, Roosevelt waved his stick at the Dominican Republic and issued a warning to other Latin American countries as well. From then on, he said, the United States would act as a bill collector for the Europeans. If necessary, it would interfere in Latin America in order to stop Europe from doing the same. This means that United States forces would move into a Latin American country that owed a European country money. U.S. troops would stay and collect taxes until the bills were paid. This new policy was called the *Roosevelt Corollary* (addition) to the Monroe Doctrine.

Under the Roosevelt Corollary, the United States interfered often in the affairs of its neighbors in Latin America. Over the years, it sent troops to the Dominican Republic, Cuba, Nicaragua, and Haiti. Latin Americans resented these actions. They argued that the United States was using the Monroe Doctrine not to protect Latin Americans but to take advantage of them. They resented Roosevelt most of all because, they said, he did not show them enough respect. To back up this claim, they pointed to the origins of the Panama Canal.

In 1902 the United States had decided to build a canal through Panama, then a part of Colombia. The United States needed a quick way to get its ships from the East to the West Coast. The canal would help the growing navy to protect U.S. possessions on both the Atlantic and Pacific sides.

A French company had started to dig a canal through Panama in the 1880's. It stopped after thousands of workers had died of malaria and yellow fever. Before it stopped, however, the French firm had lost $260 million.

The United States now offered $40 million to French investors for their digging rights. The United States also offered Colombia $10 million and a yearly rental of $250,000. The Colombian ambassador to the United States agreed to these terms, but the Colombian Senate said no. It thought that Colombia should get more money.

In our story, President Roosevelt and Secretary of State John Hay are discussing the Panama Canal. Why did the United States want to build a canal through Panama? How did it get to build the canal? Why did Latin Americans resent the United States for its actions in Panama?

Washington, D.C., 1903

"I tell you, Hay, I'm not going to let a bunch of blackmailers push me around!" said President Roosevelt.

"What can we do, Mr. President? After all, Colombia does have the right to change its mind."

"I don't agree. Those Colombian senators should not be allowed to stand in the way of one of the future highways of civilization."

"Perhaps we should offer Colombia more money," suggested Secretary Hay.

"Never!" boomed the President. "They've had their chance, and now it's my turn!"

"What do you propose?"

"I say that we should pay off the French company and just go into Panama and complete the canal."

"We can't do that, Mr. President. It would make us look like bullies to the rest of the world."

"The rest of the world will thank me when I present them with the canal."

"Still, we can't do it that way," Hay insisted.

"All right," Roosevelt agreed with a sigh, "we'll simply have to find another way."

Meanwhile, a group of Panamanians who did not like being ruled by Colombia had come to a decision. They would start a revolution against Colombia in order to make Panama an independent country. They hoped that when the shooting started, the United States would step in on their side. They knew that Roosevelt was angry with Colombia, and they hoped he would lend them his support.

The revolution began on November 3, 1903. A United States ship, sent by Roosevelt, prevented the Colombian soldiers from landing in Panama and putting down the rebellion. The revolution was a success. Less than two hours after he heard the news, Roosevelt authorized the United States government to recognize the rebels as the government of an independent Panama.

Two weeks later, the United States and Panama signed a treaty. Panama accepted the $10 million offered to Colombia. In return, Panama agreed to let the United States build and control a canal.

At another meeting, Hay turned to Roosevelt and said, "Well, Mr. President, everything turned out well after all. The new nation of Panama is grateful to us and, to show its gratitude, has agreed to give us the canal."

"Wrong, Hay," said Roosevelt with a big smile. "No one gave us the canal. I took it!"

POSTSCRIPT

Building the canal was not easy. It took ten years to master disease and to dig through the jungles and mountains.

Colonel William Gorgas cleared the Canal Zone of yellow fever and malaria. Colonel George W. Goethals supervised the building of the canal. Finally finished in 1914, just as World War I began in Europe, the project cost many lives and slightly more than $400 million.

The canal shortened the route between the Atlantic and Pacific oceans by thousands of miles. Because ships no longer had to make the long voyage around South America, the cost of shipping products dropped. Through the years, the importance of the canal has decreased in some respects. It is now too small for aircraft carriers and supertankers to pass through.

In the 1970's, the Panama Canal

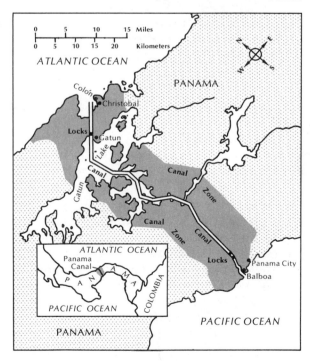

The Panama Canal

once again made headlines. For years, the people of Panama had complained about U.S. control of the canal. Since the canal slices through their country, they wanted the right to control it. In 1977 President Jimmy Carter of the United States and President Omar Torrijos of Panama agreed that Panama would take control of the canal in the year 2000. The United States Senate voted for the treaty after a long and difficult struggle.

Theodore Roosevelt insisted that a President should do more than talk about foreign policy. He should carry it out himself, boldly backed by the "Big Stick" of a powerful navy. Roosevelt's methods were often harsh, impulsive, and aggressive, as smaller nations like Colombia well knew. Yet he was the first President to be looked upon by the rulers of Europe and Asia as an equal.

In recognition of his standing in the world, Roosevelt was asked to do what he could to end a war between Russia and Japan (1904–1905). He was successful in bringing the two sides together at Portsmouth, New Hampshire, to work out a peace treaty. For his efforts, Roosevelt was awarded the Nobel peace prize.

Homework Questions

1. Why did Roosevelt decide it might be dangerous to let European powers "spank" Latin American countries that owed them money?
2. How did Roosevelt use his Big Stick in the cases of Venezuela and the Dominican Republic?
3. Why did Latin Americans object to the Roosevelt Corollary?
4. Why did the United States want to build a canal through Panama?
5. What made the Panama Canal so difficult to build?

Understanding the Story

A. Write *F* for each statement that is a fact and *O* for each statement that is an opinion.
   1. Some Latin American countries could not pay back their loans.
   2. The United States collected money from Latin Americans to pay back Europeans.
   3. The United States used the Roosevelt Corollary to interfere in Latin American affairs.
   4. Colombia was wrong to stand in Roosevelt's way.
   5. The United States bought a French company's digging rights in Panama.
   6. If Roosevelt had given in to Colombia's demands, the French would have asked for more money.
   7. The United States helped Panama with its revolution against Colombia.
   8. The Panama Canal was not worth all the lives and money it cost.

B. Study the map on page 377. Then choose the term or phrase that best completes each statement.
   1. The Panama Canal connects (*a*) the Atlantic Ocean and Caribbean Sea   (*b*) the Atlantic and Pacific oceans   (*c*) Panama and Colombia.
   2. The distance from Colón to Gatun is about (*a*) 12 kilometers   (*b*) 24 kilometers   (*c*) 30 kilometers.
   3. The distance from Gatun to Balboa is about (*a*) 34 kilometers   (*b*) 52 kilometers   (*c*) 63 kilometers.

4. To go through the Panama Canal starting from Balboa, your ship would travel (a) north (b) south (c) east.
5. To go through the canal starting from Colón, your ship would travel (a) west (b) west and north (c) southwest and southeast.

C. If you were a citizen of a Latin American country today, would you approve or disapprove of the Monroe Doctrine? Explain.

Activities and Inquiries

1. Imagine that you are the editor of a Colombian newspaper in 1903. Write an editorial describing how you feel about Roosevelt and his actions in Panama.
2. Imagine you are an American living in 1903. Write down arguments in favor of Roosevelt's methods of getting the Panama Canal started. Now write down arguments against those methods. Which arguments do you think are stronger? Why?
3. Roosevelt keeps a diary. In it he writes down the reasons he thinks Big-Stick diplomacy is good for the United States. Write the diary selection as you think Roosevelt would.
4. Roosevelt asks your advice on ways to persuade Latin Americans to warm up to the United States. Write down your ideas.
5. You meet Theodore Roosevelt. He asks you to tell him what you really think of him. Answer him and explain why you feel this way.

5 Susan B. Anthony: Fighter for Equality

Many women took an active part in the Progressive movement and in other social movements of the late 19th and early 20th centuries. Some women fought to ban the sale of liquor. Some fought to improve living conditions among the poor. Some fought corruption in government.

But, in the eyes of a large group of women, one fight seemed more important than all others. That was the struggle for woman suffrage (voting rights for women). Until women could vote in every state in the Union, many women felt, political leaders would never take women seriously.

By the turn of the century, women could vote in a few states or in certain types of elections. Wyoming Territory let some women vote in all elections as early as 1869. By 1900 a handful of Western states had woman suffrage. A few states in other parts of the country let women vote in school elections, for example, but not in most other elections.

The 15th Amendment to the United States Constitution gave voting rights to males who were former slaves. In the 1860's, when the amendment was being considered by Congress, feminists (supporters of full equality for women) asked to have women's voting rights added. Congress refused.

Susan B. Anthony was a leading feminist of the time. Disappointed by the 15th Amendment, she increased her efforts to win voting rights for women. How did she try to make her voice heard? Did she succeed?

Washington, D.C., 1906

Susan B. Anthony was tired. Her doctor had told her to stay in bed and rest. But she wanted to go to a party in her honor. Even at 86 years of age, she did not want to miss a chance to speak out for women's rights.

While dressing for the party, she thought about the many changes during her lifetime. She remembered back to the time when only one college in the United States admitted women and when there were no women doctors or lawyers in the country. If a married woman inherited money, it was not hers but her husband's. A woman was not allowed to divorce her husband even on the ground of cruelty. Even if a husband was proven to be a drunkard, he automatically gained custody of the children in the event of a divorce. In those days the working world was very harsh for most women. A woman might receive 31 cents for a working day of 14 hours. And the working woman, if married, was forced by law to turn her entire wages over to her husband. Such a woman was little more than a slave, thought Anthony.

As a young woman, Susan B. Anthony had taken a job as a teacher. She received $2.50 a week. The previous teacher, a man, had been paid $10 a week for doing the same work. This, Anthony decided, was a gross injustice. She decided to devote the rest of her life to righting what she saw as the terrible wrongs being done to women everywhere. She helped to start a feminist movement in the 1850's.

But it was a long, hard struggle. Anthony found that most people, men and women, considered women to be inferior to men. Indeed, some of the strongest critics of the feminist movement were women.

Along with Anthony, Elizabeth Stanton and Ernestine Rose became leaders of the feminist movement. They traveled around the country in an effort to organize women everywhere. Newspaper articles made fun of them. Politicians turned a deaf ear. And yet the feminists slowly began to make progress.

Other women joined the cause. As editor of *Women's Journal*, Alice Stone Blackwell proved to be an effective backer of the vote for women. Carrie Chapman Catt was called the organizing genius of the woman suffrage movement. Florence Kelley became the first woman to be appointed chief inspector of factories in Illinois and argued that working women needed the vote. Jane Addams founded Hull House in Chicago, where poor people could learn skills and have their children cared for. She played a key role in helping women win the right to vote in Chicago city elections in 1913. Belle Kearney carried the fight to the South by pushing for woman suffrage in that area.

But no one was more energetic than Susan B. Anthony. In spite of great hardships, she continued to travel around the country and speak out for feminist causes. Often her health broke down because of the long train rides, hours of speaking, and months of organizing. Still she refused to stop. She raised thousands of dollars for her cause and accepted a wage of only $12 a week for herself.

During this period, Anthony struggled to pay off a $10,000 debt brought about by the failure of her women's rights magazine. She was arrested for voting illegally and ordered to pay a heavy fine. Other women who voted were not so lucky. Several were arrested and sent to jail and workhouses. Some staged hunger strikes in protest and were fed through tubes forced down their throats.

The efforts of Anthony and others did help to bring about important changes. More universities began to admit women. Opportunities opened up for women in the fields of education, art, literature, medicine, and the law. By the end of the 19th century, married women had won the right to own and control their own property, to sue and be sued, to keep their earnings, and to exercise guardianship over their children. But women were still denied the right to vote.

Yes, the struggle was still going on, thought Anthony as she left at last for the party. When she arrived, those in the room burst into applause, honoring the woman who had fought so hard for feminist causes. Anthony held up her hand for silence. She said, "What I ask is not praise but justice. And justice is bound to come in the end. Failure is impossible!"

That was to be Anthony's final speech. After returning home she collapsed. Shortly after, she died of pneumonia. She did not live to see the triumph of her efforts to win voting rights for women.

POSTSCRIPT

Susan B. Anthony had persuaded many women and men of the need for woman suffrage. Other leaders, such as Carrie Chapman Catt, carried on her work. A new party, the National Woman's Party, was formed to fight for a constitutional amendment to grant women the right to vote.

Congress turned down the amendment in 1914 and 1915, but supporters kept up the pressure. During World War I (1917–1918), many women pitched in to help the war effort. The movement for woman suffrage picked up new support, and in 1919 Congress finally voted yes. Like all constitutional amendments, this one had to be approved by the legislatures of three fourths of the states. In 1920 Tennessee became the 36th state to approve. As a result, the 19th Amendment, granting full voting rights to women in all states, became part of the Constitution. Fittingly, it was called the Susan B. Anthony Amendment.

Homework Questions

1. What legal rights had married women won by 1900?
2. Why did feminists think it was so important for women to win the right to vote?
3. What did Susan B. Anthony do to achieve equal rights for women?
4. Why was the National Woman's Party organized?

Understanding the Story

A. List the numbers of the statements that Susan B. Anthony made or might have made.
   1. My health comes before all other things.
   2. A married woman is lucky to have someone to take care of her.
   3. I worked as hard as any man.
   4. Some American women are treated like slaves.
   5. It is always a disgrace to be arrested.
   6. Much has been accomplished in my lifetime.
   7. Everything has been accomplished in my lifetime.
   8. Failure is impossible!

B. Write *T* for each statement that is true and *F* for each statement that is false.
   1. Feminists struggled for woman suffrage for many years.
   2. The 15th Amendment included voting rights for women.
   3. The newspapers always wrote favorably about the women's rights movement.
   4. At one time, the law said women's earnings belonged to their husbands.
   5. In Susan B. Anthony's time, women received the same pay as men for equal work.
   6. Some women went to jail for casting votes.
   7. In the 19th century, no American woman could vote.
   8. The 19th Amendment gave women the right to vote.

C. Do you think the right to vote has helped improve the position of American women significantly? Why or why not?

Activities and Inquiries

1. Imagine you are reading a newspaper article that is critical of the feminist movement. What are the major criticisms included in the article?
2. Now you read an article that supports the feminist movement. What positive arguments are included in the article?
3. Assume that you are a reporter. Your assignment is to interview Susan B. Anthony. What questions will you ask?
4. What answers do you expect to get?

6 Peace or War?

Woodrow Wilson, who was elected President in 1912, was a Democrat who shared many of the Progressives' beliefs. He was a former president of Princeton University and governor of New Jersey. An expert on American government, Wilson had written a book suggesting how a President should act. Now he had a chance to put his theories into practice.

Wilson pushed a number of reform measures through Congress. Among the most important were:

An income tax. The 16th Amendment, which permitted a federal tax on income, had been approved by Congress under President Taft. It went into effect in 1913, and Congress passed an income tax law. Progressives saw the income tax both as a source of revenue and as a means of reducing the great gap between rich and poor. The tax was graduated—that is, richer people paid a higher percentage of their income than poorer people.

A national banking system. The Federal Reserve Act of 1913 set up special banks, called Federal Reserve Banks, throughout the country. It created a Federal Reserve Board with power to raise and lower the supply of credit. Such actions influenced the amount of money in use. The goal was to make the economy work more smoothly, without sudden swings from "boom" to "bust."

Regulation of business and labor. A law of 1914 set up a new body, the Federal Trade Commission, as a watchdog against unfair business practices. The Clayton Antitrust Act of 1914, besides strengthening antitrust rules, declared labor unions to be legal. Some people had argued that antitrust laws should be applied against unions and strikes.

When it came to dealing with other nations, Wilson stressed high ideals. He was particularly interested in Latin America, and he wanted to prod the people of that area toward greater democracy. Latin Americans, especially Mexicans, resented him almost as much as they had resented Theodore Roosevelt. They accused Wilson of meddling in their affairs.

In 1910 a revolution had taken place in Mexico. One Mexican leader was chased from the country in 1911, and another was murdered in 1913. That year Victoriano Huerta became Mexico's dictator, or absolute ruler. Wilson, who believed strongly in democracy, refused to recognize Huerta. He sent arms to Huerta's enemies, hoping that they would force the dictator to step down. Many Mexicans resented Wilson's interference, which created strong anti-American feelings. After a few Americans were killed, Wilson sent troops to Mexico. War seemed likely to break out. When Argentina, Brazil, and Chile offered to step in and try to settle the dispute, both the United States and Mexico accepted. Huerta left the country, and a new Mexican government was recognized by the United States.

An even more serious foreign problem soon claimed Wilson's attention. In the summer of 1914, war broke out in Europe. The conflict would later be called World War I. Germany, Austria-Hungary, Bulgaria, and the Ottoman Empire (the Central Powers) went to war against France, Britain, Russia, Japan, and Italy (the Allies).

President Wilson said that the United States would favor neither side. The President promised to keep America out of the war. But the United States found that neutrality was hard to apply in practice. Business and emotional ties linked many Americans to the Allies, especially Britain.

The British Navy, proud of its control over the seas, stopped U.S. merchant ships bound for the Central Powers and even for neutral countries. The British took care not to cause the loss of American lives. The United States made protests but did not use force.

In February, 1915, Germany declared the seas around the British Isles to be a war zone. Within this zone, German submarines would attack any ships on sight. Again, Wilson made protests. Now both sides had annoyed the United States.

In our story, the cable lines between Britain and America are buzzing with messages. Most concern the war. From London, Ambassador Walter Hines Page, the United States representative to Great Britain, wires President Wilson regularly. In Washington, D.C., the President responds to Page while dealing with pressing questions of policy. An exchange much like this actually took place between the two men. War and peace hung in the balance. How would Wilson react if the German Navy caused American deaths?

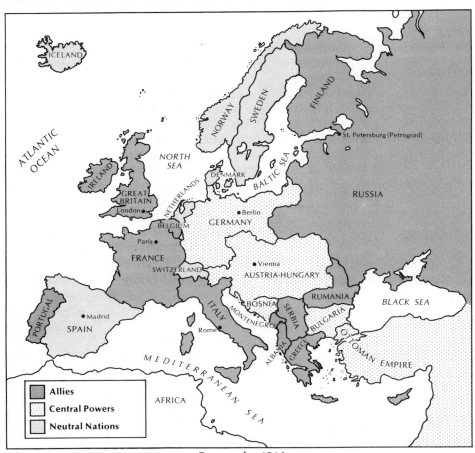

Europe in 1914

Europe in 1914

May, 1915

In his thinking, Page was as British as any English person. "Mr. President," he cabled, "Britain is fighting our fight—the battle to save civilization."

"Yes, I suppose that is true," replied President Wilson. "But our country is not prepared for war. And the people are divided. Many Americans, especially in the Midwest, hate the British. Remember—for most of our history, the British have been our enemy."

"The British are a democratic people, like us," shot back Page.

"Even so, we must remain neutral," Wilson insisted. "That means we must sell goods to Germany as well as to France and Britain. If the British stop our shipments to Europe, I must protest."

Page pressed his point: "But secretly, Mr. President, you won't protest too much if the British stop our shipments headed for Germany, will you?"

"Secretly, if I were not wary of Germany's anger, I would not protest at all."

"Then, Mr. President," cabled Page, "may I hint to the British that you are seriously thinking about joining them in the war against Germany?"

"You may tell them that your President will do everything he can to keep the United States out of the war," Wilson wrote.

"But Congress doesn't agree with you," Page responded. "Already, many members of Congress are calling for war."

The President cabled: "And many others are firmly against the war, Mr. Ambassador. Neither Congress nor the American public is ready for war. It would be dangerous to our unity to go to war at this time. And, if I may say so, dangerous to my program of reform. I am proud of the many changes that I have brought to this country. If we get into this war, many of my reforms will be lost. Some members of Congress may disagree with me, but the American people are on my side. They don't want war either."

"Unless," cabled Page, "something awful happens to change their minds and even yours."

That same day, the British passenger ship *Lusitania* was sailing ten miles off the Irish coast. It had left New York City and was now headed for England. The ship carried 1,959 men, women, and children, 197 of them Americans. In an ad in *The New York Times*, the Germans had warned that British ships sailing in a German war zone would be destroyed. The *Lusitania* was now inside a German war zone.

The first mate of the *Lusitania* turned to the captain and asked, "Do you think they'll try anything?"

The captain answered, "Of course not. This is a passenger ship carrying men, women, and children."

"But we are also carrying munitions."

"Yes, and Americans. The Germans wouldn't dare attack this ship and risk bringing the United States into the war. Besides, according to the rules of war, an unarmed passenger ship can't be sunk without warning. The attacker must also provide safety for the passengers and crew. Even the Germans must live according to the rules."

"Ah, but the rules of war were written in an earlier age," said the first mate. "A submarine is not like a battleship. Once it shows itself on the surface, it is a sitting duck. No submarine captain will take the risk of giving a warning. Modern war, I fear, is bound to be more savage than the wars of the past."

Some distance away, the captain of a German submarine, U-Boat 2, sighted the *Lusitania* through the periscope. He thought for a moment. Then he shouted, "Fire!"

The torpedoes headed for the ship and struck with tremendous force. Only a few passengers managed to get into lifeboats before the ship sank. That day 1,198 people aboard the *Lusitania* died. Of those, 128 were Americans.

Later, in a message to the President, Ambassador Page asked, "Has the sinking of the *Lusitania* changed your mind?"

President Wilson's reply was brief: "My heart, yes; my mind, no. I must have the courage to keep the United States out of a war that will kill many times the number of Americans who died on the *Lusitania*."

Page insisted: "Many Americans will call you coward."

And Wilson answered: "Then I must find the courage to wear that name. There is such a thing as a man being too proud to fight."

POSTSCRIPT

Wary of provoking the United States to enter the war, German leaders cut back on submarine attacks. Wilson kept on trying to keep America at peace. He talked to the warring nations to convince them to stop fighting. But he also began building up U.S. military might—just in case. And American ties to the Allies grew closer and closer. U.S. bankers made large loans to Britain and France. U.S. arms makers sold them munitions. The United States seemed unable to be truly neutral.

By 1917 German leaders feared defeat. To prevent this, they ordered full-scale submarine warfare to resume. German U-boats started attacking American ships that entered the war zone. Germany also tried to persuade Mexico to go to war with the United States.

Now Wilson felt forced to act, and the American public supported him. On April 6, 1917, in response to a request from the President, Congress declared war against Germany.

The United States did not have the men and equipment needed to fight a war. The army buildup had barely begun, and material was in short supply. The Selective Service Act solved the manpower shortage. It set up a military draft, and in June, 1917, more than 9 million men registered. By the end of the war in November, 1918, more than

24 million had registered, and 3 million had been inducted into the army.

United States forces arrived in Europe just as the Germans were starting an attack, a last bid for victory. The Allies had fought hard for four years and were too exhausted to stop the German advance on their own. The addition of the Americans, who fought in their own units, provided just enough extra strength to defeat the Central Powers. More than 100,000 Americans died in the war, as did more than 5 million Allied soldiers and more than 3 million soldiers of the Central Powers.

On the home front, the federal government took on broad new tasks. It channeled industry and agriculture into the war effort. Wilson created the Food Administration, headed by Herbert Hoover. High prices stimulated pork and wheat production, and the public was persuaded to observe meatless and breadless days. The War Industries Board speeded the changeover from producing autos and tractors to producing tanks and guns. Emphasizing the need for better transportation, the government took charge of the railroads through the Railway Administration. The National War Labor Board kept the nation free from serious strikes. The cost of living rose by 50 percent during the war, but wages went up even faster. With full employment there was an increase of 20 percent in real income.

Wilson also set up the Committee on Public Information. Its press releases and posters declared that the United States was fighting to "Make the World Safe for Democracy." The committee offered no kind words for the enemy. All Germans were considered evil. German spies seemed to be listening at every wall. Work stoppages were labeled as treason, and any criticism of the war or of Wilson's policies was said to show a lack of patriotism.

Partly as a result of such tactics, spy scares flourished and democratic debate withered. In some places, Americans could not play German music or teach or speak the German language. Sauerkraut became "liberty cabbage," and German shepherd dogs were called "police" dogs.

After the war, it would take time for things to return to normal. Hard feelings against "foreigners" blended with feelings against Jews, Catholics, blacks, and radicals. One result was a "Red Scare" in 1919 and 1920. U.S. authorities arrested thousands of people alleged to be "Reds," or Communists. Some were sent to jail, some deported to other countries, and others freed as innocent victims of the authorities' zeal.

Homework Questions

1. What important reform measures were passed during Wilson's Presidency?
2. What was the purpose of each of the reform laws?
3. Why did many Latin Americans resent Wilson?
4. How did Wilson react to the sinking of the *Lusitania*?
5. How did America help the Allies win World War I?

Understanding the Story

A. Write *T* for each statement that is true, *F* for each statement that is false, and *N* for each statement that is not mentioned in the story.
   1. It was easy for the United States to be neutral in World War I.
   2. Many Americans disliked the British.
   3. In the 1916 election Wilson's slogan was "He kept us out of war."

4. Wilson said that the Germans interfered with U.S. neutrality.
5. Wilson was not annoyed by German interference with U.S. shipping.
6. The *Lusitania* was a United States ship.
7. German agents tried to blow up U.S. war plants.
8. Wilson asked Congress for a declaration of war against Germany.

B. List the numbers of the statements that Wilson made or might have made.
1. Britain is against everything we stand for.
2. We must remain neutral.
3. I will do all I can to keep America out of war.
4. Congress will never declare war.
5. If we enter the war, my reforms will be lost.
6. Only a coward refuses to fight.
7. I am afraid Germany will beat us.
8. The American people are on my side.

C. While World War I raged in Europe, Woodrow Wilson asked the people of the United States to remain neutral. Do you think the United States might have succeeded in avoiding involvement in this war? If so, how? If not, why not?

Activities and Inquiries

1. Look at the map of Europe in 1914 on page 384. Then answer the following questions.
   a. What do you notice about the location of the countries called the Central Powers?
   b. What do you notice about the location of the Allies?
   c. Look at the location of both groups on the map. Which one seems to have the greater advantage? Explain.
2. Imagine that you are a British reporter aboard the *Lusitania*. Write an article for your newspaper describing the sinking of the ship.
3. Now imagine that you are a German reporter aboard the submarine. Write an article for your newspaper describing the sinking of the *Lusitania*.
4. It is April, 1917. President Wilson is thinking about making a declaration of war, and he asks for your advice. What will you say to him? Explain your answer.

7 The Fourteen Points

Before the United States entered World War I, Great Britain and France had signed secret treaties with Russia, Italy, and Japan. The treaties had promised these three powers enemy territories after victory. It is not certain whether Woodrow Wilson knew of the treaties. But he did know that the Allies would insist on taking large chunks of the losers' territories. Wilson opposed this grabbing of land by the victors. He argued instead for "peace without victory," meaning that the winners should not punish the losers severely.

To be sure that both sides understood his point of view, Wilson outlined a program for peace on January 8, 1918. It was called the Fourteen Points. Among other things, this program called for freedom of the seas, reduction of armaments, a League of Nations, and an end to secret treaties. The League was to be an organization of the nations of the world that would work to prevent future wars. Wilson also insisted that the losers of the war must be treated fairly.

About ten months later, the U.S. and the Allies had beaten back German armies and were about to invade their homeland. Germany asked President Wilson to arrange a peace treaty based on his Fourteen Points. Thinking Wilson had won the Allies' agreement, German leaders signed an armistice on November 11, 1918. The fighting stopped.

Wilson prepared to go to France to negotiate a peace treaty based on the Fourteen Points. Before leaving home, however, he found that many people—including leading Republicans—did not agree with his plan. Some wanted

Germany to be treated harshly. Others called for a declaration that the United States would have nothing more to do with European politics.

Wilson appealed to the American people to elect Democrats to Congress in 1918. He wanted to show European leaders that Americans stood solidly behind his peace plans. But the voters disappointed Wilson. They elected more Republicans than Democrats.

Smarting from this defeat, President Wilson arrived at the peace conference in Paris. He had not brought a single important Republican with him. In spite of the Republican criticism of his peace plan, Wilson was sure that the Europeans would accept his ideas. Hadn't great crowds turned out to cheer him on stops in England, Italy, and France? Wilson believed that the hopes of the world's people rested on his shoulders. Without him, there might be a harsh peace treaty that would push the losers into a war of revenge at a later date.

Did the Allied leaders whose countries had suffered so much destruction agree with Wilson's peace plans? Were

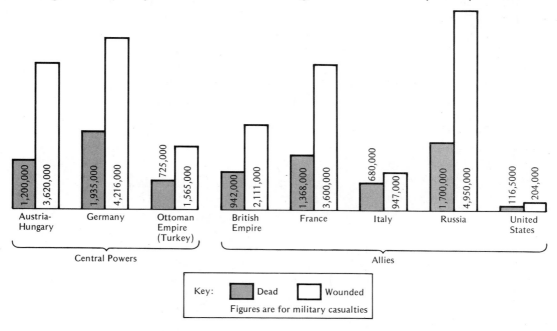

Wounded and Dead in World War I

they willing to agree to a "peace without victory"? If they disagreed, how could they change the mind of the stubborn Woodrow Wilson?

Our story involves an imaginary conversation among three Allied leaders—Vittorio Orlando of Italy, David Lloyd George of Britain, and Georges Clemenceau of France. The remarks expressed by these men reflect the positions they took in real life.

Paris, January, 1919

ORLANDO. Listen to the cheers of the crowds. How the people love that man.

CLEMENCEAU. Yes, I watched them greet Wilson as he rode through the streets of Paris. I don't think there has been anything like it in the history of the world.

ORLANDO. People think that Wilson is a god who has come to bring peace to all humankind. Do we have any choice but to go along with them?

LLOYD GEORGE. Of course we do. To go along with Wilson would be suicide. Why, that man has his head in the clouds. He would pat the Germans on the back and tell them that all is forgiven.

CLEMENCEAU. Over my dead body! Twice—in 1870 and in 1914—Germany has invaded my country and caused heavy damages. More than one million Frenchmen are dead because of those brutal murderers. I will never rest until Germany's arms and legs have been cut off. It's the only way to make sure France will not be invaded a third time.

ORLANDO. And what of my country? Britain and France have promised Italy a reward of more land for fighting on your side. I mean to collect that reward.

LLOYD GEORGE. And I, gentlemen, have promised the people of Great Britain that I will make Germany pay until it screams for mercy. The people will turn against me if I follow Wilson.

CLEMENCEAU. Then we agree. However fine Wilson's ideals may be, they are not suited to the practical world we must live in. We will find a way to show Wilson the folly of his plan.

ORLANDO. But the whole world knows of Wilson's Fourteen Points. It was his plan that convinced Germany to ask for peace.

LLOYD GEORGE. Nonsense. Our armies convinced Germany to ask for peace. We were about to cut its forces into ribbons when Wilson jumped in with his Fourteen Points.

CLEMENCEAU. Fourteen Points! Fourteen Points! I'm sick of hearing about them. Wilson has fourteen points while God has only ten!

ORLANDO. But we told Wilson that we agree with his Fourteen Points, and the whole world knows it. How can we stop him now?

CLEMENCEAU. Have no fear. Wilson can be stopped. He has some weaknesses that we can take advantage of.

ORLANDO. Such as?

CLEMENCEAU. Well, for one thing, he is one against our three. For another, his health is very poor. We have only to get him to sit down with us alone for the next few weeks. By then, he will be so weak and tired that he will give in to our demands and sign our kind of peace treaty.

ORLANDO. But what will the world say of such a peace treaty?

CLEMENCEAU. Only Germany will complain, and Germany is powerless. Britain, France, and Italy will applaud.

ORLANDO. And what of America?

LLOYD GEORGE. America will also applaud.

ORLANDO. Why do you say that?

LLOYD GEORGE. Because many important Americans laugh at Wilson behind his back.

ORLANDO. How do you know that America doesn't believe in Wilson's ideas?

LLOYD GEORGE. Because Wilson asked the Americans to elect Democrats to the Congress. Instead, more Republicans have been elected. So much for America believing in Wilson's ideas.

ORLANDO. But what of Wilson himself? How can he allow himself to sign a treaty that goes against his Fourteen Points?

CLEMENCEAU. Because Wilson wants something very badly, and we will give it to him.

ORLANDO. What is that?

CLEMENCEAU. The one thing that he thinks will put an end to all wars—a League of Nations. For this he will give up everything else.

LLOYD GEORGE. You think we should allow him to have his league?

CLEMENCEAU. Why not? It might even prove useful in keeping Germany weak.

POSTSCRIPT

The peace conference in Paris stretched from January to June, 1919. There were many disagreements. Orlando left in disgust because Italy did not get the territory promised it. Even Wilson left the conference at one point, only to return later.

True to their words, Clemenceau and Lloyd George wore Wilson down. But he proved to be a better fighter than they had imagined. When the conference finally ended, none of the top four leaders had gotten exactly what he wanted.

The main peace treaty, with Germany, was called the Treaty of Versailles. Germany was forced to admit that it alone was guilty of starting the war. All Germany's colonies were taken away. The provinces of Alsace and Lorraine were returned to France. Germany was to disarm totally and pay Allied war costs plus reparations (payment for damages) that eventually totaled $32 billion. The German economy was placed under Allied control.

Other treaties dealt with other matters. The Austro-Hungarian Empire was broken up in several ways: A new republic of Czechoslovakia was created. Poland became an independent country. Serbia was given additional land and became the kingdom of Yugoslavia. Rumania's territory was doubled at the expense of Hungary and Bulgaria.

Wilson persuaded the Allies to provide in the Treaty of Versailles for a League of Nations. Each signer of the treaty would have one vote in an Assembly. A Council with the power to make decisions would have representatives from each of the major winning nations (U.S., Great Britain, France, Italy, and Japan) plus four others chosen by the Assembly. Council decisions would require a unanimous vote.

To guarantee world peace, disputes would be sent to the Council for settlement. Or a case might be sent to the Permanent Court of International Justice for a decision. Nations refusing to agree to decisions would be punished by an economic boycott. (They would be cut off from trade.) An international army and navy were to be created as a further step against the spread of war.

The League was the first important international peacekeeping organization in modern history. Its creation gave support to Wilson's belief that the threat of war must be the concern

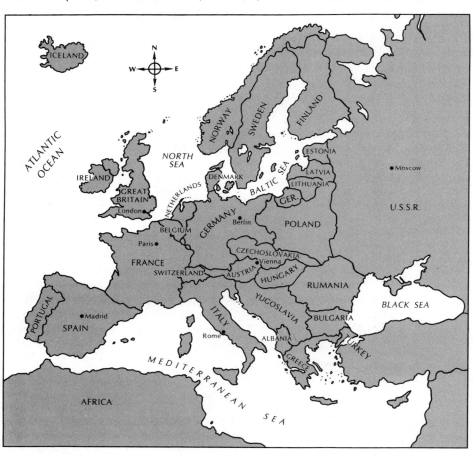

Europe in 1919

of the entire world. A great many of the world's people hoped the League would be a place where disputes could be settled and shooting wars avoided.

Wilson had used all his influence to bring the League into being. And now he returned to the United States to ask the Senate to agree to the Treaty of Versailles.

Homework Questions

1. How did the Allies' version of a peace treaty differ from Wilson's "peace without victory"?
2. Why did the Allies object to Wilson's Fourteen Points?
3. What was the purpose of the League of Nations?
4. Why did Clemenceau agree to give Wilson "his" League of Nations?
5. How were Germany and Austria-Hungary affected by the treaties ending World War I?

Understanding the Story

A. Write T for each statement that is true and F for each statement that is false.
  1. Wilson said that the losers must pay for the war.
  2. Many Republicans did not agree with Wilson's program.
  3. In 1918 more Democrats than Republicans were elected to Congress.
  4. Wilson took many Republicans with him to Paris.
  5. Wilson was very popular with the people of Europe.
  6. Germany had invaded France in two wars.
  7. Clemenceau approved of Wilson's Fourteen Points.
  8. The League of Nations was provided for in the Treaty of Versailles.

B. List the numbers of the statements that the Allied leaders made or might have made.
  1. It is suicide to agree with Wilson's Fourteen Points.
  2. Wilson is the greatest man in the world.
  3. Germany must pay for its crimes.
  4. I'm sick of hearing about Wilson's Fourteen Points.
  5. It is unfair to blame the whole war on Germany.
  6. Wilson will give in to our demands.
  7. We must give Wilson what he wants.
  8. People in America are laughing at Wilson.

C. Do you think the Allies should have accepted Wilson's peace plan? Why or why not?

Activities and Inquiries

1. Compare the maps of Europe in 1914, on page 384, and Europe in 1919, on page 392. Notice the changes in the 1919 map. Then choose the term or phrase that best completes each statement.
  a. A new country in central Europe in 1919 was (1) Czechoslovakia (2) Germany (3) France.
  b. A new country in southeastern Europe in 1919 was (1) Russia (2) Greece (3) Yugoslavia.

c. A country that lost territory in World War I was (1) Spain (2) France (3) Germany.

d. A country that gained territory in World War I was (1) Germany (2) France (3) Austria-Hungary.

e. A country divided into many new countries was (1) Great Britain (2) Austria-Hungary (3) Italy.

f. A new country in northern Europe in 1919 was (1) Estonia (2) Sweden (3) Norway.

g. A country in central Europe that did not change in size as a result of World War I was (1) Austria (2) Germany (3) Switzerland.

h. A country that lost territory to the new nation of Poland was (1) France (2) Russia (3) Bulgaria.

2. As a reporter at the peace conference, you interview the Allied leaders. What do they tell you about Wilson? Now you interview Wilson. What does he tell you about the Allied leaders?

3. You also interview the German delegate. What does he think about the conference?

4. Would you have voted for Wilson for President in 1920? Explain.

5. Study the graph on page 389. Then choose the term or phrase that best completes each statement.

a. The country with the largest number of dead was (1) Germany (2) Russia (3) France.

b. The country with the largest number of wounded was (1) Germany (2) Russia (3) France.

c. The total dead and wounded of Germany and Austria-Hungary were (1) more than that of Russia and France (2) exactly the same as that of Russia and France (3) less than that of Russia and France.

d. The nation with the second smallest number of casualties was (1) British Empire (2) Italy (3) U.S.A.

e. Russia's losses were (1) greater than those of all the others combined (2) greater than those of the British Empire, Italy, and U.S.A. (3) greater than those of Germany and Austria-Hungary.

8 The Fight Over the Treaty

President Wilson returned to the United States with the hope that the Senate would quickly ratify the Treaty of Versailles. This would make it possible for the United States to join the League of Nations.

But the Senate had ideas of its own. Republicans, led by Senator Henry Cabot Lodge of Massachusetts, opposed the treaty in its original form.

Many of these Republican senators were willing to ratify the treaty if certain changes were made. They wanted to be sure that the League would not force the United States to go to war again. They particularly wanted U.S. war-making powers to remain in the hands of Congress. And they wanted to be sure the U.S. could withdraw from the League if it saw fit to do so.

Other senators were not willing to ratify the treaty in any form. Called *isolationists*, they believed that the United States should not get involved in the politics of Europe.

Lodge did not aim to defeat the treaty altogether. He wanted to include some changes so that the Republicans could get credit for helping to shape the treaty. Lodge decided that he could best force these changes by delaying the Senate vote on the treaty. By doing this, he hoped to persuade President Wilson to give in on some items.

Wilson refused to agree to Senator Lodge's suggestions. Instead, he decided to gain support for his position by going directly to the American people. Against the advice of many of his closest friends, the President left on a speaking tour of the United States. He hoped to win so much support that the Senate would feel obliged to approve the treaty without changes.

As our story begins, President Wilson is discussing his tour and other matters with his physician, Dr. Cary T. Grayson. Ask yourself what Wilson and Lodge really wanted. Was Wilson able to get the Senate to approve the treaty?

Pueblo, Colorado, September 25, 1919

"You look tired, Mr. President. These headaches of yours worry me. Perhaps you should cancel the rest of the speaking tour and go back to Washington," said Dr. Grayson.

"I cannot do that, Doctor. The people of America are my last hope. Only they can force the Senate to pass the treaty."

"But, sir, you have enough votes in the Senate already. All you have to do is give in a little bit and—"

"I've told you, Doctor, I will never give in to that bullying Senator Lodge. He means to get at me by destroying the League of Nations. I must win approval for the treaty as it is."

"But, Mr. President, some of your own Democratic senators also believe that the treaty needs changes."

"Yes, but they are friends of the League. Lodge is its enemy."

"Why do you suppose Lodge opposes your treaty?" asked Grayson.

"He doesn't oppose the treaty so much as he hates me. Our personal relations are openly hostile. If the treaty is approved as it is now, I will win a great victory. Lodge is a Republican—a proud Republican. He doesn't want me, a Democratic President, to get the credit for making an honorable and just peace. If that happens, he fears that the people will elect another Democratic President in the next election."

"Well, isn't that what you want? You don't seem shy about asking people to vote for Democrats?"

"Of course. Party politics are part of our democratic process. But the League should be above politics because it is so important for world peace."

"Perhaps you worry too much, Mr. President. The country seems to want the League. What can Lodge do to stop you?"

"He's done much already," answered Wilson. "He has delayed a vote in the Senate for two months. I'm afraid he is forming close ties with that band of isolationist senators who believe that we should have nothing to do with Europe. They think that the same old corrupt politicians are back in power in Europe and that we helped to put them there. What the isolationist group wants is to have the United States stay out of Europe and mind its own business from now on."

"Are there other objections to the treaty?"

"Oh, yes. Some senators are afraid the League will drag us into a European war against our will. They want to make sure that only the U.S. Congress has the right to declare war."

"Are they so wrong?" asked Dr. Grayson.

"No," said Wilson. "In fact, I agree with them. In the United States, only Congress should be able to declare war."

"Then why not put that in the treaty? Even Lodge will vote for the treaty if it provides that only Congress can declare war."

"I won't agree to that. The treaty and the League must be approved as they stand right now," said the President.

"But why?" asked Grayson.

"Because if I give in on this point, Lodge will only bring up another one. He means to weaken the League. He feels that the best way to have peace is to arm ourselves and be ready for war."

"But if you don't come to some agreement with Lodge, the treaty may fail altogether," said Grayson.

Wilson answered, "That's why I have taken my case to the people. They have listened to me in the past, and they are listening to me now. They seem especially enthusiastic out here in the West. They cheer when I tell them that there will be another war unless the nations of the world learn to—"

Suddenly, Wilson closed his eyes and turned pale. Dr. Grayson sent for a glass of water. He helped Wilson to his bed.

"How serious is it, Doctor?" asked Wilson's wife, Edith.

"Right now, it's physical and emotional exhaustion. But sometimes these things can lead to a stroke."

"You mean the President might be paralyzed?"

"I'm afraid that's a possibility."

"God help us all," said Edith Wilson. "If that should happen, Americans won't only have a paralyzed President."

"What else?" asked the doctor.

"The President's dream will come to an end. The League of Nations will also be paralyzed."

POSTSCRIPT

A week later in Washington, Wilson suffered a stroke, which paralyzed one side of his body. Lying in a darkened room in the White House, he barely had the strength to listen to friends who brought him news of what was happening in the Senate and to advise them of his wishes.

On November 19, 1919, the Republican version of the treaty, carrying Lodge's amendments, came to a vote in the Senate. On Wilson's orders, Democrats joined isolationist Republicans in voting no, and the treaty failed again.

Friends told Wilson he would have to compromise if he wanted to win U.S. participation in the League of Nations. Wilson refused, and again the Senate rejected the treaty.

Other nations went ahead and set up the League, and it remained in existence for more than 20 years. But the United States never joined, and the League never became the force for peace that Wilson had expected.

As the dispute over the League faded, Americans turned to other concerns. In 1920 the voters elected a Republican, Warren G. Harding, to be President. He promised a return to "normalcy." Wilson died in 1924, a bitter and unhappy man.

Homework Questions

1. Why did many Republican senators object to the Treaty of Versailles?
2. What sort of changes did the Republicans want to make in the treaty?
3. Why did Wilson insist that the treaty be approved by the Senate with no changes?
4. How did Wilson's illness affect the chances for the approval of the League?
5. Do you think Wilson made a mistake in refusing to compromise with Lodge? Why or why not?

Understanding the Story

A. Write *T* for each statement that is true, *F* for each statement that is false, and *N* for each statement that is not mentioned in the story.
   1. The Senate voted to approve a peace treaty with Bulgaria.
   2. Isolationists favored the Treaty of Versailles.
   3. Wilson made many speeches favoring the treaty.
   4. Wilson refused to compromise with Senator Lodge.
   5. Lodge was head of the Senate Foreign Relations Committee.
   6. Some critics of the League were afraid it might drag the United States into another war without the consent of Congress.
   7. Wilson was paralyzed by a stroke.
   8. A Democrat was elected President in 1920.

B. Which of the following statements describe Wilson's thinking about the Treaty of Versailles and the Senate?
   1. The people of America are my last hope.
   2. Lodge hates me.
   3. We should stay in America and mind our own business.
   4. I don't care how the Senate votes on the treaty.
   5. I will never give in to Senator Lodge.
   6. Give Lodge credit for hard work and clear thinking.

7. The isolationists are against my treaty.
8. Lodge thinks that all nations should throw away their weapons.

C. In your opinion, what might be the advantage of an organization like the League of Nations? What might be the disadvantages? Explain.

Activities and Inquiries

1. Assume that you are Wilson's adviser. What will you suggest he do to get the Treaty of Versailles approved by the Senate?

2. You are Lodge's adviser. What will you suggest he do to get his version of the peace treaty approved by the Senate?
3. Imagine that you are a historian. How would you answer the question: "Who prevented the U.S. Senate from approving the Treaty of Versailles: Wilson or Lodge?"
4. Prepare a report card for Woodrow Wilson. Refer to chapters 6, 7, and 8 of this unit. Grade him in the following areas and justify each grade:
   a. Leadership
   b. Training and education
   c. Point of view
   d. Accomplishments while President
   e. Maturity

9 The Growth of the Constitution: Hours of Work for Women

Presidents Roosevelt, Taft, and Wilson believed that the government might interfere with the economy in certain circumstances. Each of these Presidents supported laws that regulated the activities of business with the aim of helping working people or preserving competition. In doing this, the three Presidents seemed to be acting in line with the wishes of Congress, the state legislatures, and the people.

However, one branch of government still seemed to frown on government interference with the economy.

This branch was the judicial—especially the Supreme Court of the United States. The Court took a hard look at any law or regulation that might interfere with the constitutional rights of employers or workers.

To the justices of the Court, the right to make a contract was one of the most important rights of all. It was part of the right to property that was guaranteed by the 14th Amendment. But just what did this right mean?

New York State passed a law saying that bakers could not work more than

10 hours a day or 60 hours a week. Joseph Lochner, who owned a bakery in Utica, New York, was fined $20 for overworking Frank Courvette. When Lochner continued to ignore the law, he was fined again. This time he took his case to court. In 1905 the case, *Lochner* v. *New York*, came before the United States Supreme Court.

The Court overturned the state law. It said the law took away the rights of both Lochner (the employer) and Courvette (the worker). The right of both to enter into a contract was protected by the 14th Amendment, said the Court. By taking the job Lochner offered, Courvette had freely agreed to work the longer hours that Lochner required. It was unconstitutional for a state to pass a law to limit the hours a person could work each day.

Three years later, in 1908, another state law was tested before the Supreme Court. This was a law passed by Oregon in 1903. Like the New York law about bakers, the Oregon law sought to put a limit on workers'

hours. But it dealt with a special type of worker—female.

Under the Oregon law, women employed in laundries and factories were limited to a 10-hour day. Curt Muller, who owned a laundry in Portland, Oregon, was fined $10 for having a female employee work more than 10 hours. He appealed to the federal courts.

The National Consumers League, led by Florence Kelley, played a key role in this case, known as *Muller* v. *Oregon*. The league campaigned against manufacturing in the home, child labor, and long working hours for women. Its model law to limit female working hours had been passed by the District of Columbia and 13 states. When the Oregon law was challenged, Florence Kelley asked a lawyer named Louis D. Brandeis to argue the case. Brandeis had gained a reputation as a supporter of such causes as workers' rights and civil liberties. His admirers called him "the people's attorney."

Washington, D.C., January 15, 1908

"Well, Louis, are you ready to fight the dragons?" asked Florence Kelley.

"Ready, Florence," answered Attorney Louis Brandeis.

"I don't envy you your task," said Kelley. "I'm afraid the Supreme Court has already decided this case."

"Why do you say that?" asked Brandeis.

"Oh, the way the Court has decided similar cases in the past," answered Kelley. "Muller says he has the right to ask the women employees in his laundry to work more than 10 hours a day. He says that the Court's decision in the Lochner case gives him that right."

"Well I think the Court made the wrong decision in the Lochner case," replied Brandeis, "and I think I can help the Court make the right decision in this one."

"I hope so. I'm glad you are handling the case and not Joseph Choate. When I asked him to take the case, he said he didn't see why a husky woman should not work more than 10 hours if she wanted to."

Brandeis thought for a moment. "Choate is a very important lawyer, but even important people can be wrong."

"But Choate thinks the way the Court does," said Kelley. "Can you convince the justices that they are wrong?"

"I can—by showing them the facts," answered Brandeis. "I will show them what happens to women who work in factories and laundries for more than 10 hours a day."

Attorney Brandeis argued the case before the Supreme Court that very afternoon. He presented 100 pages of statistics and reports by doctors, health officers, factory investigators, and experts in social science. These people claimed that overworked women often fell ill, turned to drink, and bore sickly children and then neglected them.

The justices of the Supreme Court were impressed. Most lawyers who argued before the Court did not talk like Brandeis. They talked mainly about the law and about precedents, or past Court decisions (like the Lochner case). By bringing in such a mass of statistics and expert advice, Brandeis was opening the Court up to new influences and feelings.

POSTSCRIPT

The Court upheld the Oregon law. In doing so, it said there was an important difference between men and women. In the eyes of the justices, women were the weaker sex and therefore might need legal protection that men did not need.

Had the Court changed its mind since the Lochner case? Not at all. The justices made a point of the fact that the earlier case had concerned a male worker, who presumably could look out for himself without help from special laws. Not until the 1930's would the Court come around to the view that states should be allowed broad leeway in regulating business and labor for the benefit of men and women alike.

Louis D. Brandeis helped to bring this change about. In 1916 he was appointed to sit on the Supreme Court as its first Jewish justice. He was noted for his outspoken defense of civil rights and for his readiness to permit government regulation of the economy.

The decision in *Muller* v. *Oregon* had important consequences. Within a few years, almost all states had adopted laws to regulate working hours of women.

Homework Questions

1. How did the case of *Lochner* v. *New York* affect New York's law about hours of work in bakeries? What was the basis for the Supreme Court's decision?
2. How was Louis D. Brandeis able to convince the Supreme Court that laws regulating working hours for women were constitutional?
3. What was Curt Muller accused of doing?
4. In what way did the Muller case differ from the Lochner case in the eyes of the Supreme Court justices?

Understanding the Story

A.   List the numbers of the statements that are true.

1. Presidents Taft and Wilson did not believe in interfering with business.
2. New York State limited the working day of bakers to 10 hours.
3. Joseph Lochner violated the 10-hour-day law.
4. The Supreme Court ruled against Lochner.
5. An Oregon law limited the working hours of women to 10 per day.
6. Louis Brandeis argued the Oregon case before the Supreme Court.
7. Brandeis convinced the justices that overlong hours were dangerous to women factory workers.
8. The Supreme Court did not agree with Brandeis.

B.   Complete each of the following sentences by filling in the missing word or words.

1. The case of *Lochner* v. *New York* was decided by the _____.
2. A New York law said that bakers could not work more than _____.
3. The Supreme Court ruled that each worker is free to make a _____ with an employer.
4. The lawyer who argued the case of *Muller* v. *Oregon* before the Supreme Court was _____.
5. Brandeis said that Joseph Choate was a very important _____.
6. Brandeis showed what happened to women who were _____.
7. Experts said that overworked women became _____ and bore _____ children.
8. The Supreme Court in *Muller* v. *Oregon* ruled that a state could limit the _____ of _____.

C.   Do you think the Supreme Court reached a wise decision in the Muller case? Why or why not?

Activities and Inquiries

1. Brandeis reads a doctors' report to the Court. What does the report say about overworked women?
2. Imagine that you are a reporter. You interview a Supreme Court justice who upheld the Oregon law. What reasons does he give for his decisions?
3. Now you interview a Supreme Court justice who opposed the Oregon law. What reasons does he give for his decision?
4. A feminist writes a letter to a newspaper about the Muller case. What does she say?

Who Built America?

Fiorello La Guardia

ROSA. I'm going to talk about Fiorello La Guardia, who was of Italian and Jewish origin. He was a member of Congress and eventually a famous mayor of New York City. He fought hard for the things he believed in.

HEINRICH. Like what?

ROSA. He was a Progressive on the side of poor people—like the Irish and Italian immigrants who lived in lower Manhattan. All his life he fought to get a better deal for working people and to end special privileges for the rich.

HEINRICH. Do you think this is what he really felt?

ROSA. Of course. He sympathized with the underdog because he was one himself. As the son of immigrants, he was called names by bullies at school. And because he was shorter than others, big boys picked on him.

JUAN. Did he fight back?

ROSA. You bet. He wouldn't take any nonsense, either from bullies in the schoolyard or from the rich and the powerful.

JOSEPHINE. What do you mean?

ROSA. Here's a "for-instance": About ten years before World War I, La Guardia was a representative of the United States government at a seaport in Austria-Hungary. His job was to help people who wanted to emigrate to the United States. One time an archduchess of Austria came to town, and local officials wanted to impress her. They wanted her to see a shipload of immigrants marching up the gangplank, preparing to sail to America.

JOSEPHINE. You mean the immigrants were supposed to "perform" for the archduchess, like trained seals?

ROSA. Yes. And what especially angered La Guardia was that, because of the archduchess's schedule, the immigrants would have to board the ship three days early and stay in the hold all that time. He wouldn't stand for it. He told the ship captain that such an outrage was a danger to the immigrants' health and that he would refuse to grant the health permit the ship needed to dock in New York. The archduchess had to do without seeing her peasants "perform."

SAM. It sounds as if La Guardia didn't mind stepping on important people's toes.

ROSA. La Guardia was a hero to many people. As a young lawyer working for poor clients, he would often settle a dispute himself and refuse to accept a fee. He wouldn't take a case unless he was sure that his client was right. In 1912 he represented a group of garment workers in a strike and marched on the picket line with them. He dared the police to arrest him. As a result of his negotiations with the employers, the workers won a victory. A reduction in working hours to 53 per week may not sound like much today, but the workers were very happy. They even won a pay increase of $1 per week.

TOM. Did he serve in World War I?

ROSA. Yes, he commanded a U.S. air squadron in Italy. He also put his career on the line by canceling a half-billion-dollar order for warplanes.

TOM. What right did La Guardia have to cancel an order?

ROSA. He had no real authority to stop the order. He just did what he thought was right. He had flown one of the planes, and it cracked up. Then another of the planes crashed and killed a close friend. La Guardia knew that the plane was dangerous.

CASIMIR. What did he do in Congress?

ROSA. He proposed laws to improve wages, hours, and factory conditions; to speed up slum clearance; and to make it more difficult to break strikes. Altogether he was elected to six terms, 12 years, in Congress.

JACK. When was he mayor of New York City?

ROSA. He was mayor from 1934 to 1945. What a colorful person he was! He loved to be in the center of action. Whenever he could, he would rush to the scene of a fire to encourage the firemen. One day he'd go on a police raid and help smash slot machines. Another day he'd be pitching for the Yankee baseball team. He was a dynamo who demanded to know everything that was happening in his city.

RICARDO. How did he find time to govern the city?

ROSA. Don't worry, the city was governed effectively! La Guardia moved around town checking on things—always asking questions. How was the food in a city lodging house or hospital? Did the storekeepers in a poor neighborhood have enough police protection? Once, during a newspaper strike, he rushed down to the city radio station to read the comic strip "Little Orphan Annie" over the air. People loved him. New York even named one of its airports after him because he helped get it built.

HEINRICH. La Guardia sounds like an unusual politician—flashy, but good and honest.

MR. MILLER. How true. We need more like him. Well done, Rosa.

MR. MILLER'S OFFICE

"Well, Jack, what did you find out?" asked Mr. Miller.

Jack thought for a moment. "For one thing, I found out that Americans had many more problems than I had realized."

"For instance?"

"I didn't know that there was so much corruption in politics. I also didn't know about places like the Triangle factory."

"Did Americans accept these things, or did they try to change them?"

"That's what impressed me the most," answered Jack. "Americans really did try to change things for the better. People like Roosevelt, Wilson, and La Guardia tried to turn things around."

"Did they succeed?" asked Mr. Miller.

"Almost," answered Jack.

"Almost?"

"Yes. They were doing fine until the war got in the way."

"You're right," said Mr. Miller, "the war did get in the way. In fact, it changed everything."

Jack seemed puzzled. "To be honest, I don't really know what you mean when you say that the war changed everything."

Mr. Miller answered, "You will, Jack, believe me, you will."

The Return to Normalcy

"Let me get this straight, Mr. Miller. You say that the war changed a great many things?"

"That's right, Jack. Wars often do."

"All I can think of is how the United States had changed already."

"In what ways?" asked Mr. Miller.

"Up to the early 1900's, the government acted as if big business could do no wrong. Then the government passed laws to regulate big business."

"How else had the United States changed?"

"The government began passing laws in favor of the workers and the farmers."

"Excellent," said Mr. Miller, "but after the United States entered World War I, Americans seemed to lose interest in reform at home. And after the war ended, the reformers seemed almost to vanish. President Warren Harding had promised a return to 'normalcy.' To many, this meant an end to worrying about other people's problems and a chance to focus on their personal needs and concerns. Workers expected to work shorter hours for higher wages. Farmers thought they should continue to get high prices for their products."

"Could life in the 1920's be as exciting as it was during World War I?" asked Jack.

"Let's find out," replied Mr. Miller.

1 Fear on Trial

The years immediately following World War I were difficult ones for the United States. A number of social problems troubled the nation.

Tensions between blacks and whites touched off riots in 1919 in such cities as Chicago and Washington, D.C. The Ku Klux Klan, largely inactive since the 1870's, sprang to life again, preaching its message of white, Protestant supremacy. Lynchings (mob murders) of blacks reached alarming numbers. In 1919 alone, some 70 blacks were lynched in the South.

Many returning soldiers could not find jobs at the end of the war. Prices rose sharply. Labor unions demanded higher wages for their members. Employers resisted, saying wage increases would drive prices even higher.

Hundreds of thousands of workers went on strike in 1919, and bitter charges flew back and forth. Union leaders accused employers of exploiting workers unmercifully. Employers accused union leaders of promoting socialism, communism, and anarchism. (Socialism is a system of government ownership of basic industry. Communism combines government ownership of industry with strict one-party rule. Anarchism is the belief that society can operate best without central control—ideally, without any government at all.)

Many Americans were fearful of the wave of strikes. They saw the strikes as threatening to the American way of life. Many of the strikers were foreign-born, which made them even more suspect.

Adding to American unease was worry over a revolution abroad. In 1917, the Russian people had overthrown their emperor, or czar. At first it seemed that Russia would become a democratic nation. But by the end of 1917 a Communist government had taken over Russia. Many Americans were alarmed. There were fears that Communists (or "Reds") would spread their revolution to other European countries and even to the United States.

In 1919 some 40 bombs exploded in different parts of the United States. Mayors, members of Congress, and judges were among the targets. An alarmed public demanded that those responsible be punished. Blame fell on foreigners. Immigrants, some said, were all dangerous radicals and should be driven out of the country.

President Wilson's attorney general, A. Mitchell Palmer, ordered a roundup of alleged "Reds" early in 1920. Thousands of people, mostly foreign-born, were arrested. They were held until authorities could decide whether to ship them out of the country. At first, hardly anyone objected to Palmer's actions even though many of those arrested had broken no laws. In time, the mass arrests came to an end, but suspicion of foreigners did not die quickly.

In April, 1920, at South Braintree, Massachusetts, two men shot and killed a factory paymaster and his guard and stole their payroll. Police arrested two immigrants, Nicola Sacco, a factory worker, and Bartolomeo Vanzetti, a fish peddler. Both men were carrying guns at the time of their arrest. They declared that they were anarchists and said they were innocent.

Their trial began in late May, 1921. In July, the jury found them guilty of murder, and the judge sentenced them to die in the electric chair. But new evidence delayed the execution. For six years, their lawyers pleaded for a new trial.

As new evidence turned up, the case attracted much attention across the nation and around the world. Thousands of people wrote to the governor of Massachusetts. Many begged the governor to call a new trial, saying that the evidence was not clear. In 1927 the governor appointed a committee of prominent men to review the case. It heard witnesses and went over the evidence.

In our story, two men are arguing about the case. Why were Sacco and Vanzetti so controversial? Did they get a fair trial?

Massachusetts, summer of 1927

ANTHONY. I get so angry when I read about Sacco and Vanzetti. Those two haven't got a chance. Everyone's against them because they're poor and foreign-born.

VINCENT. Hey, don't waste your tears, Anthony. They're guilty—the jury said so. They had a fair trial. Now they have to pay for their crime. You don't want murderers running around loose, do you?

ANTHONY. I don't think they're murderers. I think they've been railroaded. And plenty of other people think so, too.

VINCENT. Oh, sure. Plenty of left-wingers in Europe and New York. What do they know, anyway? It's just an automatic reaction, that's all.

ANTHONY. I don't think so. Some pretty important people, like Albert Einstein, the German scientist, and Anatole France, the French writer, have protested the way Sacco and Vanzetti have been treated.

VINCENT. I don't care how important you think they are. They didn't hear all the facts the jury heard.

ANTHONY. But that's just it. The jury didn't hear all the facts. And a lot of what the jurors heard was just plain false.

VINCENT. What do you mean? The jury was told that Sacco and Vanzetti lied to the police about where they were on the day of the crime. Are you denying that?

ANTHONY. No, not that. Sacco and Vanzetti admitted telling a false story at first. But why wouldn't they? They knew how the "Red Scare" was sweeping the country. They knew how the authorities had been rounding up foreign-born radicals. I'd have been scared too.

VINCENT. Why would they be scared?

ANTHONY. Because their friends had been arrested and handled roughly. They said one friend was thrown out of a window of the Department of Justice and fell to his death. They were afraid the same thing would happen to them.

VINCENT. Sure, they would say that. Listen, they were draft dodgers in the war. They're anarchists, and they admit it. The electric chair is too good for them!

ANTHONY. I'm surprised at you, Vincent. Isn't this a free country? Don't we all have a right to believe as we want to?

VINCENT. Believing is one thing. Throwing bombs and killing people is something else.

ANTHONY. Oh, you're hopeless. *All* anarchists don't go around tossing bombs! Sacco and Vanzetti certainly didn't. If they throw bombs or kill people, of course they should be punished. But as far as I know, all they ever did as anarchists was to discuss their ideas with others who believe as they do. It's a free country, Vincent. Or at least I thought it was!

VINCENT. Well, what about some other facts? They had guns when they were arrested. Are you denying that?

ANTHONY. No. They had guns, all right. But that's not necessarily a crime. Doesn't the Constitution give us a right to bear arms?

VINCENT. Oh, *owning* a gun is one thing. But experts said Sacco's gun fired the murder bullets.

ANTHONY. Well, how do you explain the other experts who said it had to be a *different* gun that fired those bullets?

VINCENT. What about the eyewitnesses to the crime? They identified Sacco and Vanzetti, didn't they?

ANTHONY. Sure. And the defense had its own witnesses who said the men were somewhere else at the time. I don't believe the eyewitnesses. They probably think all foreigners look alike anyway.

VINCENT. Well, I don't blame the jury for finding Sacco and Vanzetti guilty. What else could the jury have done?

ANTHONY. It could have found them innocent, that's what! The evidence was awfully flimsy. The cops never found any of the money the holdup men stole. And what about the getaway car? The holdup men escaped in a car, yet neither Sacco nor Vanzetti had a car.

VINCENT. I still say the jury knew enough to find them guilty.

ANTHONY. Listen, there's lots of new evidence the jury didn't get to consider. There's a fellow in jail who says someone else did it.

VINCENT. You're not going to believe some jailbird, are you?

ANTHONY. He gave the cops clues that support his story that a gang of bandits from out of state pulled the holdup.

VINCENT. I don't know. Someone's always claiming to know secrets about crimes. Who can the police believe?

ANTHONY. Who can anyone believe? But that's just the point. The evidence is so flimsy and has so many contradictions, it just doesn't seem fair to send Sacco and Vanzetti to the chair.

VINCENT. You worry too much, Anthony. If they're guilty, they've got to pay.

ANTHONY. If—if—if! How can we take their lives unless we know for sure?

POSTSCRIPT

After two months of study, the governor's committee reported its findings—the trial had been fair; the men were guilty. At midnight on August 23, 1927, Sacco and Vanzetti died in the electric chair. By this time many Americans were convinced that the two were being put to death for their political beliefs.

Up to the very end, both men insisted that they were innocent. Vanzetti, who learned to read and write English in jail, told a reporter: "If it had not been for this thing, we might have died unknowns, failures. Never could we hope to do such work for justice, for man's understanding of man. Next to this, our lives are nothing. This last moment belongs to us."

To this day the Sacco-Vanzetti case continues to stir debate. Many people now feel that one or both of the men were probably innocent. Even many who believe them guilty say they did not get a fair trial.

To compensate in part for what he called the injustice of 1927, Massachusetts Governor Michael Dukakis signed a proclamation about the Sacco-Vanzetti case in 1977. Dukakis said the men did not get a fair trial because of their foreign background and political beliefs.

During the 1920's, many members of Congress shared in the widespread distrust of foreigners. The Emergency Quota Act of 1921 limited the number of newcomers to be admitted. It set an annual quota for each European nation. This number reflected the pro-

portion of people born in that nation who lived in the United States in 1910.

Many Americans complained that the new quotas let in too many immigrants from Southern and Eastern Europe. In 1924, new quotas were set. This time they were based on the U.S. population of 1890, before many people had immigrated from Southern and Eastern Europe. The result was to close off most new immigration from those regions. Congress wanted immigrants to come mainly from Northern Europe, from countries such as England, Germany, and Sweden. Asians were barred altogether.

Beginning in 1929, immigration quotas were based on the U.S. census of 1920. The total number of immigrants was set at 150,000 a year, far below the numbers that had streamed in during the late 19th and early 20th centuries.

In 1952 the McCarran-Walter Act lifted the ban on immigrants from Asian and Pacific nations. The immigration quota system was further changed in 1965. A new immigration act established a quota of 170,000 immigrants per year from the Eastern Hemisphere. A total of 20,000 persons per year would be admitted from any one country in that area. For the Western Hemisphere, a limit of 120,000 persons per year was established, with no quota per country. These laws have encouraged immigration from Latin America, Asia, Africa, and Southern and Eastern Europe.

Homework Questions

1. What social problems troubled the United States in the years immediately after World War I?
2. Why were many Americans fearful of the strikes of 1919?
3. What evidence tended to show that Sacco and Vanzetti were guilty?
4. Why did many people think the Sacco-Vanzetti trial was unfair?
5. How did the immigration acts of 1921 and 1924 differ from each other?

Understanding the Story

A. Write *T* for each statement that is true and *F* for each statement that is false.
    1. The Ku Klux Klan grew after World War I.
    2. Socialism, communism, and anarchism are the same.
    3. Attorney General A. Mitchell Palmer had thousands of foreigners arrested in 1920.
    4. Sacco and Vanzetti claimed they were innocent.
    5. Both men were native-born Americans.
    6. Both men were anarchists.
    7. Both men carried guns.
    8. Vanzetti was freed and Sacco was executed.

B. Write *A* for each statement Anthony made or might have made and *V* for each statement Vincent made or might have made.

1. Sacco and Vanzetti had a fair trial.
2. I don't think Sacco and Vanzetti are murderers.
3. The jury didn't hear all the facts.
4. Some pretty important people have criticized the verdict.
5. Left-wingers have criticized the verdict.
6. Experts say Sacco's gun never fired those bullets.
7. Someone's always claiming to know secrets about crimes.
8. Sacco and Vanzetti are draft dodgers.

C. From what you have read of the "Red Scare," do you believe it might have made it hard for Sacco and Vanzetti to get a fair trial? Why or why not?

Activities and Inquiries

1. Assume that you are a lawyer defending Sacco and Vanzetti. Prepare your case.
2. Now assume that you are the prosecuting attorney. Prepare the case against Sacco and Vanzetti.
3. You are a member of the jury. What is your verdict? Explain.
4. Suppose that you are the governor of Massachusetts in 1927. Sacco and Vanzetti have appealed for your help. What will you do? Why?

2 Warren G. Harding

For 20 years, Americans had had strong Presidents. Theodore Roosevelt, William Howard Taft, and Woodrow Wilson had pushed for reforms at home and abroad. Roosevelt and Wilson, in particular, were influenced by the Progressive movement. All three Presidents promoted laws to correct what they saw as the wrongs of a fast-growing industrial society. They sought to make the United States a major force in world affairs. All three were popular with the voters. People seemed eager for the government to take steps to shape a better society and exert U.S. influence in the world outside.

Americans went to war in 1917 hoping to build a better world. They were making the world "safe for democracy." But things did not seem to turn out that way. The peace settlement at Versailles and the battle over the League of Nations left a bitter taste in people's mouths. Europe was thoroughly corrupt, many people felt. The less Americans had to do with the outside world, the better.

Many Americans now wanted to forget about world problems. They wanted to forget about problems of all kinds—including the problems that Presidents Roosevelt, Taft, and Wilson had been wrestling with at home. Americans turned their backs on reformers. They held out their arms to leaders who offered a different vision of the world.

In 1920, the voters elected a Republican, Warren G. Harding, to succeed Wilson as President. Harding did not want to be a strong President. He was not interested in reform. Harding had said: "The world needs to be reminded that all human ills are not curable by legislation."

What kind of President was Harding? How did he differ from Roosevelt, Taft, and Wilson?

Washington, D.C., June, 1923

You are Warren G. Harding, an Ohio farm boy who has come far. First you were a newspaper publisher. Then you were a United States Senator. Now you are the 29th President of the United States.

You are convinced that Americans are tired of cleaning up the home front and preaching to the rest of the world. They are tired of Presidents who call for self-sacrifice. The people want to have a little fun and collect some easy money. Most of all, they want a government that will let them go back to the "good old days." That is why in 1920 they chose you—an ordinary, simple, easygoing, average American—to be their President.

You never did want the job—not really. But your wife pushed you. She was ambitious and wanted to be the first lady of the land. Your friends pushed you, too. You thought that, like you, these friends were eager to serve their country. You didn't know that what several of them really wanted was to grab the riches of the land with both hands. The leaders of the Republican Party pushed you, too. They wanted a "safe" President, one they could control. When they offered you the nomination, you felt you had to accept. You could never say no.

You won by a landslide, sweeping every state outside the Democratic South. People cheered when you declared, "What we want in America is less government in business and more business in government." It was going to be back to "normalcy," you told the nation.

When you moved into the White House, you brought along your friends. They kept you company, drank with you, and played golf and poker with you. But while your back was turned, some of them stole money from the government you were trying to lead.

One friend got kickbacks from people doing business with the Veterans' Bureau. Another sold German patents and properties for the government and kept the money. Still another sold liquor permits. Secretary of the Interior Albert Fall took bribes for illegally granting leases to oil fields on publicly owned reserves in Teapot Dome, Wyoming, and Elk Hills, California.

You have begun to find out about your dishonest friends, although you still know only a small part of the scandal. Worries about your friends keep you walking the floor at night. To you the White House seems to be a prison. You moan that you are in jail. More than once you have suggested that you are not fit to handle the complicated tasks of the Presidency.

Something terrible is bound to happen. What can you do if the scandals break? Already one friend has committed suicide. Rumors about others are everywhere. To get away, you will go on a speaking trip through the West, as far as Alaska. That will take your mind off your troubles. But it can't be expected to cure them.

POSTSCRIPT

Harding never returned from his Western trip. He died in San Francisco of a stroke on August 2, 1923. He never knew the full extent of the criminal acts of his friends. But the public did learn most of the story in time, and many of Harding's cronies were disgraced. Albert Fall became the first cabinet member in history to go to jail. Harding came to be remembered as one of America's weakest Presidents.

But the Harding administration did

have its achievements. It got Congress to create a Bureau of the Budget to help the government plan its spending in an orderly way. It also took steps to cut taxes, which had gone up drastically during the war. The tax cut did not pass Congress until 1926, long after Harding was dead.

Harding also took a cautious step toward giving black people broader opportunities. President Wilson's policy had been to remove blacks from the few responsible federal jobs then open to them. Harding reversed that policy. In a speech in Birmingham, Alabama, he called for political, economic, and educational equality between the races.

Perhaps the outstanding efforts of the Harding administration were in foreign affairs. The administration won Senate approval in 1921 for a treaty with Colombia. The treaty gave that nation $25 million for the loss of Panama and opened Colombia to U.S. oil company explorations. The Harding administration also worked out peace treaties with Germany, Austria, and Hungary. (Such treaties were necessary because the Senate had rejected the Treaty of Versailles.)

Harding's able secretary of state, Charles Evans Hughes, devoted his main efforts to the problems of East Asia and the Pacific. Hughes called a conference of major nations having an interest in Asia. The Washington Conference took place in the nation's capital in 1921–1922. Hughes made a plea for major nations to disarm—or at least to reduce the size of their navies to a fixed level. The aim was to avoid an arms race that might lead to war in Asia, where a weak China was being eyed hungrily by other nations.

The United States, Britain, Japan, France, and Italy signed a treaty that did as Hughes suggested. Japan agreed to have only three major naval ships for every five such ships in the navies of the U.S. and Britain. France and Italy agreed that their navies would be even smaller. This was the first time in history that a general agreement to limit navies had been reached, and many people saw it as a first step toward disarmament. But it did not turn out that way. When the treaty expired in 1936, national rivalries were hotter than ever and war was a real threat in East Asia.

Homework Questions

1. Why did many Americans feel bitter toward Europe after World War I?
2. Why did people welcome Warren Harding's promise of a return to "normalcy"?
3. How did Harding's friends use the President for their own personal gain?
4. How much did Harding know about the corruption in his administration?
5. What did Charles Evans Hughes do to promote arms control?

Understanding the Story

A. Write *T* for each statement that is true and *F* for each statement that is false.
    1. Americans felt that they were building a better world.
    2. After World War I, most Americans worried about conditions in other countries.
    3. Warren Harding was the first President elected after World War I.

4. Many Americans were looking for easy money.
5. Harding was happy to be President.
6. Many of Harding's friends were dishonest.
7. Harding was a trustbuster.
8. Harding is viewed as one of America's great Presidents.

B. Write *A* for each statement Harding would agree with and *N* for each statement that he would not agree with.
1. I never wanted to be President.
2. I am not interested in playing golf or cards.
3. I want less government in business.
4. Not all of my friends are completely honest.
5. Good laws can solve all our problems.
6. I am well suited for the job of President.
7. Let's get America back to normal.
8. The White House is the best place to live.

C. Do you think that Warren G. Harding should be held responsible for the wrongdoing of his friends? Why or why not?

Activities and Inquiries

1. Prepare a report card for Warren Harding. Grade him in the following areas and justify each grade:
   a. Leadership
   b. Training
   c. Point of view
   d. Accomplishments while President
   e. Maturity
2. Imagine that you are a newspaper reporter assigned to investigate the corruption around President Harding. What do you find out?
3. Suppose that Harding reads your article. What will he say?
4. Harding suggested that he was not fit for the Presidency. Why do you think he felt this way?
5. Imagine that you interview a person who voted for Harding in 1920. You ask why the person supported Harding. What is the answer?

3 "What Is the World Coming to?"

The "Red Scare" and the scandals of the Harding administration got the 1920's off to a shaky start. But before long most people had forgotten such things. The 20's were a time of exciting new products—radios, automobiles, vacuum cleaners. They were a time of social experiment—it was now illegal to sell beer, wine, or liquor. They were a time of shocking fads— many women bobbed their hair (cut it short), wore short skirts, began puffing cigarettes. What was the world coming to? Many people shook their heads and wondered.

Automobiles came into widespread

use, changing the face of America. From 1919 to 1929, the number of cars went up from 6.7 million to more than 23 million. There was a growing network of highways dotted with filling stations, restaurants, and tourist homes that rented rooms to travelers. Now there had to be traffic lights, one-way streets, and complex driving rules.

More and more trucks appeared on the roads, giving new competition to railroads. During the 1920's, truckers took a growing share of the freight business. And buses began to cut into the railroads' passenger business.

The first commercial broadcasting station came on the air in 1920. By early 1922, listening to the radio had become a popular craze. The sales of radio sets jumped from $60 million in 1922 to $506 million in 1926 to $843 million in 1929. Milions of Americans gathered at home around their radios to listen to stories, news, sports, and music.

The social experiment called Prohibition had begun in 1919. In that year the 18th Amendment to the Constitution prohibited the manufacture or sale of alcoholic beverages. But drinking didn't stop—it went "underground." Many people made their own booze ("bathtub gin") or bought bootleg whiskey in illegal bars called speakeasies. Gangsters smuggled in liquor from Canada and elsewhere. In many cities there was open disregard for the liquor laws.

Many young people did things that shocked and confused their elders. They danced fast new dances like the Charleston. They went joyriding in sporty cars. They went on dates without chaperons. They smoked and drank and "got blotto," as slang-happy Americans said.

In our story, a family has gathered at the supper table. George Gillette, the father, is a salesman. Millie, the mother, keeps house. Sid, 18, and Joanna, 16, are their two children. How is the Gillette family different from families of earlier years? How is it different from families today?

Evanston, Illinois, 1924

Sid grabbed a biscuit and passed the platter to Joanna. "Hey, Dad," he said, "did you hear about Babe Ruth's home run this afternoon? That makes 39."

"Yeah, he's going great guns, isn't he?" answered George. "Maybe the Yankees will win a fourth straight pennant. Say, Millie, this is great soup."

"You think so?" Millie asked. "It's out of a can, and I was afraid it wouldn't turn out just right."

"Oh, Mom, it's swell," put in Joanna. "Say, Dad, Sarah's family just got an automobile. It's an open touring car with balloon tires. Why can't we get a car, too?"

"Honey, we will, one of these days. Right now all my money is tied up in the stock market. When the price of my stock goes up just a bit more, I'll sell out and buy a car. I have my eye on a sassy little roadster."

"Oh, wow, Dad, that's great," Joanna said. "I hope it has a rumble seat. It'd be just the thing to go to a party in."

"You've been going to a good many parties lately, Joanna," her mother said. "I wish you'd spend more time studying."

Sid snickered. "Study? Joanna? She hasn't cracked a book in weeks. She spends all her time with her beau, Eddy."

"What beau?" sputtered George, looking up from his roast beef. "I thought we told you to quit seeing that young rake."

"Yes, Joanna," her mother said. "Eddy smokes and drinks and I don't know what all. He's too wild—not the kind of boy I want you to associate with."

"Oh, you're such old fogies," Joanna blurted out. "He's not what you think. Besides, he's not my beau—he's my best friend's brother. How can I *help* seeing him?"

"'How can I *help* seeing him?'" Sid mimicked. "I notice you put on lots of lipstick to go over to Sarah and Eddy's house."

"Sid," said his mother sternly, "don't tease your sister." Then she turned to Joanna. "But it *is* disturbing to see you wearing that bright lipstick, dear. When I was a girl, I would never have thought of painting my face up like you do."

Joanna reacted with a pout. "Oh, in your day you probably wore leopard skins. Why don't you ask Sid where he was until 2 A.M. Saturday night?" She shot a challenging glance at her brother.

George looked concerned. He chewed his meat vigorously and said nothing. Millie busied herself clearing the table for dessert. She opened the refrigerator—it was so new she still called it an "icebox." "I've got a surprise for dessert," she said. "Huckleberry Roly Poly. I got the recipe from *The Ladies' Home Journal*."

"This is delicious," said Joanna and Sid and George as they cleaned their plates.

"I have my eye on a sassy little roadster."

"It'd be just the thing to go to a party in."

"What say we all go to the movies tonight?" said George, pushing back his chair.

"Can't, Dad," said Joanna as she skipped toward the door. "Gotta go see Sarah about our plans for Friday night."

"Not tonight, Dad," said Sid. "I promised my buddies I'd let them listen to dance music on our radio tonight." Sid put his dish on the sink and went out.

George looked at Millie. She smiled. "I'll go with you, George," she said. "Since you bought me that new vacuum cleaner, I don't have to finish up my housework after supper. And I can take care of the dishes when we come home."

POSTSCRIPT

During the 1920's, American factories were churning out more goods than ever before. In fact, manufacturing output grew three times faster than the population. How could businesses ever sell so many goods? New ways had to be found to persuade people to buy more.

Advertising and easy credit helped. Large ads in magazines like *The Ladies' Home Journal* urged people to buy cars, breakfast cereals, deodorants, appliances. Sellers let people buy more and more items—from living room furniture to automobiles—on credit. All the buyer had to do was make a small down payment. The rest could be paid off in easy monthly installments.

Never before had so many American families been able to buy so much. Now it was not just the rich—it was the middle classes, too, who were able to stock their homes with radios, refrigerators, and many other conveniences.

Many people, it should be noted, could not get credit and could not buy the new machines. Even by 1929 only one family in six owned an automobile. Poverty remained, especially in rural areas and among minority groups. But politicians were beginning to talk about wiping out poverty completely. Hopes for the future were high. If anyone could eliminate poverty, people said, Americans certainly could.

Homework Questions

1. How did the automobile change American life?
2. What was Prohibition? How well did it work?
*3. Why were older people shocked by the things that many young people did?
4. What new household conveniences were changing American life?
5. How could so many people afford the new conveniences?

Understanding the Story

A. List the numbers of the statements that are true.
   1. Listening to the radio was a popular craze of the 1920's.
   2. It was illegal to sell liquor in the United States during the 1920's.
   3. Prohibition put an end to the drinking of alcoholic beverages.
   4. Some Americans could not afford such new conveniences as vacuum cleaners.

5. Millie never used a vacuum cleaner.
6. George bought an automobile on credit.
7. Millie disapproved of the lipstick her daughter wore.
8. Trucks and buses took business away from railroads.

B. Choose the term or phrase that best completes each statement.
1. During the 1920's, some women wore bobbed hair—that is, hair that was (*a*) braided (*b*) cut short (*c*) dyed.
2. From 1919 to 1929 the number of cars in the United States (*a*) decreased (*b*) just doubled (*c*) more than tripled.
3. The first commercial broadcasting station went on the air in (*a*) 1914 (*b*) 1920 (*c*) 1922.
4. "Speakeasies" were (*a*) illegal bars (*b*) radio sets (*c*) telephones.
5. George planned to buy (*a*) a roadster (*b*) a pickup truck (*c*) a touring car.
6. Joanna's parents thought her boyfriend was (*a*) handsome (*b*) not very smart (*c*) wild.
7. Joanna got back at Sid by revealing that he (*a*) drank beer (*b*) got home late (*c*) was an old fogy.
8. Millie finished her housework quickly because of her new (*a*) refrigerator (*b*) vacuum cleaner (*c*) telephone.

C. Do you think such innovations as the radio and the movies brought American families closer together? Why or why not?

Activities and Inquiries

1. Imagine that Millie's mother (Joanna and Sid's grandmother) comes to visit. What does she say to Millie?
2. You ask Sid what he thinks of his father. What does he reply?
3. You ask Joanna what she thinks of her mother. What does she reply?
4. Joanna and Sid are now grandparents. What do they tell their grandchildren about life in the 1920's?
5. Do you think the Gillette family is a "typical" family of the 1920's? Why or why not?

4 Playing the Stock Market

start here

Many Americans in the 1920's thought they had discovered a shortcut to "Easy Street." They borrowed money and "played the stock market." Some who did this got rich. But the risks proved to be greater than most people imagined. *So to "In our story..."*

The stock market—especially the New York Stock Exchange on Wall Street—had long been the place where corporations went to raise money. On the Exchange, shares of a company's stock are sold to investors through brokers. Each share represents a portion of the ownership in a company. In the 1920's, stock prices seemed to be going up and up. Investors thought that they would always make a profit when buying stock.

In theory, stock prices go up or down according to the prospects of the company issuing the stock. If the company's chances of earning a profit are good, its stock sells for a high price. Many stock buyers are investing in the company's future. They hope to earn a regular *dividend*—a share of the company's profits. Others hope to make a profit by selling their stock at a higher price than they paid for it.

In the 1920's, a great many people "played the stock market" for the same reasons that gamblers play roulette. They weren't looking for dividends. They were gambling that the price of the stock would keep going up. They would reap their reward when they sold the stock for a far higher price than they had paid for it. And stock prices did keep going up—as long as many people were scrambling to

buy stocks, bidding their prices higher and higher.

Was there no limit to how high stock prices could go? Apparently not. People might pay $60 a share on Monday and sell for $65, $70, or $100 a share on Friday. It seemed so easy. At the time it was possible to buy stock by making only a small down payment. In 1927 or 1928, the down payment was as little as 10 percent. In 1929 the amount of the down payment increased to 45 or 50 percent. The rest of the purchase price could be borrowed—that is, the stock could be bought "on margin." And many people were buying stock this way. They hoped they could sell the stock for a much higher price than they had paid for it. Then they could pay off their margin debt—whatever they had borrowed—and still make a profit.

In our story, two friends are talking about the stock market. Richie wants to invest, but Steve has other uses for his money. Why does Steve disagree with Richie?

New York City, March 1, 1928

"What do you mean you're quitting school?" asked Steve. "You can't be serious."

Richie laughed. "If you had half a brain, you'd quit too."

"But in two years you'll be finished with college."

"That's two years out of my life that I can't afford to waste. There are lots of people making big money these days. I'm going to get my share."

Steve looked puzzled. "Please, Mr. Rockefeller, would you mind telling me how you're going to make your fortune?"

"I've lined up a job in a bank. I'm going to put all my earnings in the stock market."

"You've come up with some dumb ideas, Richie. But this one has to be the worst."

Richie became angry. "Grow up, Steve. Take your nose out of the books you're always reading and look at what's going on. The stock market is booming, and people are making millions of dollars."

"That's fools' gold, Richie. The experts say that most stocks aren't worth anywhere near what they're selling for. One day the buying will stop and the selling will begin. Then the whole stock market will collapse. You'll lose everything."

"Come off it, Steve. The stock market has been going strong for a long time. Sure stock prices are high. Maybe stocks are selling for more than they're worth. So what? As long as people keep buying, the market will keep going up. As for prices falling, they already have. Stock prices have fallen two or three times this year. And each time the market has come back even stronger. No, sir, this stock market is not about to collapse."

"You're taking an awful chance, Richie. You can't get something for nothing. Believe me, the best way to prepare for the future is to go to college. I'm sure that the more college training I have, the more money I can earn."

"That's old-fashioned thinking, Steve. Go ahead, stay in college. Look me up a couple of years from now when you graduate. Maybe I'll lend you some money—or I might even have a job for you. You could be my chauffeur."

As stock-market prices climbed to new highs, some investors made millions almost overnight. Their stories inspired others to put their life savings and anything they could borrow into the booming market.

But certain danger signs were appearing in the American economy. Farm prices were falling, and many farmers could no longer pay their bills or keep their farms. Industries were producing more goods than people could buy, so quantities of goods began to stack up in warehouses. As factories cut back on production, thousands were thrown out of work or had their wages cut.

The companies that owned these factories were the same ones people invested in when they bought shares on the stock market. Actually, the real value of stocks was shrinking even though the stocks were selling for higher and higher prices. Some market watchers warned that the investment market was like a time bomb. No one knew when the bomb would explode. Few seemed to worry, though— as long as they were making money.

Richie and Steve went their separate ways. Richie got a job in a bank. He invested most of his money in stocks. Steve continued his college education.

September 3, 1929

Richie called Steve on the telephone. "How's it going, Steve? Learning much from those books of yours?"

"More every day," replied Steve. "I haven't heard from you in ages. Made your first million yet?"

Richie chuckled. "Not quite a million, but I'm doing all right. I've been promoted again. And I've put my money on a real winner— Radio Corporation of America. I just checked with my stockbroker, and it's at $505 a share. When I bought the stock it was at $300, and all I had to put up was $150 a share. I borrowed the rest. Say, how about having lunch with me? My treat, of course."

They met at a fancy restaurant. Steve tried to appear as though he had such lunches every day. But he'd never been in such a swanky place before. He hardly knew which fork to use, let alone which glass.

"Boy, Richie," Steve said, "you sure know how to live in style."

"Oh, this is nothing," said Richie. "Wait till I'm *really* rich. By the way, don't forget that chauffeur's job I mentioned. I don't have a limousine yet, but when I get one, the chauffeur's job is yours—if you're ready to give up those musty books."

"Thanks a lot, but no thanks," said Steve.

During the autumn of 1929, stock-market prices slipped and then slipped some more. By late October the great Wall Street Crash had begun. Between September and November, 1929, the price of the average stock fell by half. And the bottom hadn't been reached yet. Stock prices kept falling for the next two and a half years.

People like Richie, who had bought stock "on margin," found that they now owed more money than the stock was worth. They sold their stock before it could fall even lower. But there were now more sellers than buyers, and stock prices continued to fall.

"What happened to my dreams?"

May 5, 1932

Steve had finished college with honors. He didn't find the sort of job he wanted—but he did find a job. He sat behind a big desk at an employment agency and helped other people look for jobs. It was discouraging work. There were hardly any jobs to find.

"Hello, Steve," said a voice from the other side of the desk.

Steve looked up. It was Richie, looking far from prosperous. His shirt collar was frayed. His jacket had a hole in the elbow.

"Richie, it's good to see you. Looking for work?"

"Yeah," said Richie glumly.

"What happened to your bank job? What about your stocks?"

"Forget it," replied Richie. "The bank folded. My broker sold my stocks for a song. Now I'm broke, and I don't have any way of paying back the $10,000 I borrowed for the stocks."

Steve whistled. "Golly, ten G's," he said. "That's awful. So you need a job real bad?"

"You said it," sighed Richie. "I've been out of work for two years. Please, Steve, I'll take anything."

Steve smiled feebly. "Richie, there's only one job available today, and I don't think it's what you're looking for."

"What is it?"

"A chauffeur's job."

Richie answered instantly. "I'll take it."

Homework Questions

1. Why did people like Richie think they could get rich by buying stocks?
2. What was Steve's advice to Richie?
3. What danger signs appeared before the Wall Street Crash?
4. How did the investment market in 1929 resemble a time bomb?
5. Who was smarter—Richie or Steve? Explain.

Understanding the Story

A. Write *T* for each statement that is true and *F* for each statement that is false.
   1. Some people got rich by "playing the stock market."
   2. A dividend is a share of a company's profits.
   3. Stock prices fell during most of the 1920's.
   4. Richie left school to earn money to buy stocks.
   5. Steve thought a college education was useless.
   6. Farm prices were rising in the late 1920's.
   7. Richie borrowed money to buy stocks.
   8. The Wall Street Crash occurred in October, 1929.

B. Which of these events can be connected to the Wall Street Crash of 1929 as either a cause or an effect?
   1. Steve lost all of his money.
   2. Stock prices fell sharply.
   3. Richie's fortune was completely wiped out.
   4. The American people bought more products.
   5. Factories produced less.

6. There was no change in the number of factory jobs.
7. Stock prices rose too high.
8. More people sought to hire chauffeurs.

C. What was buying on margin? Why do you think banks and stockbrokers allowed it to take place? How do you suppose that margin buying contributed to the Crash of 1929? Explain your answer.

Activities and Inquiries

1. Go to your library and prepare a report on a stock that increased greatly in value during the 1920's.

2. Look at the cartoon on page 421 and answer the following questions.
   a. What was his dream?
   b. What happened to it?
   c. Could this man have stopped his dream from falling apart? Explain.
   d. Assume that Richie is alive today. Would he still be dreaming of acquiring wealth by investing in the stock market? Explain.
3. Use library resources to prepare a report on the panic that followed the crash of 1929.
4. You meet Richie while he is working as a chauffeur. What does he tell you about the lessons he has learned?

5 The Great Depression

The Wall Street Crash of 1929 was like the straw that broke the camel's back. A new type of panic gripped Americans. Business, which had already been slowing down, came to a virtual standstill. More workers were laid off. People had less and less money to spend, which meant there were fewer buyers for the goods in American warehouses. Without buyers, there was little need for factories to keep on producing goods. So factories closed and more people lost their jobs. Without those jobs there was still less money to spend and fewer buyers. And on the cycle went.

Business and political leaders insisted that the economy was basically sound. They said the main need was to restore confidence. Political leaders such as President Herbert Hoover and Secretary of the Treasury Andrew Mellon issued a stream of optimistic statements. The worst is behind us, they said—and said again. But still business did not pick up.

In 1931 more than 8 million people were out of work. This was about 16 percent of the civilian labor force. By 1933 almost 13 million were unemployed. One worker in four had no job. Many of the unemployed drifted from place to place, seeking a job—any job. But there were few jobs of any kind. The United States was in the worst business slump it had ever known. The slump was called the Great Depression.

The Wall Street Crash was only one of many causes of the Depression. One cause lay outside the United States. There was a financial crisis in

Europe and a decline in world trade. This hurt U.S. banks and U.S. businesses that sold to other countries. Other causes grew out of serious hidden defects in the U.S. economy itself. There were too few buyers for the many goods U.S. industries turned out. This resulted from low wages, low farm prices, and a tax system that gave special advantages to rich people. It also resulted from the large investments that companies had been making in new factories to turn out more and more goods.

Banks came under severe strain as business activity dwindled. Many banks were unable to collect on loans. When depositors heard that a bank was in trouble, they rushed to withdraw their savings. This just added to the bank's difficulties. Thousands of banks collapsed (went out of business), and many depositors lost all their savings.

The Great Depression was a turning point in American life. It shook people's confidence in themselves and in the future.

Thousands of homeless people slept in subways, public parks, and abandoned factories and warehouses. Many even welcomed going to jail so they could get a free meal and a night's sleep on a bed. Hungry families walked, hitchhiked, or caught rides on trains in search of food, shelter, and work. Men who had been business executives sold newspapers, shined shoes, or sold apples. Some people even started forest fires and then hired themselves out as fire fighters.

Many stood in what were called breadlines to get free food. The places giving out meals were also called soup kitchens. A few begged money for food. People learned to live with hunger and fear of the future. All wondered why this land of plenty had suddenly become a land that offered nothing.

In our story, Jerry and Alma, recently married teenagers, join the rootless wanderers searching for food, shelter, and work. What does the Great Depression mean to them? What does it mean to America?

Alabama, 1931

Alma shivered.

"Are you cold?" asked Jerry as he drew her closer.

"I'm all right," Alma mumbled. "Just a little tired."

"We're almost there," Jerry said. "Soon we'll be on a freight car headed for Chicago. We're bound to find work there. Here's our train, Alma. Hop aboard. It should be leaving soon."

Jerry helped Alma into the freight car and climbed up after her. Alma jumped back in fright, calling, "Who's there?"

A man, a woman, and two children moved out of a dark corner and stared at Jerry and Alma. Alma whispered to Jerry, "I know things are bad, but do we have to travel with strangers?"

"Shh!" said Jerry. "At these prices we can't afford to be choosy. Besides, they were here first."

Alma walked to the far corner of the freight car, sat down, and took off her shoes. Sighing, she picked up some straw from the floor and stuffed it into the shoes to cover up the holes. Oh well, she thought, maybe things will be different once we get to Chicago.

"What kind of country is this?"

Moments later, the door flew open. A conductor flashed his light around the car. Alma, Jerry, and the other people shrank back in fear.

The conductor stared at them, hesitated, and said, "As far as I'm concerned, I didn't see you. You'll be all right as long as a railroad detective doesn't spot you. If he does, you'll have to leave the train."

The people in the freight car nodded their thanks. As the conductor slid the door shut, he shook his head. More and more people were hitching rides on freight trains. For many it was becoming a way of life. Men and women were drifting all over the United States in search of jobs and homes. Just a few years ago President Hoover and the Republicans had promised a chicken in every pot and two cars in every garage. They had predicted an end to poverty. And now this. What was happening to this country?

As soon as the train started to move, Alma took a small jar of mustard out of a paper bag and unwrapped a stale biscuit. She smeared some mustard on the biscuit and began to eat. Although he was very hungry, too, Jerry refused the piece she offered him.

"I'll get something when we reach Chicago, honey. In the meantime, eat that real slow. It's got to last you until we get there."

The other woman reached into her bag and gave the man and the two children pieces of fried chicken. The good smell made Alma and Jerry even hungrier. They could not help watching the family eat.

The woman noticed them staring and asked, "Would you like some of our chicken? We have enough to go around."

Alma wanted to say no. But she was so terribly hungry that she nodded and accepted a piece. Jerry also took some.

"Thank you," Alma said. "It's real kind of you to share with us."

The woman smiled. "We all have so little these days. I suppose it makes us feel a little better if we can share with others."

The man turned to Alma and Jerry and asked, "Where are you two headed?"

Jerry answered, "Chicago."

"We've been there. We've been to Birmingham, Nashville, and lots of other cities. It's the same everywhere. People are selling apples, sleeping in parks, standing on soup lines, begging for handouts, and looking for jobs."

Jerry asked, "What kind of people are you talking about?"

The man replied, "What kind do you think? Old people, young people, white people, black people. Men and women. People."

"I just don't understand what's happening," said Jerry. "I hear there's plenty of food in this country. Yet people are going hungry. Do you understand any of it?"

"I certainly don't," said the woman. "We've seen farmers dumping their milk, and I heard that they are killing cattle too."

Alma looked up. "How can people kill cattle while others pick through garbage cans for scraps of food?"

The man shook his head. "I used to be a farmer myself," he said. "I understand what they're trying to do. They figure the reason they get so little money for selling their beef is that there's too much beef and too little demand. By killing off cattle, they hope to make the supply smaller. They think that will drive up prices."

Alma looked puzzled. "It sounds crazy to me. They'd have to kill an awful lot of cattle to make it work. How can they ever get enough farmers to go along?"

"I doubt if they can," said the man. "Besides, even if they get the supply down, there's still the problem of demand. Who can buy beef these days? People without a job can't afford any kind of meat. They're lucky just to have beans."

Jerry spoke up again. "What kind of country lets people go without work, proper food, and homes?"

The man whispered, "All I can tell you is that people are becoming very angry. They think someone is making money while the little guys like you and me are starving. And they think the government is in on it. I tell you, if the government doesn't do something fast, we're going to have a revolution."

Alma turned to the woman and said, "I've been eating biscuits and mustard for the past two days. I never dreamed that I'd be eating fried chicken on this freight car. How did you manage to get a chicken?"

The woman looked at Alma and Jerry and said, "We found it dead on the road. My husband cleaned it and fried it. We figure we had a right to it. President Hoover promised a chicken in every pot, right? We just collected on his promise."

Alma smiled at the woman, who smiled back. Alma thought of how much she had in common with this woman. Both were poor, homeless, and searching for a better life. Alma really liked her. For the first time in her life, she was comfortable with a stranger. But what would happen in the future? Would she and Jerry have to drift like this for the rest of their lives? Why didn't the government do something to help?

Homework Questions

1. In addition to the Wall Street Crash, name three other causes of the Great Depression.
2. How did homeless families live during this period?
3. Why did Jerry and Alma want to reach Chicago?
4. How were the poor living in the big cities?
5. Why were Jerry and Alma worried about the future?

Understanding the Story

A. List the numbers of the statements that Jerry made or might have made.
   1. We're bound to find work in a big city.
   2. We can't afford to be choosy.
   3. If a detective sees you, you'll have to leave.
   4. There's plenty of food in this country.
   5. Riding in a freight car is the only way to travel.
   6. People are going hungry.
   7. I know just what caused the Depression.
   8. My government cares what happens to me.

B. Write *T* for each statement that is true, *F* for each statement that is false, and *N* for each statement that is not mentioned in the story.
   1. Thousands of people were homeless.
   2. At the start of the Great Depression, bank deposits were not insured by the government.
   3. In 1931 more than 8 million workers were unemployed.
   4. No American went hungry.
   5. Sometimes conductors called the detectives when they found people like Alma and Jerry on a train.
   6. Alma and Jerry were wanderers looking for work.
   7. Farmers who dumped milk were mainly worried that it would go sour.
   8. Alma felt that she was different from the other woman in the freight car.

C. What does this chapter tell you about the mood of the nation in 1931? What attitude did Americans seem to take about being out of work?

Activities and Inquiries

1. Look at the drawing on page 425 and answer the following questions.
   a. How would Jerry and Alma answer this question?
   b. How would the other couple answer this question?
   c. How would Richie (in Chapter 4) answer it?
   d. How would Steve (in Chapter 4) answer it?
2. Assume that you meet Jerry later, in Chicago. What does he tell you about his experiences?
3. You ask Jerry why these things are happening. What are his answers?
4. What does Alma tell you about her fears for the future?
5. You ask Jerry and Alma how the Depression can be ended. What is their answer?

6 Herbert Hoover

As the Great Depression deepened, more Americans looked to President Herbert Hoover for leadership and hope. As a person, Hoover had a fine reputation. A mining engineer by training, he became a millionaire through business operations in many parts of the world. He was also a great humanitarian (one interested in helping others). Hoover became famous for his work during and after World War I in organizing programs to feed the starving millions in Europe. Later he served as secretary of commerce under Presidents Harding and Coolidge. Now, Americans hoped that Hoover would use his talents to end the despair at home.

As President, how did Hoover try to help the American people? Were they grateful?

Washington, D.C., 1932

You are Herbert Hoover, and you are a believer. You believe in capitalism. You believe in free enterprise. You believe in progress. You believe, above all, that the American people will find a way to overcome the economic troubles that are now grinding them down.

At heart, you are an optimist. Even in the dark days of World War I, you never let problems overwhelm you. Against great odds you organized programs to house and feed millions of people in 25 countries. You were a go-getter, a doer—anything but a quitter.

What was it that made possible your successes? Cooperation—people working together. When you returned to the United States, you preached cooperation to Americans. You advised business, labor, and government to work with—not against—one another. "Collective self-help" became your motto.

As secretary of commerce during the 1920's you did everything you could to help bring order to the business world—order through cooperation. You encouraged manufacturers to use standard-sized parts. You helped small businesses set up trade associations to control "excessive" competition and improve profits. You helped large businesses grow larger in the name of greater efficiency. All the while you urged that government remain in the background, a helper of business but not a regulator. Your ways were not those of the Progressives. As you saw it, your way was the American way, the way of free enterprise.

When you were elected President on the Republican ticket in 1928,

America was riding a wave of prosperity. You gloried in that prosperity. It proved to you that the American way was working well.

But something went wrong. The wheels of prosperity ground to a halt. The Great Depression put a stranglehold on the nation. Did you lose your optimism? Not at all. You assured the public that the problems were temporary. The nation's financial system—its stock markets, its banks—had faltered, that was all. The heart of America's prosperity was its industries, and they were still sound. Recovery, you insisted, was just around the corner.

Some people, like your secretary of the treasury, Andrew Mellon, said the government should do nothing. "Let nature take its course," said Mellon. Like a fevered body, the nation's economy would sweat it out. Eventually it would recover and be the healthier for its sufferings.

You did not agree. You wanted government to step in and help bring about a cure. Your prescription was more cooperation among government, business, and labor. You persuaded business leaders to keep workers on the payroll. You persuaded labor leaders to avoid strikes. You urged people who still had jobs to donate to charities so that the hungry might be fed.

These efforts were helpful, but you decided they were not enough. So you asked Congress for further measures, and Congress agreed. It cut taxes so people had more money to spend. It started public works projects (dams, highways, buildings) to create new jobs. Federal agencies made loans to businesses and to homeowners struggling to pay off mortgages. The government bought up certain farm products that could not be sold on the open market.

To protect American industries from foreign competition, Congress passed the Hawley-Smoot Bill setting extremely high tariffs. Critics said the bill was unwise. They said other nations would raise

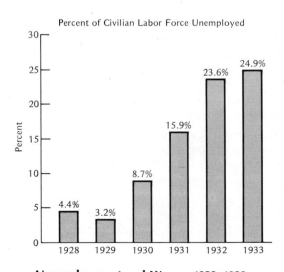

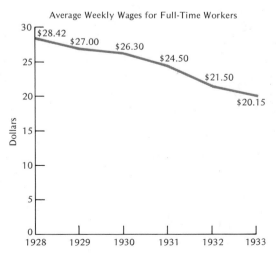

Unemployment and Wages, 1928–1933

tariffs too and that world trade would die. Perhaps the critics were right. Trade is down. The Depression has been spreading to nations in Europe and elsewhere.

Some people are calling for a federal relief program to feed the hungry. You oppose this. You insist that government aid be given to producers—not consumers. Get the economy moving again, you say, and prosperity will return. It is not the American way, you insist, for the federal government to give handouts to the hungry. That is a job for private charity and, if private charity falls short, for state and local governments. When Congress passed a bill offering direct relief to the unemployed, you vetoed it.

You insist that the government must keep its budget balanced, that spending must not exceed income. The government must pay as it goes, you say, and not borrow money for vast spending programs. We must not burden future generations with a massive debt. This is not your belief alone. It is held by prominent business people and by leaders of both the Republican and Democratic parties.

Many other Americans, however, are saying that the crisis is too desperate to worry about such things as balanced budgets. They call for sweeping government action—the sooner the better. Some people criticize you and poke fun at you. They say you don't care about the wretched people who have lost their homes. You don't care if people must live in cardboard boxes or in shacks in parks and vacant lots. They have named such places "Hoovervilles." You wince when you hear the word.

Perhaps you should be grateful that most critics still have a sense of humor. There are others who are too angry to laugh. Will they try to stir up riots? Will they attempt a revolution? These are thoughts that trouble your sleep. You don't want to take any chances.

You became concerned when thousands of army veterans camped in the nation's capital this summer. They came to urge Congress to speed up payment of a bonus for wartime service. To get rid of the "Bonus Marchers," you called out federal troops. The troops, armed with guns, bayonets, and tanks, chased the veterans away. Critics said you overreacted. But who can know for sure?

Now a presidential election is coming up. Your party has nominated you for re-election, but you know your chances are poor. You feel you are being blamed unfairly for something beyond your control. You've done more to fight a depression than any previous President. Is it your fault that your efforts haven't yet succeeded? Can you persuade the voters to give you a second chance?

POSTSCRIPT

The voters rejected Hoover in November, 1932. In his place they elected a Democrat, Governor Franklin Delano Roosevelt of New York. Roosevelt would push for a far more active role for the federal government in fighting the Great Depression. Hoover's methods came to seem pale in comparison with Roosevelt's. Many people, forgetting how vigorous Hoover's methods were in comparison with those of earlier Presidents, would think of Hoover as a heartless person. But that was unfair.

In the 1940's and 1950's, Hoover headed commissions seeking ways to make the government more efficient. At his death in 1964, he was recognized as a great American—although still a controversial one.

Homework Questions

1. What kind of reputation did Herbert Hoover have when he was elected President?
2. What did Hoover see as the proper relationship among business, labor, and government?
3. Give one reason why U.S. voters elected Hoover in 1928.
4. How did Hoover try to fight the Great Depression?
5. Why did Hoover oppose a federal relief program to feed the hungry?

Understanding the Story

A. List the numbers of the statements that are true.
1. Hoover was elected President in 1928.
2. Hoover was a Democrat.
3. Hoover believed that government should regulate business.
4. Hoover said that recovery was just around the corner.
5. Hoover favored government loans to businesses.
6. Hoover opposed government loans to homeowners.
7. The Hawley-Smoot Bill called for high tariffs.
8. The American voters re-elected Hoover in 1932.

B. Write *A* for each statement Hoover would agree with and *N* for each statement that he would not agree with.
1. I believe in capitalism.
2. I believe that the American people will overcome the Depression.
3. My beliefs are those of the Progressives.
4. Business people should cooperate with one another.
5. Government should cooperate with industry.
6. Government should do nothing to fight the Depression.
7. The American way has failed.
8. We must not burden future generations with a massive debt.

C. Do you think Herbert Hoover was to blame for the hardships that faced the American people in 1932? Why or why not?

Activities and Inquiries

1. Study the graphs on page 429. Then choose the term or phrase that best completes each statement.
   a. The year with the highest wages was (*1*) 1928 (*2*) 1929 (*3*) 1930.
   b. Unemployment was lowest in (*1*) 1933 (*2*) 1928 (*3*) 1929.

c. As weekly wages fell, unemployment *(1)* increased　*(2)* decreased　*(3)* showed no change.

d. Unemployment in 1933 was　*(1)* 8.7%　*(2)* 23.6%　*(3)* 24.9%.

e. From the graphs you can learn *(1)* the reasons for the fall in wages　*(2)* what a depression does to wages and jobs　*(3)* what caused the Great Depression.

2. Prepare a report card for Herbert Hoover. Grade him in the following areas and justify each grade:

a. Leadership
b. Training
c. Point of view
d. Accomplishments while President
e. Maturity

3. Imagine that you are a reporter and are assigned to interview Hoover about the causes of the Great Depression. What questions will you ask him? What are his answers?

4. What is Hoover's solution for the Great Depression?

7 The Growth of the Constitution: Do Workers Need Protective Laws?

During the 1920's, the American people seemed to worship at the shrine of big business. Harding, Coolidge, and Hoover, the three Presidents of the 1920's, all believed that big business would lead America to lasting prosperity. They saw little need for Congress to pass laws to regulate business. Many members of Congress agreed with them, but others pushed for various types of federal regulation. Some states also kept on trying to regulate business.

In 1923 the United States Supreme Court heard arguments about a federal law setting minimum wages for women and children working in the District of Columbia. Arizona, Arkansas, and New York had passed state laws with a similar goal. A children's hospital in the District of Columbia refused to obey the federal law. Lower federal courts upheld the law. Finally the case of *Adkins* v. *Children's Hospital* came before the Supreme Court.

Supreme Court justices Oliver Wendell Holmes and George Sutherland are discussing this case. What arguments do you think will be used to support the law? What arguments will be used against the law?

Washington, D.C., 1923

"This seems to be an open-and-shut case," said Justice Holmes. "Congress has passed a law to protect the health and morals of women and children workers by making sure they are paid a living wage. This is a perfectly valid use of the lawmaking power granted by the Constitution. I say the Court should uphold the law."

"One moment, Justice Holmes," replied Justice Sutherland. "I believe you are overlooking some key points. It is true that Congress has great power when writing laws. But it must respect the rights of the people. And the right to enter into an employment contract is one of the most basic rights. It is guaranteed by the Fifth Amendment, which says a person may not be deprived of life, liberty, or property without due process of law."

"I am perfectly aware that the Fifth Amendment protects the right to make a contract," said Holmes. "This Court has said so on many occasions."

"Of course," said Sutherland. "I'm glad you admit my point."

"Ah, but wait, Justice Sutherland. No right is absolute. Pretty much all law consists in forbidding men to do something that they want to do. The right to make a contract can be restricted in the interest of promoting the public well-being. Don't you remember the case of *Muller* v. *Oregon* back in 1908? This Court upheld a state law that kept women from working more than ten hours a day. Certainly that law interfered with their right of contract. Yet the Court agreed that the public's interest in protecting working women's health was a valid reason for limiting their working hours."

"That decision is not related to this case," Sutherland replied.

"What do you mean, 'not related'?"

"In the first place, setting a limit on hours is one thing—setting minimum wages is quite another. Hours of work are more closely related than wages to the issue of public well-being. Besides, that decision was made at a time when women suffered many disadvantages in society. But times have changed. Now the 19th Amendment has given women the vote. Women are being freed from the old idea that they must be given special protection."

Holmes shook his head. "It will take more than the 19th Amendment to convince me that there are no differences between men and women. I also believe that laws must take those differences into account."

"Mr. Holmes, women are legally just as capable as men of making contracts for themselves. This law, by forcing employers to pay a minimum wage, will make it impossible for some employers to afford to hire women at all. It will actually hurt those it is supposed to help."

"I very much doubt that that will be the case," said Holmes. "But why should it matter what you or I believe? As a matter of fact, I have my doubts about the wisdom of this particular law. But we are not asked to decide whether the law is wise—only whether it obeys the Constitution. And I believe it does."

"How can you say that, Justice Holmes? Have you fully considered all sides of this law or what it might lead to? If it is constitutional for Congress to set a *minimum* wage, then Congress also has a right to set a *maximum* wage."

"On what grounds would a maximum wage be justified?"

"Why, on grounds of the public well-being, Justice Holmes. Let's say the wages of workers in the building trades should reach a high level. The price of new houses goes way up. The average family can no longer afford a house. So Congress decides that the public well-being requires that people be well housed. Therefore, it passes a law setting a maximum wage in the building trades. The same argument used now to strip an employer of his liberty of contract will be used then to strip a worker of *his* liberty of contract."

"Justice Sutherland, it is always possible to think up extreme consequences that might—just might, mind you—flow from a case. But please, let's return to reality. This law does not force anybody to pay anything to anybody. It simply forbids employers from paying women and children less than a minimum wage. *That* is the law at issue. And that law, I say, is constitutional."

"I cannot agree," said Sutherland. "I believe this Court should bend over backwards to see things as Congress sees them. We should give the benefit of doubt to a law passed by Congress. But when a law is clearly unconstitutional, we have no choice but to say so."

POSTSCRIPT

The justices of the Supreme Court debated further and came to a decision. A majority decided that the law guaranteeing minimum wages for women and children in the District of Columbia was unconstitutional. The laws of Arizona, Arkansas, and New York eventually were struck down as well.

Prodded by Progressives, Congress and the states continued to pass laws aimed at protecting women and children. In 1924 Congress proposed a constitutional amendment to ban child labor. Not enough states ratified the amendment, so it never took effect.

During the Great Depression there was increased interest in laws that set hours and wages for women, children, and even men. In 1937 the U.S. Supreme Court in effect reversed the Adkins decision. It upheld a minimum-wage law passed by the state of Washington (*West Coast Hotel Company* v. *Parris*). In 1938 Congress passed the Fair Labor Standards Act, setting a national minimum wage of 40 cents an hour and a workweek of 40 hours. The act applied to many but not all businesses. It applied to adult males as well as women and children. It was upheld by the Supreme Court in 1941 (*U.S.* v. *Darby Lumber Company*).

Homework Questions

1. How did Justice Oliver Wendell Holmes and Justice George Sutherland feel about laws aimed at protecting women?
2. What was Holmes's main argument in favor of upholding the minimum-wage law?
3. What was Sutherland's main argument in favor of throwing out the minimum-wage law?
4. How did the Supreme Court rule on the Adkins case?
5. Is the Adkins decision still in effect? Explain.

Understanding the Story

A. Write *F* for each statement that is a fact and *O* for each statement that is an opinion.
  1. Workers do not need the protection of the federal government.
  2. Congress passed a minimum-wage law for women and children in Washington, D.C.
  3. Women had the right to vote in 1923.
  4. Women should be happy with whatever pay the boss gives them.
  5. The D.C. minimum-wage law aimed to protect the health of women and children workers.
  6. Holmes said constitutional rights are not absolute.
  7. The Supreme Court should not have declared the minimum-wage law unconstitutional.
  8. Sutherland said the minimum-wage law might hurt women.

B. Write *H* for each statement that Holmes made or might have made and *S* for each statement that Sutherland made or might have made.
  1. The right to enter into an employment contract is one of the most basic rights.
  2. The minimum-wage law is a valid use of Congress's power.
  3. No right is absolute.
  4. *Muller* v. *Oregon* is not related to this case.
  5. *Muller* v. *Oregon* supports my position.
  6. Laws that set minimum wages are quite different from laws that limit working hours.
  7. When a law goes against the Constitution, we have no choice but to say so.
  8. We are not asked to decide whether the law is wise.

C. Whose arguments do you think were more persuasive—Holmes's or Sutherland's? Why?

Activities and Inquiries

1. Justice Holmes said that men and women should be treated differently. Do you agree? Explain.
2. Sutherland said times have changed since *Muller* v. *Oregon*. What did he mean?
3. Sutherland said the D.C. minimum-wage law might actually hurt those it was supposed to help. In later years the same argument was used against minimum-wage laws for teenage workers. Do you agree that the argument is a good one? Why or why not?
4. Imagine that you are a lawyer in the Adkins case. You are defending a minimum wage for women and children. What are your arguments?
5. Suppose that you are a lawyer arguing against a minimum wage. What are your arguments?

Alfred E. Smith

MR. MILLER. Tom is going to tell us about Al Smith today.

TOM. Al Smith was an Irish-American politician who was at his peak of power in New York in the 1920's.

ROSA. Was he as good and honest as La Guardia?

TOM. He was. As a politician Smith went farther up the ladder than any Irish-American to that time. He was the first Roman Catholic governor of New York State and in 1928 the first Catholic candidate for President. Smith was a poor boy who had to leave school at age 13 to support his mother. He tried every job you can imagine: newsboy, shipping clerk, fish-market worker, laborer carrying heavy pipes. You name it; he did it. Often he worked from four in the morning to five in the afternoon. Then he helped out in his mother's store.

CASIMIR. How did he get into politics?

TOM. He spent his spare time working for the Democratic Party through its local ruling committee known as Tammany Hall. Tammany leaders saw that even though Smith was rough and uneducated, people liked him. People listened when Al Smith spoke. So he was given the chance to run for the New York State Assembly and won easily.

JUAN. Tell me, how can a school drop-out make laws?

TOM. That is what Smith asked himself. Each day he'd find a huge pile of bills, the proposed laws, on his desk. Even if he had time to read them, he couldn't understand them.

MR. MILLER. Chances are that many of the better-educated members of the Assembly couldn't understand those bills either.

TOM. Al Smith had to know what each bill was about, so he took the bills to his room at night and read every single word. He borrowed lawbooks to make sure no word or shade of meaning escaped him. He taught himself to become a great lawmaker and rose to be majority leader and speaker of the Assembly.

SAM. Great. But wasn't he just wasting his time? Wouldn't he vote the way the Tammany organization ordered?

TOM. Sure, he followed orders because he wanted to keep his

seat. But he spent time on his own interests, too. He was concerned about the working poor and wanted to improve factory conditions. I guess that the Triangle fire was a turning point in his life. He saw that new laws had to be passed to help workers.

SAM. Did Al Smith really know what was going on in factories?

TOM. You bet he did. On his travels around the state, he saw factories with mothers and their little children working seven days a week in tiny, windowless rooms. In one factory, the manager insisted that no children under seven worked there. When Smith found them hidden in an elevator, he exploded in anger. He saw to it that factory conditions improved all over the state.

RICARDO. Looks like he did good work in the legislature.

TOM. Yes, but then he kept moving up. He was chosen governor of the state for four terms, a total of eight years. He reorganized the state government and reduced hours for working men, women, and children. He even got equal pay for women teachers.

MR. MILLER. That's only fair. We should add that Al Smith turned New York into one of the best-governed states in the union.

RICARDO. If he was such a good governor, why didn't he hold on to the job?

TOM. Well, he felt that four terms were enough. Besides, he had a dream. He wanted to become the President of the United States.

JOSEPHINE. What happened?

TOM. The Democrats nominated him for President in 1928. But he lost to Hoover by a wide margin. End of dream!

JOSEPHINE. Why did he lose so badly?

TOM. I'm not completely sure. Some people opposed him because he was Irish and Catholic and from a big Eastern city. Some didn't like his New York accent and his flashy clothes.

MR. MILLER. That's prejudice any way you look at it.

TOM. Smith also made enemies by speaking out against Prohibition. He said the laws against alcoholic drinks should be changed. Hoover defended Prohibition—a popular stand in much of the country.

HANS. Well, let's suppose that Smith had been non-Irish, non-Catholic, a non-New Yorker, and a defender of Prohibition. Could he have won in 1928?

TOM. Probably not. Any Democrat would have had a tough time. It was a period of prosperity. The Republicans were in power, and the people thought, Why not keep the Republicans and the good times?

HEINRICH. If Smith didn't make it to the Presidency, you can't call him great.

TOM. I can and I do! He overcame a background of poverty to become an important person in this country. He accomplished a great deal.

MR. MILLER. You could say he was the Abe Lincoln of New York.

"How did World War I change things, Jack?"

"Well, after the war, the mood of the country shifted. Many people wanted to change America back to what it had been before. They wanted to forget the destruction and the fight over the League. They wanted to make money and enjoy themselves."

"How did people feel about foreigners after the war?" asked Mr. Miller.

"Many Americans blamed foreigners for problems like strikes, crime, and bombings. They blamed all these things on 'outsiders' and 'Reds.' Get rid of these people, they said; send them back home, or at least prevent more foreigners from coming here. Anyone with a foreign name who spoke or acted a little differently was suspect. Look what happened to Sacco and Vanzetti! I think that they were punished more for being foreigners than for the crime they were supposed to have committed."

"Good, Jack. What else were Americans interested in doing during the 1920's?"

"Mostly they seemed to be interested in making money and getting rich quick. They were turning out products faster and cheaper than ever before. Profits went higher and higher—though the profits weren't always shared by farmers and workers. People loved their cars and radios. Many people gambled on the stock market, drank illegal liquor, and looked after their own interests. And we mustn't forget the corruption of President Harding's friends. The 20's were boom times, all right!"

"What happened to the boom, Jack?"

"The balloon burst, Mr. Miller. Prices on the stock market rose much too high. When stocks fell to their true value and below, investors were wiped out in the crash. Their dreams had been as unreal as the prices of their stocks."

"How did the country react to the crash?"

"There was a loss of confidence. Manufacturers employed fewer workers and produced fewer goods. Profits fell, and still more people lost their jobs. College graduates took what low-paying jobs they could get. Others weren't so lucky and drifted around the country looking for food, a place to live, and a job."

"How did our government help?" asked Mr. Miller.

"President Hoover felt that people should be encouraged to help themselves. When that didn't work, loans were made to business people. But that wasn't enough. Sick industries didn't recover. Jobs were still hard to find. By 1932, when the presidential election was held, the voters had lost faith in Herbert Hoover. It's no wonder that he lost. But what did Franklin Roosevelt do to try to make things better?"

"You'll find out in the next unit, Jack."

Franklin Roosevelt and the New Deal

"By the way, Mr. Miller, where do we go from here?"

"I think you have the answer already," said Mr. Miller.

"What do you mean?" asked Jack.

"Well, a while back you said that Americans had had their fun and then the fun ended. What did *you* mean?"

Jack said, "That's easy. The stock market crashed, and Americans found themselves in the worst depression in their history."

"Right, Jack, it was a time of fear and gloom. A great many workers lost their jobs, and many farmers lost their land. But, worst of all, people were afraid of the future. In fact, many felt that they had no future."

"Sounds like things were pretty hopeless," said Jack.

"Ah, but there was hope. A new President, Franklin D. Roosevelt, took office in 1933. He spoke to the people on the radio and made them think things could be different. There was to be 'a new deal.' The federal government would be much more involved in American life. We didn't get out of the Great Depression right away, but America started moving again."

"Great!" exclaimed Jack. "But how did all this happen?"

"That's what we're going to find out," said Mr. Miller.

1 Franklin Delano Roosevelt

The election of a new President in November, 1932, did not end the Depression. Conditions continued to get worse. Early in 1933 there was a new wave of bank failures. Worried people lined up outside the remaining banks to withdraw their savings before those banks could also fail. Many states ordered banks to close until the panic had passed. Authorities feared that collapsing banks would topple other banks like falling dominoes.

On March 4, 1933, Herbert Hoover moved out of the White House. Franklin Delano Roosevelt took over. In his first speech as President, Roosevelt tried to break the deepening gloom with a note of hopefulness. "The only thing we have to fear," he said, "is fear itself."

Did Roosevelt have an answer to the country's mounting problems? Americans waited anxiously to find out.

Washington, D.C., March 4, 1933

You, Franklin Delano Roosevelt, are now the 31st President of the United States. Americans all over the country are praying for your success. Millions of them are unemployed, homeless, helpless. They look to you for answers. What can you do to help them?

During the campaign, you accused Hoover and the Republicans of having failed the American people. You promised "a new deal" to make conditions better. But you never said exactly what you meant by "a new deal." People are not sure what you will do.

President Hoover told a campaign audience that your "so-called new deals . . . would destroy the very foundations of our American system." He said your Democratic Party was "the party of the mob." Although Hoover lost the election, many Americans share his concerns. They are afraid you will be tempted to seize greater power and become a dictator.

World conditions seem to be ripe for dictators just now. Italy is ruled by a right-wing dictator, Benito Mussolini. The Soviet Union is ruled by a left-wing dictator, Josef Stalin. And just five weeks ago a tough-talking man named Adolf Hitler, head of the Nazi Party, took over as leader of Germany. Democracy is in deep trouble. Can it survive in America?

People wonder what kind of person you really are. They know that you have been a state senator, an assistant secretary of the navy, and a governor of New York. They also know that you have a handsome face, a charming manner, and a pleasant voice. They know you are 51 years old and come from a wealthy family. But who are you, really?

People know, by now, that your wealth has not protected you from suffering. Twelve years ago you were struck down by polio. You lost the use of both legs. With great determination you somehow overcame your handicap. You stayed active in politics, even though crutches, braces, and wheelchairs are now your constant companions. Because of your personal struggles, many people admire you as a man of courage.

Those who have dealt with you say you can be as tough as steel. But are you of the material of which dictators are made? You scoff at the very idea. You see yourself as a defender of democracy and of capitalism. You, like Hoover, are a champion of the American way.

But your idea of the American way is not precisely that of Hoover. You believe that government should right the wrongs of society and act to protect people. Your teachers about reform were Theodore Roosevelt, your distant cousin, and Woodrow Wilson. You intend to put into practice what you learned from them. You have promised to help business people, bankers, and "the forgotten man at the bottom."

Even you are not quite sure how you will go about your task. You don't have any pat answers, you have said. But you are ready to experiment. You will try something, and if that doesn't work, you will try something else.

Because of your willingness to experiment, many people will think of you as a liberal. (In American politics, a liberal is one who is willing to break with tradition and try new ways.) But you have a streak of the conservative in you too. (A conservative is one who seeks to preserve the best of the past and thus tends to be more suspicious of change.) In the months and years to come, you will propose many changes in the ways government operates. But you will argue constantly that the changes you seek are necessary to preserve the American way—to save both capitalism and democracy.

You know that you will never be able to please everyone. Some people will call you the savior of your country; others, a traitor to the American way. Some will respect and love you. Others will hate you. Few people will be indifferent to you.

You are Franklin Delano Roosevelt, "FDR," and you will leave a lasting mark upon this nation.

POSTSCRIPT

FDR wasted little time in giving the American people a glimpse of his style. Before he had been in office two days, Roosevelt had called a special session of Congress and moved to close the nation's banks. The brief "bank holiday," as it was called, was to keep more banks from failing while Roosevelt worked out a solution to the banking crisis. On his sixth day in office, Roosevelt had his plan ready. Congress passed it within a few hours.

Under Roosevelt's plan, the government kept the shakiest banks closed and allowed other banks to reopen. Government loans helped keep reopened banks in business. When people saw that the banks were not going to fail, they stopped trying to withdraw their money. The banking crisis soon came to an end.

Roosevelt's moves won praise from bankers and members of Congress. FDR had not acted like a dictator, but he had accomplished what he set out to do. His Presidency was off to a flying start. A new era had begun—the era we know as the New Deal.

Homework Questions

1. What immediate problem did FDR face upon taking office? How did he deal with it?
2. How did Herbert Hoover respond to Roosevelt's call for "a new deal"?
3. Why did many people fear that Roosevelt might act like a dictator?
4. How was Roosevelt's approach to the Presidency different from Hoover's?
5. What did Roosevelt say his goal as President would be?

Understanding the Story

A. Write *T* for each statement that is true, *F* for each statement that is false, and *N* for each statement that is not mentioned in this chapter.
  1. Franklin Delano Roosevelt said the United States should have a balanced budget.
  2. Many banks failed early in 1933.
  3. Roosevelt succeeded Herbert Hoover as President.
  4. Hoover promised Americans "a new deal."
  5. Roosevelt ran for Vice President in 1920 and lost.
  6. Roosevelt saw himself as a defender of democracy and of capitalism.
  7. Roosevelt entered the Presidency with a clear plan to end the Great Depression.
  8. Roosevelt maintained that the Democrats should "break foolish traditions."

B. List the numbers of the statements that describe Roosevelt's thinking.
  1. Recovery is just around the corner.
  2. I will help "the forgotten man" of America.
  3. I believe in the American way.
  4. Herbert Hoover is one of my heroes.
  5. Hoover and the Republicans failed the American people.
  6. I will let the banking crisis work itself out.
  7. I have known struggle and suffering.
  8. The only thing we have to fear is fear itself.

C. Do you think that a dictator might sometimes be needed to solve a nation's problems? Explain why you believe as you do.

Activities and Inquiries

1. Assume that you voted for Franklin D. Roosevelt in 1932. Explain why.

2. Assume that you voted against Roosevelt. Explain why.
3. Suppose that Roosevelt has just become President and you are his speechwriter. Prepare his first speech to the nation, or outline its major points.
4. Suppose that Herbert Hoover had won the election of 1932. Describe what might have happened.

2 The New Deal

President Roosevelt began at once to introduce the New Deal. He sent dozens of programs to Congress—programs to wage war against the Great Depression. Congress said yes to nearly all of them. At the end of 100 days, the United States found itself with a vastly expanded federal government.

The New Deal programs fell under three broad categories—"the three R's." The most urgent programs were for *relief* of people's suffering. Others were to help promote the *recovery* of business activity. Still others were to bring about *reform*.

Relief programs aimed at feeding and housing the victims of the Depression. A Federal Emergency Relief Administration (FERA) was created. It gave money to state and city relief agencies. A Civilian Conservation Corps (CCC) set up work camps where young men could find jobs fighting soil erosion, replanting forests, and improving national parks. Special agencies offered loans to people who had fallen behind on mortgage payments for their homes and farms.

Recovery programs sought to pump new life into lagging businesses. The National Industrial Recovery Act (NIRA) set up a massive public works program to build dams, airports, and other projects. It also made government a partner with business groups in enforcing rules against unfair competition. In return, labor unions won new rights to bargain for better wages and working conditions. To help farmers, an Agricultural Adjustment Administration (AAA) was created. Using money from a new tax on canners, millers, and other processors, the AAA paid farmers to produce less. The goal was to reduce supply so that the prices farmers got for their products would rise.

Reform programs aimed to correct abuses such as the sale of phony securities (stocks and bonds). The Truth-in-Securities Act set rules about the sale of stocks and bonds.

Still other important measures were passed during those first 100 days. One repealed the 18th Amendment, putting an end to Prohibition. Another set up a Tennessee Valley Authority (TVA). One of the TVA's aims was to control floods and promote conservation in parts of seven states in the South. Another was to build government-owned power plants to furnish cheap electricity to farms, homes, and industries in the region of the Tennessee River.

After 100 days the pace slacked off, but New Deal measures still kept pouring out of Congress. It continued to be concerned about how the stock market crash contributed to the Depression. A series of congressional hearings brought to light stories of business leaders who had rigged stock prices for their own profit. In June, 1934, Congress created a Securities and Exchange Commission (SEC) to stop such abuses and to curb the use of credit in buying stocks.

Roosevelt's programs affected almost every part of American life. Some people felt that even more should be done to solve the country's problems. Others were afraid that the government was becoming too strong.

In our story, a banker and a factory worker meet at a family reunion. They are talking about the New Deal and its effect on their lives. Why do you suppose each feels as he does? How do you think other Americans felt about Roosevelt and his program?

Michigan, July, 1934

"Hi, Alvin. How're the wife and kids?" asked Earl as he spooned out another helping of potato salad.

"Doing fine, now," replied Alvin. "I've got a job and we've got meat on the table again. The factory called back half of us workers when business picked up."

"Glad to hear it," said Earl. "Let's hope business keeps getting better. I'm a bit worried, though. I'm afraid that man in the White House is going to ruin things."

"You mean Roosevelt? Come on—he's the reason things are looking up. His New Deal is just what this country needs to pull us out of the Depression."

"I can't agree," Earl responded. "Oh, sure, some of what Roosevelt did at first was right on target. He helped save my bank, you know. We would have gone under if it hadn't been for the bank holiday last year. But the man seems to want the federal government to stick its nose into every little thing. I say he's going too far. He's lost the confidence of business people, and he'll never end the Depression without that."

"How can you say such a thing?" Alvin exclaimed. "He sure has *my* confidence. Why, we would have lost our home if we hadn't been able to refinance our mortgage. The only way we could do that was through the home loan program that Roosevelt set up."

"Oh, don't get me wrong," said Earl. "Some of those programs were good ones—even necessary. Take the idea of federal insurance

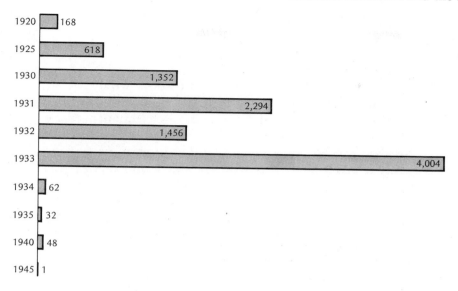

Year	Bank Failures
1920	168
1925	618
1930	1,352
1931	2,294
1932	1,456
1933	4,004
1934	62
1935	32
1940	48
1945	1

Bank Failures Before and After the Banking Act of 1933

for bank deposits up to $2,500. Now that people know they won't lose their money even if my bank fails, I don't have to worry that they'll withdraw their savings in a sudden panic."

"That's the idea. And what about the way Roosevelt has helped our young people find jobs? Our Tommy is 19 now, and he's at a CCC camp. He's not earning much, just $30 a month. But he's out in the open air, and he's doing something useful. He says every tree he plants is an investment in America's future."

"Tommy may like it, but the CCC sounds to me like something you'd find in a dictatorship. I don't like the idea of putting young men to work in camps run by army officers."

"Earl, all I know is that this country was in desperate shape. In almost every community people were hunting for food in garbage cans, sleeping in the streets, begging for handouts. You can't imagine how ashamed I was two years ago when I lost my job and couldn't put food on my family's table. Even after our savings ran out, it took me weeks to work up the courage to apply for county relief—just a little help to tide us over. Without a job, I felt worthless. I didn't get my self-respect back until I was called back to work last fall. And I think I have Roosevelt to thank for better times."

"Listen, Alvin. I don't care how much you like the man, he's dangerous. You think he's up there tinkering with our American system to make it better. But he's tinkering too much. With his alphabet soup of new agencies, his CCC's and TVA's and so on, he's changing the system into something completely different—something un-American. It's like that editorial in the paper the other day said: Roosevelt is more communistic than the Communists."

"Honestly, Earl, Roosevelt is *saving* the American way—not destroying it. Without Roosevelt's New Deal our whole system of democracy and free enterprise might have collapsed. We could have ended up with a dictatorship."

"Maybe we will yet—a New Deal dictatorship! You know what opened my eyes to the dangers? It was the way the New Dealers pressured the business community with that bill to give the government control over the stock markets. Mark my words, that's just the first step. Roosevelt and his wild-eyed New Dealers are going to wrap us business people so tightly in red tape that we won't be able to move."

"Earl, aren't you getting all worked up about nothing? So the government decided to regulate the stock market. You know that should have been done long ago. Maybe then we wouldn't have had the Wall Street Crash and all that followed."

"But the government isn't stopping with rules for just one organization," said Earl. "The bureaucrats are trying to control the whole private enterprise system. Soon we'll have a government so big and powerful that you and I and people all over the country won't have any say in our own lives."

"I can see we'll never see eye to eye, Earl," Alvin said with a wink. "We'd better stop this discussion before one of us gets mad and says something he'll regret."

"You're right, Alvin. Let's have another talk at next year's reunion. Maybe you'll have changed your mind."

"Or maybe you'll have changed yours."

Homework Questions

1. What were the three main categories of New Deal programs?
2. How did the National Industrial Recovery Act (NIRA) seek to promote recovery?
3. What were the goals of the Tennessee Valley Authority (TVA)?
4. Why did Earl dislike the New Deal?
5. Why was Alvin grateful to Roosevelt and the New Deal?

Understanding the Story

A. List the numbers of the statements that are true.

1. Congress refused to go along with Roosevelt's New Deal.
2. The Civilian Conservation Corps (CCC) put young men to work on outdoor jobs.
3. The New Deal greatly expanded the federal government.
4. The National Industrial Recovery Act (NIRA) provided for the government to take over private industries.
5. The New Deal did not affect the stock markets.
6. The Tennessee Valley Authority (TVA) aimed to control floods and furnish cheap electricity.
7. Much New Deal legislation was passed in Roosevelt's first 100 days.
8. Alvin and Earl worked together in a factory.

B. Write *A* for each statement Alvin made or might have made and *E* for each statement Earl made or might have made. If both would agree with a statement, write *A-E*.
1. Business is picking up.
2. The New Deal is just what this country needs.
3. Roosevelt is going too far.
4. The New Deal has helped me personally.
5. Roosevelt has helped me recover my self-respect.
6. Roosevelt is changing the American system into something un-American.
7. The government is getting too big and powerful.
8. Without the New Deal our democracy might have collapsed.

C. Alvin and Earl disagree about whether the New Deal is saving or harming the American system. What do you think? Explain your answer.

Activities and Inquiries

1. Prepare a report card for Franklin Roosevelt. Grade him in the following areas and justify each grade.
   a. Leadership
   b. Training
   c. Point of view
   d. Accomplishments while President
   e. Maturity
2. Imagine that you are spending a day with Alvin. What questions will you ask him?
3. How will Alvin answer your questions?
4. You ask Earl what he thinks of Franklin Roosevelt. What will he tell you?
5. Study the graph on page 445. Then choose the term or phrase that best completes each statement.
   a. The number of bank failures in 1933 was (*1*) about the same as in other years (*2*) greater than the total in 1932 and 1931 (*3*) not much worse than the number in 1930.
   b. The Banking Act of 1933 resulted in (*1*) an increase in bank failures (*2*) a great decrease in bank failures (*3*) no change in the number of bank failures.
   c. The year with the fewest bank failures was (*1*) 1945 (*2*) 1934 (*3*) 1920.
   d. The Depression brought about (*1*) more bank failures (*2*) fewer bank failures (*3*) no change in the number of bank failures.
   e. The graph does *not* tell you (*1*) the years in which bank failures occurred (*2*) the number of banks that failed (*3*) the number of banks that stayed in business.

3 The Farm Auction

Farmers were among the Americans who suffered the most in the Great Depression. They had faced severe problems even in the 1920's. The need for expensive farm machinery helped drive them into debt. With their many machines, farmers could produce great quantities of crops. But they often grew more than they could find buyers for. Prices dropped lower and lower, sometimes so low that farmers burned crops for fuel rather than try to sell them. The average farm income fell from $162 per family member in 1929 to $48 in 1932.

Mortgage debts were a special problem. Many farmers were paying off mortgages they had taken on when prices were higher. As farm income fell, farmers were hard pressed to keep up their payments. Some fell behind. Some could not even pay their taxes. Many lost everything.

In our story, Ed and Martha Jones face the loss of their farm. How do their neighbors try to help them?

Wisconsin, 1934

Ed and Martha Jones held hands and waited for the auction to begin. They were not here to bid on anything. They were saying good-bye to their life's work. The Jones farm was to be sold today.

About 50 people gathered to wait for the sheriff. They were neighbors of Ed and Martha. The men stood with clenched fists and grim faces. They understood only too well that what was happening to the Joneses could also happen to them. Some muttered things to their wives and to other men. Others gripped their shotguns and stared at the empty platform.

Suddenly the sheriff appeared. He moved to the platform, glanced briefly at Ed and Martha, and began the auction. "Ladies and gentlemen, it is my sad duty to auction off the Jones farm. I don't enjoy this any more than you—"

"Then why are you doing it?" shouted a farmer. "Why are you helping the vultures pick the bones of our neighbors?"

The sheriff reddened. He looked away from the farmer and said, "I'm only doing my job. Wouldn't you do the same if you were in my place?"

The crowd murmured among themselves. The sheriff was right. He was simply doing his job. It couldn't be helped.

"Wait a minute!" shouted the farmer. "Your job is to uphold law and order. It's not to sell people's belongings just because they've fallen on hard times. These people are not guilty of a crime. They just can't pay their taxes. Is that a reason to take away their home?"

Many in the crowd nodded. They, too, were having a hard time paying their taxes. Their farms might be the next to be sold on the auction block.

The sheriff was beginning to lose patience. "Like it or not," he said, "this auction is going to continue. Now, let's hear some bids. What am I bid for this tractor?"

"One dollar!" shouted the farmer.

The crowd gasped.

The sheriff's face tightened. "Okay, fun is fun. Let's get down to some serious bidding. This tractor is worth a lot of money. What am I bid?"

Again the farmer called out, "One dollar!"

You could hear the rustle of women's dresses. No one else offered a bid. The sheriff looked around anxiously. A well-dressed man at the edge of the crowd began to raise his hand, then thought better of it when he saw the scowls on the faces of the men and women around him.

"Not for one dollar," said the sheriff.

"What am I bid for this tractor?"
"One dollar!"

"For one dollar, unless you can get a higher bid," the farmer answered.

Some of the men shifted restlessly from one foot to the other. A few with shotguns gripped them tightly. It seemed to the sheriff that this crowd had the makings of a violent mob.

The sheriff thought for a moment and said, "All right, the tractor is sold for one dollar. Now let's get on with the other items."

Item for item, the livestock, and the furniture, and the equipment, and the land, and the house were put up for sale. Each was sold to the same farmer for one dollar. There were no other bidders.

At the end, the farmer walked to the platform and took the deed to the farm from the sheriff. He said, "As the new owner of the Jones farm, I have something I want to do. I'm making a gift of my farm and all of its belongings to my good friends, Ed and Martha. Sheriff, I want you to deliver this deed to them."

The sheriff took the deed and walked toward the Joneses. He handed them the deed and quickly elbowed his way through the crowd. Ed and Martha looked at their friends and then at one another and wept.

POSTSCRIPT

Incidents such as this, before and after Roosevelt took office, helped convince him that farmers were indeed desperate. In a few places farmers turned to open violence. A mob in Iowa kidnapped a judge and threatened to hang him for taking away people's farms. Were farmers on the verge of revolution?

New Deal farm programs tried to strike at the roots of the trouble. Federal agencies were set up to lend money to help farmers meet their debts. In 1934 the Farm Bankruptcy Act protected farmers for five years against having their farms sold for failing to meet mortgage payments. The Supreme Court declared this act unconstitutional, but a 1935 act protecting farmers for three years was upheld.

Other New Deal programs sought to reduce farm output and thus raise crop prices (see page 443). The government paid farmers not to cultivate part of their land. It also helped them to plant crops that would enrich and conserve the soil. It guaranteed them a fair price for their goods.

The Rural Electrification Administration (REA) was set up in 1935 to help bring electricity to rural areas. At that time, only one farm in ten was on a power line. Private companies had determined that it wouldn't pay to try to serve widely scattered farms. By making low-interest loans to farmer-owned electrical cooperatives, the REA made such service possible.

Nature dealt a new blow to farmers from 1933 to 1936, when states in and near the Great Plains were struck by a severe drought. High winds blew away millions of tons of dusty topsoil, creating a "Dust Bowl." In five years, 350,000 farmers from Oklahoma and Arkansas (Okies and Arkies) fled to California to escape the drought. In 1935 Congress established the Resettlement Administration to help farmers move from poor to better land.

Some people complained that the various farm programs were pouring millions of dollars "down a rathole." The farm surplus bought by the government and stored in warehouses sometimes rotted. Farmers still produced too much. According to critics, the program helped big farmers at the expense of small farmers. It was ex-pensive, wasteful, and unworkable.

But defenders said the New Deal farm program saved American farmers from disaster. They said it boosted prices, halted erosion, and kept farmers at work producing food that the country needed. Supporters said the program was well worth its cost.

Homework Questions

1. In what ways did the Great Depression add to the problems of farmers?
2. How did the New Deal help farmers keep their land?
3. How did New Deal laws help farmers get a better return for their crops?
4. Why did many farmers leave their land and move to California?
5. Why were New Deal laws criticized by some people?

Understanding the Story

A. Write *T* for each statement that is true and *F* for each statement that is false.
1. Farmers often produced more than they could sell.
2. Many farmers lost all they owned.
3. The New Deal encouraged farmers to grow more.
4. The New Deal farm program was expensive.
5. The sheriff auctioned off the Jones's farm.
6. Neighboring farmers encouraged the sheriff.
7. The Joneses had paid their taxes.
8. The sheriff was afraid that the farmers might become violent.

B. List the numbers of the statements that give results of the farm auction.
1. The sheriff had to accept very low bids.
2. The sheriff was uncomfortable, but he carried out his job.
3. No farmer made an offer for the farm.
4. The other farmers were less afraid of losing their farms.
5. The farm and machines were sold to a real estate dealer.
6. Farm prices no longer went down.
7. The farm was returned to the Joneses.
8. The Depression ended for farmers.

C. Do you think Ed and Martha Jones's neighbors did the right thing? What arguments can you think of in favor of their actions? What arguments can you think of against their actions?

Activities and Inquiries

1. Imagine that you are a reporter interviewing Ed and Martha. You ask them why their farm is being auctioned off. What do they tell you?
2. You speak to the sheriff. What are his feelings about auctioning off the farm?

3. Assume that you are at the auction. Will you bid for anything? Explain.
4. Interview the farmer who is doing the bidding. How does he explain what he is doing?

5. Imagine that it is 1934 and you are living in a city. How do you think New Deal farm programs might affect you? Explain.

4 Huey Long

By 1935 President Roosevelt had been in office two years and his New Deal was taking effect. Economic conditions had improved, but the Great Depression was far from over. Millions still had no jobs. Factory output was less than three fourths of its 1929 levels.

Conservatives, including many business leaders, grew more and more critical of Roosevelt. They argued that the New Deal was bankrupting the government, undermining free enterprise, and tearing the Constitution to shreds.

But not all the criticism came from the right—from conservatives. Some was from the left—from liberals, progressives, and others. Some people argued that the New Deal favored big business at the expense of labor and small business. New Deal programs, they said, helped to create monopolies that drove out competition and forced workers to accept wage cuts and longer hours. Some thought the New Deal had not gone far enough. They called for federal pensions for old people, high taxes on the rich, federal ownership of banks and utilities.

Three critics of the New Deal drew large followings, composed mainly of poor and middle-class people. One critic was Charles E. Coughlin, a Roman Catholic priest who had a weekly radio program heard all over the country. Father Coughlin wanted the government to put more money into circulation and guarantee everyone a "living annual wage." A second critic was Dr. Francis E. Townsend, a California physician. His remedy for the nation's ills was for the government to pay $200 each month to everyone over the age of 60.

Our story concerns a third critic of the New Deal—Huey Long. At first a supporter of President Roosevelt, Long became impatient with what he thought was the timidity of Roosevelt's program. Why did Long break with Roosevelt? What did he offer in place of the New Deal?

Baton Rouge, Louisiana, 1935

Your name is Huey Long, and you want to be President of the United States. With your razzle-dazzle style, you are confident you can make it to the top. President Roosevelt's advisers are afraid you may be right.

Your parents were poor farmers in Louisiana. As a boy, you got up before the sun and worked until after dark. You hated the farm, the work, and most of all the boredom. You knew you were meant for better things, so you left the farm and became a traveling salesman. You could sell anything. Once people heard you speak, they simply couldn't say no. You sold enough to afford to get married and to put yourself through law school.

A man in a hurry, you finished three years of law school in eight months. By the time you were 35 years old, you had been elected governor of Louisiana.

You went a long way in a short time by promising the poor and the forgotten a better life. You built them roads, bridges, hospitals, and schools and gave them free textbooks and relief from high taxes. To do this, you slapped high taxes on the telephone company, power companies, railroads, oil companies, and other businesses.

No man in Louisiana was more popular—or more feared—than you. By fair means and foul you controlled the lawmakers, the state militia, the police, the election commission, even the state supreme court. You were the boss, it seemed, and everyone had to obey or suffer the consequences.

But you wanted more. To see how the federal government worked, you got yourself elected a United States Senator in 1930. It was time to let the rest of America know about Huey Long.

With your showy clothes and breezy manner, you made quite a splash in Washington. You made political points by telling funny stories with a down-home style. Reporters quoted your stories in the newspapers. They made people laugh. You laughed too—at the senators who thought they were smarter than Huey Long. You laughed at the reporters who thought you were just another small-town politician. You laughed at President Roosevelt, who thought he could control you. You know that behind your clown's mask lay a determined mind. You were a match for anyone. You were intelligent, shrewd, cunning, hard, and if necessary, mean. When you wanted something, you got it, and you wanted to be President of the United States.

Some people attacked you, saying you ran Louisiana from Washington. Your enemies said you took bribes from corporations and turned the state police loose on your enemies. According to critics, you allowed racketeers to operate in return for payoffs and prevented state workers from holding jobs without your permission. People called you a dictator.

You fought back, claiming that Louisiana was a true democracy. No governor had ever done more for the people than you had. Roosevelt, you said, was nothing more than a stooge for bankers and corporations. The New Deal was a rotten deal, and Roosevelt would make slaves of the American people. Under his policies, the common people would have to beg the government for handouts while big business did whatever it pleased. You, Huey Long, had a different program, a real "new deal" for the American people.

The people listened as you told them your ideas. You would take money from the rich and give it to the poor. Every family would have a house, a car, and an income of at least $5,000 a year. Education would be free from kindergarten through college. The workday would be cut. Everyone over 60 would receive a pension. Critics said your plan was impossible, but it attracted great attention, and why not? The Depression is still raging, and some people are still desperate.

Millions of people have joined your Share-Our-Wealth clubs. They represent millions of potential votes when you run for President. Now you are someone to be taken seriously. President Roosevelt cannot afford to ignore you. Your enemies aren't laughing any more.

POSTSCRIPT

Huey Long never got to run for President. In September, 1935, he was assassinated in the Louisiana state capitol by a relative of a man he had ruined.

Many were relieved by Long's death, but in Louisiana he was not forgotten. Poor people, black and white, remembered that he had built schools, enlarged the state university, and built hard-top roads. They remembered that he had abolished the poll tax that kept many blacks from voting. It was easy to forget the brutal and dictatorial methods he had used in accomplishing these goals. Singers celebrated Long in popular ballads, and his family remained prominent in Louisiana politics.

Critics like Long, Coughlin, and Townsend had an impact on the nation. President Roosevelt tried to win over their supporters by expanding the New Deal. He did not go so far as many critics wanted him to go, but he went far enough to undercut the critics.

During 1935, Congress passed several laws that expanded the New Deal. The National Labor Relations Act sought to protect the rights of workers to join unions and engage in collective bargaining. The Social Security Act set up a system of old-age pensions paid for by taxes on workers and employers. The act also created a system of unemployment insurance. The Wealth Tax Act raised taxes on rich people and put into effect a graduated tax on corporations. Before this, all corporations had paid at the same percentage rate. Now, bigger corporations paid at a higher rate.

Supporters of Long, Coughlin, and Townsend put up a joint candidate for President in 1936. He got less than 2 percent of the popular vote and no electoral votes. The Republican candidate, Governor Alfred M. Landon of Kansas, won only two states. Roosevelt won a second term by an overwhelming majority.

Homework Questions

1. What criticisms did conservatives make of the New Deal?
2. What other criticisms did people make?
3. Why do you think Huey Long's Share-Our-Wealth clubs won a large following?
4. How did Roosevelt react to critics such as Long?
5. Why do you suppose Roosevelt won such a big victory in 1936?

Understanding the Story

A. Write *F* for each statement that is a fact and *O* for each statement that is an opinion.
   1. Too many people criticized the New Deal programs.
   2. The Great Depression was not over in 1935.
   3. The New Deal programs should have ended the Depression.
   4. Huey Long wanted to be President.
   5. Long kept many of the promises he made to the poor.
   6. Long should have stayed in Louisiana.
   7. Some people called Long a dictator.
   8. Long had no reason to attack Roosevelt's New Deal.

B. List the numbers of the statements that describe Huey Long's thoughts and actions.
   1. I could sell anything.
   2. I was not in a hurry to climb to the top.
   3. I built roads, bridges, hospitals, and schools.
   4. I could not control the state legislature.
   5. I was just another small-town politician.
   6. Louisiana is a true democracy.
   7. Franklin D. Roosevelt is my idol.
   8. The New Deal is a rotten deal.

C. Do you think Huey Long would have made a good President? Why or why not? How do you think the United States might be different today if Long had become President?

Activities and Inquiries

1. Prepare a report card for Huey Long. Grade him in the following areas and justify each grade:

   a. Leadership
   b. Training
   c. Point of view
   d. Political accomplishments
   e. Maturity

2. Imagine that you are a reporter. You ask Huey Long why he thinks he will be a good President. What does he say?
3. Now you ask one of Long's critics how Long would have hurt the United States if he had become President. What does the critic tell you?
4. You are the editor of a Louisiana newspaper. Write Huey Long's obituary (death notice).
5. Next, interview Roosevelt about Long's death. What does he say about Huey Long?

5 Sit-Down Strike!

The New Deal gave a boost to labor unions, which had gone through troubled times since World War I. During the 1920's there were many unsuccessful strikes, and unions competed with one another for members. Union membership declined from more than 5 million in 1920 to about 3.6 million in 1929.

The Great Depression dealt a new blow to labor unions. In a single year more than 12 million workers lost their jobs. Many who continued to work turned their backs on the unions. They were afraid of being fired, and union membership was no protection against unemployment.

Congress gave unions some help in 1932, before Roosevelt became President. It passed the Norris-La Guardia Act, sponsored in part by Representative Fiorello La Guardia of New York (see pages 402–403). This act sought to keep courts from unfairly siding with employers against unions.

The first New Deal measure to aid labor was the National Industrial Recovery Act (NIRA) of 1933. Under it American workers for the first time were guaranteed the right to join a union of their choice. If the workers in a company decided to join a union, the workers had a right to have a union representative meet with management to bargain over such issues as pay, hours, and working conditions. This process is known as *collective bargaining*.

The Supreme Court in 1935 declared the NIRA to be unconstitutional (see page 461). But the National Labor Relations Act of that same year restated the right to collective bargaining and put teeth into the law. Now employers were required to bargain in good faith. Workers were guaranteed the right to choose a union in a secret election. A National Labor Relations Board (NLRB) was created to supervise these elections and enforce the law.

Encouraged by such measures, unions rushed to sign up new members. But a split occurred in the labor movement. The biggest labor organization, the American Federation of Labor (AFL), was made up mostly of *craft unions*—unions organized according to skills. However, some leaders within the AFL favored *industrial unions*—unions that grouped all workers in a single industry, skilled and unskilled. They reasoned that a union that spoke for all auto workers or all steel workers would be more powerful than a union that spoke only for painters within the auto industry or for welders within the steel industry.

After losing a power struggle within the AFL, a number of leaders broke away to form a rival organization of industrial unions. This organization came to be known as the Congress of Industrial Organizations (CIO). The AFL and the CIO staged vigorous drives in many industries, fighting each other as well as management.

One of the growing new industrial unions was the United Automobile Workers (UAW). The UAW met stiff resistance from auto companies, especially General Motors (GM). GM had its own company union, and it insisted that this union already represented the workers. GM executives refused to bargain with the UAW on a company-wide basis.

In the closing days of 1936, members of the UAW began what was called a sit-down strike against GM. Rather than refusing to come to work, they refused to *leave* the work place. Instead of working, they barricaded themselves in the factories and dared management and the police to kick them out. Workers were aware that this tactic was probably illegal. But they hoped that public opinion would be on their side.

In our story, two workers inside a GM plant are discussing the strike. What do they hope to gain by their sit-down strike? How does General Motors respond? Why does the strike turn out as it does?

Flint, Michigan, 1937

STAN. How long have we been at it?

PETE. This is our 44th day.

STAN. We can't go on like this much longer.

PETE. Neither can they.

STAN. I hope you're right. I'm tired of playing cards, standing guard, and sleeping on the floor. As far as I'm concerned, General Motors can have its plant back right now.

PETE. A couple of months ago you didn't feel that way. We were nothing more than hired slaves, you said. General Motors didn't give us enough work in a year to feed our families properly.

STAN. Nothing's changed. I still feel the same. It's just that I'm not sure what we'll get out of all this.

PETE. So far, we've gotten lots of headlines and been pushed around. Soon General Motors will have to bargain with us, and we'll have a strong union.

STAN. I've heard that before. But I'm still waiting for it to happen.

PETE. You and 40,000 workers like you. We're all waiting, and we're going to win. We're never going back to a speeded-up assembly line that doesn't even let a person stop for a drink of water or go to the restroom. We're never going back to jobs that make us old before our time—jobs that leave us so tired that we barely have the strength to crawl into bed. Never!

STAN. I wish I could be so sure.

PETE. Why shouldn't you be? This is a war, and we haven't lost a battle yet. We took over this plant a month and a half ago, and we're still here. General Motors turned off the heat. Then the police stormed the plant, but we beat them back. Next the governor called out the National Guard, and it looked as if we had lost. But the governor didn't want bloodshed, so he held the troops back. When President Roosevelt asked us to leave the plant, we refused. We're here, and we're going to stay.

STAN. I don't know. I don't like defying the courts. I've been worried ever since that judge signed a court order telling us to leave the factories.

PETE. Wasn't that a farce, though? The judge turned out to be a big stockholder in GM.

STAN. It doesn't really matter. Now another judge has threatened to fine the union $15 million if we don't get out. That would really cripple the union.

PETE. I'm not worried. I'm ready to stay here until General Motors bargains with our union.

STAN. Listen, if it has to deal with the union, GM is going to end up paying out lots more money. Why should it agree to that?

PETE. Because this sit-down strike is costing it even more money. While we sit here, no cars are being made and sold. GM's custom-

"We're going to stay until the company recognizes our union and agrees to bargain with us."

ers are buying cars from other manufacturers. Believe me, the GM stockholders aren't going to stand for this much longer. They're going to want this strike settled.

STAN. But General Motors has already tried to settle the strike. Didn't it agree to talk with the union?

PETE. Sure. It said that it would also sit down with the company union. GM wants two unions to represent the workers—the United Auto Workers and the company union. You know we can't stand for that.

STAN. Why not?

PETE. The company union is led by a bunch of puppets. They do everything the company wants and nothing the workers want. As long as there is a company union, our own union will suffer. Workers will be fired for joining our union or for asking others to join. No, the UAW will not end this strike until GM agrees to bargain only with the UAW.

STAN. Pete, I'm trying hard to believe that what you say will happen. But I'm scared it won't.

PETE. It will happen. It's got to happen.

Suddenly, a worker bursts into the factory and shouts, "We've won! We've won! General Motors has agreed to recognize the United Auto Workers as the only bargaining agent for the workers. The strike is over!"

POSTSCRIPT

Pressure from public officials, including the governor of Michigan, helped persuade General Motors to give in. Sit-down strikes spread to other industries. The turmoil in labor-management relations continued for several years.

A number of large companies, including United States Steel, decided it was better to deal with the new industrial unions than to fight them and suffer the consequences. Other companies resisted, and in many cases strikes ended in failure. Also, in 1939 the Supreme Court ruled that sit-down strikes were illegal.

Nonetheless, labor unions grew in strength, and by 1941 union membership had reached 9.5 million. Much later, in 1955, the AFL and the CIO merged to form a giant union called the AFL-CIO.

Homework Questions

1. How were labor unions affected by the Great Depression?
2. In what ways did New Deal laws help the unions?
3. How did the American Federation of Labor (AFL) differ from the Congress of Industrial Organizations (CIO)?
4. Why did the workers in the story stage a sit-down strike?
5. Why was Pete opposed to a company union?

Understanding the Story

A. Write *F* for each statement that is a fact and *O* for each statement that is an opinion.
1. Labor unions lost members during the 1920's.
2. Unions competed with each other for members.
3. The NIRA should not have been declared unconstitutional.
4. The CIO organized skilled and unskilled workers.
5. Sit-down strikes are unfair to factory owners.
6. Stan and Pete were part of a sit-down strike.
7. The sit-down strikers were very brave.
8. The UAW won a victory in the sit-down strike in the story.

B. Write *P* for each statement that Pete made or might have made and *S* for each statement that Stan made or might have made.
1. General Motors can have its plant back right now.

2. You said we were hired slaves.
3. We're going to win.
4. I don't like defying the courts.
5. The stockholders want this strike settled.
6. The company union is led by puppets.
7. GM won't deal with the union because it will cost too much.
8. I'm trying hard to believe what you say.

C. Imagine that you are the governor of Michigan in 1937. What arguments can you think of for having the National Guard evict the strikers? What arguments can you think of for holding the Guard back? What would you have done?

Activities and Inquiries

1. Visit your local library to find books about labor unions. Prepare a report on any other sit-down strike.
2. Check your local newspaper for stories about strikes. Prepare a report on any recent one.
3. Interview a union member and a person in the management side of a business. Ask each to give the good and bad points of dealing with unions.
4. Imagine that you are a member of the UAW strike committee. What are your plans for a successful sit-down strike?
5. Imagine that you are a factory owner in 1937. Your workers are planning to join a union. What will you do about it?

6 The Growth of the Constitution: Packing the Court

New Deal programs faced rough going in the courts. Some were thrown out by the Supreme Court. The Court said that these programs went against the Constitution.

The National Industrial Recovery Act (NIRA) was declared unconstitutional in 1935. In a unanimous decision in the Schechter Poultry Case, the Court said Congress had violated the Constitution in a number of ways. It had given too much power to the executive branch—power to make laws, in effect, by setting rules for industry. Lawmaking powers could be used only by Congress. Also, the Court said Congress had exceeded its own powers in another way. It had tried to regulate businesses that operated wholly within one state. Under Article I, Section 8, of the Constitution, only interstate commerce (business between states) can be regulated by Congress.

In 1936, a six-to-three majority of the Court ruled that the Agricultural Adjustment Act was also unconstitutional. The Court said Congress had gone beyond its rightful power of taxation (Article I, Section 8). Also, Congress had invaded rights of the states that are guaranteed by the 10th Amendment. This case was called *U.S. v. Butler*.

In 1936 the Court gave approval to part of the New Deal, the Tennessee Valley Authority (TVA). But President Roosevelt and his supporters were unhappy. They said the justices were "nine old men" who were out of tune with the will of the people. Roosevelt wanted to do something about the judicial branch—the one branch of government that stood in the way of New Deal laws.

Late in 1936, Roosevelt thought he saw his chance to act. Voters had elected him to a second term by a wide margin. Roosevelt interpreted the Democrats' big victory as a sign of great public support for the New Deal.

How did Roosevelt propose to deal with the Supreme Court? Was he successful?

Washington, D.C., December, 1936

President Roosevelt turned to his attorney general, Homer Cummings. "Homer, that Court means to destroy us. We must do something."

Cummings nodded. "Nearly 28 million people voted for you in the last election. They knew that a vote for you was a vote for the New Deal. If the New Deal is good enough for all those voters, why isn't it good enough for the nine old men on the Supreme Court?"

"I wish I knew."

"It does seem unfair, Mr. President. You have a majority in Congress passing laws the country desperately needs. Yet five men, a simple majority of the nine justices, have the power to declare these laws unconstitutional."

"I'm afraid the justices are living in another age, Homer. They think we're still in the horse-and-buggy era, and they read the Constitution as if nothing had changed since George Washington's day. But now we live in an age of automobiles and airplanes, with giant businesses that have dealings all over the country. Our nation's economy has grown vastly more complex. Only the federal government has the scope and the power to take effective action."

"Perhaps we need to write a new constitution to take the new conditions into account."

"No, Homer, our present Constitution can still do the job. The founders provided room for growth. They made the Constitution a statement of broad principles, not a list of detailed rules. Those principles are just as true today as they ever were. And I believe our New Deal is fully in line with constitutional principles. What we need are Supreme Court justices who can keep our new needs in mind as they read the Constitution."

"But how can we get any new justices? Not one justice has retired since you took office four years ago. You can't appoint your own men until some of the old justices retire."

"Ah, but perhaps I can," the President answered.

Roosevelt had thought the problem over carefully. He knew that Article II, Section 2, of the Constitution gave the President the power to appoint justices to the Supreme Court with the approval of a majority of the Senate. Under Article I, Section 8, Congress had the power to determine the size of the Court. The President knew that the number of justices had been changed by Congress many times: from six in 1789 to five in 1801, seven in 1807, nine in 1837, ten in 1863, seven in 1866, and nine in 1869. Since then the number had not changed. But, obviously, changes could be made in the make-up of the Court.

"Why don't we ask Congress to enlarge the size of the Court?" Roosevelt asked Cummings. "See if you can't come up with a plan that Congress will pass."

February, 1937

Quickly and in secret, Roosevelt and Cummings worked on a plan. Early in February, 1937, Roosevelt described the plan to Congress. The President announced that he was asking Congress to pass a law to permit him to add a new justice to the Supreme Court for every member over the age of 70 who did not retire. Since six of the nine justices were over 70, the membership of the Court might rise to 15.

The President said that the Supreme Court had fallen behind in its work and needed extra help, which "younger blood" could provide. Privately, everyone knew why Roosevelt wanted this law: to get a more friendly court. Adding justices who supported New Deal ideas would keep the Court from declaring Roosevelt's laws unconstitutional.

Congress reacted sharply.

Senator Burton K. Wheeler of Montana turned to Senator William Borah of Idaho and said, "He'll never get away with this."

Borah nodded. "I agree, but I understand why he wants the law passed."

"It doesn't matter why he wants it," snapped Wheeler. "The law is a bad one. If Roosevelt wins, all Americans will lose."

"Why?" asked Borah.

"Because the Court is a check against the President and the Congress. Right or wrong, the Supreme Court is the Constitution's watchdog. If the President's bill passes, the watchdog will die."

Wheeler, Borah, and many other members of Congress spoke out against the President's bill. They were joined by many newspapers and by groups of private citizens. All of these critics accused the President of trying to pack the Supreme Court with his own followers. They said that Roosevelt was trying to destroy the system of checks and balances. Some even said that the President was preparing to become a dictator.

These charges shocked Roosevelt. He never dreamed that the reaction to his plan would be so strong. He watched gloomily as Congress—even though it was controlled by Democrats—refused to pass the bill.

POSTSCRIPT

Roosevelt lost the "battle," but he did not lose the "war." The pressure of the Supreme Court fight had some effect on the justices. During the debate over the bill, the Court voted to uphold several New Deal laws. Over the next few years, deaths and resignations gave Roosevelt the opportunity to make nine appointments to the Court.

But while Roosevelt began to have better luck with the Supreme Court, he had worse luck with Congress. Economic conditions took a turn for the worse in 1937, and in congressional elections the next year, voters defeated many supporters of the New Deal. No longer could Roosevelt count on heavy support in Congress. The New Deal was at an end.

The New Deal had brought great and lasting changes to American life. It had greatly enlarged the size of the federal government and set the nation on a new course. But it had not achieved its main goal, ending the Great Depression. In 1940, when Roosevelt was re-elected to an unprecedented third term, 7.6 million people were unemployed. One worker in seven still had no job.

Homework Questions

1. What objections did the Supreme Court make to some New Deal laws?
2. Why did President Roosevelt think the New Deal was constitutional? Explain.
3. How did President Roosevelt try to overcome the Supreme Court's resistance to the New Deal?
4. Why did Congress object to Roosevelt's plan for adding new justices to the Court?
5. How did Roosevelt lose the Supreme Court "battle" but win the "war"?

Understanding the Story

A. Write *T* for each statement that is true, *F* for each statement that is false, and *N* for each statement that is not mentioned in this chapter.
1. In 1937 the Supreme Court upheld the National Labor Relations Act.
2. Roosevelt was re-elected in 1936.
3. The Republicans controlled Congress after the election of 1936.
4. President Roosevelt appointed Hugo Black to the Supreme Court.
5. Roosevelt wanted to add up to six justices to the Supreme Court.
6. The Supreme Court is called the Constitution's watchdog.
7. Most members of Congress supported Roosevelt's Supreme Court proposal.
8. Justice George Sutherland resigned from the Supreme Court in 1938.

B. Complete each of the following sentences by filling in the missing word or words.
1. In 1935 and 1936, important New Deal laws were declared _____.
2. Roosevelt proposed to increase the number of justices to a maximum of _____.
3. Roosevelt said the Court needed extra _____.
4. Senator Wheeler thought the proposed law was _____.
5. He said that if the bill passed, the _____ would die.
6. Critics accused Roosevelt of destroying the system of _____.
7. Some people said Roosevelt was preparing to become a _____.
8. Roosevelt's bill was _____, but he made many appointments to the Court because of _____ and _____.

C. Suppose that Congress had agreed to enlarge the Supreme Court as President Roosevelt suggested. Do you think this would have been good or bad for the country? Why?

Activities and Inquiries

1. Imagine you are Franklin Roosevelt. You write a letter urging Congress to pass your bill to enlarge the Supreme Court. What do you say?
2. Imagine you are Justice George Sutherland (see Chapter 8 in Unit Eleven). You write a letter telling a friend why you oppose Roosevelt's plan. What do you say?
3. Visit your local library. Prepare a report on a New Deal law that was declared unconstitutional. Tell what the law was supposed to accomplish. Why did the majority of the Court find the law unconstitutional? Do you think the Court did the right thing? Why or why not?
4. If there was a minority decision, read it and then write a summary. Do you agree or disagree with it? Would this minority opinion be acceptable to President Roosevelt? Explain.

Eleanor Roosevelt

MR. MILLER. All right, Hans. This is your big day.

HANS. I'm going to talk about Eleanor Roosevelt, the wife of President Franklin Roosevelt. Her ancestors were Dutch. The character of Eleanor Roosevelt appealed to me. Besides, she's the most unusual First Lady in American history.

ROSA. What makes Eleanor Roosevelt so different?

HANS. She was the first President's wife to have an active political career of her own.

CASIMIR. You mean she sought election to public office.

HANS. No, not that. But she took stands on controversial issues and supported lots of social causes.

JUAN. Why is that such a big deal?

HANS. Well, the President is always in the spotlight. His wife, the First Lady, helps him—but usually quietly. She's a charming hostess who greets people and chooses the White House menus and perhaps takes part in a charity drive now and then. You know she's there, but you can't always see her.

CARLA. But that wasn't the life for Eleanor. She wasn't going to sit in her husband's shadow, right?

HANS. Right. She lived her own life, not her husband's. She felt that the worst thing in the world was to be idle. She was an outspoken defender of the rights of women, blacks, and young people. Eleanor Roosevelt never wasted a moment. She even wrote a daily newspaper column.

RICARDO. She must have annoyed the President.

HANS. Sometimes, but not very often. She was careful not to argue with him in public about how to run the country. She defended the New Deal with vigor. She traveled about 50,000 miles each year in this country and overseas and reported back to the President. She became his eyes and ears.

ROBERT. She must have loved to travel.

HANS. That wasn't why she did it. The President asked her to find out information for him. She was terribly concerned about the sufferings of the poor. One day she might pop in unannounced at a federal housing project, ring doorbells, and speak to the surprised residents. Another day, you might find her visiting a coal mine or speaking out on behalf of black people's rights.

TOM. She must have stirred up a lot of controversy.

HANS. Oh, she did. A lot of people despised her. They called her names like do-gooder, meddler, and worse.

HEINRICH. Sounds to me as if she was minding everyone's business but her own.

HANS. You miss the whole point, Heinrich. The life of the nation *was* Eleanor Roosevelt's business. She devoted her life, her career, to helping others.

SAM. How did she get started on this active life?

HANS. Well, she married Franklin Roosevelt when she was 20 years old and he was in law school. After he got into politics, she did too—I guess it just seemed natural. She really plunged into things after his attack of polio in 1921. She was a leader of women's activities for the Democratic Party and took part in political campaigns. Why, without her help FDR might never have been elected President.

JUAN. You mean she didn't wait until he was in the White House to start being a public figure?

HANS. Oh, no. But she really became well known once she was First Lady. Then, after Roosevelt died in 1945, she was appointed a United States delegate to the United Nations and served for several years. She was always speaking out on behalf of world peace and human rights.

JOSEPHINE. She sounds like a remarkable woman.

HANS. You said it, Josephine. Even if she hadn't married a man destined for fame, she still would have made her mark. Harry Truman, Roosevelt's successor as President, was right when he called Eleanor Roosevelt the "First Lady of the World."

MR. MILLER'S OFFICE

"Mr. Miller, I never realized how serious the Great Depression was. How did people have the courage to live through it?"

"People didn't really have a choice, Jack. They had to get up every morning and face the day, whatever its hardships."

"Well, it sounds as if Franklin Roosevelt's New Deal helped ease those hardships."

"Most people would agree with that, Jack. One of Roosevelt's three R's was relief, and the New Deal did provide that. It put an end to the worst of the suffering by providing food for the hungry and shelter for the homeless."

"Another R was reform, wasn't it, Mr. Miller? I'd say the New Deal brought about a number of reforms. It made it harder for dishonest people to manipulate the stock market. And it set up some major new government programs—help for farmers, Social Security, unemployment insurance, TVA—"

"Don't forget the boost the New Deal gave to labor unions, Jack. The federal government stepped in to insure the right of collective bargaining."

"Yes, Mr. Miller. But reforms like this were controversial. Lots of people opposed them because they made the federal government bigger than ever. Some people said Roosevelt was destroying the American way of life."

"That's what some people said, all right. But Roosevelt saw things differently. He insisted he was saving capitalism and democracy by bringing about needed reforms. And millions of voters seem to have agreed with him."

"What was the third R, then, Mr. Miller?"

"It was recovery, and Roosevelt had more trouble with that one. Oh, business picked up during the New Deal, all right, but it never really got healthy again. The Depression was still around in 1941 when the United States suddenly faced a new challenge."

"I know what that was, Mr. Miller—World War II."

"Right, Jack. Let's look at the next unit to see how we got into— and out of—that war."

From World War II to the 1950's

"World War II must have been exciting, Mr. Miller."

"More destructive than exciting, Jack. Wars result in new weapons that kill more effectively. No war brought forth a more awesome weapon than World War II."

"You mean the atomic bomb?"

"Yes," replied Mr. Miller, "and everything that goes along with nuclear power—both good and evil."

"Then future wars would all be nuclear wars?" asked Jack.

"Not necessarily. In this unit we'll have a more or less traditional war—World War II—and something called the 'Cold War.' In the Cold War, military force did not usually come into actual use."

"I thought that a war had to include shooting—otherwise it wouldn't be a real war," said Jack.

"The Cold War was just as intense as a shooting war—and in the early 1950's it did erupt into a shooting war, in Korea. But for most of the time, the Cold War was a war of nerves. It was sort of a face-off between two social systems—our system of democracy and capitalism and the Soviet Union's system of one-party rule and communism."

"Then this unit mainly points up Americans' concern with communism."

"The nation was concerned about other things, too," said Mr. Miller. "It continued, or renewed, the debate over the meaning of equal rights under the law. In this period black Americans made major gains in the struggle for equality and full civil rights."

"Sounds more interesting than I thought," said Jack.

"Fine, then let's move on into World War II and the 1950's."

1 World War Comes Again

The world of the 1930's was a dangerous place. The Great Depression, worldwide in scope, was causing unemployment and hunger in many nations. War clouds loomed over Europe, Africa, and Asia.

In Europe, the peace settlement that followed World War I was unraveling. Two nations, Germany and Italy, seemed especially restless and eager to expand.

Adolf Hitler came to power in Germany in 1933, vowing to revive German strength and erase the "shame" of the Treaty of Versailles. Hitler called for a Greater Germany that would include German-speaking people in nearby countries such as Austria, Czechoslovakia, and Poland.

Backed by German business leaders and by his own Nazi Party, Hitler created a dictatorship. In his speeches, Hitler promised jobs, housing, new roads, cars, law and order, and prosperity for all Germans. At the same time, he preached hatred for democracy and especially for Jews, whom he blamed for most of Germany's troubles. A Nazi army of brown-shirted brawlers attacked Jews and anyone who spoke out against the party.

Italy too was a dictatorship seeking to expand. Its ruler, Benito Mussolini, had come to power in 1922 with the backing of armed, black-shirted bands organized by his Fascist Party. Italian

business leaders supported him in an attempt to stop the spread of socialism and communism.

Although Italy had been on the winning side in World War I, it had not received the territories it wanted. Many Italians were unhappy with the peace settlement. Now Mussolini had his eyes on Ethiopia, next door to Italy's African colony of Eritrea. Ruled by its own Christian king, Ethiopia was an independent country.

On the other side of the world, the island nation of Japan was also growing restless. Lacking natural resources of its own, Japan needed iron, coal, and oil from other places. Japan got some supplies from its East Asian colony of Korea. But it depended heavily on foreign trade for most raw materials. The Great Depression caused many nations to erect tariff barriers, and this had a devastating effect on Japanese trade.

The restless nations began grabbing new territory in the 1930's. Japan took Manchuria from China in 1931. Four years later Italy invaded Ethiopia. In 1937 new fighting broke out in China, developing into a major war as Japan seized more and more territory. Hitler marched his troops into Austria in 1938 and merged that country with Germany. By early 1939 he had also taken over Czechoslovakia. The two leading powers of Europe, Britain and France, did not think their forces were strong enough to stop Hitler's armies. The League of Nations looked on helplessly.

The American public, disappointed with the outcome of World War I, seemed eager to keep the United States out of any new war. Congress passed a series of neutrality laws to block the sale of arms and the lending of money to countries at war. The goal of these laws was to avoid the situation that developed in World War I. Then the U.S. had become so closely tied to one side that it was drawn into the fighting. To the dismay of many, however, the neutrality laws tended to hurt the better-armed attacking nations far less than they hurt the victim nations.

On September 1, 1939, Nazi Germany attacked Poland. This time Britain and France did not stay on the sidelines. They had promised to stand by Poland, and they did, by declaring war on Germany. World War II had begun.

While the United States continued to try to stay out of the war, it backed away from neutrality and began selling arms to Britain and France. But arms were not enough. In June, 1940, Italy joined the war on Germany's side, and German troops conquered France. German bombs began to rain down on British cities.

Seriously worried now, Congress approved a new type of aid to Britain in March, 1941. This was called "Lend-Lease." The U.S. "lent" war materials to Britain, which promised to pay them back after the war. Ships carrying the materials to Britain were escorted by U.S. warships.

In June, 1941, Germany attacked the Soviet Union, and the U.S. began sending Lend-Lease aid to the Communist government of Soviet ruler Joseph Stalin. Undeclared war developed between Germany and the U.S., as each side tried to sink the other's ships. All the while, however, many Americans hoped it would be possible for the United States to avoid full involvement in the war.

In Asia, meanwhile, Japan faced some fateful decisions. The war in China had given military leaders a growing voice in the Japanese government. Control was slipping out of the hands of civilian leaders such as Prince Fumimaro Konoye, the prime minister. Descuil the

In our story, Japanese leaders debate their next moves. The United States, hoping to prevent Japan from taking over all of China, had been sending money and supplies to the Chinese government. At the same time, the U.S. was selling such war materials as scrap iron and aviation gasoline to Japan. By 1940, the U.S. was considering a cutoff in trade with Japan. What options (choices) did the Japanese and the U.S. governments have? What decisions did they make, and what were the results?

Tokyo, Japan, June, 1940

General Hideki Tojo, the minister of war, turned to Prince Konoye, the prime minister. Tojo said, "Now that France and the Netherlands have fallen to Germany, we must move into French Indochina. If we don't do this, others will."

Konoye protested. "The United States will not stand for such an action. It is very angry over our war with China. It has done much to hurt us there. If we move against Indochina, the Americans might send their fleet to attack us."

Tojo flared, "We cannot show weakness at a time like this. The French and Dutch are not strong enough to hold onto their Asian colonies. It is our duty to take them. We will use them to help make Japan the great power it is destined to become."

Konoye bowed his head and said nothing.

In July, 1940, the United States restricted the sale of petroleum products and scrap metal to Japan. U.S. leaders hoped that this would force the Japanese to see that they were too weak to fight a major war.

September, 1940

Prince Konoye looked at Tojo and said, "I told you the Americans would punish us."

Tojo answered, "We too can take strong steps. Germany and Italy have asked us to sign a military agreement with them. They promise to come to our aid if the United States goes to war against us. In return, we would help Germany and Italy if the United States declares war on them. I think we should sign the treaty."

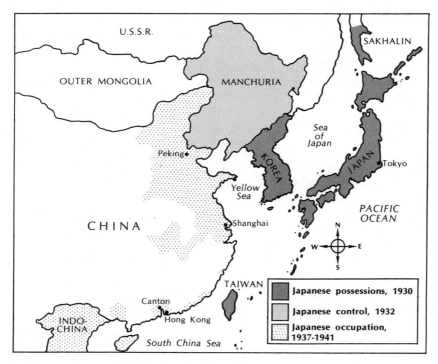

Japanese Expansion in East Asia, 1930–1941

"But," protested Konoye, "wouldn't such a move push us closer to war with the United States?"

"I don't think so," said Tojo. "I think it will convince the United States to stay out of other nations' wars."

On September 27, 1940, Japan signed the treaty with Germany and Italy, thus joining what were called the Axis Powers. One day earlier the United States announced that it would put a total embargo on sales of scrap metal to Japan.

Japan moved troops into French Indochina. In July, 1941, Roosevelt put a hold on Japanese economic interests in the United States. The British and Dutch did the same in territories they controlled, including the oil-rich Dutch East Indies.

Now Japan's supplies of oil were almost entirely cut off. Japanese leaders saw two possible choices. They could go to war and seize the resources they needed. Or they could try to work out some sort of compromise with the United States and its friends.

Prince Konoye and other civilian leaders sought a compromise that would allow Japan to take over China. In September, 1941, Konoye offered to meet with Roosevelt to discuss their differences. Roosevelt refused. He felt that such a meeting would only convince the Japanese that Americans wanted peace at any price. This, he thought, would make the Japanese behave even more boldly in Asia.

October, 1941

General Tojo smiled and said, "I see your American friends have turned their backs on you. Their President has refused to meet with you. What more proof do you need that the Americans hold us in contempt?"

"I had no choice but to try to reason with them," said Prince Konoye.

"As you know, there is another way—one that we have long been considering. We can take our foes by surprise. We can attack the American fleet in the Pacific. Before they know what has happened to them, we can seize the Dutch oil fields, the British colonies, and the American territory of the Philippines. This will bring our foes to their knees and make them agree to our peace terms."

"Your idea is suicide," said Konoye. "The Americans are divided over the question of war. Your plan will unify them and encourage them to fight us to the death. I will never agree to such a plan."

Tojo became angry. "Japan will not become an American lap dog. We must put the United States in its place. We need a courageous person to lead us. I am afraid that you are not that person."

Konoye asked, "Are you that person?"

Tojo smiled and did not answer.

On October 16, 1941, Konoye was forced out of office. Tojo replaced him as prime minister.

Now, while continuing negotiations with U.S. diplomats, the Japanese made final plans for an attack on the American fleet. That fleet was based at Pearl Harbor in Hawaii. On November 25, 1941, a Japanese aircraft-carrier task force secretly began to move closer to Hawaii. The United States had broken a Japanese code and knew that Japan was preparing an attack. But it did not know when or where the attack would take place. Roosevelt sent a note to Emperor Hirohito of Japan, asking him to help avoid war between the two countries. Japanese army officials kept the note from the emperor.

Early Sunday morning, December 7, 1941, a large group of Japanese planes attacked the U.S. fleet at Pearl Harbor. The Japanese sank 19 ships, destroyed more than 150 planes, and killed 2,335 U.S. soldiers and sailors.

The next day, Congress declared war on Japan. Three days later, Germany and Italy declared war on the United States. Once again, Americans found themselves in a world war they had hoped to avoid. For four long years, the nation concentrated on winning World War II.

Provide 3 reasons why Gen. Tojo wanted Japan to put the U.S. in its place.

POSTSCRIPT

The war brought great changes to the United States. Industries quickly tooled up to turn out materials of war, and suddenly the economy was booming. The Great Depression came to an end at last.

It took time, however, to switch from a peacetime to a wartime economy. Food, clothing, and arms had to be supplied not only to American fighting forces but to the troops of Allied nations as well. The effort succeeded beyond all expectations. By 1945, the United States was turning out massive quantities of war materials.

In the first months of the war, Japan took over British and Dutch colonies in East Asia and evicted U.S. forces from the Philippines. This cut the United States off from much of its normal supply of rubber, tin, and quinine (an anti-malaria drug). Substitutes had to be found, and were. Before long, for example, U.S. factories were making large quantities of synthetic (artificial) rubber from petroleum.

A War Production Board (WPB) was set up to supervise the output of war materials. It decided which items must come first. The WPB ordered a halt to all nonessential building to save materials for the war effort. An Office of Price Administration (OPA) tried to keep rents and prices from climbing too high. Strikes were considered a threat to the war effort and were restricted by the Smith-Connally Antistrike Act, passed over President Roosevelt's veto in 1943.

Farm production increased, and farm income more than doubled. Unemployment disappeared, and the CCC and WPA were disbanded. Shortages of many goods on the home front made rationing necessary. Coupons were issued to limit the amount of butter, meat, gasoline, and certain types of clothing a person could buy.

Some 16 million Americans entered the armed forces, including 216,000 women in noncombat units. The total spending of government during the war came to $330 billion, which was 15 times as much as in World War I.

World War II was not as idealistic a crusade as World War I, and there was less interference with people who spoke out against the war. But one group of people suffered special penalties. This group was composed of some 110,000 people of Japanese ancestry who lived along the West Coast. About one third of them were Japanese

citizens, and two thirds were American citizens.

For many years, Japanese immigrants had faced harsh treatment from whites. After the attack on Pearl Harbor, some Americans feared that such people might give help to Japan, especially if Japan invaded the West Coast. The federal government ordered people of Japanese ancestry living along the coast to leave their homes and businesses. They were moved to internment camps, where many of them were housed for most of the war. Eventually, some Japanese-Americans were allowed to join the U.S. armed forces and take part in the war.

Homework Questions

1. What did Adolf Hitler promise the German people?
2. How did Benito Mussolini rise to power in Italy?
3. How was Japan affected by the Great Depression of the 1930's?
4. What happened to Japanese-Americans during World War II?
5. How did Americans cope with World War II on the home front?

Understanding the Story

A. List the numbers of the statements that are true.
1. Germany and Italy were dictatorships in the 1930's.
2. Civilian leaders held firm control of Japan's government in the late 1930's.
3. The United States passed neutrality laws.
4. Lend-Lease helped Britain and the Soviet Union.

5. Japan had enough iron and oil of its own.
6. Prince Fumimaro Konoye tried to reach a compromise with the United States.
7. The United States cut off sales of scrap metal to Japan.
8. Japan became an ally of France and Britain in the 1940's.

B. Number the following events in the order in which they took place.
1. Germany attacked Poland.
2. Congress passed the Lend-Lease Act.
3. Japan took over Manchuria.
4. Britain and France declared war on Germany.
5. The U.S. restricted sales of petroleum products and scrap metal to Japan.
6. Japan attacked Pearl Harbor.
7. Germany conquered France.
8. Major war began between Japan and China.

C. President Roosevelt refused to meet with Prince Konoye late in 1941. Do you think Roosevelt did the right thing? Why or why not?

Activities and Inquiries

1. Study the map on page 472. Then choose the term or phrase that best completes each statement.
   a. An area in Japan's possession in 1930 was (1) Hong Kong (2) Korea (3) Outer Mongolia.
   b. A country in Asia that does not touch Manchuria is (1) Japan (2) Korea (3) the U.S.S.R.
   c. North of Manchuria is (1) Outer Mongolia (2) the U.S.S.R. (3) Korea.
   d. South of Peking is (1) Manchuria (2) Outer Mongolia (3) Hong Kong.
   e. An area controlled by Japan in 1932 was (1) Indochina (2) Hong Kong (3) Manchuria.
2. Imagine that you are writing a book about the Japanese attack on Pearl Harbor. Prepare the table of contents.
3. It is 1941. Interview General Tojo. What does he tell you about his feelings toward the United States? What does he plan to do?
4. Now interview Prince Konoye. What does he think of Tojo and his plans?

2 The Atomic Bomb

The United States faced war in two regions—in Europe and the Mediterranean and in the Pacific and East Asia. In spite of pressure for revenge against Japan for Pearl Harbor, U.S. leaders agreed that Hitler's Germany must be defeated first. Thus the main U.S. forces were concentrated on the European war. But enough ships and planes were sent to the Pacific to keep the Japanese off balance and prevent them from winning.

The United States became an ally of Great Britain, the Soviet Union, and other nations. At first the U.S. had a hard time supplying these Allies. German U-boats (submarines) controlled the Atlantic and sank many ships. Not until the spring of 1943 did the Allies overcome Hitler's "wolf packs of the sea" and win the Battle of the Atlantic.

There were many fronts, or zones of battle, in the European war. On the eastern front, German troops were invading the Soviet Union. On the southern front, Germans and Italians were advancing across North Africa toward Egypt and the vital Suez Canal.

In October, 1942, British troops led by General Bernard Montgomery stopped German Field Marshal Erwin Rommel and drove his forces back from Egypt. American and other Allied troops pushed across North Africa from Morocco. Thus Rommel came under attack from two sides. By May, 1943, Axis forces had retreated from North Africa to Europe. Germans were retreating on the eastern front as well because Soviet forces had turned them back at Stalingrad.

From the beginning, Soviet troops had faced the heaviest German attacks. Josef Stalin, the Soviet dictator, wanted the Allies to start a major second front in western Europe to take some of the pressure off his troops. The U.S. high command agreed with Stalin that a large Allied force should cross the English Channel to attack the Germans in France. But the attack was put off, first because of the fighting in North Africa, then to allow an invasion of Italy.

From North Africa, British and American forces invaded the Italian island of Sicily in the Mediterranean. Sicily fell in August, 1943. Next Allied troops attacked the Italian mainland. Although Mussolini fell from power and Italian leaders sought peace, German troops fought doggedly in Italy. The Allied invasion made very slow progress. Finally, the Italian capital of Rome fell on June 4, 1944.

Two days later the long-awaited invasion of France began. On D-Day, the sixth of June, Allied troops under the direction of U.S. General Dwight D. Eisenhower landed on the beaches of Normandy in northwest France. Against fierce German resistance, the Allies pushed forward—Americans and British from the west, Soviets from the east. Eleven months later, on May 7, 1945, the Germans surrendered.

Horrified Allied soldiers discovered concentration camps in which the Nazis had put to death some six million Jews. (Some four million others—Poles, Slavs, Russians, Gypsies—had also been killed.) The Germans had been carrying out what Hitler called his "final solution" to "the Jewish problem." This destruction of Jews has come to be called the Holocaust.

Meanwhile, the Allies had made slow gains in the Pacific war after a string of early setbacks. They pushed the Japanese back, one island at a time. Tiny specks of land like Guadalcanal, the Solomon Islands, and the Gilberts became the scenes of bloody battles. U.S. General Douglas MacArthur, who had withdrawn from the Philippines in 1942, returned at the head of invading Allied forces in October, 1944. In the Battle of Leyte Gulf, the biggest naval engagement of the war, much of Japan's seapower was destroyed. By early 1945 MacArthur and his troops had recaptured the Philippines.

From newly built bases in the Mariana Islands, U.S. B-29's began steady bombing attacks on the Japanese mainland in November, 1944. Within months, much of Tokyo, Japan's capital, had been destroyed by fire bombs. But Japan refused to admit defeat.

As our story opens, the European war is almost over. United States leaders are beginning to turn greater attention to the Pacific war. A new man has replaced President Roosevelt, who died on April 12, 1945. That man is Harry Truman, elected Vice President when Roosevelt won a fourth term in 1944. The job of bringing the war to a close fell on President Truman's shoulders.

Advisers told Truman that an invasion of Japan might cost more than one million American lives. They also told him of a deadly new weapon that could end the war quickly and thus save American lives. What was this weapon? How did it work? How would it change the course of world events?

Washington, D.C., April, 1945

"Come in, gentlemen," said President Truman to Secretary of War Henry Stimson and General Leslie Groves.

The men had come to see the new President for a special reason: to tell him about a top-secret experiment.

Stimson spoke first. "Mr. President, a team of experts has been working to develop a new device that may be the most terrible weapon ever known in human history."

General Groves added, "Since the beginning of the war, the best scientific minds in the world have worked on this project. It has cost more than $2 billion."

"Now this weapon is almost ready," said Stimson.

"What exactly is it?" asked President Truman.

Stimson answered, "It is an atomic bomb. It works on a simple principle—when an atom is split, energy is released. Scientists say that the splitting of many uranium atoms in a chain reaction will create an extremely powerful explosion. Such an explosion could destroy an entire city in a flash. A single atomic bomb will cause as much destruction as hundreds of conventional bombs."

"Has this bomb been tested?" Truman asked.

"No," replied Stimson, "and until it is tested, we cannot be sure it will really work. We propose to test it in the New Mexico desert. The first bomb will be ready in a few months, and two more bombs should be available soon after."

"This atomic bomb may be just what we need to bring the war with Japan to a rapid end!" exclaimed Truman.

"It may very well be, Mr. President," Stimson said. "If it works, it will also greatly affect our dealings with the Soviet Union."

Truman looked thoughtful. The Soviet Union had been much on his mind. As the war in Europe neared an end, the Allies seemed to be splitting up. U.S. and British leaders deeply distrusted the Soviet Union, and Soviet leaders distrusted the Western powers. Each side had its own ideas about the way postwar Europe should look, and the ideas were very different. Some sort of diplomatic showdown seemed likely. A powerful weapon like the atomic bomb would give the United States a strong bargaining position.

"This matter is too serious to be dealt with in a haphazard way," said Truman. "I will appoint a committee to consider the consequences of our having this new bomb."

The committee's job was not to decide whether to use the bomb against Japan. It was generally assumed that the bomb would be used. The committee's job was to decide *how* the bomb should be used.

Committee members thought the bomb should be used to shock Japan into surrender. They recommended that the bomb be dropped without warning on a big city that contained war industries. Some scientists thought this would kill too many Japanese civilians. They suggested that the bomb be dropped in a part of Japan where few people lived. The committee rejected this idea. With so few atomic bombs available, the committee felt that only great destruction could be counted on to persuade the Japanese that further fighting was useless. In everyone's mind was the fear that if the war dragged on, more U.S. soldiers would die.

There was also another consideration. If Japan surrendered quickly, the war might end before the Soviet Union declared war on Japan. So far, the Soviet Union had been involved only in the European war. But it had promised to go to war against Japan as soon as possible after Germany's defeat. At one time, U.S. leaders wanted Soviet help to defeat Japan. Now they were no longer sure they needed it. In fact, they worried that Soviet aid might allow the Soviets to gain a voice in any East Asian peace settlement.

President Truman postponed a meeting with Soviet leader Stalin. He ordered plans for testing the atomic bomb to go ahead.

It was 5:25 A.M., on July 16, 1945, in the desert near Alamogordo, New Mexico. A scientist and a general were pacing nervously in an underground shelter. The bomb to be tested was 10 feet long and weighed 9,000 pounds. Most of the weight was cushioning material. The explosive part weighed 22 pounds.

The minutes ticked away. At exactly 5:30 A.M., the bomb would be exploded. Three seconds, two seconds, one second—

The blast was frightening. A force equal to 20,000 tons of dynamite exploded in a flash of atomic fire. Winds of hurricane force swept through the area. A great ball of fire rose and touched the clouds. The temperature at the center of the blast soared to 100 million degrees Fahrenheit. This was 10,000 times the heat on the surface of the sun. All plant and animal life within a mile of the blast vanished, and the sand near the blast turned into beads of glass.

The general looked at the scientist and said, "The war is over."

Truman learned of the successful test in Potsdam, Germany, where he had gone to meet with Stalin and British Prime Minister Winston Churchill. Without using the term "atomic bomb," Truman told Stalin that the U.S. had developed a startling new weapon. Stalin showed no sign that he understood just how startling the weapon might be.

The United States warned the Japanese to surrender or face complete destruction. Japanese leaders disagreed about how to deal with the warning and did not surrender. But the threat was vague—there was no mention of an atomic bomb.

On August 5, 1945, three U.S. B-29 bombers flew over the Japanese city of Hiroshima. One plane carried the atomic bomb. It was dropped on the city at 8:15 A.M. In a flash, 60,000 people were dead or missing. The city became a furnace. This atomic bomb had the explosive power of 20,000 tons of dynamite and killed or injured 130,000 people. It destroyed 60 percent of Hiroshima and caused more damage than a raid of 2,000 bombers with conventional bombs.

The Japanese still refused to surrender. On August 8, the Soviet Union declared war on Japan. On August 9, a U.S. plane dropped a second atomic bomb, this time on the Japanese city of Nagasaki. More than 50,000 people were killed. Five days later, Japan agreed to surrender.

The Second World War was over. The atomic age had begun.

POSTSCRIPT

Possession of the atomic bomb gave the United States a major advantage in military strength, but it was a temporary advantage. United States leaders knew it was only a matter of time before the Soviet Union made its own bomb. Would it take five years? Seven? As it turned out, it took four. The Soviet Union exploded its first atomic bomb in 1949.

Since then, other nations have joined the ranks of atomic, or nuclear, powers. Britain made the breakthrough in 1952, France in 1960, China in 1964, India in 1974. Far more powerful versions of "The Bomb" have become available. The hydrogen bomb, so powerful that it made the first atomic bomb seem scarcely bigger than a firecracker, was first tested by the United States in 1952. In the early 1980's the United States decided to produce a neutron bomb. It would cause less physical destruction but emit more deadly radiation.

People all over the world were awed by the power unleashed by the new weapons. Nuclear bombs did not merely kill and destroy by the force of the blast. They also released radioactive particles that could poison the air and cause illness and death over a vast area and for long periods of time. Efforts to establish international controls over the new weapons began in the late 1940's. But the efforts made very slow progress. Nations simply did not trust one another enough to give up their deadly new weapons.

Homework Questions

1. Why was it difficult for the United States to supply the Allies during the early years of World War II?
2. Why did Stalin insist on a major second front in western Europe?
3. In what ways did U.S. officials hope the atomic bomb would be useful to the United States?
4. How did the first atomic bomb compare with conventional bombs?
5. How has the development of nuclear weapons affected all the peoples of the world?

Understanding the Story

A. Write *T* for each statement that is true and *F* for each statement that is false.
1. The United States decided to concentrate on defeating Germany first.
2. The Allies won victories in North Africa in 1942 and 1943.
3. President Truman told General Groves about a top-secret experiment.
4. Truman appointed a committee to consider the consequences of the atomic bomb.
5. The atomic bomb was tested near Los Angeles.
6. The test was a failure.
7. The U.S. gave the Japanese advance warning that an atomic bomb would be used against them.
8. An atomic bomb was dropped on the city of Hiroshima.

B. Which of the following happened as the result of the dropping of the atomic bombs?
1. World War II ended.
2. The Japanese still refused to surrender.
3. Many thousands of Japanese were killed in Hiroshima and Nagasaki.
4. The war continued for many years.
5. The world was awed by the destructive power of nuclear weapons.
6. The Japanese surrendered.
7. The world would never need to worry about another war.
8. The nuclear age began.

C. From the first, American officials assumed that the United States would use the atomic bomb against Japan. Do you think the U.S. did the right thing? Why or why not?

Activities and Inquiries

1. Assume that you are a newspaper reporter. You interview General Leslie Groves. What questions will you ask him?
2. How will General Groves answer your questions?
3. Now you are a reporter at the bomb-testing site. Describe what you see.
4. It is September, 1945. Write an editorial for your newspaper: Should the United States share the secret of its atomic bomb with other nations? Why or why not?

3 The Cold War

As long as they were fighting a common enemy, the Allies could bury their differences. But as the war came to an end, old rivalries and new ambitions arose to divide the Western powers and the Soviet Union.

A major dispute centered on Poland, a flat land dividing Germany from the Soviet Union. German tanks had crossed Poland to invade the Soviet Union in 1941. Early in 1945 Soviet troops drove the Germans back and occupied Poland. Stalin, the Soviet leader, insisted that Poland must have a "friendly" government, to protect the Soviet Union against any future invasion. He helped set up a Polish government dominated by Communists.

Western leaders called for free elections in Poland. At first Stalin agreed to work for such elections. But they never took place. Poland became a full-fledged Communist state, a close ally of the Soviet Union. To many Americans, Poland became a symbol. It was cited as proof that Soviet leaders could not be trusted to keep their promises.

Each side viewed the other with deep suspicion. In Soviet eyes, the United States was forcing its way into Europe and posing a threat to Soviet security. In U.S. eyes, the Soviet Union was seeking to create a new Russian Empire, larger than that of the czars.

Relations between the two sides worsened, and Europe was split into two parts. In the East were countries with pro-Soviet governments, run mainly by Communists. In the West were countries with pro-American governments, hostile to Communists. Separating the two parts was what Winston Churchill, the British leader, called an "iron curtain."

In talks during the war, Allied leaders had agreed on the need for a new world organization to replace the League of Nations. The new body, called the United Nations, came into existence in 1945. Rather than staying aloof, as it had from the League of Nations, the United States joined the UN immediately. The vote in the U.S. Senate in favor of membership was 89-2. In time, the UN made New York City its headquarters.

The United Nations had a number of separate parts, but there were two main bodies. In one, called the General Assembly, each member nation had an equal voice. The General Assembly could give advice, but it could not make decisions that were binding on member states. A second and smaller body, the Security Council, had the power to make binding decisions. For example, it could form a joint military force to fight an aggressor (a nation or group that started a war).

The Allied leaders agreed that the UN could work only if the major powers cooperated. They gave a special role to five powers—the United States, Britain, the Soviet Union, China, and France. These nations became permanent members of the Security Council, with a right of veto. The veto was considered essential to protect the vital interests of the major powers. Americans and Soviets alike insisted on it. (The Soviets, often outnumbered, cast many vetoes in the early years of the UN. In recent years the United States has been the main user of the veto.)

The cooperation that the UN's founders had counted on never developed. The tension between the Western powers and the Soviet Union came to dominate the world organization. As time passed, that tension came to be referred to as "the Cold War."

By early 1947 one main focus of tension was Greece, a Mediterranean nation bordering on three Communist countries. During the war Greece had been occupied by German troops. British troops moved in at the end of the war and imposed order on armed Greek groups that were struggling for power. The British then brought the Greek king back from exile. Soon a rebellion broke out, with leftist rebels receiving arms from nearby Communist countries. At first Britain aided the Greek government with money and military forces. But Britain had its own problems and decided it could not afford to get deeply involved in the Greek struggle. The Greek government turned to the United States for help.

To American leaders, the Greek civil war was no isolated struggle. It had been stirred up by the Soviet Union, these leaders felt, and showed that the Soviets were seeking to expand their empire.

Our story tells of an imaginary meeting between two State Department officials. They are discussing their worries about the Soviet Union. What are their views on Soviet expansion? What reasons do they give for those views?

Washington, D.C., 1947

"I understand that President Truman's former secretary of commerce, Henry Wallace, has charged that the President is being too tough on the Soviets," said Earl Block. "Truman fired Wallace for going public with his opinions, but Wallace is not the only one who feels Truman is too tough."

"Wallace knows more about farming than about world politics," said Adam Morris. "He was a good secretary of agriculture for Franklin Roosevelt and not a bad Vice President either. But I'm glad Roosevelt switched from Wallace to Truman in 1944.

"Henry believes that the Soviets are acting out of fear. They don't trust the outside world to leave them alone. Most of all, they don't trust Germany. Twice in 30 years Germany invaded Russia, and the Soviets want to make sure it doesn't happen again."

"Of course the Soviets distrust the Germans," said Morris. "But does that give them any right to take over Eastern Europe?"

"Wallace says that the Russians want to put some room between themselves and the non-Communist countries. If we let them do this, he says, we'll have no further trouble with them."

Morris shook his head. "I disagree. If we let them do this, we are only going to increase their appetite for more of the same. I've been talking with a member of our department's policy-planning staff, George Kennan. George knows Russian history and a great many Soviet officials. He tells me he doesn't believe that they mean to live in peace with the non-Communist world. I agree with him."

Block looked puzzled. "But does he mean that we must prepare to go to war against Russia?"

"Yes and no," replied Morris.

"What sort of an answer is that?"

"Kennan doesn't exactly believe that the Soviet Union wants war. But he thinks they will take any action short of war to get whatever they do want."

"Is there anything we can do?"

Morris answered slowly. "There is a lot. The Russians respect strength. Kennan thinks we have to show them great strength."

"What kind of strength?"

"Military and moral strength. Right now the Russians think that our only interest is what happens at home because we are tired of fighting Europe's wars. They are fairly sure that we will not get involved in what seems to be a strictly European affair. Kennan says we must find a way to prove to them that Europe and indeed the rest of the world are very much our business. They also have to know that we have the power to stop them, to contain them, and that we have the will to use that power."

"That's fine, but it isn't very concrete. How do we get this message across to the Russians?"

"We must help many of the weakened countries around the world to help themselves. We should also deal very firmly with the Russians whenever they decide to test us. We must keep reminding ourselves of the need for containment of Soviet expansion. We must never let ourselves seem to be backing down."

"How do you know they will back down?" asked Block.

"I really don't know for sure. No one does."

Block thought for a long time. Finally he spoke. "The United States has fought in two world wars—two very hot wars. This war of nerves that you are talking about may be the hardest of all to fight."

"Let's hope that the American people are up to fighting this kind of cold war."

"They'll have to be," said Block. "There is no one else to fight it."

POSTSCRIPT

President Truman decided that the Soviet Union was testing the United States by backing the Greek rebels. He saw Turkey, too, as threatened. The President decided to ask Congress for $400 million in military and economic aid to Greece and Turkey. In a message to Congress on March 12, 1947, Truman said that United States policy must be "to support free peoples who are resisting armed subjugation [conquest] by armed minorities or by outside pressures." This policy became known as the Truman Doctrine.

Critics argued that the Truman Doctrine was a mistake. They said the United States was undercutting the United Nations and meddling in other nations' affairs, just like the Soviet Union. But Congress strongly backed the President. With U.S. help, the Greek government put down the rebellion within two years, and Turkey stood up to Soviet pressures.

Soon the United States adopted George Kennan's policy of containment in its broader outlines. At the same time, U.S. officials committed themselves to another idea. In mid-1947 Secretary of State George C. Marshall suggested a plan, the Marshall Plan, to revive the war-torn nations of Europe. Hunger and poverty were widespread in Europe. U.S. leaders feared that some countries might turn in desperation to communism. Also, U.S. officials believed that a poverty-stricken Europe could not afford to buy U.S. exports. Helping Europe was seen as a way of helping U.S. businesses to find new customers and thus of creating jobs for American workers.

Marshall announced his plan in a speech at Harvard University on June 5, 1947. He proposed that European nations draw up a plan of recovery and then let the United States know what it could do to help. Britain and France eagerly accepted the idea. The Soviet Union, after a brief hesitation, bluntly rejected it and insisted that Eastern European nations take no part. Soviet leaders condemned the Marshall Plan as a cover for the expansion of U.S. military and economic influence in Europe.

Great Britain, France, and 14 other non-Communist nations then prepared estimates of their needs. They told the United States they would need $22.4 billion for assistance.

At first Congress was reluctant to approve the Marshall Plan. Conservatives said it might be the start of a worldwide "New Deal." But Soviet dislike of the plan and a Communist takeover of Czechoslovakia in February, 1948, eased the way for congressional approval.

For the next four years, the United States and Western Europe worked hand in hand toward the economic rebuilding of Europe. By July, 1951, the 16 nations that took part in the Marshall Plan had raised their industrial production 40 percent above the level of 1938. They were well on their way to recovery from World War II. Between 1948 and 1951, the United States spent $12.5 billion on aiding European recovery—about 40 percent less than expected. As a result of improved economic conditions, the influence of Communist parties in the 16 nations decreased.

Homework Questions

1. How did the Cold War begin?
2. How was the attitude of the United States toward the rest of the world after World War II different from its attitude after World War I?
3. In what ways did Henry Wallace and George Kennan differ in their attitudes toward the Soviet Union?
4. What was the Truman Doctrine? Was it successful?
5. What was the Marshall Plan? Was it successful?

Understanding the Story

A. Write *T* for each statement that is true, *F* for each statement that is false, and *N* for each statement that is not mentioned in this chapter.
   1. After World War II, the Soviet Union came to control much of Eastern Europe.
   2. In 1947 the Soviet Union was pressing Turkey to give up some territory.

3. Germany did not invade the Soviet Union in the 1940's.
4. George Kennan said that the Soviet Union was eager for war.
5. President Truman asked Congress for aid for Greece and Turkey.
6. Bulgaria did not join the Marshall Plan.
7. The Marshall Plan improved economic conditions in Western Europe.
8. The Marshall Plan was the largest U.S. foreign aid program up to that time.

B. Write *A* for each statement that George Kennan would agree with and *N* for each statement that he would not agree with.
1. The Soviets trust the outside world.
2. The Russians will not live in peace with the non-Communist world.
3. The Soviet Union does not want war.
4. Let the nations of Europe stand on their own feet.
5. The Russians respect strength.
6. Don't be firm with the Russians.

7. We don't have the power to stop the Russians.
8. The U.S. should help weak nations to help themselves.

C. Imagine that you are a member of Congress in 1948. What arguments can you think of in favor of the Marshall Plan? What arguments can you think of against it? How will you vote on the plan?

Activities and Inquiries

1. Imagine that Henry Wallace appears before the Senate Foreign Relations Committee. What will he say about how the United States should deal with the Soviet Union?
2. George Kennan appears before the Foreign Relations Committee. What will he say about how the United States should deal with the Soviet Union?
3. Assume that you are a member of the Foreign Relations Committee in 1947. Would you follow Wallace's or Kennan's advice? Explain your choice.

4 The Berlin Airlift

When World War II ended, Germany was a conquered nation. Allied troops occupied its soil. Its government, its industries, and many of its cities were destroyed.

The Allies divided Germany into four zones. Each of the major Allies, plus France, had its own zone of occupa-

tion. Berlin, the capital, was also divided into four zones. However, Berlin lay deep within the Soviet zone. All roads and railroads into Berlin passed through Soviet-held areas.

The zones of occupation were supposed to be temporary. But as the Cold War deepened, the former Allies could not agree on what to do about Germany. One proposal was to tear down German industries and make the country into a nation of farmers. Although U.S. leaders had once favored this plan, they gave it up by war's end. Later, the United States and Britain proposed to revive German industry. At the same time, they planned to create safeguards to prevent the rise of war industries.

France and the Soviet Union, stung by recent German invasions, favored harsher policies. The Soviets, in particular, demanded that Germany pay for the damage its invasions had done. They began to tear down factories in the Soviet zone of Germany and move them to the Soviet Union. Over Western protests, they seized goods produced at German factories and sent the goods to the Soviet Union.

To make decisions about Germany, the four occupying powers had to set up a council. But the council often split three against one: the Western powers against the Soviet Union. Frustrated with the council's inability to make decisions, the three Western powers went ahead on their own. They made plans for a new German government in the three Western zones and for West German participation in the Marshall Plan. They put a new German money into circulation. The Soviets protested, in vain.

Suddenly, in June, 1948, the Soviet Union forced a showdown. Saying that the West did not have written authority to use the land routes to Berlin, the Soviet Union closed those routes to all except Soviet vehicles. How would the West react to this Berlin Blockade? Would there be war?

Berlin, Germany, 1948

Two American soldiers were driving a truck filled with supplies to Berlin. On a highway bridge in the Eastern zone of Germany, a Soviet guard ordered them to stop. The driver braked the truck to a halt. The guard approached.

"What's going on?" asked one of the Americans.

"You will have to turn back," said the guard.

"Why?"

"The bridge is being repaired. All traffic must turn back."

One American pointed and said, "But traffic is moving over the bridge. I don't see any repairmen."

The Soviet guard stood his ground and repeated, "You must turn back."

After some hesitation, the Americans turned the truck around and headed back to the Western zones.

On that day and the next, the Soviets stopped all traffic from Western Germany to Berlin. Now the Soviets were ready for an even bigger move. They announced that road and railway traffic from Western Germany to Berlin would no longer be permitted. The Soviets had decided to force the West either to leave Berlin or to give up the plans for a West German government.

The Western powers faced a tough decision. Without supplies, West Berlin would die. Its 2.5 million people needed 4,000 tons of goods a day just to keep alive and 8,000 tons a day to keep the city running normally. How should the Western powers deal with this Soviet challenge?

President Truman decided it was too risky to send tanks and troops to clear the way to Berlin. But there was another way: use cargo planes to carry supplies into the city. An airlift would not place U.S. and Soviet forces in a direct confrontation.

The flights began in late June. Lumbering planes headed for West Berlin's two airports. Wiping the sleep from their eyes, the pilots and crews flew mission after mission. Often Soviet fighter planes flew close to the supply planes, but the Soviets did not shoot.

Working around the clock, the airlift at first averaged slightly more than 1,000 tons a day. Berlin was running short of food and coal. Would the airlift fail?

The Western Powers refused to give up. They brought in larger planes, and American, British, and French fliers began to deliver 4,000 tons a day. The people of West Berlin also refused to give up. They ate less, used less fuel, and patched their clothing. German workers toiled 24 hours a day to build a third airstrip. The Berliners believed they were fighting for their freedom, maybe even for their lives.

Eventually the airlift delivered 8,000 tons a day. Planes landed supplies every three minutes. Berlin's warehouses bulged, and Berliners began to breathe easier.

The Soviets were beaten. They had not counted on the will of the Americans, British, French, and the West Berliners. In May, 1949, the Soviets once again permitted road and railway traffic from West Germany to Berlin.

Thirty-one Americans lost their lives in airplane crashes during

"Only a miracle could have saved the city of West Berlin."

the airlift. In 15 months, 300,000 flights had delivered 2.5 million tons of supplies. The people of West Berlin, overjoyed by the success of the airlift, spoke of it as a miracle. West Berlin, immersed in a Communist-ruled Eastern Europe, had kept its links with the West.

POSTSCRIPT

Alarmed by the Soviet blockade of West Berlin and the earlier Communist takeover of Czechoslovakia, Western leaders saw a need to strengthen their military power. In April, 1949, the United States, Canada, and ten nations of Western Europe formed the North Atlantic Treaty Organization (NATO). An attack against any one member would be considered an attack against them all. Just as the United States had supplied food and materials under the Marshall Plan, it now supplied Western European nations with arms.

For the first time since the 1770's, the United States had joined a military alliance with a European nation in peacetime. A few Americans protested, but a large majority approved.

It was widely believed that the United States had a duty to defend what was called "the free world" against the challenge of communism. In the 1950's the Soviet Union and other Communist states formed a rival military alliance, known as the Warsaw Pact.

By the end of 1949, Germany's division into two separate states had become formal. The republic of West Germany eventually became a member of NATO. The republic of East Germany, ruled by a Communist government, eventually joined the Warsaw Pact. Both became members of the United Nations in 1973. In spite of its location within East Germany, West Berlin was part of the West German republic.

Homework Questions

1. How did the former Allies differ on the treatment to be given to conquered Germany?
2. Why did the Soviet Union begin the Berlin Blockade?
3. For what reasons did President Truman respond as he did?
4. Why was the Berlin airlift successful?
5. How did Americans feel about the forming of NATO?

Understanding the Story

A. List the numbers of the statements that are true.
 1. Germany was divided into four zones of occupation.
 2. Berlin was in the American zone.
 3. After the war, U.S. leaders wanted to make Germany a nation of farmers.
 4. The Soviet Union removed factories from its zone in Germany.
 5. The Soviet Union sent troops into Western Germany in 1948.
 6. West Berlin was supplied by an airlift.
 7. The Soviet blockade of Berlin was a failure.
 8. Western powers gave up their plan to create a republic in West Germany.

B. Complete each of the following sentences by filling in the missing word or words.
 1. The Soviets tried to force the West out of _____.

2. The Soviet guard said the bridge was closed for _____.
3. If the airlift had failed, West Berlin would have fallen under the control of the _____.
4. West Berliners believed they were fighting for their _____.
5. The airlift lasted for _____ months.
6. In 1949, 12 Western nations formed an alliance called _____.
7. A Communist military alliance is called the _____.
8. Germany was divided into _____ separate republics.

C. Assume that West Berlin is again cut off from land contact with West Germany. You are the President of the United States. Would you order another airlift? Why or why not?

Activities and Inquiries

1. Look at the drawing on page 488 and answer the following questions.
   a. Why was saving West Berlin called a "miracle"?
   b. Why did the United States save West Berlin?
   c. Do you think the United States did the right thing? Why or why not?
2. Imagine that you are producing a movie about the Berlin airlift. What scenes will you include?
3. Assume that a Soviet critic reviews your film. What does the critic say?
4. Imagine that you are the President's adviser. He tells you that the airlift is too expensive and dangerous and asks for another plan. What are your suggestions?
5. You decide that the airlift is the best way, after all. How will you convince the President?

5 War in East Asia

Even after Japan's defeat, East Asia remained a region of great tension. United States armed forces occupied Japan. Soviet and U.S. troops occupied Japan's former colony of Korea, which was split into two parts. And China was torn by civil war.

The Chinese fighting pitted the Communist forces of Mao Zedong against the Nationalist government of Chiang Kai-shek. In 1949 the Communists won out. Chiang and the Nationalists retreated to the Chinese island of Taiwan. Now two governments claimed to speak for all of China—a Communist one, which ruled most of China's 500 million people, and a Nationalist one, which ruled some 7 million people on Taiwan and other nearby islands. In February, 1950, Communist China signed an alliance with the Soviet Union.

Korea, meanwhile, remained divided. The United States pushed for elections to unify the country under United Nations supervision. It won approval for such a plan in the UN General Assembly, where friends of the U.S. were in a majority. The Soviet Union boycotted the elections. It argued that UN rules required such important matters to be dealt with by the Security Council, where the big powers had a veto. Elections in the U.S. zone, under UN supervision, resulted in the creation of an independent government for South Korea in 1948. A rival government, run by Communists, was quickly set up in North Korea.

The Soviet Union and the United States pulled their troops out of Korea, but the area remained tense. Both Korean governments claimed to speak for all Koreans. Both threatened to reunify the country by force if necessary.

U.S. leaders discussed whether the United States should support South Korea in case of war. Public statements indicated the U.S. would not do so. That is how matters stood on the morning of June 25, 1950, when North Korean troops poured across the 38th parallel (the border) into South Korea. They seemed likely to overrun all of South Korea in a short time.

In our story, U.S. leaders take a new look at their policies. Was the North Korean invasion a Soviet-inspired move, a challenge to "the free world"? Should the U.S. respond with military force? If so, how?

June 25, 1950

NORTH KOREA INVADES SOUTH; REDS ADVANCE RAPIDLY

President Truman was on a weekend visit to Independence, Missouri, his hometown, when he got word of the invasion. The President flew back to Washington on June 25, a Sunday.

That afternoon, the United Nations Security Council passed a resolution ordering a ceasefire. It accused North Korea of starting the war and ordered it to withdraw its forces from South Korea. The Soviet Union did not veto this resolution, as it might have been expected to do. Soviet diplomats were refusing to attend Council meetings until China's Communist government was allowed to take over the Chinese seat on the Council. (Nationalists still held the seat in China's name. The U.S. was backing the Nationalists.)

Back in Washington that evening, Truman met with Secretary of State Dean Acheson. "What are we going to do about the invasion of South Korea?" Acheson asked.

President Truman slowly cleaned his glasses. He replied, "We've got to stop it no matter what. I think the Soviets may be using their North Korean ally to test our strength. We can't allow the Communists to take over independent nations by armed invasion. If we did, we might soon have another world war on our hands."

"Should we ask Congress for a declaration of war?"

"There's no time," the President said. "As commander in chief, I have authority to order our troops into action to defend the free world."

June 27, 1950

TRUMAN COMMITS U.S. FORCES IN KOREA

At first, President Truman ordered only air and sea forces into action in South Korea. On June 30, after North Koreans had captured the South Korean capital of Seoul, Truman sent in U.S. ground troops. With the Soviets still absent, the United Nations Security Council readily backed the United States. It asked members of the UN to help South Korea "repel the armed attack."

In July the Security Council went further. It asked nations sending troops to Korea to place them in "a unified command under the United States." The troops would fight under a UN flag. They would be responsible to an American commander. The next day, President Truman named General Douglas MacArthur to lead the UN forces. In time, some 17 nations would fight under the UN flag. Americans and South Koreans made up nine tenths of the total.

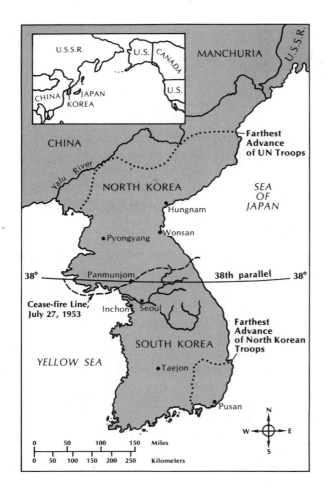

The Korean War, 1950–1953

For a while it appeared that the North Koreans might sweep all the way to the southern tip of Korea. The South Koreans and their allies retreated.

September 15, 1950

UN MAKES DARING LANDING AT INCHON

The UN landing did not take place in the far south, where North Koreans and UN forces were slugging it out. Instead, the landing took place at Inchon, near Seoul. Sweeping eastward, the UN troops threatened the Communists' lines of support. North Korean troops beat a hasty retreat. By the end of September, the Communists were crossing the 38th parallel into North Korea.

October 1, 1950

SOUTH KOREAN TROOPS CROSS 38TH PARALLEL

On October 7, U.S. ground troops entered North Korea for the first time. Their goal seemed to be a quick drive to reunify Korea under one, non-Communist, government.

By now, General MacArthur was a hero to many people. But his relations with President Truman were shaky. MacArthur thought Truman's policies were too cautious. In his view, if the UN was going to fight the Communists, it shouldn't be cautious; it should let them have it with both barrels. In a public statement in late August, MacArthur warned against "appeasement and defeatism." MacArthur had some powerful supporters in Congress.

Truman was reluctant to speak out against such a popular general. But he was afraid the general might take some rash action that would bring Soviet or Communist Chinese troops into the war in force. Truman decided to fly to Wake Island in the Pacific to meet MacArthur face to face.

October 15, 1950

TRUMAN, MACARTHUR CONFER

In a private meeting, the President was blunt. "I am the commander in chief. I expect you to obey my orders—not make policy on your own." MacArthur was apologetic, saying, "It won't happen again."

Then the President turned to the progress of the war. "Your troops are pushing north. What happens now? North Korea borders on both the Soviet Union and Communist China. Will the Soviets and the Chinese stand by, or will they enter the war?"

"They won't dare risk war with us," MacArthur replied. "Let me do it my way, and the war will be over by Thanksgiving. Our troops will be out by Christmas."

"All right," said Truman. "But you must make sure that no U.S. troops get any closer than 40 miles from the Soviet and Chinese borders. Only South Korean troops must be used to secure this territory."

October 26, 1950

UN FORCES REACH YALU RIVER

North Korea's capital, Pyongyang, fell to UN troops on October 20. By October 26, the retreat seemed almost complete. The first UN forces had reached the Yalu River, the border between China and North Korea. Other UN forces were approaching a major complex of dams on the Yalu—dams that provided hydroelectric power for North Korea, China, and the Soviet Union. A few thousand Chinese troops had moved into North Korea to protect these dams. Against orders, MacArthur sent U.S. troops into the border regions.

November 26, 1950

MASSIVE CHINESE ATTACK ACROSS YALU

On November 24, the day after Thanksgiving, UN forces began a "final drive" to mop up North Korean resistance along the Yalu. Two days later, 300,000 Chinese troops smashed south across the river. The surprised UN troops stumbled back across snow-covered hills toward the 38th parallel. By Christmas, the retreating troops were crossing back into South Korea.

According to some, MacArthur deliberately provoked the Chinese. In this view, he sought a wider war that would allow U.S. forces to wipe out communism in Asia once and for all. Another view is that MacArthur simply made a mistake. In any event, the result was a bigger war and a major setback for UN forces.

Retreating in the face of what were called "hordes" of North Koreans and Chinese, the UN forces pulled behind the 38th parallel. Seoul fell to the Communists but was recaptured by the UN forces in mid-March. This brought the front lines once again near the 38th parallel, where the war had begun. Britain and other U.S. allies were pressing for peace talks. By early April, President Truman seemed ready to enter negotiations.

April 5, 1951

MACARTHUR CRITICIZES U.S. POLICY SEES "NO SUBSTITUTE FOR VICTORY"

It was no secret that General MacArthur did not see eye to eye with Truman and other U.S. leaders. MacArthur agreed with those who said Nationalist Chinese forces on Taiwan should be "unleashed" to attack Communist China. He had repeatedly criticized rules that prevented U.S. bombing within China itself. But MacArthur had kept his criticisms more or less to himself since his meeting with Truman at Wake Island.

Then, on April 5, the Republican leader in the House of Representatives stood up to speak in Congress. He read a letter from MacArthur. The general restated his criticisms of Truman's policies and concluded, "There is no substitute for victory."

President Truman was outraged. In the first place, he felt, MacArthur was making a direct challenge to the President's authority as commander in chief. "It is my job to make policy," he stormed. "If he can't follow orders and keep his mouth shut, he's not suited to command our military forces."

In the second place, Truman felt, MacArthur seemed bent on expanding the Korean War. "If that fool isn't careful, we'll be fighting not only the Red Chinese but also the Soviets themselves."

"I'm going to get rid of him," Truman exclaimed. "He has embarrassed me for the last time."

Dean Acheson urged caution. "You'd better clear it first with the Joint Chiefs of Staff," Acheson said. "MacArthur's a popular hero. Firing him will cause a storm among the Republicans and much of the public. You need the military leaders firmly on your side." Truman took Acheson's advice, and all the members of the Joint Chiefs backed the President.

April 11, 1951

TRUMAN SACKS MAC; NATION IN SHOCK

General MacArthur returned at once to the United States, where much of the public treated him as a hero. There were parades, speeches, and 21-gun salutes. Congress invited the general to speak and interrupted him 30 times with applause. Some people hoped that MacArthur would become a political leader and run for President, but his popularity soon faded.

Peace talks began July 10, 1951, but the war did not end. While the two sides argued back and forth for months, their troops kept on fighting. Many Americans were angry at what appeared to be a stalemate. Had MacArthur been right? Should the United States go all-out for victory?

The truce talks and the fighting dragged on. Truman did not run for re-election in 1952. His war policies, defended by Democratic candidate Adlai Stevenson, contributed to a Republican victory. The winning candidate was General Dwight D. Eisenhower, a leader of Allied forces in World War II. He had promised during the campaign to "go to Korea" to bring the war to an early end. Eisenhower did visit Korea, and his administration continued the peace talks.

July 26, 1953

TRUCE ENDS KOREA FIGHTING; 38TH PARALLEL IS TRUCE LINE

In July, 1953, an agreement was reached and the fighting stopped. Korea remained divided at the 38th parallel, with a Communist North Korea and a U.S.-backed South Korea. But this was only a truce and not a peace treaty. Hostile armies continued to face each other across a narrow neutral area known as the demilitarized zone.

POSTSCRIPT

In the midst of the Korean War, the United States signed a peace treaty with Japan. The treaty ended the U.S. occupation. Japan allowed the U.S. to keep military bases on Japanese territory.

The Korean War cost the United States some 54,000 dead and 103,000 wounded. South Korea suffered close to a million casualties. One and half million North Koreans and Chinese were dead or wounded. Much of Korea lay in ruins. And the Cold War was more frigid than ever.

By the 1980's, three decades after the Korean truce agreement, no peace treaty had been signed. Some 39,000 U.S. troops remained in South Korea. Another 47,000 U.S. troops were in Japan.

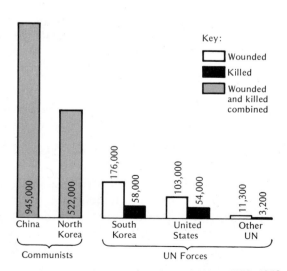

Military Casualties in the Korean War, 1950–1953

Homework Questions

1. How did the Chinese civil war turn out?
2. Why did President Truman believe the United States had to send help to South Korea?
3. Why did the Soviet Union fail to veto the UN Security Council's call for action against North Korea?
4. What were Truman's reasons for concern as UN troops neared the Yalu River?
5. Why did Truman fire General Douglas MacArthur?

Understanding the Story

A. Write *F* for each statement that is a fact and *O* for each statement that is an opinion.
1. The Communists won a civil war in China in 1949.
2. The Soviet Union should have been kept out of Korea.
3. Korea was occupied by the United States and the Soviet Union.
4. It was a mistake to give General MacArthur command in Korea.
5. United Nations troops crossed into North Korea in late 1950.
6. Chinese Communist soldiers joined the North Koreans in late 1950.
7. Truman was too severe with MacArthur.
8. Truman fired MacArthur.

B. Which statements describe Truman's ideas about the Korean War?
1. We must stop the Communists in Korea.
2. The people elected me—not General MacArthur.
3. MacArthur is disliked by the American people.
4. MacArthur must stay in Korea.

5. Let MacArthur make the decisions in Korea.
6. I don't agree with MacArthur's actions.
7. MacArthur might drag the Soviet Union and Communist China into the war.
8. MacArthur has embarrassed me for the last time.

C. Imagine that you are the President. A general tells you that war should be left to the generals. What is your answer?

Activities and Inquiries

1. Study the map on page 492. Then choose the term or phrase that best completes each statement.
   a. The Yalu River is a northern boundary of (*1*) China (*2*) North Korea (*3*) the U.S.S.R.
   b. The body of water west of Korea is the (*1*) Sea of Japan (*2*) Pacific Ocean (*3*) Yellow Sea.
   c. The distance from Pyongyang to Seoul is about (*1*) 120 kilometers (*2*) 375 kilometers (*3*) 180 kilometers.
   d. The distance from Pusan to the Yalu River is about (*1*) 660 kilometers (*2*) 240 kilometers (*3*) 500 kilometers.
   e. A city in South Korea is (*1*) Taejon (*2*) Hungnam (*3*) Wonsan.
   f. 38° on the map refers to (*1*) the number of miles from Korea to Japan (*2*) a line separating North from South Korea (*3*) the average temperature in Korea during February.
2. Visit your local library. Prepare a report on President Truman's views about his difficulties with General MacArthur.
3. Using library resources, prepare a report on MacArthur's views about his difficulties with Truman.

4. Re-read the stories about President Truman in this unit. Prepare a report card for Harry Truman. Grade him in the following areas and justify each grade:
   a. Leadership
   b. Point of view
   c. Accomplishments while President
   d. Maturity
5. Study the graph on page 496. Then choose the term or phrase that best completes each statement.
   a. The other side had (*1*) about the same number of casualties as UN forces (*2*) much greater casualties than the UN forces (*3*) fewer casualties than the UN forces.
   b. The South Koreans had (*1*) more casualties than all other UN forces (*2*) fewer casualties than all other UN forces (*3*) more casualties than the North Koreans.
   c. Among the UN forces, the U.S. suffered (*1*) greater casualties than South Korea (*2*) fewer casualties than South Korea (*3*) about the same number of casualties as the other UN forces.
   d. The total North Korean casualties were (*1*) more than those of the Chinese (*2*) greater than the combined total of the UN forces (*3*) about the same as those of the South Koreans.
   e. This graph tells you (*1*) why the United States fought the Korean War (*2*) why the casualties were so heavy on both sides (*3*) the number of military people killed and wounded on both sides.

6 Point of Order

The Cold War had stirred up a great fear among the American people. U.S.-Soviet tensions seemed to grow ever tighter. There was a feeling that atomic war might break out at any moment.

The danger seemed all the greater because the Soviet Union was not just a major power. It was also the leader of a worldwide Communist movement. To Americans of the 1940's and early 1950's, that movement seemed to be on the march. First Eastern Europe, then China had "fallen" to communism. What country would be next?

Political leaders, especially conservatives, had long warned against Communist influence in government within the United States. They said Communists in high places might be able to subvert (undermine) U.S. policies. Liberals such as Presidents Roosevelt and Truman did not want to seem "soft on communism." To prevent subversion, Roosevelt called for loyalty checks on key government workers during World War II. After the war, Truman established a much broader system of loyalty checks. He set up loyalty boards to inquire into the political beliefs of all people who held federal jobs. Critics said such procedures were undemocratic and un-

American. But most people supported the loyalty boards as necessary in what seemed a time of national peril.

Some people thought U.S. leaders were still too lax. Committees in Congress held investigations, and in 1948 there were sensational charges that a Communist spy had held a key post in the State Department during World War II. The alleged spy, Alger Hiss, was convicted in 1949 of lying to a grand jury. (However, he was never convicted of spying.)

In February, 1950, Senator Joseph McCarthy of Wisconsin began to make headlines. In a speech in Wheeling, West Virginia, the Republican senator claimed to have a list of 205 Communists working in the State Department. These Communists, he said, shaped foreign policy for the United States. How had McCarthy obtained his list? He refused to say. When questioned, he changed the number on his list from 205 to 57.

A Senate subcommittee investigated McCarthy's charges and found no real evidence to prove them. Still McCarthy went on making charges about Communists in government, and many Americans believed him. McCarthy became a powerful figure as newspapers and radio and television networks reported his new charges day after day.

Some politicians spoke out against McCarthy. They said he was using "smear tactics" and making reckless charges that hurt the reputations of innocent people. But large numbers of voters looked upon McCarthy as an American hero, a leader in the fight against communism. Several members of Congress were voted out of office after criticizing McCarthy.

McCarthy and other members of Congress led investigations of Communist influence in American life. While McCarthy focused mainly on the State Department, others looked into charges of Communist influence in education and the motion picture industry. Many people were summoned before congressional committees and asked to describe their political beliefs and actions.

Some people refused to talk. They said it was their right as Americans to keep their beliefs to themselves. In some cases, such people were sent to jail for contempt of Congress. Others testified. Only a few said they believed in communism, but many said they had joined Communist-led groups in the past. Some named others as having taken part in Communist-influenced activities. In the fearful atmosphere of the time, anyone who had ever flirted with communism became suspect. Many whose names were mentioned lost their jobs. Some were ruined.

The series of investigations stirred controversy. Some people criticized the methods used by the investigators, especially McCarthy. They said "McCarthyism" (as they called such methods) went against the Constitution. They said McCarthyism was making Americans afraid to speak out for fear that they too would be accused of communism. Others defended the investigators. They said Communists had wormed their way into sensitive jobs and must be removed before they could destroy the American way of life.

In 1954 McCarthy turned his attention to the U.S. Army. He charged the Army with being riddled with Communists and trying to hide that fact. The Army countercharged that McCarthy had used improper influence on behalf of one of his assistants who had been drafted into the Army. A hearing began, and the battle moved before television cameras. How did this hearing affect McCarthy's future and the hunt for Communists in the government? Why do you think many people admire Joseph Welch?

Washington, D.C., June, 1954

"Point of order! Point of order!" called out Senator McCarthy, leaping to his feet.

For 30 days the senator had been using these words, and by now they were familiar to Americans all across the country. McCarthy would jump to his feet, take the microphone, make a speech, and smile for the television cameras. When he cross-examined witnesses, he spoke roughly, angrily. Most of the millions of people who watched this hearing on their television screens saw the senator in action for the first time. Many did not like what they saw.

McCarthy represented one side in the Senate hearing. Joseph Welch represented the other. Welch, a lawyer from Boston, was the chief attorney for the Army.

Already Welch had gotten in a few licks at McCarthy. He had asked the senator about an FBI document.

"Where did you get this letter?" Welch asked.

"I won't answer that," said McCarthy.

For years, McCarthy had been badgering people who refused to answer his questions. "Do you have something to hide?" he would ask. "Why don't you answer?" Now it was he who refused to answer. Score one for Welch.

One of McCarthy's assistants took the stand. Welch asked him about Communists in the Army. Senator McCarthy interrupted. He knew of someone who might be working for the Communists. "His name is Fisher. He works for Mr. Welch's law firm. For years he has been a member of an organization that was named, oh, years ago, as a Communist front." Welch tried to interrupt.

McCarthy kept talking. "I am not asking you, Mr. Welch, if you knew Fisher was a member of a Communist organization. I assume you did not. You are quite an actor, but I don't think you realize just how dangerous the Communist Party really is. I don't think you would knowingly aid the Communist cause. But you are unknowingly aiding it by the way you are carrying on at this hearing."

The senator sat down, with a look of triumph on his face. He turned and spoke to an aide. Welch stared at him and waited to get his attention. Every eye in the audience was on the Army's lawyer.

"Until this moment, Senator, I had never really understood how cruel you are. You are trying to ruin a decent young man by smearing him in front of millions of people. This young man joined a Communist organization out of ignorance. He resigned from the organization as soon as he learned more about it. You could have asked me about this privately. Instead, you chose to try to assassinate this lad in public. You are a cruel and reckless man, and what you have done is unforgivable."

McCarthy tried to interrupt. Welch kept talking.

"Senator McCarthy, have you no sense of decency?"

"Senator, you have done enough. Have you no sense of decency, sir, at long last? Have you no sense of decency?"

Many of the people in the hearing room rose and applauded. Senator McCarthy was confused. Why were people turning away from him? What had he done?

POSTSCRIPT

Even before Welch's attack, McCarthy had made enemies. President Eisenhower had been angered by McCarthy's campaign against the Army. Without naming names, the President denounced "demagogues thirsty for personal power and public notice." Others called McCarthy a bully.

When the Army-McCarthy hearings came to an end, the Senate set up a new committee. Its job was to look into charges against Senator McCarthy. In December, 1954, by a vote of 67–22, the Senate formally condemned McCarthy for conduct unworthy of a senator. McCarthy's career as a hunter of Communists was over, although he remained in the Senate until his death three years later.

The effects of the McCarthy period were in some cases long-lasting. Many actors, writers, and scientists who had been accused of disloyalty remained under a cloud for years, even when there was no evidence to support the charges. Some were placed on employers' blacklists and could not find work in their professions.

Looking back, many people came to think of the early 1950's as a time of excesses—of "witch-hunts" against communism. Such excesses flourished in a time of international danger. By 1954, however, the Korean War had ended in a truce. Cautious attempts were being made to find a way to ease the tensions of the Cold War.

Homework Questions

1. Why were Americans afraid of the Soviet Union?
2. By what methods did Senator Joseph McCarthy attack communism?
3. How did the public respond at first to McCarthy's hunt for Communists?
4. Why did Joseph Welch say McCarthy was cruel and reckless?
5. In what way did the Army-McCarthy hearings help bring about the senator's downfall?

Understanding the Story

A. Write *M* for each statement that McCarthy made or might have made and *W* for each statement that Welch made or might have made.
1. Point of order.
2. I won't answer that.
3. Where did you get this letter?
4. I assume you are not a Communist.
5. You are trying to ruin a decent young man.
6. You don't realize just how dangerous the Communist Party really is.
7. You are a cruel and reckless man.
8. Have you no sense of decency?

B. Write *T* for each statement that is true and *F* for each statement that is false.
1. Senator McCarthy warned the American people about communism.
2. McCarthy always offered proof of his charges of communism in high places in government.
3. McCarthy became a powerful figure.
4. Many people were accused of being Communists and lost their jobs.
5. Only actual Communists were accused of wrongdoing in the McCarthy period.
6. The chief lawyer for the Army at the hearings was Joseph Welch.
7. McCarthy answered all questions at the Army hearings.
8. The Senate condemned McCarthy for conduct unworthy of a senator.

C. Why do you think Senator Joseph McCarthy became so powerful? If he were alive today and resumed his hunt for Communists, do you think many people would support him? Why or why not?

Activities and Inquiries

1. Look at the drawing on page 501 and answer the following questions.
   a. Who is saying this? Why?
   b. What does he mean?
   c. How should McCarthy have answered?
2. Assume that you support McCarthy. Re-read the story and list all the points favorable to him.
3. Now assume that you are opposed to McCarthy. List all the points unfavorable to him.
4. Suppose that McCarthy holds a press conference. How does he justify his actions?
5. Joseph Welch holds a press conference. What arguments does he offer against McCarthy?

7 Jackie Robinson

In the years after World War II, the United States took a new look at laws and customs that kept black Americans apart from other Americans.

For years blacks had complained that they were second-class citizens. In many parts of the United States, blacks were required to attend separate, racially segregated schools. They were barred from "white" hotels, restaurants, and places of worship. They were confined mainly to low-paying jobs, often the hard and dirty jobs that no one else wanted to take. In both North and South, blacks lived mostly in "black" neighborhoods, because "white" neighborhoods were often closed to them. In parts of the South, blacks were not allowed to vote or even to register to vote. In the army, blacks were placed in separate units apart from whites.

During World War II, some Americans, black and white, had spoken out against such practices. How could the United States claim to be fighting for basic freedoms abroad, they asked, when it denied full rights to black Americans at home? In 1946 President Truman appointed a committee on civil rights to look into the question of race relations. What problems existed? How could they be resolved?

About this time, a white baseball executive was making a move that would have lasting effects. The executive's name was Branch Rickey, and he was head of the Brooklyn Dodgers. Rickey hired a baseball player named Jackie Robinson—the first black American to be hired for a major league team. What challenges did Robinson face? How did he meet them?

Brooklyn, New York, 1947

You are Jackie Robinson, a man of many talents. Even as a college student you commanded attention. You excelled at track, football, basketball, and baseball. After serving in the army, you began a career as a professional baseball player. You played for an all-black team, the Kansas City Monarchs.

Then came your big chance. You got a call from Branch Rickey. He wanted the best players for the Brooklyn Dodgers, and he didn't care whether they were black or white. He picked you as his first black player because he thought you had two basic qualities—skill and "guts." He wanted a player, he said, "with guts enough not to fight back."

You knew you would face abuse and not just name-calling. Players would come at you with spikes flashing. Pitchers would aim some of their fastest pitches at your head. All ballplayers, whatever their race, must face this sort of abuse, you knew. So what if you had to face more than others do? You had guts. You could take it—and keep your temper.

It hasn't been easy, this first year. Even on your own team, many players resented you. They looked on you as an alien, an outsider. But you had support. During tense situations, the team captain, Kentucky-born Pee Wee Reese, moves to your side. To show that he supports you, he often puts his hand on your shoulder. You are grateful to Pee Wee. You and he will be lifelong friends.

When a pitcher throws a ball at your head, you feel deep anger. But you don't take out that anger on the pitcher. You pick yourself up, dig in your heels, and smash the next pitch for a hit. It's the same when you're playing first base. If you get angry, you just play harder. You're going to make even those who hate you admit that you're a great ballplayer. And many do, in the end.

By the end of 1947, you've become a star. Most of your teammates now accept you. *Sporting News* names you rookie of the year, and the Dodgers win the National League pennant. People are beginning to forget the color of your skin. The only thing that really matters is how well you play baseball, and you play very well indeed.

POSTSCRIPT

Once Jackie Robinson had broken the color line, other black players entered the major leagues. Within a few years blacks were leading players on many of the teams.

Meanwhile, new efforts were made to end discrimination against blacks. (Discrimination, in this sense, means treatment that is not equal.) In 1948, President Truman asked Congress to pass a variety of civil rights laws. He wanted laws to protect blacks' rights to vote, travel, and get good jobs. He also wanted a law against lynching and a law to end discrimination in the armed forces.

When Congress failed to act, Truman went ahead on his own. He ordered equality in the armed services and in federal hiring. He also set up a committee to make sure that companies doing work for the government did not discriminate against blacks.

Jackie Robinson continued to be a star. In 1949 he led the National League in batting. Off the field he began to speak out on issues such as civil rights. On the field he became more assertive, occasionally arguing with umpires. Now and then he flashed his own spikes when he felt he needed to "fight back" against a player who had abused him.

Robinson retired from baseball in 1957 to become a business executive. He also devoted more time to the civil-rights movement. In 1972 he died of a heart attack at the age of 53.

Homework Questions

1. Why did blacks feel they were being treated unfairly in the 1940's?
2. Why was Jackie Robinson's role as a major league baseball player so difficult?
3. What qualities did Branch Rickey admire in Robinson?
4. How did Robinson's behavior change after a few years in the major leagues?
5. How did President Truman try to end discrimination against blacks?

Understanding the Story

A. List the numbers of the statements that are true.
   1. Many blacks had to go to all-black schools.
   2. Blacks had no trouble getting high-paying jobs.
   3. President Truman wanted laws to protect blacks' rights.
   4. Truman did not do anything about discrimination in the armed forces.
   5. There were many black baseball players in the major leagues before Jackie Robinson.
   6. After a while, Robinson was accepted by his teammates.
   7. At first, Robinson took abuse without fighting back.
   8. Robinson never argued with an umpire.

B. Which of the following statements might have been made by Jackie Robinson?
   1. I never went to college.
   2. I did pretty well at track and football.
   3. I knew if I joined the Dodgers I would face abuse.
   4. Pitchers never aim fast pitches at white players' heads.
   5. I have to hold my temper.
   6. All of my teammates resent me.
   7. I guess I'm not much of a hitter.
   8. I'll play hard and win over even those who hate me.

C. Assume that you are Jackie Robinson in 1947, and Branch Rickey says he hopes you have the guts not to fight back. What will you say to him? Why?

Activities and Inquiries

1. Imagine that you are writing a book about Jackie Robinson's life. Prepare the table of contents.
2. Which chapter of the book will be the most important? Explain.
3. Someone asks why you think it is important to write about a baseball player. How will you answer?
4. Suppose that Jackie Robinson reads your book. What will he say about it?

8 Nine Students Face a Mob

The actions of people like Jackie Robinson helped to bring racial equality a step closer. But civil rights leaders felt that more had to be done. They turned to the government and the courts to aid in the fight for equal rights.

In 1954, help came from the United States Supreme Court. In the case of *Brown* v. *Board of Education of Topeka*, the Court ruled that it was unconstitutional to have separate schools for white and black students. It ordered steps to end segregation in public schools (see pages 514 to 516).

Many whites in the South strongly opposed the Court's decision. They argued that it went against local customs and ignored the principle of states' rights. In some places local officials flatly refused to put an end to segregation. When this happened, court battles began, with civil rights leaders asking courts to order officials to integrate schools.

Some communities, facing court orders to desegregate, closed all public schools. White parents formed private schools to educate their children—sometimes using tax money. Once again civil rights leaders went to court, arguing that such use of public money went against the Constitution. In time, courts stopped the practice.

Emotions ran high, and violence broke out in many places. Sometimes armed groups of whites gathered outside schools to prevent blacks from entering. In classrooms, fights sometimes occurred between whites and blacks.

In 1957, the school board in the Arkansas capital of Little Rock announced that the upper grades of high school would be desegregated. State officials tried to block the move. A federal court ordered desegregation to go ahead. Just before school was to open, Arkansas Governor Orval Faubus called out the National Guard. He used the troops to keep nine black students from entering Central High School. He said his actions were necessary to prevent mob violence.

Our story tells what happened to one of those nine students. What problems did she face? How did the federal government help her?

Little Rock, Arkansas, September, 1957

Her name was Elizabeth, and she was 15 years old. On the first day of school, she was more nervous than usual. She was getting ready to go to a new school, Central High in Little Rock. Central High had been all-white, but that was about to change.

Elizabeth's parents were afraid that something awful would happen to her. They agreed to let her go to Central High only because it was the best high school in town.

Elizabeth told her parents not to worry. The 400 white students would hardly notice nine black ones. The worst that would probably happen was that the white students would have nothing to do with the newer ones. She hoped she was right.

On the first day, she decided to go to school by herself in order to attract as little attention as possible. As she walked toward the school building, she saw a large crowd of students near it. She had to pass through the crowd to get to the entrance. All the faces looked angry and seemed to be staring at her. Someone shouted an ugly name. Other voices joined in. Elizabeth kept moving. At last she reached the entrance, but it was blocked. National Guardsmen stood in front of the door. One of them told Elizabeth that she must turn back. She started to cry. All she wanted was a chance to get a good education. Why were people trying so hard to keep her out of a school?

She turned and walked back through the crowd. The ugly names followed her, and the crowd began to move closer. One of the guardsmen stopped them from hurting her. He escorted her to a bus-stop bench. The crowd continued to yell at her. A white woman came to her aid, calling the crowd a bunch of cowards for picking on a frightened girl. Some in the crowd looked ashamed. Then the school bell rang, and the white students walked into the school. Elizabeth stared at the school for a little while and then started for home.

The eight other black students got the same treatment. News of what happened to them made headlines across the nation. Many people were on their side. Some of these people wrote letters to their representatives in Congress demanding federal action to protect the

"I thought grown-ups wanted kids to go to school."

students' civil rights. Finally a federal court ordered Governor Faubus to remove the National Guard.

Once again Elizabeth prepared to go to school. This time her friends and she agreed that they would all go together. They expected some name-calling. But they knew that no guardsmen would be at the doors to turn them back.

As they approached the school, they saw an angry crowd milling about. Every eye was on them. People jeered and cursed the black teenagers as they walked. Finally, they reached the door and entered the school. A crowd of white students followed. They moved closer. Elizabeth looked around for help. There was none.

She heard a scream. Pieces of glass were thrown at one of her friends. A can opener was thrown at another. Elizabeth was kicked. Another black student was pushed out of the school and down the steps. Finally, the police came and restored order.

Embarrassed school officials told the black students to go home for their own safety because the school could not protect them. The law of the land had said that the students had the right to enter Central High. The mob had said no. It looked as if the mob had won.

Later that day, the nine young people and their parents met with civil rights leaders. The parents said the students must not go back to Central High. The civil rights leaders argued that a retreat now would be a serious blow to the movement for black rights. If the mob succeeded here, mobs elsewhere would be encouraged to oppose the law. The students joined the leaders in trying to convince their parents to let them go back. Reluctantly, their parents agreed.

In the meantime, President Dwight Eisenhower had decided to send federal troops to Little Rock to protect the students. He made a speech against "mob rule." The law of the land, he said, would be enforced.

Once again Elizabeth and her friends started for school. Troops met them and escorted them through the shouting crowd. As the students entered the school with the federal soldiers at their side, they knew they were there to stay.

POSTSCRIPT

In time the mobs went away. By the end of November most federal troops had been withdrawn. Only a handful of soldiers stayed on to protect the nine students.

But President Eisenhower's actions had stirred a storm of controversy. Southern leaders accused him of sabotaging states' rights and stirring up racial hatred. Many Southern whites complained about what they called "federal tyranny." Nonetheless, the President won strong support from blacks and from many whites. They praised the President for upholding the principle of equal rights under the law. Outside of the South, according to an opinion poll, three out of four people who were questioned supported Eisenhower's actions.

Homework Questions

1. How did some Southern communities try to get around the Supreme Court ruling in the case of *Brown* v. *Board of Education?*
2. What reason did Governor Orval Faubus give for barring nine black students from a school in Little Rock?
3. What happened when these students tried to enter the school?
4. How did President Eisenhower react to the events in Little Rock?
5. Why did Eisenhower's actions stir controversy?

Understanding the Story

A. Write *F* for each statement that is a fact and *O* for each statement that is an opinion.
1. Local officials in the South often tried to stop desegregation.
2. Some white students were enrolled in segregated private schools.
3. The Supreme Court went too far in the Brown case.
4. The Little Rock schools were ordered to go ahead with desegregation.
5. Black students should not have been afraid.
6. Governor Orval Faubus ordered that no black students be admitted to Central High.
7. The National Guard did the best job it had ever done.
8. General Eisenhower ordered federal troops to Little Rock.

B. Which statements describe Elizabeth's situation?
1. She was more nervous than usual on the first day of school in 1957.
2. Her parents were afraid that something awful would happen to her.
3. The crowd around the school was happy to see her.
4. The National Guard escorted her into the school.
5. The school officials said that she must go home for her own safety.
6. It looked as if the mob had won.
7. The federal troops were not so helpful as the National Guardsmen.
8. Elizabeth asked her parents to let her go back to Central High.

C. Do you think President Eisenhower did the right thing in sending federal troops to Little Rock? Why or why not?

Activities and Inquiries

1. Look at the cartoon on page 507 and answer the following questions.
   a. Why are these young people barred from the school?
   b. Suppose you talk to a National Guardsman. What do you think he would say?
   c. How would the blacks answer him?
   d. With whom would you agree? Explain.
2. Imagine that you are a reporter. You ask Elizabeth why she is going to Central High even though there may be trouble. What is her answer?
3. Next, you interview the principal of Central High. What does he say about the admission of blacks to the school?
4. Next, you ask Governor Orval Faubus and President Eisenhower why they took the actions they did. What do they tell you?
5. What were your feelings as you read about Elizabeth's experiences?

9 Boycott Power

As we have seen, blacks were seeking to gain an equal place in American society. Legal action through the courts was one method of seeking equality. But were other ways needed too? Many blacks thought they were.

One path to equality seemed to lie through state legislatures and the United States Congress. Civil rights leaders pushed for new laws to guarantee equal rights, but they met fierce resistance. In the South, especially, where voting was difficult, if not impossible, for blacks, legislators were not inclined to pass civil rights laws.

Instead, many states passed laws aimed at strengthening racial segregation. In Congress, too, civil rights laws ran into trouble. Southern Democrats held key positions of leadership, and many used their power to keep civil rights laws from passing.

Some blacks came to believe that other types of action would be needed to win equality. In 1955, the black community in Montgomery, Alabama, began a campaign to end segregation on local buses. What methods did the community use? Did the campaign succeed?

Montgomery, Alabama, December, 1955

Rosa Parks was tired. She had finished work and done some shopping. Now, on her way home, she stood with her parcels waiting for a bus. When it came, Parks got on and took the first empty seat she could find.

As the bus moved along its route, it began to fill up. Soon all the seats were taken. When two white passengers got on, the driver called to Rosa Parks to stand and give one of them her seat. She refused. Under local law, bus riders were supposed to obey a driver's orders, and bus seating was supposed to be segregated.

The driver called out again. Parks still remained in her seat. The driver stopped the bus and walked up to her. "Move back, you hear?" Rosa Parks said nothing. The police were called, and they arrested her.

A railroad porter named E. D. Nixon was told about the arrest. Nixon was a local leader of the NAACP, the National Association for the Advancement of Colored People. Ever since 1910 the NAACP had been going to court to argue for black rights. At Nixon's urging, the NAACP agreed to defend Parks' challenge of the local law and the system of segregated bus seating.

Nixon and other black leaders wanted to win national attention for their lawsuit. They also wanted to show the white people of Montgomery that blacks were fed up with the system of segregated seating on buses. It was decided to ask the 50,000 black residents of Montgomery to stay off city buses, to boycott them for one day. For many blacks, this would cause hardship. A great many blacks used the buses to go to and from work and could not afford to be late or absent. But it would be worth the hardship, black leaders argued. If whites saw that blacks were united, perhaps they would give in.

More than 40 black ministers and civil rights leaders agreed to support the one-day boycott. That agreement was reached on a Friday. Over the weekend leaflets were passed out, and ministers announced the boycott in their churches.

Monday came. Only a few blacks rode buses, while most others walked, hitched rides, or rode in horse-drawn wagons to get to work. Buses rolled by half empty. The boycott succeeded beyond anyone's expectations.

Monday evening a mass meeting was held at a Baptist church. Every seat was taken, and thousands stood on the sidewalk near the church. Loudspeakers on the roof of the church let the people outside hear what went on inside.

Speakers said they were tired of being treated as second-class citizens. What had happened to Rosa Parks had happened to other black people over and over. Blacks were ready to do something about this. All they needed was a person to inspire and lead them.

Nixon warned that the work had just begun and that there might be violence. The white community would resent any attempt to do away with segregation. Anyone who wanted to leave was welcome to do so now. No one rose to go.

Then Nixon introduced a new speaker, Martin Luther King, Jr., a 26-year-old Baptist minister with a doctor's degree from Boston University. King said, "We have been amazingly patient. We can no longer be patient with anything less than freedom and justice. We are tired of being segregated and humiliated. Still we must not become bitter. We must not hate our white brothers. We must protest with Christian love so that future historians will say of us, 'There lived a great people.'"

The audience rose and cheered. Nixon smiled. He had found the person he had been looking for. King would lead this movement.

Other members of the audience rose to speak. They did not want to end the boycott. But how long would they stay off the buses? Until the buses were no longer segregated, people agreed.

Plans were made to get the black workers to and from their jobs. The community would use its own cars. Volunteer drivers would help people get around town.

News of the boycott spread, and money poured into Montgomery from outside supporters. Many people, white and black, saw the boycott as a struggle for freedom and dignity. They wanted to help the blacks of Montgomery win their struggle.

Months passed. The black community kept on walking or riding in cars. Acts of violence took place. The homes of King and other leaders were bombed. Some blacks wanted to fight back, but King cooled them down. The way to victory, he said, was through love—not hate.

In the meantime, a three-judge federal court heard the Parks case. The court ruled that segregation on buses was unconstitutional. The State of Alabama appealed, and the case went before the Supreme Court.

The Supreme Court's decision was a swift one. It declared Alabama's state and local laws requiring segregation on buses to be unconstitutional. The black community had won, just over one year after Rosa Parks lost her seat.

POSTSCRIPT

The Montgomery bus boycott brought fame to the Reverend Dr. Martin Luther King, Jr. With his powerful voice and eloquent words, he helped to organize a broad, national civil rights movement. Some called King a radical, and the FBI kept a close watch on his activities. But others admired him as a leader who could stir black Americans to action while winning support from many whites for equal rights.

King encouraged his followers to take a stand against laws they felt were unfair to blacks. In some cases, he openly broke such laws and peacefully accepted arrest. As King saw it, such nonviolent methods served to arouse public sympathy for his movement's goals. Court cases were all well and good, King felt, but public sympathy was necessary if Congress was to be persuaded to pass new laws to promote full equality.

Homework Questions

1. What methods did civil rights leaders use in challenging segregation?
2. Why did blacks in Montgomery, Alabama, decide to boycott city buses?
3. How did Martin Luther King, Jr., want the blacks in Montgomery to conduct their boycott?
4. What brought an end to the Montgomery boycott?

Understanding the Story

A. Write *T* for each statement that is true and *F* for each statement that is false.
   1. In 1955 the buses in Montgomery, Alabama, were segregated.
   2. Rosa Parks took the first empty seat on the bus.
   3. Parks quickly agreed to move to the back of the bus.
   4. The NAACP defended the system of bus segregation.
   5. The bus boycott failed.

6. Martin Luther King, Jr., told blacks that the way to victory was through love.
7. King changed his mind after his house was bombed.
8. The Supreme Court ruled that segregated buses were unconstitutional.

B. Complete each of the following sentences by filling in the missing word or words.
1. The police came and _____ Rosa Parks.
2. The NAACP decided to take the Parks case to _____.
3. Black leaders agreed to _____ city buses.
4. Speakers said they were tired of being treated as _____.
5. King said that blacks must not become _____.
6. Blacks agreed to stop riding until the buses were no longer _____.
7. The boycott _____ beyond most people's expectations.
8. King became leader of a national _____.

C. Black Americans used three main methods in seeking an equal place in American society. Of the three—court suits, pressure for new laws, and direct actions such as the bus boycott—which do you think was the most important? Why?

Activities and Inquiries

1. Rosa Parks was arrested for breaking a local law. Assume that you are her lawyer. State your defense.
2. Now pretend that you are the prosecutor. State your case.
3. Martin Luther King, Jr., was arrested many times and charged with breaking the law. Go to your library and write a report on one such arrest. Do you think King was in the right? Explain.
4. Do you think the bus boycott helped the black community of Montgomery? Why or why not?

10 The Growth of the Constitution: *Brown* v. *Board of Education*

The 13th Amendment abolished slavery. The 14th Amendment guaranteed citizenship to black Americans. The 15th Amendment gave voting rights to blacks. By the early 1950's, nearly 100 years had passed since these amendments had become part of the United States Constitution. Many blacks felt that the nation had yet to fulfill the promises they contained.

Civil rights leaders began to zero in on certain targets. Education was one of them. Many blacks had to send their children to segregated schools. They complained that their children received an inferior education—that the black schools were not the equals of white ones. Besides, they said, the very existence of segregated schools implied that blacks and whites should be kept apart, and true equality was impossible under such conditions.

Blacks decided to challenge the segregated education system by testing local and state school laws in the courts. They expected to lose at the local and state levels, but they would keep appealing until one or more cases came before the United States Supreme Court. Blacks hoped that the Supreme Court would strike down the school segregation laws. They thought the laws violated the 14th Amendment, which provides that no state can take away from any person the equal protection of its laws. What arguments would be used against segregated schools? What arguments would be used in favor of segregated schools? What would the Supreme Court say?

Topeka, Kansas, 1951

The Reverend Oliver Brown was angry. He had tried to register his eight-year-old daughter Linda for school, but the principal of the all-white school had refused to let her in.

The minister met with his congregation and told them that his daughter was not allowed to go to a school only four blocks away from her home. Because she was black, she would have to travel more than 20 blocks by school bus to another school, one that was badly overcrowded. The congregation agreed to help him bring his case to court.

In the local and state courts, the judges said separate schools for blacks and whites were legal so long as the schools were equal to one another. These judges said they were following *precedents* (past examples). In 1896, in the case of *Plessy* v. *Ferguson*, the Supreme Court had ruled that separate but equal facilities for whites and blacks were permitted under the Constitution. Brown was determined to challenge this precedent, which concerned railroad seating—not public schools.

Washington, D.C., 1954

At last, Brown's case and three similar ones came before the Supreme Court. Lawyers favoring separate schools argued that there was nothing in the Constitution against segregation. They said school policy was a matter for each state to decide for itself. Also, they argued that all-white and all-black schools were equal in the kind of education they offered. In many cases, these lawyers claimed, more money had been spent on black schools than on white ones. They also warned that integrating (desegregating) schools would cause terrible problems. Riots might break out. Whites might pull their children out of public schools and place them in private ones. Communities would refuse to support integrated schools, causing all education to suffer.

Lawyers of the NAACP, led by Thurgood Marshall, argued that segregated schools were not equal at all. Many black schools were poorly equipped compared with white ones. Blacks suffered many inconveniences to attend school. Sometimes they had to travel to the far end of a town to attend an all-black school when a white school was nearby. But the worst damage was being done to society, the lawyers said. From the example of segregated schools, black and white students were being taught that they must be separated from one another.

The Court heard all of the arguments. The justices thought a good deal about what had been said and discussed the case among themselves. Other Americans did the same. The case dragged on for a long time. Finally, on Monday, May 17, 1954, came the opinion in *Brown* vs. *Board of Education of Topeka*.

Chief Justice Earl Warren started reading the decision: "We must look at the important place that education holds in American life today. No child can hope to succeed in life if he is denied the opportunity of an education. This opportunity must be made available to all on equal terms."

Reporters who had followed the case leaned forward to listen.

Chief Justice Warren continued, "We come then to the most important question. Are children in segregated schools denied equal educational opportunities?" Speaking for all of the justices, he went on to say: "We conclude that in the field of public education the doctrine of 'separate but equal' has no place. Separate educational facilities are inherently unequal."

The courtroom exploded in a roar. Reporters rushed to call in the news to their papers. Some lawyers looked very unhappy. Others jumped for joy. Everyone understood that the Supreme Court had ruled that segregated schools were unconstitutional because such action went against the 14th Amendment. This was the most important ruling of the Supreme Court since the Dred Scott decision of 1857, many people said.

A black civil rights leader watching the joyful demonstration smiled at the thought that blacks had made a major step toward equality in education. But he told himself that this was only a first step. A long, hard struggle lay ahead.

Homework Questions

1. Why did civil rights leaders complain about the education of black children?
2. How did the case of *Plessy* v. *Ferguson* serve as a precedent in segregation cases?
3. What arguments were used to support the system of segregated schools?
4. What arguments were used to challenge this system?
5. How did the Supreme Court rule in the Brown case?

Understanding the Story

A. Write *T* for each statement that is true, *F* for each statement that is false, and *N* for each statement that is not mentioned.
   1. The 14th Amendment guaranteed citizenship to blacks.
   2. In 1952 few schools were segregated.
   3. Kansas was one of 21 states that either permitted or required school segregation in 1954.
   4. All-black schools were generally as good as all-white schools, everyone agreed.
   5. In 1896 the Supreme Court ruled that facilities for whites and blacks could be separate if they were equal.
   6. The Supreme Court based its ruling in the Brown case on the First Amendment.
   7. Chief Justice Warren said that segregated schools deny children equal educational opportunities.
   8. President Eisenhower was not happy with the Court's decision in the Brown case.

B. Match each item in Column *A* with its description in Column *B*.

Column A

1. 14th Amendment
2. racial segregation
3. 15th Amendment
4. Chief Justice Earl Warren
5. *Plessy* v. *Ferguson*
6. The Reverend Oliver Brown
7. racial integration
8. 13th Amendment

Column B

a. approved separate but equal facilities
b. brought a case against segregated education
c. gave voting rights to blacks
d. announced the decision against school segregation
e. guaranteed citizenship to blacks
f. the separation of blacks and whites
g. abolished slavery
h. the bringing together of blacks and whites

C. Assume that Chief Justice Earl Warren is alive today. He travels around the country and looks at the racial makeup of public schools. Is he pleased with what he sees? Why or why not?

Activities and Inquiries

1. Interview several of your fellow students. Ask them how they feel about integration in high schools.

2. Imagine that you are a lawyer for Oliver Brown. Prepare the arguments you will offer to support Brown's court case.

3. Imagine that you are a judge in a lower court. Prepare a ruling in the Brown case, citing *Plessy* v. *Ferguson* as a precedent.

4. Visit your local library. Prepare a report on a community that was ordered to integrate its schools. Describe what happened. What is your personal opinion about the situation?

Who Built America?

Albert Einstein

SAM. I've chosen to tell you about Albert Einstein, a Jewish scientist.

HEINRICH. Wasn't Einstein a German?

SAM. Yes, but the Nazis took away his German citizenship. Einstein was in the United States when Hitler came to power in 1933. He stayed here.

MR. MILLER. Let's just say that Einstein was a Jewish scientist born in Germany.

SAM. Einstein was one of the greatest scientists of all time.

ROBERT. You're not going to make this too complicated are you, Sam?

SAM. Oh, no. Einstein said that we shouldn't clutter our minds with facts. I agree. You can find the details about his theory of relativity in science books.

JANET. Did Einstein really say that about not cluttering our minds?

SAM. Yes, and he said something else you'd like. He was against exams because he remembered how he suffered through so many of them in his youth.

CASIMIR. Did he say anything else about school?

SAM. Yes. He said that children should go to school to learn to think.

MR. MILLER. Very interesting, Sam. But I think you'd better move on to Einstein's contributions in science.

SAM. Okay. He worked out theories that helped give us the photo-electric eye.

CARLA. I didn't know that he invented the gadget for opening doors and counting things.

SAM. He didn't invent it, Carla. His ideas helped the person who did invent it.

HANS. I'm not saying that the electric eye isn't important. But is there something that Einstein did that I can appreciate?

518

SAM. Sure, Hans. Have you ever heard of television?

HANS. You mean?

SAM. Right! Einstein's discoveries helped lead to the transmission of pictures over the air.

ROSA. Do you think Einstein would be surprised at how television has developed?

SAM. I really can't answer that. But I do know that he would be very unhappy about the nuclear arms race. He said so himself.

JUAN. I can see why atomic weapons would concern him. Did Einstein have anything to do with the first atomic bomb?

SAM. Einstein predicted that we would be able to split the atom and turn atomic energy to various uses. In the 1930's, German scientists proved that Einstein was right. They became the first to split the atom artificially and release its energy. The question was: How would this energy be used?

JOSEPHINE. What happened?

SAM. World War II hadn't started yet, but many believed that the Germans might build an atomic bomb. Scientists outside of Germany asked Einstein to send a letter to President Roosevelt urging him to start an atomic bomb project at once. Einstein was a pacifist—he was against war. Yet he agreed that the United States should develop this weapon. So he wrote the letter.

TOM. In a way, then, Einstein might be called the father of the A-bomb.

SAM. Not exactly. He helped to show the way, but he didn't actually take part in making the bomb.

RICARDO. You said that Einstein wouldn't be happy about nuclear weapons. Why not? The atom bomb helped win World War II.

SAM. True, but Einstein regretted its use against Japan. I'm sure that he was unhappy about his part in it all.

MR. MILLER. Can you summarize what Einstein did?

SAM. He changed our ideas about the vast universe and the tiny atom. The paths of thinking he opened up took us into a new scientific age.

JACK. He was a great man—and a great scientist.

"Mr. Miller, you said that World War II had a different effect on America than World War I."

"That's right Jack, and you agree, of course."

"Surprisingly enough, I do."

"Good," said Mr. Miller. "Explain yourself."

"After World War I, the United States decided to mind its own business. It lost interest in the rest of the world and refused to join the League of Nations."

"And what happened after World War II?" prodded Mr. Miller.

"The United States did just the opposite. It joined the United Nations and became involved with countries all over the world."

"How do you account for this difference?" asked Mr. Miller.

"I guess Americans had learned a lesson. They had learned that problems don't go away simply because you ignore them."

"What made Americans begin to think that way?" asked Mr. Miller.

"The atomic bomb for one," said Jack. "Now an ordinary war could become an atomic war. Such a war could easily destroy the United States as well as the rest of the world."

"What else?"

Jack continued. "After World War I, the United States had no real enemies. After World War II, the U.S. became locked in a cold war with the Soviet Union. Air travel made the world seem smaller. Nations became more dependent on one another than ever before. We needed friends as much as others needed us."

"Jack, that's good."

"Thanks. By the way, there is something else. After World War I, the United States turned away from reform. After World War II, it didn't. In fact, it kept most of the New Deal ideas and even went a step further."

"What step was that?" asked Mr. Miller.

"Americans began to pay attention to their civil rights problems. They began to make good on promises more than 100 years old."

"It sounds like everything was rosy," said Mr. Miller.

"Oh, no, you're not trapping me. When you say that things are rosy, that's when it's time to watch out."

"Let's turn to the next unit to find out."

The 1960's

"I take it everything wasn't rosy in the 1960's," said Jack.

"Well, the decade started on an upbeat note," said Mr. Miller. "Americans had a new President, a man noted for his youthfulness and his optimism. Many people hoped that a new age was dawning."

"So what happened?"

"Many things, Jack. The United States almost came to blows with the Soviet Union. It got bogged down in a major war in Southeast Asia. At home, Americans were at odds with themselves. And assassins took the lives of three prominent Americans."

"Sounds like pretty heavy going."

"It was, Jack. For a time Americans seemed to be losing confidence in themselves and their leaders."

"What a gloomy picture!"

"It wasn't all gloomy, Jack. The United States sent men to the moon and made new commitments to bring about a better life for Americans of all races and backgrounds."

"That's more like it. Let's find out how it all happened."

1 The Cuban Missile Crisis

A sudden thaw in the Cold War in the late 1950's raised hopes for smoother relations between the United States and the Soviet Union. President Eisenhower invited the Soviet leader, Nikita Khrushchev, to come to the United States. Khrushchev came in 1959, met with the President, and invited him to visit the Soviet Union the next year. But Khrushchev withdrew the invitation at the last minute. The Soviets had just captured a U.S. pilot after shooting down his specially equipped spy plane far inside Soviet borders. The Cold War was on again.

A new President, John F. Kennedy, a Democrat, took office in 1961. Kennedy was a young man—at 43, the youngest ever to be elected President. He was a Roman Catholic—the first Catholic President. In his inaugural speech, Kennedy warned Americans that they faced a long, hard struggle in the days and years ahead. Their courage, he said, would be tested many times.

U.S.-Soviet tensions in the early 1960's focused in part on Cuba. This island nation 90 miles off the coast of Florida had had a revolution in the late 1950's. Its new ruler, Fidel Castro, was a leftist who was making vast changes in Cuban society and seeking help from the Soviets. Many Cubans cheered for Castro, but many others went into exile (left the country). Some of the exiles vowed to overthrow Castro. U.S. leaders offered to help.

In great secrecy the United States supplied military training and equipment to the exiles. Advisers to both Eisenhower and Kennedy said an exile invasion would spark a broad uprising in Cuba. They said Castro was so unpopular that the invasion would bring him down. Kennedy gave the green light.

On April 17, 1961, some 2,000 Cuban exiles landed at a place in Cuba called the Bay of Pigs. Castro's forces smashed the invasion and captured many of the invaders. No uprising took place. Castro angrily denounced the United States, declared himself to be a Communist (something he had earlier denied), and asked the Soviet Union for increased military aid.

Meanwhile, Kennedy and Khrushchev met in Vienna, Austria, in June, 1961. Their meeting was stormy. Kennedy thought the Soviet leader was trying to bully him. Kennedy told Khrushchev, "It will be a cold winter."

A new crisis was brewing over Germany. Although World War II had been over for 16 years, no German peace treaty had been signed. The former Allies still could not agree about Berlin. Khrushchev wanted to end the special rights of the Western powers in Berlin. If the United States would not agree to join in a peace treaty by the end of 1961, said Khrushchev, the Soviet Union would sign a treaty with East Germany. Then East Germans, not Soviets, would control the land that surrounded West Berlin.

Once again, as in 1948, there could be a confrontation over Berlin.

West Berlin was an annoyance to the Communist bloc. Many East Germans had crossed into West Berlin, seeking better living conditions or greater freedom or both. Suddenly in August, 1961, the East Germans built a wall to seal off East Berlin from West Berlin. Clearly, Khrushchev and his East German partners were trying to stop East Germans from fleeing to the West. Were they also trying to test the courage of the United States to stand up to Communist pressure?

Kennedy thought they were. He sent more U.S. troops to West Berlin. He stepped up an overall military buildup begun earlier that summer. Were the two powers headed for a showdown?

Not yet. In October, 1961, Khrushchev took back his deadline over the peace treaty. He would not force a showdown. The Berlin crisis was over.

But there was to be a second and more dangerous crisis, this time over Cuba. As the Soviets and the Cubans moved closer together, the United States stepped up its watch on Cuba. U.S. planes flying more than 13 miles above the earth's surface made regular trips over the island nation, snapping photos to be studied by experts. On October 15, 1962, the experts spotted a medium-range nuclear missile being set up in western Cuba. Such a missile could reach targets as far away as Dallas, Texas, and Washington, D.C. There were signs that even longer-range missiles were to be installed too.

American officials were stunned. Instead of the 15-minute warning that could be expected if a missile were fired from the Soviet Union, the Cuban missiles would give the United States less than three minutes' warning of any attack. What should the United States do? What could it do?

Washington, D.C., October, 1962

President Kennedy called together his top advisers. He said, "This is a grave moment for the United States. Unless we act soon, the Soviet Union will have its missiles on our very doorstep."

A cabinet official was the first to speak. "Mr. President," he said, "do we really need to do anything at all? The Soviets have had missiles aimed at us for years. What difference does it make whether their missiles are in Russia or in Cuba? Remember, we have our own nuclear missiles in Turkey, which is right on the Soviet border, and the Soviets have learned to live with them."

The President shook his head. He said, "Even so we must stop the Soviets from installing their missiles in Cuba. First, the missiles present us with a much greater danger than missiles based in Russia. Second, to allow the Soviets to get away with this would be to permit a sudden, drastic change in the world balance of power. The suddenness makes this move all the more dangerous, both to our prestige and to our safety."

A military leader spoke up. "I agree. Our bombers can hit the missile sites in a surprise attack. We can destroy them before they are ready."

A civilian at the end of the table said, "That's too risky. It might force the Soviets to strike back—in Berlin, perhaps, where our troops

The Caribbean, 1962

are surrounded. We must act firmly, but we must leave the Soviets room to back down. Why not use our ships to blockade Cuba? We can keep the Soviets from bringing in more missiles while giving them time to remove the ones already there."

"A blockade is risky too," said the cabinet official. "It would be considered an act of war. Khrushchev couldn't back down without losing face."

"What makes you think the Soviets would back down at all?" asked the military leader. "They must have known that putting their missiles into Cuba would force a showdown. Maybe they're just itching to start a war."

"I don't think the Soviets are any more eager than we are to have a war," said the President. "I think it is more likely that they have miscalculated. But we must let them know in no uncertain terms: Their missiles in Cuba are a serious threat to the United States. And we will not permit such threats to go unchallenged, even if it means risking a nuclear war."

A grim silence followed. Those at the table had the feeling that this was the most serious crisis since the start of the nuclear age. How would it end?

Attorney General Robert Kennedy, the President's brother, spoke up. "Now I know how Tojo felt when he was planning Pearl Harbor. I don't like the feeling at all. It would be a great mistake for our nation to attack a small country without warning. We must think of the blow to our reputation as a peace-loving nation—and the blow to our consciences."

"Our reputation won't be worth a darn if we let the Soviets get the upper hand," said another adviser. "We must do whatever it takes to get those missiles out."

The President turned to the military man. "What would a strike at the missiles involve?"

"We can't just hit the missile bases. We would have to hit storage bases and air defenses, too. We probably would have to send in backup troops to finish the job."

The President frowned. "I don't like it. We would be killing not only Cubans but Russian soldiers as well. Let's come back to the idea of a blockade."

"Why not start with a blockade," said a civilian, "and leave our other options open? If the blockade does the job, fine. If it doesn't, we can still send in the bombers."

"That sounds better," said the President. "We want to keep this thing under control. We can increase the pressure step by step, until the Soviets either back down or—"

He left the sentence unfinished.

"Let's work out the details of the blockade," said the President. "And let's hope that Khrushchev is a reasonable man who knows when it's time to back down."

POSTSCRIPT

The President appeared on television the night of October 22 to announce the blockade, although the word he used was "quarantine," which sounded less warlike. The U.S. Navy would station ships in a ring around Cuba, he said. It would stop and inspect all ships headed for Cuba that were suspected of carrying medium- or long-range missiles. Any ship trying to run (evade) the blockade would be sunk. The President warned that the blockade might be followed by stronger measures.

The news came as a shock to the public and to world leaders. Suddenly the world seemed to teeter on the brink of nuclear war. U.S. nuclear bombers went on a round-the-clock alert.

In a few days came reports that the Soviet Union had turned many of its ships around. That was a first step. It would avoid a showdown at sea.

In a message to Kennedy, Khrushchev offered to remove the missiles already in Cuba—but only if the United States pledged not to invade Cuba. Kennedy made the pledge. Secretly, he also told Khrushchev that the United States would take its missiles out of Turkey. On October 28, Khrushchev announced that the Soviet missiles would be withdrawn. The crisis was over.

President Kennedy did not boast that he had won a victory over the Soviet Union. Instead, he wrote Khrushchev suggesting that the two leaders make a new effort to end the nuclear arms race. An agreement to stop above-ground testing of nuclear weapons was signed in 1963. But underground testing and the development of new weapons continued. The rivalry between the two powers throughout the world did not stop.

Homework Questions

1. Why did President Kennedy approve the exiles' invasion of Cuba?
2. How did the Berlin crisis of 1961 come about?
3. What arguments were made against the proposal to attack the missile bases in Cuba?
4. Why did Kennedy decide on a blockade instead?
5. How did the Soviet Union respond to the U.S. blockade?

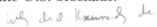

Understanding the Story

A. Write *T* for each statement that is true and *F* for each statement that is false.
   1. The Soviets built missile bases in Cuba.
   2. President Kennedy did nothing about the Cuban missile bases.
   3. Khrushchev and Kennedy agreed that both nations should build bases in Cuba.
   4. Kennedy hoped that Khrushchev would back down.
   5. Kennedy ordered the U.S. Navy to sink ships that tried to run the blockade.
   6. The Soviet ships refused to stop.
   7. Both sides wanted to avoid a nuclear war.
   8. Khrushchev refused to withdraw the missiles from Cuba.

B. Number the following events in the order in which they took place.
   1. Kennedy meets Khrushchev in Vienna.
   2. Soviet ships turn around.
   3. Castro comes to power in Cuba.

4. The Soviet Union builds missile bases in Cuba.
5. The Soviet Union withdraws missiles from Cuba.
6. Exiles defeated at Bay of Pigs.
7. U.S. sets up blockade of Cuba.
8. East Germans build Berlin Wall.

C. Imagine that the United States did not discover the Soviet missiles in Cuba until they were all in place and ready to fire. You are an adviser to President Kennedy. What will you suggest that he do?

Activities and Inquiries

1. Study the map on page 524. Then choose the term or phrase that best completes each statement.
   a. The distance from Havana, Cuba, to Key West, Florida, is about (*1*) 100 miles   (*2*) 250 miles   (*3*) 375 miles.
   b. The distance from Havana to the Panama Canal is about (*1*) 500 kilometers   (*2*) 1,600 kilometers   (*3*) 2,400 kilometers.
   c. Cuba is west of (*1*) Mexico   (*2*) Haiti   (*3*) the Panama Canal.
   d. An island directly south of Cuba is   (*1*) Puerto Rico   (*2*) the Dominican Republic   (*3*) Jamaica.
   e. Study the map once again. Why was the United States concerned about Soviet missiles being in Cuba?
2. Imagine that Khrushchev issues a statement to the press about the Cuban missile crisis. Write the statement.
3. Now, write a statement that Kennedy issues to the press.

2 Death of a President

President Kennedy's actions in the Cuban missile crisis were widely supported by the American people. But many of his domestic policies stirred controversy.

Race relations had become a tense national issue by the 1960's. A broad civil rights movement was making headlines with such tactics as "sit-ins" and "freedom rides." In 1962 riots occurred at the University of Mississippi when whites tried to stop a black student, James Meredith, from entering classes. President Kennedy sent federal troops to the university to put down the riots. In 1963 Kennedy backed a civil rights bill that aimed at greater equality for blacks. In the South, especially, many whites disliked Kennedy for these actions.

A Kennedy proposal to land a man on the moon by 1970 also caused controversy. Some people saw the proposal as a necessary step in beginning the exploration of the universe. Others denounced it as a waste of money.

In foreign policy, Kennedy set up a Peace Corps that recruited Americans to work in less developed countries where their skills were needed. He also turned his attention to Indo-China, which had become independent from France in the 1950's.

Indo-China consisted of three nations—Cambodia, Laos, and Vietnam. Since the 1950's, the situation in Vietnam had alarmed U.S. leaders. A strong nationalist movement, led by a Communist named Ho Chi Minh, had fought to prevent the French from re-gaining control of Vietnam after World War II. After years of warfare, an agreement was signed in 1954. Vietnam was now independent, but it was divided into two parts. The North was a Communist state ruled by Ho Chi Minh. South Vietnam was a non-Communist state that kept close ties to France and the United States.

Elections were planned for 1956 to unify Vietnam. When the elections did not take place, leftists took up arms against the South Vietnamese government. The United States sent a few hundred military advisers to help the government, claiming that North Vietnam was controlling the rebellion and that the rebels were mostly Communists. President Eisenhower said it was important that South Vietnam not be taken over by Communists.

Kennedy continued the Eisenhower policy, but the war was going badly for South Vietnam. Kennedy decided to send several thousand U.S. soldiers to serve as advisers. He rejected a suggestion that he send U.S. combat troops. He said he did not want the United States to get bogged down in another war like the Korean War.

By November, 1963, Kennedy had been President for roughly 1,000 days. He was looking ahead to 1964, when he would be running for re-election. Seeking to gain support from leaders within his Democratic Party who were unhappy with some of his policies, Kennedy made a trip to Texas. Our story tells what happened on that trip.

Dallas, Texas, November 22, 1963

President Kennedy smiled and waved to the cheering crowds. Large open cars were carrying the presidential party through the streets of Dallas, the second largest city in Texas. With Kennedy in one car were his wife, Jacqueline, and the governor of Texas. In another car was Vice President Lyndon B. Johnson, a Texan. The motorcade wound slowly through the downtown section.

Many were surprised at the warm welcome the President was receiving. Kennedy was not considered popular in Dallas. The city, a major center of finance and industry, contained many conservatives who thought Kennedy was just too liberal. One month earlier, angry people in a crowd in Dallas had spat upon a high official in Kennedy's administration.

Kennedy had come to Dallas to make a speech and to meet political leaders. Earlier that day he had made a speech in the nearby city of Fort Worth. "We live in a dangerous and uncertain world," the President had said.

The President smiled and waved at the Dallas crowds. There were so many things Kennedy wanted to do—about civil rights, about world problems. And he needed time to do them. Kennedy had asked Congress to pass many new laws—not only a civil rights law but also a tax cut, a new health program, and a boost in aid to education. Many of the bills seemed unlikely to pass in 1963. That was one reason Kennedy thought it important to smooth over political differences and build support for the 1964 election. He wanted to be re-elected, to keep pushing for passage of his program.

The motorcade was almost through the downtown section. Suddenly shots rang out. John Kennedy slumped down in the back seat of the car, struck at the base of the neck and in the head. Within a matter of minutes, the President was dead. The Texas governor was also shot, although not fatally.

The shots appeared to have come from a tall building on the edge of downtown. Lee Harvey Oswald, a 24-year-old man who worked in the building, was arrested several miles away later the same day. Oswald was charged with the killing. Possible reasons why Oswald might have wanted to shoot the President were unclear. Two days after the assassination Oswald himself was shot and killed by a Dallas nightclub owner in the basement of the Dallas police headquarters. To this day, questions about why and how Kennedy and Oswald were shot continue to be debated.

POSTSCRIPT

Before flying back to Washington, D.C., Lyndon B. Johnson took the oath of office as President. Johnson had had long years of experience in Congress, where he served from 1937 to 1960. He had risen to the position of majority leader of the Senate. He had also become a master of the political process of making compromises to get bills passed.

As President, Johnson proved more effective than Kennedy at pushing bills through Congress. He persuaded Congress to pass most of Kennedy's program and much more. For example, Johnson got Congress to declare "war on poverty" by setting up several programs to train poorer Americans for jobs and to help them in other ways. Another program, Medicare, provided federal health insurance for older people as part of the Social Security system. Johnson said his aim was to create a "Great Society."

Prodded by Johnson, Congress passed major civil rights bills in 1964, 1965, and 1968. The new laws aimed to bar discrimination in voting, in the use of public facilities such as restaurants and hotels, and in the sale and rental of housing.

Homework Questions

1. Why did President Kennedy's domestic program stir controversy?
2. How did Kennedy respond to events in Vietnam?
3. What was the reason for Kennedy's trip to Dallas?
4. Did Lyndon Johnson carry on Kennedy's policies or change them? Explain.

Understanding the Story

A. Write *T* for each statement that is true, *F* for each statement that is false, and *N* for each statement that is not mentioned in the story.
   1. President Kennedy liked to play touch football.
   2. Kennedy was popular with all Americans.
   3. Kennedy favored a new civil rights bill.
   4. Lee Harvey Oswald once tried to give up his U.S. citizenship.
   5. Kennedy was the first U.S. President to aid South Vietnam.
   6. Kennedy worried about the next election.
   7. Kennedy had trouble getting his bills through Congress.
   8. Kennedy thought a tax cut was a bad idea.

B. Which of the following statements describe Kennedy's thinking?
   1. I want Congress to pass a civil rights bill.
   2. The United States should land a man on the moon.
   3. Americans should help people in less developed lands.
   4. The United States has nothing to worry about in Vietnam.
   5. I don't want Vietnam to become another Korea.
   6. I don't care if I am re-elected.
   7. I must smooth over differences with my Democratic critics.
   8. Congress is doing what I want it to do.

C. From what you have read of President Lyndon Johnson's policies, do you think they would have been popular with conservatives? Why or why not?

Activities and Inquiries

1. Prepare a report card for President Kennedy. Grade him in the following areas and justify each grade:
   a. Leadership
   b. Point of view
   c. Accomplishments while President
   d. Maturity
2. Assume that you are a reporter assigned to interview Lyndon B. Johnson. He has just been sworn in as President following Kennedy's death. What questions will you ask him?
3. How will Johnson answer your questions?
4. Go to the library and read about what happened in Vietnam after World War II. Write a report telling how the United States got involved there.

3 Martin Luther King, Jr.

For more than a decade after the Montgomery bus boycott (pages 510–512), Martin Luther King, Jr., dominated the civil rights movement in the United States. There were many other leaders in the movement. Some were older than King and some were younger, some more conservative and some more radical. But King had the attention of the nation's press. He also had the support of a broad range of Americans, black and white, who believed in racial equality.

Not that King was universally popular. Many blacks disagreed with his methods and called him an "Uncle Tom," a black man who was too eager to please whites. And many whites despised him, calling him a troublemaker and worse.

In our story, we take a closer look at King. What kind of vision did this man have for America? How did he try to make his vision a reality? What was the result?

Memphis, Tennessee, 1968

You are Martin Luther King, Jr., and you have a dream for America. It is a dream of a future in which race no longer matters, in which blacks and whites live as equals—full equals. In your preacher's voice, with rich sentences rolling off your tongue, you have tried to describe this dream to others.

"I have a dream," you have said, "that one day this nation will rise up and live out the true meaning of its creed: '. . . that all men are created equal.' I have a dream that one day on the red hills of Georgia the sons of former slaves and the sons of former slaveowners will be able to sit down together at the table of brotherhood."

You have traveled around this nation telling others of your dream. But you don't just talk. You also act. You lead your supporters in defying laws that you believe to be unfair.

What sort of laws? Laws that allow a restaurant to serve whites but not blacks, for example, and that allow restaurant owners to have blacks arrested for trespass. For years it was common for Southern "white" restaurants to refuse to let blacks sit down to eat a meal. Blacks might buy food at a take-out counter, but they could not sit down and eat it there.

The sit-in was one technique used to fight such customs. Blacks would sit down at a restaurant or lunch counter, order a meal or a cup of coffee, and wait. They would not be served. They would keep their seats and wait. Sometimes all the seats would fill up with blacks waiting to be served. Often the restaurant owners would call the police and have the blacks arrested.

It was college students who first used sit-ins, in 1960, but you soon joined in. In 1962 you were sentenced to four months at hard labor for refusing to leave a restaurant in a department store in Atlanta, Georgia. You appealed and were released on bail.

The next year you went to Birmingham, Alabama, to lead several hundred people in street marches and sit-ins. You said Birmingham was the most segregated city in the United States, and you wanted to bring change. The police used snarling dogs and fire hoses against your supporters. Pictures of these activities were printed in newspapers around the world. Again you were arrested and put in jail. Again you were released. Seeing the pictures from Birmingham, President Kennedy declared, "I can well understand why the Negroes of Birmingham are tired of being asked to be patient."

That was your point, after all. By your method of civil disobedience—breaking the law to court arrest, then submitting quietly to the police—you were trying to show that black Americans were suffering under unjust laws. You believed that nonviolent protest was the way to convince white Americans to change those laws. And many whites, including President Kennedy, came to agree.

In August, 1963, you and other civil rights leaders walked at the head of a "march on Washington." Some 200,000 or more people joined the march through the streets of the nation's capital. It was a peaceful parade, with whites and blacks walking arm in arm. The march ended at the Lincoln Memorial. It was from the steps of this monument that you declared, "I have a dream."

You had hope and your dream, but in the ghettos (slum neighborhoods) of many cities lived blacks who had lost both. Equality seemed to be forever out of reach. Beginning in the summer of 1964, riots tore through many of these ghettos. Often set off by an incident such as the shooting of a black person by a white police officer, these riots

The Reverend Martin Luther King, Jr., giving his "I Have a Dream" speech

caused many deaths and great destruction to property. At times, heavily armed U.S. troops moved in to put down the rioting. Most of those killed were blacks.

You publicly deplored the riots. Again you spoke of the power of love over hatred and called for nonviolent methods of protest. But many blacks no longer listened to you. They turned to new leaders, young men who used terms like "black power" and who carried guns.

Appalled at what was happening, you took a new tack. You continued your work in the civil rights movement, but you also began to speak out on other issues. You said that blacks and other Americans, especially the poor, were suffering because the nation used too much money for war and not enough to fight poverty and discrimination. You made headlines by criticizing U.S. policies in Vietnam, where full-scale war raged from 1965 on. (For more on the Vietnam War, see Chapter 5 in this unit.)

Of course, this made you more of a controversial figure than ever. But you were winning wider recognition. You were awarded the 1965 Nobel Prize for Peace. And you continued to voice your dream for America.

"I just want to do God's will," you said. "And He's allowed me to go to the mountain. And I've looked over, and I've seen the promised land. I may not get there with you, but I want you to know tonight that we as a people will go to the promised land."

POSTSCRIPT

In April, 1968, an assassin's bullet struck and killed Martin Luther King, Jr., as he stood on the balcony of a motel in Memphis, Tennessee. A white man named James Earl Ray was convicted of killing King and sentenced to prison. Accusations that someone had hired Ray to kill King were investigated, but no other suspects were arrested or tried.

The night King died, riots tore through black neighborhoods in 125 American cities. It seemed that 1968 was a year for riots. Besides the riots in black ghettos, there were riots on college campuses and a riot on the streets of Chicago as the Democratic National Convention met nearby. Some blamed youthful protesters for the Chicago riot; others called it "a police riot." In any case it was part of a wave of violence that swept American life that year.

A second assassination was part of 1968's violence. In June a gunman killed John Kennedy's brother, Robert Kennedy, who was in Los Angeles campaigning for the presidential nomination.

To some it seemed that King's methods of nonviolence were outdated, forgotten. But others kept the faith and carried on in King's footsteps. By 1968 the civil rights movement could claim credit for a series of federal civil rights measures that had struck down many of the legal barriers to racial equality. King's followers now set their sights on a new goal—finding ways to attack the poverty that kept many blacks from sharing fully in the American dream.

Homework Questions

1. What criticisms did some people make of Martin Luther King, Jr.?
2. How did King describe his dream for America?
3. Why did King and his followers defy certain laws?
4. How did King respond to the rioting in black ghettos?
5. What kinds of violence swept the United States in 1968? Give examples.

Understanding the Story

A. Write *F* for each statement that is a fact and *O* for each statement that is an opinion.
   1. Martin Luther King, Jr., was a leading figure in the civil rights movement.
   2. King was an "Uncle Tom."
   3. King had a dream of brotherhood.
   4. Blacks and whites should live as equals.
   5. King said that unjust laws should not be obeyed.
   6. There were riots in many cities in the mid-1960's.
   7. King should not have gone to Memphis.
   8. King spoke against U.S. policies in Vietnam.

B. Write *A* for each statement that Martin Luther King would agree with and *N* for each statement that he would not agree with.
   1. Racial segregation must end.
   2. We must meet violence with violence.
   3. We must obey all laws, good or bad.
   4. We can win without violence.
   5. The United States uses too much money for war.

6. Peaceful sit-ins are a waste of time.
7. Let us work harder to end poverty and discrimination.
8. We will reach the promised land.

C. Assume that you are a leader seeking to advance a cause in the United States today. Do you think the methods of Martin Luther King, Jr.—nonviolent protest and civil disobedience—would be effective? Explain.

Activities and Inquiries

1. Describe the changes that would have to take place in American society if Martin Luther King's dream of racial equality were to come true.

2. Prepare a report card for Martin Luther King. Grade him in the following areas and justify each grade.
   a. Leadership
   b. Training
   c. Point of view
   d. Accomplishments
   e. Maturity
3. Assume that Martin Luther King, Jr., kept a diary. Write an account of one day in his life as described in his diary.
4. Visit a library. Prepare a report about another black leader of the 1960's.
5. Interview people in your community. Ask what they remember about Martin Luther King, Jr., or what his life has meant to them.

4 The Fish-In

The decade of the 1960's was a time of protest. Blacks were not the only ones calling for change. American Indians, or Native Americans, also had grievances and voiced them strongly.

Unlike black Americans, Indians could back up their grievances by citing solemn treaties signed by the United States government. The United States had made treaties with one Indian nation after another in the 19th century and earlier. The United States was not keeping its word, Indians asserted. It was breaking its treaties.

By the 1960's, many people had forgotten those dusty treaties. Didn't the Indians live on reservations now?

Wasn't the federal government trying to help them adjust?

Over the years the government had followed a variety of policies toward the Indian tribes. For a time it divided tribal lands among Indian families and encouraged such practices as farming. This tended to break up tribal cultures. It did not, however, achieve its goal of "assimilating" (absorbing) Indians into the dominant American culture. It did not turn Indians into "white people."

Congress ordered a new Indian policy in 1934. The goal now was to build up the tribes, to promote self-government for each tribe, and to keep tribal lands together.

Again in 1953, Congress shifted gears. It went back to the earlier policy of trying to bring Indians into the American "melting pot." It proposed to terminate (end) federal programs for tribes. This goal was called "termination."

Through all the shifts of policy one thing was constant, and that was poverty. Indians on reservations had the lowest standard of living of all Americans. Many Indians left reservations to look for jobs in cities.

During the 1960's, a new generation of young Indians, many of them college students, decided it was time for Indians to reassert themselves. They talked of Indian traditions with pride and of "white" culture with scorn. They said Indians must again become self-reliant, like their ancestors of long ago. But how?

In our story, a young man and his father differ about a direct-action campaign to claim a treaty right. In what ways do the Indians' tactics and goals resemble those of blacks in the civil rights movement? In what ways are they different?

Near Tacoma, Washington, 1966

The game wardens were waiting in boats at the river's edge, along with the fisheries patrol officers and the deputy sheriffs. Jack pushed his small boat off from shore and began to row. As he went, he unreeled a large fishing net. He was going to catch salmon, even though he knew he was breaking the state's fishing regulations. Indians had been catching salmon in these waters for centuries. To Jack, the state's regulations were an insult and a challenge.

The officers watched and waited. Jack was not alone. There were dozens of other boats, all containing Indians who wanted to catch salmon. On the shores were Indian women and children, watching silently. The Indians had publicized their plan for a "fish-in," patterned after the sit-ins of the civil rights movement. Reporters were there, and curious onlookers.

As the nets unfurled, the officers moved into action. They seized the fishing boats. They made arrests. There were scuffles, angry words, and blows. Some bystanders threw rocks or sticks at the officers. Jack was among those arrested. He spent the night in jail.

The next morning Jack's father came to bail him out. At the police station he was silent. But on the way home he exploded.

"You are a fool, Jack," he said. "It makes no sense to break the law and go to jail. What will it get you? A fine, perhaps a jail term— and you'll lose your boat. Then how will you catch fish?"

"Father, we have to stand up for our rights," said Jack. "Our people have always fished for salmon. Every year at spawning time we have gone to the river. We have cast our nets and caught the fish as they swam upstream to lay their eggs."

"That is so," said the father. "But in the old days our people needed salmon for food. You do not eat the salmon you catch. You sell them to big companies, and they end up in cans on the shelves of supermarkets."

"What difference does that make, Father? The salmon are my livelihood. I don't want to work in a shop, like you. I want to work outdoors, like your father and his father before him."

"You must obey the laws, Jack. Haven't I taught you that an honest person obeys the laws?"

"Father, it is the state that is breaking the law, not I. We Indians have a right to fish in these waters—as long as the grass shall grow and the stream shall run. Our right is spelled out in the treaties that our ancestors signed with 'the Great White Father.'" Jack spat out the final words with contempt.

"How can you make the government keep a promise that was made more than a century ago?"

"A promise is a promise, Father. If the government is honest, it will keep its word."

"But times have changed, Jack. How many Indians are there in the state of Washington? Twenty, twenty-five thousand? We are just a tiny minority in a sea of non-Indians. How can we make our voice heard?"

"Father, the blacks are a minority in this country, too, yet they have found ways to make their voice heard. They have protested to claim their rights, and so must we. Our fish-ins are like the sit-ins of the civil rights movement. The regulations that tell Indians they can fish freely only on reservations are unjust. They are as unjust as the laws that tell blacks they can't enjoy the same rights as whites."

"No, Jack, it is not that simple. The blacks want equal rights, and whites can understand that. But to most non-Indians, you seem to be demanding special privileges. You demand the right to fish when and where you want, and yet non-Indians must obey the fishing regulations of the state. They think you will take all the fish and leave none for them. They think you will destroy the salmon by overfishing."

"That's just an excuse, Father. We Indians will not destroy the salmon—we need them. Besides, we are not demanding special privileges. We are only asking that the government respect our treaty rights. We should not need anyone's permission to fish. I am proud of being a Nisqually, an Indian. Fishing is part of my heritage. If I want to preserve that heritage for my children and my children's children, then I must insist on my rights. *All* my rights."

POSTSCRIPT

The fish-ins caused a split in the Indian community. Many Indians, and some well-known non-Indians, took part in them. Some tribal leaders supported them. But other tribal leaders opposed them, arguing that they might cause the government to halt programs that aided Indians.

Besides holding fish-ins and protest marches, Indian groups filed court suits asking that state governments respect various treaty rights. A federal judge in

Tacoma, Washington, ruled in 1974 that many of Washington State's fishing regulations could no longer be applied to Indians. He said the regulations violated treaty rights dating back to the 1850's. Although the state of Washington sought to appeal, the U.S. Supreme Court in 1976 said it would not review the case.

Other court cases have also given new life to Indian treaty rights. In the West, Indians have won recognition of tribal water claims. In South Dakota, New York, and Maine, tribal groups have won tens of millions of dollars for lands that were illegally taken. The efforts to sort out the many claims and counterclaims have caused complicated problems for the states, the federal government, and private individuals. Legal disputes are likely to go on for many years.

Homework Questions

1. How did the Indians' tactics resemble those of the blacks?
2. In what way were Indian claims different from those of blacks?
3. Why did Jack's father oppose the fish-ins?
4. What were Jack's arguments in favor of the fish-ins?
5. How did court rulings give new life to Indian treaty rights?

Understanding the Story

A. Write *T* for each statement that is true and *F* for each statement that is false.
  1. The United States made many treaties with Indian tribes.
  2. Indians were satisfied that the United States was respecting its treaties.
  3. Congress always tried to keep Indian tribes from breaking up.
  4. Indians on reservations had the lowest standard of living of all Americans.
  5. Jack purposely broke the state's fishing regulations.
  6. Jack was fishing for tuna.
  7. Because of court rulings, Indian treaty rights no longer matter.
  8. Federal judges sometimes sided with Indians against state governments.

B. Write *J* for each statement Jack made or might have made and *F* for each statement Jack's father made or might have made.
  1. Indians must ignore the state's fishing regulations.
  2. By going to jail we can make our voice heard.
  3. It is foolish to break the law.
  4. Indians are a tiny minority in a sea of non-Indians.
  5. Indians can learn from the tactics of blacks.
  6. We cannot make the government keep its promises.
  7. To preserve my heritage, I must insist on my rights.
  8. Non-Indians think we are demanding special privileges.

C. Do you think it would be better for Indians to preserve tribal cultures or to blend into the American "melting pot"? Why?

Activities and Inquiries

1. Go to a library to find information about Native Americans. Write a description of life on an Indian reservation today.

2. Imagine that you are Jack. Write a letter to a newspaper explaining the purpose of your fish-in.
3. Imagine that you are a state fisheries officer. Write a letter to a newspaper telling why you think Indians should obey state regulations.
4. Pretend you are a judge in a case in which Indians claim treaty rights against a state government or the federal government. What information would you want before making a decision?
5. Pretend you own some land that an Indian tribe is claiming under an old treaty. You must defend your claim to the land in court. What arguments will you make?

5 War Policies Are Questioned

In the mid-1960's, the United States again went to war. Hundreds of thousands of U.S. troops poured into South Vietnam to defend the non-Communist government there. U.S. leaders argued that the war was necessary to block the spread of communism. But many Americans disagreed, and the war touched off a stormy debate in the United States.

President Johnson at first continued the policy of Presidents Eisenhower and Kennedy. He sent only noncombat troops to South Vietnam. But the war was not going well for South Vietnam's government. One reason, U.S. leaders felt, was that the rebels fighting in South Vietnam were getting massive help from Communist North Vietnam.

In 1964 and early 1965, U.S. planes bombed parts of North Vietnam. Still, conditions in South Vietnam kept getting worse. So Johnson ordered U.S. combat troops into action while stepping up the bombing. By 1968 the United States had half a million troops in South Vietnam. They faced not only rebel forces but also large numbers of North Vietnamese troops.

In public statements, U.S. officials were optimistic. They said they saw "the light at the end of the tunnel," that South Vietnamese forces were getting stronger, that the war would soon be won. News reports from the scene, however, told a different story. The reports said South Vietnam's government was unpopular. They said the war was bogging down with no end in sight.

At first, President Johnson kept pushing for his Great Society programs while stepping up military spending to pay for the war. But both the Great Society and the war were expensive. Could the United States afford them both? In time the President had to cut back many of his Great Society programs.

Day after day, Americans watched the war on their television screens. Much of what they saw was grisly and bloody. Many were shocked by the ugliness. Many were also shocked by the gap between what U.S. officials said and what reporters said. Whom could one believe?

At first, most people believed the U.S. government. Polls showed wide support for Johnson's policies. But as the war dragged on, more and more people came to question those policies. An antiwar movement took to the streets in protest. Some members of Congress questioned Johnson's policies, too, accusing him of misleading both Congress and the public. Debate over the war grew shrill and often violent.

In our story, two students discuss the issues raised by the war and the protest movement. Why did the war stir such strong feelings? How could individuals make their opinions known?

San Francisco, California, 1968

JESSICA. What are you doing with that big piece of cardboard?

BRUCE. Making a sign. I'm going to carry it in the antiwar march tomorrow.

JESSICA. What does it say?

BRUCE. It's a message to Lyndon B. Johnson. It says, "Hey, hey, LBJ, how many kids did you kill today?"

JESSICA. That's gross, Bruce. And it's unfair. President Johnson hasn't killed any kids. He's trying to make sure Vietnamese people of all ages can live in peace—and in freedom.

BRUCE. Who do you think you're kidding? It's Johnson's war. He started it, and he's responsible for all the babies and other people who are being killed.

JESSICA. Come on, Bruce. Johnson didn't start the war. The Communists did. They went to war against South Vietnam's government. It was only when South Vietnam asked for help that the United States got involved. What else could we do? You don't want Communists to take over a free country, do you?

BRUCE. Free country—hah! South Vietnam is a dictatorship. Its people are no freer than the Germans were under Hitler. And I don't think the people fighting against the South Vietnamese government are all Communists, either. Lots of them are just nationalists who want their own Vietnamese government, not one that's run by puppets of the United States.

JESSICA. Puppets indeed! If the Communists win, the South Vietnamese won't have a shred of freedom. They'll be ruled by puppets of the Soviet Union. And neighboring countries in Southeast Asia will fall to the Communists, too.

BRUCE. You seem to have swallowed Johnson's whole line. How can you believe the U.S. government after all the lies it's told? Remember how officials said we were bombing only military targets in North Vietnam? So, what did American reporters find when they went there? That our bombs were falling on hospitals and homes, too!

JESSICA. I'm sure our pilots did their best to hit only military targets. What I want to know is: Why do so many of the reporters in Vietnam seem to delight in reporting bad news? They're only harming the American cause. Can't you see that?

BRUCE. They're doing what a free press is supposed to do—keep the public informed. They have to report both the good and the bad. If our troops are doing bad things, we ought to know. The more people learn about what's really happening, the stronger the antiwar movement will get.

JESSICA. Your antiwar movement is just a bunch of scruffy kids and draft-dodgers who like to march around shouting nasty things.

BRUCE. Scruffy kids, are we? My mom and dad are going with me tomorrow, and lots of distinguished people will be there. There'll be speeches by a senator, a professor, and a movie star, and music by some of the country's most popular singers.

JESSICA. You make it sound almost respectable. What about the kids who burn American flags and wave Communist banners? I bet they'll be there too.

BRUCE. Maybe they will. It's a free country, isn't it?

JESSICA. Well, I'm going to be there myself. I'll join the countermarchers—the people who support the President. I'm going to carry my own sign with a message for you protesters: "America— Love It or Leave It!"

BRUCE. We do love America, Jessica. That's why we're marching. We don't want our country to be carrying on an unjust war.

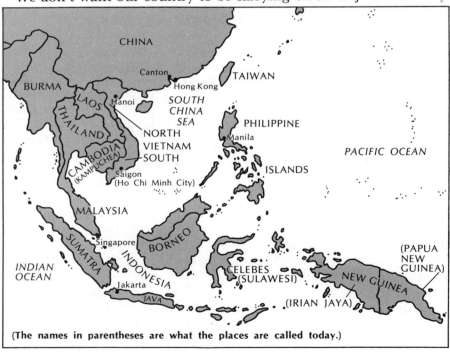

(The names in parentheses are what the places are called today.)

Southeast Asia in 1968

JESSICA. Listen, Bruce, there's a right way to do things, and there's a wrong way. Marching around calling the President a killer is the wrong way. If you don't like what your government is doing, you should work to change the government's policies. Write your representatives in Congress. Get out and campaign for a candidate who thinks the way you do. But don't give aid and comfort to the enemy. Don't tear down America!

BRUCE. People tried those traditional methods, Jessica, and nothing happened. The government went right on sending American boys and bombs to Vietnam. By marching in the streets we can make people realize what an atrocity this war is. We have to arouse the people. That's the only way to stop the war.

JESSICA. You've certainly got me aroused—against you! I think Johnson should go all out to win this war. Up to now our troops have been fighting with one hand tied behind their backs. We ought to bomb the tar out of North Vietnam and then invade it.

BRUCE. Even Johnson wouldn't do that. It might cause the Soviets or the Chinese to get into the war. Then we really would have a mess on our hands.

JESSICA. I don't see how we could have a bigger mess than right now. All this dissent and turmoil! I'm afraid it's tearing our country apart.

BRUCE. I can agree with you there, Jessica. And the way to end it is to stop the war.

JESSICA. No, the way to end it is to win the war.

POSTSCRIPT

Those who wanted the United States to get out of the war were known as "doves." Those who wanted to step up the war were known as "hawks." Caught between doves and hawks, President Johnson announced that he would not run for re-election in 1968. A Republican, Richard Nixon, was elected President after promising to achieve "peace with honor" in Vietnam.

Nixon began to reduce the number of U.S. troops in Vietnam. He tried to build up the South Vietnamese forces so they could take over most of the fighting. At the same time, he stepped up U.S. bombing, trying to put pressure on the other side.

After more than four years of negotiations, a ceasefire was announced in January, 1973. It was signed by four parties—the United States and South Vietnam on one side and North Vietnam and the rebels on the other. The United States agreed to withdraw its troops from South Vietnam within 60 days. Both sides agreed to turn over prisoners of war. Both sides agreed that free elections should be held, under outside supervision, to decide the future of South Vietnam.

President Nixon said the accord met his pledge of "peace with honor." But still there was no peace. After U.S. forces had left, the Vietnamese resumed fighting. Finally, in April, 1975, the fighting ended in defeat for the South Vietnamese government. The following year, all of Vietnam was united under a single government. It was a Communist government. Communist governments also took control of Laos and Cambodia (Kampuchea), the other countries of Indo-China.

The Vietnam War had caused great destruction. More than 55,000 Americans were killed in the war. Another 300,000 were wounded. It is estimated that about 1,200,000 Vietnamese died.

It was widely agreed that the United States had suffered a defeat, but Americans differed about the meaning of that defeat. Some said it showed the limits to U.S. power. They said the United States should never have become involved in Vietnam in the first place. Others said the defeat showed what could happen if the United States lost its will and failed to use its power effectively. They said it was more important than ever to stand firm against the spread of communism.

Homework Questions

1. Why did President Johnson send combat troops to South Vietnam?
2. How did the American public feel about the Vietnam War?
3. What reasons did Bruce give for opposing Johnson's policies?
4. How did Jessica feel about the President's policies?
5. What lessons did Americans draw from the Vietnam War?

Understanding the Story

A. Write *T* for each statement that is true and *F* for each statement that is false.
   1. Americans held sharply different opinions about the Vietnam War.
   2. President Johnson refused to send combat soldiers to South Vietnam.
   3. Troops from North Vietnam fought in South Vietnam.
   4. The war did not affect Johnson's Great Society programs.
   5. Some members of Congress spoke out against the war.
   6. News reports from Vietnam sometimes conflicted with official reports on the war.
   7. President Nixon increased the number of U.S. troops in South Vietnam.
   8. The United States won the Vietnam War.

B. Write *J* for each statement Jessica made or might have made and *B* for each statement Bruce made or might have made.
   1. The Vietnam War is Johnson's war.
   2. The Communists started the war.
   3. Some reporters in Vietnam are harming the American cause.
   4. South Vietnam is a dictatorship.
   5. There are lots of draft-dodgers in the antiwar movement.
   6. A free press must report both the good and the bad.
   7. Don't give aid and comfort to the enemy.
   8. The only way to stop the war is to arouse the people.

C. In your opinion, what is the main lesson Americans should learn from the Vietnam War? Explain.

Activities and Inquiries

1. Assume that you are a reporter. You interview Bruce at an antiwar march. What does he say about the Vietnam War?
2. Assume that you interview Jessica at a countermarch. What does she say about the Vietnam War?
3. Assume that it is 1968 and you are writing a letter about the war to a senator in Washington. What do you say?
4. Visit a library. Look up information about life in South Vietnam in the 1960's. Look up information about life in Vietnam today. Write a report telling of your findings.
5. Interview an older member of your family. Ask that person to recall memories of the Vietnam War years. Make a class report on your findings.

6 A Giant Leap

The 1960's were a time of war and disagreement, but they were also years of excitement. The space age had dawned. Humans were on their way to the moon.

The opening of the Space Age came in 1957, when the Soviet Union put a small sphere into orbit around the earth. Americans were shocked. Wasn't the United States the richest, most advanced country in the world? Why hadn't the United States been the first into space? The United States speeded up its space program. The first of a series of American space satellites went into orbit early in 1958.

A space race was on. By 1961, the United States had launched 32 satellites to 7 for the Soviets. In April, 1961, however, the Soviets scored another first by putting a man into earth orbit. The following February, an American named John Glenn shot into orbit. His space capsule circled the earth three times.

The moon was next. President Kennedy had vowed that an American must get there first. He believed, and Congress agreed, that U.S. prestige was at stake. The moon program was named Project Apollo. One after another, teams of Americans rocketed into space as scientists perfected the equipment that would be needed for a moon trip. By 1969 all was ready. Americans were set to go to the moon for the first time.

In our story, two technicians at the space control center in Houston, Texas, follow the moon shot known as Apollo 11. What made the event so exciting? Why was it important?

Houston, Texas, July, 1969

For months Ed and Gary had been looking forward to this day, and now it was here, July 16, 1969. All systems were "go." The flight of Apollo 11 was about to begin.

Ed and Gary sat at control panels in the Houston space center. On television screens above their heads they could see the 36-story-high space rocket, sitting on the launching pad several hundred miles away at Cape Kennedy (now Cape Canaveral) in Florida. Millions of people in the United States and other countries were also watching over live television.

"This is it," said Ed.

Gary nodded. "After 10 years and $25 billion."

At Cape Kennedy, three astronauts settled into their seats and began checking switches. Their names were Neil Armstrong, Edwin Aldrin, Jr., and Michael Collins. They had been picked to be the first humans to go to the moon.

It was time for takeoff. A tongue of flame pushed down from the rocket. With a roar, the giant spacecraft rose from the launch pad. It climbed slowly at first, then faster. Soon it was just a speck in the sky, a speck headed for the moon some 250,000 miles away.

Columbia, as the command craft was called, sped away from the earth at an initial speed of 24,000 miles an hour. Television viewers listened in on conversations between the astronauts and Houston Control. Ed and Gary concentrated on their work as computers in Houston quietly guided the spacecraft on its historic journey.

"So far, so good," said Ed.

"They're not there yet," replied Gary. "The landing will be the tricky part."

On the fourth day, *Columbia* went into orbit around the moon. Armstrong and Aldrin had crawled into a smaller capsule called *Eagle* that would take them to the moon. Collins would stay in moon orbit in the command craft.

The descent began on the morning of the fifth day. At an altitude of less than 10 miles, trouble struck. The computers were not working right. Armstrong took over the manual controls. With guidance from Houston, he eased the capsule toward the moon.

Almost too late, Armstrong realized that the ground below was extremely rocky. He didn't want to risk a crash. Moving *Eagle* to a new and smoother landing site, Armstrong used up precious fuel. There was barely enough fuel left to set down and take off. Would he play safe and head back to the command craft? No. The craft settled slowly, safely to the moon's surface.

The two astronauts put on spacesuits to protect them on the airless moon. They opened the hatch. Armstrong was the first to step down. "That's one small step for a man," he said, "one giant leap for mankind." In Houston and in homes around the world, television viewers shared in and enjoyed the historic moment.

Ed clapped Gary on the back. "They did it!" he shouted. "They did it!"

Gary smiled and then looked concerned. "Now let's hope they can get off the moon safely and get back to the command craft. They're still 250,000 miles from home."

Aldrin joined Armstrong, and for two hours the men walked the moon's surface. At times they seemed to bounce, so light were they in the moon's gravity, which is only one sixth as strong as earth's. The astronauts collected rock and dust samples. They took photographs and made scientific measurements. In the sunlight it was 234°F. above zero; in the shade it was 279°F. below zero.

On the soft, powdery surface the two astronauts left a plaque for future visitors to see. It read, "Here men from planet Earth first set foot upon the moon, July, 1969, A.D. We came in peace for all mankind."

Back aboard *Eagle,* the men prepared to take off. Just over 21 hours after touchdown, they roared into space again. Without a hitch they

"Christopher Columbus, move over!"

got back to *Columbia*. Collins greeted them warmly. The three said a last farewell to the moon and headed for home.

Again they reached a top speed of 24,000 miles an hour. At last the spacecraft plunged into the earth's atmosphere. Scorching heat seared the craft. Exactly 8 days, 3 hours, 18 minutes, and 21 seconds after leaving Cape Kennedy, the command capsule splashed into the Pacific Ocean. The voyage had been a success. Humans had walked on the moon—and Americans had got there first.

POSTSCRIPT

Five more moon trips followed in the next three and a half years. Then the Apollo program ended. The United States turned to different goals—studying distant planets, for example, and perfecting a space station.

To save money, many space shots carried no passengers. Instead, space capsules were fitted with instruments that could make precise measurements and perform useful tasks. A series of satellites placed in earth orbit did such tasks as studying the weather, making more accurate maps, and relaying television signals and telephone calls. Other satellites had military uses. Still other spacecraft traveled to distant parts of the solar system. They landed on Mars and Venus and passed close enough to other planets to provide detailed information about them and their moons.

More astronauts, both male and female, were trained for trips into space. In the 1970's a project known as Skylab put humans into earth orbit to study methods of working in space. The United States and the Soviet Union forgot their rivalry long enough to undertake a joint space venture. In 1975 two spacecraft, one from each country, linked together and exchanged crews. In the 1980's attention focused on a reusable U.S. space shuttle that could make repeated trips between earth and space.

Would the day come when humans could live permanently in space, taking advantage of reduced gravity to manufacture products such as drugs and metals in new ways? No one could say for sure. But the human adventure in space was off to a strong start.

Homework Questions

1. How did the space race develop?
2. What problems did Neil Armstrong and Edwin Aldrin, Jr., face as they approached the moon?
3. What did Armstrong and Aldrin bring back from the moon?
4. Why did many space shots carry no passengers? How were such shots useful?
5. How does a space shuttle differ from other spacecraft?

Understanding the Story

A. Write *T* for each statement that is true, *F* for each statement that is false, and *N* for each statement that is not mentioned in the story.
1. The Soviet Union put the first satellite made by humans into orbit.
2. The first man in space was named Yuri Gagarin.
3. John Glenn was the first American to land on the moon.
4. The United States moon program cost $25 billion.

5. The Soviet Union put the first humans on the moon.
6. Neil Armstrong and Edwin Aldrin, Jr., walked on the moon.
7. Michael Collins stayed in the command craft while Armstrong and Aldrin landed on the moon.
8. Apollo shots put a total of 12 Americans on the moon.

B. List the numbers of the statements that give results of the United States space program.
1. The United States finished second in the race to the moon.
2. Americans walked on the moon.
3. The United States entered the space age.
4. The United States set up a colony on the moon.
5. The United States spent billions of dollars on space flights.
6. The space capsule *Eagle* crashed while trying to land.
7. Women were trained as astronauts.
8. Americans placed a plaque on the moon.

C. Suppose you have a chance to be the first person to visit Mars. Would you go? Why or why not?

Activities and Inquiries

1. Look at the cartoon on page 545 and answer the following questions.
   a. Turn back to Unit Two, Chapter 1, pages 26 to 30. Compare the perils of the astronauts with the perils Columbus faced.
   b. Which journey was more difficult? Why?
   c. Which journey would you prefer? Why?
2. Assume that you are on a moon voyage. You keep a log of the trip. What will you include?
3. Write an editorial about the United States space program. What do you think the goal of the program should be now?
4. Some people feel that the money spent on the space program could be used in better ways. What is your opinion? Why?
5. Assume that it is the year 2020 and that the United States has decided to send astronauts to visit another planet. Write a story about how you imagine the trip might go.

7 The Growth of the Constitution: Gideon Gets a Lawyer

If you were accused of a crime, you would want the courts to do everything possible to protect your constitutional rights. Not all people accused of crimes are guilty. At times, innocent people have been punished unjustly. One duty of our courts is to protect the individual's rights against such miscarriages of justice.

But there is another side to the question. If the courts go too far in protecting the accused, some guilty people may go free. This would be unfair to the victims of crime. It would be unfair to society at large. Thus, a second duty of our courts is to uphold the rights of society—to protect the rights of life, liberty, and property that belong to all.

Throughout American history, the courts have tried to strike a balance between those two duties. At times the stress has fallen on the rights of society. At times it has fallen on the rights of individuals. During the 1960's, a time when civil rights and other rights were major issues in American life, the United States Supreme Court made a number of decisions that were widely seen as strengthening individual rights. These were controversial decisions, and they led to major changes in the way police agencies and the courts dealt with crime.

In our story, we read of one such decision. How did the decision strengthen the rights of the accused? How did it affect society as a whole? Was it a wise decision?

Florida, 1963

Clarence Earl Gideon paced back and forth in his prison cell. It seemed that he had been behind bars forever. How much longer would he have to wait? How would the U.S. Supreme Court decide his case?

Gideon was no stranger to jails and prisons. He had been convicted four times of crimes. Now he was behind bars for a fifth conviction, and this time Gideon was determined not to stay there. He was innocent, he insisted, and he wanted to be free.

The state of Florida claimed that Gideon had broken into a poolroom one night in 1961. Gideon lived in a hotel near the poolroom, and a man told police he had seen Gideon inside the closed poolroom at 5:30 in the morning. At his trial, Gideon said he had no money to hire a lawyer. He asked the judge to appoint one. The judge refused, saying that Florida law provided for free lawyers only in cases that call for the death penalty.

So Gideon served as his own lawyer. Considering his lack of legal experience, he did a pretty good job. He called witnesses and cross-examined his accuser, while declining to testify himself. But the jury found him guilty. The judge sentenced him to five years in prison.

Gideon wouldn't give up. He wondered how the trial would have gone if he'd had a lawyer. Perhaps he hadn't used the right words.

Visiting the prison library, Gideon began to read up on the law. Hadn't there been cases like his before? Didn't the Constitution protect the right of the accused to have a lawyer? From law books and court rulings, Gideon decided that he had a strong case. He would ask the U.S. Supreme Court for a hearing.

In pencil, Gideon wrote out his plea. It covered five pages. It didn't look fancy, and it might have had a few misspelled words, but it was enough. The Court agreed that Gideon had raised some important issues. It would hear the case, known as *Gideon* v. *Wainwright*. (Louie L. Wainwright was the director of Florida's prison system.)

The Supreme Court appointed a lawyer to argue for Gideon. He was a prominent Washington lawyer named Abe Fortas, and he had studied constitutional law. Fortas would know the right words.

In presenting the case, Fortas tried to show that Gideon had made mistakes while serving as his own lawyer. The jury never learned that Gideon and his accuser had previously quarreled. Perhaps Gideon had not realized the importance of the point. Or perhaps he had not known how to raise it. But a lawyer would have known. If Gideon had had a lawyer, Fortas said, the jury might well have found in Gideon's favor.

Fortas also quoted the Constitution. He pointed to the 14th Amendment. This says that a state must not "deprive any person of life, liberty, or property without due process of law." He also pointed to the 6th Amendment. This says, "In all criminal prosecutions, the accused shall enjoy the right . . . to have the assistance of counsel [a lawyer] for his defense."

Over the years, the Court had considered these amendments in similar cases. It had paid special attention to two questions: Did different rules apply to federal cases and to state cases? How serious did a case have to be before a free lawyer might be required?

The 6th Amendment was part of the Bill of Rights, which originally applied only to the federal government. The 14th Amendment applied only to state governments. Piece by piece, the Court had decided that parts of the Bill of Rights were so important that they must apply to both the federal and state governments. They were an essential part of the "due process of law" required by the 14th Amendment. Was the right to a lawyer one of those important parts?

In 1932, the Court decided that it was. It ruled in *Powell* v. *Alabama* that a state must supply a lawyer in cases that carry the death penalty.

But what about cases that don't carry the death penalty? Here the Court had made a distinction between federal cases and state cases. In federal courts, people accused of crimes were entitled to a lawyer in all cases (*Johnson* v. *Zerbst*, 1938). In state courts, people accused of lesser crimes were *not* entitled to a free lawyer (*Betts* v. *Brady*, 1942). The Betts case was similar to the Gideon case. It looked as if the Court would rule against Gideon—unless the Court had changed its mind.

To Gideon's relief, the Court *had* changed its mind. Justice Hugo Black, speaking for seven of the justices, said that the Betts decision had been wrong. Without a lawyer, said Black, an accused person could not be assured of a fair trial—in a state court just as much as in a federal court. All nine justices agreed that Gideon deserved a new trial, this time with a lawyer.

POSTSCRIPT

For a second time, Gideon went on trial. Aided by a lawyer, he was found not guilty.

The Gideon case was only one of many during the 1960's that spelled out greater rights for people accused of crimes. In *Escobedo* v. *Illinois* (1964), the Court ruled that a suspect was entitled to have a lawyer present while being questioned by the police. In *Miranda* v. *Arizona* (1966), it ruled that the police must tell all suspects of their right to a lawyer and their right to remain silent.

Such Court decisions were applauded by many Americans. Supporters of the decisions argued that the police and other agents of the state (the government) had enormous powers to hurt individuals and deny them their freedom. In order to keep society free,

they said, individuals must be protected against abuse of such powers.

But many other Americans criticized the Court's decisions. They argued that the Court was making it more difficult to convict people who had committed serious crimes. They said the Court's rulings posed a danger to the safety of society at large.

The Court of the 1960's was known as the Warren Court, after Earl Warren, who served as Chief Justice from 1953 to 1969. When Earl Warren retired, Warren Burger was appointed to take his place. The Burger Court of the 1970's and 1980's tended to place greater stress on the rights of society as a whole. It seemed less inclined than the Warren Court to spell out broader rights for individuals.

Homework Questions

1. How did the Supreme Court in the 1960's strengthen the rights of individuals?
2. Why did the state of Florida refuse to provide a lawyer for Clarence Earl Gideon?
3. How did Gideon try to convince the Supreme Court that he deserved a new trial?
4. How are the 6th and 14th Amendments different?
5. What decision did the Supreme Court make in the Gideon case?

Understanding the Story

A. List the numbers of the statements that are true.
1. The Florida court refused to appoint a lawyer for Clarence Earl Gideon.
2. Gideon did not have the money to hire a lawyer.
3. Gideon defended himself as well as a lawyer would have.
4. Gideon asked the Supreme Court to hear his case.
5. The Supreme Court refused to hear Gideon's case.
6. Abe Fortas tried to show that Gideon made mistakes at his trial.
7. Justice Hugo Black said that a lawyer is not necessary in a criminal trial.
8. Gideon was given a new trial.

B. Complete each of the following sentences by filling in the missing word or words.
1. The courts must balance the rights of the individual with the rights of _____.
2. Gideon was accused of breaking into a _____.
3. Gideon and his accuser had previously _____.
4. The Supreme Court agreed to appoint a _____ to defend Gideon.
5. The right to a lawyer is mentioned in the _____ Amendment to the Constitution.
6. In Gideon's second trial, the jury found him _____.
7. In the Escobedo case, the Supreme Court decided that a suspect has a right to a lawyer while being _____ by the police.
8. In the Miranda case, the Supreme Court decided that a suspect must be told of his or her right to _____.

C. Do you approve or disapprove of the decision in *Gideon* v. *Wainwright*? Explain.

Activities and Inquiries

1. Imagine that Gideon has just been sentenced to jail. He tells you that he plans to get a new trial. Describe his plans.
2. Assume that you are a lawyer and that you have agreed to help Gideon. List all the reasons you will give in arguing that Gideon did not get a fair trial.
3. Gideon had committed crimes in the past; he was not a model citizen. Should he have been given all this attention? Why or why not?
4. "The Gideon case shows that the Warren Court cared more for the rights of criminals than for the rights of society." Do you agree with this statement? Why or why not?
5. "It is better for nine guilty people to go free than for one innocent person to be convicted." Do you agree with this statement? Why or why not?

Who Built America?

Roberto Clemente

JUAN. My report is on Roberto Clemente, *el Orgullo de Puerto Rico*, the Pride of Puerto Rico. He was one of the greatest baseball players who ever lived.

HEINRICH. Was he as great as Babe Ruth?

JUAN. He didn't hit as many homers as Babe Ruth, but he was a great hitter and fielder. In 1972, Clemente became the 11th player in baseball history to reach a lifetime total of 3,000 hits. And his deadly right arm was legendary. He could make a leaping catch against the right-field wall, spin around, and without pausing, fire the ball straight to home plate on the fly.

SAM. Big deal. What's so important about being a hot-shot baseball player?

JUAN. Clemente wasn't just a baseball player. He was also a great human being. He threw himself into all sorts of projects to help children and to fight misery. In 1972 he organized a relief program to get food and medical goods to Nicaragua after a devastating earthquake. He was killed when his plane crashed on the way to Nicaragua.

RICARDO. He wanted to help his Latin brothers and sisters.

JUAN. Yes, Clemente took great pride in his Latin heritage—and in his black heritage.

CARLA. Did he face as much discrimination as a black person in the United States might face?

JUAN. Whoa! Don't think that Clemente was some kind of foreigner. Puerto Rico is a U.S. commonwealth in the Caribbean, and its people are as much United States citizens as people born on the mainland. Just because we have Spanish-sounding names and speak Spanish among ourselves doesn't mean we're outsiders.

CARLA. Sorry, I didn't mean to offend. But what about discrimination?

JUAN. Oh, there was plenty of that. Clemente knew what it was like to be turned away from a restaurant or hotel because of his skin. And he faced other kinds of discrimination too. It made him angry that black and Latin ball players rarely got the chance that other players did to make extra money by endorsing commercial products. He spoke out in public about such practices. Finally, in the late 1960's and early 1970's, things began to change.

ROBERT. Sounds like he was touchy.

JUAN. Some sportswriters thought so. They were always making fun of Clemente's great pride. And they made fun of his injuries, too—especially the bad back that troubled him all through his career. Sportswriters called Clemente a hypochondriac. They implied that he faked his injuries.

RICARDO. If he had been a faker, wouldn't his team have gotten rid of him?

JUAN. Of course. But he was no goldbrick. He played hard—even when it meant enduring great pain. And he was a star. He helped the Pittsburgh Pirates win two pennants and two World Series, won the National League batting championship four times, and was named the league's most valuable player once. After his tragic death, he was named immediately to the Baseball Hall of Fame—the first Latin American ever chosen. Ordinarily, the rules say that no one may be considered for the Hall of Fame until five years after quitting the game.

SAM. Did Clemente come from a poor family?

JUAN. Not exactly. His family was poor by today's standards, all right. But they were a notch up the ladder from the bottom. Clemente's father was a foreman who helped to supervise the cutters in the sugarcane fields. The family had a modest home.

ROBERT. I suppose when Clemente became a star he didn't want to spend time with the kind of people he had grown up with.

JUAN. Not at all. He made a point of helping to teach other young Puerto Ricans the fine points of baseball. Between seasons he'd take part in baseball clinics for youth. When he died, he was trying to get the Puerto Rican government to set up a "sports city" to train young people in many kinds of sports.

CARLA. All in all, he sounds like an unusual man.

JUAN. He certainly was. He wanted young people to believe in themselves—to have pride in their accomplishments. His own pride contributed to his great sense of dignity. "Lose everything else," he once said, "but never lose your dignity."

MR. MILLER. I'd say Roberto Clemente had something to teach us all, Juan. Thanks for your report.

"You were right, Mr. Miller," said Jack. "This unit did have some heavy moments."

"What disturbed you most about the period?" asked Mr. Miller.

"The assassinations and the constant worries about war. It seemed as if violence was everywhere."

"And did you find some bright spots?"

"Oh, yes. The trip to the moon was like a tonic to help lift Americans' spirits. And the United States made progress in civil rights and in fighting poverty."

"How would you sum up the period, Jack?"

"I'd say it showed that Americans were committed to finding ways to improve their society—even while admitting that it wasn't yet as 'great' as it could be."

"Did the period leave you hopeful about the future?"

"As hopeful as ever, Mr. Miller. Is the next unit all good times and happy days?"

"Hardly, Jack. Like the 1960's, the 1970's and 1980's brought a new set of challenges. Let's see how Americans met them."

The 1970's and 1980's

"You said the United States faced new challenges in the 1970's and 1980's, Mr. Miller. What kinds of challenges?" asked Jack.

"Many kinds," replied Mr. Miller. "There was a scandal in the White House that raised distrust of our leaders to new heights. That was the Watergate scandal, and it led to the first resignation by a President in our history. There were also a number of other jolts—worries about pollution, energy shortages, price rises, and so on."

"Weren't there any bright spots, Mr. Miller?"

"Of course, Jack. In the first place, Americans worked hard to answer the many challenges. They reacted to Watergate by calling for laws aimed at preventing such abuses of power in the future. They took steps to cut down pollution. They explored new sources of energy while making oil and coal resources stretch further."

"Sounds as though Americans weren't going to take those challenges lying down."

"That's right. And Americans kept their eyes out for new opportunities, too. In the 1970's, they found ways to take advantage of the growing differences between the leading Communist powers, China and the Soviet Union. President Nixon restored U.S. ties with China and signed some important agreements with the Soviet Union. Later in the 1970's, U.S. leaders helped to cool down quarrels in the Middle East by getting Egypt and Israel together for talks."

"What happened then? Did the Cold War come to an end and peace come to the Middle East?"

"Not at this time, Jack. By the early 1980's, U.S.-Soviet relations had chilled again. And the Middle East was still a powder keg. But President Carter encouraged the Israelis to return the Sinai to Egypt in return for a peace treaty between the two nations. Israel agreed, and Egypt thus became the first Arab nation to recognize Israel as a nation."

"I'd say American history resembles a roller coaster. It's up and down, up and down, all the time."

"That's a good way to think of it, Jack. History never stands still."

"Well, if it did, it might get dull—and it's more fun the way it is. Let's get into the 70's and 80's."

1 Cleaning Up the Environment

Alarms were sounded during the 1960's about dangers posed by pollution in the air and waters of the United States. Smoggy air and oily rivers were part of the problem, but only a part. Strange chemicals were turning up in humans' bodies. Birds, fish, and wildlife were dying of mysterious causes. Human activities, it seemed, were causing serious changes in the environment—in people's surroundings.

Those who urged immediate action to protect the environment were known as "environmentalists." By the late 1960's a strong environmentalist movement was making its voice heard. Congress responded in 1969 by pass-ing the National Environmental Policy Act. For the first time, protecting the environment became a central goal of the U.S. government.

In late 1970, President Nixon set up an Environmental Protection Agency (EPA) to lead the fight against pollution. The EPA was given the job of working out regulations to enforce the anti-pollution laws passed by Congress.

In our story, three imaginary Americans discuss the drive to improve the environment. Why did this drive cause controversy? How do Sludge, Allbright, and Maybe differ in their opinions about the many kinds of environmental problems?

Somewhere in the United States, 1972

SLUDGE. The environmentalists have gone too far. These new anti-pollution laws are going to drive my factory out of business.

ALLBRIGHT. Come, come, Sludge. How will they do that?

SLUDGE. For years I've just dumped the waste water into the river. And why shouldn't I? We only use a few mild chemicals in the factory. Nothing that would harm anyone. Now they tell me I'll have to put in filters and other equipment to get rid of the chemicals before the waste water is dumped. I can't afford it.

ALLBRIGHT. I know about those chemicals. Under certain conditions they can kill fish. That's not what I call "mild."

SLUDGE. Oh, who cares about some silly fish?

ALLBRIGHT. If you kill off the fish, you'll harm the birds and raccoons and other animals that eat those fish. Haven't you heard of the chain of food? We humans may be at the top of the chain, but anything that breaks the chain can harm us. "Some silly fish" may not seem important to you, but they're part of our environment and ought to be protected.

SLUDGE. You sound like a person of high ideals, Allbright. I admire you for that. But I'm talking about dollars and cents. If I have to close my factory, all my workers will be out of jobs. Would you protect a few fish at the expense of those workers' jobs?

ALLBRIGHT. I think both should be protected.

MAYBE. Maybe you could just raise your prices and pass the costs on to your customers, Sludge.

SLUDGE. Up to a point, I suppose I could. But why should my customers have to pay extra to save a handful of fish?

ALLBRIGHT. If you keep dumping chemicals into the river, Sludge, we'll all have to pay—by living in a filthier environment. Dirty air and dirty water cost us Americans millions of dollars every year. We pay in lost opportunities for fishing and swimming, in higher doctors' bills for unnecessary illnesses, and in many other ways.

SLUDGE. Now Allbright, how many dollars is it worth to you to be able to swim in my river? Are you willing to pay for my anti-pollution equipment?

ALLBRIGHT. Not by myself, no, but as a member of the public, yes. Of course it will cost money to clean up the environment, but we really have no choice. Pollution is a threat to human as well as animal life. Many of the chemicals being put into our air and water can contribute to cancer and other diseases. How many dollars is a human life worth to you, Sludge?

SLUDGE. Let's put things in perspective, Allbright. Life is full of risks. You wake up in the morning, and you get into your car and drive to work. You're taking a risk—you may be killed in an accident. Yet you drive to work anyway. Why? Because you figure the risks are small. It's the same with pollution. Sure, a few people may get hurt by *some* pollution, *somewhere, sometime*. But the risks are small that those people will include you, or me, or anybody we know.

MAYBE. Maybe Sludge has a point. Maybe we should just try to get rid of the very worst types of pollution—the things that we know are dangerous.

SLUDGE. It's a matter of dollars and cents, Allbright. Let someone calculate how much a certain pollutant costs us in illness or injury or whatever. Then calculate how much it would cost to eliminate the pollutant from the environment. Compare the two figures and you have your answer. If you can save money by fighting pollution, do it. If you can't save money, forget it.

ALLBRIGHT. It's not that simple, Sludge. There's no way to put a dollars-and-cents tag on every effect of pollution. And besides, some effects won't be known for years to come. When farmers started using the pesticide DDT to kill insects in the 1940's, they didn't know that DDT would find its way into animals' bodies and then into humans too. As a nerve poison, DDT could become a deadly danger. The effects of DDT worked their way up the food chain until they became too obvious to ignore. Thank goodness the government has finally banned the use of DDT. Hidden dangers, like those of DDT, can't be figured into your calculations.

MAYBE. Maybe we should require lots of tests on new chemicals *before* they are put into use.

SLUDGE. The government already does, Maybe—too many tests, if you ask me. Listen, no respectable business firm would use a chemical it knew to be unsafe. But you can't stop progress. If we held back on new products for years while we waited for all the test results to come in, we'd never have *any* progress. A company can't afford to spend millions of dollars developing a new product and then wait a decade before putting it on sale.

ALLBRIGHT. More important, we as a people can't afford to fill our bodies with dangerous chemicals we know so little about.

MAYBE. Maybe you're both part right and part wrong. Anyway, it's a good thing we finally brought these questions out into the open and started to talk about them.

POSTSCRIPT

During the 1970's a massive environmental cleanup began. Among the many new laws were the following:

The Clean Air Act of 1970. Set strict standards for cleaning up air pollution.

The Occupational Safety and Health Act of 1970. Aimed to protect people against pollutants and unsafe conditions at work.

The Clean Water Act of 1972. Set up a goal of "fishable, drinkable, swimmable" waters in the nation's rivers and lakes.

The Endangered Species Act of 1973. Required new efforts to save plant and animal species in danger of extinction.

The Toxic Substances Control Act of 1976. Required stricter tests on new chemicals that might be toxic, or harmful.

The Strip Mine Act of 1977. Aimed to halt erosion and pollution caused by surface mines.

As anti-pollution devices appeared in cars, factories, and sewage plants, reports of a cleaner environment began to appear. Fish returned to rivers in which they had not been sighted for years. The air over major cities became less polluted. Levels of DDT found in human bodies dropped by half. At the same time, however, new problems turned up. Poisonous wastes were found to be leaking into the air and water from certain dumps. And pollution levels in many areas remained well above national standards.

A debate about the pros and cons of environmental laws continued into the 1980's. Some said that the laws were still not strict enough and that

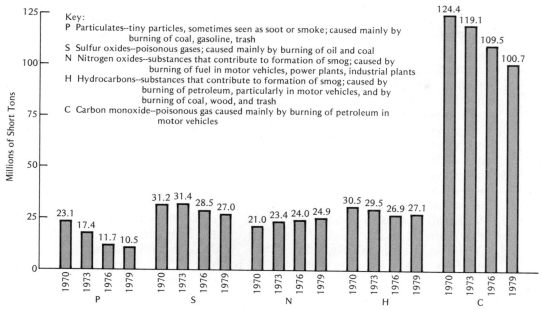

Cleaner Air to Breathe

government agencies were slow to enforce the laws. Others said that the laws were too strict, that they put unnecessary burdens on industry and forced consumers to pay much higher prices than necessary. In the 1980's, steps were taken to ease some of the stricter provisions of anti-pollution measures.

Homework Questions

1. Why did environmentalists call for laws to protect the environment?
2. How did Congress respond?
3. What was the role of the Environmental Protection Agency?
4. What were the main laws passed to protect the environment?
5. Why did some people criticize the environmental laws?

Understanding the Story

A. List the numbers of the statements that are true.
1. In the 1960's the only important pollution problems were smoggy air and oily rivers.
2. Environmentalists called for strict laws to stop pollution.
3. The U.S. government paid little attention to pollution in the 1970's.
4. Sludge thought anti-pollution measures were too costly.
5. Allbright thought a dirty environment was too costly.
6. DDT was used by farmers to kill insects.
7. DDT was harmless to humans.
8. Extensive testing of new chemicals can be very costly.

B. Complete each of the following sentences by filling in the missing word or words.
1. Congress voted in 1969 to make protecting the _____ a national goal.

2. The chief agency in charge of fighting pollution is the _____.
3. Allbright thought pollution from Sludge's factory would harm _____.
4. Sludge thought that progress shouldn't be slowed down by too many _____.
5. Congress passed a law to protect plant and animal species that were in danger of _____.
6. Congress passed a law to require stricter tests on chemicals that might be harmful, or _____.
7. Poisonous wastes sometimes leak from _____.
8. Critics said anti-pollution laws would put too heavy a burden on _____ and _____.

C. Do you agree or disagree with this statement: "We should clean up the environment no matter how much it costs"? Explain your answer.

Activities and Inquiries

1. Go to a library and look through recent issues of a newsmagazine. Write a report on pollution problems that are currently in the news.
2. Look up DDT in an encyclopedia. Write a report discussing its benefits and its dangers.

3. Assume that you are interviewing Allbright today. What does Allbright say about efforts made since 1972 to protect the environment?
4. Assume that you are interviewing Sludge today. What does Sludge say about efforts made since 1972 to protect the environment?
5. Study the graph on page 559. Then choose the term or phrase that best completes each statement or answers each question.
   a. Which substance in the air showed the most dramatic decrease between 1970 and 1979? (1) Particulates (2) Nitrogen (3) Carbon Monoxide
   b. When it is burned, which substance seems to cause the greatest amount of air pollution? (1) Petroleum (2) Wood (3) Trash
   c. Between 1970 and 1979 the amount of nitrogen oxides in the air (1) remained the same (2) increased (3) decreased.
   d. By 1973 the Clean Air Act of 1970 had lowered the amount of which substances in the air? (1) Particulates and Carbon Monoxide (2) Sulfur oxides and Nitrogen oxides (3) Hydrocarbons and Nitrogen oxides
   e. After looking carefully at the graph, what advice would you give to your representative in Congress about the need for regulating the amount of poisonous substances in the air?

2 Tearing Down Walls

The world had changed since the height of the Cold War in the 1950's and early 1960's. On the Communist side, the Soviet Union and China had quarreled. The Communist bloc was no longer united. On the American side, problems had multiplied. The war in Vietnam was not going well in the early 1970's.

President Nixon and his top foreign policy adviser, Henry Kissinger, saw an opportunity. They wanted to take advantage of the quarrel between the Soviets and the Chinese, both of whom were supporting the enemy in Vietnam. Perhaps U.S. officials could persuade them to help bring the Vietnam War to an end.

Nixon's first goal was to break down the wall that separated the United States and China. It was an invisible wall, but a solid one. For years Chinese leaders had used such terms as "gangsters" and "mad dogs" to refer to U.S. leaders. On their side, U.S. leaders had tried to pretend the Chinese Communists did not exist.

Why such hostility? It all dated back to the Chinese civil war, which began in the 1920's. For years China was torn between two groups, the Nationalists (who ruled) and the Communists (who wanted to drive out the Nationalists). The Nationalists got help from the United States. The Communists got help from the Soviet Union.

The civil war came to a halt in the late 1930's when Japan invaded China. The Chinese united to fight their common enemy, Japan. The United States helped China in this fight. After Japan was defeated and World War II ended, the Chinese civil war resumed. The United States again sided with the Nationalists. In 1949 the Communists won the civil war, and the Nationalists fled to the island of Taiwan.

Backed by the United States, the Nationalists claimed they were still the rightful rulers of China. They kept China's seat in the United Nations and vowed to recapture "mainland China." The United States gave protection to the Nationalists, pledging to keep the Communists from taking over Taiwan.

The Chinese Communists, led by Mao Zedong, ruled the rest of China from their capital in Peking. The United States did not trust the Communists and did not have diplomatic or trade relations with them.

Nixon and Kissinger thought the time was ripe for better relations between the United States and China. They believed that the Chinese leaders might want some U.S. help in their quarrel with the Soviets. And they thought China, in return, might be willing to help end the Vietnam War by putting pressure on North Vietnam to agree to U.S. terms.

Our story tells of the steps that led to a thaw in U.S.-Chinese relations. How did the United States and China manage to overcome so many years of hostility? What were the results?

Nagoya, Japan, April, 1971

You are Glen Cowan, a college sophomore from California, and at the age of 19 you are a crack player of table tennis—Ping-Pong, as most people say. You have come to Nagoya as part of a team of Americans to compete in the world championships of table tennis. With your shoulder-length hair and casual clothes, you look like anything but a diplomat. But you are about to play a part in a dramatic diplomatic breakthrough.

In Nagoya you became friendly with the Chinese team. Now the tournament has ended. Here come the Chinese players. They have smiles on their faces. They want you and your teammates to come to China for more games of Ping-Pong. They'll even pay your expenses. Will you go?

You know right away that this is something big. The Chinese don't take their Ping-Pong—or their politics—lightly. Your team's leader wants to check with the U.S. embassy in Tokyo. The embassy wants to check with Washington.

Word comes back—go ahead, play Ping-Pong in China. The leaders in Washington think China is giving a signal. For a number of months President Nixon has been sending his own signals. He has eased the restrictions on U.S. trade with China. He has lifted a ban on travel to China. Nixon wanted the Chinese to know that the United States was ready for friendlier relations. Now the Chinese seem to be signaling that they are ready too. "Ping-Pong diplomacy" has opened a new chapter in U.S.-Chinese relations.

Islamabad, Pakistan, July, 1971

You are Henry Kissinger, and you have a secret. You have just returned from China, where you have spent two days in secret talks with the leaders of the Communist government in Peking. Now you are heading home to tell President Nixon of the great breakthrough you have made.

The news media know nothing of all this. Reporters think you have spent the past two days in Pakistan in bed with a stomachache. As far as they know, Pakistan is just a convenient stopping point on your way home from Vietnam, Thailand, and India.

You have come far in the 48 years since you were born in Germany, a Jew in a nation that would soon explode in hostility toward Jews. With your family, you came to the United States in the late 1930's. You became a U.S. citizen, a student of international relations, a professor, and finally a top adviser to President Nixon. From your title, "assistant to the President for national security affairs," it is hard to tell that you hold greater responsibilities than the secretary of state himself. (Later, in 1973, you will be "promoted" to secretary of state.)

You are well aware that your trip to China was a historic one. For years China and the United States have been enemies. But time has brought changes. China is worried about its giant neighbor, the Soviet Union. Once the two Communist nations were allies. Now they are feuding over their common borders. They disagree about "true" Communist doctrine. China needs new partners. It needs the United States.

You believe that China and the United States can cooperate. This does not mean that they can ever be true friends. "Friendship" is not something that applies among nations, in your view. You believe that nations are brought together only when they share common interests. If those interests change, the nations then drift apart. History is full of examples of nations that once were enemies and then became partners—and then, perhaps, enemies again.

You have met with China's premier, Zhou Enlai. You and Zhou have agreed on a plan for President Nixon to visit China early in 1972 to open a new era in U.S.-Chinese relations. This is the news you have brought back from your secret trip to Peking. Five days from now, when President Nixon announces the news, shock waves will be felt all over the world—and nowhere more than in the Soviet Union and North Vietnam. You smile at the thought.

Shanghai, China, February, 1972

You are Richard Nixon, and you are bursting with pride. For a week you have been in China, meeting Chinese leaders, visiting historic places, making public speeches. "This was the week that changed the world," you told your smiling hosts.

Perhaps that's a bit of an exaggeration. But it certainly was an important week. In Peking, you sat down for a chat with Chairman Mao, China's top leader, a man U.S. leaders had once called an agitator of worldwide revolution. Then you visited the Great Wall. It was built in ancient times to keep invaders out of China. Moved by the sight, you declared: "We do not want walls of any kind between people."

In the course of your visit you got many glimpses of Chinese society. You saw reminders of the imperial past, like the Forbidden City where Chinese emperors once reigned in splendor. You saw signs of the Communist present, including a ballet in which a peasant girl leads Communist troops to victory over an evil enemy.

But the purpose of your trip was not tourism. It was "tearing down walls." Each day you met with top Chinese officials to discuss U.S.-Chinese relations. While you dealt with the "big picture," Henry Kissinger hammered out the details in endless sessions with Chinese diplomats.

There was not—there could not be—complete agreement on all questions. The biggest stumbling block was Taiwan. The Chinese insisted on restating their claim that "the liberation of Taiwan is China's internal affair." You and Kissinger wanted to avoid the appearance of abandoning the Nationalists on Taiwan. In Shanghai you insisted on keeping up U.S. ties to Taiwan—including military ties. (Still, the United States in October, 1971, joined in voting to seat China's Communist government in the United Nations. Over the opposition of the United States, Taiwan was expelled.)

In effect, the Americans and the Chinese have agreed to disagree. They have started on the road to better relations. But no one can tell how long or twisted that road might be.

POSTSCRIPT

As expected, Soviet leaders were not happy about the new relations between the United States and China. But they were eager for a thaw in the Cold War. Three months after his trip to China, President Nixon made a historic visit to the Soviet Union. He was the first U.S. President to have gone there since World War II.

In Moscow, Nixon signed a major arms-control treaty with Soviet leaders. It put limits on strategic arms—that is, long-range nuclear weapons. The treaty had an odd name: SALT. The letters stood for Strategic Arms Limitation Treaty.

The treaty slowed but did not stop the arms race between the two major powers. The main result of SALT was to take the chill off the Cold War. In describing U.S.-Soviet relations, people began to use a new term: "détente." It is a French word meaning relaxation—a relaxation of tensions.

The period of détente lasted for several years. It helped to make possible the 1973 agreement that ended the

U.S. role in the Vietnam War. Later in the 1970's, U.S. and Soviet leaders negotiated a second treaty, SALT II, designed to take arms control a step further.

But détente was in trouble. Within the United States, there was strong opposition to SALT II. The treaty went to the Senate for approval in 1979. A number of senators criticized the document, saying it would hurt the United States and help the Soviet Union. Just then the Soviet Union sent troops across its southern border into Afghanistan, to take sides in a civil war. U.S. leaders strongly condemned the Soviet action. They withdrew SALT II from Senate consideration. The era of détente had come to an end, and U.S.-Soviet relations once more frosted over.

With China, however, the new warmth continued. American tourists poured into China, and there was growing trade between the United States and China. In 1979 the United States moved closer to China by breaking official relations with the Nationalist government on Taiwan. This pleased the Chinese government in Peking. But it greatly angered the Nationalists and their supporters in the United States. The United States continued to sell military supplies to the Nationalists. Even so, American

critics charged that the United States had "sold out" its anti-Communist allies. Others, however, said the steps begun by Nixon and Kissinger had served U.S. interests by opening new prospects for trade and diplomacy in East Asia.

Homework Questions

1. How did relations between the United States and China change after World War II?
2. Why did President Nixon and Henry Kissinger seek closer ties with China?
3. What issue was the biggest obstacle to bringing the United States and China together?
4. How did U.S.-Soviet relations change after Nixon's trip to China?
5. What was détente, and why did it end?

Understanding the Story

A. Write *T* for each statement that is true, *F* for each statement that is false, and *N* for each statement that is not mentioned in this chapter.
   1. The United States helped China during World War II.
   2. Mao Zedong was the leader of the Chinese Nationalists.
   3. In the early 1970's, the Soviet Union moved troops into border regions near China.
   4. "Ping-Pong diplomacy" signaled a thaw in U.S.-Chinese relations.
   5. Henry Kissinger did not want reporters to know about his visit to China in July, 1971.
   6. The idea that Soviet leaders might be angry about the thaw

in U.S.-Chinese relations worried Kissinger.
   7. President Nixon was the first U.S. President to visit China.
   8. There was a thaw in the Cold War in the 1970's.

B. Choose the term or phrase that best completes each statement.
   1. President Nixon and Henry Kissinger hoped their dealings with China might help end (*a*) détente (*b*) the Vietnam War (*c*) the Chinese civil war.
   2. The Chinese civil war ended in (*a*) 1949 (*b*) 1971 (*c*) 1979.
   3. The Chinese Nationalists fled to (*a*) Shanghai (*b*) Taiwan (*c*) Peking.
   4. Kissinger made his secret trip to China from (*a*) Vietnam (*b*) Taiwan (*c*) Pakistan.
   5. At the time he made his secret trip, Kissinger was (*a*) secretary of state (*b*) President (*c*) an adviser to the President.
   6. Nixon said his visit to China (*a*) changed the world (*b*) ended U.S. ties with Taiwan (*c*) was not important.
   7. The term "SALT" describes a (*a*) Soviet-American alliance (*b*) treaty to limit nuclear weapons (*c*) pact ending the Vietnam War.
   8. Détente ended after Soviet troops went into (*a*) Afghanistan (*b*) China (*c*) Taiwan.

C. From what you have read, do you think the thaw in U.S.-Chinese relations was a good thing for the Chinese? For the Americans? Explain.

Activities and Inquiries

1. Using your library, prepare a report on one of the following: Mao Zedong, Zhou Enlai, the Great Wall, SALT I.
2. On the basis of library research, compare China with the United States with regard to:
   a. Geography and resources
   b. Government
   c. Industry
   d. Agriculture
   e. Dress and manners
   f. Labor
3. Ask an older member of your family to recall the Nixon-Kissinger "opening" to China. Write an account of your interview.
4. Pretend that you have interviewed an official of the Nationalist government on Taiwan. What are the official's reactions to the changes in U.S.-Chinese relations?
5. "True friendship among nations is impossible." Do you agree or disagree with that statement? Write a brief essay explaining your opinion.

3 Watergate: A Scandal

President Nixon's trips to China and the Soviet Union in 1972 came shortly before a presidential election. Nixon was the Republican candidate. The Democrats chose a liberal senator, George McGovern of South Dakota, an outspoken critic of the Vietnam War. Many Democrats were unhappy about McGovern's antiwar stance and about some of his domestic proposals. With the Democrats split, Nixon easily won re-election. The President got 61 percent of the total vote.

But Nixon's victory was a hollow one. An incident that took place during Nixon's campaign touched off an explosive scandal. The scandal was slow to build, but it finally brought Nixon's disgrace.

Our story relates this scandal, known as "the Watergate affair," as a drama in five acts. Who was mainly responsible for the affair? What did they do wrong? What was the penalty? How did this "national nightmare" (as it was called) come to an end?

ACT I: The Burglary

Scene: The Watergate, a complex in Washington, D.C., that includes offices, apartments, and a hotel.

Time: Shortly after midnight, June 17, 1972.

Five men in business suits creep through the corridors. They wear surgical gloves. They carry a walkie-talkie, a camera, lock picks, and electronic bugging equipment. They stop in front of a door. Behind that door is the headquarters of the Democratic National Committee of the Democratic Party. Cautiously, one of the men picks the lock.

FIRST MAN. What's that noise?

SECOND MAN. Shush!

THIRD MAN (in a whisper). It's the guard. Quick—head for the stairway!

The men vanish. A guard approaches. He notices a piece of tape on a door latch that keeps it from locking. He removes the tape. He goes on about his rounds. The five men return.

FIRST MAN. Get that lock open. Then go into the office. Put the tap on the telephone, and let's get out.

THIRD MAN. Uh, oh. The guard's coming back.

The guard walks by again and sees tape on the door latch. Hadn't he already removed that tape? Suspicious, he calls the police. The police arrive quickly, find the five men, and arrest them for burglary. In the pocket of one is an address book. It contains a phone number for an office in the White House. An investigation begins.

ACT II: The Cover-up

Scene: The White House.

Time: Six days later.

H. R. HALDEMAN (*the President's chief of staff*). Mr. President, we're back in the problem area. It's that burglary at the Democratic headquarters. Investigators are trying to tie it to your re-election committee and its head, John Mitchell.

PRESIDENT NIXON. Did Mitchell know about the burglary?

HALDEMAN. Apparently.

NIXON. And can it be pinned on the committee?

HALDEMAN. It might very well be.

NIXON. All right. We won't second-guess Mitchell and the rest. Thank goodness we didn't know about it ourselves.

HALDEMAN. It won't look good for us if the investigators pin it on the re-election committee. The Federal Bureau of Investigation can be pretty thorough when it wants to be.

NIXON. Can't we stop the FBI?

HALDEMAN. The FBI is not under our control. The way to handle this is to contact the Central Intelligence Agency. Have the CIA ask the FBI to stay out of this. Say it's a matter of national security—CIA secrets. We don't want to risk letting out secrets that could help our enemies.

NIXON. Well, fine. You handle it. I'm not going to get involved.

ACT III: The Pursuit

The plot was thickening. It is a criminal offense to try to interfere with the investigation of a crime. Would the cover-up work? Or would the facts come out anyway?

A few facts dribbled out. Tantalizing facts. For instance:

One of those arrested inside the Watergate, James McCord, was chief of security for the President's re-election committee.

Money carried by the burglars came from a secret fund controlled by the re-election committee.

The fund contained hundreds of thousands of dollars collected in violation of federal campaign laws.

The Watergate burglary was only one of many projects financed by the fund. Other projects included efforts to disrupt the primary campaigns of Democratic candidates for President.

High officials in the administration controlled the fund.

Reporters kept digging to find more facts. None dug with more zeal than two young reporters for *The Washington Post*, Bob Woodward and Carl Bernstein. Day after day *The Post* printed new information. Administration officials shrugged off the story. They accused *The Post* of "shabby journalism" and of blowing up a "third-rate burglary attempt" far out of proportion.

Scene: A federal courtroom in Washington, D.C.
Time: February, 1973.

Five men (including McCord) have pleaded guilty to the Watergate burglary. Two others, charged with aiding in the crime, have been convicted by a jury. Despite charges in the press, no evidence was introduced in court to link higher officials such as John Mitchell directly to the burglary.

JUDGE JOHN J. SIRICA. I do not think we have heard the entire truth. All the facts have not come out.

PROSECUTOR. Your Honor, the prosecution has done its best. We have proved that these men were guilty of a serious crime.

JUDGE SIRICA. So they were. But I am not satisfied with the questions you asked the witnesses. What was behind this crime? *Who* was behind it? The American people need to have answers to these questions.

PROSECUTOR. As you know, Your Honor, the Senate is opening its own investigation of the case.

JUDGE SIRICA. I earnestly hope that Congress can get to the bottom of things.

On the day he sentenced the seven men, Judge Sirica read in court a letter from McCord. The letter said some witnesses at the trial had committed perjury—had lied under oath. It said that more than seven people were involved in the crime.

Now the case began to break. A Senate committee, led by Senator Sam Ervin, a Democrat from North Carolina, developed new leads. It called witnesses from high up in the administration. They said the administration had tried desperately to cover up the trail of responsibility for the Watergate crime. The Nixon administration feared that investigators would uncover other illegal activities.

Details of those other activities began to come out. They included wiretaps on reporters, illegal collection of campaign funds from large corporations, a burglary of a psychiatrist's office. The acting head of the FBI, it turned out, had personally burned some of the evidence in the Watergate case.

It was becoming clear that a cover-up had been organized at the White House. But by whom? How high in the administration did the cover-up go? President Nixon said he was doing all he could to find out the truth. Voicing regret, he accepted the resignations of Haldeman and other high officials.

ACT IV: The Tapes

Scene: A room in Washington, D.C.
Time: July, 1973.

Staff investigators for the Senate Watergate committee are interviewing a former White House employee.

INVESTIGATOR: One of your colleagues has testified about a puzzling event. He was meeting at the Executive Office Building with the President. The President suddenly got up, went behind your colleague's chair, and lowered his voice. He kept talking, quietly. Your colleague suspected that the room might be bugged. What do you think?

EMPLOYEE (*hesitantly*). I probably shouldn't talk to you about this.

INVESTIGATOR. Please tell us what you know.

EMPLOYEE. Well, yes, the room probably was bugged. You see, the President has had hidden tape recorders installed in his main offices. He wants a record for history. Almost all of his conversations are on tape. Only a few people know about this.

INVESTIGATOR. Are you sure? How long has this been going on?

EMPLOYEE. Since 1970 or 1971.

The news, made public a few days later, hit like dynamite. This might blow the case wide open. If tapes for certain conversations existed, they could help the investigators learn just how high in the White House the cover-up went. They might even answer the explosive question: Was the President himself involved?

Investigators went to court to force the President to turn over certain tapes. The President resisted. Vigorously denying any wrongdoing, Nixon asserted a right to keep the tapes secret on grounds of "executive privilege." A President must be able to conduct the nation's affairs without worrying that his conversations will later be made public, Nixon said.

As the court battle went on, the House of Representatives set up a committee to consider impeaching the President. Not since Andrew Johnson, a century before, had a President been impeached. (See pages 305–306). The seriousness of the process made many representatives hold back. They did not want to impeach a President, they said, unless the evidence against him was airtight.

The President had many defenders. They argued that the activities he was accused of were not really very serious. Other administrations, it was said, had spied on political rivals. Other Presidents—Democrats—had used the FBI for political purposes.

But the ranks of the critics were growing. Many people were shocked at the vast scope of the administration's illegal activities. Even more shocking to many was the argument of one of Nixon's assistants—that a President was virtually above the law. Such an attitude, critics said, showed contempt for democracy.

Court decisions went against the President. Taped conversations were made public. One conversation revealed that the President had discussed payoffs to the Watergate burglars to keep them quiet. In July, 1974, a House committee voted three counts of impeachment, to be submitted to the full House.

Still, some representatives stood by the President. Then more conversations were made public. Included was the conversation related in Act II. That did it. Even the President's firmest defenders deserted him. For the good of the country, said one, the President should resign. It was either that or impeachment. There was widespread agreement that the President had betrayed his public trust—his duty to uphold the laws and the Constitution.

ACT V: The Resignation

Scene: The White House.
Time: The night of August 8, 1974.

PRESIDENT NIXON (*appearing before TV cameras to speak to the American people*). Good evening. I have felt it was my duty to complete the term of office to which you elected me. But I cannot. I no longer have the support in Congress that I need. I have never been a quitter. But as President I must put the interests of America first. I shall resign the Presidency effective at noon tomorrow. By doing this I hope to start the process of healing that is so desperately needed in America.

Nixon's Vice President had been Spiro Agnew. But in 1973 Agnew had been accused of bribe-taking and had resigned. In Agnew's place, Nixon had appointed Representative Gerald Ford of Michigan to be Vice President. Thus, it was Ford who became President when Nixon resigned. Ford was the first President in United States history who reached the office through appointment instead of election.

POSTSCRIPT

In September, 1974, President Ford issued a pardon for any crimes President Nixon might have committed. This meant there would be no criminal trial for Nixon. But many of his associates, including Mitchell and Haldeman, were convicted of crimes and sent to prison.

The Watergate affair had ended. It had proved that no one, not even a President, is above the law. But it had also revealed some serious problems in the American political system. In trying to solve such problems, Congress passed laws that brought a variety of changes.

Campaign spending. Nixon's helpers had broken existing laws in taking secret gifts for his campaign. In 1974, Congress decided that future presidential campaigns should be partly paid for with public tax money. Private gifts to presidential nominees after the political conventions had been

held were forbidden. In addition, Congress set limits on the amount an individual could give to a candidate for Congress or to a candidate in a presidential primary. It also required that names of major givers be made public.

FBI and CIA. Both the FBI and CIA had a part in the Watergate cover-up. More abuses by those agencies came to light later, some dating to before the Nixon administration. For example, a presidential committee in 1975 reported that the CIA had engaged in such illegal activities as opening people's mail and otherwise invading privacy. It was also revealed that the CIA had plotted to assassinate foreign leaders, including Cuba's Premier Fidel Castro. Leaders of the FBI and CIA promised to stop such activities.

Special prosecutor. In the Ethics-in-Government Act of 1978, Congress set up a new method of investigating charges against high officials. The law provided for the naming of a special prosecutor, independent of the regular government.

Some said the Watergate reforms had not gone far enough. They called for additional steps, such as federal financing of congressional elections. Others argued that the reforms had gone too far. They said, for example, that the work of intelligence agencies had been hampered. Debate on the reform efforts continued into the 1980's.

Homework Questions

1. How did the Watergate affair begin?
2. Why was the Watergate cover-up considered a crime?
3. How was Nixon involved in the cover-up?
4. What part did the courts play in the Watergate affair?
5. In your opinion, what was the chief lesson of the Watergate affair?

Understanding the Story

A. List the numbers of the statements that are true.
1. The Watergate burglars planned to tap a telephone at the Democrats' headquarters.
2. The burglars carried money from President Nixon's campaign committee.
3. When he learned of the burglary, Nixon insisted that the whole truth be made public.
4. Judge John J. Sirica thought the conviction of seven burglary suspects solved the case.
5. White House officials worried that other illegal activities would be found out.
6. President Nixon refused at first to turn over his tapes.
7. The courts said Nixon did not have to turn over the tapes.
8. The House of Representatives impeached Nixon.

B. Choose the term or phrase that best completes each statement.
1. President Nixon and H. R. Haldeman decided to (a) cooperate with (b) block (c) ignore the FBI investigation.
2. Administration officials called Watergate (a) the crime of the century (b) a Democratic hoax (c) a third-rate burglary attempt.
3. The head of the Senate Watergate committee was (a) John Sirica (b) Sam Ervin (c) H. R. Haldeman.
4. In refusing to turn over his tapes, Nixon claimed a right of (a) executive privilege (b) habeas corpus (c) personal privacy.
5. Critics of Nixon said the President had (a) betrayed his public trust (b) aided the Communists (c) been betrayed by his helpers.
6. Gerald Ford was the first President who (a) resigned (b) granted a pardon (c) reached office through appointment.
7. In July, 1974, a House committee voted to (a) ask the President to resign (b) destroy the tapes (c) submit three counts of impeachment to the full House.
8. Since 1974, presidential campaigns have been partly paid for by (a) lottery tickets (b) public tax money (c) unlimited private contributions.

C. A number of Presidents have secretly taped their conversations in the White House. Why do you suppose they have done so? Do you think such White House tapings are a good thing? Why or why not?

Activities and Inquiries

1. Read a book dealing with the Watergate affair. Prepare a report on the book.
2. Prepare a report card on Richard Nixon. Grade him in the following areas and justify each grade:
   a. Leadership
   b. Accomplishments while President
   c. Point of view
   d. Maturity
3. In a reference book, look up the three counts of impeachment voted against President Nixon by the House committee. Pretend you are a member of the House of Representatives. Would you vote to impeach Nixon? Why or why not?
4. Assume you are Gerald Ford. What reasons can you think of for pardoning Richard Nixon? What reasons can you think of for not pardoning him?
5. In your opinion, who was mainly responsible for the Watergate affair? Explain.

4 The Gas Line

From its earliest days, the United States has been rich in sources of energy. Early settlers found vast forests that provided wood for fuel. Later, new fuels were put to use—coal, oil, natural gas. Such resources lay under the surface of the United States in great abundance. They helped to build American industries and keep American factories humming.

As the years went by, the U.S. appetite for energy grew and grew. But production of fuel did not keep pace. Oil, in particular, had to be imported from overseas, mainly from the Middle East. A sharp rise in oil imports began in the mid-1960's. By 1973, one third of the oil used in the United States came from outside the country. And U.S. oil production had begun to drop.

To most Americans, the changing pattern of energy supply was unimportant. Fuel seemed plentiful. Gasoline prices had remained fairly steady for years. One could find stations selling gasoline for as little as 30 cents a gallon.

But that was about to change. In October, 1973, a war broke out in the Middle East—another round in the Arab-Israeli feud. For the first time, Arab nations decided to use oil as a weapon. They cut output and declared a boycott of the United States and other countries that were aiding Israel.

At first, U.S. oil companies dipped into their storage tanks. But the boycott dragged on even after the Middle East fighting had ended, and serious shortages developed. There was not enough fuel for winter heating. There was too little gasoline for driving.

In our story, a double line of automobiles stretches for half a mile outside a filling station. Because of the shortages, the station is open only four hours a day. Three other stations in the area are closed. Motorists are waiting for a chance to buy a few gallons of gasoline. Whom do they blame for their troubles? What solutions do they propose?

[handwritten: Who do motorist to blame for the gas crisis and what sol. do they propose?]

Teaneck, New Jersey, March, 1974

MOLLY (*through her open car window*). Hey, mister, have you got the time?

JERRY (*from the next car*). Six-thirty.

MOLLY. Oh, my, I'll never get to work on time. I've been in this line for more than an hour.

JERRY. Me too. And with my luck they'll close the pumps just when I get up there. They did that to my friend Joe just yesterday. He was so mad he almost hit the guy pumping gas.

MOLLY. I don't blame your friend for getting mad. This gas shortage is getting on everyone's nerves.

JERRY. The gas business isn't the half of it. It's the shortage of heating oil that gets me. I've turned my thermostat down to 62, and I'm still worried I won't make it through the month. My supplier said I could have only three fourths of my normal supply of oil That Arab boycott had better end soon.

MOLLY. I know a lot of people blame the Arabs, but I think it's the big oil companies that are behind this. Look at how the price of gasoline has gone up. This station is charging 47 cents a gallon— can you imagine? The oil companies want shortages so they can raise the prices. They're probably in cahoots with the Arabs. After all, many American oil companies operate in the Arab world.

JERRY. Personally, I think the oil companies are as much victims as we are. But I'll tell you one thing. Once oil and gas prices get up high, they'll never come down.

MOLLY. You're probably right. And me with this old gas-guzzling station wagon. How can I afford to keep it running?

JERRY. Better get a four-cylinder foreign compact like I've got. This one gets 30 miles to the gallon.

MOLLY. I don't know. I've always bought American cars.

JERRY. I'll bet the American companies will be putting out their own mini-compacts before long. The days of the gas guzzler are over.

MOLLY. I guess we'll all be paying more attention to how much energy we use. My husband says if we put more insulation in the

Energy* Use Per Person in the United States, 1970–1980

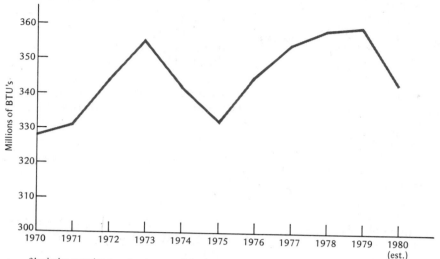

*Includes petroleum, natural gas, coal, hydropower, nuclear power, geothermal power.

attic floor, we can cut our heating bill by a fourth. But who can afford all that insulation?

JERRY. Who can afford to waste all that heat? The insulation will probably pay for itself in a few years. Especially if fuel prices keep going up.

MOLLY. Do you think they can go higher? Seems to me they're already in orbit.

JERRY. Some guys on TV said we'll be paying $1 a gallon for gasoline in a few years.

MOLLY. I hope it never comes to that.

JERRY. Me too, but I won't place any bets. Well, we've finally gotten to the head of the line. (To attendant:) Ten gallons, please.

ATTENDANT. Sorry, mister, we just ran out. Come back tomorrow.

POSTSCRIPT

The Arab boycott ended later that same month. Already the price of crude oil had quadrupled—multiplied by four. And it would quadruple again by the early 1980's. Gasoline prices passed the $1-a-gallon mark in 1979.

As the cost of oil rose, so did the price of other types of energy. And that was not all. Products like steel, which require large amounts of energy to make, also became more costly.

Airlines raised ticket prices to cover the higher costs of jet fuel. Other businesses increased prices too. The effects of the oil-price increases rippled through the whole economy. Inflation (rising prices) would be a major problem of the 1970's and 1980's.

Rising energy prices had many causes. One obvious cause was an effort by oil-producing countries to limit the output of oil. An association called OPEC, the Organization of

Petroleum Exporting Countries, led the effort. But there were other causes as well. Energy consumption was rising in nations all over the world. Demand was going up—and prices depend as much on demand as on supply.

Within the United States, a debate began about the double energy challenge—the rising prices and limited supply. The first thing we must do, U.S. leaders said, is to boost production of energy. This would make the United States less vulnerable to actions by OPEC. Just as important, said some, was finding ways to make energy resources stretch farther by cutting down waste. Thus, U.S. leaders also called for energy conservation.

Here are some of the things the government did to try to boost U.S. energy production:

• Gradually phased out price controls that had been placed on oil and gas in 1971. The idea was that if the companies could charge more, they could make higher profits. Then they would be more likely to invest in new oil and gas wells.

• Opened more federal land to energy production.

• Encouraged exploration for oil and gas under the oceans near U.S. shores.

• Set up a Department of Energy (1977) to encourage research in "alternative" (other) energy sources. Two areas that received attention were solar energy (from the sun) and "synfuels." Synfuels, or synthetic fuels, are new types of fossil fuels—for example, gasoline from coal or oil made by crushing shale (a type of rock).

• Encouraged expanded production of nuclear power. By the early 1980's, nuclear plants were producing about 12 percent of U.S. electricity and accounted for 4 percent of total energy output.

Some of these actions were controversial. For example, critics questioned the safety of nuclear power plants. And critics argued that offshore drilling was a danger to the environment. In reply, supporters of such projects said their risks were limited. They said such limited risks were justified in the interest of boosting energy supplies and strengthening the U.S. economy.

Here are some of the things the government did to promote the conservation of energy:

• Gave tax breaks to homeowners who took energy-saving steps such as installing more insulation.

• Set a maximum speed of 55 miles an hour on the nation's highways. Previously, speed limits had been as high as 70 miles an hour in some states.

• Directed that stores and other public buildings set thermostats lower in winter (to use less heat) and higher in summer (to use less air conditioning). This policy was ended in the early 1980's.

Many Americans acted on their own to conserve energy. Some people bought smaller cars. (U.S. car-makers introduced new models to meet the demand.) Some people bought wood or coal stoves to furnish extra heat in winter. Some began to dry clothes on clotheslines rather than in dryers that burned large amounts of electricity or natural gas. Americans found many ways to cut down on energy use— partly because they thought it was the right thing to do, and partly because energy had become so costly.

The efforts of the government, of businesses, and of individuals did have an effect. New sources of energy went into production. Energy consumption rose more slowly than in the past. But the United States did not end its dependence on foreign energy supplies. In the early 1980's, the United States still imported about one third of the oil it used.

In the 1970's for the first time, the "energy crisis" (a widely used term) was a major topic of national debate. Some people warned that the world was "running out of energy." Others said there was plenty of energy—people just had to develop it. By the early 1980's the debate had quieted down. But U.S. energy policies had changed significantly, and Americans had become more aware of the vital role of energy in a modern society.

Homework Questions

1. Why did gas lines form in the early months of 1974?
2. What causes contributed to the "energy crisis" of the 1970's?
3. How did the U.S. government respond to the energy challenge?
4. Why were some of the government's actions controversial?
5. What did individuals do to meet the energy challenge?

Understanding the Story

A. Write *T* for each statement that is true, *F* for each statement that is false, and *N* for each statement that is not mentioned in the story.
 1. The Arab oil boycott of 1973–1974 was touched off by a war between Iraq and Iran.
 2. The boycott caused serious disruptions in U.S. fuel supplies.
 3. U.S. oil production was higher in 1970 than in any year before or since.
 4. Molly drove a station wagon that used a lot of gasoline.
 5. The average car built in the United States in 1974 got 13.2 miles per gallon.
 6. OPEC sought to raise prices by increasing the supply of oil.
 7. The Department of Energy was created in 1977.
 8. Solar energy is an example of a "synfuel."

B. Choose the term or phrase that best completes each statement.
 1. In 1973 the United States imported about (*a*) one fourth (*b*) one third (*c*) one half of the oil it used.
 2. The Arab oil boycott was directed at countries that (*a*) aided Israel (*b*) had Communist governments (*c*) had no oil of their own.
 3. Molly's husband wanted to save fuel by using (*a*) more insulation (*b*) solar heat (*c*) clotheslines.
 4. During the Arab oil boycott the price of crude oil (*a*) doubled (*b*) tripled (*c*) quadrupled.
 5. Measures taken by the U.S. government to boost energy production included (*a*) price controls (*b*) lower speed limits (*c*) the encouragement of nuclear power.
 6. In the early 1980's nuclear plants produced about (*a*) 12 (*b*) 15 (*c*) 25 percent of U.S. electric power.
 7. Americans tried to conserve energy by buying (*a*) longer clotheslines (*b*) smaller cars (*c*) cheaper thermostats.
 8. By conserving energy, Americans could (*a*) help Israel (*b*) save money (*c*) boost oil imports.

C. Suppose you are President of the United States. All foreign supplies of oil have been cut off. What will you ask the government and the people to do to meet the crisis?

Activities and Inquiries

1. Study the graph on page 575. Then choose the term or phrase that best completes each statement or answers each question.

   a. According to the information given in the chapter, what caused the change in energy use between 1973 and 1976? (1) warm winters throughout the United States (2) a decrease in petroleum supplies imported from the Middle East (3) rationing of supplies by the federal government

   b. In which year was the use of energy the highest? (1) 1979 (2) 1978 (3) 1973

   c. In which year was the least amount of energy used? (1) 1980 (2) 1975 (3) 1970

   d. Hydropower is the same as (1) wind power (2) water power (3) electric power.

   e. What probably accounts for the drop in energy use between 1979 and 1980? (1) high cost of energy and increased use of conservation measures (2) federal regulations on energy use (3) greater use of solar power

2. Would you say that the United States is solving its energy problems? Why or why not?

3. Outline a program that you and the members of your household can follow to save energy.

4. Assume that you are preparing a script for a television film on the energy crisis. Describe your major scenes. List the characters you would use, and show how you would fit them into the scenes.

5. Prepare a newspaper article, advertisement, or poster suggesting ways to save energy.

5 Woman's Place

"Women's issues" faded from the front pages after women won voting rights in 1920. But behind the scenes, many changes were going on. Women were becoming more and more independent. They started assuming a new place in American life.

Increasing numbers of women began taking jobs outside the home. The big jump came during World War II. As men went off to war, women replaced them in factories, in offices, and on the farm. After the war, many women stayed in the work force. In 1960, about 23.2 million U.S. women over 16 years of age were in the labor force. They represented 37.7 percent of the work force. (In 1940 14.2 million women 14 years of age and older were in the labor force. They represented 27.9 percent of the work force.)

"Equality of the sexes" became a major issue—just like "equality of the races." Many civil rights laws applied to both minority groups and women. During the 1960's laws made it illegal to discriminate against women in hiring. In the 1970's more laws were passed to bar sex discrimination in other areas—in bank loans, in apartment rentals, in school sports, for example.

The most sweeping proposal called for adding an amendment to the Constitution guaranteeing equal rights to people of both sexes. This was called ERA—the Equal Rights Amendment. Congress voted in 1972 to submit it to the states for ratification. The debate on ratification lasted into the 1980's.

Americans were deeply divided by the issue of sex equality. Many women worked hard to get equal-rights provisions put into laws and the Constitution. They joined organizations like the National Organization for Women (NOW), formed in 1966 to promote women's rights. But other women opposed such groups and the trend they represented. Critics said equal-rights efforts were causing more problems for women than they were solving.

How were women's roles in society changing? What lay behind the debate over equality for the sexes? In our story, an imaginary television personality interviews two imaginary women about their lives and their beliefs. How do the women differ? What do they have in common?

New York City, 1975

A sign flashed—"On the Air"—and the studio audience clapped and whistled. Malcolm Morgan, the dapper host, smiled his million-dollar smile and held up a hand for silence.

"Welcome to 'Mornings with Malcolm,'" he purred. "Today we have with us two charming ladies. Alice is a mother of two. She's a coal miner."

The audience snickered. Alice, a trim woman in her late 20's or early 30's, nodded shyly. A ripple of applause greeted her gesture.

"Alice is also an author," the host said with a smile. "Her book, *It's the Pits*, tells what it's like to work in a coal mine."

Alice spoke up. "Actually, it's not all that bad, Malcolm—once the men learn you're there to work and once they know you can keep up the pace."

"Alice has what you might call a 'non-traditional' job," said Malcolm. "Our other guest, Nancy, has a more 'traditional' job. She's a housewife."

Again there was laughter from the audience, and some applause. Nancy smiled. She too was trim and thirtyish.

"Nancy is president of an organization called Home and Family First. Tell us about your organization, Nancy."

"Certainly, Malcolm. We try to promote a warm family life. We believe a mother should be in the home, taking care of her children and her husband. We act as a support group for mothers who want to resist the pressure in our society for women to take a job."

"Does that mean you think working mothers can't meet their family responsibilities?"

"Yes, it does, Malcolm. Being a mother is a full-time job. I've seen too many mothers trying to juggle a job and run a home at the same time. What usually happens is that the kids are left to take care of themselves after school. And that can be tragic. Unsupervised children may be hurt or killed in an accident. Or they may engage in the kinds of activities that are becoming so awfully common nowadays—drugs, alcohol, and all that.''

''I take it, Alice, that you would disagree,'' said Malcolm. ''How do you square your working life with your family responsibilities?''

''Well, Malcolm, first of all, running a family is a responsibility that my husband and I share. He works a day shift, and I work a night shift. I'm at home when the kids get back from school, and I fix their supper and help them with their homework. After I leave for work, my husband puts them to bed and does the dishes.''

''So your husband wears the apron in the family,'' said Malcolm with a grin. ''What do his friends say about that?''

''Listen, there may have been a time when doing housework was considered not to be 'manly,' but that time is way in the past. Most of the men I know change diapers, and most of the women I know change the oil in their cars. That doesn't make the men sissies or the women tomboys. Why should jobs be divided into 'men's work' and 'women's work'?''

''What kind of work would you call coal mining, Alice?''

''Hard work, Malcolm—plain old hard work. I have to lug heavy equipment around, I get my eyes and throat filled with coal dust, and I'm pretty well worn out when I get home.''

''So why do you do it?''

''The same reason men do it—for the money. I can make three times what most women make, and that means something. When my husband was laid off for three months last year, our family depended on *me* to bring home the bacon. I couldn't have done that if I'd been an 'office girl.' ''

"But don't the men you work with give you trouble? They must resent the presence of a woman in the mines."

"Oh, sure, some men do—but most just ignore me. Of course," Alice went on, "the mining company isn't too happy about us women miners. A friend and I had to go to court to get our jobs in the first place. But the law says 'equal hiring,' and they had to hire us if we could do the work. I think the laws have changed for the better in recent years, and I'm all for it. Once we get the ERA in the Constitution, we women will be truly equal."

Part of the audience erupted in cheers. Others booed loudly. Malcolm raised a hand to silence them.

"I'm afraid Alice is going to be disappointed," Nancy declared. "ERA isn't going to get into the Constitution—"

The audience interrupted her with more cheers and boos.

"—and even if it did, women and men would not be equal. We are different, as most people can tell for themselves."

The audience snickered, and Malcolm nodded his head.

"The trouble with all these laws and amendments," said Nancy, "is that they go against human nature. For centuries we humans got along fine with a traditional family structure. Men went out and earned a living. Women stayed home and took care of the kids. But somewhere we got off the track. Some women wanted to be different. They went off in search of 'fulfillment,' ignoring their responsibilities to their husbands and children. And what did that lead to? Rising divorce rates, broken homes, juvenile delinquency—the list goes on and on."

Alice interrupted. "I think you've got your history a bit confused. The 'traditional family' that you describe, with men 'going out' and women 'staying home,' is really quite recent. Until less than two centuries ago, *both* men and women usually worked at home—together. Only after the rise of industry did their roles in society get separated. And nowadays rising divorce rates and delinquency and such things have more to do with changes in the economy and in society than they do with women taking jobs."

"You ignore the main point, Alice," said Nancy. "It's just against human nature for women and men to be exactly the same. I'm proud to be a woman, to be feminine. I like to have men open the door for me or offer me a seat. Men *like* to treat women with respect. I don't understand women who act as if a man has committed a crime when he tells her how lovely she looks."

"By putting women on a pedestal," said Alice, "men can control them—'keep them in their place.' That's what men have done for ages. I think it's time women demanded a different kind of respect—a respect based on true equality. I just want to be treated like a whole person, a real human being, an equal."

Malcolm flashed his famous smile. "You're both just great human beings. Really. But I'm afraid our time is up."

POSTSCRIPT

During the 1970's and 1980's women were more widely accepted in "non-traditional" roles. More women than ever before moved into jobs as coal miners, lawyers, road workers, doctors, TV newscasters. Women became ministers and rabbis. The U.S. Army recruited women for a wide variety of new tasks, although not for combat. By 1980, 44.6 million women 16 years old and over were in the labor force. They represented 51.6 percent of the work force.

Many women welcomed the widening opportunities. They claimed that women were being "liberated" (freed) from second-class roles in society. But many others continued to encourage "traditional" roles for women. They strongly regretted the trends that were bringing great changes to relations between the sexes.

After prolonged and bitter debate, the Equal Rights Amendment died. Only 35 of the required 38 states had approved it by 1982, when the deadline for ratification passed. But many states had added equal-rights amendments to their own constitutions. And debate continued on the pros and cons of the national ERA.

Homework Questions

1. How did World War II affect the role of women in American society?
2. What forms of discrimination against women were banned by laws of the 1960's and 1970's?
3. Why did the Equal Rights Amendment stir controversy?
4. How did Alice and Nancy feel about the ERA?
5. What changes took place during the 1970's and 1980's in job opportunities for women?

Understanding the Story

A. List the numbers of the statements that are true.
1. A larger proportion of American women held jobs in 1940 than in 1960.
2. Many laws bar discrimination against women.
3. The Equal Rights Amendment sought to guarantee equal rights for both sexes.
4. Alice had a "non-traditional" job.
5. Nancy was unhappy being a housewife.
6. Nancy opposed the Equal Rights Amendment.
7. Alice blamed working women for high divorce rates.
8. It was harder than ever in the 1970's for women to get jobs as lawyers.

B. Write *A* for each statement that Alice made or might have made and *N* for each statement that Nancy made or might have made.
1. Being a mother is a full-time job.
2. My husband and I share in running the family.
3. It's good for a woman to know how to change the oil in her car.
4. Above all, a woman should take care of her children and her husband.
5. Men don't annoy me on the job.
6. It is human nature for men to work and women to stay home.
7. I like it when a man opens the door for me.
8. I don't like it when men put women on a pedestal.

C. Assume that you are a legislator in a state that is considering its own equal-rights amendment. Will you vote for or against the measure? Why?

Activities and Inquiries

1. Prepare questions to ask Alice about her job as a coal miner. What answers does she give?
2. Prepare questions to ask Nancy about her organization. What answers does she give?
3. Ask a woman you know to tell you what she thinks about the women's rights movement. Make a class report.
4. Consult an almanac or other reference book to find the average pay levels for men and women in a number of recent years. Plot the figures on a graph. What reasons can you think of for the gap between men's pay and women's pay?
5. Write a TV commercial for a wash-day product. Pay attention to the way you picture women in your commercial. Do you think Alice would approve of your commercial? Do you think Nancy would approve of your commercial? Explain.

6 Compromise at Camp David

From the 1940's on, the Middle East had been a hotspot of world trouble. War had erupted there four times—in 1948, 1956, 1967, and 1973. Behind the tension was a dispute over who should rule the biblical land of Palestine. Both Arabs and Jews had historical ties to Palestine, and both claimed it as a homeland.

For centuries Palestine was under Moslem rule as part of the Ottoman Empire of the Turks. After World War I, the British took control. Many Jews immigrated to Palestine, fleeing persecution in Europe and elsewhere. Zionists—that is, Jews who wanted to set up a Jewish state in Palestine—pressed Britain to allow such a state.

Finally the British government turned the question over to the United Nations. In November, 1947, the U.N. General Assembly approved a plan to split Palestine into two states—one Arab, one Jewish. Arabs, who made up two thirds of Palestine's people, bitterly rejected this plan, insisting that Palestine should remain one country. Open warfare broke out between Arabs and Jews in Palestine. A few months later, when Jewish leaders announced creation of the state of Israel, nearby Arab states went to war on the side of the Palestinian Arabs. From 1948 on, Arab states refused to recognize Israel's right to exist as a nation and considered themselves to be at war with Israel.

Israeli armies fought well, and the new state survived. But hatred and bitterness poisoned the atmosphere of the Middle East. Large numbers of Palestinian Arabs fled to nearby countries and settled in refugee camps. Many Palestinian Arabs joined military units working to recapture what Arabs considered to be *their* homeland.

Leaders of the United States were greatly concerned about the tensions in the Middle East. On the one hand, the United States had formed close ties to Israel. Israel was a democracy; many Americans had gone to live there; investments and weapons from the United States helped build up Israel's strength. On the other hand, the United States depended increasingly on oil from the Middle East—from Arab nations such as Saudi Arabia and Kuwait and from the non-Arab nation of Iran. Any new flareup of war in the Middle East might cut off U.S. supplies of oil, as happened in 1973 (see pages 573–574). Or, worse, a new Middle East war might explode into a wider war, perhaps into World War III.

U.S. leaders had a variety of goals. They wanted to assure Israel's survival. They wanted to stay on good terms with Israel's neighbors. They wanted to avoid a disastrous war. And they wanted to keep Soviet influence in the Middle East from growing. As long as tensions were high, U.S. leaders reasoned, Arabs would be tempted to turn to the Soviet Union for arms and other help—as many Arab states had already done.

The Arab effort to recapture their homeland from the Israelis resulted in a number of wars that backfired. The 1973 war marked the fourth time that Israel had been victorious in battle. The Israelis had captured land (mainly in 1967) on four sides. In the northeast, they took the Golan Heights from Syria. In the east, they took a large Palestinian area called the West Bank (of the Jordan River). On the southwest, they took the much larger Sinai Peninsula from Egypt. On the west, they took a stretch of Palestinian land called the Gaza Strip.

Israelis looked on the new lands as a buffer, a protective zone, between Israel and the Arab states. They wanted such a buffer to help protect against attacks by terrorists and Arab armies. Israel gave up a small part of the Sinai in 1974 but said it would give other lands back only after the Arabs made peace and recognized Israel's right to exist.

Israel insisted on dealing only with Arab states—not with Palestinian groups like the Palestine Liberation Organization (PLO). The PLO and similar groups were terrorists, Israeli leaders said. Arab governments, on the other hand, insisted that Israel must come to terms first of all with the Palestinian Arabs and their wish for a homeland. Arab states refused to deal directly with Israel.

After the 1973 war, U.S. leaders tried hard to bring Israeli and Arab officials to the peace table. Henry Kissinger, the U.S. secretary of state from 1973 to 1977, shuttled back and forth by plane from one Middle East capital to another. This "shuttle diplomacy" began to make headway. It was backed up by promises of U.S. economic and military aid both to Israel and to Israel's enemy, Egypt.

Late in 1977, after Kissinger had left office, came a stunning breakthrough. Anwar Sadat, president of Egypt, flew to Israel and spoke before the Israeli parliament in Jerusalem. He called for peace between Egypt and Israel. Many Arab leaders angrily denounced Sadat. But Egyptians and Israelis began difficult face-to-face negotiations.

In our story, Sadat meets with the Israeli prime minister, Menachem Begin. The two leaders have been invited to the United States by Jimmy Carter, who became President in 1977. They are meeting at Camp David, Maryland. What obstacles stand in the way of peace in the Middle East? How will President Carter try to break the deadlock?

Camp David, Maryland, September, 1978

President Carter prepared to greet his two guests, men whom he had met before but did not know well. He had invited them to the United States to try to revive their dragging talks.

Carter had mixed feelings about the task that faced him. On the one hand, he admired the Israeli people and was committed, like U.S. Presidents before him, to help Israel obtain secure boundaries. On the other hand, he suspected that Menachem Begin was going to be a difficult man to deal with—a man who would not want to budge once he took a stand. Anwar Sadat had impressed Carter as a man who was both warm and flexible. The President hoped he could get both men to make concessions for peace.

Carter knew there was no way the Israeli-Egyptian talks could please everyone. Other Arabs suspected Egypt's motives. They accused Egypt of "selling out" the Palestinian Arabs by seeking a separate peace with Israel. Arab critics did not want Egypt to make a separate peace. They feared that such a peace would reduce the pressure on Israel to come to terms with the Palestinians themselves.

But Carter saw things differently. To him, the most important thing was to prevent another Arab-Israeli war. A fifth such war, Carter feared, might lead to a showdown between the United States, backing Israel, and the Soviet Union, backing the Arabs. The United States had close ties to both Israel and Egypt. Carter might be able to nudge them closer together at a crucial step in the bargaining.

Carter's role was to serve as a mediator, a middle-man. He was ready to make proposals of his own if he thought he could bridge a gap between the Israelis and the Egyptians. It would take all his skills as a negotiator and his resources as President to help these two leaders come to an agreement.

It was the first day at Camp David. Anwar Sadat stared at Menachem Begin. "Premier Begin," he said, "if you want peace you must give us back our land."

Sadat was determined to recover the Sinai Peninsula from Israel. He wanted every bit of Egyptian land back. He also wanted Israel to give up the West Bank and the Gaza Strip.

Begin stared at Sadat. "If you want your land back," he declared, "you must give us peace."

Begin was prepared to strike a bargain. He would give back the Sinai if Egypt would agree to sign a peace treaty. One of Israel's chief goals over the years had been to get the Arab states to admit that Israel existed—that it had a right to exist.

But the West Bank and the Gaza Strip were a different matter. The Egyptians believed that these areas were part of Palestine. According to them, there was no state of Palestine, no government to speak for the Palestinian Arabs. The Israelis disagreed. They claimed that Jordan was the Palestinian homeland.

As the Camp David talks continued, the lines of a possible agreement began to take shape—or rather, the lines of two possible agreements. One would deal with the Sinai and with Egyptian-Israeli relations. The other would deal with occupied parts of Palestine.

Israel was willing to work out some sort of "self-rule" for the Palestinian Arabs. But "self-rule" did not mean independence. Israel insisted on keeping a degree of authority within the West Bank and Gaza, at least for the time being for reasons of security.

The talks went on and on. There were points of agreement, but also many points of disagreement. In private, Carter tried to persuade both leaders to be more flexible. Carter told them: "If you lose this opportunity for peace, it may never come again."

Day after day the leaders met, but still they could not settle their differences. On the 11th day, Sadat sent word to Carter that he was going home. Sadat said he had given up hope that an agreement could be reached. Carter persuaded Sadat to stay for one last try.

On the 12th day there was a breakthrough. With the help of a dictionary, President Carter found a way to say "self-rule" without using the exact words proposed by the Israelis. This pleased Sadat. The Egyptian was even more pleased when Begin gave up his insistence that 2,000 Israeli settlers must be allowed to stay in the Sinai. Begin agreed to ask the Israeli parliament if the settlers could be removed.

Overnight, the final touches were put on an agreement. On the 13th day the leaders met. Begin, Sadat, and Carter embraced one another. At last they had found an agreement both sides could accept.

POSTSCRIPT

In effect, what the leaders agreed on at Camp David was only a framework for peace. Final details still had to be added. Israeli and Egyptian officials worked for several more months before a peace treaty was signed in March, 1979.

Egypt became the first Arab nation to open diplomatic relations with Israel. Israel gave back the rest of the Sinai Peninsula, with a peacekeeping force from other nations in the eastern Sinai serving as a buffer between Israeli and Egyptian troops. Israel agreed to enter negotiations on the future of the West Bank and the Gaza Strip.

The Camp David agreements and the resulting peace treaty brought both great praise and bitter criticism. Begin and Sadat were given a high honor—the Nobel Peace Prize for 1978—for their role in the accords. Arab nations, on the other hand, accused Sadat of being a traitor to the Palestinian cause. Almost all Arab nations broke off relations with Egypt.

As the years passed, true peace remained out of reach. Negotiations on "self-rule" for the Palestinian Arabs made little progress. Large numbers of Israelis moved into the West Bank and Gaza and settled there. The Egyptians and Jimmy Carter claimed that Begin had gone back on a promise at Camp David not to allow new settlements of this sort. Begin denied that he had made any such promise. Israel's relations with the Palestinians and with other Arab nations remained hostile. In 1982, after numerous attacks by PLO terrorists, Israel launched a major invasion of Lebanon. The Begin government said its aim was to remove bases from which armed Palestinian groups had attacked Israel.

In 1981, Egypt's President Sadat had been assassinated by a group of Egyptians. The new president of Egypt promised to continue Sadat's policies toward Israel.

The Israeli-Palestinian conflict showed no sign of abating in the 1980's. In 1993, after much international diplomatic effort, Israel and the Palestinians took a major step toward permanent peace in the Middle East. They signed an agreement in which Israel agreed to return the Gaza Strip and the town of Jericho to the Palestinians. In return the latter recognized the existence of Israel as a nation.

Despite strong opposition from some Palestinians, who rejected any treaty with Israel, and Israeli settlers in occupied territories, who feared the loss of their homes, the treaty went into effect in 1994.

Homework Questions

1. How did the tensions in the Middle East begin?
2. What reasons did U.S. leaders have for their concern about Middle East troubles?
3. What was the agreement that Israel and Egypt reached at Camp David?
4. Why were the Camp David agreements hailed by some as a breakthrough for peace?
5. Why did other Arab nations denounce Egypt for making peace with Israel?

Understanding the Story

A. Write T for each statement that is true and F for each statement that is false.
   1. The United Nations voted to split Palestine into an Arab state and a Jewish state.
   2. Both Arabs and Jews welcomed the U.N.'s plan.
   3. Arabs and Israelis fought wars in 1948, 1956, 1967, and 1973.
   4. Arab armies occupied the Sinai Peninsula after the 1967 war.
   5. President Carter wanted to avoid a breakdown in the talks between Menachem Begin and Anwar Sadat.
   6. Israel refused to give any territory back to Egypt.
   7. Egypt was the first Arab state to sign a peace treaty with Israel.
   8. Other Arab states praised Sadat for his courage.

B. Choose the term or phrase that best completes each statement.
   1. The Golan Heights were part of (a) Jordan (b) Syria (c) Egypt.
   2. The West Bank was part of (a) Egypt (b) Lebanon (c) Palestine.
   3. Israel agreed to return to Egypt the (a) Gaza Strip (b) West Bank (c) Sinai Peninsula.
   4. The Camp David meetings were held in (a) Israel (b) the United States (c) Egypt.
   5. An Arab state from which the United States buys oil is (a) Iran (b) Saudi Arabia (c) Israel.

6. Begin wanted Sadat to sign a treaty because (*a*) Israel needed Egyptian loans (*b*) Israel wanted an Arab state to admit Israel's right to exist (*c*) Israel wanted Egyptian land.

7. In regard to the West Bank, Begin agreed to (*a*) negotiate its future (*b*) keep Israeli settlers out (*c*) give it to Jordan.

8. Sadat agreed to (*a*) open diplomatic relations with Israel (*b*) make a military alliance with Israel (*c*) let Israel keep Egyptian land.

C. Imagine that you have been asked to draw up a peace agreement that would be fair to all sides in the Middle East. Is such an agreement possible? What do you recommend?

Activities and Inquiries

1. You are President Carter's biographer. You are writing the chapter about his role in helping Egypt and Israel agree to a treaty. Outline the chapter.

2. You are about to interview the Israeli prime minister. List the questions you would like to ask. What answers do you think you will get?

3. Do the same for the president of Egypt.

4. You visit the Arab countries and Israel. You find that many people in these lands sincerely want peace. You ask if they believe peace will ever come. What do they answer? Do you agree? Explain.

5. Using a library, find how much aid the United States gave to Israel and to Egypt in a recent year. What reasons can you think of in favor of such aid? What reasons can you think of against it? Do you approve of the U.S. policy of aiding both countries? Why or why not?

MR. MILLER'S OFFICE

"You were right, Mr. Miller. There was more to the 1970's and 1980's than just the Watergate scandal and the Cold War."

"Lots of ups and downs, weren't there, Jack?"

"Yes, Mr. Miller. But I saw lots of positive things."

"Go on, Jack."

"Well, I especially liked our spirit. Whatever the problem— pollution, Watergate, the Middle East—we were always trying to solve it."

"And do you believe that, in the next decade, the 1990's, the American people will try to solve all the problems that confront them, no matter how difficult?"

Jack smiled. "I would like to answer 'yes,' but I have the feeling that you are about to challenge me."

"Yes, Jack, in a way I am. Let's turn to the 1990's."

UNIT SIXTEEN

The 1990's

"We've reached the 1990's at last," smiled Jack. "Should I be excited about this new decade?"

"I don't know whether you should be excited," replied Mr. Miller. "But you have to realize that there have been many changes in the United States and in the world."

"Such as?"

"In the United States, we have seen the election of Bill Clinton, a Democrat, as President, after twelve years of Republican presidency. Abroad, there have been a great many changes."

"What happened, Mr. Miller?"

"Our long-time Cold War enemy, the Soviet Union, no longer exists. Political and economic turmoil brought about its collapse in the early 90's. We'll have more to say about Russian-American relations in the unit."

"Are there any other pluses?" Jack asked.

"In South Africa, in 1994, blacks voted in national elections for the first time, and the nation elected a black president. In the Middle East, Israel and the Palestinians signed an agreement that may bring them closer to peace. But poverty, starvation, and violence continue to plague many people throughout the world."

"What about the problems in our own country, Mr. Miller?"

"We have many long-standing problems too, Jack. The President and Congress set out to try to find a solution to one of them—the crisis in health care."

"I'm interested in finding out what they did, Mr. Miller."

"Then let's get into the unit and see what happened."

1 After the Cold War

In 1991, it became clear that the long Cold War between the United States and the Soviet Union was finally coming to an end. The once-mighty Soviet empire was breaking up. The Soviet Union's East European satellites had declared their independence and formed non-Communist governments. East Germany was united with West Germany. The three Soviet Baltic states had also declared their independence, and other Soviet republics were also breaking away.

The Soviet economy was in a shambles. Industrial output had been falling year by year, farm production was declining alarmingly, and consumer goods were practically nonexistent. Many feared they might not survive the next harsh Russian winter.

In the 1980's, Soviet leaders, under President Mikhail Gorbachev, had attempted to stop the decline on the national level by encouraging more personal economic initiative and allowing more freedom of speech. On the international level, Gorbachev signed arms-reduction treaties with the United States, thus lessening the threat of nuclear war between the two superpowers. But the Soviet Union was involved in a costly and futile war to maintain a Communist government in Afghanistan, and it supported at great cost Communist movements in other parts of the world.

At the end of 1991, realizing that the Soviet Union was no longer functioning, Gorbachev resigned as President and declared the end of both the Soviet Union and the Communist party. Boris Yeltsin, the President of the Russian parliament, assumed leadership.

The Soviet Union broke up into a loose confederation of most of its former republics, called the Commonwealth of Independent States (CIS). Many of these states, however, remained dependent on Russia for political leadership and economic assistance. A dispute over territory led to war between Armenia and Azerbaijan.

As compared to the United States, Japan, and Western European nations, the standard of living in much of Russia and other CIS members was low. Salaries were only a fraction of those in other developed nations. The new Russian government abolished price controls, which sent prices soaring because production did not increase to meet the demand, as had been hoped. Black markets flourished, and street crimes rose dramatically. The Russians were quick to seek economic aid and technical assistance from the developed nations.

What policy should the United States adopt regarding its former enemy? There was much debate in government circles and the media. Some advocated a hands-off policy, arguing that the former Soviet Union would soon return to its militaristic, Communist ways. In 1993, reactionaries won many seats in the Russian parliamentary elections because voters were dissatisfied with economic conditions and political leadership. Other Western observers advocated substantial aid to Russia in the belief that this would improve the conditions of the people and check political turmoil.

Which side was right? The United States watched as civil wars and violent ethnic rivalries broke out around the globe. Could they be contained or ended by diplomatic means, military intervention, or both? Would economic aid forestall such events in the CIS?

In our story, two diplomats, one Russian and the other American, are having a conversation. They had often faced one another in the past as Cold War enemies. Now they speak as old friends who wonder about the future.

Washington, D.C. April 1994

"American-Russian relations have changed a great deal since the days of the Cold War," said the American.

"You are absolutely right," said the Russian, smiling. "Not too long ago, we could not have had an open, friendly conversation like this one for fear of what we might reveal of our governments' secret plans."

"I hope that those days of suspicion and deceit are gone forever," replied the American.

"We had many disagreements, but I knew that I could always count on you for a just and reasonable answer," said the Russian.

"We personally were on good terms," said the American, "but our governments did not trust each other. Yet we had helped you with military and civilian aid during the terrible days of World War II when the Germans invaded your country."

"You helped us because it was to your advantage to do so," said the Russian. "But after the war, you turned against us."

"You forget that after 1945 the Soviet Union took over Eastern Europe and made the countries its satellites," replied the American. "And you encouraged and promoted Communist movements in China, Vietnam, and North Korea. The United States fought terrible wars against the Communist forces that your government had armed and trained in Korea and Vietnam."

"That was your fault, for meddling in the affairs of people you wanted to control yet did not understand," retorted the Russian.

"We used nonmilitary means whenever possible to stop the spread of totalitarian government," countered the American. "We spent billions of dollars on economic aid to help the war-devastated and poor nations of the world. And we did this while our people at home were demanding an end to inequality, racism, and poverty."

"Let us not argue about the past," sighed the Russian. "We Russians spent untold amounts of our wealth and resources trying to catch up to you in industrial and military power. Millions of our people struggled and sacrificed to help build a mighty Soviet empire.

Those who opposed this effort were exiled to labor camps or killed! There was no choice; we could not have enemies of the state in our midst! And you forget that in the late 19th century and early 20th century, the United States aimed at dominating large areas of its own hemisphere and setting up governments that obeyed its wishes."

The American laughed. "How you rewrite history! We have indeed made mistakes in our relations with our neighbors, but we have made much effort to redress these wrongs. And in recent decades, we have opened our doors to great numbers of people from this hemisphere and from all over the world who wish to live here.

"We know that the political and economic freedoms that most Americans take for granted are just not available to people in many parts of the world. We have shown the rest of the world that our system, although imperfect and subject to abuse, is probably the best that has ever been devised for providing the greatest good for the greatest number."

"Perhaps only history will judge whether our countries' goals and ambitions were very different," said the Russian. "Right now, the forces of reaction and fascism are at work in my land. They seek a return to the old ways of ethnic hatred and militarism, of rigid control over people's lives, of poverty for most people and riches for a few.

"Our industries are old-fashioned and inefficient. We have great natural resources but lack the ability to use them properly. And we cannot produce enough consumer goods to satisfy our people's wants and needs. Our farmers often cannot grow enough food, and when they do, they cannot get the crops harvested fast enough before they rot! In the postwar years, we spent the greater part of our national wealth on our army and on weapons. We knew how to produce the machinery of war, but we did not know how to create a peaceful life for our people.

"We see great problems in the world. Across our borders is China, the world's largest Communist nation. There, a dictatorship oppresses the people who disagree with it, but permits some free enterprise when it suits its purpose. In North Korea, a Communist government is readying nuclear weapons. When and where will it use them?

"Within our borders are the people of Russia and other republics, who are crying out for assistance. We need the help of the West to get our economies rolling, to feed and clothe our people."

"But my friend," said the American, "you have already received an aid package amounting to $1.6 billion from us! That was in 1993. Our people complain that this money should be spent on needy projects and people at home."

"We need more—much more!" exlaimed the Russian. "We need loans, which we will repay, to buy modern farming equipment. We need assistance to stop industrial pollution and clean up our air, water, and land. We need investments from Western businesses in factories that will provide new manufacturing jobs. Many of our industries once produced war materials. Now the industries produce little or nothing, but the people still go to work and receive their salaries every week. The government still supports these industries because it cannot throw hundreds of thousands of people out of work. The costs of converting these industries to money-making peacetime ones are immense, and we do not have the money. And we need help in retraining our people for new jobs in civilian industries.

"And, don't forget, there are over 285 million people in the Commonwealth. As our economy improves and people have more money to spend, they will be able to buy the goods that you produce so abundantly. This will provide more business and income for your industries and more jobs for your people. Everyone will benefit."

"What about all those people who, the newspapers say, are getting rich in the 'new Russia'?"

"Bah! Many 'new capitalists' are operating just this side of the law—and sometimes they're on the other side! We have little understanding of how your Western free-market economies operate. Making a profit from other people's work was forbidden by the Communist government. Even today, people who earn large incomes by their own efforts are looked at with suspicion. We need to educate our people and encourage them to be enterprising, to take risks. For so long, we expected the state—the government—to make major personal and economic decisions for us. It told us where to go to school, what to study, where we would work after we graduated, and how much we would earn. Now that system has fallen apart, and many people don't know what to do. They long for the old ways, when everything seemed simpler. Some are looking to the people who are advocating a return to the old ways."

There was a pause. The American finally replied, "My friend, freedom, peace, and justice cannot simply be bought. The United States learned that lesson many times over when it tried to help other nations in which there was little democracy or freedom. The United States has faced and continues to face many new challenges around the globe in the 1990's. We joined with the United Nations when it sent troops to Somalia to feed people who were starving to death. In 1990, we joined with an international force to stand up to Iraq and help establish the principle that no country can take the territory of another without facing severe consequences. In other areas, terrible civil wars have broken out, and there is great suffering. We have done much negotiating to try to stop the fighting and bring peace. People from all over the world are seeking refuge in our land from governments that oppress them. Are we to be the world's banker, policeman, and teacher?"

"Can you afford *not* to be all those things?" asked the Russian.

"My country will always act according to its best interests in the world, and it will place the well-being and security of its own people first. We will always seek peace in the world and oppose strife and war. If your country shows that it has the same goals, our best interest will be to offer you more aid. But if you fall back to the old ways—'' The American stopped.

The Russian nodded. The American, who could always be counted upon for an honest answer, had delivered a clear message. The Russian would have much to discuss with his government.

POSTSCRIPT

The Cold War was over, but the United States continued to be challenged by crises all over the globe. After having successfully intervened in the Persian Gulf to thwart Iraq's takeover of Kuwait, the United States found itself confronted by new problems in many other areas of the world. The question arose: Should the United States intervene to stop aggression, civil war, and ethnic strife? Should it use military force, even if its allies did not wish to do so? There seemed to be no simple answers.

There were many other global problems that needed attention. These included poverty, illiteracy, and starvation in the Third World; the unequal distribution of the world's resources; and the pollution and possible decline of the global environment. These were concerns that everyone, both the rich and the poor nations, shared. As the world approached the 21st century, the need for international cooperation and for some lessening of national self-interest was becoming increasingly apparent.

Homework Questions

1. Why has the Cold War ended?
2. Why did the United States and the Soviet Union distrust each other?
3. What were the causes of the collapse of the Soviet Union?
4. What are some of the international challenges that confront the United States even though the Cold War has ended?
5. How was the American diplomat's question, ''Are we to be the world's banker, policeman, and teacher?'' answered?

Understanding the Story

A. Write T for each statement that is true, F for each statement that is false, and O for each statement that is an opinion.
   1. The United States and the Soviet Union had many disagreements after World War II.
   2. The American government has refused aid to Russia and the former Soviet republics in order to punish them.
   3. The fear, hatred, and suspicion between Russia and the

United States will continue even though the Cold War is over.

4. The Soviet Union tolerated people who disagreed with its philosophy and methods.
5. The American diplomat felt that economic aid by itself was not enough to guarantee freedom and peace.
6. The nations of the world are in agreement on how to stop military aggression in the 1990's.
7. The American warned the Russian that the United States would not lend assistance if Russia and the CIS republics fell back on the old Soviet ways.
8. The need for international cooperation is not very great.

B. Write R for each statement the Russian made or might have made and A for each statement the American made or might have made.
1. You needed our help to repel the German invasion in World War II.
2. The policies of your country had much to do with its collapse.
3. Many of our people are suspicious of capitalism and free markets.
4. We fought terrible wars against forces that you had trained and armed.
5. In 1990, my country joined with an international force to help establish the principle that no country can take the territory of another without facing severe consequences.
6. We are looking to your government for technical and economic aid.
7. Your country took over East-

ern Europe after World War II.
8. We face possible challenges from Communist nations across our borders.
9. The forces of reaction are at work in my country.

C. Suppose that the President of the United States asked you if the United States should continue to use its resources to try to solve problems around the world. How would you respond? Explain your answer. What goals would you recommend for American foreign policy in the next decade?

Activities and Inquiries

1. Prepare a report on the Cold War. Include both positive and negative events from the viewpoint of the United States.
2. Imagine that, in preparing your report on the Cold War, you are reading books published in the former Soviet Union. How do you think the Soviet Union viewed the events of the Cold War?
3. Suppose that you are an American reporter in Moscow. You are about to interview the head of the Russian government. What questions will you ask him or her? How might the Russian leader answer your questions?
4. The Russian leader asks whether you favor United States aid to Russia. How will you answer the question?
5. Prepare a report on President Clinton's foreign policy. What events or actions do you approve of? Why? What do you disapprove of? Why? What message has the President's foreign policy sent to other world leaders? Explain.

2 What Price Health Care?

The United States faced many challenges at home in the 1990's. Crime, domestic violence and the breakup of families, drug use, poverty, unequal pay and fewer opportunities for women and minorities, and threats to the environment were among the major national problems. Americans were also deeply concerned with another problem, which threatened the lives and well-being of millions of people. This was the growing crisis in health care coverage and spending.

Health care costs were the single fastest growing item in consumer budgets in the 1980's and 1990's. Yearly national health expenditures had tripled in little over a decade—rising from $250 billion in 1980 to over $750 billion in 1991. (The figure was expected easily to pass $1 trillion in the 1990's.) Rising medical costs usually meant higher insurance premiums and higher deductibles for medical services.

Americans as a whole spent about $1 out of every $7 they earned for health care. But nearly 39 million persons out of the total population of 255 million had no health insurance coverage at all in 1992. Millions more were underinsured or risked losing their insurance if they lost their jobs.

President Bill Clinton had won election in 1992 in part because he promised to put a program in place that would bring medical costs under control and extend comprehensive medical coverage to all. In our story, two members of Congress, a senator and a congressperson, are meeting privately to discuss the proposed health care reform act.

Washington, D.C. May 1994

"Many of us on my Senate committee are prepared to vote 'yes' for a health care bill that controls costs and guarantees adequate medical care for every man, woman, and child in the country," said the senator. "Are you and your colleagues on the health care committee in the House of Representatives prepared to join with us and vote 'yes' as well?"

The congressperson shook her head. "Senator, I share your concern about the problem of health care for the American people. But I don't agree that the present health care bill is the solution that everyone has been seeking."

"Aren't you concerned that rising health care costs and poor coverage or none at all pose a grave threat to millions of Americans?" the senator asked.

"Yes, of course, I'm concerned, but I don't agree that the present bill, as I understand it, will solve the problem. In fact, I believe that, if anything, it will increase health care costs and will cause a decline in the quality of health services.''

''Can you support these statements with facts?'' asked the senator.

''Every time the government creates a new social program, it also sets up a huge agency to run it. The rules and regulations are enormous and costly to follow. Taxes rise to keep paying the costs of the program. In the end, the government does not keep down the costs of services or the number of persons employed to run the program,'' answered the congressperson. ''And this health care program is doubly costly, since it requires all employers to pay for their employees' health care. Many small businesses claim that they cannot afford to do so. Are we going to drive them out of business?''

''Are you saying that there is nothing for us to do but sit back and watch helplessly as health care costs continue to rise and tens of millions of people have inadequate care or none at all?''

''No, I'm not saying that, Senator. I too want to see our nation's medical costs brought under control and every American receive adequate health care coverage.''

''But what are we to do?'' asked the senator.

The congressperson shook her head. ''We in the Congress must look at the health care programs that are currently in place and are considered successful. I've been reading about the statewide health program in Hawaii, where the federal government is *not* involved. There, nearly 96 percent of the people have medical coverage. A high percentage are both healthy and satisfied with the care they get. Hawaii ranks near the top in the United States in low infant mortality and in long-lived citizens, and near the bottom in the number of early deaths from heart and lung disease and cancer.''

''How is this done?'' asked the senator. ''Who pays for this care?''

''Hawaii requires employers to provide health insurance for their employees and to pay most of the costs.''

''And have health costs been rising rapidly in Hawaii?'' asked the senator.

''Actually, because so many people in Hawaii have health insurance and receive good preventive care and early treatment when they become ill, health costs have been kept down. Health insurance is about 30 percent cheaper in Hawaii than on the mainland, even though almost everything else is more expensive,'' said the congressperson.

''Have many jobs been lost and companies forced out of business because employers were required to cover their workers?''

''Much to everyone's surprise,'' the congressperson answered, ''this did not happen in 1975, when the program was introduced. Nor did it happen during the recession of the 1980's. Nor is it happening today. I should add that doctors are not leaving Hawaii to practice elsewhere. We in Washington have to learn from state programs like this one, which does not add to people's burdens.''

''What works in Hawaii may not work as well or at all in other states,'' replied the senator. ''It seems unlikely that Congress can devise a national health care act that will not impose some financial burden on everybody except the very poor. In providing medical care for all, we must guarantee access to a very wide range of care and treatment. And we must continue to conduct basic research and seek new treatments. This will cost a great deal of money.''

''But most Americans are covered by health plans, and those who are not can still get treatment and care when they are ill,'' said the congressperson. ''If we continue to improve the services that government now provides, and if we encourage private enterprise to improve its insurance plans and keep costs down, don't you feel that we will solve the health care problem?''

The senator replied, ''Improving the current system is fine for those who have coverage. But what about those with heart disease or diabetes who can't get any medical coverage because the insurance companies say it is too risky to insure them? And those who need very expensive or long-term treatment for serious illnesses? And the millions who are about to lose their coverage because they have lost their jobs? And don't forget the millions who are working in low-wage or part-time jobs that offer no coverage at all. You are very optimistic if you think that the health care system will reform itself to include all those it now excludes.''

''What solution do you see, then?'' asked the congressperson.

''It is going to take a great deal of money to buy health care for all the people with special needs. Where is the money going to come from? Are the nation's employers going to have to pay for each worker? Are employees going to see money taken from their paychecks for their medical insurance? Are we going to need new federal taxes on some goods and services? The answer is probably 'yes' to all three questions. One way or another, many people are going to have to make some sacrifices. They will either have to pay more for what they now receive or pay less and make do with less. Our real job is to present the facts to the American people and listen carefully to what they say. Their wishes will help us make the decisions that are in their best interests.''

''I'm not sure that I agree with everything you just said, Senator,'' said the congressperson. ''But I certainly agree with one thing: The people must have the facts so they can help us make the right decisions.''

The meeting was over and both hurried away. Each returned to a busy office and to further meetings with other lawmakers who were grappling with one of the major problems of the 1990's.

POSTSCRIPT

As the debate on national health care goes on, important questions are being asked. Will the government try to set up price controls on medical services? Will new taxes be needed to pay for services? Will medical treatment be denied to some persons because of their age or condition? Will people be denied access to the doctors of their choice because of costs? Will jobs be lost because some employers cannot afford to cover their employees? Will medical research suffer because of a lack of funds? Even if a national health care bill is enacted in the mid-1990's, it may take some time before all these questions are resolved.

Health care is only one of the issues facing the United States in the 1990's. Nearly every solution to these problems requires spending large sums of money. Each year, Congress and the state governments tackle the question of raising taxes to pay for all the services that are needed and demanded in our society. It has been estimated that today's teenagers will pay some 38 percent of their lifetime earnings in taxes, up from 32 percent for their parents. In some nations that provide many social services for the entire population, the people pay two to three times what Americans pay in social security and other taxes. Are we prepared to do the same for the same protections?

It will, of course, take more than money to solve the nation's problems. It will take personal imagination, determination, cooperation, and sacrifice. Americans have found these resources within themselves throughout their history. They will have to rediscover these resources if they are to move confidently into the 21st century.

Homework Questions

1. What are some of the challenges that the United States faces at home in the 1990's?
2. Why is there a health care crisis?
3. Why did the congressperson in the story fear that the health care crisis would worsen if the federal government became involved in overseeing health care for all Americans?
4. Why did Hawaii have less of a problem with health care than the mainland states?
5. What will the people of the United States need to begin solving the many problems that confront them?

Understanding the Story

A. Write T for each statement that is true, F for each statement that is false, and O for each statement that is an opinion.
1. The growing health care crisis is the most serious of all the problems that confront the American people.
2. In the early 1990's, 39 million Americans had no medical coverage at all, and millions more were underinsured.
3. President Bill Clinton won election in part because he promised to rely on private

businesses to solve the health care crisis.

4. The government should not become involved in trying to provide full health care for all citizens.

5. Hawaii pays for its health care program by levying a special tax on all its residents.

6. In Hawaii, many jobs were lost and companies forced out of business when employers were required to pay for health insurance for their workers.

7. In the 1990's, health insurance costs were about 30 percent higher in Hawaii than in other states.

8. In 1994, all but a small number of Americans were covered by health care insurance.

B. Complete each of the following sentences by filling in the missing word or words.

1. In the 1990's, the United States faced _____ _____ at home.

2. Americans spent $_____ of every $_____ they earned on health care.

3. Hawaii ranks near the top in the nation in low _____ _____.

4. Hawaii's health care program requires _____ to provide health insurance for their _____ and to pay most of the cost.

5. The senator said that to get medical care for everyone, people would have to make some _____.

6. People will either have to pay _____ or make do with _____.

7. Both the congressperson and the senator agreed on this: The people needed _____ _____.

8. It will take more than _____ to solve national problems.

C. You have just learned that you will probably have to pay higher taxes to help support a government program under which all Americans will have medical coverage. How do you feel about this? Do you have any suggestions about how the problem of paying for medical care should be solved?

Activities and Inquiries

1. Write letters to your U.S. Senators and congressperson. Ask them to state their positions on national health care. Compare their responses and decide which position you agree with most.

2. Interview members of your family. Ask them whether they are satisfied with the health care they now receive. Make notes of their comments. What would they like to see changed?

3. You are asked to speak about a national problem before a Congressional committee. Which national problem do you believe is most serious today? Explain your answer.

4. Take a poll among your friends and family. Ask if they are willing to pay insurance premiums and higher taxes in order to receive lifetime health care. Make notes of their comments.

5. If you were a member of Congress, would you vote for a health care bill in which the federal government has the power to specify what kind of health care every citizen receives, and when and how this care is given? Explain your answer.

MR. MILLER'S OFFICE

"Tell me, Jack, what have you learned after a full year of studying American history?"

Jack thought for a moment. "For one, I learned that I didn't know nearly as much about American history as I thought I did. More important, I learned that I had never really understood American history before."

"What do you mean?"

"I mean that I knew about America's problems, but I really didn't understand America's strengths. Now I know better. Now I know that as long as the American people are free to express themselves and to better themselves, this country will continue to be great."

"What about America's future?" asked Mr. Miller. "Do you still believe that Americans will try to solve all the problems that confront them, no matter how difficult?"

"A band of rebel Americans won this country's independence from Great Britain. This band was outnumbered and often out-fought. It had nothing going for it except hope. Well, the United States has come a long way since that time. I believe it will continue to go far as long as the American people don't lose hope and the desire for freedom. My answer is 'yes.'"

"Do you sincerely believe that, Jack?" asked Mr. Miller.

Jack nodded. "America's future is my future. I have to believe it."

Appendix

The Declaration of Independence

(Adopted in Congress July 4, 1776)

The Unanimous Declaration of the Thirteen United States of America

When, in the course of human events, it becomes necessary for one people to dissolve the political bands which have connected them with another, and to assume among the powers of the earth, the separate and equal station to which the laws of nature and of nature's God entitle them, a decent respect to the opinions of mankind requires that they should declare the causes which impel them to the separation.

We hold these truths to be self-evident, that all men are created equal, that they are endowed by their Creator with certain unalienable rights, that among these are life, liberty and the pursuit of happiness. That to secure these rights, governments are instituted among men, deriving their just powers from the consent of the governed. That whenever any form of government becomes destructive of these ends, it is the right of the people to alter or to abolish it, and to institute new government, laying its foundation on such principles and organizing its powers in such form, as to them shall seem most likely to effect their safety and happiness. Prudence, indeed, will dictate that governments long established should not be changed for light and transient causes; and accordingly all experience hath shown that mankind are more disposed to suffer, while evils are sufferable, than to right themselves by abolishing the forms to which they are accustomed. But when a long train of abuses and usurpations, pursuing invariably the same object evinces a design to reduce them under absolute despotism, it is their right, it is their duty, to throw off such government, and to provide new guards for their future security.—Such has been the patient sufferance of these colonies; and such is now the necessity which constrains them to alter their former systems of government. The history of the present King of Great Britain is a history of repeated injuries and usurpations, all having in direct object the establishment of an absolute tyranny over these states. To prove this, let facts be submitted to a candid world.

He has refused his assent to laws, the most wholesome and necessary for the public good.

He has forbidden his governors to pass laws of immediate and pressing importance, unless suspended in their operation till his assent should be obtained; and when so suspended, he has utterly neglected to attend to them.

He has refused to pass other laws for the accommodation of large districts of people, unless those people would relinquish the right of representation in the legislature, a right inestimable to them and formidable to tyrants only.

He has called together legislative bodies at places unusual, uncomfortable, and distant from the depository of their public records, for the sole purpose of fatiguing them into compliance with his measures.

He has dissolved representative houses and repeatedly, for opposing with manly firmness his invasions on the rights of the people.

603

He has refused for a long time, after such dissolutions, to cause others to be elected; whereby the legislative powers, incapable of annihilation, have returned to the people at large for their exercise; the state remaining in the meantime exposed to all the dangers of invasion from without, and convulsions within.

He has endeavored to prevent the population of these states; for that purpose obstructing the laws for naturalization of foreigners, refusing to pass others to encourage their migration hither, and raising the conditions of new appropriations of lands.

He has obstructed the administration of justice, by refusing his assent to laws for establishing judiciary powers.

He has made judges dependent on his will alone, for the tenure of their offices, and the amount and payment of their salaries.

He has erected a multitude of new offices, and sent hither swarms of officers to harass our people, and eat out their substance.

He has kept among us, in times of peace, standing armies without the consent of our legislature.

He has affected to render the military independent of and superior to the civil power.

He has combined with others to subject us to a jurisdiction foreign to our constitution, and unacknowledged by our laws; giving his assent to their acts of pretended legislation:

For quartering large bodies of armed troops among us;

For protecting them, by a mock trial, from punishment for any murders which they should commit on the inhabitants of these states;

For cutting off our trade with all parts of the world;

For imposing taxes on us without our consent;

For depriving us in many cases, of the benefits of trial by jury;

For transporting us beyond seas to be tried for pretended offenses;

For abolishing the free system of English laws in a neighboring province, establishing therein an arbitrary government, and enlarging its boundaries so as to render it at once an example and fit instrument for introducing the same absolute rule into these colonies;

For taking away our charters, abolishing our most valuable laws, and altering fundamentally the forms of our governments;

For suspending our own legislatures, and declaring themselves invested with power to legislate for us in all cases whatsoever.

He has abdicated government here, by declaring us out of his protection and waging war against us.

He has plundered our seas, ravaged our coasts, burned our towns, and destroyed the lives of our people.

He is at this time transporting large armies of foreign mercenaries to complete the works of death, desolation and tyranny, already begun with circumstances of cruelty and perfidy scarcely paralleled in the most barbarous ages, and totally unworthy the head of a civilized nation.

He has constrained our fellow citizens taken captive on the high seas to bear arms against their country, to become the executioners of their friends and brethren, or to fall themselves by their hands.

He has excited domestic insurrections amongst us, and has endeavored to bring on the inhabitants of our frontiers, the merciless Indian savages, whose known rule of warfare, is an undistinguished destruction of all ages, sexes and conditions.

In every stage of these oppressions we have petitioned for redress in the most humble terms: our repeated petitions have been answered only by repeated injury. A prince whose character is thus marked by every act which may define a tyrant is unfit to be the ruler of a free people.

Nor have we been wanting in attention to our British brethren. We have warned them from time to time of attempts by their legislature to extend an unwarrantable jurisdiction over us. We have reminded them of the circumstances of our emigration and settlement here. We have appealed to their native justice and magnanimity, and we have conjured them by the ties of our common kindred to disavow these usurpations, which would inevitably interrupt our connections and correspondence. They too have been deaf to the voice of justice and of consanguinity. We must, therefore, acquiesce in the necessity, which denounces our separation, and hold them, as we hold the rest of mankind, enemies in war, in peace friends.

We, therefore, the representatives of the United States of America, in General Congress, assembled, appealing to the Supreme Judge of the world for the rectitude of our intentions, do, in the name, and by the authority of the good people of these colonies, solemnly publish and declare, that these united colonies are, and of right ought to be free and independent states; that they are absolved from all allegiance to the British Crown, and that all political connection between them and the state of Great Britain, is and ought to be totally dissolved; and that as free and independent states, they have full power to levy war, conclude peace, contract alliances, establish commerce, and to do all other acts and things which independent states may of right do. And for the support of this declaration, with a firm reliance on the protection of Divine Providence, we mutually pledge to each other our lives, our fortunes and our sacred honor.

Signed by John Hancock of Massachusetts as President of the Congress and by the fifty-five other Representatives of the thirteen United States of America.

Presents and Vice Presidents of the United States

No.	President	Years in office	Party	Home state when elected	Vice President	Home state when elected
1	George Washington (b. 1732–d. 1799)	1789–1797	*none*	Virginia	John Adams	Massachusetts
2	John Adams (b. 1735–d. 1826)	1797–1801	Federalist	Massachusetts	Thomas Jefferson	Virginia
3	Thomas Jefferson (b. 1743–d. 1826)	1801–1809	Democratic-Republican	Virginia	Aaron Burr George Clinton	New York New York
4	James Madison (b. 1751–d. 1836)	1809–1817	Democratic-Republican	Virginia	George Clinton Elbridge Gerry	New York Massachusetts
5	James Monroe (b. 1758–d. 1831)	1817–1825	Democratic-Republican	Virginia	Daniel D. Tompkins	New York
6	John Quincy Adams (b. 1767–d. 1848)	1825–1829	National Republican	Massachusetts	John C. Calhoun	South Carolina
7	Andrew Jackson (b. 1767–d. 1845)	1829–1837	Democratic-Republican	Tennessee	John C. Calhoun Martin Van Buren	South Carolina New York
8	Martin Van Buren (b. 1782–d. 1862)	1837–1841	Democratic	New York	Richard M. Johnson	Kentucky
9	William H. Harrison (b. 1773–d. 1841)	1841 (*died in office*)	Whig	Ohio	John Tyler	Virginia
10	John Tyler (b. 1790–d. 1862)	1841–1845	Whig	Virginia	*vacant*	
11	James K. Polk (b. 1795–d. 1849)	1845–1849	Democratic	Tennessee	George M. Dallas	Pennsylvania
12	Zachary Taylor (b. 1784–d. 1850)	1849–1850 (*died in office*)	Whig	Louisiana	Millard Fillmore	New York
13	Millard Fillmore (b. 1800–d. 1874)	1850–1853	Whig	New York	*vacant*	
14	Franklin Pierce (b. 1804–d. 1869)	1853–1857	Democratic	New Hampshire	William R. King	Alabama

#	President	Term	Party	State	Vice President	State
15	James Buchanan (b. 1791–d. 1868)	1857–1861	Democratic	Pennsylvania	John C. Breckinridge	Kentucky
16	Abraham Lincoln (b. 1809–d. 1865)	1861–1865 (died in office)	Republican	Illinois	Hannibal Hamlin Andrew Johnson	Maine Tennessee
17	Andrew Johnson (b. 1808–d. 1875)	1865–1869	Republican	Tennessee	*vacant*	
18	Ulysses S. Grant (b. 1822–d. 1885)	1869–1877	Republican	Illinois	Schuyler Colfax Henry Wilson	Indiana Massachusetts
19	Rutherford B. Hayes (b. 1822–d. 1893)	1877–1881	Republican	Ohio	William A. Wheeler	New York
20	James A. Garfield (b. 1831–d. 1881)	1881 (died in office)	Republican	Ohio	Chester A. Arthur	New York
21	Chester A. Arthur (b. 1830–d. 1886)	1881–1885	Republican	New York	*vacant*	
22	Grover Cleveland (b. 1837–d. 1908)	1885–1889	Democratic	New York	Thomas A. Hendricks	Indiana
23	Benjamin Harrison (b. 1833–d. 1901)	1889–1893	Republican	Indiana	Levi P. Morton	New York
24	Grover Cleveland (b. 1837–d. 1908)	1893–1897	Democratic	New York	Adlai E. Stevenson	Illinois
25	William McKinley (b. 1843–d. 1901)	1897–1901 (died in office)	Republican	Ohio	Garret A. Hobart Theodore Roosevelt	New Jersey New York
26	Theodore Roosevelt (b. 1858–d. 1919)	1901–1909	Republican	New York	*vacant 1901–1905* Charles W. Fairbanks	Indiana
27	William H. Taft (b. 1857–d. 1930)	1909–1913	Republican	Ohio	James S. Sherman	New York
28	Woodrow Wilson (b. 1856–d. 1924)	1913–1921	Democratic	New Jersey	Thomas R. Marshall	Indiana
29	Warren G. Harding (b. 1865–d. 1923)	1921–1923 (died in office)	Republican	Ohio	Calvin Coolidge	Massachusetts
30	Calvin Coolidge (b. 1872–d. 1933)	1923–1929	Republican	Massachusetts	*vacant 1923–1925* Charles G. Dawes	Illinois

Presidents and Vice Presidents of the United States (*Continued*)

No.	President	Years in office	Party	Home state when elected	Vice President	Home state when elected
31	Herbert C. Hoover (b. 1874–d. 1964)	1929–1933	Republican	California	Charles Curtis	Kansas
32	Franklin D. Roosevelt (b. 1882–d. 1945)	1933–1945 (*died in office*)	Democratic	New York	John N. Garner Henry A. Wallace Harry S. Truman	Texas Iowa Missouri
33	Harry S. Truman (b. 1884–d. 1972)	1945–1953	Democratic	Missouri	*vacant 1945–1949* Alben W. Barkley	Kentucky
34	Dwight D. Eisenhower (b. 1890–d. 1969)	1953–1961	Republican	New York	Richard M. Nixon	California
35	John F. Kennedy (b. 1917–d. 1963)	1961–1963 (*died in office*)	Democratic	Massachusetts	Lyndon B. Johnson	Texas
36	Lyndon B. Johnson (b. 1908–d. 1973)	1963–1969	Democratic	Texas	*vacant 1963–1965* Hubert H. Humphrey	Minnesota
37	Richard M. Nixon (b. 1913–d. 1994)	1969–1974 (*resigned*)	Republican	New York	Spiro T. Agnew Gerald R. Ford	Maryland Michigan
38	Gerald R. Ford (b. 1913–)	1974–1977	Republican	Michigan	Nelson A. Rockefeller	New York
39	James E. Carter, Jr. (b. 1924–)	1977–1981	Democratic	Georgia	Walter F. Mondale	Minnesota
40	Ronald W. Reagan (b. 1911–)	1981–1989	Republican	California	George H. W. Bush	Texas
41	George H. W. Bush (b. 1924–)	1989–1993	Republican	Texas	James D. Quayle	Indiana
42	William J. Clinton (b. 1946–)	1993–	Democratic	Arkansas	Albert H. Gore, Jr.	Tennessee

Facts About the States

State	Entered Union	Population (1992)	Rank in population	Area (sq. mi.)	Rank in size	Capital
Alabama	1819	4,136,000	22	51,609	29	Montgomery
Alaska	1959	587,000	49	589,757	1	Juneau
Arizona	1912	3,832,000	23	113,909	6	Phoenix
Arkansas	1836	2,399,000	33	53,104	27	Little Rock
California	1850	30,867,000	1	158,693	3	Sacramento
Colorado	1876	3,470,000	26	104,247	8	Denver
Connecticut	1788*	3,281,000	27	5,009	48	Hartford
Delaware	1787*	689,000	46	2,057	49	Dover
Dist. of Columbia†	1790–1791	589,000	48	67	51	Washington
Florida	1845	13,488,000	4	58,560	22	Tallahassee
Georgia	1788*	6,751,000	11	58,876	21	Atlanta
Hawaii	1959	1,160,000	40	6,450	47	Honolulu
Idaho	1890	1,067,000	42	83,557	13	Boise
Illinois	1818	11,631,000	6	56,400	24	Springfield
Indiana	1816	5,662,000	14	36,291	38	Indianapolis
Iowa	1846	2,812,000	30	56,290	25	Des Moines
Kansas	1861	2,523,000	32	82,264	14	Topeka
Kentucky	1792	3,755,000	24	40,395	37	Frankfort
Louisiana	1812	4,287,000	21	48,523	31	Baton Rouge
Maine	1820	1,235,000	39	33,215	39	Augusta
Maryland	1788*	4,908,000	19	10,577	42	Annapolis
Massachusetts	1788*	5,998,000	13	8,257	45	Boston
Michigan	1837	9,437,000	8	58,216	23	Lansing
Minnesota	1858	4,480,000	20	84,068	12	St. Paul
Mississippi	1817	2,614,000	31	47,716	32	Jackson
Missouri	1821	5,193,000	15	69,686	19	Jefferson City
Montana	1889	824,000	44	147,138	4	Helena
Nebraska	1867	1,606,000	36	77,227	15	Lincoln
Nevada	1864	1,327,000	38	110,540	7	Carson City
New Hampshire	1788*	1,111,000	41	9,304	44	Concord
New Jersey	1787*	7,789,000	9	7,836	46	Trenton
New Mexico	1912	1,581,000	37	121,666	5	Santa Fe
New York	1788*	18,119,000	2	49,576	30	Albany
North Carolina	1789*	6,843,000	10	52,586	28	Raleigh
North Dakota	1889	636,000	47	70,665	17	Bismarck
Ohio	1803	11,016,000	7	41,222	35	Columbus
Oklahoma	1907	3,212,000	28	69,919	18	Oklahoma City
Oregon	1859	2,977,000	29	96,981	10	Salem
Pennsylvania	1787*	12,009,000	5	45,333	33	Harrisburg
Rhode Island	1790*	1,005,000	43	1,214	50	Providence
South Carolina	1788*	3,603,000	25	31,055	40	Columbia
South Dakota	1889	711,000	45	77,047	16	Pierre
Tennessee	1796	5,024,000	17	42,244	34	Nashville
Texas	1845	17,656,000	3	267,338	2	Austin
Utah	1896	1,813,000	34	84,916	11	Salt Lake City
Vermont	1791	570,000	50	9,609	43	Montpelier
Virginia	1788*	6,377,000	12	40,817	36	Richmond
Washington	1889	5,136,000	16	68,192	20	Olympia
West Virginia	1863	1,812,000	35	24,181	41	Charleston
Wisconsin	1848	5,007,000	18	56,154	26	Madison
Wyoming	1890	466,000	51	97,914	9	Cheyenne

*One of the original thirteen states. The date is that of the state's ratification of the Constitution.
†For the purposes of this table, Washington, D.C., is listed among the states.

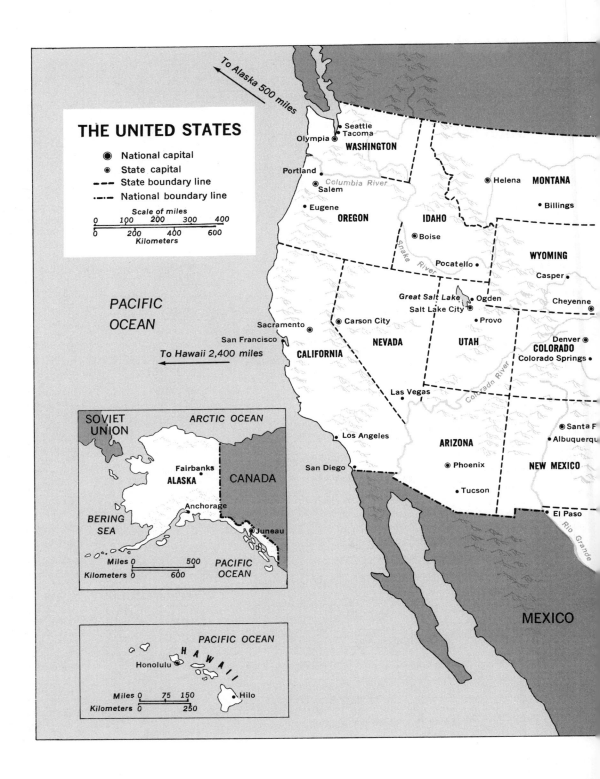

THE UNITED STATES

- ◉ National capital
- ◎ State capital
- – – – State boundary line
- –·–·– National boundary line

Scale of miles
0   100   200   300   400
0   200   400   600
Kilometers

To Alaska 500 miles

PACIFIC
OCEAN

To Hawaii 2,400 miles

Seattle
Tacoma
Olympia ◎
WASHINGTON

Portland
Salem ◎   Columbia River
Eugene
OREGON   IDAHO
Boise ◎

Helena ◉   MONTANA
Billings

Snake River

Pocatello   WYOMING
Casper

Great Salt Lake   Ogden
Salt Lake City ◎   Cheyenne
Carson City ◎   Provo
San Francisco   NEVADA   UTAH   Denver ◉
CALIFORNIA   Colorado River   COLORADO
Colorado Springs

Las Vegas

Los Angeles   Santa F
Albuquerqu
San Diego   ARIZONA   NEW MEXICO
Phoenix ◎
Tucson   El Paso

Rio Grande

MEXICO

SOVIET
UNION   ARCTIC OCEAN

Fairbanks
ALASKA   CANADA

BERING
SEA   Anchorage

Juneau

Miles 0   500   PACIFIC
Kilometers 0   600   OCEAN

PACIFIC OCEAN

Honolulu   HAWAII
Hilo

Miles 0   75   150
Kilometers 0   250

610

CANADA

NORTH DAKOTA
⊙ Bismarck
Fargo •

Duluth •

Lake Superior

MAINE
• Augusta

MINNESOTA

MICHIGAN

Montpelier ⊙
VERMONT

NEW HAMPSHIRE
⊙ Concord

SOUTH DAKOTA
⊙ Pierre

Minneapolis •
St. Paul ⊙

WISCONSIN

Lake Huron

Lake Ontario

Albany ⊙
Hudson River

MASSACHUSETTS
Boston ⊙
⊙ Providence
RHODE ISLAND

Sioux Falls •

Madison ⊙
Milwaukee •

Lake Michigan

Lansing •

Buffalo •

NEW YORK

Hartford ⊙
CONNECTICUT

IOWA
Cedar Rapids •

Lansing

Lake Erie

Detroit

Harrisburg ⊙
Pittsburgh •

NEW YORK CITY
Newark •
⊙ Trenton

NEBRASKA

Des Moines ⊙

Chicago •
Gary •

Cleveland •

PENNSYLVANIA

Philadelphia •
NEW JERSEY

Omaha •

ILLINOIS

INDIANA

OHIO
Columbus ⊙

Baltimore •
Washington, D.C.

• Dover
DELAWARE

Missouri River

Lincoln ⊙

Springfield ⊙

Indianapolis ⊙

Cincinnati •

WEST VIRGINIA

Annapolis ⊙
MARYLAND

Platte River

KANSAS
Topeka ⊙

Kansas City •
Jefferson City ⊙
St. Louis •

Ohio River

Frankfort ⊙
• Louisville

Charleston
Richmond ⊙

Norfolk •

Wichita •

MISSOURI

KENTUCKY

VIRGINIA

Arkansas River

Raleigh •

Tulsa •
Oklahoma City ⊙
OKLAHOMA
Little Rock ⊙

ARKANSAS
Fort Smith •

TENNESSEE
Memphis •

Nashville •

NORTH CAROLINA
• Charlotte

Columbia ⊙

Mississippi River

Birmingham •

• Atlanta

Charleston •
SOUTH CAROLINA

Dallas •

MISSISSIPPI
Jackson ⊙

ALABAMA

GEORGIA

ATLANTIC OCEAN

TEXAS

Montgomery ⊙

Columbus •

LOUISIANA

Austin ⊙

Baton Rouge ⊙

Tallahassee ⊙

Houston •

Gulfport •
New Orleans

San Antonio •

FLORIDA

Gulf of Mexico

Lake Okeechobee

• Miami

BAHAMAS

CUBA

611

Glossary

(The page number is the one on which the term first appears.)

Abolitionism. The movement in the early 1800's to end slavery immediately, with no compensation to owners. (p. 240)

Alien. A person who is not a citizen of the country in which he or she lives. (p. 189)

Ally. A friendly nation that sides with another against a common enemy. (p. 85)

Amendment. An addition or change in a document. It refers particularly to changes in the U.S. Constitution. (p. 149)

Amnesty. A pardon given to a group of people. (p. 291)

Anarchism. Belief that all government is unnecessary and should be eliminated. (p. 406)

Antifederalist. A person who was opposed to the ratification of the Constitution. (p. 148)

Aristocratic. Belonging to the upper class of society. (p. 73)

Armistice. A temporary end to wartime fighting by agreement among opposing groups. (p. 389)

Artisan. A skilled worker. (p. 238)

Assembly. A lawmaking body; a group of people. (p. 80)

Bail. A sum of money left with a court to guarantee that the accused will appear in court. (p. 169)

Bankruptcy. The state of being without funds to meet one's debts; the process of having one's assets administered by the courts. (p. 450)

Big Stick. Theodore Roosevelt's policy of policing the Western Hemisphere and other parts of the world with U.S. military power. (p. 375)

Black Codes. Laws to limit the rights of slaves and freedmen. (p. 266)

Blacklist. A list of people barred from holding jobs. (p. 501)

Blockade. The preventing of ships from moving in and out of a nation's ports. (p. 284)

Bond. A certificate of government or corporate debt. (p. 180)

Boom. A period of great prosperity. (p. 215)

Boycott. A refusal to buy or use a product or service as a protest. (p. 96)

Bull Moose. The nickname for the Progressive political party formed by Theodore Roosevelt in his unsuccessful bid for the Presidency in 1912. (p. 373)

Budget. A plan for matching income and expenses. (p. 413)

Bust. A period of financial and business failures. (p. 326)

Cabinet. The heads of federal departments who advise the President. (p. 162)

Candidate. A person who runs for political office. (p. 140)

Capitalism. An economic system in which the means of production are privately owned. (p. 428)

Carpetbagger. A Northerner who moved to the South during the post-Civil War period of Reconstruction. (p. 307)

Census. A count of the population of the United States taken every ten years (at the beginning of each decade). (p. 350)

Checks and balances. The system that prevents any branch of the federal government from gaining too much power over another part. It relates particularly to the executive, legislative, and judicial branches. (p. 144)

Citizen. A person who owes loyalty to a nation and is guaranteed rights by that nation. (p. 162)

Civil disobedience. The refusal to obey local or national laws. (p. 281)

Civil rights. Those rights guaranteed to a citizen of a country. (p. 302)

Civil war. A war between opposing groups in the same nation. (p. 73)

Cold War. An economic and political struggle between nations that does not involve the use of military war. Term applied particularly to relations between the United States and the Soviet Union. (p. 469)

Collective bargaining. Negotiations between representatives of workers and their employers about working conditions and benefits. (p. 456)

Communism. An economic system in which the means of production are owned in common and goods are given to all as needed. In the 20th century, the term refers to the system of government in which the state is all powerful, owning and controlling the means of production. (p. 406)

Conservative. One who wants to keep the best of the past and who may be suspicious of change. (p. 441)

Constitution. A written framework of government. The U.S. Constitution includes the powers, duties, and basic principles of government and the rights belonging to the people. (p. 66)

Corporation. A type of business organization that is authorized by the government to exist, has a life independent of its owners, and sells shares of ownership, called stocks, to raise money. (p. 322)

Crash. A sudden downward plunge in stock values or prices. (p. 421)

Culture. The special way of life of a group of people or a nation. Culture includes language, government, education, music, and fine arts. (p. 19)

Debate. A formal argument or discussion. (p. 216)

Delegate. A person selected to represent a group in a convention or lawmaking body. (p. 66)

Democracy. A form of government in which the people have power and select their lawmakers through elections. (p. 1)

Desegregate. To put an end to the separation of different races or groups of people. (p. 506)

Détente. The easing of tensions between nations. (p. 564)

Dictator. One holding absolute control of the government of a country. (p. 440)

Direct democracy. The handling of governmental affairs (the passing of laws or rules) by the citizens themselves rather than by elected representatives. (p. 66)

Direct primary. An election to choose political party candidates for public office. (p. 369)

Discrimination. The favoring or punishing of people because of their membership in a particular group. (p. 353)

Dissenter. One who disagrees with the decisions or way of life of a majority of the people. (p. 64)

Double jeopardy. The process of trying a person twice for the same crime. (p. 168)

Due process of law. The procedures and protections that govern all criminal and civil cases in the United States. (p. 352)

Economy. The structure of the industrial and business life of a country. (p. 326)

Elastic Clause. The section of the U.S. Constitution that gives Congress powers in addition to those specifically listed. (p. 159)

Electoral College. The group of people chosen every four years to elect the President and Vice President. (p. 142)

Emancipation. The act of freeing slaves. (p. 241)

Embargo. A stoppage of commerce and trade. (p. 199)

Empire. A group of nations, territories, or peoples governed by one nation or ruler. (p. 36)

Environment. The natural, social, or physical surroundings that affect our daily life. (p. 556)

Executive. The president or head of government who carries out the laws. (p. 124)

Excise taxes. Taxes on the manufacture, sale, or use of a product. (p. 158)

Exports. Goods shipped out of a country. (p. 160)

Factory. A building in which products are manufactured by machines. (p. 236)

Federal. The central or national government. (p. 182)

Federalist. One who favored the ratification of the Constitution. Also, a member of an important political party in the early years of the United States. (p. 148)

Feminist. A believer in equal rights for women. (p. 380)

Freedmen. Former slaves. (p. 288)

Free enterprise. The freedom of private business to operate at a profit under capitalism without great interference by the government. (p. 428)

Government. The authority in an area that passes and administers laws, keeps the peace, and promotes the well-being of the people in the area. (p. 3)

Grand jury. A group of people who determines whether the accused should be indicted and stand trial. (p. 151)

Grange. A national organization of farmers. (p. 342)

Great Depression. The economic crisis in the 1930's. (p. 423)

Great Society. The social and economic program of President Lyndon Johnson. (p. 529)

Habeas corpus. The right of the accused to a hearing in open court. (p. 159)

Holocaust. The Nazi effort to exterminate the Jews during the 1930's and 1940's. (p. 477)

Homestead. Land occupied and cultivated under the terms of the Homestead Act of 1863. (p. 322)

Immigration. The coming of foreigners into a country for the purpose of settling there. (p. 51)

Impeach. To accuse a public official of misconduct in office. In the United States, a formal impeachment takes place in the House of Representatives. (p. 145)

Imperialism. The policy of seeking to extend a nation's control over foreign territory. (p. 359)

Implied power. A power that is assumed to be held by the federal government even though it is not specifically listed in the Constitution. (p. 195)

Imports. Goods that are brought into a country for purpose of sale. (p. 94)

Impressment. The practice by the British of forcing U.S. sailors to serve in the British Navy in the early 1800's. (p. 199)

Indentured servant. One who contracts to work for another for a specific number of years. (p. 48)

Independence. Freedom from control by another person or government. (p. 101)

Inflation. A rise in prices, an increase in the money supply, an easing of credit terms, and a decrease in the amount of goods for sale. (p. 290)

Initiative. A procedure by which citizens may require lawmakers to consider a bill. (p. 348)

Insurgent. A rebel who refuses to accept the policies of a government or organization. (p. 290)

Internment camp. An area where people who are considered dangerous are imprisoned, especially during wartime or civil unrest. (p. 475)

Interstate commerce. Trade among the states. (p. 130)

Intervention. Interference in the affairs of another nation. (p. 209)

Iron Curtain. An imaginary line in Europe after World War II that separated the Communist and non-Communist nations. (p. 482)

Isolationist. One who believes that the United States should not become involved in the problems of foreign nations. (p. 395)

Judiciary. A system of courts. (p. 131)

Labor union. An organization of workers formed to improve conditions of work. (p. 238)

Laissez-faire. A policy whereby government does not interfere with business. (p. 324)

Landslide. An overwhelming political victory. (p. 412)

League of Nations. An international organization formed after World War I to guarantee world peace. (p. 389)

Legislature. A lawmaking body such as the United States Congress or its counterpart in each of the states. (p. 66)

Libel. A published statement that presents an untrue and harmful view of a person, organization, or government. (p. 80)

Liberal. A person who believes in progress or change. (p. 441)

Loyalty check. Investigation of a person thought to be a Communist sympathizer. (p. 498)

Majority. More than half. (p. 57)

Manifest Destiny. The belief that the United States had a God-given mission to expand from the Atlantic Ocean to the Pacific Ocean. (p. 250)

Massacre. The killing of a number of people who can offer little resistance. (p. 99)

Migrant workers. Workers who move from place to place in response to the need for labor usually in harvesting crops. (p. 318)

Militia. A citizen army equipped by state governments. (p. 105)

Minority. Less than half. Also, a group that is different from the majority of the population and that may be discriminated against by the majority. (p. 578)

Minutemen. Armed civilians pledged to fight at very short notice before and during the Revolutionary War. (p. 105)

Misdemeanor. A minor crime. (p. 305)

Missile. Weapon that can be propelled to distant targets. (p. 523)

Monarchy. A government headed by a king or queen. (p. 73)

Monopoly. Control of a product or service by one company. (p. 322)

Mortgage. A loan made to individuals and businesses that uses land and buildings as security. (p. 444)

Muckrakers. Writers who searched out and exposed misconduct and disregard for the public interest by well-known corporations and government officials in the early 1900's. (p. 366)

Nation. A group of people living in a definite territory with an organized government. (p. 2)

Naturalization. The process whereby an alien becomes a citizen. (p. 189)

Neutrality. The policy of not taking sides in a contest or a war. (p. 185)

New Deal. Franklin Roosevelt's program of social and economic reform in the 1930's. (p. 439)

Nominate. To name candidates to run for political office. (p. 59)

Nonviolence. Peaceful protest against laws or government. (p. 512)

Northwest Passage. A much looked-for but nonexistent waterway through North America from the Atlantic to the Pacific oceans. Europeans hoped to use the waterway as a shortcut to Asia. (p. 40)

Nuclear. Refers to the power generated by the splitting of the atom for both industrial and military use. (p. 469)

Nullification. The process by which a state disobeys or disregards a federal law. (p. 202)

Orbit. The path in space of a natural object, such as a planet around the sun, or of a manufactured object, such as a space craft around the earth. (p. 543)

Parliament. The British lawmaking body. (p. 91)

Patent. The exclusive right given to a company or individual to manufacture and sell an invention; a grant of public lands. (p. 59)

Patriot. A person who loves his or her country. One loyal to the American cause at the time of the Revolutionary War. (p. 107)

Petition. A written request that officials follow a certain course of action. (p. 109)

Pilgrim. A person who travels to foreign lands, often for religious reasons. In American history, the people who settled in Plymouth, Mass., in 1620. (p. 57)

Pocket veto. Rejection of a bill by the President after Congress has adjourned. (p. 158)

Plantation. A large agricultural estate. In the U.S. South before 1865, it was generally worked by slave labor. (p. 55)

Plurality. The number of votes cast for a candidate in an election with three or more candidates that is more than anyone else receives but is less than a majority. (p. 212)

Political party. An organization of people with shared beliefs working for the election of their candidates. (p. 183)

Pollution. The creation of a dirty or unhealthy environment or atmosphere. (p. 555)

Popular sovereignty. A system developed before the Civil War to allow settlers in a territory to decide whether to accept or reject slavery. (p. 256)

Potlatch. A ceremonial feast of the Indians of the Northwest in which the host distributes lavish gifts. (p. 8)

Prejudice. Strong feeling for or against a person or group without a firm basis in reason. (p. 1)

Progressive. A person who believes in reforming society and politics by gradual action. (p. 360)

Prohibition. The banning of the manufacture and sale of alcoholic beverages. (p. 415)

Proprietor. An owner of something. In colonial times, proprietors owned certain American colonies. (p. 70)

Protective tariff. A tax on imports designed to eliminate the competition of foreign goods. (p. 322)

Public works. Construction projects financed and owned by the government— for example, schools, highways, dams, docks. (p. 429)

Puritan. A member of the Church of England who broke with the church because of an insistence on reforms. The people who settled in New England in the 1630's and after. (p. 57)

Quota. The number of persons from other countries permitted to enter the United States yearly according to immigration laws. (p. 335)

Radical. A person favoring drastic changes. (p. 101)

Ratify. To approve. (p. 145)

Rebellion. An uprising against a government. (p. 125)

Recall. The removal of an elected official by the voters before the official's term of office is up. (p. 348)

Recession. A period of mild or temporary economic decline. (p. 592)

Reconstruction. The period of rebuilding the South following the Civil War. (p. 283)

Red Scare. A period of national panic in the United States after World War I. Fears centered on the possibility of a Communist takeover of the United States. (p. 407)

Reform. An attempt to improve or change those portions of society that people feel must be upgraded or replaced. (p. 245)

Referendum. A procedure by which laws may be accepted or rejected by voters. (p. 348)

Relief. Financial assistance given to the poor. (p. 443)

Reparations. Payments for war damages made by the losers of a war to the winners. (p. 391)

Representative democracy. A system of government in which legislative decisions are made by elected representatives rather than by the voters themselves. (p. 66)

Republic. A representative democracy. (p. 204)

Reservation. Land set aside by the federal government for the use of an Indian tribe. (p. 348)

Revolution. A major change in government or in society. (p. 1)

Scalawags. Southern whites who supported congressional Reconstruction. (p. 307)

Search warrant. A court order authorizing police to search a person's property. (p. 151)

Secret ballot. A method of voting that keeps the individual voter's choices secret. (p. 343)

Sectionalism. An emphasis on the importance of a region rather than on the welfare of the entire nation. (p. 229)

Sedition. Activities designed to stir up resistance to the authority of the government. (p. 189)

Segregation. Keeping people apart because of their race, class, or ethnic background. (p. 503)

Separatist. An English Protestant who preferred to separate from the Church of England rather than try to reform it. (p. 57)

Sit-down strike. The stopping of work as a protest by workers who stay in their place of employment. (p. 457)

Sit-in. A protest device, particularly in the 1960's, whereby a restaurant or other building was occupied in order to force the people in power to make a policy change. (p. 531)

Slave. A person who is owned by another and who is treated like property. (p. 6)

Socialism. An economic system in which the government owns and controls the means of production. (p. 406)

Social justice. The idea that all citizens should be treated fairly without distinction or discrimination. (p. 366)

Social security. A system of social welfare legislation providing for the economic protection of the individual. Currently, Social Security means federal old age insurance. (p. 454)

Speaker. The presiding officer of the United States House of Representatives or of the lower house of a state legislature. (p. 155)

Speculator. One who takes risks in investments in the hope of realizing a large profit. (p. 181)

Square Deal. Theodore Roosevelt's program of social and economic reform. (p. 372)

States' rights. The belief that state powers are superior to those of the federal government. (p. 202)

Stock. Shares of ownership in a corporation. (p. 322)

Strike. A stoppage of work or other activity as a protest. (p. 238)

Suffrage. Right to vote. (p. 379)

Tariff. A tax on imports levied by the federal government. (p. 124)

Territory. An area of land owned or run by a government. In U.S. history, a government possession not yet admitted to statehood. (p. 124)

Tolerance. The acceptance of others' differences. (p. 64)

Tory. Supporter of Great Britain during the American Revolution—also referred to as a Loyalist. (In Great Britain, the political party supporting the king; later called the Conservative Party.) (p. 101)

Treason. An attempt to overthrow or undermine a government by a citizen of that country. (p. 110)

Tribe. A group of people united by common background, language, customs, and leaders. (p. 2)

Truce. A temporary halt in fighting a war, comparable to armistice. (p. 262)

Trust. A combination of businesses for the purpose of creating a monopoly by the elimination of competition. Now illegal in the U.S. (p. 324)

Tyranny. A government controlled by a harsh, all-powerful ruler; oppressive power. (p. 84)

Unanimous. Having the agreement of all. (p. 180)

Unconstitutional. Against the Constitution; a law may be declared unconstitutional by the Supreme Court. (p. 193)

Underground Railroad. A system of helping runaway slaves escape to the North and Canada before the Civil War. (p. 233)

Union. The combination of states that make up the United States; the North during the Civil War. *See also* Labor Union. (p. 134)

United Nations. An international organization formed in 1945 to promote peace in the world. (p. 482)

Veto. The rejection by the President of a congressional bill. (Congress can override a veto by a two-thirds majority.) (p. 80)

War Hawks. Members of Congress who, before the War of 1812, favored war with Britain so that the United States could take over Canada and also defeat the Indians armed by British officials in Canada. (p. 200)

Watergate Affair. Name for the series of wrongdoings that caused Richard Nixon to resign from the Presidency in 1974. (p. 566)

Women's rights. Political, legal, and social rights equal to those of men. (p. 245)

Writs of assistance. Court orders allowing officials, during colonial times, to enter buildings at any time to search for smuggled goods. (p. 96)

Index